Major Conservation and Recreation Areas

10 0174533 7

THIS PUBLICATION MAY NOT BE BORROWED FROM THE LIBRARY

D0590730

Orkney Islands

Shetland Islands

Legend
- ...nal Parks (...cotland)
- ...st Parks ...creation Areas
- Community Forests (England)
- Areas of Outstanding Natural Beauty (National Scenic Areas in Scotland)
- Heritage Coasts (England and Wales)
- National Trails (Long Distance Routes in Scotland)
- World Heritage Sites

SCOTLAND

West Highland Way

Loch Lomond

Fife

Clyde Muirshiel

Pentland Hills

Southern Upland Way

NORTHERN IRELAND

Proposed

Northumberland

Hadrian's Wall Path

Cleveland Way

North York Moors

Lake District

Yorkshire Dales

Wolds Way

Pennine Bridleway

Pennine Way

World Heritage Sites

1. Canterbury Cathedral
2. Maritime Greenwich
3. Palace of Westminster, etc.
4. Tower of London
5. Stonehenge and Avebury
6. City of Bath
7. Blenheim Palace
8. Ironbridge Gorge
9. Castles of King Edward 1
10. Durham Cathedral and Castle
11. Studley Royal Gardens and Fountains Abbey
12. Hadrian's Wall
13. Edinburgh Old and New Towns
14. Giant's Causeway
15. St Kilda

Peak District

Snowdonia

Offa's Dyke Path

Peddars Way and Norfolk Coast Path

The Broads (Special protected area)

WALES

ENGLAND

Pembrokeshire Coast

Pembrokeshire Coast Path

Brecon Beacons

Cotswold Way

Ridgeway

Thames Path

North Downs Way

South Downs Way

South West Coast Path

Exmoor

Dartmoor

South West Coast Path

New Forest Heritage Area

| 0 | 40 | 80 | 120 km |
| 0 | 20 | 40 | 60 | 80 miles |

BRITAIN
2 0 0 0
THE OFFICIAL YEARBOOK
OF THE UNITED KINGDOM

THE UNIVERSITY OF NOTTINGHAM
UNIVERSITY LIBRARY
HAL
17 NOV 1999

Prepared by the Office for National Statistics

London: The Stationery Office

Published with the permission of the Office for National Statistics on behalf of the Controller of Her Majesty's Stationery Office.

© Crown Copyright 1999.

All rights reserved.

If you wish to reproduce any items in this publication, please contact ONS Copyright Enquiries, Zone B1/04, 1 Drummond Gate, London, SW1V 2QQ. Tel 020 7533 5671 or fax 020 7533 5689.

While every attempt has been made to ensure that the information in this yearbook is up to date at the time of publication, the publisher cannot accept responsibility for any inaccuracies.

First published 1999

ISBN 0 11 621098 2

Published by The Stationery Office and available from:

The Publications Centre
(mail, telephone and fax orders only)
PO Box 276, London SW8 5DT
Telephone orders/General enquiries 0870 600 5522
Fax orders 0870 600 5533

www.tso-online.co.uk

The Stationery Office Bookshops
123 Kingsway, London WC2B 6PQ
020 7242 6393 Fax 020 7242 6394
68–69 Bull Street, Birmingham B4 6AD
0121 236 9696   Fax 0121 236 9699
33 Wine Street, Bristol BS1 2BQ
0117 9264306 Fax 0117 9294515
9–21 Princess Street, Manchester M60 8AS
0161 834 7201 Fax 0161 833 0634
16 Arthur Street, Belfast BT1 4GD
028 9023 8457 Fax 028 9023 5401
The Stationery Office Oriel Bookshop
18-19 High Street, Cardiff CF1 2BZ
029 2039 5548 Fax 029 2038 4347
71 Lothian Road, Edinburgh EH3 9AZ
0131 228 4181   Fax 0131 622 7017

The Stationery Office's Accredited Agents
(see Yellow Pages)

and through good booksellers

Printed in the UK for The Stationery Office.

J87259 C110 11/99

Contents

List of Illustrations

Diagrams

Maps

Photographs

Acknowledgments for photographs

Cover photograph: Photofusion.

Devolution: p. 3, Overseas Press and Pictures Service, Foreign & Commonwealth Office, and PA Photos (large interiors).

Then and Now—1900 and 1999: p. 1, top—Carlisle Library, bottom—Carmarthenshire County Museum; p. 2, top left—Norfolk Record Office, top right—Norwich Area Tourism Agency, bottom left—Westcountry Studies Library, Devon Library Services, Exeter, bottom right inset—Economy and Tourism, Exeter City Council; p. 3, top—Lawrence (Royal 2548) Collection, National Library of Ireland, top inset—Derry Visitor and Convention Bureau, bottom—Warwickshire County Council Libraries and Heritage, bottom colour picture—Flamingo Photography; p. 4, top upper right and lower left—Inverness Museum and Art Gallery, top upper left and lower right—Ian Rhind, bottom—Huddersfield Daily Examiner.

The Chelsea Flower Show 1999—of the Royal Horticultural Society (RHS): p. 1, top—Theresa Donaghey, bottom—RHS/James Ross; p. 2, top left—RHS/Sue Snell, top right—RHS/John Glover, bottom left—RHS/Mark Bolton, bottom right—Theresa Donaghey; p. 3, top and bottom left—RHS/Jerry Harpur, top right—RHS/Derek Harris, bottom right—RHS/Liz Eddison; p. 4, top left—RHS/Derek Harris, top right—RHS/Mark Bolton, middle right—RHS/Sue Snell, bottom left—RHS/James Ross, bottom right—RHS/Mark Bolton.

Abbeys and Priories: p. 1, English Heritage Photo Library; p. 2, Crown Copyright, Historic Scotland; p. 3, Lester Tipton; p. 4, Northern Ireland Tourist Board.

Millennium Products: Design Council; p. 2, TX1 taxi—Edmund Clark, Europa XS—Keith Wilson.

Sport: PA Photos and: p. 1, top—EPA, bottom—Gerry Penny; p. 2, top—EPA, bottom—Neil Munns; p. 3, top left and right—EPA, bottom—Paul Barker; p. 4, all photos—EPA, except middle right inset—Yoav Lemmer.

The International Festival of the Sea and the National Glass Centre: pp. 1 and 2, Nigel Huxtable; p. 3, top—National Glass Centre; p. 3, bottom and p. 4, top right, Bridget Jones at the National Glass Centre; p. 4, top left—National Glass Centre, bottom—Kaleidoscope Gallery at the National Glass Centre.

Science and Space: p. 2, top—John Innes Centre, bottom—Dr Peter Mertens, Institute of Animal Health, Pirbright Laboratory and Professor David Stuart, University of Oxford; p. 3, top—Brian Moss, middle and bottom—Centre for Analytical Sciences, University of Sheffield; p. 4, top and middle—Professor C. S. Frenk, Dr E. Branchini and Dr L. Teodoro, University of Durham, bottom—Anglo-Australian Telescope/David Malin.

Jubilee Line Extension: QA Photos/Jubilee Line Extension Project.

The Office for National Statistics works in partnership with others in the Government Statistical Service to provide Parliament, government and the wider community with the statistical information, analysis and advice needed to improve decision-making, stimulate research and inform debate. It also administers the registration of key life events. It aims to provide an authoritative and impartial picture of society and a window on the work and performance of government, allowing the impact of government policies and actions to be assessed.

Foreword

Britain 2000 is the 51st edition of an official annual reference book that was first published in the 1940s. Since 1997 it has been produced by the Office for National Statistics (ONS). Drawing on a wide range of official and other authoritative sources, *Britain 2000* provides a factual and up-to-date overview of the state of the United Kingdom, while also covering every aspect of current government policy. It is a widely used work of reference, both in the United Kingdom itself, and overseas, where it is an important element of the information service provided by British diplomatic posts.

Coverage and Geographical Terms

Every effort is made to ensure that the information given in *Britain 2000* is accurate at the time of going to press. The text is generally based on information available up to the end of August 1999.

The term 'Britain' is sometimes used as a short way of expressing the full title of the country: the United Kingdom of Great Britain and Northern Ireland (or, more simply again, the United Kingdom or the UK). 'Great Britain' comprises England, Wales and Scotland only. The adjectives 'British' and 'UK' have the same meaning and cover the whole of the United Kingdom. As far as possible, the book applies to the UK as a whole, as the title suggests. However, sometimes the information given refers to just: Great Britain; England and Wales; or, in some instances, England, Scotland, Wales or Northern Ireland alone.

Special Features

The 51st edition has more charts and tables than ever before, and 40 colour pages including some new and redrawn maps. The text is 285,000 words long and has been fully updated and revised. Although it is the 2000 edition, it cannot be truly 'millennial', since official figures are not yet available and will follow on, as they normally do, between one and four years after the year itself. However, we have made historical comparisons throughout the book (in highlighted boxes) with life in Britain in the early part of the 20th century. At that time official statistics were relatively limited and additional sources have therefore been used. There is also an introductory chapter on the millennial celebrations in the UK, which are remarkably extensive, together with photographs of Millennium Products.

One of the most significant changes to have occurred since the publication of *Britain 1999* is that the Scottish Parliament and National Assembly for Wales are now in existence and are exercising their responsibilities. The separate chapters on Scotland and Wales reflect these changes. Coverage in other chapters has also been updated, but it is not always possible to set out all the differences where these exist.

The five Parts of *Britain 2000* align with their equivalents in another ONS publication, the *Annual Abstract of Statistics*, so that the two books can be consulted as complementary volumes, painting a picture of the UK in words and figures.

Sources

To help the reader seeking further information, at the end of each chapter there is a brief further reading section, which lists the main ONS statistical publications and other important documents, such as recent White Papers. A selection of websites is included at the end of most chapters. The main government websites are listed in the entry for Government Departments and Agencies in Appendix 1.

ONS issues a number of important statistical publications, many of which have been used in the compilation of *Britain 2000*, including:

Annual Abstract of Statistics
Business Monitors/Sector Reviews
Family Spending
Labour Market Trends
Living in Britain: Results from the General
  Household Survey
Monthly Digest of Statistics
Population Trends
Regional Trends
Social Trends
Travel Trends
United Kingdom Balance of Payments—
  the Pink Book
United Kingdom National Accounts—
  the Blue Book

A full list of ONS publications is available from: ONS Direct Sales, Room D.140, Office for National Statistics, Cardiff Road, Newport NP10 8XG.

In compiling *Britain 2000*, information about particular companies has been taken only from company reports and news releases, or from other publicly available sources. No information about individual companies has been taken from returns submitted in response to ONS statistical inquiries. Very strict arrangements operate within ONS to ensure that such data remain confidential.

Acknowledgments

Britain 2000 has been compiled with the full co-operation of around 250 organisations, including other government departments and agencies. The editor would like to thank all the people from these organisations who have taken so much time and care to ensure that the book's high standards of accuracy have been maintained. Their contributions and comments have been extremely valuable.

The book was researched, written and edited by a combination of in-house authors and freelances. The main in-house team comprised Nigel Pearce, John King, Derek Tomlin, David Harper, Conor Shipsey, Paul Webb and John Chrzczonowicz; individual chapters were also written by Catherine Hill and Craig Myers. The freelance writers were Henry Langley, Richard German (who also compiled the index), John Collis and Oliver Metcalf, and most of the design work, including the maps and colour sections, was done by Ray Martin. Jane Howard, Jole Cosgrove and Rosemary Hamilton proofread the text. The cover was designed by The Stationery Office.

Readers' Comments

We welcome readers' comments and suggestions. These should be sent to: The Editor, *Britain Yearbook*, Room B4/02, Office for National Statistics, 1 Drummond Gate, London SW1V 2QQ, UK.

Symbols and Conventions

Units of Measurement. In most cases, metric measurements are used, although for certain measurements, such as for speed limits, the imperial measurement is given first.

Billion. 1 billion = 1,000 million.

Rounding of Figures. In tables where figures have been rounded to the nearest final digit, the constituent items may not sum to the total.

The Millennium in the UK

The United Kingdom's plans to celebrate the millennium are among the most ambitious in the world. More than £2 billion of proceeds from the National Lottery have been devoted to projects and award schemes all over the country, which will ensure that a lasting legacy remains once the celebrations are over.

Although the year 2000, according to traditional dating, marks two millennia of Christian faith since the birth of Jesus Christ, it is of great significance to all people—religious and secular alike—who use the Gregorian calendar. The UK today is a multi-faith society, and the Government wants to make the celebrations equally relevant and accessible to people of all faiths and none.[1]

In 1994 it set up the Millennium Commission, one of the 'good causes' funded by National Lottery proceeds (see p. 122), to help communities throughout the UK celebrate the year 2000. Since then the Commission has been distributing funds to four main areas: the Millennium Experience, centred on Greenwich in London; the nationwide Millennium Festival of events; the Millennium Awards to individuals; and a programme of major capital projects around the country.

The Millennium Experience

The Millennium Experience consists of the 'experience' itself at the Millennium Dome in Greenwich and an associated National Programme of events and activities. Both are being organised and delivered by a public sector company especially set up for the purpose in 1997—the New Millennium Experience Company (NMEC)—whose budget is £758 million. This is made up of a Lottery grant of £399 million from the Millennium Commission and a forecast income of £359 million from private sector sponsorship, visitor revenues and other forms of commercial income.

The Dome itself is the biggest such structure ever built. It is one kilometre in circumference and has 80,000 square metres of floor space. Inside it is divided into 14 exhibition zones, sponsored by such well-known companies as BT, Marks & Spencer, and Tesco. By June 1999 the NMEC had exceeded its sponsorship target of £150 million, the largest amount of sponsorship ever raised for any single event in the UK. The 14 zones are:

- Body
- Faith
- Home Planet
- Journey
- Talk
- Learning
- Living Island
- Mind
- Money
- Work
- Play
- Rest
- Self Portrait
- Shared Ground

The Body Zone, for example, which is sponsored by Boots, includes the largest ever representation of the human form, measuring 64 metres from elbow to foot and 27 metres high. Visitors will be able to travel inside the body, viewing exhibits on medical discoveries, lifestyle, health and beauty. The Mind Zone, sponsored by British Aerospace and GEC, explores the human brain, senses and perceptions through a combination of traditional art and advanced technology.

In addition, the 500-seat 'Our Town Stage' will host performances from more than 200 different UK towns and cities, and from countries around the world. Outside the Dome,

---

[1] The plans of the religious communities for the millennium in the UK are described in more detail in chapter 15, p. 246.

'Skyscape' will consist of two 2,500-seat cinemas by day (one of which can convert into a 3,300-seat venue for concerts and other live events), and visitors will be able to enjoy a specially commissioned half-hour film of *Blackadder,* which will reunite the original cast of the 1980s comedy show and feature a series of cameos by famous international stars.

The Dome will be opened by HM The Queen on 31 December 1999. Over 12 million people are expected to visit the Dome before it closes on 31 December 2000. The Millennium Experience could contribute an additional £300–£500 million of overseas tourist revenue to the UK economy and create 10,000–15,000 new tourist-related jobs. The public will have many means of public transport available to them to reach the site. London Underground's Jubilee Line Extension links the Dome to central London (see photographs between pp. 484 and 485), and the NMEC has constructed a new pier for river buses and ferry services from central London and historic Greenwich. In addition, there will be a park and ride facility at Woolwich, and a bus transit link to the North Kent Rail line (Charlton station). An on-site coach park was completed by April 1999.

The Dome has been built on a large tract of previously derelict land on the Greenwich peninsula, an eyesore for more than 20 years. But the regeneration of the area does not stop there. Seven of the most deprived boroughs in the UK surround the Dome site, and current plans also include the construction on adjacent land of 5,000 new homes, a business district, and industrial and retail developments.

The Millennium Experience does not, however, by any means confine itself to London. The NMEC has 12 regional offices throughout the UK whose staff are working with voluntary groups, schools, churches, local authorities and businesses to get everyone involved in the National Programme of activities. For example, over 90,000 schoolchildren have already composed and submitted their songs for the millennium as part of a unique music project called Voices of Promise, sponsored by Marks & Spencer. The same company is supporting an imaginative fundraising campaign, called the Children's Promise, in which the nation's workforce is being asked to give the value of their final hour's earnings of this millennium to help the children of the next. The idea is being taken up around the world. Meanwhile, the nationwide Our Town Story project, sponsored by McDonald's, will feature more than 200 British towns in the Dome on different days of the year 2000.

The Millennium Festival

The Millennium Festival Fund is providing £100 million to enable people throughout the UK to celebrate the millennium with a programme of events at national, regional and local level, in partnership with the NMEC. The scale, number and variety of celebrations will be the greatest since the Queen's Silver Jubilee in 1977, and will also include sporting and artistic activities, and religious, charitable and heritage events throughout the year 2000. The Millennium Commission is contributing £25 million towards the Fund, and other National Lottery distributors for 'good causes' (the Arts Councils, Sports Councils, Heritage Lottery Fund and National Lottery Charities Board) are providing the rest.

Many events are planned for the millennium weekend itself. For example, an initiative has been launched to help local communities to light Millennium Beacons at over 2,500 locations. Church bells will ring all around the UK and many churches will be floodlit. Some of the largest celebrations will be in the four capitals and other major cities.

- The focus of Liverpool's New Year's Eve event is to be the Pier Head, by the Royal Liver building, where there will be a large-scale musical festival with special lighting and laser displays. The River of Light Initiative will illuminate prominent buildings on both sides of the river, constructing light and water bridges across the Mersey and staging 'light spectaculars' with water screens in docks near the millennium eve parties.

- The 'Millennium Dawn' will launch Dundee's year-long millennial celebrations on hogmanay (New Year's Eve). A laser-lit *son et lumière* depicting Dundee's heritage will herald the year 2000, and live entertainments are planned throughout the city centre. A week-long festival will follow, featuring performances from a complete cross-section of the community—including schoolchildren, disabled groups and ethnic minorities.

- The centrepiece of Swansea's first weekend celebrations will be a Bio-Diversity Carnival as part of the Green Futures Eco-Festival, which will comprise demonstration projects and exhibits. Costumes, masks and giant puppets depicting plants, animals and habitats are being made by volunteers and schools, with help from local artists, for a procession through the city centre on New Year's Eve, accompanied by a firework display.

- Londonderry/Derry City Council in Northern Ireland is planning a two-day city-wide outdoor extravaganza to mark the first weekend of the third millennium. The city's chosen theme ('Derry—Londonderry 2000 Living Our Lives') will be reflected in a range of events involving local, national and international figures, and will include a cross-border dimension with the Irish Republic. Beacons will be lit throughout the Council area, culminating in 'a procession of light' to the city's famous 17th century city walls.

Millennium Awards

The Millennium Commission has allocated £200 million for a scheme to provide individuals with bursaries that will allow them to fulfil a personal aspiration while bringing benefit to their local communities. On successful completion of their project, they become members of the Millennium Awards Fellowship.

The awards, ranging from about £2,000 to £15,000, are made through organisations with a strong track record in grant-making. These organisations are known as Millennium Award Partners. By June 1999, £60 million had been offered to 57 schemes, offering opportunities to 20,000 individuals across the UK. In June alone over 4,000 individuals were taking part in schemes promoting, among other things, science and technology, the arts, conservation, health, education and religious understanding. Awards have been given to set up a community radio station, for instance, drama workshops, pond construction, a bowls project, and research into contemporary attitudes about, and knowledge of, Islam. By the year 2004 more than 40,000 people will have participated in one of over 100 award schemes. So far the youngest award winner has been 12 years old and the oldest 92. Among other examples:

- A couple from Louth in Lincolnshire both received a £3,300 Arthritis Care Millennium Volunteer Award. The awards enabled them to participate in a unique training programme to learn how to self-manage their arthritis. Having completed their training, they are now helping others by taking them through the same course, which includes relaxation techniques and other ways of overcoming the difficulties of living with arthritis.

- A local development officer from Alloway in South Ayrshire received an award of £2,605 through the Millennium Forest for Scotland Millennium Awards. First of all she engaged young people in woodland and environmental issues by exploring traditional tales of woodlands and trees. She then helped them to use multimedia and theatre workshop techniques to present the information they had gathered to the local community in Dalmellington, through performances at local community groups and schools.

- A university lecturer received a Techniquest/PanTecnicon Millennium Award of £10,170 to create posters for display by bus companies operating in Cardiff that would stimulate passengers' interest in science. Having been inspired by the successful 'Poems on the Underground' poster campaign in London, he designed a number of posters which intrigued bus passengers with their eye-catching information about the science behind topics which were already familiar to them.

- An international computer systems analyst from Enniskillen has received an award of £2,950 through the Building Sustainable Communities Millennium Award Scheme. She wants to create a community-led organisation committed to redeveloping a sense of identity for Enniskillen and creating a vision for its future. She will set up a preliminary website, distribute flyers, hold presentations and convene three open meetings to discuss her proposals across the communities living in the town.

Capital Projects

By September 1999 the Millennium Commission had awarded grants totalling £1.26 billion to 187 capital projects at 3,037 sites across the UK. These range from village greens and community halls in rural locations around the country, to major flagship projects such as the new national stadiums in Scotland and Wales, and the new Tate Gallery in Bankside, London. Nearly everyone in the UK lives within about 30 miles (48 kilometres) of the site of a millennium capital project. The following are examples of larger projects, one from each country:

The Norfolk and Norwich Millennium Project

Total cost £61 million; Millennium Commission grant £30 million
This project links three facilities—a Millennium Library, a Business and Learning Centre and a Heritage Attraction—around a new urban square, creating a major new civic meeting place within the historic city centre of Norwich. The complex will also include a multimedia auditorium, a learning shop and a range of café bars and restaurants.

Millennium Link, Forth & Clyde and Union Canals

Total cost £78.4 million; Millennium Commission grant £32.2 million
This project will reopen the Forth & Clyde Canal and the Union Canal to navigation, linking not only Scotland's major east and west coast rivers, but also the cities of Glasgow and Edinburgh. Obstacles such as infilled sections and low bridges will be removed, locks refurbished and a transfer mechanism, the Millennium Wheel, will be built to allow boats to pass between the two canals at Falkirk.

The National Botanic Garden of Wales

Total cost £43.4 million; Millennium Commission grant £21.7 million
A national botanic garden and research centre for Wales is to be developed on a 230-hectare (570-acre) site on the Middleton Hall estate at Llandeilo in Dyfed. It will be dedicated to the protection of threatened plant species and will be a centre of international significance. The project is backed by a consortium of public and private organisations and individuals.

The Odyssey Project, Belfast

Total cost £90 million; Millennium Commission grant £45 million
This project will provide a mixture of education, entertainment and sporting facilities, including the Science Centre, the IMAX (a two- and three-dimensional film theatre), an indoor arena, pavilion and public open space. It will be the first major development on the east side of the river Lagan in Belfast and is seen as a catalyst for future regeneration.

Websites

Millennium Commission: www.millennium.gov.uk
New Millennium Experience Company: www.dome2000.co.uk
British Tourist Authority: www.visitbritain.com

1 Introduction

The establishment in 1999 of the Scottish Parliament, the National Assembly for Wales and (subject to the outcome of a formal Implementation Review) the Northern Ireland Assembly, is bringing about the most significant change in the constitution in the United Kingdom since its formation in 1801.[1] In addition, eight new Regional Development Agencies have been set up in England while a separate development agency for London will be formed under the Greater London Authority in 2000.

Physical Features

The United Kingdom (UK) constitutes the greater part of the British Isles. The largest of the islands is Great Britain, which comprises England, Scotland and Wales. The next largest comprises Northern Ireland, which is part of the UK, and the Irish Republic. Western Scotland is fringed by the large island chains known as the Inner and Outer Hebrides, and to the north east of the Scottish mainland are the Orkney and Shetland Islands. All these, along with the Isle of Wight, Anglesey and the Isles of Scilly, have administrative ties with the mainland, but the Isle of Man in the Irish Sea and the Channel Islands between Great Britain and France are largely self-governing, and are not part of the United Kingdom. The UK is one of the 15 member states of the European Union (EU).

With an area of about 243,000 sq km (93,000 sq miles), excluding inland water, the United Kingdom is just under 1,000 km (about 600 miles) from the south coast to the extreme north of Scotland and just under 500 km (around 300 miles) across at the widest point.

The population of the UK increased from 38.2 million in 1901 to 59.2 million in 1998.

Channel Islands and Isle of Man

Although the Channel Islands and the Isle of Man are not part of the United Kingdom, they have a special relationship with it. The Channel Islands were part of the Duchy of Normandy in the 10th and 11th centuries and remained subject to the English Crown after the loss of mainland Normandy to the French in 1204. The Isle of Man was under the nominal sovereignty of Norway until 1266, and eventually came under the direct administration of the British Crown in 1765, when it was bought for £70,000. Its parliament, 'Tynwald', was established more

---

[1] When the UK was the United Kingdom of Great Britain and *Ireland*. The Irish Free State (now the Irish Republic) was created in 1922, leaving Northern Ireland in the Union. The devolution of political power in 1999 is discussed in greater detail in chapters 2, 3, 4, 5 and 6.

Table 1.1: Area and Population of the Four Countries of the United Kingdom, mid-1998

	Area (sq km)[a]	Population (million)	Population density (people per sq km)
England	130,395	49.5	380
Scotland	78,313	5.1	65
Wales	20,754	2.9	141
Northern Ireland	13,843	1.7	122
United Kingdom	**243,305**	**59.2**	**243**

Source: Office for National Statistics
[a] Including inland water, with some exceptions in Scotland and Northern Ireland.

Table 1.2: Area and Population of some Islands around the United Kingdom, 1996

Island	Area (sq km)	Population	Population density (people per sq km)
England			
Isle of Wight	380	125,000	328
Isles of Scilly	15	2,000	124
Wales			
Anglesey (Ynys Môn)	714	67,000	94
Scotland			
Eilean Siar (Western Isles)	3,134	29,000[a]	9
Shetland Islands	1,438	23,000	16
Orkney Islands	992	20,000	20
Skye[b]	1,676	8,800	5
Bute[b]	124	7,400	60
Arran[b]	431	4,500	10
Islay[b]	615	3,500	6
Mull[b]	918	2,700	3
Channel Islands[c]			
Jersey	116	85,000	734
Guernsey	63	59,000	928
Isle of Man	573	72,000	125

Sources: Office for National Statistics, General Register Office for Scotland, Guernsey Economics and Statistics Department, Isle of Man Tourist Office
[a] Of which Lewis and Harris accounted for nearly three-quarters.
[b] 1991 data.
[c] Of the other Channel Islands, Alderney had a population of 2,147, Sark about 650, Herm 97 and Jethou 3.

than 1,000 years ago and is the oldest legislature in continuous existence in the world. Today the territories have their own legislative assemblies and systems of law, and their own taxation systems. The British Government is responsible for their international relations and external defence.

The relationship of the Channel Islands and the Isle of Man with the EU is limited to trading rights only. Rules on customs matters

- Highest mountain: Ben Nevis, in the Highlands of Scotland, 1,343 m (4,406 ft)
- Longest river: the Severn, 354 km (220 miles) long, which rises in central Wales and flows through Shrewsbury, Worcester and Gloucester in England to the Bristol Channel
- Largest lake: Lough Neagh, Northern Ireland, 396 sq km (153 sq miles)
- Deepest lake: Loch Morar in the Highlands of Scotland, 310 m (1,017 ft) deep
- Highest waterfall: Eas a'Chual Aluinn, from Glas Bheinn, also in the Highlands of Scotland, with a drop of 200 m (660 ft)
- Deepest cave: Ogof Ffynnon Ddu, Wales, 308 m (1,010 ft) deep
- Most northerly point on the British mainland: Dunnet Head, north-east Scotland
- Most southerly point on the British mainland: Lizard Point, Cornwall
- Closest point to mainland continental Europe: Dover, Kent. The Channel Tunnel, which links England and France, is a little over 50 km (31 miles) long, of which nearly 38 km (24 miles) are actually under the English Channel.

apply to the Islands under the same conditions as they apply to the UK. However, the free movement of persons and services within the EU as a whole only extends to the Islanders if they have close ties with the UK, although they do still enjoy their traditional rights in the UK.

Climate and Wildlife

The climate in the United Kingdom is generally mild and temperate. Prevailing winds are south-westerly and the weather from day to day is mainly influenced by depressions and their associated fronts moving eastwards across the Atlantic, punctuated by settled, fine, anticyclonic periods of a few days to weeks. In general, there are few extremes of temperature; it rarely rises above 32°C (90°F) or falls below –10°C (14°F). However, as with other countries, the UK has experienced unusual weather in recent years—for example, the period between summer 1995 and winter 1997 was the driest in England and Wales since weather records began in the 18th century, while April 1998 was the wettest since 1818.

Average annual rainfall is more than 1,600 mm (over 60 inches) in the mountainous areas of the west and north but less than 800 mm (30 inches) over central and eastern parts. Rain is fairly well distributed throughout the year but, on average, March to June are the driest months and September to January the wettest. During May, June and July (the months of longest daylight) the mean daily duration of sunshine varies from five hours in northern Scotland to eight hours in the Isle of Wight. During the months of shortest daylight (November, December and January) sunshine is at a minimum, with an average of an hour a day in northern Scotland and two hours a day on the south coast of England.

According to the Hadley Centre for Climate Prediction and Research, global warming may cause annual average UK temperatures to be about 1.5°C warmer by the

Anecdotal evidence of climate change over the past 100 years can be found in such sources as the London County Council Statistics for 1900–01. In the winter of 1899–1900, 'permanent cleansing staff' and other regular employees together spent 37,687 hours of work, and casual labourers 17,792 hours, removing snow from the streets of the London Borough of Wandsworth alone. In recent years snow has rarely settled for long enough in central London to warrant removal. Harder evidence of climate change in the UK comes from the Central England Temperature, an instrument record going back to the mid-18th century, which has shown an increase of about 0.6°C since the last century.

2050s compared with the 1961–90 average (three times the rise between 1881–1910 and 1968–1997). Such an increase could also result in a rise in average sea levels of 25–35 centimetres. A recent report commissioned by Scottish Natural Heritage, taking a 1.8°C rise in average temperature in Scotland by 2100 as one scenario, forecasts that Scottish pine forests will be gradually replaced by oak trees. It suggests that various mountain birds, plants and insects will be threatened by higher temperatures, but some species and habitats will thrive or expand, including lowland flowers, over-wintering birds, bats, butterflies and peat bogs.

The UK is home to a great variety of wildlife, with an estimated 30,000 animal species, as well as marine and microscopic life; about 2,800 species of 'higher' plants; and many thousands of mosses, fungi and algae. However, the unusual weather of recent years—together with changes in farming methods, urban development and other factors—has put pressure on a number of species, such as the song thrush, dormouse and great crested newt, while over 50 different mosses are already thought to be on the verge of extinction. A new £100,000 project launched in February 1999, and run by English Nature and the Royal Botanic Gardens, is aiming to find new ways to halt the decline of these species, both in the wild and through propagation, freezing and culture (see also p. 325).

Historical Outline

The name 'Britain' derives from Greek and Latin names probably stemming from a Celtic original. Although in the prehistoric timescale the Celts were relatively late arrivals in the British Isles, only with them does Britain emerge into recorded history. The term 'Celtic' is often used rather generally to distinguish the early inhabitants of the British Isles from the later Anglo-Saxon invaders.

After two expeditions by Julius Caesar in 55 and 54 BC, contact between Britain and the Roman world grew, culminating in the Roman invasion of AD 43. Roman rule was gradually extended from south-east England to include Wales and, for a time, the lowlands of Scotland. The final Roman withdrawal in 409 followed a period of increasing disorder during which the island began to be raided by Angles, Saxons and Jutes from northern Europe. It is from the Angles that the name 'England' derives. The raids turned into settlement and a number of small English kingdoms were established. The Britons maintained an independent existence in the areas now known as Wales and Cornwall. Among the Anglo-Saxon kingdoms more powerful ones emerged, claiming overlordship of the whole of England, first in the north (Northumbria), then in the midlands (Mercia) and finally in the south (Wessex). However, further raids and settlement by the Vikings from Scandinavia occurred, although in the 10th century the Wessex dynasty defeated the invading Danes and established a wide-ranging authority in England. In 1066 England was invaded by the Normans (see p. 7), who then settled along with others from France.

Dates of some of the main events in Britain's history are given below. The early histories of England, Wales, Scotland and Northern Ireland are included in chapters 2 to 5.

Significant Dates

55 and 54 BC: Julius Caesar's expeditions to Britain

AD 43: Roman conquest begins under Claudius

122–38: Hadrian's Wall built

c.409: Roman army withdraws from Britain

450s onwards: foundation of the Anglo-Saxon kingdoms

597: arrival of St Augustine to preach Christianity to the Anglo-Saxons

664: Synod of Whitby opts for Roman Catholic rather than Celtic church

789–95: first Viking raids

832–60: Scots and Picts merge under Kenneth Macalpin to form what is to become the kingdom of Scotland

Population Density, 1997

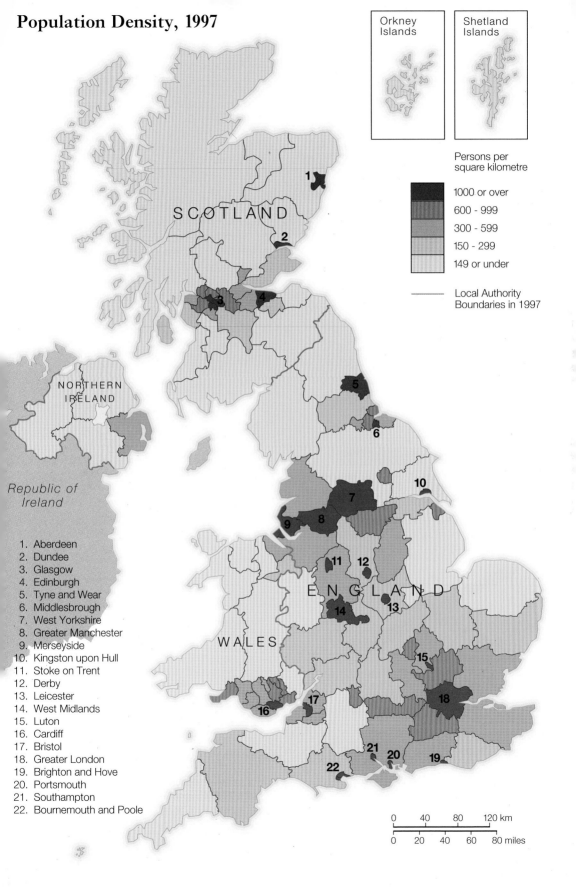

Orkney
Islands

Shetland
Islands

Persons per
square kilometre

- 1000 or over
- 600 - 999
- 300 - 599
- 150 - 299
- 149 or under

— Local Authority
  Boundaries in 1997

SCOTLAND

NORTHERN
IRELAND

Republic of
Ireland

ENGLAND

WALES

1. Aberdeen
2. Dundee
3. Glasgow
4. Edinburgh
5. Tyne and Wear
6. Middlesbrough
7. West Yorkshire
8. Greater Manchester
9. Merseyside
10. Kingston upon Hull
11. Stoke on Trent
12. Derby
13. Leicester
14. West Midlands
15. Luton
16. Cardiff
17. Bristol
18. Greater London
19. Brighton and Hove
20. Portsmouth
21. Southampton
22. Bournemouth and Poole

| 0 | 40 | 80 | 120 km |

| 0 | 20 | 40 | 60 | 80 miles |

THE UNION FLAG

The flag of the United Kingdom of Great Britain and Northern Ireland is officially called the Union Flag, because it embodies the emblems of three countries united under one Sovereign.
It is commonly known as the Union Jack. The term 'jack' was first used in the Royal Navy during the 17th century to describe the Union Flag, a little smaller than the other ensigns worn by ships at that time, which was flown at the main masthead of a ship.

The Union Flag

The emblems that appear on the Union Flag are the crosses of three patron saints:

the red cross of St George, for England, on a white ground;

the white diagonal cross or saltire of St Andrew, for Scotland, on a blue ground; and

the red diagonal cross attributed to St Patrick, for Ireland, on a white ground.

Wales is not represented in the Union Flag
because when the first version of the flag appeared, Wales was already united with England.

The first Union Flag, in 1606, combined the national flag of England –
the cross of St George – and that of Scotland – the cross of St Andrew.

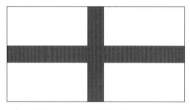

The cross of St George

The cross of St Andrew

The cross of St Patrick

The final version of the Union Flag appeared in 1801, following the union of Great Britain with Ireland, with the inclusion of the cross of St Patrick.
The cross remains in the flag although now only Northern Ireland is part of the United Kingdom; southern Ireland is a separate republic.

The national flag of Wales, a red dragon on a field of white and green, dates from the 15th century, and is in widespread use throughout the Principality.

The Welsh flag

DEVOLUTION

Scottish Parliament
The new Scottish Parliament is initially meeting in the
General Assembly Hall of the Church of Scotland in Edinburgh.
Holyrood, at the foot of Edinburgh's Royal Mile, will be the
Parliament's permanent site (see p. 22).

National Assembly for Wales
The temporary home of the National Assembly for Wales in Cardiff Bay—
a new assembly building next to the present one is due to open in 2001
(see p. 29).

UK Postal Areas

Orkney Islands

KW

Shetland Islands

ZE

L	Liverpool	PL	Plymouth
LA	Lancaster	PO	Portsmouth
LD	Llandrindod Wells	PR	Preston
LE	Leicester	RG	Reading
LL	Llandudno	RH	Redhill
LN	Lincoln	RM	Romford
LS	Leeds	S	Sheffield
LU	Luton	SA	Swansea
M	Manchester	SE	London South East
ME	Medway	SG	Stevenage
MK	Milton Keynes	SK	Stockport
ML	Motherwell	SL	Slough
N	London North	SM	Sutton
NE	Newcastle-upon-Tyne	SN	Swindon
NG	Nottingham	SO	Southampton
NN	Northampton	SP	Salisbury
NP	Newport	SR	Sunderland
NR	Norwich	SS	Southend-on-Sea
NW	London North West	ST	Stoke-on-Trent
OL	Oldham	SW	London South West
OX	Oxford	SY	Shrewsbury
PA	Paisley	TA	Taunton
PE	Peterborough	TD	Galashiels
PH	Perth	TF	Telford
		TN	Tonbridge
		TQ	Torquay
		TR	Truro
		TS	Cleveland
		TW	Twickenham
		UB	Southall
		W	London West
		WA	Warrington
		WC	London West Central
		WD	Watford
		WF	Wakefield
		WN	Wigan
		WR	Worcester
		WS	Walsall
		WV	Wolverhampton
		YO	York
		ZE	Lerwick

AB	Aberdeen	E	London East
AL	St Albans	EC	London East Central
B	Birmingham	EH	Edinburgh
BA	Bath	EN	Enfield
BB	Blackburn	EX	Exeter
BD	Bradford	FK	Falkirk
BH	Bournemouth	FY	Blackpool
BL	Bolton	G	Glasgow
BN	Brighton	GL	Gloucester
BR	Bromley	GU	Guildford
BS	Bristol	HA	Harrow
BT	Belfast	HD	Huddersfield
CA	Carlisle	HG	Harrogate
CB	Cambridge	HP	Hemel Hempstead
CF	Cardiff	HR	Hereford
CH	Chester	HS	Outer Hebrides
CM	Chelmsford	HU	Hull
CO	Colchester	HX	Halifax
CR	Croydon	IG	Ilford
CT	Canterbury	IM	Isle of Man
CV	Coventry	IP	Ipswich
CW	Crewe	IV	Inverness
DA	Dartford	KA	Kilmarnock
DD	Dundee	KT	Kingston-upon-Thames
DE	Derby	KW	Kirkwall
DG	Dumfries	KY	Kirkcaldy
DH	Durham		
DL	Darlington		
DN	Doncaster		
DT	Dorchester		
DY	Dudley		

Central London Area

860s: Danes overrun East Anglia, Northumbria and eastern Mercia
871–99: reign of Alfred the Great in Wessex
1066: William the Conqueror defeats Harold Godwinson at Hastings and takes the throne
1086: *Domesday Book* completed: a survey of English landholdings undertaken on the orders of William I
c.1136–39: Geoffrey of Monmouth completes *The History of the Kings of Britain*
1215: King John signs Magna Carta to protect feudal rights against royal abuse
13th century: first Oxford and Cambridge colleges founded
1301: Edward of Caernarvon (later Edward II) created Prince of Wales
1314: Battle of Bannockburn ensures survival of separate Scottish kingdom
1337: Hundred Years War between England and France begins
1348–49: Black Death (bubonic plague) wipes out a third of England's population
1381: Peasants' Revolt in England, the most significant popular rebellion in English history
c.1387–c.1394: Geoffrey Chaucer writes *The Canterbury Tales*
1400–c.1406: Owain Glyndŵr (Owen Glendower) leads the last major Welsh revolt against English rule
1411: St Andrews University founded, the first university in Scotland
1455–87: Wars of the Roses between Yorkists and Lancastrians
1477: first book to be printed in England, by William Caxton
1534–40: English Reformation; Henry VIII breaks with the Papacy
1536–42: Acts of Union integrate England and Wales administratively and legally and give Wales representation in Parliament
1547–53: Protestantism becomes official religion in England under Edward VI
1553–58: Catholic reaction under Mary I
1558: loss of Calais, last English possession in France
1588: defeat of Spanish Armada
1558–1603: reign of Elizabeth I; moderate Protestantism established

c.1590–c.1613: plays of Shakespeare written
1603: union of the crowns of Scotland and England under James VI of Scotland
1642–51: Civil Wars between King and Parliament
1649: execution of Charles I
1653–58: Oliver Cromwell rules as Lord Protector
1660: monarchy restored under Charles II
1660: founding of the Royal Society for the Promotion of Natural Knowledge
1663: John Milton finishes *Paradise Lost*
1665: the Great Plague, the last major epidemic of plague in England
1666: the Great Fire of London
1686: Isaac Newton sets out his laws of motion and the idea of universal gravitation
1688: Glorious Revolution; accession of William and Mary
1707: Acts of Union unite the English and Scottish Parliaments
1721–42: Robert Walpole, first British Prime Minister
1745–46: Bonnie Prince Charlie's failed attempt to retake the British throne for the Stuarts
c.1760s–c.1830s: Industrial Revolution
1761: opening of the Bridgewater Canal ushers in Canal Age
1775–83: American War of Independence leads to loss of the Thirteen Colonies
1801: Act of Union unites Great Britain and Ireland
1805: Battle of Trafalgar, the decisive naval battle of the Napoleonic Wars
1815: Battle of Waterloo, the final defeat of Napoleon
1825: opening of the Stockton and Darlington Railway, the world's first passenger railway
1829: Catholic emancipation
1832: first Reform Act extends the franchise (increasing the number of those entitled to vote by about 50%)
1833: abolition of slavery in the British Empire (the slave *trade* having been abolished in 1807)
1836–70: Charles Dickens writes his novels
1837–1901: reign of Queen Victoria
1859: Charles Darwin publishes *On the Origin of Species by Means of Natural Selection*

1868: founding of the Trades Union Congress (TUC)
1907: Henry Royce and C.S. Rolls build and sell their first Rolls-Royce (the Silver Ghost)
1910–36: during the reign of George V, the British Empire reaches its territorial zenith
1914–18: First World War
1918: the vote given to women over 30
1921: Anglo-Irish Treaty establishes the Irish Free State; Northern Ireland remains part of the United Kingdom
1926: John Logie Baird gives the first practical demonstration of television
1928: voting age for women reduced to 21, on equal terms with men
1928: Alexander Fleming discovers penicillin
1936: Jarrow Crusade, the most famous of the hunger marches in the 1930s
1939–45: Second World War
1943: Max Newman, Donald Michie, Tommy Flowers and Alan Turing build the first electronic computer, Colossus I, which was used for breaking enemy communications codes in the Second World War
1947: independence for India and Pakistan: Britain begins to dismantle its imperial structure

1948: the National Health Service comes into operation, offering free medical care to the whole population
1952: accession of Elizabeth II
1953: Francis Crick and his colleague James Watson of the United States discover the structure of DNA
1965: first commercial natural gas discovery in the North Sea, by the British Petroleum Company
1969: first notable discovery of offshore oil in the North Sea
1973: the UK enters the European Community (now the European Union)
1979–90: Margaret Thatcher, the UK's first woman Prime Minister
1994: Channel Tunnel opened to rail traffic
1997: General Election: the Labour Party returns to power with its largest ever parliamentary majority
1999: Scottish Parliament and National Assembly for Wales assume their devolved powers, while a formal Implementation Review to give devolved powers to the Northern Ireland Assembly begins

Further Reading

Annual Publications

Annual Abstract of Statistics, Office for National Statistics. The Stationery Office.
Regional Trends, Office for National Statistics. The Stationery Office.
Social Trends, Office for National Statistics. The Stationery Office.

Websites
Office for National Statistics: www.ons.gov.uk
Government Statistical Service: www.statistics.gov.uk
The Meteorological Office: www.met-office.gov.uk

2 England

England is predominantly a lowland country, although there are upland regions in the north (the Pennine Chain, the Cumbrian mountains and the Yorkshire moorlands) and in the South West (in Cornwall, Devon and Somerset). The greatest concentrations of population are in London and the South East, South and West Yorkshire, Greater Manchester and Merseyside, the West Midlands conurbation, and the north-east conurbations on the rivers Tyne and Tees. England's population is expected to rise from 49.9 million in 2001 to 52.5 million in 2021.

Early History

The name 'England' is derived from the Angles, one of the Germanic tribes which established monarchies in lowland Britain in the 5th century, after the final withdrawal of the Romans in 409. The Anglo-Saxon kingdoms were initially fairly small and numerous, but gradually larger entities emerged. Eventually Wessex came to dominate, following its leading role in resisting the Danish invasions of the 9th century. Athelstan (924–39) used the title of 'King of all Britain', and from 954 there was a single Kingdom of England. The present Royal Family is descended from the old royal house of Wessex.

In 1066 the last successful invasion of England took place. Duke William of Normandy defeated the English at the Battle of Hastings and became King William I. Many Normans and others from France came to settle; French became the language of the nobility for the next three centuries; and the legal and social structures were influenced by those prevailing across the Channel.

When Henry II, originally from Anjou, was king (1154–89), his 'Angevin empire' stretched from the river Tweed on the Scottish border, down through much of France to the Pyrenees. However, almost all the English Crown's possessions in France, after alternating periods of expansion and contraction, were finally lost during the late Middle Ages.

England and Wales were integrated administratively and legally in 1536–42 during the reign of Henry VIII, and the union of England and Scotland took place in 1707, when Queen Anne was Sovereign.

Government

In contrast to Wales, Scotland and Northern Ireland, England has no separate elected national body or a department exclusively

England: Counties and Unitary Authorities, since April 1998

Counties

Unitary Authorities

D   Darlington
H   Hartlepool
M   Middlesbrough
RC   Redcar and Cleveland
ST   Stockton-on-Tees

Bn   Blackburn
Bpl Blackpool
H   Halton
W   Warrington
S   Stoke-on-Trent

De   Derby
KH Kingston upon Hull
Lr   Leicester
NEL North East Lincolnshire
Nt   Nottingham
Pe   Peterborough
R   Rutland

B   City of Bristol
BS Bath and North East Somerset
NS North Somerset
SG South Gloucestershire
Sw Swindon

L   Luton
MK Milton Keynes
Mtn Medway Towns
SS Southend-on-Sea
Tk   Thurrock

BF   Bracknell Forest
BH Brighton and Hove
Po   Portsmouth
Re   Reading
Sl   Slough
So   Southampton
W   Wokingham
WM Windsor and Maidenhead

Bo   Bournemouth
Pl   Poole
Py   Plymouth
Ty   Torbay

responsible for its central administration. Instead, there are a number of government departments, whose responsibilities in some cases also cover aspects of affairs in Wales and Scotland (see Appendix 1). A network of nine Government Offices for the Regions (GOs— see p. 10) is responsible for the implementation of several government programmes in the English regions.

There are 529 English parliamentary constituencies represented in the House of Commons. After the General Election of May 1997, England had 328 Labour Members of Parliament (MPs), 165 Conservative, 34 Liberal Democrat and one independent.[1] By August 1999 there had been six by-elections, but in each case the political party that had been representing the constituency retained the seat. Conservative support tends to be strongest in suburban and rural areas, and the party has a large number of parliamentary seats in the southern half of England. The Labour Party has tended in the past to derive its main support from the big cities and areas associated with traditional industry, but it won many seats in the last General Election that had previously been considered safe Conservative constituencies. The Liberal Democrats, who are traditionally strong in the South West, now have a third of their 34 English seats in Greater London and the South East.

Local government is administered in many areas through a two-tier system of county and district councils. However, there are also a number of single–tier, or unitary, authorities—especially in the larger cities.

England elects 71 representatives (MEPs) to the European Parliament (see p. 70). In the June 1999 election, the Conservatives won 33 seats, Labour 24, the Liberal Democrats nine, the UK Independence Party three and the Green Party two.

The English legal system comprises on the one hand a historic body of conventions known as 'common law' and 'equity', and, on the other, parliamentary and European Community legislation ('statute law'). In the formulation of common law since the Norman Conquest, great reliance has been placed on precedent. Equity law—law outside the scope of the common law or statute law—derives from the practice of petitioning the Lord Chancellor in cases not covered by common law.

The Church of England, which was separated from the Roman Catholic Church at the time of the Reformation in the early 16th century, is the Established Church (that is, the official religion of England). The Sovereign must always be a member of the Church and appoints its two archbishops and 42 other diocesan bishops (see p. 240).

A London Mayor and Assembly

In a referendum in 1998, 72% of those who voted said yes to having a directly elected Mayor for the capital, and a separately elected assembly of 25 members.[2] The Mayor and Assembly will form a new Greater London Authority (GLA), the first elected London-wide body since the Greater London Council was abolished in 1986.

The first elections for the Mayor and Assembly will be on 4 May 2000, and the GLA will assume its responsibilities on 3 July 2000, subject to parliamentary approval. Thereafter, elections will take place every four years. The GLA will not duplicate the work of the boroughs, but will have responsibility for London-wide issues: transport, economic development, strategic planning, culture, health, the environment, the police, fire and emergency planning. It will be housed in a new building to be constructed on a 'brownfield' (that is, previously developed) site between London Bridge and Tower Bridge, on the south bank of the river Thames.

---

[1] The Speaker of the House of Commons, who presides over the debates there (see p. 43), traditionally does not vote along party lines and so is not counted towards the strength of the party for which he or she was originally elected. The independent MP is the former journalist Martin Bell, who won what had been the safe Conservative seat of Tatton in Cheshire.

[2] Of the 25 members, 14 will represent constituencies covering two or more London boroughs; the rest will be 'London-wide Members' divided among the political parties according to their share of the vote for these 11 seats. The new arrangements will not affect the continuance of the separate post of Lord Mayor of London (first established in 1191), whose role is restricted to the City of London, the financial 'Square Mile' at the heart of the capital.

Four other administrative bodies will come into being at the same time as the GLA, and will be accountable to it: a new Metropolitan Police Authority; the London Fire and Emergency Planning Authority; Transport for London; and the London Development Agency, one of nine regional agencies covering the whole of England.

> Work is starting during 1999 on construction of the first footbridge (for pedestrians *only*) across the river Thames probably since Roman times. The 'Millennium Bridge' will span the river from St Paul's steps on the north bank to the new Tate Gallery of Modern Art at Bankside on the south bank. It is expected to open in April 2000.

The Regions of England

The Government wishes to see a more accountable system of regional government in England where there is demand for this. Eight of the nine Regional Development Agencies (RDAs) in England have now been created under the Regional Development Agencies Act 1998 (see p. 11) and the London Development Agency will be established as part of the arrangements for the Greater London Authority. Regional chambers—working within the present democratic structure—will provide a measure of regional responsiveness in what RDAs do and will help build up the voice of the regions and enhance regional identities. The first eight chambers were designated between May and July 1999.

The economic performance of the nine English regions (see map), and subregions within them, varies quite considerably. For example, Inner London had the highest average gross domestic product (GDP) per head in 1994–96 in the European Union (EU), even though it also contains some of the worst pockets of deprivation in the UK. On the other hand, in March 1999 South Yorkshire and Cornwall and the Scilly Isles qualified for the highest level of European funding ('Objective 1'—see p. 395)[3] because their GDP per head

---

[3] Merseyside was already an Objective 1 area and remains so.

Regions of England Covered by the Regional Development Agencies and Government Offices for the Regions (GOs)

was less than 75% of the EU average. According to the latest figures, total household disposable income per head in 1996 was above the England average in London, the South East and East; and the same three regions had the highest gross hourly earnings for full-time employees in 1998. The North East had the lowest disposable income and hourly earnings, as well as the lowest GDP per head, in 1997, for a whole region (as opposed to a subregion).

Some of the consequences of economic success in the wealthier English regions are higher residential and industrial property prices, and higher rental costs for offices. Average journey times to work are far longer in London than elsewhere, ranging from 30 minutes in Outer London to 55 minutes into Central London, compared with an average in Great Britain of just 24 minutes. In autumn 1997 the number of people entering Central London between 7.00 a.m. and 10.00 a.m. on each working day was nearly 1.1 million, a 5% increase on the previous year. Of those working in Central London, 76% used public transport, compared with the average of 13% for Great Britain as a whole.

Regional Development Agencies

The RDAs aim to improve the economic performance and competitiveness of the English regions and tailor national policies to regional needs. Among other things, they are bringing together the regional regeneration work previously carried out by English Partnerships and the Rural Development Commission (see pp. 356–7), and by the GOs, and are responsible for co-ordinating inward investment in their own regions.

RDAs are accountable through ministers to Parliament. Their boards of around 12 members, plus chairman, are business-led, but also reflect the broad range of groups that have an interest in the regional economy. Four positions on each board are filled by local councillors and one by a leading trade unionist. In addition, RDAs are required to take account of the views of new voluntary regional chambers in preparing their strategies and corporate plans, and to give them an account of their activities. The combined budget for the eight RDAs operating in 1999–2000 is £967 million, although their initiatives are also expected to attract private finance.

The Agencies are required to prepare their first strategies by October 1999. These should show how they are going to develop an integrated and *sustainable* approach to increasing business competitiveness and productivity, and to addressing the underlying problems in their regions of unemployment, skills shortages, inequalities, social exclusion and environmental decay.

Rural Areas

There are over 16,700 rural towns, villages and hamlets in England with populations of 10,000 or fewer.[4] According to this definition, one in five people live in a rural area. Over three-quarters of rural settlements have populations of under 500. In many respects, the rural economy is vibrant and healthy. Although small firms dominate the rural economy, where larger firms do exist, local employment is particularly vulnerable to any

downturn in their performance: larger companies comprise just 1.4% of rural firms, but account for 31% of employment. Earnings are generally low. National policies such as the New Deals for the unemployed and the national minimum wage are intended to help tackle these problems. As elsewhere in the country, the advances in telecommunications are allowing more people in isolated areas to work from home.

Car ownership is greater in rural households (84%) than nationally (69%), but it needs to be, since the countryside often lacks services that urban dwellers take for granted.

The comparative lack of public transport, of such importance for access to other services, is one of the issues which the Government is particularly keen to address. In 1998 it allocated an extra £150 million over three years to improve rural transport in the UK as a whole. A further £10 million a year for the next two years was announced in the 1999 Budget. By April 1999 the first £50 million of funding had already led to the creation of over 550 new, and 700 enhanced, rural bus services in England. The provision of some other services, such as childcare facilities, has also improved, and the Government is increasingly ensuring that the rural dimension is fully reflected in its wider policy-making—in its preparation, for example, of a White Paper on the future of rural England.

The Environment

Despite its high population density and degree of urbanisation, England has many unspoilt rural and coastal areas. There are eight National Parks (including the Norfolk Broads), nine forest parks, 37 designated Areas of Outstanding Natural Beauty, 22 Environmentally Sensitive Areas, over 200 country parks recognised by the Countryside Agency, and more than 1,043 km (648 miles) of designated heritage coastline. At the end of March 1999, there were 197 National Nature Reserves, 612 Local Nature Reserves and 4,045 Sites of Special Scientific Interest. (See also chapter 20.)

---

[4] The data in this section come from the Countryside Agency (see p. 319).

Table 2.1: Population and Population Density Mid-1997

GO[a]	Population	Area (sq km)[b]	People per sq km	% change in population, 1981–97
North East	2,594,364	8,528	304	−1.6
North West and Merseyside	6,884,632	14,014	491	−0.8
Yorkshire and the Humber	5,036,980	15,319	329	2.4
East Midlands	4,156,346	15,507	268	7.9
West Midlands	5,320,784	12,932	411	2.6
East	5,334,204	19,087	279	9.9
London	7,122,171	1,560	4,565	4.7
South East	7,958,788	18,962	420	9.8
South West	4,875,973	23,712	206	11.3
England	**49,284,242**	**129,621**	**380**	**5.3**

Source: *Regional Trends*, Office for National Statistics

[a] The region in England covered by each regional Government Office.

[b] Excluding inland water.

Since 1996 the Countryside Character initiative has been mapping the landscape character of the whole English countryside, not just those parts of it that have special protection. The countryside has been divided into 159 separate, distinctive character areas, and these are described in detail in eight regional volumes that are being published by the Countryside Agency. The purpose of this work is to enable proper account of the widely varying character of England's countryside to be taken in all decisions, national and local, which should lead to far more sustainable management of the English landscape.

Culture

London and the other large cities have a wealth of cultural centres, including major art galleries, renowned museums, theatres, ballet and opera houses, and concert halls. Many theatres outside London are used for touring by the national theatre, dance and opera companies. Popular culture also thrives in England, as elsewhere in Britain: there are numerous kinds of pop music, theatre styles such as pantomime and musicals, jazz festivals and performances by comedians. Safari, wildlife and theme parks all offer family activities and entertainment. A proportion of the proceeds from the National Lottery (see p. 122) is allocated to arts projects, which are also featuring strongly in the millennial celebrations (see pp. ix–xii).

Many regions and towns have associations with great English writers, artists and musicians: such as Stratford-upon-Avon (William Shakespeare), the Lake District (William Wordsworth), Stoke-on-Trent (Arnold Bennett), Haworth (the Brontë sisters) and Dorset (Thomas Hardy); Essex and Suffolk (John Constable) and Salford (L.S. Lowry); and Worcestershire (Edward Elgar), Aldeburgh (Benjamin Britten) and Liverpool (The Beatles).

Further Reading

Regional Trends (annual publication), Office for National Statistics. The Stationery Office.

Regional Competitiveness Indicators, Department of Trade and Industry, 1999.

3 Northern Ireland

About half of the 1.7 million people in Northern Ireland live in the eastern coastal region, the centre of which is the capital, Belfast. Northern Ireland is, at its nearest point, only 21 km (13 miles) from Scotland. It has a 488-km (303-mile) border with the Irish Republic. A comprehensive agreement on a political settlement for Northern Ireland—the Good Friday Agreement—was reached in April 1998 and a referendum held the following month which endorsed its proposals. Elections to a new Northern Ireland Assembly took place in June and it met for the first time in July 1998. Efforts to achieve the full implementation of the agreement are continuing.

The Northern Ireland Continuous Household Survey (CHS)[1] reported that 54% of the population regarded themselves as Protestants and 42% as Roman Catholics. Most of the Protestants are descendants of Scots or English settlers who crossed to north-eastern Ireland; they are British by culture and have traditionally been committed to remaining part of the UK. The Roman Catholic population is mainly Irish by culture and history, and many are nationalist in political aspiration, favouring union with the Irish Republic. Northern Ireland has a younger population with proportionately more children and fewer pensioners than any other region in the UK.

---

[1] Northern Ireland Statistics and Research Agency: CHS sample 1995–96 to 1997–98.

History

During the 10th century Ireland was dominated by the Vikings. In 1169 Henry II of England invaded Ireland, having been granted its overlordship by the English Pope Adrian IV, who was anxious to bring the Irish Church into full obedience to Rome. Although a large part of the country came under the control of Anglo-Norman nobles, little direct authority was exercised from England during the Middle Ages.

The Tudor monarchs showed a much greater tendency to intervene in Ireland. During the reign of Elizabeth I, a series of campaigns was waged against Irish insurgents. The main area of resistance was the northern province of Ulster. After the collapse of this resistance in 1607 and the flight of its leaders, Protestant immigrants from Scotland and England settled in Ulster.

Northern Ireland Districts

Cf   Carrickfergus
Cr   Castlereagh
ND   North Down
Nta   Newtownabbey

The English civil wars (1642–51) led to further uprisings in Ireland, which were crushed by Oliver Cromwell. More fighting took place after the overthrow of the Roman Catholic James II in 1688. During the Battle of the Boyne in 1690 the forces of James II, who was trying to regain the throne, starting in Ireland, were defeated by those of the Protestant William of Orange (William III).

Throughout most of the 18th century there was uneasy peace. In 1782 the Irish Parliament (dating from medieval times) was given legislative independence; the only constitutional tie with Great Britain was the Crown. The Parliament, however, represented only the privileged Anglo-Irish minority, and the Roman Catholic majority was excluded from it. Following the abortive rebellion led by Wolfe Tone's United Irishmen movement in 1798, Ireland was unified with Great Britain under the 1800 Act of Union. The Irish Parliament was abolished in 1801 and Irish members sat in both Houses of the Westminster Parliament.

The Irish question was one of the major issues of British politics during the 19th century. In 1886 the Liberal Government introduced a Home Rule Bill designed to give a new Irish Parliament devolved authority over most internal matters while Britain maintained control over foreign and defence policy. This failed as did a second Bill introduced in 1893.

The issue returned to the political agenda in 1910 because the Liberal Government was dependent for its political survival on support from the pro-Home Rule Irish Parliamentary Party. The controversy intensified as unionists and nationalists in Ireland formed private armies. In 1914 Home Rule was approved in the Government of Ireland Act. Implementation, however, was suspended by the outbreak of the First World War.

A nationalist rising in Dublin in 1916 was suppressed and its leaders executed. Two years later the nationalist Sinn Féin party won a large majority of the Irish seats in the general election to the Westminster Parliament. Its members refused to attend the House of Commons and, instead, formed the Dáil Éireann in Dublin. A nationalist guerrilla force called the Irish Republican Army began operations against the British administration in 1919.

In 1920 the Government of Ireland Act provided for separate Parliaments in Northern and Southern Ireland, subordinate to Westminster. The Act was implemented in Northern Ireland in 1921, giving six of the nine counties of the province of Ulster their own Parliament with powers to deal with internal affairs. However, the Act proved unacceptable in the South, and in 1922, following negotiations between the British Government and Sinn Féin, which led to the Anglo-Irish Treaty of 1921, the 26 counties of Southern Ireland left the UK to become the Irish Free State (now the Irish Republic).

Recent History

From 1921 until 1972 Northern Ireland had its own Parliament in which the Unionists, primarily representing the Protestant community, held a permanent majority and formed the regional government. The nationalist minority resented this persistent domination and their effective exclusion from political office and influence.

Between the late 1960s and early 1970s, the civil rights movement and responses to it led to serious inter-communal rioting. This led to the introduction in 1969 of British Army support for the police. These sectarian divisions were subsequently exploited by militant nationalists (principally the Provisional Irish Republican Army—IRA) and 'Loyalist' paramilitary groups.

Because of increased terrorism and inter-communal violence, the British Government took over direct responsibility for law and order in 1972. The Northern Ireland Unionist Government resigned in protest at this decision, the regional government was abolished, and direct rule from Westminster began. A Secretary of State was appointed with a seat in the UK Cabinet and with overall responsibility for the government of the Province.

Government

The Secretary of State for Northern Ireland currently has overall responsibility, through the Northern Ireland Office, for political and constitutional matters, law and order, policing and criminal justice policy and community relations. The Secretary of State and a ministerial team also control the work of the Northern Ireland government departments (see p. 537). All laws are approved by the UK Parliament. When devolution takes place, different arrangements will apply (see p. 18), but the Secretary of State will remain responsible for Northern Ireland Office matters not devolved to the Assembly, and the Westminster Parliament (whose power to make legislation for Northern Ireland would remain unaffected) will legislate for non-devolved issues.

Northern Ireland elects 18 Members of Parliament (MPs) to the House of Commons and, by proportional representation, three of the 87 UK representatives to the European Parliament.

Northern Ireland Representation in the House of Commons

General Election May 1997: Results by Party

Party	Seats
Ulster Unionist	10
Social Democratic & Labour	3
Democratic Unionist	2
Sinn Féin	2[a]
United Kingdom Unionist	1

[a]The Sinn Féin members have not taken their seats.

The Alliance Party, offering an alternative to Unionists and Nationalists, received 8% of the vote but no seats.

The Province's 26 local government district councils have limited executive functions (see p. 64). The councils nominate locally elected representatives to sit as members of the various statutory bodies set up to administer regional services, such as education and libraries, health and personal social services, drainage and fire services (see p. 64).

Political Change

The system of direct rule was never intended to be permanent. Over the years, successive British and Irish Governments have worked closely together to bring peace to Northern Ireland, recognising the need for new political arrangements acceptable to both communities in the Province.

Recent Developments

- *1985.* The Anglo-Irish Agreement provided a new basis for relations between the UK and the Irish Republic, creating an Intergovernmental Conference in which to discuss issues such as improved cross-border co-operation and security.

- *1991–92.* The British and Irish Governments held a series of talks with the four main constitutional parties (Ulster Unionists, Democratic Unionists, Alliance Party, and Social Democratic & Labour Party) to try to find a settlement, but no agreement was reached. The British Government continued bilateral talks with the Northern Ireland parties and separately with the Irish Government on matters of mutual interest under the auspices of the Anglo-Irish Intergovernmental Conference.

- *1993.* The Downing Street Declaration, signed by the British and Irish Governments, set out their views on how a future settlement might be achieved. The declaration restated the fundamental principle that any constitutional change would require the consent of a majority of people in Northern Ireland.

- *1995–96.* The two Governments set up an independent International Body to examine the decommissioning of illegally held arms by paramilitary groups. Chaired by former US Senator George Mitchell, the International Body set out six principles of democracy and non-violence (the Mitchell Principles) to which it said all parties should adhere.

- *1997.* Following the British General Election in May, the new Government confirmed its intention of making the talks process as inclusive as possible. It maintained that any agreement reached would have to have the broad support of the parties representing each of the main communities. In September the British and Irish Governments set up the Independent International Commission on Decommissioning to make proposals for taking terrorist arms out of action and to monitor implementation. This body comprises Commissioners and staff from the United States, Canada and Finland.

- *1998.* Multi-party talks in Belfast concluded in April with what became known as the 'Good Friday Agreement'. Legislation was passed at Westminster authorising a referendum on the settlement in Northern Ireland and permitting elections to a new Northern Ireland Assembly. The Irish Parliament also considered the Agreement and passed legislation authorising a concurrent referendum in the Irish Republic. In May referendums were held in both parts of Ireland, and the Agreement received a clear endorsement. Northern Ireland voted 71.1% in favour and 28.8% against, while in the Irish Republic the result was 94.3% and 5.6% respectively. A new Northern Ireland Assembly of 108 members was elected in June and met for the first time the following month (see p. 18). Legislation to implement the whole settlement, and formally institute devolved administrative powers, was introduced in the Westminster Parliament in July 1998 and received Royal Assent the following November (see p. 17).

- *1999.* Almost all aspects of the Agreement have been implemented. An independent Policing Commission started a year-long review of the future policing needs in Northern Ireland; a scheme for the early release of prisoners was established and measures to normalise the security situation have been introduced (see below). Steps towards the establishment of new Equality and Human Rights Commissions—as provided for in the

Good Friday Agreement—have also been taken.

The one remaining area awaiting implementation is the linked issues of the decommissioning of all paramilitary weapons (see below) and the formation of a cross-community Executive to which power can be devolved. Despite attempts by both the British and Irish Governments and the political parties in Northern Ireland, the latest attempt occurring in July 1999, it has so far not proved possible to secure consensus on how the difficulties surrounding these issues can be practically resolved to enable the full implementation of the Agreement to occur.

On 20 July, both Governments initiated a formal Implementation Review, provided for in the Agreement, and asked the former chairman of the multi-party talks, Senator George Mitchell, to act as facilitator. The review, which is limited to the resolution of the decommissioning/formation of an Executive question, aims to reach a speedy conclusion.

The Northern Ireland Act 1998

The Act, which received Royal Assent in November 1998, is intended to give legal effect to the Good Friday Agreement. It sets out the principle of consent to change in constitutional status and makes the detailed provision necessary for the future administration of Northern Ireland, new Intergovernmental bodies, and new arrangements on human rights and equality.

Intergovernmental Dialogue

A North/South Ministerial Council has been set up to bring together those with executive responsibilities in Northern Ireland and the Irish Government, to work on matters of mutual interest. All decisions will be by agreement between the two sides. Those participating in the Council will be mandated by, and remain accountable to, the Northern Ireland Assembly and to the Irish Parliament. Six 'implementation bodies' have been identified to put decisions taken by the Council into effect. Their specific areas are:

inland waterways; food safety; trade and business development; special European Union (EU) programmes; language; and marine matters.

A British-Irish Council will be set up to bring together the two Governments, representatives of the Northern Ireland Assembly, the Welsh Assembly and the Scottish Parliament, and delegates from the Channel Islands and the Isle of Man, to address issues of mutual interest.

A new British-Irish Agreement to replace the 1985 Anglo-Irish Agreement, outlining the shared understanding on constitutional matters, and a new British-Irish Intergovernmental Conference, to promote co-operation between the two Governments, are also due to be established.

Decommissioning

The Good Friday Agreement committed all participants to the total disarmament of all paramilitary organisations. The participants also confirmed their intention to continue to work constructively and in good faith with the Independent International Commission and to use any influence they may have to achieve the decommissioning of all paramilitary arms, in the context of the implementation of the whole settlement, within two years of the May 1998 referendum.

The Independent International Commission will monitor, review and verify progress on decommissioning and will report regularly to both Governments. Both Governments have agreed to take all necessary steps to facilitate the decommissioning process and to ensure that decommissioning occurs by May 2000. To this end it is expected that the Implementation Review under Senator Mitchell will seek to address how best this objective can be achieved in a manner determined by the Independent International Commission, alongside that of establishing an inclusive Executive.

Policing and Justice

An Independent Commission on Policing was set up in June 1998 under the Chairmanship of Chris Patten, former Governor of Hong

Kong and former Northern Ireland Minister. The Commission considered the appropriate role the police service should play in a society free from the threat of terrorist violence, while fully commanding the support of both communities. The UK Government is considering the recommendations made in the Commission's report, which was published in September 1999. There is a parallel review of the criminal justice system, which will report by autumn 1999 (see p. 232).

Release of Prisoners

The Agreement committed both Governments to making arrangements for an accelerated programme for the release of paramilitary prisoners. Legislation was passed in the Westminster Parliament in July 1998 establishing the independent Sentence Review Commission, which looks at individual prisoners' cases to determine eligibility for release on licence. The first prisoners to qualify under these new arrangements were released in September 1998.

The New Northern Ireland Assembly

Following the referendum held in May 1998 (see p. 16), which resulted in a majority voting in favour of the Good Friday Agreement, the new Northern Ireland Assembly was constituted under the Northern Ireland (Elections) Act 1998.

Assembly Elections June 1998: Results by Party	
Party	Seats
Ulster Unionist	28
Social Democratic & Labour	24
Democratic Unionist	20
Sinn Féin	18
Alliance	6
United Kingdom Unionist	5
Progressive Unionist	2
Northern Ireland Women's Coalition	2
Others	3

In June 1998, 108 members were elected to the Assembly by proportional representation (single transferable vote) from the existing 18 Westminster constituencies.

The Assembly met for the first time in July 1998 and elected the First Minister (Designate) and Deputy First Minister (Designate) on a cross-community basis. It has since established several committees, including one to advise on Standing Orders for the future operation of the body and another to advise the initial Presiding Officer of the new Assembly. Other cross-party committees have advised on the procedural consequences of devolution and the future of Belfast Port.

Human Rights

Economic and social deprivation persists on both sides of the Northern Ireland community. However, on all major social and economic indicators, Roman Catholics generally experience higher levels of disadvantage than Protestants, leading to feelings of discrimination and alienation which in turn influence attitudes to political and security issues. Government guidelines aim to promote fair treatment by ensuring that policies and programmes do not discriminate unjustifiably against, for example, people of different religious beliefs or political opinion, women, disabled people, ethnic minorities and people of different sexual orientation. The Government provides funding for local government programmes designed to encourage mutual understanding and appreciation of cultural diversity; support is also given to the Cultural Traditions Programme, which attempts to show that different cultures do not have to lead to division. The aim of these initiatives is to encourage a more pluralistic and tolerant society with equal esteem for unionist and nationalist traditions.

Equality Commission

Under the Fair Employment and Treatment (Northern Ireland) Order 1998, which came into operation in March 1999, a new Equality Commission has been set up, taking over the functions of the Fair Employment Commission, the Equal Opportunities

Commission, the Commission for Racial Equality and the Disability Council. It aims to ensure that public authorities meet the new statutory obligation to promote equality of opportunity in all the services they provide to the public. Direct or indirect discrimination in employment on grounds of religious belief or political opinion is unlawful and there is compulsory monitoring of the religious composition of workforces, continual review of recruitment, training and promotion procedures, and affirmative action if fair employment is not provided.

Human Rights Commission

The Northern Ireland Human Rights Commission, established under legislation in 1998, met for the first time in March 1999. The Commission's role is to consult and advise on the scope for defining rights supplementary to those in the European Convention on Human Rights, which the Government is incorporating into UK law (see p. 212).

The Parades Commission

The Parades Commission was set up in 1997 and given full statutory powers in March 1998 to help implement new legislation over contentious parades in Northern Ireland. In the absence of local agreement on contentious parades, the Commission may make legally binding determinations, such as imposing route conditions. The Commission imposed conditions on 119 such parades in the year to 31 March 1999 out of a total of 3,211.

The vast majority of parades each year are organised by the Protestant/Unionist community, especially the 'Loyal Orders'. Most take place during the six months from around Easter to the end of September.

Victims of Violence Commission

A Commission to look at possible ways of providing greater recognition of the suffering felt by victims of violence arising from the events of the last 30 years was set up in 1997. The Commission, chaired by Sir Kenneth Bloomfield, reported in May 1998 and the

Government has since announced a number of support measures for victims, including an independent review of criminal injuries compensation arrangements (also chaired by Sir Kenneth Bloomfield).

Security Policy

The authorities have exceptional powers to deal with and prevent terrorist activities, including special powers of arrest for those suspected of certain serious terrorist offences, non-jury courts to try terrorist offences (see p. 232) and the banning of terrorist organisations. The relevant legislation is subject to annual independent review and to annual approval by Parliament (see p. 216).

An Independent Commissioner observes and reports on the conditions under which terrorist suspects are detained by the security forces in police offices known as Holding Centres. Statutory codes of practice apply to the detention, treatment, questioning and identification of suspects. A breach of any of the codes' provisions by a police officer is a disciplinary offence.

At present an independent Commission supervises police investigations into the more serious complaints against police officers and, at its discretion, the investigation of other matters. Under legislation passed in July 1998, the Commission is to be replaced with a new office of Police Ombudsman.

The Economy

Throughout the 1990s the Northern Ireland economy has performed well. Gross domestic product (GDP) rose by 16.4% between 1990 and 1996, compared with 9.6% for the UK as a whole. Manufacturing output rose by 28% between 1991 and 1998, compared with the UK rate of 9%. Employment has grown throughout the decade and unemployment has declined since 1993. However, the Labour Force Survey for March to May 1999 showed that 66.3% of those people of working age in Northern Ireland were in employment, compared to 73.9% in the rest of the UK. Comparable rates for unemployment were 7.2% and 6.2% respectively.

A substantial increase in new inward investment in growth industries such as computer software, telecommunications and network services contributed to the 5,434 new jobs generated by the Industrial Development Board in 1998 in difficult world economic conditions.

Northern Ireland's economic strategy has been reviewed to take account of changing needs by a largely private sector-led steering group which drew on the input of 18 working groups. The steering group report—*Strategy 2010*—will be presented to the new Northern Ireland Assembly for its consideration.

The public expenditure allocation within the Secretary of State for Northern Ireland's responsibility for 1999–2000 is £8.4 billion.

Economic Assistance

In 1986 the British and Irish Governments established the International Fund for Ireland. Some three-quarters is spent in Northern Ireland, the rest going to border areas in the Irish Republic. Programmes cover business enterprise, tourism, community relations, urban development, agriculture and rural development. Donors include the United States, Canada, New Zealand and the European Union. The Berlin EU summit at the end of March 1999 agreed a Special Programme for Northern Ireland in support of peace worth about £260 million between the years 2000 and 2004. It also confirmed the renewal for three years of EU support of approximately £10 million a year for the International Fund for Ireland.

Northern Ireland currently receives around £1.3 billion under the EU Structural Funds Programme (see p. 395). Over the period 1995–99 some £200 million of this has come from the Special Support Programme for Peace and Reconciliation. The five areas eligible for funding are employment; urban and rural regeneration; cross-border development; social inclusion; and productive investment and industrial development. Up to 80% of funds are allocated to Northern Ireland, and the remainder must be spent on cross-border activities.

The Irish Language

In June 1998, the Government announced its intention to sign the Council of Europe Charter for Regional or Minority Languages, and to specify Irish for the purposes of part III of the charter at an early date. In July 1998, a statutory duty was placed on the Department of Education in Northern Ireland to encourage and facilitate Irish-medium education.

A new branch within the Northern Ireland civil service is being established to develop policy on linguistic diversity, including the Irish language. Estimates suggest that around 142,000 people in Northern Ireland have some ability to use Irish as a means of communication, either orally or in writing. A cross-border implementation body is being set up with responsibility for promoting the Irish language and facilitating and encouraging its use; £108,000 has also been spent on a study of the Ulster-Scots language.

Numbers of Pupils Taught in Irish Medium Schools in Northern Ireland[a]	
Year	Pupils
1985–86	198
1990–91	378
1995–96	1,038
1998–99	1,512

[a] Out of a total number of 332,000 primary and secondary school pupils.

Further Reading

Northern Ireland Expenditure Plans and Priorities. The Government's Expenditure Plans 1999–2002. The Stationery Office, 1999.

The Belfast Agreement. Cm 3883. The Stationery Office, 1998.

Partnership for Equality. Cm 3890. The Stationery Office, 1998.

Northern Ireland Office website: www.nio.gov.uk

4   Scotland

Three-quarters of the population of Scotland live in the central lowlands. The chief cities are Edinburgh (the capital), Glasgow, Aberdeen and Dundee. Scotland contains large areas of unspoilt and wild landscape, and many of the UK's mountains, including its highest peak, Ben Nevis (1,343 m, 4,406 ft).

Scotland's first Parliament for almost 300 years was officially opened by the Queen on 1 July 1999. It has taken over responsibility for many functions formerly exercised by the Parliament at Westminster (London).

Early History

At the time of the Roman invasion of Britain, what is now Scotland was mainly inhabited by the Picts. Despite a long campaign, Roman rule was never permanently extended to most of Scotland. In the sixth century, the Scots from Ireland settled in what is now Argyll, giving their name to the present-day Scotland.

War between the kingdoms of England and Scotland was frequent in the Middle Ages. Despite reverses such as the defeat of William Wallace's uprising in 1298, Robert the Bruce's victory over Edward II of England at Bannockburn in 1314 ensured the survival of a separate kingdom of Scotland.

The two crowns were eventually united when Elizabeth I of England was succeeded in 1603 by James VI of Scotland (James I of England), who was her nearest heir. Even so, England and Scotland remained separate political entities during the 17th century, apart from an enforced period of unification under Oliver Cromwell in the 1650s, until in 1707 the English and Scottish Parliaments agreed on a single parliament for Great Britain.

Population

Scotland's population has changed relatively little in the last 50 years. In June 1998 the population was 5.12 million (see Table 4.1), compared with 5.24 million in 1971. Population density averages 66 people per sq km, the lowest density in the UK.

Scottish Parliament and Executive

The Scotland Act 1998 provided for the establishment of the Scottish Parliament and Executive, following endorsement of the UK Government's proposals on devolution in a referendum in 1997 when the proposal to establish a Scottish Parliament was supported by 1,775,045 votes (74.3%) to 614,400

Table 4.1: Population

	Population at 30 June 1998	Population density (people per sq km)	Population change 1991–98 (%)
Cities			
Aberdeen	213,070	1,146	−0.9
Dundee	146,690	2,257	−6.1
Edinburgh	450,180	1,718	2.4
Glasgow	619,680	3,541	−1.9
Least densely populated areas			
Argyll and Bute	89,980	13	−3.9
Eilean Siar[a]	27,940	9	−5.0
Highland	208,300	8	2.1
Orkney Islands	19,550	20	−0.1
Scottish Borders	106,300	22	2.1
Shetland Islands	22,910	16	1.6
Scotland	**5,120,000**	**66**	**0.3**

Source: General Register Office for Scotland
[a] Formerly Western Isles.

(25.7%); and a second question, on the Parliament's tax-raising powers (see p. 24), was also supported, by 1,512,889 votes (63.5%) to 870,263 (36.5%).

In the first election to the Parliament, in May 1999, 129 Members of the Scottish Parliament (MSPs) were elected for a fixed four-year term: 73 MSPs for single-member constituencies and 56 MSPs representing eight regions, based on the European parliamentary constituencies, each with seven members. The latter were allocated so that each party's overall share of seats in the Parliament, including the constituency seats, reflected its share of the regional vote. Under the 'additional member system' of proportional representation (PR), each elector had two votes: one for a constituency MSP and a 'regional' vote for a registered political party or an individual independent candidate.

The Labour Party, which has traditionally done well in elections in Scotland, became the largest single party, with 56 MSPs (see Table 4.2), winning 53 of the 73 constituency seats, including nearly all those in central Scotland. The Scottish National Party is the second largest party, with 35 MSPs. Most of its seats came from the 'top-up' PR system, as did all the 18 seats won by the Conservative Party, the third largest party in the Parliament.

Responsibilities

The Scottish Parliament's responsibilities include health; education and training; local government; housing; economic development; home affairs and many aspects of civil and criminal law; transport; the environment; agriculture, fisheries and forestry; and sport and the arts. In these areas, the Scottish Parliament is able to amend or repeal existing Acts of Parliament and to pass new legislation.

The Parliament is meeting initially at the General Assembly Hall in Edinburgh's Old Town. A new permanent site for the Parliament is planned at Holyrood, at the other end of the Royal Mile. The area is in the historic centre of Edinburgh, and the previous Scottish Parliament met from 1640 to 1707 in Parliament House on the Royal Mile. The new building is expected to be completed by the end of 2001.

The Scottish Executive is headed by a First Minister, normally the leader of the party able to command majority support in the

Scotland: Council Areas

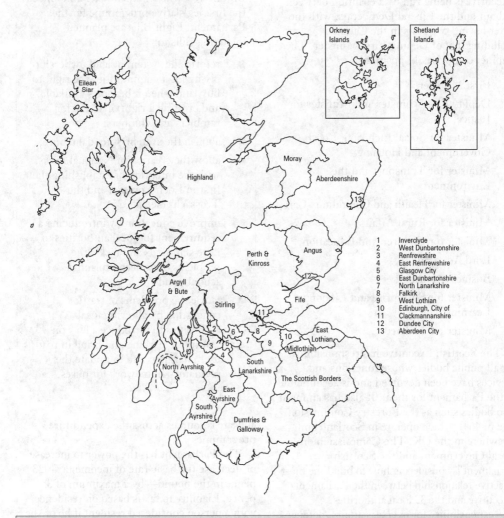

1. Inverclyde
2. West Dunbartonshire
3. Renfrewshire
4. East Renfrewshire
5. Glasgow City
6. East Dunbartonshire
7. North Lanarkshire
8. Falkirk
9. West Lothian
10. Edinburgh, City of
11. Clackmannanshire
12. Dundee City
13. Aberdeen City

Table 4.2: Electoral Representation in Scotland—Number of Seats

	Scottish Parliament			Westminster Parliament (MPs)	European Parliament (MEPs)
	Constituency MSPs	Additional MSPs	Total MSPs		
Labour	53	3	56	55	3
Scottish National Party	7	28	35	6	2
Conservative	—	18	18	—	2
Liberal Democrats	12	5	17	10	1
Independent[a]	1	—	1	1	—
Scottish Socialist Party	—	1	1	—	—
Green	—	1	1	—	—
Total seats	73	56	129	72	8

[a] Dennis Canavan, who was elected as a Labour MP in the 1997 General Election, but stood as an independent in the election to the Scottish Parliament after failing to secure nomination as an official Labour candidate.

Parliament. Following the 1999 election, the Executive is being run by a coalition between Labour and the Liberal Democrats, with the latter having two seats in the Cabinet, including that of Deputy First Minister. The Cabinet comprises 11 positions:

- First Minister;
- Deputy First Minister and Minister for Justice;
- Minister for Social Inclusion, Local Government and Housing;
- Minister for Transport and the Environment;
- Minister for Health and Community Care;
- Minister for Rural Affairs;
- Minister for Children and Education;
- Lord Advocate;
- Business Manager;
- Minister for Enterprise and Lifelong Learning; and
- Minister for Finance.

The Scottish Executive has responsibility for all public bodies whose functions and services have been devolved and is accountable to the Parliament for them. It also has an input into bodies such as the Forestry Commission (see p. 464), which operate in Scotland and elsewhere in the UK. The Commission on Local Government and the Scottish Parliament is considering how to build the most effective relationship between the Parliament/ Executive and the 32 local authorities.

Responsibility for overseas affairs, defence and national security, overall economic and monetary policy, employment legislation and social security remains with the UK Government and Parliament. The position of Secretary of State for Scotland continues, with the responsibility of representing Scottish interests within the UK Government.

Finance

The Scottish Parliament has a budget broadly equivalent to that formerly controlled by the Secretary of State—nearly £16 billion in 1999–2000. Once the amount of the budget has been determined, the Parliament is free to

In June 1999 the First Minister announced the first legislative programme for the Parliament. Eight Bills are planned, including Bills to:

- reform the system of land ownership, giving local communities the right to buy land when it becomes available, and creating a right of access for ramblers and climbers;
- abolish the system of feudal tenure;
- allow the creation of National Parks, with the intention of establishing the first in Loch Lomond and the Trossachs (see p. 321);
- improve education by introducing a requirement for local authorities to raise standards and tackle the problems of underperforming schools; and
- tackle the problems of traffic congestion by allowing local authorities to introduce a levy on workplace parking and bring in road user charging, and to update the regulatory framework for buses.

allocate resources across the expenditure programmes.

The Parliament has the power to increase or decrease the basic rate of income tax—23 pence in the pound—by a maximum of 3 pence. Liability to tax is based on residence, with a person considered resident if he or she is a UK resident for tax purposes and either spends 50% or more of the tax year in Scotland or has his or her only or principal home in Scotland.

The Parliament is responsible for determining the form of local taxation and, if it wishes, is able to alter both the council tax and business rates.

The Economy

In the last 50 years the economy has moved away from the traditional industries of coal, steel and shipbuilding, with the establishment of the offshore oil and gas industry, growth in services and, more recently, developments in high-technology industries, such as chemicals, electronic engineering and information technology. Manufacturing remains important, and Scotland's manufacturing exports were provisionally estimated at £19 billion in 1998, 6.7% higher than in 1997, with above average increases in exports of metals and metal products, transport equipment, and paper, printing and publishing.

Notable features of the Scottish economy include:

- *Electronics.* Scotland has one of the biggest concentrations of the electronics industry in Western Europe, with around 660 units (some 420 companies) employing about 40,300 workers. Electrical and instrument engineering exports were worth £10 billion in 1998, 54% of Scotland's manufacturing exports.

- *Oil and gas.* Offshore oil and gas production has made a significant contribution to the Scottish economy in the last 30 years. Many of the UK's 109 offshore oilfields are located to the east of Shetland, Orkney or the east coast of Scotland (see map, opposite p. 420).

- *Whisky.* Whisky continues to be one of Scotland's most important industries. There are 92 whisky distilleries in operation, mostly in the north east. Whisky exports dominate exports by the drinks industry, which were valued at £1.8 billion in 1998.

- *Tourism.* Tourism is a major industry, supporting about 177,000 jobs. In 1998 expenditure by tourists in Scotland was valued at £2.47 billion; there were 11.8 million tourist trips, including those originating in Scotland.

- *Financial services.* Funds managed by financial institutions in Scotland were some £224.9 billion in 1999, of which £96.5 billion were in long-term life insurance funds and £66.9 billion in pension funds. Several financial institutions are based in Scotland, including insurance companies, fund

managers, unit trusts and investment trusts. There are four Scottish-based clearing banks, which have limited rights to issue their own banknotes.

> One of Scotland's leading financial concerns, the insurance company Scottish Widows, is being acquired by Lloyds TSB (one of the UK's biggest banks). However, as part of the takeover, Lloyds TSB is to transfer its own savings business into Scottish Widows, and this combined operation will be based in Edinburgh.

- *Forestry.* Scotland accounts for just under half of the UK's timber production. In the last ten years there has been significant international and local investment in wood-based panel production and in pulp and paper processing.

- *Fishing.* Fishing remains significant, particularly in the north east, and the Highlands and Islands. In 1998, Scotland accounted for 67% by weight and 60% by value of the fish landed in the UK by British vessels. Fish farming, particularly of salmon, has become much more important, and Scotland produces the largest amount of farmed salmon in the EU. However, some fish farms have recently been affected by a viral disease, Infectious Salmon Anaemia (see p. 462), and measures are being taken to eradicate it.

Support for industry and commerce is managed by two bodies: Scottish Enterprise and Highlands and Islands Enterprise (see p. 394). Inward investment is encouraged by Locate in Scotland, a joint operation between the Scottish Executive and Scottish Enterprise. In 1998–99, 78 inward investment projects were recorded, which are expected to lead to investment of £760 million and the creation or safeguarding of nearly 11,000 jobs.

Legal System

The principles and procedures of the Scottish legal system (see p. 228) differ in many respects from those of England and Wales. These differences stem, in part, from the adoption of elements from medieval canon law and selective borrowing from other European legal systems, based on Roman law, during the 16th century. Preservation of Scots law and the Scottish Courts was provided for in the 1707 Treaty of Union. In addition to separate courts and a separate legal profession, Scotland has its own prosecution, prison and police services.

Education and Culture

The Scottish education system has a number of distinctive features (see chapter 10), including a separate system of examinations and differences in the curriculum. A new system of courses and awards for education after 16, 'Higher Still', is being phased in from August 1999, and is expected to be fully implemented in 2003. Record numbers of students are entering post-compulsory education—about 533,000 students were enrolled in vocational, further or higher education in 1997–98.

Gaelic, a language of ancient Celtic origin, is spoken by some 70,000 people, many of whom live in the Hebrides. The Scottish Executive is providing £13 million to support Gaelic in 1999–2000. Broadcasting is the largest single area, accounting for £8.5 million. In 1998–99 there were 1,816 children in Gaelic-medium education in 56 primary schools and 235 pupils in 14 secondary schools. Extra resources are being allocated to supporting Gaelic education and cultural organisations. Research carried out in connection with the possible inclusion of a question on the Scots language in the next Census, in 2001, found that 30% of the population claimed to be able to speak Scots or a dialect of Scots.

The annual Edinburgh International Festival is one of the world's leading cultural events. Held in August and September, it brings about £70 million into the Scottish economy each year, and is the largest arts festival in the UK. Scotland possesses several major collections of the fine and applied arts, such as the Burrell Collection in Glasgow and the Scottish National Gallery of Modern Art, in Edinburgh. A new Museum of Scotland has been built in Edinburgh to house the National Museums' Scottish Collection.

Further Reading

Scotland Act 1998. The Stationery Office, 1998.
Scotland's Parliament. Cm 3658. The Stationery Office, 1997.

Websites

Scottish Executive: www.scotland.gov.uk
Scottish Parliament: www.scottish.parliament.uk

5   Wales

The population of Wales is 2.9 million. About two-thirds live in the southern valleys and the lower-lying coastal areas. The chief urban centres are Cardiff (with a population of 321,000), Swansea and Newport in the south and Wrexham in the north. Much of Wales is hilly or mountainous. The highest peak is Snowdon (1,085 m, 3,560 ft). The Welsh name of the country is Cymru.

The National Assembly for Wales has been set up to give the people of Wales greater control over their own affairs. It was officially opened by the Queen in May 1999.

Early History

After the collapse of Roman rule (see p. 7), Wales remained a Celtic stronghold, although often during Norman times within the English sphere of influence. In 1282 Edward I completed a successful campaign to bring Wales under English rule. The great castles that he built in north Wales remain among the UK's finest historic monuments (see p. 329). Edward I's eldest son—later Edward II—was born at Caernarfon in 1284 and was given the title Prince of Wales, which continues to be borne by the eldest son of the reigning monarch.

Continued strong Welsh national feeling culminated in the unsuccessful rising led by Owain Glyndŵr at the beginning of the 15th century. The Tudor dynasty, which ruled England from 1485 to 1603, was of Welsh ancestry. The Acts of Union of 1536 and 1542 united England and Wales administratively, politically and legally.

National Assembly for Wales

Government proposals for devolution in Wales were endorsed in a referendum in 1997 by 559,419 votes (50.3%) to 552,698 (49.7%). The Government of Wales Act 1998 provided for the establishment of the Assembly.

In the first election to the Assembly, held in May 1999, electors had two votes: one for a candidate in their local constituency and one for a party list. The Assembly has 60 members: 40 from local constituencies (which are the same as the House of Commons constituencies) and 20 elected by the additional member system of proportional representation from electoral regions—four for each of the five European parliamentary constituencies.

The Labour Party has traditionally been strong in Wales, and won the largest number of seats in the Assembly (see Table 5.2), although it did not obtain an overall majority. It is now running the Assembly as a minority administration.

Table 5.1: Population Mid-1998

	Population (thousands)	Population density (people per sq km)	Change in population 1991–1998 (%)
Cardiff (Caerdydd)[a]	321	2,285	7.0
Newport (Casnewydd)	139	722	1.7
Torfaen (Tor-faen)	90	716	−1.3
Blaenau Gwent	72	664	−1.4
Caerphilly (Caerffili)	170	614	−1.1
Swansea (Abertawe)	230	604	−0.9
Rhondda, Cynon, Taff (Rhondda, Cynon, Taf)	240	569	1.3
Bridgend (Pen-y-bont ar Ogwr)	131	535	1.6
Merthyr Tydfil (Merthyr Tudful)	57	514	−5.0
Vale of Glamorgan (Bro Morgannwg)	121	363	1.7
Flintshire (Sir y Fflint)	147	338	3.0
Neath Port Talbot (Castell-nedd Port Talbot)	139	314	−0.5
Wrexham (Wrecsam)	125	252	1.8
Denbighshire (Sir Ddinbych)	91	108	−1.3
Monmouthshire (Sir Fynwy)	86	102	7.3
Conwy	112	99	3.1
Isle of Anglesey (Sir Ynys Môn)	65	91	−5.8
Pembrokeshire (Sir Benfro)	114	71	0.6
Carmarthenshire (Sir Gaerfyrddin)	169	71	−0.9
Gwynedd	117	46	1.2
Ceredigion (Sir Ceredigion)	71	39	6.2
Powys	126	24	4.9
Wales (Cymru)	**2,933**	**141**	**1.4**

Sources: Office for National Statistics and National Assembly for Wales

[a] Welsh-language local authority names are given in parenthesis if there are differences between the English and Welsh names.

Table 5.2: Electoral Representation in Wales—Number of Seats

	National Assembly			Westminster Parliament[a] (MPs)	European Parliament[a] (MEPs)
	Constituency seats	Additional seats	Total seats		
Labour	27	1	28	34	2
Plaid Cymru	9	8	17	4	2
Conservative	1	8	9	—	1
Liberal Democrat	3	3	6	2	—
Total seats	40	20	60	40	5

[a] Elections in May 1997 for the Westminster Parliament and June 1999 for the European Parliament.

Wales: Unitary Authorities

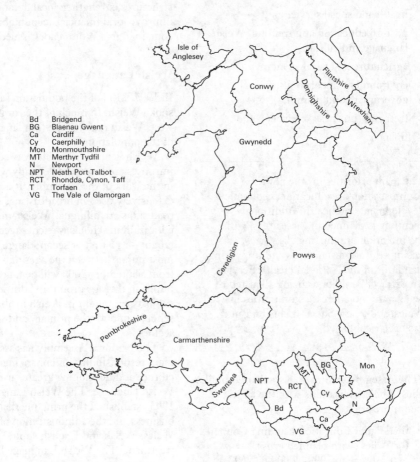

Bd   Bridgend
BG   Blaenau Gwent
Ca   Cardiff
Cy   Caerphilly
Mon   Monmouthshire
MT   Merthyr Tydfil
N   Newport
NPT   Neath Port Talbot
RCT   Rhondda, Cynon, Taff
T   Torfaen
VG   The Vale of Glamorgan

Responsibilities

On 1 July 1999 the Assembly took over virtually all the functions formerly held by the Secretary of State for Wales in the Parliament in London. These include economic development; agriculture, forestry, fisheries and food; education and training; industry; local government; health and personal social services; housing; the environment; planning; transport and roads; arts, culture and the Welsh language; ancient monuments and historic buildings; and sport and recreation. It has acquired responsibility for most of the annual £7 billion budget formerly exercised by the Welsh Office.

Foreign affairs, defence, taxation, overall economic policy, social security and broadcasting are the main functions for which responsibility has remained with the Government in London. The office of Secretary of State for Wales is continuing, with a seat in the Cabinet and responsibilities for primary legislation, giving the Assembly its budget and for matters in the Westminster Parliament that relate to Wales. Wales retains full representation in the Parliament in London.

The Assembly has powers to make secondary legislation (see p. 49) to meet distinctive Welsh circumstances. It is based in Cardiff Bay, initially meeting in a temporary chamber until a new Chamber and associated facilities are opened in 2001.

The First Secretary heads the Assembly and in May 1999 he appointed a Cabinet of eight secretaries. Their responsibilities are:

- economic development;
- education (up to 16);
- health and social services;
- post-16 education and training, Welsh language and culture;
- agriculture and rural economy;
- environment (incorporating local government and planning);
- trefnydd (business secretary); and
- finance.

The main priorities for the new administration are education, economic development and health. Additional spending is planned in these areas, with the intention of reducing class sizes, raising education standards and improving standards in the National Health Service. An extra £87 million is being allocated to regenerate the poorest communities in Wales, and a new Social Inclusion Fund has been established.

The Assembly controls 38 sponsored public bodies. The organisations with the largest expenditure are:

- the Higher Education Funding Council for Wales (with planned gross expenditure in 1999–2000 of £269 million);
- the Welsh Development Agency (WDA, see p. 395) (£200 million), which was enlarged in 1998 when it incorporated the Development Board for Rural Wales and the Land Authority for Wales; and
- the Further Education Funding Council for Wales (£200 million).

Local Government

The 22 unitary local authorities (see map on p. 29) spend nearly half of the total Welsh budget. The Assembly is required to respect the powers of local government, with the emphasis on local decisions being taken at a local level. A Partnership Council will be set up, comprising members from the Assembly and from the unitary authorities. Measures to modernise local authority management structures, strengthen local democracy and improve local financial accountability were contained in a White Paper issued in 1998.

Welsh Language

In 1997, 21% of the population said that they spoke Welsh. In much of the rural north and west, Welsh remains the first language of most of the population.

Welsh is now more widely used for official purposes, and is treated equally with English in the work of the Assembly. It is also quite extensively used in broadcasting, while most road signs are bilingual. Welsh-medium education in schools is encouraged. Welsh is taught—as a first or second language—to most pupils between the ages of 5 and 16, and from September 2000 will be taught to all pupils in this age group. In addition, other subjects are taught in Welsh in about 500 schools, in both the primary and secondary sectors.

The National Assembly has assumed the main responsibility for enhancing Welsh culture and developing greater use of the Welsh language. The Welsh Language Act 1993 established the principle that, in public business and the administration of justice in Wales, Welsh and English should have equal treatment. The Welsh Language Board aims to promote and facilitate the use of the Welsh language; in 1999–2000 its gross expenditure will be £6 million.

Economy

Recent decades have seen fundamental changes in the Welsh economy, which traditionally used to be based on coal and steel. Wales now has a more diverse range of manufacturing industries, including many at the forefront of technology, and a growing number involved in electronic commerce. However, the steel industry remains important, and crude steel production in Wales was around 7.7 million tonnes in 1997, accounting for 42% of UK steel output.

Manufacturing accounts for 29% of gross domestic product (GDP) in Wales, well above the UK average. Wales is an important centre for consumer and office electronics, information technology, automotive components, chemicals and materials, aerospace, and food and drink. Around 39,200 people are employed in the optical and electrical industries, and 13,800 in the automotive components sector. In the service sector, tourism and leisure services are significant, with Wales accounting for 8% of UK visitor expenditure, while call centre activity is becoming more important and prevalent.

A key feature of the economy has been the success in attracting investment from overseas companies and from elsewhere in the UK. Since 1983, 1,932 inward investment projects have been recorded in Wales, bringing in total investment of £12.6 billion and promising the creation and safeguarding of over 188,000 jobs. Overseas-owned manufacturing companies in Wales employ over 75,000 people.

In July 1998 the Government set out its views on the economic future for Wales in *Pathway to Prosperity: A New Economic Agenda for Wales*. It envisages spreading prosperity throughout Wales, through a more coherent approach to indigenous and inward investment, to be undertaken by the expanded WDA. The Agency now has broader functions and powers, so that it is better placed to contribute to economic regeneration across the whole of Wales. Increased resources are being provided to support business development, and a new Entrepreneurship Action Plan for Wales is being co-ordinated by the WDA, to develop a stronger business culture. A new

The area of West Wales and the Valleys, which has been affected by the decline in traditional industry (especially coalmining), qualified in 1999 for the first time for 'Objective 1' status from the European Union (EU) as its GDP was below 75% of the EU average. The area covers large parts of south, west, mid and north Wales. It is eligible for the highest levels of aid from the EU's structural funds (see p. 395) and will qualify for up to £1.3 billion of aid between 2000 and 2006.

Rural Partnership for Wales, which brings together a range of public and private sector organisations, has prepared a statement on rural issues for consideration by the National Assembly for Wales.

Environment

Wales has a rich and diverse natural heritage. About one-quarter is designated as a National Park or Area of Outstanding Natural Beauty (see p. 320). As well as three National Parks—Snowdonia, the Brecon Beacons and the Pembrokeshire Coast—and five Areas of Outstanding Natural Beauty, there are two national trails, 36 country parks and large stretches of heritage coast. There are also 62 National Nature Reserves, over 900 Sites of Special Scientific Interest and a number of internationally important nature conservation sites in Wales. For example, 44 sites are proposed for designation as Special Areas of Conservation under the European Community (EC) Habitat Directive, 13 Special Protection Areas are classified under the EC Wild Birds Directive, and ten wetlands of international importance are designated under the Ramsar Convention (see p. 326). There are six Environmentally Sensitive Areas (see p. 455), representing about 25% of the land in Wales, while a new scheme, Tir Gofal, is being introduced in 1999–2000 to replace most of the current agri-environment schemes. Tir Gofal aims to encourage agricultural practices that will help to protect and enhance the landscape and wildlife of the Welsh countryside.

Cultural and Social Affairs

Welsh literature has a long tradition and can claim to be one of the oldest in Europe. The Welsh people have strong musical traditions and Wales is well known for its choral singing, while both the Welsh National Opera and the BBC National Orchestra of Wales have international reputations. Special festivals, known as eisteddfodau, encourage Welsh literature and music. The largest is the annual Royal National Eisteddfod, consisting of competitions in music, singing, prose and poetry entirely in Welsh. Artists from all over the world come to Llangollen for the annual

International Musical Eisteddfod. The biennial 'Cardiff Singer of the World' competition has established itself as one of the world's leading singing competitions.

The National Museums and Galleries of Wales include the Museum of Welsh Life at St Fagans, near Cardiff; and the recently rebuilt Welsh Slate Museum at Llanberis. The main building in Cardiff contains many paintings by Welsh artists, including Augustus John, Gwen John and Kyffyu Williams as well as a representative collection of other important artistic works. A new Industrial and Maritime Museum is to be built in Swansea. The National Library of Wales at Aberystwyth contains over 4 million books.

An active local press includes several Welsh and English language publications. The fourth television broadcaster, Sianel Pedwar Cymru (S4C), has recently been broadcasting in Welsh for 12 hours a day on its new digital channel.

Among many sporting activities, there is particular interest in rugby union football, which has come to be regarded as the Welsh national game. Wales will stage the final of the Rugby World Cup in November 1999 at the Millennium Stadium in Cardiff—Cardiff Arms Park Stadium, which has been rebuilt, at a cost of some £114 million. The Sports Council for Wales is preparing a new strategy for sport in Wales.

Further Reading

Pathway to Prosperity: A New Economic Agenda for Wales. Welsh Office, 1998.

A Voice for Wales: The Government's Proposals for a Welsh Assembly. Cm 3718. The Stationery Office, 1997.

Website

National Assembly for Wales: www.wales.gov.uk

6 Government

A major programme of constitutional reform is under way. Its aim is to decentralise power, open up government, reform Parliament and increase individual rights. In July 1999 the Scottish Parliament and the National Assembly for Wales came into being, with powers to govern affairs in those parts of the United Kingdom. A new Northern Ireland Assembly will begin to function fully when the final elements of a cross-community agreement are in place. Other plans include: setting up a city-wide authority and directly elected mayor for London; increasing the openness of government through a Freedom of Information Act; holding a referendum on the voting system for the House of Commons; and reforming the House of Lords.

The Constitution

The system of parliamentary government in the United Kingdom is not based on a written constitution, but is the result of gradual evolution over many centuries. The constitution, unlike that of most other countries, is not set out in any single document. Instead it is made up of statute law, common law and conventions.[1]

The constitution can be altered by Act of Parliament, or by general agreement, and is thus adaptable to changing political conditions.

The component parts of UK government overlap but can be clearly distinguished:

Parliament is the legislature and the supreme authority. The *executive* consists of: the Government—the Cabinet and other ministers responsible for national policies; government departments and agencies, responsible for national administration; local authorities, responsible for many local services; public corporations, responsible for operating particular nationalised industries; independent bodies responsible for regulating the privatised industries; and other bodies subject to ministerial control.

The *judiciary* (see chapter 14) determines common law and interprets statutes.

Origins of Government

The origins of government in the UK are to be found in each of the four geographical areas

[1] Conventions are rules and practices which are not legally enforceable but which are regarded as indispensable to the working of government.

it comprises: England, Wales, Scotland and Northern Ireland. England was united as a kingdom over a thousand years ago, and Wales became part of the kingdom during the Middle Ages (see p. 27). The thrones of England and Scotland were dynastically united in 1603, and in 1707 legislation passed in the two countries provided for the establishment of a single Parliament of Great Britain with supreme authority both in England and Wales, and in Scotland (see p. 21). Ireland had had links with the kingdom of England since the 13th century, and in 1801 the creation of the United Kingdom was completed by a union joining the Irish Parliament to that of Great Britain (see p. 14). In 1922 Southern Ireland (now the Irish Republic) became an entirely separate and self-governing country. The six counties of Northern Ireland had been given their own subordinate Parliament in 1920, and voted to remain within the United Kingdom. The UK Parliament at Westminster in London, with an elected chamber comprising members from English, Scottish, Welsh and Northern Ireland constituencies, thus represents people sharing very varied backgrounds and traditions. It has had ultimate authority for government and law-making, but takes account of the particular needs of different areas.

Administration of Scottish, Welsh and Northern Ireland Affairs

England and Wales on the one hand and Scotland on the other have different systems of law, a different judiciary, different education systems and different systems of local government. In Scotland, prior to devolution, departments dealing with most domestic issues were grouped under a Secretary of State with a seat in the Cabinet who had policy responsibility for these matters in Scotland. The administration of Welsh affairs was also formerly the responsibility of a Secretary of State and a ministerial team working through the Welsh Office. The powers of the Secretaries of State for Scotland and for Wales have been reduced since the Scottish Parliament and Executive and the Welsh Assembly began to exercise their devolved authority in July 1999.

The UK Government assumed direct responsibility for Northern Ireland in 1972 (see p. 15), and a Secretary of State for Northern Ireland has been in charge of the Northern Ireland Office since then. As with Scotland and Wales, the powers of the Northern Ireland Secretary will be reduced when the new Northern Ireland Assembly begins to exercise its full authority for domestic affairs in the Province.

Background to Devolution

Referendums held in Scotland and Wales in 1997 endorsed proposals to devolve power from Parliament at Westminster to a Scottish Parliament (see p. 21) and a National Assembly for Wales (see p. 27). Legislation was passed in 1998 to establish these bodies, and elections to the Scottish Parliament and the National Assembly for Wales were held in May 1999.

The Scottish Parliament has law-making powers, including defined and limited financial powers to vary revenue. It has taken democratic control over many of the responsibilities formerly exercised by The Scottish Office. The National Assembly for Wales provides democratic control over the former Welsh Office functions. It has secondary legislative powers and can reform and control the non-departmental public bodies (NDPBs—see p. 56) in Wales. The Scottish and Welsh bodies are each elected by a combination of a simple majority system and proportional representation.

A comprehensive agreement on a political settlement for Northern Ireland—the Good Friday Agreement—was reached in 1998. Following a referendum endorsing the Agreement, elections to a new Northern Ireland Assembly were held in June that year. The Assembly has been operating in shadow form since then. Negotiations between the political parties on all sides of the community have been taking place to finalise arrangements which will allow the new Northern Ireland Assembly to exercise its devolved powers to the full (see pp. 17–18).

The responsibilities of the UK Parliament remain unchanged over economic and monetary policy, overseas affairs, defence and national security.

Human Rights Act 1998

The Human Rights Act 1998 incorporates the European Convention on Human Rights into domestic law. This enables people in the UK to secure decisions on their human rights from British courts and not just from the European Court of Human Rights in Strasbourg.

The legislation makes it unlawful for public authorities to act in a way that is incompatible with the Convention rights, and enables the courts to award whatever remedy within their jurisdiction they see fit in the event of a breach (see chapter 14).

At the turn of the century, the present Queen's great-great-grandmother, Queen Victoria, was still on the throne. When she died in 1901, aged 81, she had reigned for 63 years, having served as Monarch longer than any other member of the Royal Family before or since. The political stage looked very different then. In the 1906 General Election, the Liberals won a landslide victory over the Conservatives, reversing the two parties' fortunes from the election held six years earlier. However, the Liberal Party's political strength was subsequently to decline, a process that was accelerated by the rise of the Labour Party (founded in 1900) on the strength of universal adult suffrage and its trade union base.

Number of Seats Won

	1900	1906
Conservative	402	157
Liberal	184	400
Labour	2	30
Irish Nationalist	82	83

The Monarchy

The Monarchy is the oldest institution of government. Queen Elizabeth II is herself directly descended from King Egbert, who united England under his rule in 829. The only interruption in the history of the Monarchy was the republic, which lasted from 1649 to 1660.

Today the Queen is not only Head of State, but also a symbol of national unity. The Queen's title in the UK is: 'Elizabeth the Second, by the Grace of God of the United Kingdom of Great Britain and Northern Ireland and of Her other Realms and Territories Queen, Head of the Commonwealth, Defender of the Faith'.

In the Channel Islands and the Isle of Man the Queen is represented by a Lieutenant-Governor.

The Commonwealth

Although the seat of the Monarchy is in the UK, the Queen is also Head of State of a number of Commonwealth states.[2] In each of these states the Queen is represented by a Governor-General, appointed by her on the advice of the ministers of the country concerned and completely independent of the British Government.

In UK Overseas Territories (see p. 77) the Queen is usually represented by governors, who are responsible to the British Government for the administration of the countries concerned.

Succession, Accession and Coronation

The title to the Crown is derived partly from statute and partly from common law rules of descent. Despite interruptions in the direct line of succession, the hereditary principle upon which it was founded has always been preserved. Sons of the Sovereign still have precedence over daughters in succeeding to the throne. When a daughter succeeds, she becomes Queen Regnant, and has the same powers as a king. The consort of a king takes her husband's rank and style, becoming

[2] The other Commonwealth states of which the Queen is Head of State are: Antigua and Barbuda; Australia; the Bahamas; Barbados; Belize; Canada; Grenada; Jamaica; New Zealand; Papua New Guinea; St Kitts and Nevis; St Lucia; St Vincent and the Grenadines; Solomon Islands; and Tuvalu.

The Royal Family from the Reign of Queen Victoria to July 1999

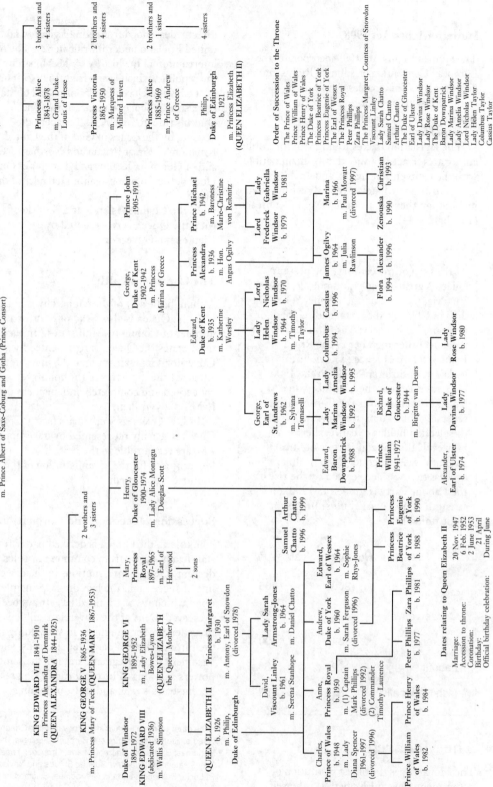

QUEEN VICTORIA 1819-1901
m. Prince Albert of Saxe-Coburg and Gotha (Prince Consort)

Princess Alice 1843-1878 m. Grand Duke Louis of Hesse — 3 brothers and 4 sisters

Princess Victoria 1863-1950 m. Marquess of Milford Haven — 2 brothers and 4 sisters

Princess Alice 1885-1969 m. Prince Andrew of Greece — 2 brothers and 1 sister

Philip, Duke of Edinburgh b. 1921 m. Princess Elizabeth (QUEEN ELIZABETH II) — 4 sisters

Order of Succession to the Throne

The Prince of Wales
Prince William of Wales
Prince Henry of Wales
The Duke of York
Princess Beatrice of York
Princess Eugenie of York
The Earl of Wessex
The Princess Royal
Peter Phillips
Zara Phillips
The Princess Margaret, Countess of Snowdon
Viscount Linley
Lady Sarah Chatto
Samuel Chatto
Arthur Chatto
The Duke of Gloucester
Earl of Ulster
Lady Davina Windsor
Lady Rose Windsor
The Duke of Kent
Baron Downpatrick
Lady Marina Windsor
Lady Amelia Windsor
Lord Nicholas Windsor
Lady Helen Taylor
Columbus Taylor
Cassius Taylor

KING EDWARD VII 1841-1910 m. Princess Alexandra of Denmark (QUEEN ALEXANDRA 1844-1925)

KING GEORGE V 1865-1936 m. Princess Mary of Teck (QUEEN MARY 1867-1953) — 2 brothers and 3 sisters

Duke of Windsor 1894-1972 KING EDWARD VIII (abdicated 1936) m. Wallis Simpson

KING GEORGE VI 1895-1952 m. Lady Elizabeth Bowes-Lyon (QUEEN ELIZABETH the Queen Mother)

Mary, Princess Royal 1897-1965 m. Earl of Harewood — 2 sons

Henry, Duke of Gloucester 1900-1974 m. Lady Alice Montagu Douglas Scott

George, Duke of Kent 1902-1942 m. Princess Marina of Greece

Prince John 1905-1919

QUEEN ELIZABETH II b. 1926 m. Philip, Duke of Edinburgh

Princess Margaret b. 1930 m. Antony, Earl of Snowdon (divorced 1978)

Prince William 1941-1972

Richard, Duke of Gloucester b. 1944 m. Birgitte van Deurs

Princess Alexandra b. 1936 m. Hon. Angus Ogilvy

Prince Michael b. 1942 m. Baroness Marie-Christine von Reibnitz

Edward, Duke of Kent b. 1935 m. Katherine Worsley

George, Earl of St. Andrews b. 1962 m. Sylvana Tomaselli

Lord Nicholas Windsor b. 1970

Lady Helen Windsor b. 1964 m. Timothy Taylor

James Ogilvy b. 1964 m. Julia Rawlinson

Marina b. 1966 m. Paul Mowatt (divorced 1997)

Lord Frederick Windsor b. 1979

Lady Gabriella Windsor b. 1981

Edward, Baron Downpatrick b. 1988

Lady Marina Windsor b. 1992

Lady Amelia Windsor b. 1995

Columbus b. 1994

Cassius b. 1996

Flora b. 1994

Alexander b. 1996

Zenouska b. 1990

Christian b. 1993

Alexander, Earl of Ulster b. 1974

Lady Davina Windsor b. 1977

Lady Rose Windsor b. 1980

Charles, Prince of Wales b. 1948 m. Lady Diana Spencer 1961-1997 (divorced 1996)

Anne, Princess Royal b. 1950 m. (1) Captain Mark Phillips (divorced 1992) (2) Commander Timothy Laurence

Andrew, Duke of York b. 1960 m. Sarah Ferguson (divorced 1996)

Edward, Earl of Wessex b. 1964 m. Sophie Rhys-Jones

David, Viscount Linley b. 1961 m. Serena Stanhope

Lady Sarah Armstrong-Jones b. 1964 m. Daniel Chatto

Prince William of Wales b. 1982

Prince Henry of Wales b. 1984

Peter Phillips b. 1977

Zara Phillips b. 1981

Princess Beatrice of York b. 1988

Princess Eugenie of York b. 1990

Samuel Chatto b. 1996

Arthur Chatto b. 1999

Dates relating to Queen Elizabeth II

Marriage:	20 Nov. 1947
Accession to throne:	6 Feb. 1952
Coronation:	2 June 1953
Birthday:	21 April
Official birthday celebration:	During June

Queen. The constitution does not give any special rank or privileges to the husband of a Queen Regnant.

Under the Act of Settlement of 1700, only Protestant descendants of Princess Sophia, the Electress of Hanover (a granddaughter of James I of England and VI of Scotland) are eligible to succeed. The order of succession can be altered only by common consent of the countries of the Commonwealth of which the Monarch is Sovereign.

The Sovereign succeeds to the throne as soon as his or her predecessor dies: there is no interregnum. He or she is at once proclaimed at an Accession Council, to which all members of the Privy Council (see p. 38) are summoned. Members of the House of Lords (see p. 41), the Lord Mayor and Aldermen and other leading citizens of the City of London are also invited.

The Sovereign's coronation follows the accession after a convenient interval. The ceremony takes place at Westminster Abbey in London, in the presence of representatives of the Houses of Parliament and of all the major public organisations in the UK. The Prime Ministers and leading members of the other Commonwealth nations and representatives of other countries also attend.

The Monarch's Role in Government

The Queen personifies the State. In law, she is head of the executive, an integral part of the legislature, head of the judiciary, the commander-in-chief of all the armed forces of the Crown and the 'supreme governor' of the established Church of England. As a result of a long process of evolution, during which the Monarchy's absolute power has been progressively reduced, the Queen acts on the advice of her government ministers. The UK is governed by Her Majesty's Government in the name of the Queen.

Within this framework, and in spite of a trend during the past hundred years towards giving powers directly to ministers, the Queen still takes part in some important acts of government. These include summoning, proroguing (discontinuing until the next session without dissolution) and dissolving

Parliament; and giving Royal Assent to Bills passed by Parliament. The Queen formally appoints important office holders, including the Prime Minister and other government ministers (see pp. 53–4), judges, officers in the armed forces, governors, diplomats, bishops and some other senior clergy of the Church of England. She is also involved in pardoning people wrongly convicted of crimes; and in conferring peerages, knighthoods and other honours.[3] In international affairs the Queen, as Head of State, has the power to declare war and make peace, to recognise foreign states and governments, to conclude treaties and to annex or cede territory.

With rare exceptions (such as appointing the Prime Minister), acts involving the use of 'royal prerogative' powers are now performed by government ministers, who are responsible to Parliament and can be questioned about particular policies. It is not necessary to have Parliament's authority to exercise these prerogative powers, although Parliament may restrict or abolish such rights.

The Queen holds Privy Council meetings (see p. 38), gives audiences to her ministers and officials in the UK and overseas, receives accounts of Cabinet decisions, reads dispatches and signs state papers. She must be consulted on every aspect of national life, and must show complete impartiality.

The law provides for a regent to be appointed to perform the royal functions if the monarch is totally incapacitated. The regent would be the Queen's eldest son, the Prince of Wales, then those, in order of succession to the throne, aged 18 or over. In the event of her partial incapacity or absence abroad, the Queen may delegate certain royal functions to the Counsellors of State (her husband the Duke of Edinburgh, the four adults next in line of succession, and the Queen Mother). However, Counsellors of State may not dissolve Parliament (except on the Queen's instructions) or create peers.

---

[3] Although most honours are conferred by the Queen on the advice of the Prime Minister, a few are granted by her personally—the Order of the Garter, the Order of the Thistle, the Order of Merit and the Royal Victorian Order.

Ceremonial and Royal Visits

Ceremony has always been associated with the British monarchy, and many traditional ceremonies continue to take place. Royal marriages and funerals are marked by public ceremony, and the Sovereign's birthday is officially celebrated in June by Trooping the Colour on Horse Guards Parade. State banquets take place when a foreign monarch or head of state visits the UK and investitures are held at Buckingham Palace and the Palace of Holyroodhouse in Scotland to bestow honours.

Each year the Queen and other members of the Royal Family visit many parts of the UK. They are also closely involved in the work of many charities. For example, the Prince of Wales is actively involved in The Prince's Trust, set up to encourage small firms and self-employment in inner cities, while the Princess Royal is President of the Save the Children Fund. The Queen pays state visits to foreign governments, accompanied by the Duke of Edinburgh. She also tours the other countries of the Commonwealth.

> On 19 June 1999, Prince Edward, the Queen's youngest son and seventh in line of succession to the throne, married Miss Sophie Rhys-Jones in St George's Chapel, Windsor Castle. Before the wedding the Queen created Prince Edward the Earl of Wessex, reviving a title which died out when the last holder, King Harold II, was killed in the Battle of Hastings in 1066. His wife therefore became the Countess of Wessex.

Royal Income and Expenditure

The expenditure arising from the Queen's official duties is met by the Civil List and by government departments, which meet the cost of, for example, royal travel (£9.3 million in 1999–2000) and the upkeep of the royal palaces and media and information services (£15 million in 1999–2000). The Civil List is a payment from public funds approved by Parliament to meet the costs of running the Royal Household.

In 1991 Civil List payments were fixed at £7.9 million a year for ten years. In July 2000 a Royal Trustee's Report will make recommendations on the Civil List for the period 2001–2010. About three-quarters of the Queen's Civil List provision is required to meet the cost of staff. Under the Civil List, the Queen Mother and the Duke of Edinburgh receive annual parliamentary allowances (together amounting to £1 million) to enable them to carry out their public duties. Each year the Queen refunds the Government for all parliamentary allowances received by other members of the royal family. The Prince of Wales does not receive a parliamentary annuity, since as Duke of Cornwall he is entitled to the annual net revenues of the estate of the Duchy of Cornwall.

The Queen's private expenditure as Sovereign is met from the Privy Purse, which is financed mainly from the revenues of the Duchy of Lancaster;[4] her expenditure as a private individual is met from her own personal resources.

Since 1993 the Queen has voluntarily paid income tax on all personal income and on that part of the Privy Purse income which is used for private purposes. The Queen also pays tax on any realised capital gains on her private investments and on the private proportion of assets in the Privy Purse. In line with these changes, the Prince of Wales pays income tax on the income from the Duchy of Cornwall so far as it is used for private purposes.

The Privy Council

The Privy Council was formerly the chief source of executive power in the State; its origins can be traced back to the King's Court, which assisted the Norman monarchs in running the government. As the system of Cabinet government developed in the 18th century, however, much of the role of the Privy Council was assumed by the Cabinet,

---

[4] The Duchy of Lancaster is a landed estate which has been held in trust for the Sovereign since 1399. It is kept quite apart from his or her other possessions and is separately administered by the Chancellor of the Duchy of Lancaster.

although the Council retained certain executive functions. Some government departments originated as committees of the Privy Council.

Nowadays the main function of the Privy Council is to advise the Queen on the approval of Orders in Council (which are made under prerogative powers, such as Orders approving the grant of Royal Charters of incorporation, and under statutory powers, which enact subordinate legislation). Responsibility for each Order, however, rests with the minister answerable for the policy concerned, regardless of whether he or she is present at the meeting where approval is given.

The Privy Council also advises the Sovereign on the issue of royal proclamations, such as those summoning or dissolving Parliament. The Council's own statutory responsibilities, which are independent of the powers of the Sovereign in Council, include supervising the registration authorities of the medical and allied professions.

There are about 500 Privy Counsellors at any one time, consisting of all members of the Cabinet, other senior politicians, senior judges and some appointments from the Commonwealth. Membership of the Council, with the style of 'Right Honourable', is retained for life, except for very occasional removals. It is accorded by the Sovereign on the recommendation of the Prime Minister. A full Council is summoned only on the accession of a new Sovereign or when the Sovereign announces his or her intention to marry.

Committees of the Privy Council

There are a number of Privy Council committees. These include prerogative committees, such as those dealing with legislation from the Channel Islands and the Isle of Man, and with applications for charters of incorporation. Committees may also be provided for by statute, such as those for the universities of Oxford and Cambridge and the Scottish universities. Except for the Judicial Committee, membership is confined to members of the current administration.

The Judicial Committee of the Privy Council is primarily the final court of appeal from courts in UK Overseas Territories and those Commonwealth countries which retained this avenue of appeal after independence. The Committee also hears appeals from the Channel Islands and the Isle of Man, and from the disciplinary and health committees of the medical and allied professions. It has a limited jurisdiction to hear certain ecclesiastical appeals.

The members of the Judicial Committee include the Lord Chancellor, the Lords of Appeal in Ordinary, other Privy Counsellors who hold or have held high judicial office and certain judges from the Commonwealth. Administrative work is carried out in the Privy Council Office under the President of the Council, a Cabinet minister.

Parliament

Origins of Parliament

The medieval kings were expected to meet all royal expenses, private and public, out of their own revenue. If extra resources were needed for an emergency, such as a war, the Sovereign would seek to persuade his barons in the Great Council—a gathering of leading men which met several times a year—to grant aid. During the 13th century several English kings found the private revenues and baronial aids insufficient to meet the expenses of government. They therefore summoned not only the great feudal magnates but also representatives of counties, cities and towns, primarily to get their assent to extraordinary taxation. In this way the Great Council came to include those who were summoned by name (those who, broadly speaking, were to form the House of Lords) and those who were representatives of communities—the Commons. The two parts, together with the Sovereign, became known as 'Parliament' (the term originally meant a meeting for parley or discussion).

Over the course of time the Commons began to realise the strength of their position. By the middle of the 14th century the formula had appeared which in substance was the same as that used nowadays in voting supplies to the Crown—that is, money to the government— namely, 'by the Commons with the advice of the

Lords Spiritual and Temporal'. In 1407 Henry IV pledged that henceforth all money grants should be approved by the House of Commons before being considered by the Lords.

A similar advance was made in the legislative field. Originally the King's legislation needed only the assent of his councillors. Starting with the right of individual commoners to present petitions, the Commons gained the right to submit collective petitions. During the 15th century they gained the right to participate in giving their requests—their 'Bills'—the form of law.

The subsequent development of the power of the House of Commons was built upon these foundations. The constitutional developments of the 17th century led to Parliament securing its position as the supreme legislative authority.

The Powers of Parliament

The three elements which make up Parliament—the Sovereign, the House of Lords and the elected House of Commons—are constituted on different principles. They meet together only on occasions of symbolic significance such as the State Opening of Parliament, when the Commons are summoned by the Sovereign to the House of Lords. The agreement of all three elements is normally required for legislation, but that of the Sovereign is given as a matter of course.

Parliament can legislate for the UK as a whole, or for any parts of it separately. It can also legislate for the Channel Islands and the Isle of Man, which are Crown dependencies and not part of the UK. They have local legislatures which make laws on island affairs (see p. 2).

As there are no legal restraints imposed by a written constitution, Parliament may legislate as it pleases, subject to the UK's obligations as a member of the European Union (see p. 69). It can make or change any law, and overturn established conventions or turn them into law. It can even prolong its own life beyond the normal period without consulting the electorate.

In practice, however, Parliament does not assert its supremacy in this way. Its members bear in mind the common law and normally act in accordance with precedent. The House of Commons is directly responsible to the electorate, and in the 20th century the House of Lords has recognised the supremacy of the elected chamber. The system of party government helps to ensure that Parliament legislates with its responsibility to the electorate in mind.

The Functions of Parliament

The main functions of Parliament are:

- to pass laws;
- to provide (by voting for taxation) the means of carrying on the work of government;
- to scrutinise government policy and administration, including proposals for expenditure; and
- to debate the major issues of the day.

In carrying out these functions Parliament helps to bring the relevant facts and issues before the electorate. By custom, Parliament is also informed before important international treaties and agreements are ratified. The making of treaties is, however, a royal prerogative exercised on the advice of the Government and is not subject to parliamentary approval.

The Meeting of Parliament

A Parliament has a maximum duration of five years, but in practice General Elections are usually held before the end of this term. The maximum life has been prolonged by legislation in rare circumstances such as the two world wars. Dissolution of Parliament and writs for a General Election are ordered by the Sovereign on the advice of the Prime Minister.

The life of a Parliament is divided into sessions. Each usually lasts for one year—normally beginning and ending in October or November. There are 'adjournments' at night, at weekends, at Christmas, Easter and the late Spring Bank Holiday, and during a long summer break usually starting in late July. The average number of 'sitting' days in a session is about 168 in the House of Commons and about 146 in the House of Lords. At the start of each session the Sovereign's speech to Parliament outlines the Government's policies and proposed legislative programme. Each session is ended by prorogation. Parliament then 'stands prorogued' for about a week until the new session opens. Prorogation brings to an end nearly all parliamentary business: in particular, public Bills which have not been passed by the end of the session are lost.

The House of Lords

The House of Lords consists of the Lords Spiritual and the Lords Temporal. The Lords Spiritual are the Archbishops of Canterbury and York, the Bishops of London, Durham and Winchester, and the 21 next most senior diocesan bishops of the Church of England. Pending new legislation before Parliament (see below), the Lords Temporal consist of:

- all hereditary peers of England, Scotland, Great Britain and the United Kingdom (but not peers of Ireland);
- life peers created to assist the House in its judicial duties (Lords of Appeal or 'law lords);[5] and
- all other life peers.

Hereditary peerages carry a right to sit in the House provided holders establish their claim and are aged 21 years or over. However, anyone succeeding to a peerage may, within 12 months of succession, disclaim that peerage for his or her lifetime. Disclaimants lose their right to sit in the House but gain the right to vote and stand as candidates at parliamentary elections. When a disclaimant dies, the peerage passes on down the family in the usual way.

Both hereditary and life peerages are created by the Sovereign on the advice of the Prime Minister. They are usually granted in recognition of service in politics or other walks of public life or because one of the political parties wishes to have the recipient in the House of Lords. The House also provides a place in Parliament for people, including cross-benchers, who offer useful advice but do not wish to be involved in party politics.

Reforming the House of Lords

The Government is committed to a step-by-step reform of the House of Lords. It proposes to make the second chamber more democratic and representative by:

- removing the right of hereditary peers to sit and vote in the second chamber;
- establishing a transitional House with reformed arrangements for the nomination of life peers; and
- initiating wide-ranging longer-term reform.

In January 1999, following a White Paper detailing its proposed changes, the Government introduced the House of Lords Bill. When enacted, the legislation would remove the right of some 750 people to sit and vote in Parliament solely on the basis that they inherited their seats. Ninety-two existing hereditary peers would be allowed to sit temporarily in the transitional chamber until a full reform programme is in place. During that time non-political appointments would be made on the recommendation of an independent Appointments Commission.

A Royal Commission was set up in February 1999 to make recommendations on the role, functions and composition of a reformed second chamber and to report by the end of 1999. It is intended that a joint committee of the House of Commons and the House of Lords would then be established to consider those recommendations. The Government has said that it will make every effort to ensure that the second stage of reform has been approved by Parliament by the next General Election.

Three main political parties are represented in the Lords; the number of peers eligible to sit and declaring party allegiance is shown in Table 6.1.

---

[5] The House of Lords is the final court of appeal for civil cases in the UK and for criminal cases in England, Wales and Northern Ireland.

Table 6.1: House of Lords Composition: by Party Strength, 4 January 1999

Party	Lords Temporal		Lords Spiritual	Total
	Hereditary peers	*Life peers*		
Conservative	304	172		476
Labour	18	157		175
Liberal Democrat	24	45		69
Cross-bench	198	119		317
Other	92	10	26	128
Total	**636**	**503**	**26**	**1,165**

Source: House of Lords
Note: Excludes peers without writ of summons or on leave of absence (130).

Members of the House of Lords (the average daily attendance is about 386) receive no salary for their parliamentary work, but can claim for expenses incurred in attending the House (for which there are maximum daily rates) and certain travelling expenses.

In January 1999 there were 1,165 members of the House of Lords, including the two archbishops and 24 bishops. The Lords Temporal consisted of 627 hereditary peers who had succeeded to their titles, nine hereditary peers who had had their titles conferred on them (including the Prince of Wales), and 503 life peers, of whom 28 were 'law lords', created under the Appellate Jurisdiction Act 1876. There were 103 women peers.

The total potential membership of the House is reduced by about 60 by a scheme which allows peers who do not wish to attend to apply for leave of absence for the duration of a Parliament. In addition, some hereditary peers do not receive a writ of summons entitling them to sit in the House, for example, because they have not established their claim to succeed or because they are minors.

Officers of the House of Lords

The House is presided over by the Lord Chancellor, who takes his place on the woolsack[6] as *ex-officio* Speaker of the House. In the Lord Chancellor's absence, his place is taken by a deputy.

As Clerk of the House of Lords, the Clerk of the Parliaments is responsible for the records of proceedings of the House of Lords and for the text of Acts of Parliament. He is the accounting officer for the House, and is in charge of its administrative staff, known as the Parliament Office. The Gentleman Usher of the Black Rod, usually known as 'Black Rod', is responsible for security, accommodation and services in the House of Lords' part of the Palace of Westminster.

The House of Commons

The House of Commons is elected by universal adult suffrage (see p. 43) and consists of 659 Members of Parliament (MPs). In May 1999 there were 121 women MPs and nine MPs from ethnic minorities. Of the 659 seats, 529 are for England, 40 for Wales, 72 for Scotland, and 18 for Northern Ireland. The number of Scottish seats is to be reviewed now that the Scottish Parliament has been set up (see chapter 4).

General Elections are held after a Parliament has been dissolved and a new one summoned by the Sovereign. When an MP dies or resigns,[7] or is given a peerage, a by-election takes place. Members are paid an annual salary of £47,008 (from 1 April 1999 to 31 March 2000) and an office costs allowance (from April 1999) of up to £50,264. Other allowances include travel allowances, a

---

[6] The woolsack is a seat in the form of a large cushion stuffed with wool from several Commonwealth countries; it is a tradition dating from the medieval period, when wool was the chief source of the country's wealth.

[7] An MP who wishes to resign from the House can do so only by applying for an office under the Crown as Crown Steward or Bailiff of the Chiltern Hundreds, or Steward of the Manor of Northstead.

supplement for London members and, for provincial members, subsistence allowances and allowances for second homes. (For ministers' salaries see p. 54.)

Officers of the House of Commons

The chief officer of the House of Commons is the Speaker, elected by MPs to preside over the House. Other officers include the Chairman of Ways and Means and two deputy chairmen, who act as Deputy Speakers. They are elected by the House on the nomination of the Government but are drawn from the Opposition as well as the government party. They, like the Speaker, neither speak nor vote other than in their official capacity (when deputising for the Speaker). Responsibility for the administration of the House rests with the House of Commons Commission, a statutory body chaired by the Speaker.

Permanent officers (who are not MPs) include the Clerk of the House of Commons, who is the principal adviser to the Speaker on the House's privileges and procedures. The Clerk's other responsibilities relate to the conduct of the business of the House and its committees. The Clerk is also accounting officer for the House. The Serjeant at Arms, who waits upon the Speaker, carries out certain orders of the House. He is also the official housekeeper of the Commons' part of the building, and is responsible for security. Other officers serve the House in the Library, the Department of the Official Report (*Hansard*), the Finance and Administration Department, and the Refreshment Department.

Parliamentary Electoral System

For electoral purposes the UK is divided into constituencies, each of which returns one member to the House of Commons. To ensure that constituency electorates are kept roughly equal, four permanent Parliamentary Boundary Commissions, one each for England, Wales, Scotland and Northern Ireland, keep constituencies under review. They recommend any adjustment of seats that may seem necessary in the light of population movements or other changes. Reviews are conducted every eight to 12 years. The recommendations in the Commissions' last general reviews were approved by Parliament in 1995.

Voters

British citizens, together with citizens of other Commonwealth countries and citizens of the Irish Republic resident in the UK, may vote provided they are:

- aged 18 or over;
- included in the annual register of electors for the constituency; and
- not subject to any legal incapacity to vote.

People not entitled to vote include people under 18, members of the House of Lords, foreign nationals (other than Commonwealth citizens or citizens of the Irish Republic), some patients detained under mental health legislation, sentenced prisoners and people convicted within the previous five years of corrupt or illegal election practices. Members of the armed forces, Crown servants and staff of the British Council employed overseas (together with their wives or husbands if accompanying them) may be registered for an address in the constituency where they would live but for their service. British citizens living abroad may apply to register as electors for a period of up to 20 years after they have left the UK.

Voting Procedures

Each elector may cast one vote, normally in person at a polling station. Electors who cannot reasonably be expected to vote in person at their local polling station on polling day—for example, electors away on holiday—may apply for an absent vote at a particular election. Electors who are physically incapacitated or unable to vote in person because of the nature of their work or because they have moved to a new area may apply for an absent vote. People entitled to an absent vote may vote by post or by proxy, although postal ballot papers cannot be sent to addresses outside the UK.

Voting is not compulsory; 71.5% of a total electorate of 44.2 million people voted in the General Election in May 1997. The simple majority system of voting is used. Candidates are elected if they have more votes than any of the other candidates (although not necessarily an absolute majority over all other candidates).

The Government proposes to hold a referendum on the voting system for the House of Commons. The Independent Commission on the Voting System was set up in 1997 to identify an alternative to the present 'first-past-the-post' system for Westminster and it produced a report in 1998. A Ministerial Working Group has been set up to examine a number of aspects of electoral law and practice, with the aim of modernising electoral procedures. The Working Group issued a summary of recommendations in July 1999 and the final report is expected to follow shortly.

Candidates

British citizens and citizens of other Commonwealth countries, together with citizens of the Irish Republic, may stand for election as MPs provided they are aged 21 or over and are not disqualified. Those disqualified include undischarged bankrupts; people who have been sentenced to more than one year's imprisonment; clergy of the Church of England, Church of Scotland, Church of Ireland and Roman Catholic Church; peers; and holders of certain offices listed in the House of Commons Disqualification Act 1975.

A candidate's nomination for election must be proposed and seconded by two electors registered as voters in the constituency and signed by eight other electors. Candidates do not have to be backed by a political party. A candidate must also deposit £500, which is returned if he or she receives 5% or more of the votes cast.

The maximum sum a candidate may spend on a general election campaign is £4,965 plus 4.2 pence for each elector in a borough constituency, or 5.6 pence for each elector in a county constituency. Higher limits have been set for by-elections in order to reflect the fact that they are often regarded as tests of national opinion in the period between General Elections. The maximum sum is £19,863 plus 16.9 pence for each elector in borough seats, and 22.2 pence for each elector in county seats. A candidate may post an election communication to each elector in the constituency free of charge. All election expenses, apart from the candidate's personal expenses, are subject to the statutory maximum.

The Political Party System

The party system, which has existed in one form or another since the 18th century, is an essential element in the working of the constitution. The present system depends upon the existence of organised political parties, each of which presents its policies to the electorate for approval; in practice most candidates in elections, and almost all winning candidates, belong to one of the main parties. A system of voluntary registration for political parties in the UK was introduced in 1998. However, registration is necessary for the proportional representation electoral systems which involve 'lists' of candidates, used in elections to the Scottish Parliament, the National Assembly for Wales and, for the first time nationally in June 1999, for electing UK members to the European Parliament. Registration helps prevent the use of misleading candidates' descriptions on ballot papers at election, since only candidates representing a registered or political party are permitted to have the name and emblem of the party printed on the ballot paper.

For the last 150 years a predominantly two-party system has existed in Britain. Since 1945 either the Conservative Party, whose origins go back to the 18th century, or the Labour Party, which emerged in the last decade of the 19th century, has held power. A new party— the Liberal Democrats—was formed in 1988 when the Liberal Party, which traced its origins to the 18th century, merged with the Social Democratic Party, formed in 1981. Other parties include two nationalist parties, Plaid Cymru (founded in Wales in 1925) and the Scottish National Party (founded in 1934). Northern Ireland has a number of parties. They include the Ulster Unionist Party, formed in the early part of the 20th century; the Democratic Unionist Party, founded in 1971 by a group which broke away from the Ulster Unionists; the Social Democratic and Labour Party, founded in 1970; and Sinn Féin.[8]

Since 1945 eight General Elections have been won by the Conservative Party and seven by the Labour Party; the great majority of members of the House of Commons have belonged to one of these two parties.

Table 6.2: General Election Results by Party, 1997

	Number of MPs elected	% share of vote
Labour	418	43.2
Conservative	165	30.7
Liberal Democrats	46	16.8
Plaid Cymru	4	0.5
Scottish National	6	2.0
Northern Ireland parties	18	2.1
Others	1	0.5

The General Election, May 1997

The May 1997 general election was notable in a number of ways:

- The Labour Party's 13.5 million votes were exceeded only in 1951, and the party's share of 43.2% of the vote was its highest since 1966. The 418 seats won were the party's largest number ever.

- The Conservative Party's 9.6 million votes were its fewest since 1929, and its share of 30.7% of the vote was the lowest since 1832. The 165 seats won were its smallest number since 1906. The Conservatives won no seats in Scotland, Wales or Northern Ireland.

- The Liberal Democrats' 5.2 million votes were fewer than in 1992, as was the

---

[8] Sinn Féin is the political wing of the IRA.

party's share of the total vote, but the 46 seats won represented the party's highest number since 1929, when it won 59 as the Liberal Party.

- Turnout at the election was relatively low, at 71.5%—the lowest national level of turnout since 1935.

- A record number of women were elected in 1997. In all 120 women MPs were returned, double the number in 1992. Of the women MPs, 101 were Labour, 13 Conservative, three Liberal Democrat, two SNP and one was the Speaker.

The party which wins most seats (although not necessarily the most votes) at a General Election, or which has the support of a majority of members in the House of Commons, usually forms the Government. By tradition, the leader of the majority party is asked by the Sovereign to form a government. About 100 of its members in the House of Commons and the House of Lords receive ministerial appointments (including appointment to the Cabinet—see p. 55) on the advice of the Prime Minister. The largest minority party becomes the official Opposition, with its own leader and 'shadow cabinet'.

The Party System in Parliament

Leaders of the Government and Opposition sit on the front benches of the Commons with their supporters (the 'backbenchers') sitting behind them. Similar arrangements for the parties apply to the House of Lords; however, a significant number of Lords do not wish to be associated with any political party, and sit on the 'cross-benches'.

The effectiveness of the party system in Parliament rests largely on the relationship between the Government and the opposition parties. Depending on the relative strengths of the parties in the House of Commons, the Opposition may seek to overthrow the Government by defeating it in a vote on a 'matter of confidence'. In general, however, its aims are to contribute to the formulation of policy and legislation by constructive criticism; to oppose government proposals it considers objectionable; to seek amendments to Government Bills; and to put forward its own policies in order to improve its chances of winning the next General Election.

The detailed arrangements of government business are settled, under the direction of the Prime Minister and the Leaders of the two Houses, by the Government Chief Whips of each House in consultation with the Opposition Chief Whips. The Chief Whips together constitute the 'usual channels' often referred to when the question of finding time for a particular item of business is discussed. The Leaders of the two Houses are responsible for enabling the Houses to debate matters about which they are concerned.

Parliamentary party control is exercised by the Chief Whips and their assistants, who are chosen within the party (usually by the Leader). Their duties include keeping members informed of forthcoming parliamentary business, maintaining the party's voting strength by ensuring members attend important debates, and passing on to the party leadership the opinions of backbench members. Party discipline tends to be less strong in the Lords than in the Commons, since peers have less hope of high office and no need of party support in elections.

Financial Assistance to Parties

The Government plans to make party funding more transparent, control spending on elections and ensure the fair conduct of referendums. In July 1999 it published a White Paper—*The Funding of Political Parties in the United Kingdom*—setting out its response to the 1998 report by the Committee on Standards in Public Life (see p. 59). The White Paper includes a draft Bill—the Political Parties, Elections and Referendums Bill—which contains provisions for:

- a registration scheme to bring parties under specified funding controls;
- a requirement on parties to disclose the source and amount of donations above £5,000;
- a ban on the acceptance of donations made from outside the UK;
- national spending limits on parties determined by the number of constituencies and/or regions contested in an election—in a General Election, a party with candidates in all 659 seats could spend up to £19.77 million;
- a framework for the fair conduct of referendums; and
- a new Electoral Commission to supervise the financial restrictions on parties and oversee referendums—it would take over the functions of the Boundary Commissions and the Local Government Commission for England, and have broad responsibility for electoral law, provide guidance on party political broadcasts and promote understanding of electoral and political matters.

Parliamentary Procedure

Parliamentary procedure is based on custom and precedent, partly codified by each House in its Standing Orders. The system of debate is similar in both Houses. Every subject starts off as a proposal or 'motion' by a member. After debate, in which each member (except the mover of the motion) may speak only once, the motion may be withdrawn: if it is not, the Speaker or Chairman 'puts the question' whether to agree with the motion or not. The question may be decided without voting, or by a simple majority vote. The main difference in procedure between the two Houses is that the Speaker or Chairman in the Lords has no powers of order; instead such matters are decided by the general feeling of the House, which is sometimes interpreted by the Leader of the House.

In the Commons the Speaker has full authority to enforce the rules of the House and must guard against the abuse of procedure and protect minority rights. The Speaker has discretion on whether to allow a motion to end discussion so that a matter may be put to the vote, and has powers to put a stop to irrelevance and repetition in debate. In cases of grave disorder the Speaker can adjourn or suspend the sitting. The Speaker may order members who have broken the rules of behaviour of the House to leave the Chamber or can initiate their suspension for a number of days.

The Speaker supervises voting in the Commons and announces the final result. In a tied vote the Speaker gives a casting vote, without expressing an opinion on the merits of the question. Voting procedure in the House of Lords is broadly similar, although the Lord Chancellor may vote but does not have a casting vote.

Modernisation of the House of Commons

A Select Committee on Modernisation of the House of Commons was set up in 1997 to consider how its practices and procedures should be modernised. Its first report, on the legislative process, called for greater flexibility in the way legislation is handled and suggested that it should be possible in defined circumstances to carry forward Bills from one session to the next. The Committee is now looking at other issues, including the structure of the parliamentary year, the process for scrutinising European legislative proposals, and the ability of MPs to make the Government accountable for its actions.

Measures to modernise debating procedures were approved in the Commons in 1998. These include abolishing the preference given to Privy Counsellors' speeches in debates and the rule preventing MPs from quoting from speeches made in the Lords.

Financial Interests

The Commons has a public register of MPs' financial (and some non-financial) interests. Members with a financial interest must declare it when speaking in the House or in Committee and must indicate it when giving notice of a question or motion. In other proceedings of the House or in dealings with other members, ministers or civil servants, MPs must also disclose any relevant financial interest. MPs cannot advocate matters in the House which are related to the source of any personal financial interest.

The House of Lords also has a Register of Interests, on lines similar to that for MPs. It, too, is open to public inspection.

Parliamentary Commissioner for Standards

The post of Parliamentary Commissioner for Standards was created in 1995, following recommendations of the Committee on

Standards in Public Life (see p. 59). The Commissioner, who is independent of government, can advise MPs on matters of standards, and conduct a preliminary investigation into complaints about alleged breaches of the rules by Members. The Commissioner reports to the House of Commons Select Committee on Standards and Privileges.

Public Access to Parliamentary Proceedings

Proceedings of both Houses are normally public. The minutes and speeches (transcribed in Hansard, the Official Report) are published daily.

The records of the Lords from 1497 and of the Commons from 1547, together with the parliamentary and political papers of a number of former members of both Houses, are available to the public through the House of Lords Record Office.

The proceedings of both Houses of Parliament may be broadcast on television and radio, either live or, more usually, in recorded or edited form. Complete coverage is available on cable and satellite television.

The Law-making Process

Statute law consists of Acts of Parliament and delegated legislation made by ministers under powers given to them by Act (see p. 49). While the interpretation of the law undergoes constant refinement in the courts (see p. 211), changes to statute law are made by Parliament.

Draft laws take the form of parliamentary Bills. Proposals for legislation affecting the powers of particular bodies (such as individual local authorities) or the rights of individuals (such as certain proposals relating to railways, roads and harbours) are known as Private Bills, and are subject to a special form of parliamentary procedure. Bills which change the general law and which constitute the more significant part of the parliamentary legislative process are Public Bills.

Public Bills can be introduced into either House, by a government minister or by an ordinary ('private' or 'backbench') member (or peer). Most Public Bills that become Acts of Parliament are introduced by a government minister and are known as 'Government Bills'. Bills introduced by other MPs or Lords are known as 'Private Members' Bills'.

The main Bills which constitute the Government's legislative programme are announced in the Queen's Speech at the State Opening of Parliament, which usually takes place in November, and the Bills themselves are introduced into one or other of the Houses over the succeeding weeks.

Before a Government Bill is drafted, there may be consultation with professional bodies, voluntary organisations and other agencies interested in the subject, and with interest and pressure groups seeking to promote specific causes. 'White Papers', which are government statements of policy, often contain proposals for legislative changes; these may be debated in Parliament before a Bill is introduced. From time to time consultation papers, sometimes called 'Green Papers', set out government proposals which are still taking shape and seek comments from the public.

Passage of Public Bills

Public Bills must normally be passed by both Houses. Bills relating mainly to financial matters are almost invariably introduced in the Commons. Under the provisions of the Parliament Acts 1911 and 1949, the powers of the Lords in relation to 'money Bills' are very restricted. The Parliament Acts also provide for a Bill to be passed by the Commons without consent of the Lords in certain (very rare) circumstances.

The process of passing a Public Bill is similar in each House. On presentation the Bill is considered, without debate, to have been read for a first time and is printed. After an interval, which may be between one day and several weeks, a Government Bill will receive its second reading debate, during which the general principles of the Bill are discussed.

If it obtains a second reading in the Commons, a Bill will normally be committed to a standing committee (see p. 50) for detailed examination and amendment. In the Lords, the committee stage usually takes place on the floor of the House, and this procedure may also be followed in the Commons if that House so decides (usually in cases where there

is a need to pass the Bill quickly or where it raises matters of constitutional importance).

The committee stage is followed by the report stage ('consideration') on the floor of the House, during which further amendments may be made. In the Commons, the report stage is usually followed immediately by the third reading debate, when the Bill is reviewed in its final form. In the Lords, the third reading debate usually takes place on a different day; a Bill may be further amended at third reading.

After passing its third reading in one House, a Bill is sent to the other House, where it passes through all its stages once more and where it is, more often than not, further amended. Amendments made by the second House must be agreed by the first, or a compromise reached, before a Bill can go for Royal Assent.

In the Commons the House may vote to limit the time available for consideration of a Bill. This is done by passing a 'timetable' motion proposed by the Government, commonly referred to as a 'guillotine'. There are special procedures for Public Bills which consolidate existing legislation or which enact private legislation relating to Scotland.

Royal Assent

When a Bill has passed through all its parliamentary stages, it is sent to the Queen for Royal Assent, after which it is part of the law of the land and becomes an Act of Parliament. The Royal Assent has not been refused since 1707. In the 1997–98 session 62 Public Bills were enacted.

Limitations on the Power of the Lords

Most Government Bills introduced and passed in the Lords go through the Commons without difficulty, but a Lords Bill which was unacceptable to the Commons would not become law. The Lords, on the other hand, do not generally prevent Bills insisted upon by the Commons from becoming law, though they will often amend them and return them to the Commons for further consideration.

By convention, the Lords pass Bills authorising taxation or national expenditure without amendment. A Bill that deals only with taxation or expenditure must become law within one month of being sent to the Lords, whether or not the Lords agree to it, unless the Commons directs otherwise. If no agreement is reached between the two Houses on a non-financial Commons Bill, the Lords can delay the Bill for a period which, in practice, amounts to at least 13 months. Following this the Bill may be submitted to the Queen for Royal Assent, provided it has been passed a second time by the Commons. There is one important exception: any Bill to lengthen the life of a Parliament requires the full assent of both Houses.

The limits to the power of the Lords are based on the belief that nowadays the main legislative function of the non-elected House is to act as a chamber of revision, complementing but not rivalling the elected House.

Private Members' Bills

Early in each session backbench members of the Commons ballot (draw lots) for the opportunity to introduce a Bill on one of the Fridays during the session when such Bills have precedence over government business. The first 20 members whose names are drawn win this privilege, but it does not guarantee that their Bills will pass into law. Members may also present a Bill on any day without debate, while on most Tuesdays and Wednesdays on which the Commons is sitting there is also an opportunity to seek leave to present a Bill under the 'ten minute rule'. This provides an opportunity for a brief speech by the member proposing the Bill (and by one who opposes it).

Few of these Bills make further progress or receive any debate, but in most sessions some do become law (ten in the 1997–98 session). Private Members' Bills do not often call for the expenditure of public money; but if they do they cannot proceed to committee stage unless the Government decides to provide the necessary money. Peers may introduce Private Members' Bills in the House of Lords at any time. A Private Member's Bill passed by one House will not proceed in the other unless taken up by a member of that House.

Private and Hybrid Bills

Private Bills are promoted by people or organisations outside Parliament (often local authorities) to give them special legal powers. They go through a similar procedure to Public Bills, but most of the work is done in committee, where procedures follow a semi-judicial pattern. Hybrid Bills are Public Bills which may affect private rights, for example, the Channel Tunnel Rail Link Bill, which was passed in 1996. As with Private Bills, the passage of Hybrid Bills through Parliament is governed by special procedures which allow those affected to put their case.

Delegated Legislation

In order to reduce unnecessary pressure on parliamentary time, primary legislation often gives ministers or other authorities the power to regulate administrative details by means of secondary or 'delegated' legislation (usually in the form of 'statutory instruments'). To minimise any risk that delegating powers to the executive might undermine the authority of Parliament, such powers are normally delegated only to authorities directly accountable to Parliament. Moreover, Acts of Parliament which delegate such powers usually provide for some measure of direct parliamentary control over proposed delegated legislation, by giving Parliament the opportunity to affirm or annul it. Certain Acts also require that organisations affected must be consulted before rules and orders can be made.

A joint committee of both Houses reports on the technical propriety of these 'statutory instruments'. In order to save time on the floor of the House, the Commons uses standing committees to debate the merits of instruments; actual decisions are taken by the House as a whole. In the Lords, debates on statutory instruments take place on the floor of the House. The House of Lords has appointed a delegated powers scrutiny committee which examines the appropriateness of the powers to make secondary legislation in Bills.

Parliamentary Committees

Committees of the Whole House

Either House may pass a resolution setting itself up as a Committee of the Whole House to consider Bills in detail after their second reading. This permits unrestricted discussion: the general rule that an MP or peer may speak only once on each motion does not apply in committee.

Standing Committees

House of Commons standing committees debate and consider Public Bills at the committee stage. The committee considers the Bill clause by clause, and may amend it before reporting it back to the House. Ordinary standing committees do not have names but are referred to simply as Standing Committee A, B, C, and so on; a new set of members is appointed to them to consider each Bill. Each committee has between 16 and 50 members, with a party balance reflecting as far as possible that in the House as a whole. The standing committees currently still include two Scottish standing committees, and the Scottish, Welsh and Northern Ireland Grand Committees.

The Scottish Grand Committee comprises all 72 Scottish MPs (and may be convened anywhere in Scotland as well as at Westminster). It may consider the principle of any Scottish Bill at the second and third reading stages, where such a Bill has been referred to the Committee by the House for that purpose. It also debates other matters concerning Scotland. In addition, its business includes questions tabled for oral answer, ministerial statements and other debates, including those on statutory instruments referred to it.

The Welsh Grand Committee, consisting of all 40 Welsh MPs and up to five others who may be added from time to time, considers Bills referred to it at second reading stage, questions tabled for oral answer, ministerial statements, and other matters relating exclusively to Wales.

The Northern Ireland Grand Committee considers Bills at the second and third stages, takes oral questions and ministerial statements, and debates matters relating specifically to Northern Ireland. It includes all 18 Northern Ireland MPs and up to 25 others who may be added from time to time.

The House of Commons is considering whether the Grand Committees, and the Scottish, Welsh and Northern Ireland Select Committees (see below) should have a continuing role at Westminster following the establishment of the Scottish Parliament and the Welsh and Northern Ireland National Assemblies.

There is a Standing Committee on Regional Affairs, consisting of all Members sitting for constituencies in England, plus up to five others. It has not met since 1977, but its revival is being considered.

There are also standing committees to debate proposed European legislation, and to scrutinise statutory instruments and draft statutory instruments brought forward by the Government.

In the Lords, various sorts of committees on Bills may be used instead of, or as well as, a Committee of the Whole House. Such committees include Public Bill Committees, Special Public Bill Committees, Grand Committees, Select Committees and Scottish Select Committees.

Select Committees

Select committees are appointed for a particular task, generally one of enquiry, investigation and scrutiny. They report their conclusions and recommendations to the House as a whole; in many cases their recommendations invite a response from the Government, which is also reported to the House. A select committee may be appointed for a Parliament, or for a session, or for as long as it takes to complete its task. To help Parliament with the control of the executive by examining aspects of public policy, expenditure and administration, 16 committees, established by the House of Commons, examine the work of the main government departments and their associated public bodies. The Foreign Affairs Select Committee, for example, 'shadows' the work of the Foreign & Commonwealth Office. The Environmental Audit Committee was set up in 1997 (see p. 313). The committees are constituted on a basis which is in approximate proportion to party strength in the House.

Other regular Commons select committees include those on Public Accounts, Standards and Privileges, and European Legislation. 'Domestic' select committees also cover the internal workings of Parliament.

Each House has a select committee to keep it informed of European Union (EU) developments, and to enable it to scrutinise and debate EU policies and proposals, while two Commons standing committees debate specific European legislative proposals. Ministers also make regular statements about EU business.

In their examination of government policies, expenditure and administration, committees may question ministers, civil servants, and interested bodies and individuals. Through hearings and published reports, they bring before Parliament and the public an extensive body of fact and informed opinion on many issues, and build up considerable expertise in their subjects of inquiry.

In the House of Lords, besides the Appeal and Appellate Committees in which the bulk of the House's judicial work is transacted, there are two major select committees: on the European Community and on Science and Technology. *Ad hoc* committees may also be set up to consider particular issues (or, sometimes, a particular Bill), and 'domestic' committees—as in the Commons—cover the internal workings of the House.

Joint Committees

Joint committees, with a membership drawn from both Houses, are appointed in each session to deal with Consolidation Bills[9] and statutory instruments (see p. 49). The two Houses may also agree to set up joint select committees on other subjects.

Unofficial Party Committees

The Parliamentary Labour Party comprises all members of the party in both Houses. When the Labour Party is in office, a parliamentary committee, half of whose members are elected and half of whom are government

representatives, acts as a channel of communication between the Government and its backbenchers in both Houses. When the party is in opposition, the Parliamentary Labour Party is organised under the direction of an elected parliamentary committee, which acts as the 'shadow cabinet'.

The Conservative and Unionist Members' Committee (the 1922 Committee) consists of the backbench membership of the party in the House of Commons. When the Conservative Party is in office, ministers attend its meetings by invitation and not by right. When the party is in opposition, the whole membership of the party may attend meetings. The leader appoints a consultative committee, which acts as the party's 'shadow cabinet'.

Other Forms of Parliamentary Control

In addition to the system of scrutiny by select committees, both Houses offer a number of opportunities for the examination of government policy by both the Opposition and the Government's own backbenchers. In the House of Commons, the opportunities include:

1. Question Time, when for 55 minutes on Monday, Tuesday, Wednesday and Thursday, ministers answer MPs' questions. The Prime Minister's Question Time takes place for half an hour every Wednesday when the House is sitting. Parliamentary questions are one means of seeking information about the Government's intentions. They are also a way of raising grievances brought to MPs' notice by constituents. MPs may also put questions to ministers for written answer; the questions and answers are published in *Hansard*. There are about 60,000 questions every year.

2. Adjournment debates, when MPs use motions for the adjournment of the House to raise constituency cases or matters of public concern. There is a half-hour adjournment period at the end of the business of the day, and opportunities for several adjournment debates on Wednesday mornings. In

---

[9] A Consolidation Bill brings together several existing Acts into one, with the aim of simplifying the statutes.

addition, an MP wishing to discuss a 'specific and important matter that should have urgent consideration' may, at the end of Question Time, seek leave to move the adjournment of the House. On the very few occasions when leave is obtained, the matter is debated for three hours in what is known as an emergency debate, usually on the following day.

3. Early day motions (EDMs) provide a further opportunity for backbench MPs to express their views on particular issues. A number of EDMs are tabled each sitting day; they are very rarely debated but can be useful in gauging the degree of support for the topic by the number of signatures of other MPs which the motion attracts.

4. Opposition days (20 each session) when the Opposition can choose subjects for debate. Of these days, 17 are at the disposal of the Leader of the Opposition and three at the disposal of the second largest opposition party.

5. Debates on three days in each session on details of proposed government expenditure, chosen by the Liaison Committee (a select committee largely made up of select committee chairmen, which considers general matters relating to the work of select committees). Procedural opportunities for criticism of the Government also arise during the debate on the Queen's Speech at the beginning of each session; during debates on motions of censure for which the Government provides time; and during debates on the Government's legislative and other proposals.

Similar opportunities for criticism and examination of government policy are provided in the House of Lords at daily Question Time, during debates and by means of questions for written answer.

Control of Finances

The main responsibilities of Parliament, and more particularly of the House of Commons, in overseeing the revenue of the State and public expenditure, are to authorise the raising of taxes and duties, and the various objects of expenditure and the sum to be spent on each. Parliament also has to satisfy itself that the sums granted are spent only for the purposes which it intended. No payment out of the central government's public funds can be made, and no taxation or loans authorised, except by Act of Parliament. However, limited interim payments can be made from the Contingencies Fund.

The Finance Act is the most important of the annual statutes, and authorises the raising of revenue. The legislation is based on the Chancellor of the Exchequer's Budget statement (see p. 389). Scrutiny of public expenditure is carried out by House of Commons select committees (see p. 50).

Forcing the Government to Resign

The final control is the ability of the House of Commons to force the Government to resign by passing a resolution of 'no confidence'. The Government must also resign if the House rejects a proposal which the Government considers so vital to its policy that it has declared it a 'matter of confidence' or if the House refuses to vote the money required for the public service.

Parliamentary Commissioner for Administration

The Parliamentary Ombudsman—officially known as the Parliamentary Commissioner for Administration—investigates complaints from members of the public (referred through MPs) alleging that they have suffered injustice arising from maladministration. The Ombudsman is independent of government and reports to a Select Committee of the House of Commons. The Ombudsman's jurisdiction covers central government departments and agencies and a large number of non-departmental public bodies (NDPBs). He cannot investigate complaints about government policy, the content of legislation or relations with other countries.

In making investigations, the Commissioner has access to all departmental papers, and has powers to summon those from whom he wishes to take evidence. When an investigation is completed, he sends a report with his findings to the MP who referred the complaint (with a copy for the complainant). When a complaint is justified, the Ombudsman normally recommends that the department or other body provides redress (which can include a financial remedy for the complainant in appropriate cases). There is no appeal against the Ombudsman's decision. He submits an annual report to Parliament, and publishes selected cases three times a year.

The Ombudsman received 1,506 new complaints in 1998–99 (an increase of 3% over the previous year), and completed 372 investigations. Complaints against the Department of Social Security accounted for 647 of the total received.

The Parliamentary Ombudsman also monitors the Code of Practice on Access to Government Information (see p. 58).

Separate arrangements for a Scottish Parliamentary Commissioner for Administration have been set up to deal with complaints about the Scottish Executive and devolved public bodies. Complaints to the Scottish Commissioner are referred through Members of the Scottish Parliament.

Parliamentary Privilege

Each House of Parliament has certain rights and immunities to protect it from obstruction in carrying out its duties. The rights apply collectively to each House and to its staff and individually to each member. They include freedom of speech; first call on the attendance of its members, who are therefore free from arrest in civil actions and exempt from serving on juries, or being compelled to attend court as witnesses; and the right of access to the Crown, which is a collective privilege of the House. Further privileges include the rights of the House to control its own proceedings (so that it is able, for instance, to exclude 'strangers'[10] if it wishes); to decide upon legal disqualifications for membership and to declare a seat vacant on such grounds; and to

punish for breach of its privileges and for contempt. Parliament has the right to punish anybody, inside or outside the House, who commits a breach of privilege—that is, offends against the rights of the House.

The privileges of the House of Lords are broadly similar to those of the Commons. The law of privilege has been examined by a Joint Committee of both Houses of Parliament, which published its report in March 1999. The committee's main recommendation was to call for a Parliamentary Privileges Act codifying parliamentary privilege as a whole and explaining its relevance, both to MPs and to the electorate as a whole.

Her Majesty's Government

Her Majesty's Government is the body of ministers responsible for the conduct of national affairs. The Prime Minister is appointed by the Queen, and all other ministers are appointed by the Queen on the recommendation of the Prime Minister. Most ministers are members of the Commons, although the Government is also fully represented by ministers in the Lords. The Lord Chancellor is always a member of the House of Lords.

The composition of governments can vary both in the number of ministers and in the titles of some offices. New ministerial offices may be created, others may be abolished, and functions may be transferred from one minister to another.

Prime Minister

The Prime Minister is also, by tradition, First Lord of the Treasury and Minister for the Civil Service. The Prime Minister's unique position of authority derives from majority support in the House of Commons and from the power to appoint and dismiss ministers. By modern convention, the Prime Minister always sits in the Commons.

The Prime Minister presides over the Cabinet (see p. 55), is responsible for allocating functions among ministers and informs the Queen at regular meetings of the general business of the Government.

---

[10] All those who are not members or officials of either House.

The Prime Minister's other responsibilities include recommending a number of appointments to the Queen. These include: Church of England archbishops, bishops and deans and some 200 other clergy in Crown 'livings'; senior judges, such as the Lord Chief Justice; Privy Counsellors; and Lord-Lieutenants. He or she also recommends certain civil appointments, such as Lord High Commissioner to the General Assembly of the Church of Scotland (after consultation with the First Minister), Poet Laureate, Constable of the Tower, and some university posts; and appointments to various public boards and institutions, such as the BBC (British Broadcasting Corporation), as well as various royal and statutory commissions. Recommendations are likewise made for the award of many civil honours and distinctions and of Civil List pensions (to people who have achieved eminence in science or the arts and are in financial need). The Prime Minister also chooses the trustees of certain national museums and institutions.

The Prime Minister's Office at 10 Downing Street (the official residence in London) is staffed by civil servants. The Prime Minister may also appoint special advisers to the Office to assist in the formation of policies (see p. 60).

Departmental Ministers

Ministers in charge of government departments are usually in the Cabinet; they are known as 'Secretary of State' or 'Minister', or may have a special title, as in the case of the Chancellor of the Exchequer.

Non-departmental Ministers

The holders of various traditional offices, namely the President of the Council, the Chancellor of the Duchy of Lancaster, the Lord Privy Seal, the Paymaster General and, from time to time, Ministers without Portfolio, may have few or no departmental duties. They are thus available to perform any duties the Prime Minister may wish to give them. In the present administration, for example, the President of the Council is Leader of the House of Commons, and the

Chancellor of the Duchy of Lancaster is Minister for the Cabinet Office.

Lord Chancellor and Law Officers

The Lord Chancellor holds a special position, as both a minister with departmental functions and the head of the judiciary (see p. 220). The three Law Officers of the Crown advising the UK Government are the Attorney General and the Solicitor General (for England and Wales) and the Advocate General for Scotland.

Other Ministers

Ministers of State are middle-ranking ministers. They normally have specific responsibilities, and are sometimes given titles which reflect these functions, for example, 'Minister for School Standards' and 'Minister for Energy and Industry'.

The most junior ministers are Parliamentary Under-Secretaries of State (or, where the senior minister is not a Secretary of State, simply Parliamentary Secretaries). They may be given responsibility, directly under the departmental minister, for specific aspects of the department's work.

Ministerial Salaries

The salaries of ministers in the House of Commons (from April 1999) range from £25,319 a year for junior ministers to £64,307 for Cabinet ministers. In the House of Lords salaries range from £55,631 for junior ministers to £83,560 for Cabinet ministers. The Prime Minister is entitled to a salary of £107,179.[11] The Lord Chancellor receives £160,011.

In addition to their ministerial salaries, ministers in the Commons, including the Prime Minister, receive a full parliamentary salary of £47,008 a year in recognition of their constituency responsibilities and can claim the other allowances which are paid to all MPs.

---

[11] The present Prime Minister and his Cabinet colleagues have declined the full salary to which they are entitled; the Prime Minister draws instead a salary of £62,760, while Cabinet ministers in the Commons draw £47,149 and in the Lords £70,608.

The Leader of the Opposition in the Commons receives a salary of £58,949 (and also the full parliamentary salary of £47,008); two Opposition whips in the Commons and the Opposition Leader and Chief Whip in the Lords also receive additional salaries.

The Cabinet

The Cabinet is composed of about 20 ministers (the number can vary) chosen by the Prime Minister and may include both departmental and non-departmental ministers. The Cabinet reconciles ministers' individual responsibilities with their collective responsibilities as members of the Government. It is the ultimate arbiter of all government policy.

Cabinet Meetings

The Cabinet meets in private and its proceedings are confidential, although after 30 years Cabinet papers may be made available for inspection in the Public Record Office at Kew, Surrey.

Normally the Cabinet meets weekly during parliamentary sittings, and less often when Parliament is not sitting. Cabinet Committees relieve the pressure on Cabinet itself by settling business in a smaller forum or at a lower level, when possible, or at least by clarifying issues and defining points of disagreement. Committees enable decisions to be fully considered by those ministers most closely concerned in a way that ensures that the Government as a whole can be expected to accept responsibility for them. They act by implied devolution of authority from the Cabinet and their decisions therefore have the same formal status as decisions by the full Cabinet.

There are Cabinet Committees dealing, for example, with defence and overseas policy, economic policy, home and social affairs, the environment, and local government. A new committee set up by the present Government, the Joint Consultative Committee, became the first to involve politicians from a party outside the Government—the Liberal Democrats. The Committee considers constitutional issues.

The membership and terms of reference of all ministerial Cabinet Committees are published. Where appropriate, the Secretary of the Cabinet and other senior Cabinet Office officials attend meetings of the Cabinet and its Committees.

The Cabinet Office

The Cabinet Office, together with HM Treasury and the Prime Minister's Office, is at the centre of the UK government.

The Secretary of the Cabinet (a civil servant who reports directly to the Prime Minister) manages the Cabinet Secretariats, which serve ministers collectively in the conduct of Cabinet business and in the co-ordination of policy at the highest level. Since 1983, the Cabinet Secretary has had the additional role of Head of the Home Civil Service.

The current Chancellor of the Duchy of Lancaster is a Cabinet minister with the title Minister for the Cabinet Office and has ministerial responsibility for all parts of the Cabinet Office except the Cabinet Secretariats.

The Cabinet Office is responsible for:

- modernising and simplifying government so that it works more effectively for the benefit of the people;
- implementing a government programme to improve the accessibility and quality of public services; and
- providing the central strategic management of the Civil Service.

Ministerial Responsibility

'Ministerial responsibility' refers both to the collective responsibility for government policy and actions which ministers share, and to ministers' individual responsibility for their own departments' work.

The doctrine of collective responsibility means that all ministers unanimously support government policy once it has been settled. The policy of departmental ministers must be consistent with the policy of the Government as a whole. Once the Government's policy on a matter has been decided, each minister is expected to support it or resign. On rare occasions, ministers have been allowed free votes in Parliament on important issues of principle or conscience. For example, free votes were allowed in 1997 on prohibiting the private ownership of handguns, and in 1998 on lowering the age of consent to homosexual sex from 18 to 16.

The individual responsibility of ministers for the work of their departments means that they have a duty to Parliament to account, and to be held to account, for the policies, decisions and actions of their departments.

Departmental ministers normally decide all matters within their responsibility. However, many issues cross departmental boundaries and require agreement between different ministers. Proposals require consideration by Cabinet or a Cabinet Committee where the issue is one that raises major policy concerns, is likely to lead to significant public comment or criticism, or where the departmental ministers concerned have been unable to agree.

On taking up office ministers must generally resign directorships in private and public companies, and must ensure that there is no conflict between their public duties and private interests.

Government Departments

Government departments and their agencies are the main instruments for implementing government policy and for advising ministers. They are staffed by politically impartial civil servants and generally receive their funds out of money provided by Parliament. They often work alongside local authorities, non-departmental public bodies, and other government-sponsored organisations.

The structure and functions of departments sometimes change to meet the needs of major changes in policy. A change of Government does not necessarily affect the functions of departments.

The work of some departments (for instance, the Ministry of Defence) covers the UK as a whole. Other departments, such as the Department of Social Security, cover England, Wales and Scotland, but not Northern Ireland. Others again, such as the Department of the Environment, Transport and the Regions (DETR), are mainly concerned with affairs in England. (For changes in responsibilities associated with devolution, see chapters 3, 4 and 5.)

The nine Government Offices for the Regions in England (see pp. 9–10) are responsible for administering some of the main programmes of the DETR, the Department of Trade and Industry, and the Department for Education and Employment. They also link these where appropriate to the programmes of other departments, some of which have seconded staff to the Government Offices. Some departments or agencies which have direct contact with the public throughout the country also have local offices.

Regional Development Agencies (RDAs) were formally launched in eight English regions on 1 April 1999. The ninth, in London, will follow in 2000. They will provide effective, properly co-ordinated regional economic development and regeneration, and enable the English regions to improve their competitiveness relative to their European counterparts.

Voluntary regional chambers have been established in each region (see p. 10). The chambers will provide a mechanism through which the RDAs can consult on their proposals and give an account of their activities.

Most departments are headed by ministers. However, some non-ministerial departments are headed by a permanent office holder and ministers with other duties are accountable for them to Parliament. For instance, the Secretary of State for Education and Employment accounts to Parliament for the work of the Office for Standards in Education (OFSTED). OFSTED is headed by HM Chief Inspector of Schools in England, who is largely independent of the Secretary of State.

The functions of the main government departments and agencies are set out in Appendix 1, pp. 531–9.

Non-departmental Public Bodies

A non-departmental public body (NDPB) is a national or regional public body, operating independently of ministers, but for which ministers are ultimately accountable. Such bodies are commonly referred to as 'quangos'.

There are two main categories of NDPB:

- **Executive NDPBs** are those with executive, administrative, commercial or regulatory functions. They are typically engaged in a wide variety of activities and are established in a number of different ways. Executive NDPBs carry out prescribed functions within a government framework but the degree of operational independence varies. Examples include the Arts Council of England, the Environment Agency and the Health and Safety Executive.

- **Advisory NDPBs** are those set up by ministers to advise them and their departments on particular matters. They are normally set up by administrative action and are typically staffed by officials from within the department whose minister they advise. Examples include the Committee on Standards in Public Life and the Low Pay Commission. Some Royal Commissions are also classified as advisory NDPBs.

Other categories of NDPB include certain tribunals and boards of visitors to penal establishments.

There are currently over 1,000 NDPBs in the UK, spending around £24 billion (in the 1997–98 financial year). A list of all NDPBs is held centrally by the Cabinet Office and is issued annually in the publication *Public Bodies*. An electronic directory of NDPBs is also maintained on the Cabinet Office website (www.cabinet-office.gov.uk/quango).

The Lobby

As press adviser to the Prime Minister, the Prime Minister's Official Spokesman and other staff in the Prime Minister's Press Office have direct contact with the parliamentary press through regular meetings with the Lobby correspondents. The Lobby correspondents are a group of political journalists with the special privilege of access to the Lobby of the House of Commons, where they can talk privately to government ministers and other members of the House.

The Prime Minister's Official Spokesman is the accepted channel through which information about parliamentary business is passed to the media.

Modernising Government

The *Modernising Government* White Paper was published in March 1999. It sets out key policies and principles underpinning the Government's long-term programme of reform to modernise public services. It is based on five key commitments:

- developing policies to achieve lasting results rather than reacting to short-term pressures;

- delivering public services to meet the needs of citizens, rather than for the convenience of service providers;

- providing efficient, high-quality public services;

- 'information age' government using new technology to meet the needs of citizens and business; and

- valuing those who work in the public service.

The *Modernising Government* Action Plan, published in July 1999, lists 62 commitments that were in the White Paper and the targets which need to be met in order to achieve them. New public service agreements (PSAs) with government departments (see p. 402) will be a way of measuring and monitoring the effective implementation of these commitments. Information on progress against the PSAs will be published in March 2000. The Government has already begun to implement a number of significant measures to improve public services. These include:

- the establishment of the Centre for Management and Policy Studies which will be responsible for Civil Service-wide training and development, and act as a source of best practice in public service governance. One of its priorities is to design a joint training programme for ministers and senior civil servants;

- a new system to ensure that the Cabinet Office Regulatory Impact Unit must now be consulted on any policy proposal likely to impose a significant regulatory burden;

- appointment of an 'information age' Government representative at Board level in each department and agency;

- electronic delivery of services—38% of services are now available electronically and a 100% target has been set for the year 2008;

- a second round of the Invest to Save budget has been launched which allows public service organisations to bid for money to develop projects to deliver better services to their users;

- new 'learning labs' are to be established to encourage front-line staff who deal with the public to test new ways of working by suspending rules that stifle innovation; and

- new arrangements to encourage diversity (including ethnic background, disability, level of qualification, and gender) in Civil Service staffing.

Open Government

The Code of Practice on Access to Government Information commits government departments, agencies and executive public bodies within the jurisdiction of the Parliamentary Ombudsman to volunteer information, such as facts and analysis behind major policy decisions, and to answer requests for information.

The Parliamentary Ombudsman (see p. 52) offers an independent appeals mechanism for those seeking information under the Code who are dissatisfied with the response to their enquiry and with the results of any internal review of the original decision. Complaints to the Parliamentary Ombudsman must be referred through an MP.

Freedom of Information

As a major step towards fulfilling its commitment to greater openness in the public sector and involving people more in decisions which affect their lives, the Government published a draft Freedom of Information Bill and consultation paper in May 1999. The proposals in the draft Bill follow the general principles set out in the 1997 White Paper *Your Right to Know*, but depart from it in some respects: a more open environment than envisaged is proposed in certain areas, while the legislation would go slightly less far in others where the original proposals were later felt to be detrimental to the effective conduct of government.

The draft Bill is intended to supersede the non-statutory Code of Practice on Access to Government Information, creating a statutory right of access to recorded information held by public authorities. It also aims to weight the scales decisively in favour of openness and preserve confidentiality only where disclosure would be against the public interest.

The main provisions of the draft Bill are:

- a right of wide general access, subject to clearly defined exemptions and conditions;

- a requirement to consider discretionary disclosure in the public interest even when an exemption applies;

- a duty to publish information; and

- strong powers of enforcement through an independent information commissioner and Information Tribunal.

There will also be a requirement imposed on:

- police forces to give out information about the conduct of inquiries (provided it does not prejudice law enforcement);

- schools to explain how they apply their admissions criteria;

- health authorities to provide details of how they allocate resources between different treatments;

- the Prison Service to provide information on the performance of different regimes;

- hospitals and general practitioners to explain how they prioritise their waiting lists; and

- National Health Service (NHS) Trusts and health authorities to provide information on the administrative procedures that govern their private finance initiatives.

Independent National Statistical Service

A further element in the government programme of constitutional reform is the creation of an independent national statistical service. A Green Paper was published in 1998 with the intention of opening up debate on the best arrangements for ensuring high-quality statistics, driven by the requirements of all users and which are efficiently produced, compiled and presented free from political interference. The Government is proposing to follow up this consultation with a White Paper.

Service First

In 1998, following a wide-ranging review, the Government launched Service First as part of its agenda to modernise government. Service First defines the principles of good public service delivery, including: setting clear standards of service; consultation with users; a well-publicised and easy-to-use complaints procedure; and closer working with other providers to ensure better services which are simple to use and well co-ordinated.

Service First applies to all public services, at both national and local level, and to those privatised utilities retaining a monopoly element. In support of the programme, a range of guides has been produced covering issues such as drawing up a charter, consultation, and complaints handling. Other key elements of the programme include:

- the *Charter Mark Award Scheme*, which rewards excellence in delivering public services;
- *The People's Panel*, which consists of 5,000 members of the public randomly selected from across the UK, to provide views on public service delivery from a cross-section of the population; and

- *Better Government for Older People*, which aims to improve public services for older people by better meeting their needs, listening to their views, and recognising their contribution to society.

Committee on Standards in Public Life

This Committee was set up in 1994 against a background of increasing public concern about standards in many areas of public life. The Committee's terms of reference are 'to examine current concerns about standards of conduct of all holders of public office, including arrangements relating to financial and commercial activities, and make recommendations as to any changes in present arrangements which might be required to ensure the highest standards of propriety in public life'.

The Committee has published five reports (see Further Reading). The first, in 1995, was about MPs, ministers and civil servants, and NDPBs. This led to the appointment of a Parliamentary Commissioner for Standards (see p. 52) and a Commissioner for Public Appointments (see p. 60).

Reports in 1996 and 1997 examined standards of conduct in local public spending bodies and conduct in local government, and called for a radical change in the ethical framework within which local government operates. A proposal was made for a new statutory criminal offence of misuse of public office and progress on implementing some of its earlier recommendations was reviewed.

In 1997 the Prime Minister gave the Committee additional terms of reference to review the funding of political parties. The Committee's report, published in 1998, called for a new regulatory regime, overseen by an independent Election Commission, for political party funding in the UK, and in July 1999 the Government published a White Paper (see p. 46), containing proposals to make party funding more transparent and control spending on elections.

In March 1999, the Committee published a consultation paper setting out some of the issues and questions it proposed to consider in its review of recommendations in its First

Report. The review will cover MPs, ministers and civil servants, and procedures in making public appointments which are appropriate to the nature of the post and weight of responsibility. The report will be published towards the end of 1999.

Commissioner for Public Appointments

The Commissioner for Public Appointments, who is independent of government, is responsible for monitoring, regulating and auditing approximately 16,000 ministerial appointments to a range of public bodies including NDPBs, public corporations, nationalised industries and NHS Trusts. The Commissioner has issued a Code of Practice which encompasses the seven principles to be applied to these appointments—ministerial responsibility, merit, independent scrutiny, equal opportunities, probity, openness and transparency, and proportionality. An annual report is published.

Civil Service Commissioners

The Civil Service Commissioners are responsible for upholding the fundamental principle, in the context of recruitment to the Civil Service, that selection should be solely on merit on the basis of fair and open competition. The Commissioners, who are independent of government, produce a mandatory Recruitment Code and audit the recruitment policies and practices of departments and agencies to ensure compliance. They are also responsible for approving appointments through external recruitment to the Senior Civil Service, and for hearing and determining appeals in cases of concern about propriety and conscience under the Civil Service Code. The Commissioners publish an annual report.

The Civil Service

The constitutional and practical role of the Civil Service is to assist the duly constituted Government of the United Kingdom, the Scottish Executive or the National Assembly for Wales in formulating their policies, carrying out decisions and administering public services for which they are responsible.

Civil servants are servants of the Crown; in effect this means the Government of the United Kingdom, the Scottish Executive and the National Assembly for Wales. The executive powers of the Crown are generally exercised by ministers of the Crown, Scottish ministers and secretaries of the National Assembly for Wales, who are in turn answerable to the appropriate Parliament or Assembly. The Civil Service as such has no separate constitutional personality or responsibility. The duty of the individual civil servant is first and foremost to the minister or Assembly secretary in charge of the department in which he or she is serving. A change of minister, for whatever reason, does not involve a change of staff.

Cabinet ministers may appoint special advisers from outside the Civil Service. (There are about 70 such advisers in the present administration.) The advisers are normally paid from public funds, but their appointments come to an end when the Government's term of office finishes, or when the appointing minister leaves the Government or moves to another appointment.

The Civil Service Code, first introduced in 1996, is a concise statement of the role and responsibilities of civil servants. It was revised in May 1999 to take account of devolution. The Code includes an independent line of appeal to the Civil Service Commissioners on alleged breaches of the Code.

Civil servants constitute about 2% of the working population in employment, and about 10% of all public sector employees. The number of permanent civil servants fell from 751,000 in 1976 to 463,000 in April 1998 (a decrease of 38%). These figures include the Senior Civil Service, which comprises around 3,000 of the most senior managers and policy advisers.

About half of all civil servants are engaged in providing services to the public. These include paying benefits and pensions, running employment services, staffing prisons, issuing driving licences, and providing services to industry and agriculture. A further quarter are employed in the Ministry of Defence and its agencies. The rest are divided between central administrative and policy duties; support services; and largely financially self-supporting services, for instance, those provided by the Royal Mint. Four-fifths of civil servants work outside London. Roughly 13,000 civil servants work in the Scottish Executive and 2,000 in the National Assembly for Wales.

Northern Ireland Civil Service

The Northern Ireland Civil Service (NICS) is modelled on its counterpart in Great Britain, and has its own Civil Service Commission. There were 22,600 civil servants in the NICS at 1 April 1998. There is a degree of mobility between the NICS and the Home Civil Service.

The Diplomatic Service

The Diplomatic Service, a separate service of some 5,450 people, provides staff for the Foreign & Commonwealth Office (FCO—see p. 96) in London and at British diplomatic missions abroad.

Terms and conditions of service are comparable, but take into account the special demands of the Service, particularly the requirement to serve abroad. Home civil servants, members of the armed forces and individuals from the private sector may also serve in the FCO and at overseas posts on loan or attachment.

Equality and Diversity

The Civil Service aims to create a culture in which the different skills, experience and expertise that individuals bring are valued and used. Its equal opportunities policy provides that there must be no unfair discrimination on the basis of age, disability, gender, marital status, sexual orientation, race, colour, nationality or (in Northern Ireland) community background. The Civil Service is committed to achieving greater diversity, particularly at senior levels, where women, people from ethnic minorities and those with disabilities are still under-represented. Addressing this is a top priority.

In April 1998, the overall proportion of women in the Civil Service was 51%; ethnic minority representation was 5.7%, compared with 5.4% in the economically active population; and at least 4.1% of staff employed were disabled. Progress is monitored and reported on regularly by the Cabinet Office.

Central Management

Responsibility for central co-ordination and management of the Civil Service lies with the Prime Minister as Minister for the Civil Service, supported by the Cabinet Office. The Cabinet Office oversees the central framework for management of the Civil Service. Day-to-day responsibility for a wide range of terms and conditions is delegated to departments and agencies under the Civil Service (Management Functions) Act 1992.

The function of official Head of the Home Civil Service is combined with that of Secretary of the Cabinet.

Executive Agencies

Executive agencies were introduced to deliver government services more efficiently and effectively within available resources for the benefit of taxpayers, customers and staff. This involved setting up, as far as is practicable, separate units or agencies to perform the executive functions of government. Agencies remain part of the Civil Service, but under the terms of individual framework documents they enjoy greater delegation of financial, pay and personnel matters. Agencies are headed by chief executives who are normally directly accountable to ministers but are personally responsible for day-to-day operations. A chief executive's pay is normally directly related to the agency's performance.

No organisation carrying out a government function can become an agency until the 'prior options' of abolition, privatisation and contracting out have been considered and ruled out. These 'prior options' are reconsidered when agencies are reviewed, normally after five years of operation.

By April 1998, 355,900 civil servants (77%) were working in executive agencies.

Local Government

Local Authorities' Powers

Local authorities derive their power from legislation. They can act only under powers conferred on them by Acts of Parliament. If these powers are exceeded, the local authority concerned can be challenged in a court of law. Local authorities' functions are far-reaching. Some are mandatory, which means that the authority must do what is required by law; others are purely permissive, allowing an authority to provide services if it wishes. In certain services, ministers have powers to secure a degree of uniformity in standards in order to safeguard public health or to protect the rights of individual citizens.

The main link between local authorities and central government in England is the Department of the Environment, Transport and the Regions. However, other departments, such as the Department for Education and Employment, the Department of Health and the Home Office, are also concerned with various local government functions. In Scotland and Wales, local authorities now deal mainly with the new devolved Parliament and Assembly. In Northern Ireland they continue to deal with the Department of the Environment for Northern Ireland until the new Northern Ireland Assembly begins to function fully.

Closer links between central and local government in England have been promoted through the Central-Local Partnership Meeting, which brings together Cabinet ministers and senior local government leaders to discuss major issues affecting local government.

In 1998 the Government ratified the Council of Europe's Charter of Local Self Government. This lays down standards for protecting and developing the rights of local authorities.

Reform of Local Government Structure

A major reform of local government took place in 1974 in England and Wales and in 1975 in Scotland. This created two main tiers of local authority throughout England and Wales: counties and the smaller districts. Local government in London had been reorganised along the same lines in 1965. In Scotland functions were allocated to regions and districts on the mainland; single-tier authorities were introduced for the three Islands areas. In Northern Ireland changes were made in 1973 which replaced the two-tier county council and urban/rural council system with a single-tier district council system.

The Local Government Act 1985 abolished the Greater London Council and the six metropolitan county councils in England. Most of their functions were transferred to the London boroughs and metropolitan district councils respectively in 1986 (see below).

Recent Changes

Further restructuring of local government has since taken place in non-metropolitan England and in Scotland and Wales. In 1992 the Local Government Commission was established to review the structure, boundaries and electoral arrangements of local government in England and to undertake periodic electoral reviews. In its structural reviews of local government in non-metropolitan England, the Commission considered whether the two-tier structure should be replaced by single-tier ('unitary') authorities in each area; for the most part it recommended the retention of two-tier government, but suggested unitary authorities for some areas, especially the larger cities. Parliament approved reorganisation in 25 counties, creating a total of 46 new unitary councils (see map on p. 8). Implementation was completed in 1998.

In Scotland 29 new unitary councils replaced the previous system of nine regional and 53 district councils in 1996; the three Islands councils have remained in being. In Wales, 22 unitary authorities replaced the previous eight county councils and 37 district councils, again in 1996.

In 1998 the Government published White Papers for modernising local government in England (*Modern Local Government: In Touch with the People*) and Wales (*Local Voices: Modernising Local Government in Wales*). The

White Papers contained proposals for: creating new political structures for councils (see p. 64); improving local democracy (see p. 64); strengthening local financial accountability; establishing a new ethical framework; improving local services through best value (see p. 66); simplifying capital finance; and introducing some local discretion in business rates. The Local Government Act 1999 abolished compulsory competitive tendering (CCT) and imposed a new duty on authorities to make arrangements to achieve best value (see p. 66). The Act also repealed the existing legislation to cap local authority budgets, replacing it with more discriminating reserve powers.

Principal Types of Local Authority

Greater London

Greater London is made up of the 32 London boroughs and the City of London, each with a council responsible for all local government services in its area. Exceptions include public transport, responsibility for which lies with London Transport (see p. 367), and London's Metropolitan Police force, which at present is responsible to the Home Secretary. (For details of the police service, which is financed by central and local government, see p. 217.)

Proposals for London Government

At present London is the only Western capital without an elected city-wide government. In 1997 the Government issued proposals for establishing a Greater London Authority made up of an elected Mayor and a separately elected Assembly. The proposed Authority, which would encompass the whole of Greater London, would not duplicate the work of the London boroughs, but would take responsibility for London-wide issues such as transport, economic development, environmental protection, strategic planning, police and fire services. The Corporation of the City of London has produced its own proposals for reforming its existing franchise in order to prevent abuse of power and to extend the electoral system to give a wider variety of bodies and organisations voting rights within the City.

In a referendum held in Greater London in 1998, a majority of those who voted cast their votes in favour of the Government's proposals. The new Authority will be set up, subject to parliamentary approval, under the provisions of the Greater London Authority Bill, with a view to holding the first elections for the Mayor and Assembly in May 2000 and assuming its responsibilities in July that year. Subsequent elections will take place every four years.

English Metropolitan County Areas

The six metropolitan county areas—Tyne and Wear, West Midlands, Merseyside, Greater Manchester, West Yorkshire and South Yorkshire—have 36 district councils, but no county councils. The district councils are responsible for all services apart from those which require a statutory authority over areas wider than the individual boroughs and districts—namely, waste disposal (in certain areas); the fire services, including civil defence; and public transport. These are run by joint authorities composed of elected councillors nominated by the borough or district councils.

English Non-metropolitan Counties

Before the recent reforms, local government in England—outside Greater London and the metropolitan areas—was divided into counties and sub-divided into districts. All the counties and districts had locally elected councils with separate functions. County councils provided large-scale services, while district councils were responsible for the more local ones. These arrangements are broadly continuing in areas where two-tier local government remains.

County councils are responsible for transport, planning, highways, traffic regulation, education,[12] consumer protection, refuse disposal, the fire service, libraries and

---

[12] Under the Education Reform Act 1988, schools were able to 'opt out' of local education authority control by obtaining grant-maintained (GM) status. However, the School Standards and Framework Act 1998 introduced a new framework under which GM schools returned to the local authority sector: from April 1999 they have been funded by local education authorities and they will move to their chosen new status—foundation, voluntary or community—from September 1999 (see p. 125).

the personal social services. District councils are responsible for environmental health, housing, decisions on most local planning applications, and refuse collection. Both tiers of local authority have powers to provide facilities such as museums, art galleries and parks; arrangements depend on local agreement. In areas where the new unitary authorities have been set up, county and district level functions have merged.

In addition to the two-tier local authority system in England, over 10,000 parish councils or meetings provide and manage local facilities such as allotments and village halls, and act as agents for other district council functions. They also provide a forum for discussion of local issues.

Fire Services in the UK

Every part of the UK is covered by a local authority fire service. Each of the 64 fire authorities must by law make provision for firefighting and maintain a brigade to meet efficiently all normal firefighting requirements. Each fire authority appoints a Chief Fire Officer (Firemaster in Scotland) who exercises day-to-day control from brigade headquarters. The fire services in England and Wales employ some 50,000 staff and spend around £1.4 billion each year. In 1998 local authority fire brigades attended about 865,000 fires or false alarms in the UK.

Scotland, Wales and Northern Ireland

In Scotland the 32 single-tier councils are responsible for the full range of local government services. In Wales the 22 single-tier councils have similar functions, except that fire services are provided by three combined fire authorities. In addition, about 750 community councils in Wales have functions similar to those of the parish councils in England (see above); in Scotland community councils exist to represent the views of their local communities to local authorities and other public bodies in the area.

In Northern Ireland 26 district councils are responsible for local environmental and certain other services, such as leisure and the arts. Responsibility for planning, roads, water supply and sewerage services is currently exercised in each district through a divisional office of the Department of the Environment for Northern Ireland. Area boards, responsible to central departments, administer education, public libraries, and the health and personal social services locally.

Election of Councils

Local councils consist of elected councillors. In England and Wales each council elects its presiding officer annually. Some districts have the ceremonial title of borough, or city, both granted by royal authority. In boroughs and cities the presiding officer is normally known as the Mayor. In the City of London and certain large cities, he or she is known as the Lord Mayor. In Scotland the presiding officer of the council of each of the four cities— Aberdeen, Dundee, Edinburgh and Glasgow—is called the Lord Provost.

Councillors are elected for four years. All county councils in England, borough councils in London, and about two-thirds of non-metropolitan district councils are elected in their entirety every four years. In the remaining districts (including all metropolitan districts) one-third of the councillors are elected in each of the three years when county council elections are not held. In the interests of greater accountability, the recent White Paper (see p. 62) proposes that all unitary authorities in non-metropolitan districts and London boroughs should adopt a pattern of elections similar to that in metropolitan districts. It also proposes that other authorities should adopt arrangements where, in alternate years, elections take place for half of the district council and then, in the following year, half of the county council.

In Scotland whole council elections are held every three years, with the next elections due in 2002. In Wales whole council elections are held every fourth year, with the next due in 2003. The Government has given the National Assembly for Wales a power to determine the frequency of council elections.

County, district and unitary authority councillors are paid a basic allowance but may also be entitled to additional allowances and expenses for attending meetings or taking on special responsibilities. The Government proposes to abolish attendance allowance and make possible the payment of pensionable salaries to some councillors in executive positions in the proposed new political management structures.

Voters

Anyone may vote at a local government election in the UK provided he or she is:

- aged 18 years or over;
- a citizen of the UK or of another Commonwealth country, or of the Irish Republic, or a citizen of a member state of the European Union;
- not subject to any legal incapacity to vote; and
- on the electoral register.

To qualify for registration a person must be resident in the council area on the qualifying date.

Candidates

Most candidates at local government elections stand as representatives of a national political party, although some stand as independents. Candidates must be British citizens, other Commonwealth citizens or citizens of a member state of the European Union, and aged 21 or over. In addition, they must also either:

- be registered as local electors in the area of the relevant local authority; or
- have occupied (as owner or tenant) land or premises in that area during the whole of the preceding 12 months; or
- have had their main place of work in the area throughout this 12-month period.

No one may be elected to a council of which he or she is an employee. All candidates for district council elections in Northern Ireland are required to make a declaration against terrorism.

Electoral Areas and Procedure

Counties in England are divided into electoral divisions, each returning one councillor. Districts in England and Northern Ireland are divided into wards, returning one councillor or more. In Scotland the unitary councils are divided into wards and in Wales into electoral divisions; each returns one councillor or more. Parishes (in England) and communities (in Wales) may be divided into wards, returning at least one councillor.

The procedure for local government voting in Great Britain is broadly similar to that for parliamentary elections. In Northern Ireland district councils are elected by proportional representation on the grounds that it allows for the representation of sizeable minorities.

The electoral arrangements of local authorities in England are kept under review by the Local Government Commission (see p. 62), and in Wales and Scotland by the Local Government Boundary Commissions. Under legislation passed in 1997, electoral arrangements in England and Wales for parishes and communities can be reviewed by local councils.

Provision of Local Services

In recent years, there has been a move away from direct service provision, to a greater use of private contractors, and an increase in what is often called the 'enabling' role. Local authorities now carry out many functions in partnership with both public and private organisations. For example, under community care arrangements (see p. 164), councils with social services responsibilities draw up care plans for those who need them, but the care is often provided by the private or voluntary sectors funded by the council rather than directly by the local authority itself.

The previous administration introduced legislation in the 1980s aimed at encouraging local authorities to contract out the services they provide. It introduced a practice known as compulsory competitive tendering (CCT), under which many services traditionally provided by the council's own staff, such as refuse collection and leisure management, had to be put out to tender and won in open competition.

In a departure from the approach of its predecessor, the Government has devised a new system designed to achieve best value in the delivery of local government services. It considers that councils should not be forced to put their services out to tender, but equally it sees no reason why a service should be delivered directly if more efficient means are available elsewhere. The Government has incorporated provisions in the Local Government Act 1999 to replace CCT with a duty on local authorities to achieve best value.

The Best Value programme aims to encourage local accountability and involve local communities in deciding the quality, level and cost of local services. Local authorities will be expected to set themselves challenging targets for the improvement of services following regular reviews of their performance. Local people will be able to see how well their authority is performing through the publication of annual performance plans.

A White Paper containing proposals for modernising local government in Wales was published in 1998. The Government of Wales Act (see p. 27) requires the National Assembly to set up a Partnership Council to oversee relations between the Assembly and local government. A Commission to establish effective relations between local government and the new Scottish Parliament has been set up (see chapter 4).

Internal Organisation of Local Authorities

Local authorities have considerable freedom to make arrangements for carrying out their duties. Some decisions are made by the full council; many other matters are delegated to committees composed of members of the council, although certain powers are legally reserved to the council as a whole. Parish and community councils in England and Wales are often able to do their work in full session, although they appoint committees from time to time as necessary.

In England and Wales committees generally have to reflect the political composition of the council (although the legislation governing this specifically excludes parish or community councils). In practice, this is the case in Scotland, although it is not enforced by legislation. People who are not members of the council may be co-opted onto decision-making committees and can speak and take part in debates; they cannot normally vote. Legislation also prevents senior council officers and others in politically sensitive posts from being members of another local authority or undertaking public political activity. Some, but not all, of these provisions have been introduced in Northern Ireland.

The recent local government White Papers (see p. 62) criticised these arrangements for producing a lack of openness, for being inefficient, and for preventing councillors from spending more time with those they represent. The Government has proposed a separation between the executive and the back bench role of councillors, and has suggested a range of models which would achieve this, including ones featuring directly elected mayors.

Public Access

The public (including the press) are admitted to council, committee and sub-committee meetings, and have access to agendas, reports and minutes of meetings and certain background papers. Local authorities may exclude the public from meetings and withhold these papers only in limited circumstances.

Employees

About 1.9 million people[13] are employed by local authorities in Great Britain. These include administrative, professional and technical staff, teachers, fire-fighters and manual workers, but exclude those in law and order services. Education is the largest service. Councils are individually responsible, within certain national legislative requirements, for deciding the structure of their workforces.

Senior staff appointments are usually made by the elected councillors. More junior

---

[13] Full-time equivalents.

appointments are made by heads of
departments. Pay and conditions of service are
usually a matter for each council, although most
authorities follow the scales recommended as a
result of national negotiation between
authorities and trade unions.

Local Authority Finance

Local government expenditure accounts for
about 25% of public spending. In 1998–99
expenditure by local authorities in the UK was
about £79.1 billion. Current expenditure
amounted to £70.7 billion; capital
expenditure, net of capital receipts, was £5.6
billion; and debt interest £4.4 billion. Local
government capital expenditure is financed
primarily by borrowing within limits set by
central government and from capital receipts
from the disposal of land and buildings.

Local authorities in Great Britain raise
revenue through the council tax (see chapter
24), which meets about 20% of their revenue
expenditure. Their spending is, however,
financed primarily by grants from central
government and by the redistribution of
revenue from the national non-domestic rate,
a property tax levied on businesses and other
non-domestic properties.

District councils in Northern Ireland
continue to raise revenue through the levying
of a domestic rate and business rates.

Financial Safeguards

Local councils' annual accounts must be audited
by independent auditors appointed by the Audit
Commission in England and Wales, or in
Scotland by the Accounts Commission for
Scotland. In Northern Ireland this role is
exercised by the chief local government auditor,
who, at present, is appointed by the
Department of the Environment for Northern
Ireland. Local electors have a right to inspect
the accounts to be audited. They may also ask
questions and lodge objections with the auditor.

Local Government Complaints System

Local authorities are encouraged to resolve
complaints through internal mechanisms, and
members of the public will often ask their own
councillor for help in this. Local authorities
must also appoint a monitoring officer, whose
duties include ensuring that the local authority
acts lawfully in the conduct of its business.

Complaints of alleged local government
maladministration leading to injustice may be
investigated by independent Commissions for
Local Administration, often known as 'the
Ombudsman service'. There are three
Ombudsmen in England, and one each in
Wales and Scotland. A report is issued on each
complaint fully investigated and, if injustice
caused by maladministration is found, the

Local Authority Expenditure and Funding in England, 1999–2000

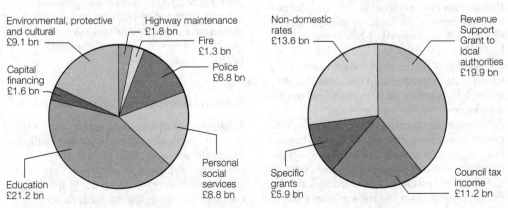

Source: Department of the Environment, Transport and the Regions

local Ombudsman normally proposes a remedy. The council must consider the report and reply to it. In 1998–99 the local government Ombudsmen for England received 15,869 complaints, 6% more than in 1997–98. Compensation or redress was obtained or recommended in 4,268 cases (27%). In Wales there were 1,134 complaints, 8% more than in 1997–98.

In Northern Ireland a Commissioner for Complaints deals with complaints alleging injustices suffered as a result of maladministration by district councils and certain other public bodies.

Pressure Groups

Pressure groups are informal organisations which aim to influence the decision-making of Parliament and Government, to the benefit of their members and the causes they support. There is a huge range of groups, covering politics, business, employment, consumer affairs, ethnic minorities, aid to developing countries, foreign relations, education, culture, defence, religion, sport, transport, social welfare, animal welfare and the environment. Some have over 1 million members, others only a few dozen. Some exert pressure on a number of different issues; others are concerned with a single issue. Some have come to play a recognised role in the way the UK is governed; others seek influence through radical protest.

Pressure Groups and Policy

Pressure groups operating at a national level have a number of methods for influencing the way the UK is governed. Their action may highlight a particular problem, which is then acknowledged by the Government. Groups whose scale of membership indicates that they are broadly representative in their field may then be consulted by a government department, or take part in Whitehall working groups or advisory councils. Ministers have a duty to give fair consideration and due weight to informed and impartial advice from civil servants, so pressure groups often seek to inform civil servants and thus influence the advice given to ministers.

Pressure Groups and Government

The principle of consultation to gain the consent and co-operation of as wide a range of organisations as possible, and ensure the smooth working of laws and regulations, plays an important part in the relationship between government departments and interested groups.

In some instances a department is under legal obligation to consult interested groups. The Government has a duty to consult organised interests, providing the pressure groups involved have a broad enough membership for them to represent a majority view, and that they observe confidentiality about their discussions with the department. Members of pressure groups often have direct expertise, and an awareness of what is practicable, and can give advice and information to civil servants engaged in preparing policy or legislation. In return, the pressure groups have the opportunity to express their opinions directly to the Government. The contacts between civil servants and pressure group representatives may be relatively informal—by letter or telephone—or more formal, through involvement in working parties or by giving evidence to committees of inquiry.

Administration by Pressure Groups

The Government also makes grants to pressure groups which, as well as speaking on behalf of their members or for an issue, provide a service. For example, Relate: National Marriage Guidance has received grants for the advice centres it runs, and government departments make grants to a number of pressure groups for research relating to public policy.

Pressure Groups and Parliament

Lobbying—the practice of approaching MPs or peers, persuading them to act on behalf of a cause, and enabling them to do so by providing advice and information—has substantially increased in recent years. A common pressure group tactic is to ask members of the public to write to their MP

CARLISLE

CARMARTHEN

NORWICH

EXETER

LONDONDERRY/
DERRY

RUGBY

INVERNESS

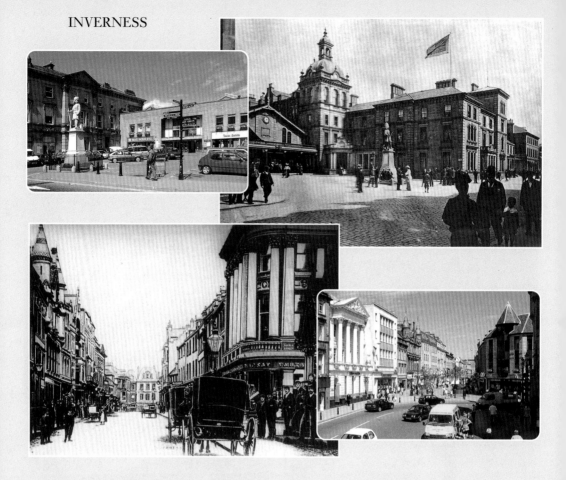

HUDDERSFIELD

about an issue—for example, the Sunday trading laws, or the plight of political prisoners in particular countries—in order to raise awareness and persuade the MP to support the cause.

Parliamentary Lobbyists

Many pressure groups employ full-time parliamentary workers or liaison officers, whose job is to develop contacts with MPs and peers sympathetic to their cause, and to brief them when issues affecting the group are raised in Parliament.

There are also public relations and political consultancy firms specialising in lobbying Parliament and Government. Such firms are employed by pressure groups—as well as by British and overseas companies and organisations—to monitor parliamentary business, and to promote their clients' interests where they are affected by legislation and debate.

Raising Issues in Parliament

Other ways through which pressure groups may exert influence include:

- suggesting to MPs or peers subjects for Private Members' Bills (see p. 49); many pressure groups have ready-drafted legislation waiting to be sponsored;
- approaching MPs or peers to ask parliamentary questions as a means of gaining information from the Government and of drawing public attention to an issue;
- suggesting to MPs subjects for Early Day Motions (see p. 52) and suggesting to peers subjects for debates; and
- orchestrating public petitions as a form of protest against government policy, or to call for action.

The UK in the European Union

As a member of the European Union (EU), the UK is bound by the various types of European Community (EC) legislation and wider policies (for policies, see chapter 7). Almost all UK government departments are involved in EU-wide business, and EU legislation is an increasingly important element of government.

The Community enacts legislation which is binding on the national governments of the 15 member states or, in certain circumstances, on individuals and companies within those states. British government ministers take part in the discussions and decision-making, and the final decision is taken collectively by all the member states.

The UK Representative Office (UKREP), based in Brussels, conducts most of the negotiations on behalf of the UK Government. The devolved administrations of Scotland and Wales are also represented by UKREP, although in October 1999 a new office specifically aimed at helping to promote Scotland's interests within the EU will be opened in Brussels.

The EU has three legislative bodies:

The Council of the European Union is the main decision-making body. Member states are represented by the ministers appropriate to the subject under discussion. When, for instance, education matters are being discussed, the UK's Secretary of State for Education and Employment attends with his or her European counterparts. The Presidency of the Council changes at six-monthly intervals and rotates in turn among the 15 member states of the Union.

The European Council, which is not a legislative body and which usually meets twice a year, comprises the heads of State or Government accompanied by their foreign ministers and the President of the European Commission and one other Commissioner. The Council defines general political guidelines and has an important role in common foreign and security policy.

The European Commission is the executive of the EU. It implements the Council's decisions, initiates EC legislation and ensures that member states put it into effect. Each of the 20 Commissioners, who are drawn from all member states (there are two from the UK), is responsible for a specific policy area, for example, education, transport or agriculture. The Commissioners are entirely independent of their countries, and serve the EU as a whole.

The European Parliament, which plays an increasingly important role in the EU legislative process, has 626 directly elected members (MEPs), including 87 from the UK. The Parliament is consulted about major decisions and has substantial shared power with the Council of the European Union over the EC budget. In areas of legislation, its role varies between: *consultation*, where it can influence but does not have the final say in the content of legislation; the *co-operation and assent* procedures, where its influence is greater; and *codecision* (introduced by the Maastricht Treaty and extended in the Amsterdam Treaty—see chapter 7), where a proposal requires the agreement of both the Council and the European Parliament.

Elections to the Parliament take place every five years, most recently in June 1999. In the UK, these were held under a proportional voting system,[14] bringing the country in line with the other member states.

The European Parliament meets in full session in Strasbourg for about one week every month, although its committee work normally takes place in Brussels.

EC legislation is issued in some areas jointly by the Council of the European Union and the European Parliament, by the Council in other areas, or by the Commission under delegated powers. It consists of Regulations, Directives and Decisions.

European Parliament Elections, June 1999	
UK Results by Party—MEPs elected	
Conservative	36
Labour	29
Liberal Democrat	10
UK Independence Party	3
Green	2
Plaid Cymru	2
Scottish National Party	2
Democratic Unionist Party	1
Ulster Unionist Party	1
Social Democratic and Labour Party	1

- Regulations are directly applicable in all member states, and have the force of law without the need for implementing further measures;
- Directives are equally binding as to the result to be achieved but allow each member state to choose the form and method of implementation; and
- Decisions, like Regulations, do not normally need national implementing legislation. They are binding on those to whom they are addressed.

Other EU Institutions

Each member state provides one of the judges to serve in the European Court of Justice, which is the final authority on all aspects of Community law. Its rulings must be applied by member states, and fines can be imposed on those failing to do so. The Court is assisted by a Court of First Instance, which handles certain cases brought by individuals and companies. The UK is also represented on the Court of Auditors, which examines Community revenue and expenditure, to see that it is legally received and spent.

[14] The regional list system is used for England, Scotland and Wales, under which an elector may cast his or her vote for a party list of candidates. England is divided into nine regions while Scotland and Wales each constitute one region. These 11 regions each return between four and 11 MEPs, depending on the size of the electorate of each region. Northern Ireland, which also constitutes one region, continues to use the single transferable vote system to return its three MEPs.

Further Reading

Committee on Standards in Public Life:

—First Report: *MPs, Ministers and Civil Servants, Executive Non-departmental Public Bodies.* Cm 2850. HMSO, 1995.

—Second Report: *Local Public Spending Bodies.* Cm 3270. The Stationery Office, 1996.

—Third Report: *Standards in Public Life—Standards of Conduct in Local Government in England, Scotland and Wales.* Cm 3702. The Stationery Office, 1997.

—Fourth Report: *Review of Standards of Conduct in executive NDPBs, NHS Trusts and local public spending bodies.* Cm 3701. The Stationery Office, 1997.

—Fifth Report: *The Funding of Political Parties in the United Kingdom.* Cm 4057. The Stationery Office, 1998.

The Funding of Political Parties in the United Kingdom. Cm 4413. The Stationery Office, 1999.

Modernising Government. Cm 4310. The Stationery Office, 1999.

Modernising Parliament: Reforming the House of Lords. Cm 4183. The Stationery Office, 1998.

Public Services for the Future: Modernisation, Reform, Accountability. Cm 4181 (1998) and supplement Cm 4315 (1999). The Stationery Office.

Modern Local Government: In Touch with the People. Cm 4014. The Stationery Office, 1998.

Local Voices: Modernising Local Government in Wales. Cm 4208. The Stationery Office, 1998.

Statistics: A Matter of Trust. Cm 3882. The Stationery Office, 1998.

Freedom of Information: Consultation on Draft Legislation. Cm 4355. The Stationery Office, 1999.

The British System of Government (3rd edn). Aspects of Britain series, The Stationery Office, 1996.

Honours and Titles (2nd edn). Aspects of Britain series, HMSO, 1996.

Parliament (3rd edn). Aspects of Britain series, The Stationery Office, 1996.

Websites

Central government: www.open.gov.uk

Houses of Parliament: www.parliament.uk

British Monarchy: www.royal.gov.uk

7 Overseas Relations

The aims of British foreign policy are to promote the interests of the United Kingdom abroad and to contribute to a strong international community. The UK is one of the 15 member states of the European Union, and a founding member of NATO (the North Atlantic Treaty Organisation). It also has a central position in the Commonwealth and in the United Nations Security Council.

In 1999 the UK played an important role in NATO's military action in the Federal Republic of Yugoslavia to stop Serbian repression and displacement of the ethnic Albanian population in the province of Kosovo, and in the subsequent establishment of a safe environment in which Albanian Kosovar refugees could return to their homes.

INTERNATIONAL ORGANISATIONS

Active membership of the United Nations (UN), the European Union (EU), the Commonwealth, NATO, the Western European Union (WEU) and other major international organisations remains central to the British Government's foreign policy objectives.

United Nations

The UK is a founder member of the UN and one of the five permanent members of the Security Council, along with China, France, Russia and the United States. It supports the purposes and principles of the UN Charter, including the maintenance of international peace and security, the development of friendly relations among nations, the achievement of international co-operation on economic, social, cultural and humanitarian issues and the protection of human rights and fundamental freedoms.

The UK is the sixth largest contributor to the UN regular budget (just over 5% in 1998) and the fifth largest contributor to peacekeeping operations (see p. 88). In order to enhance the UN's effectiveness, the UK is pressing for comprehensive institutional and financial reform. It encourages all member states to pay their contributions promptly and

The European Union

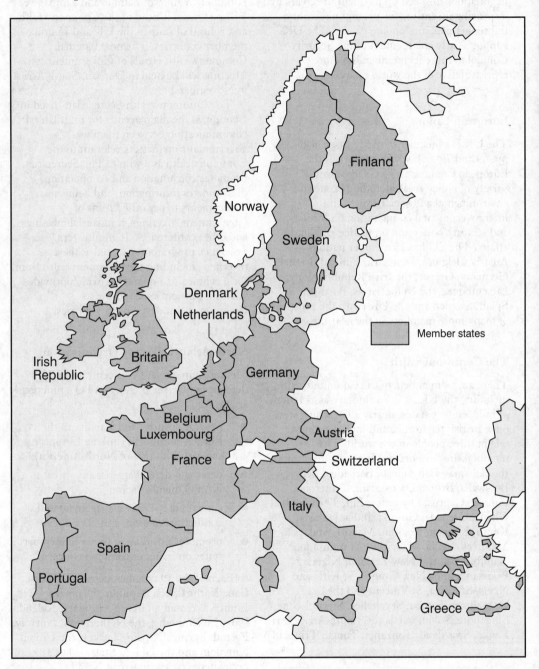

Finland

Norway

Sweden

Denmark

Netherlands

Member states

Irish
Republic

Britain

Germany

Belgium
Luxembourg

Austria

France

Switzerland

Italy

Spain

Portugal

Greece

in full, and has also taken a leading role in negotiations to speed up payment of arrears by improving incentives for prompt payers and tightening penalties on late payers. The UK supports early enlargement of the Security Council to make its membership more representative of the world today.

European Union

The UK is a member of the EU (see also pp. 69 and 79–83), which comprises the European Community (EC—covering a variety of policy areas including economic, environmental and social issues) and intergovernmental co-operation on foreign and security policy and on justice and home affairs. The EU has 15 member nations— Austria, Belgium, Denmark, Finland, France, Germany, Greece, the Irish Republic, Italy, Luxembourg, the Netherlands, Portugal, Spain, Sweden and the UK (with the prospect of many more members in the near future).

The Commonwealth

There are 54 members of the Commonwealth, including the UK. It is a voluntary association of independent states, nearly all of which were once British territories, and includes almost one in three people in the world. The members are Antigua and Barbuda, Australia, the Bahamas, Bangladesh, Barbados, Belize, Botswana, Brunei Darussalam, Cameroon, Canada, Cyprus, Dominica, Fiji, The Gambia, Ghana, Grenada, Guyana, India, Jamaica, Kenya, Kiribati, Lesotho, Malawi, Malaysia, Maldives, Malta, Mauritius, Mozambique, Namibia, Nauru,[1] New Zealand, Nigeria,[2] Pakistan, Papua New Guinea, St Kitts and Nevis, St Lucia, St Vincent and the Grenadines, Samoa, Seychelles, Sierra Leone, Singapore, Solomon Islands, South Africa, Sri Lanka, Swaziland, Tanzania, Tonga, Trinidad and Tobago, Tuvalu,[3] Uganda, United Kingdom, Vanuatu, Zambia and Zimbabwe.

The Queen is head of the Commonwealth and is head of state in the UK and 15 other member countries. The next biennial Commonwealth Heads of Government Meeting will be held in Durban, South Africa, in November 1999.

The Commonwealth Secretariat, based in London, is the main agency for multilateral communication between member governments on matters relevant to the Commonwealth as a whole. The Secretariat promotes consultation and co-operation, disseminates information, and helps host governments to organise Heads of Government Meetings, ministerial meetings and other conferences. It administers assistance programmes agreed at these meetings, including the Commonwealth Fund for Technical Co-operation, which provides advisory services and training to Commonwealth developing countries.

North Atlantic Treaty Organisation

Membership of NATO is central to UK defence policy (see p. 99). NATO's functions are to:

- provide security and stability in the Euro-Atlantic area (linking European security with that of North America);

- deter and defend against any threat to a NATO member state;

- contribute to crisis management and conflict prevention; and

- promote consultation between member states on issues of common concern.

Each of the 19 member states—Belgium, Canada, the Czech Republic, Denmark, France, Germany, Greece, Hungary, Iceland, Italy, Luxembourg, the Netherlands, Norway, Poland, Portugal, Spain, Turkey, the United Kingdom and the United States—has a permanent representative at NATO headquarters in Brussels. The Czech

---

[1] Nauru became a full member of the Commonwealth in May 1999.

[2] Having been suspended from the Commonwealth in 1995 because of political repression and human rights abuses, Nigeria resumed full membership in May 1999 upon the completion of its transition to democracy.

[3] Tuvalu is a 'special' member, entitled to take part in all Commonwealth activities, with the exception of the biennial Commonwealth Heads of Government Meetings.

The Commonwealth

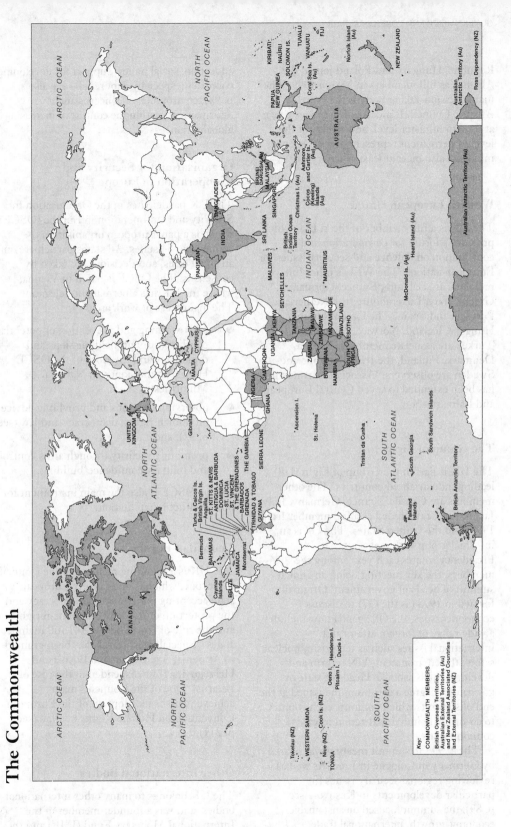

Republic, Hungary and Poland joined the Alliance as full members in March 1999. The main decision-taking body is the North Atlantic Council. It meets at least twice a year at foreign minister level, and weekly at the level of permanent representatives. Defence ministers also meet at least twice a year.

Western European Union

The UK is a full member of the WEU, which provides a forum for co-operation and consultation on defence and security issues for European nations. The WEU's other full members are Belgium, France, Germany, Greece, Italy, Luxembourg, the Netherlands, Portugal and Spain. The Czech Republic, Hungary, Iceland, Norway, Poland and Turkey are associate members; Austria, Denmark, Finland, the Irish Republic and Sweden are observers. 'Associate partnership' has been extended to seven Central European and Baltic states.

The Group of Eight

The UK is part of the Group of Eight (G8) leading industrialised countries. The other members are Canada, France, Germany, Italy, Japan, Russia (included as a full member from 1998) and the United States. The G8 is an informal group with no secretariat. Its Presidency rotates each year among the members, the key meeting being an annual summit of heads of government. Originally formed in 1975 (as the G7) to discuss economic issues, the G8 agenda now includes a wide range of foreign affairs and international issues such as terrorism, nuclear safety, the environment, UN reform and development assistance. Heads of state or government agree a communiqué issued at the end of summits which commits each country to co-ordinate individual action towards common goals.

The 1999 G8 summit meeting was hosted by Germany in Cologne in June. As well as reviewing regional security issues (in particular developments in Kosovo—see p. 89), the summit focused on sustainable economic growth, international trade, education, social policy, support for developing countries (especially debt relief—see also p. 94), environmental concerns and disarmament, within the context of increasing globalisation.

Organisation for Security and Co-operation in Europe

The UK participates in the Organisation for Security and Co-operation in Europe (OSCE), which is a pan-European organisation comprising 54 states. All states participate on an equal basis, and decisions are taken by consensus. The OSCE is based in Vienna, where the UK has a permanent delegation. The main areas of work are:

- early warning and prevention of potential conflicts through field missions and diplomacy and the work of the OSCE High Commissioner on National Minorities;
- observing elections and providing advice on human rights, democracy and law (see p. 92); and
- promoting security through arms control and military confidence-building.

The OSCE is also the main instrument for post-conflict rehabilitation.

Council of Europe

The UK is a founding member of the Council of Europe, which is open to any European state accepting parliamentary democracy and the protection of fundamental human rights and the rule of law. There are 41 full member states. 'Special guest status' has been granted to Armenia, Azerbaijan, and Bosnia and Herzegovina (but suspended in the case of Belarus). One of the Council's main achievements is its adoption of the European Convention on Human Rights in 1950 (see p. 211).

Other International Bodies

The UK belongs to many other international bodies, and was a founder member of the International Monetary Fund (IMF) and the

World Bank. The IMF regulates the international financial system and provides credit for member countries facing balance-of-payments difficulties. The World Bank provides loans to finance economic and social projects in developing countries.

The UK is also a member of the World Trade Organisation (WTO—see p. 419), and of the Organisation for Economic Co-operation and Development (OECD), which promotes economic growth, support for less developed countries and worldwide trade expansion. Other organisations to which Britain belongs or extends support include the regional development banks in Africa, the Caribbean, Latin America and Asia, and the European Bank for Reconstruction and Development.

OVERSEAS TERRITORIES

The UK's Overseas Territories (formerly the Dependent Territories) have a combined population of nearly 180,000. The territories are listed on p. 78. Most have considerable self-government, with their own legislatures. Governors appointed by the Queen are generally responsible for external affairs, internal security and defence. Certain responsibilities are delegated to locally elected representatives but the ultimate responsibility for government rests with British ministers. The British Indian Ocean Territory, the British Antarctic Territory, and South Georgia and the South Sandwich Islands have non-resident Commissioners, not Governors. The UK aims to provide the Overseas Territories with security and political stability, ensure efficient and honest government, and help them achieve economic and social advancement. None of the territories has yet expressed a desire for independence from Britain.

A new Overseas Territories Department within the Foreign & Commonwealth Office (FCO—see p. 96) provides a single focus and direct point of contact with the UK Government, although Gibraltar, because of its EU status (see p. 79), is dealt with primarily by the FCO's European Departments. The Department for International Development (DFID—see

In March 1999 the Government published a White Paper, *Partnership for Progress and Prosperity*, setting out the results of a review of the relationship between the UK and the Overseas Territories. The White Paper proposes offering British citizenship to all those residents of the Overseas Territories who do not already have it and who wish to take it up,[4] and confirms that the reasonable assistance needs of the territories are a first call on the UK development aid programme (see p. 93). Overseas Territories are required to match high international standards in the regulation of financial services by the end of 1999, and must abide by the same standards of human rights and good governance to which the UK subscribes. The Government also proposes an Environment Charter between the UK and the Overseas Territories to build their capacity to protect their environment, manage their resources and ensure that Britain can fully reflect their interests in international agreements.

p. 93) has also set up an Overseas Territories Unit, which administers aid to Anguilla, the British Virgin Islands, Montserrat, the Turks and Caicos Islands, St Helena (and its dependencies) and Pitcairn. A new Council of the Territories, including the Chief Minister or equivalent in each territory and chaired by the relevant FCO minister, convenes its first meeting later in 1999.

Falkland Islands

The Falkland Islands are the subject of a territorial claim by Argentina. The UK Government does not accept the Argentine claim and is committed to defending the

---

[4] The offer of right of abode will be on a non-reciprocal basis, as the territories do not have the capacity to absorb uncontrolled numbers of new residents. The UK Government's decision on this follows the precedent set by Gibraltar and the Falkland Islands whose existing right of abode is also non-reciprocal.

The Overseas Territories at a Glance

Anguilla (capital: The Valley)
Area: 96 sq km (37 sq miles) (Sombrero, 5 sq km).
Population: 10,700 (1996).
Economy: tourism, construction, offshore banking, fishing and farming.
History: British territory since 1650.

Bermuda (capital: Hamilton)
Area: 53.3 sq km (20.6 sq miles).
Population: 60,144 (1996).
Economy: financial services and tourism.
History: first British settlers in 1609–12. Government passed to Crown in 1684.

British Antarctic Territory
Area: 1.7 million sq km (660,000 sq miles).
Population: no permanent inhabitants. There are two permanent British Antarctic Survey stations staffed by 40 people in winter and 150 in summer. Scientists from other Antarctic Treaty nations have bases within the territory.
History: the Antarctic Peninsula was discovered in 1820. The British claim to the British Antarctic Territory dates back to 1908. The UK is one of 44 signatories to the 1961 Antarctic Treaty, which states that the Antarctic continent should be used for peaceful purposes only.

British Indian Ocean Territory
Area: 54,400 sq km (21,000 sq miles) of ocean.
Land area: the Chagos Archipelago with no permanent inhabitants.
Economy: territory used for defence purposes by the UK and United States; 1,500 military personnel plus 1,500 civilians.
History: archipelago ceded to Britain by France under 1814 Treaty of Paris.

British Virgin Islands (capital: Road Town)
Area: 153 sq km (59 sq miles).
Population: 19,100 (1997).
Economy: tourism and financial services.
History: discovered in 1493 by Columbus and annexed by Britain in 1672.

Cayman Islands (capital: George Town)
Area: 259 sq km (100 sq miles).
Population: 36,600 (1997).
Economy: tourism and financial services.
History: 1670 Treaty of Madrid recognised Britain's claim to islands.

Falkland Islands (capital: Stanley)
Area: 12,173 sq km (4,700 sq miles).
Population: 2,220 (1996), plus British garrison.
Economy: fishery management and sheep farming.
History: first known landing in 1690 by British Naval Captain, John Strong. Since 1833 they have been under continuous British occupation and administration.

Gibraltar
Area: 6.5 sq km (2.5 sq miles).
Population: 27,192 (1997).
Economy: financial services, tourism, port services.
History: ceded to Britain in 1713 under Treaty of Utrecht.

Montserrat (capital: Plymouth)
Area: 102 sq km (39 sq miles).
Population: 3,500 (mid-1998).
Economy: agriculture and fishing.
History: colonised by English and Irish settlers in 1632.

Pitcairn, Ducie, Henderson and Oeno (capital: Adamstown)
Area: 35.5 sq km (13.7 sq miles).
Population: 54 (end-1998).
Economy: fishing, agriculture and postage stamp sales.
History: occupied by mutineers from the British ship *Bounty* in 1790; annexed as a British colony in 1838.

St Helena (capital: Jamestown)
Area: 122 sq km (47 sq miles).
Population: 5,000 (1998).
Economy: fishing and agriculture.
History: taken over in 1661 by British East India Company.

Ascension Island (St Helena Dependency)
Area: 88 sq km (34 sq miles).
Population: 1,123 (1998).
Economy: communications and military base.
History: British garrison dates from Napoleon's exile on St Helena after 1815.
Government: Governor of St Helena with local administration.

Tristan da Cunha (St Helena Dependency)
Area: 98 sq km (38 sq miles).
Population: 285 (1998).
Economy: fishing.
History: occupied by British garrison in 1816.
Government: Governor of St Helena with local administration and elected Island Council.

South Georgia and the South Sandwich Islands
No indigenous population. First landing by Captain Cook in 1775. Small British military detachment on South Georgia, plus British Antarctic Survey all-year research station on Bird Island.

Turks and Caicos Islands (capital: Cockburn Town)
Area: about 500 sq km (193 sq miles).
Population: 20,000 (1997).
Economy: tourism, financial services and fishing.
History: Europeans from Bermuda first occupied the islands from about 1678, then planters from southern states of America settled after the War of Independence in the late 18th century.

Islanders' right to live under a government of their own choice. The inhabitants wish to remain under British sovereignty and this right of self-determination is enshrined in the 1985 Falkland Islands Constitution.

In 1982 Argentina invaded and occupied the Islands, but its forces were expelled by British troops following Argentina's failure to abide by UN resolutions requesting its forces to withdraw. The UK and Argentina, while sticking to their respective positions on sovereignty, maintain diplomatic relations and continue to discuss their common interests in the South Atlantic region, such as fisheries conservation and the exploitation of oil reserves.

Gibraltar

Spain ceded Gibraltar to Britain in perpetuity under the 1713 Treaty of Utrecht but has long sought its return. However, the UK is firmly committed to the principle, set out in the preamble to the 1969 Gibraltar Constitution, that it will never enter into arrangements under which the people of Gibraltar would pass under the sovereignty of another state against their freely and democratically expressed wishes.

Gibraltar has an elected House of Assembly, and responsibility for a wide range of 'defined domestic matters' is devolved to elected local ministers. The territory is within the EU, as part of the United Kingdom member state, although it is outside the common customs system and does not participate in the Common Agricultural or Fisheries Policies or the EU's value added tax arrangements. The people of Gibraltar have been declared UK nationals for EU purposes.

EUROPEAN UNION POLICY

The UK Government aims to play a leading role in Europe and increase the UK's political influence in the EU. Relationships with other member states have been reinforced (see box) and the UK has recently launched joint initiatives with Germany, France, Spain, Italy and Sweden. The Government is also keen to make the EU and its institutions more accessible and relevant to the public in the UK. Britain's priorities in Europe include creating jobs, enlargement and institutional reform.

Step Change Initiative

In September 1998 the Prime Minister called for a stepping up of the UK's relations with the rest of Europe, to form ever stronger links with the EU and applicant countries in order to emphasise Britain's central place in the Union. The aims of this longer-term initiative are to maximise British influence in Europe, build alliances to promote British interests, and highlight the UK's positive approach towards Europe. A key element is to intensify contacts at all levels by all UK government departments and to encourage joint initiatives.

The Treaties

The Union had its origins in the post-Second World War resolve by Western European nations, particularly France and Germany, to prevent further conflict and establish lasting peace and stability.

Rome Treaty

The 1957 Rome Treaty, establishing the European Community, defined its aims as the harmonious development of economic activities, a continuous and balanced economic expansion and an accelerated rise in the standard of living. These objectives were to be achieved by the creation of a common internal market, including the elimination of customs duties between member states, free movement of goods, people, services and capital, and the elimination of distortions in competition within this market. These aims were reaffirmed by the 1986 Single European Act, which agreed measures to complete the single market (see p. 81). The UK joined the European Community in 1973.

Under the Rome Treaty, the European Commission speaks on behalf of the UK and the other member states in international trade negotiations. The Commission negotiates on a mandate agreed by the European Council.

(For further information on overseas trade, see chapter 25.)

Maastricht Treaty

The 1992 Maastricht Treaty amended the Rome Treaty and made other new commitments, including moves towards economic and monetary union. It established the EU, which comprises the European Community and intergovernmental arrangements for a Common Foreign and Security Policy (CFSP—see p. 83) and for increased co-operation on interior/justice policy issues (see p. 84). The Maastricht Treaty also codified the principle of subsidiarity under which, in areas where the Community and member states share competence, action should be taken at European level only if its objectives cannot be achieved by member states acting alone and can be better achieved by the Community. In addition, the Treaty introduced the concept of EU citizenship as a supplement to national citizenship.

Amsterdam Treaty

Following the Maastricht Treaty, an intergovernmental conference was convened in 1996 to consider further amendments. This resulted in the Amsterdam Treaty, which was signed by member states in 1997 and entered into force in May 1999. Among the main points are:

- provisions for the Council to take action to combat discrimination on the basis of gender, race, religion, sexual orientation, disability or age;
- more co-ordination by member states of measures designed to cut unemployment;
- integration of the social chapter (see p. 82) into the Treaty, following its adoption by the UK;
- new mechanisms to improve the co-ordination and effectiveness of the CFSP;
- an increase in the areas subject to co-decision between the Council of Ministers and European Parliament, and simplification of the co-decision procedure (see p. 70);

- a binding protocol on subsidiarity; and
- measures to enhance openness in the EU institutions.

Treaty Ratification

Any amendments to the Treaties must be agreed unanimously and must then be ratified by each member state according to its own constitutional procedures. In the UK, Treaty ratifications must be approved by Parliament before they can come into force.

Economic and Monetary Union

The Maastricht Treaty envisaged economic and monetary union in three stages. The first, establishment of the single market (see pp. 81 and 418–19), was largely achieved at the end of 1993. The second stage included the establishment of a European Monetary Institute (EMI) responsible for technical preparations for stage 3 and for strengthening co-ordination of member states' monetary policy. Stage 3, beginning on 1 January 1999, was the adoption of a single currency (the euro).

In May 1998 a meeting of EU heads of state and government agreed that 11 of the 15 EU member states (excluding the UK, Denmark, Greece and Sweden) would take part in the single currency from its launch date. It also agreed the establishment of the European Central Bank (ECB) from June 1998.

On 1 January 1999 conversion rates between currencies of qualifying countries and the euro were legally fixed. The euro became the legal currency in those countries and the ECB assumed responsibility for formulating the monetary policy of the euro area. Since no euro banknotes or coins will be available until 1 January 2002, national currencies will continue to exist in parallel to the euro and national banknotes and coins will be used for all cash transactions.

The UK Government's policy towards joining the single currency is described in chapter 23 (p. 388).

Enlargement

Enlargement of the EU—to include those European nations sharing its democratic values and aims, which are functioning market economies, able to compete in the EU and to take on the obligations of membership—is a key policy objective for the Union. In March 1998, an accession process with ten European applicant states and Cyprus was launched and formal accession negotiations started with Poland, Hungary, Slovenia, Estonia, Cyprus and the Czech Republic. Substantive negotiations opened in November 1998 and are progressing. Preparations for future negotiations with Bulgaria, Latvia, Lithuania, Romania and Slovakia to join the EU continue, with the examination of their national laws alongside the body of EU legislation.

The EU is also preparing institutional changes to take account of enlargement. An important stage in this process was the agreement reached at the Berlin European Council in March 1999 on internal policy reforms and a financial settlement for 2000–06 (see below). The Cologne European Council in June 1999 agreed that an intergovernmental conference in 2000 would decide the remaining institutional changes necessary for enlargement. These include the number of Commissioners in an enlarged Union, the weighting of votes in the Council and a review of the issues which might be decided by qualified majority voting.

The EU has recognised Turkey's eligibility for membership. It is pursuing closer political and economic co-operation on the basis of a strategy to prepare Turkey for membership endorsed at the European Council in June 1998.

European Community Budget

The Community's revenue consists of levies on agricultural imports from non-member countries, customs duties, the proceeds of value added tax receipts and contributions from member states based on gross national product (GNP).

In March 1999 the European Council agreed on budgetary amendments. The 'own resources' system for financing the EU will maintain the current ceiling of 1.27% of GNP; but, progressively from 2001, more revenue will be raised from contributions linked to GNP and less from VAT receipts and customs payments. It was also agreed that the UK's annual budget rebate (in place since 1984, and without which the British net contribution would be far greater than that justified by its share of Community GNP) would remain.

Single Market

The single market, providing for the free movement of people, goods, services and capital within the EU, came into effect in 1993 (see also p. 418). Largely complete in legislative terms, it covers, among other benefits, the removal of customs barriers, the liberalisation of capital movements, the opening of public procurement markets and the mutual recognition of professional qualifications.

Measures to improve the operation and effectiveness of the single market were approved by the European Council in 1997. These sought to ensure the removal of remaining obstacles, with better implementation and enforcement of existing rules, and action to simplify single market legislation. By February 1999 the proportion of single market Directives not yet implemented by all member states had fallen to just under 14% of the total.

Under the European Economic Area (EEA) Agreement, which came into force in 1994, most of the EU single market measures have been extended to Iceland, Norway and Liechtenstein. EEA member states comprise the world's largest trading bloc, accounting for 40% of all global trade.

Transport, Energy and Telecommunications

The concept of a common transport policy was laid down in the Treaty of Rome (see also chapter 22). EU objectives in energy policy are security of supply, liberalised energy markets and environmental protection. Most of the legislation on liberalisation of the telecommunications market was in force by 1998.

The EU is also working towards the completion of trans-European networks in transport, energy and telecommunications. The aim is to improve the interconnection and interoperability of national networks.

Agriculture, Fisheries and the Environment

The Common Agricultural Policy (CAP) was designed to secure food supplies and to stabilise markets. It also, however, created overproduction and unwanted food surpluses, placing a burden on the Community's budget. The Common Fisheries Policy is concerned with the conservation and management of fishery resources. See chapter 27 for further details of these policies, and of the UK's support for CAP reform (agreement on which was reached by EU member states in March 1999).

Environmental considerations are integrated into all areas of EU policymaking. See chapter 20 for more information about EU environmental protection measures.

Regional and Infrastructure Development

The economic and social disparities within the EU are considerable, and will become more evident with further enlargement. To address the problem of regional imbalances there are a number of Structural Funds designed to:

- promote economic development in underdeveloped regions;

- regenerate regions affected by industrial decline;

- combat long-term unemployment and help young people into the labour market;

- help workers adapt to industrial changes and to advances in production systems;

- speed up the adjustment of production, processing and marketing structures in agriculture; and

- promote development in rural areas.

Infrastructure projects and industrial investments are financed by the European Regional Development Fund. The European Social Fund supports training and employment measures for the unemployed and young people. The Guidance Section of the European Agricultural Guidance and Guarantee Fund supports agricultural restructuring and some rural development measures. The Financial Instrument of Fisheries Guidance promotes the modernisation of the fishing industry. A Cohesion Fund, set up under the Maastricht Treaty, provides financial help to reduce disparities between EU members' economies. Other initiatives promote new economic activities in regions affected by the restructuring of traditional industries, such as steel, coal and shipbuilding.

New funding levels for the Structural and Cohesion Funds in the period 2002–06 (£141 billion) were agreed by the European Council in March 1999.

The European Investment Bank, a non-profit-making institution, lends at competitive interest rates to public and private capital investment projects.

Employment and Social Affairs

The UK accepted the social chapter (a separate protocol to the Maastricht Treaty) at the European Council in 1997 and agreed to implement the measures already adopted under it by the other 14 member states.[5] Also in 1997, EU member states agreed demanding guidelines to shape their national employment policies and committed themselves to producing national action plans to show progress towards implementation.

A European Employment Pact, aimed at a substantial reduction of unemployment, was approved at the European Council in Cologne in June 1999. The pact, bringing together all the EU's employment policy measures, involves three long-term interlinked processes, namely:

---

[5] In 1998 the UK implemented EU Directives on working time and young workers, which provide that employees do not have to work more than an average of 48 hours a week without their consent (see chapter 11). The Government intends to implement other Directives relating to parental leave and worker consultation in December 1999 and employment rights of part-time workers in April 2000.

- co-ordination of economic policy and improved interaction between wage developments and monetary, budget and fiscal policy, aimed at preserving non-inflationary growth;
- greater efficiency of the labour markets by improving employability, entrepreneurship, adaptability of businesses and employees, and equal opportunities; and
- structural reform and modernisation to improve innovative capacity and efficiency of the labour market and the markets in goods, services and capital.

For details of EU education and youth programmes see chapter 10 (p. 142).

Research and Development

EU spending on research and development (R&D) plays an increasingly important role in enabling Europe to maintain the science and technology base necessary to remain competitive in world markets. Research collaboration among member states is promoted mainly through a series of framework programmes defining priorities and setting out the level of funding. The Government actively encourages UK companies and organisations to participate in collaborative R&D with European partners (see pp. 434–5).

The Fifth Framework Programme (for the period 1999–2002) covers information technology, sustainable development, energy and environment, international research, innovation and small and medium-sized enterprises, improving research potential, and management of living resources.

Common Foreign and Security Policy

The CFSP is intergovernmental and, since 1993, has provided for EU member states to agree unanimously a common foreign and security policy. Common policies and/or joint actions have been agreed on a wide range of international issues. Recent examples include punitive measures against Serbia over violence in Kosovo (see p. 89) and the resumption of dialogue with Iran.

The Amsterdam Treaty (see p. 80) is introducing several key changes to make the policy more effective, including the appointment of a High Representative to help with the formulation, preparation and presentation of CFSP policy decisions, and the establishment of a Policy Planning and Early Warning Unit in the Council Secretariat to sharpen the preparation and focus of common foreign policy decisions.

There are also new decision-making rules. The Treaty preserves the principle that all policy should be decided by unanimity, but states that decisions implementing common strategies, which are themselves agreed by unanimity, will be by qualified majority voting. A member country may prevent a vote being taken by qualified majority voting for 'important and stated reasons of national policy'. Also, a member state may abstain and stand aside from an EU decision/action when its interests are not affected.

The EU continues to look to the Western European Union (see p. 76) to handle defence issues under the CFSP. The Amsterdam Treaty provides for the 'progressive framing of a common defence policy', in which the WEU would support the EU. The WEU also provides the EU with access to an operational military capacity. The Treaty recognises that NATO provides common defence for the UK and its allies.

In December 1998 the European Council called for the preparation of EU common

In late 1998, the UK launched an initiative to strengthen the EU's capacity to respond to crises, on the basis that, if the Union is to play a coherent and effective political role, this needs to be underpinned by a credible European military capability. The initiative envisages that the EU should have the capacity for autonomous action, backed up by appropriate military forces, the means to decide to use them and a readiness to do so, in order to respond to international crises without prejudice to actions by NATO (which would remain the foundation of collective security). This approach was endorsed by the European Council summit in Cologne in June 1999.

strategies on Russia, on Ukraine, on the Mediterranean region and on the western Balkans. The first such strategy, to strengthen the strategic partnership between Russia and the EU, was adopted by the Council in June 1999.

Justice and Home Affairs

The Maastricht Treaty established intergovernmental arrangements for increased co-operation among EU states on justice and home affairs issues. Conventions agreed under these arrangements have included those on EUROPOL (see p. 92), extradition and the protection of EU financial interests.

In 1997 the European Council endorsed an action plan to fight organised crime and to increase international police and customs co-operation (which is due for full implementation by the end of 1999). In addition, EU member states and the candidate member nations agreed in 1998 to step up joint action to combat organised crime.

CENTRAL AND EASTERN EUROPE AND CENTRAL ASIA

European Security

Since the disintegration of the Warsaw Pact and the formation of new governments in Central and Eastern Europe and Central Asia, the European security situation has been transformed. The UK and its NATO allies, together with former Warsaw Pact states, set up the North Atlantic Co-operation Council (NACC) in 1990 to foster co-operation and understanding. In 1994 a NATO summit meeting invited the non-NATO states in Central and Eastern Europe and Central Asia to join a Partnership for Peace, which, among other things, enlists the Partners' assistance in peacekeeping operations and guides their armed forces towards compatibility with those of NATO countries. Then, in 1997, the Euro-Atlantic Partnership Council was established to develop closer political and military co-operation between NATO countries and non-members.

The UK played a major role in negotiations leading to:

- the signature in 1997 of a Founding Act between NATO member states and Russia, introducing new mechanisms for a close and permanent relationship;

- a NATO-Ukraine Charter for a Distinctive Partnership, also signed in 1997; and

- the accession to NATO, in March 1999, of the Czech Republic, Hungary and Poland.

Economic Help

The UK and other Western countries continue to help deal with the economic problems following the fall of Communism, and to promote the development of market economies. The IMF and World Bank, with the UK's active support, provide advice and finance to nearly all countries in the region, while the European Bank for Reconstruction and Development channels Western investment. The EU's PHARE scheme[6] is primarily devoted to aiding Central European countries in the process of reform and development of their infrastructure. Countries of the former Soviet Union and Mongolia receive help through a parallel programme (TACIS),[7] which concentrates on financial services, transport, energy (including nuclear safety) and public administration reform. The UK's Export Credits Guarantee Department (ECGD) provides insurance cover for exporters to a number of these countries.

Know How Fund

The Know How Fund is the UK's programme of bilateral technical assistance to the countries of Central and Eastern Europe and Central Asia. It aims to support their transition to democracy and a market economy by the flexible provision of British skills in a range of key sectors, such as finance, energy

---

[6] An aid programme for economic restructuring in Central Europe, which consists of many individual projects and operations to underpin the process of reform. It was initially applicable to Poland and Hungary, but has since been extended to other countries in Central Europe.
[7] An EU aid programme providing technical assistance to recipient countries.

and public administration, and by encouraging UK investment in the region. Since 1990 the Know How Fund has spent nearly £300 million in the candidate countries.

Association and Co-operation Agreements

The EU has strengthened relations with Bulgaria, the Czech Republic, Estonia, Hungary, Latvia, Lithuania, Poland, Romania, Slovakia and Slovenia by signing Europe (Association) Agreements with them. The agreements provide an institutional framework to support the process of integration, and anticipate accession of these countries to the EU when they are able to assume the obligations of membership (see p. 81).

EU Partnership and Co-operation Agreements have entered into force with Russia (in 1997), Ukraine and Moldova (in 1998), and Kazakhstan, Kyrgyzstan, Georgia, Armenia, Azerbaijan and Uzbekistan (in 1999). A Trade and Co-operation Agreement with Albania and a Co-operation Agreement with Macedonia are in force. The purpose of these agreements is to reduce trade barriers, develop wide-ranging co-operation and increase political dialogue.

EU plans to develop closer links through Stabilisation and Association Agreements with states in south-eastern Europe, providing that they meet the EU's conditions, were endorsed in June 1999.

OTHER REGIONS

Middle East

Peace Process

The UK supported the breakthrough in the Middle East peace process in 1993, when Israel and the Palestine Liberation Organisation (PLO) agreed to mutual recognition and signed a Declaration of Principles on interim self-government for the Palestinians in Israeli-held territories occupied in 1967. The first stage of the Declaration was implemented in 1994, when the Palestinians adopted self-government in the Gaza Strip

and the Jericho area. A peace treaty between Israel and Jordan was also signed in that year. The UK has continued to encourage peace negotiations between Israel, Syria and Lebanon.

In 1995 Israel and the PLO reached an agreement providing for a phased Israeli troop withdrawal from occupied Palestinian areas of the West Bank and for elections to a new Palestinian Council with legislative and executive powers. The UK took part in the international observation of the Palestinian elections in 1996 co-ordinated by the EU.

Subsequent progress has been far from smooth, aggravated by continuing expansion of Israeli settlements in the occupied territories and terrorist bomb attacks in Israel. The UK has sought to complement the peace efforts of the United States, based on the conviction that a lasting resolution must both protect Israel's security and provide a just exchange of land for peace. In October 1998 a further agreement was reached—the Wye River Memorandum (brokered by the US)—providing for a phased Israeli redeployment from the West Bank in parallel with Palestinian achievement of security objectives. However, deadlock once again ensued. In March 1999 the UK and its EU partners called for a resumption of negotiations on 'final status' issues, and reaffirmed the Palestinian right to self-determination including the option of statehood. A new Israeli Prime Minister was elected in May 1999 and the European Council, meeting in June, welcomed his plans to resume talks with the Palestinians and Syrians and to address the withdrawal of Israeli forces from Lebanon. The new Israeli Government and the Palestinians agreed revisions to the Wye River deal in early September 1999.

British assistance to projects related to the peace process (covering, for example, education, social welfare, environmental concerns, human rights, economy and gender issues) through all bilateral and multilateral sources amounts to about £25 million a year. In November 1998 the Government announced a bilateral programme of UK assistance to the Palestinians of £50 million over three years.

Gulf Conflict

The UK, a permanent member of the UN Security Council, condemned Iraq's invasion of Kuwait in August 1990 and supported all Council resolutions designed to force Iraqi withdrawal and restore international legality. Because of Iraq's failure to withdraw, its forces were expelled in February 1991 by an international coalition led by the United States, the UK, France and Saudi Arabia, acting under a UN mandate.

The UN Security Council imposed sanctions on Iraq in August 1990. In April 1991 the Council formalised the ceasefire in the Gulf War and stipulated conditions for Iraqi acceptance, including measures to prevent the development of weapons of mass destruction, recognition of the border with Kuwait and the payment of compensation to those who suffered as a result of the invasion of Kuwait. Sanctions remain in force (although with substantial humanitarian exemptions) because Iraq has failed to comply with the relevant Security Council resolutions. The UK has led efforts to bring relief to the Iraqi people, principally through the 'oil-for-food' programme (under which Iraq may sell oil in exchange for food, medicines and other essential humanitarian supplies).

As part of the agreement ending hostilities, the Security Council authorised the establishment of a Special Commission (UNSCOM) to supervise the elimination of Iraq's weapons of mass destruction. The UK has provided considerable support to UNSCOM and the International Atomic Energy Authority in the form of personnel, equipment and information since the first inspection in 1991.

Continuing failure by the Iraqi regime to co-operate with UNSCOM, and its unwillingness to heed repeated warnings, led to a four-day campaign of air attacks against strategic targets by the United States and the UK in December 1998. Since then, Iraqi forces have persistently tried to shoot down US and UK planes patrolling 'no-fly' zones over southern and northern Iraq, forcing them to respond against Iraqi air defences in line with their rights of self-defence.

The British Government has tabled a draft UN Security Council resolution, proposing a new body to address outstanding Iraqi disarmament issues, as well as further measures to improve the humanitarian situation in Iraq and to deal with Iraq's continued failure to meet its obligations on Kuwaiti detainees and stolen property.

Relations with Iran

In May 1999 the UK and Iranian Governments exchanged ambassadors for the first time since the Iranian revolution in 1979, bringing years of dispute to a close.

Mediterranean

The UK and its EU partners are developing, on the basis of the Barcelona Declaration of 1995, closer links with 11 southern Mediterranean states (and the Palestinian Authority) with the aim of establishing a free trade area by 2010.

Asia-Pacific Region

The UK has well-established relations with Japan, China, the Republic of Korea, many South East Asian nations, Australia and New Zealand, and has defence links with some countries in the region. British commercial activity has developed through increased trade and investment and the setting up of business councils, joint commissions or industrial co-operation agreements. The UK is also taking advantage of increased opportunities for English language teaching, co-operation in science and technology, and educational exchanges.

The Asia-Europe Meeting (ASEM) process was inaugurated in 1996. ASEM is intended to foster closer economic and political ties between EU countries and Brunei, Cambodia, China, Indonesia, Japan, the Republic of Korea, Malaysia, Singapore, the Philippines, Thailand and Vietnam. The UK, which hosted the second ASEM conference in London in 1998, has played a leading role in the establishment of the ASEM Trust Fund and the European Financial Expertise Network (EFEX); the objective of the fund and EFEX is to help the Asian ASEM countries find effective ways to recover from recent serious financial instability in Asia and help prevent future recurrences.

In May 1998 India and Pakistan conducted nuclear tests, disregarding the global non-proliferation regime (see p. 90) and undermining regional security. As President of the EU and G8 at that time, the UK sought to ensure an effective international response to the tests, and both South Asian countries have since indicated their willingness in principle to adhere to the Comprehensive Test Ban Treaty. Serious bilateral tension surfaced again from May 1999 over the disputed territory of Kashmir, prompting the UK and its G8 partners at their June summit meeting to call for an immediate end to military confrontation and a resumption of dialogue.

In 1998 Britain rejoined the South Pacific Commission, having withdrawn from membership in 1995. The Commission provides technical advice and assistance to its Pacific Island members, with which the UK has long-standing and Commonwealth ties. Links with the Pacific are also reinforced by the Lomé Convention (see pp. 420–1).

Hong Kong

In 1997 the UK returned Hong Kong to Chinese sovereignty under the provisions of the 1984 Sino-British Joint Declaration, which contains guarantees about Hong Kong's way of life until at least 2047. Hong Kong's return to China was necessary because of the expiry of the 99-year lease under which the greater part of the territory was transferred by China to Britain under the 1898 Peking Convention.

As set out in the Joint Declaration, Hong Kong is a Special Administrative Region (SAR) of China. Apart from in foreign affairs and defence, the Hong Kong SAR enjoys a high degree of autonomy, maintaining its own government. Its capitalist economy and freedoms, including its social systems, will remain intact for at least 50 years from the date of the handover. The Sino-British Liaison group will remain in existence until 2000 to discuss matters relating to the implementation of the Joint Declaration.

The UK is represented in Hong Kong by the largest British consulate-general in the world. It will continue to have strong responsibilities towards Hong Kong and the 3.5 million British passport holders living there. In addition, Hong Kong is the UK's second largest export market in Asia.

The Americas

The Government believes that the close transatlantic links between the UK, the United States and Canada remain essential to guarantee the security and prosperity of Europe and North America.

The UK and the US co-operate very closely on nuclear, defence and intelligence matters. As founding members of NATO, Britain and the US are deeply involved in Western defence arrangements and, as permanent members of the UN Security Council, work closely together on major international issues. There are also important economic links. The UK is the largest foreign investor in the US, where about 1 million jobs have been created by British investment worth £82.5 billion—nearly one-quarter of all overseas investment in the US. Over 40% of US investment in Europe comes to the UK, a share far bigger than to any other European country. In 1998 the EU and US agreed a formula for resolving differences over extraterritorial trading sanctions against Iran and Cuba. They are also pursuing a programme (through the Transatlantic Economic Partnership and Action Plan) to break down barriers to trade across the Atlantic and to pursue multilateral liberalisation.

Strong links are maintained with Canada, with which the UK shares membership of the Commonwealth, NATO and other key international organisations. In 1997 the Prime Ministers of Britain and Canada issued a joint declaration to modernise and broaden the bilateral relationship. The UK is the second largest foreign investor in Canada and its third largest trading partner.

Important British connections with Latin America date from the participation of British volunteers in the wars of independence in the early 19th century. Greater democracy and freer market economies in the region have enabled Britain to strengthen its relations with Latin American governments. The UK is now one of the largest investors in the region after the United States. The first summit of EU, Latin American and Caribbean heads of state and government was held in Rio de Janeiro at the end of June 1999, with the aim of building a strategic partnership between the two regions based around a political, economic and cultural dialogue.

Africa

The objective of British policy towards Africa is to promote positive change throughout the continent, by building peace, prosperity and democracy. The UK Government is giving political and practical support to efforts to prevent or end African conflicts (for example, in Sierra Leone—see below); promoting trade, reducing debt and supporting development for lasting prosperity; and supporting African governments, organisations and individuals espousing the principles of democracy, accountability, the rule of law and human rights (for example, promoting democratic transition in Nigeria).

Since the abolition of apartheid and the election of an African National Congress government in 1994, South Africa's relations with the UK have broadened into areas ranging from development assistance to military advice, and from sporting links to scientific co-operation. There has also been a steady flow of state and ministerial visits to and from South Africa. The UK is South Africa's largest single trading partner, and largest foreign investor. Both countries are committed to build on this relationship by promoting the further expansion of bilateral trade and investment. A trade, development and co-operation agreement with South Africa was approved by EU leaders in March 1999, providing for the creation of a free trade area.

PEACEKEEPING AND CONTAINMENT

The UN is the principal body responsible for the maintenance of international peace and security. In mid-1999 there were some 10,000 troops from 73 nations deployed to 17 peacekeeping operations around the world.

Britain and UN Peacekeeping

In 1998 the UK was the fifth largest contributor to the UN's peacekeeping costs, meeting 6.2% of the £560 million total. It deploys peacekeeping troops in Cyprus, military observers in Georgia, Sierra Leone and on the Iraq/Kuwait border, and police officers in Bosnia. A small number of British military officers have been seconded to the UN Secretariat's Department of Peacekeeping Operations in New York.

Cyprus

The UK has a contingent of about 315 troops in the UN Force in Cyprus, established in 1964 to help prevent the recurrence of fighting between Greek and Turkish Cypriots. Since the hostilities of 1974, when Turkish forces occupied the northern part of the island, the Force has been responsible for monitoring the ceasefire and control of a buffer zone between the two communities.

Iraq/Kuwait

In 1991, UN Security Council Resolution 687 established a demilitarised zone extending 10 km into Iraq and 5 km into Kuwait to deter violations of the boundary and to observe hostile or potentially hostile actions. The UK, with the other permanent members of the Security Council, contributes 11 personnel to the UN Iraq/Kuwait observer mission (UNIKOM).

Georgia

The UK contributes seven military personnel to the UN Observer Mission in Georgia, which was established in 1993. Its mandate includes monitoring a ceasefire between Georgian government troops and rebels in the Georgian region of Abkhazia.

Sierra Leone

Nine British military observers are deployed to the UN observer mission in Sierra Leone (UNOMSIL). Its role is to monitor and report on the security situation and on

Crisis in Kosovo

From early 1998 there was increasing international concern over the deteriorating situation in the province of Kosovo in the Federal Republic of Yugoslavia (FRY—comprising Serbia and Montenegro) and its implications for regional stability in south-eastern Europe. Excessive repression by Serbian security forces against the overwhelmingly ethnic Albanian population, and terrorism by elements of the Kosovar population, prompted widespread condemnation and calls for a peaceful solution based on the territorial integrity of the FRY and autonomy for Kosovo. The UN Security Council adopted an arms embargo against the FRY, and the EU imposed economic sanctions in response to the repression in Kosovo. In September 1998 the UN Security Council adopted a resolution demanding a ceasefire and the start of real dialogue to secure long-term peace and stability. The UK and its NATO partners threatened to intervene militarily if the Serbian offensive in Kosovo was not stopped.

In October 1998 a ceasefire was agreed which enabled thousands of Kosovar refugees to find shelter, averting a humanitarian crisis over the winter. A verification mission was deployed under the auspices of the OSCE. However, violence continued and the situation worsened significantly in January 1999. A peace conference, held in Paris, broke up in mid-March with the refusal of the Yugoslav delegation to accept a peaceful settlement. On 24 March the UK and other NATO countries began intensive air operations against targets in the FRY in pursuit of a resolution to the Kosovo crisis and to try to prevent an imminent humanitarian catastrophe.

On 3 June 1999 the Yugoslav Parliament and Government (under President Slobodan Milosevic, who has been indicted for war crimes) finally accepted peace terms presented by special EU and Russian envoys. These entailed a verifiable withdrawal of Serbian security forces from Kosovo and deployment of an international security presence (with NATO participation at its core), enabling the return of displaced persons and refugees to their homes in what would become a substantially autonomous province.

NATO and Serbian military commanders reached agreement on the implementation of the Serbian withdrawal on 9 June and the UK and its G8 partners agreed a resolution to put to the UN Security Council on the terms for the deployment of the international mission in Kosovo. With the subsequent authorisation (on 10 June) of the UN, NATO and other forces (including around 10,000 British troops) began deploying into Kosovo on 12 June to begin the task of restoring peace to the province.

As well as military support, the UK is contributing £90 million in humanitarian and emergency assistance to alleviate the consequences of the Kosovo crisis.

progress with disarmament and demobilisation programmes.

Bosnia and Herzegovina

The UK supports the establishment of a peaceful, multi-ethnic and democratic Bosnia and Herzegovina, and is helping to implement the 1995 Dayton Peace Agreement. The Stabilisation Force (SFOR), around 33,000-strong in mid-1999, comprises troops from NATO nations and other contributing countries, including Russia and a number of other Partnership for Peace members (see p. 84). The UK contributes about 4,500 troops to SFOR. In addition, 80 UK police officers are with the UN International Police Task Force in Bosnia.

The main task of SFOR is to ensure continuing compliance with the military aspects of the Dayton Agreement, including monitoring the actions of the armed forces and inspecting weapon sites. It also provides broad support to the main organisations responsible for the civil aspects of the Agreement, including the Office of the High

Representative, the International Police Task Force, the UN High Commissioner for Refugees and the OSCE. Although the Dayton military requirements have largely been met, some of the civil aspects have yet to be fully implemented.

The UK is assisting the International Criminal Tribunal in The Hague, which was set up to try those indicted for war crimes in the former Yugoslavia. With other SFOR contributors, British forces have detained several of those indicted. Although governments in the region are responsible for arresting suspects and handing them over to the Tribunal, in most cases they have failed to do so. As well as supporting the Tribunal through the provision of staff, information and forensic science expertise, the UK has provided funds to establish a second courtroom in The Hague.

The UK has provided over £400 million in humanitarian and reconstruction aid (bilaterally and through the EU) to Bosnia since 1992.

ARMS CONTROL

Because of the global reach of modern weapons, the UK has a clear national interest in preventing proliferation of weapons of mass destruction and promoting international control.

Weapons of Mass Destruction

Nuclear Weapons

The main instrument for controlling nuclear weapons is the 1968 Nuclear Non-Proliferation Treaty (NPT). The UK took an active part in securing its indefinite extension in 1995. It also played an important role in negotiations on the Comprehensive Test Ban Treaty (CTBT), which it signed in 1996 and ratified in 1998. The CTBT, with its permanent verification system, will come into force when it has been ratified by 44 named states. The British Government is pressing for negotiation of a treaty banning future production of fissile material for use in nuclear weapons.

While large nuclear arsenals and risks of proliferation remain, the Government considers that the UK's minimum nuclear deterrent (see p. 102) remains a necessary and continuing element of British security.

Biological Weapons

The 1972 Biological Weapons Convention provides for a worldwide ban on such weapons, but there is no effective verification mechanism. The UK has taken a leading role in international negotiations to strengthen the Convention with a Protocol containing measures to verify compliance, including mandatory declarations of key facilities and challenge inspections.

Chemical Weapons

The 1993 Chemical Weapons Convention, which came into force in 1997, provides for a worldwide ban on chemical weapons. The Organisation for the Prohibition of Chemical Weapons is responsible for verification. During the negotiations the UK made major contributions to drawing up extensive and effective verification provisions. All the necessary British legislation is in place to license the production, possession and use of the most toxic chemicals and to implement the Convention's trade controls.

Conventional Armed Forces

The UK and its NATO partners have reached a number of agreements whose purpose is to enhance security and stability in Europe. The UK is working with its allies and other European countries to develop and improve these agreements in the light of the changing security environment.

The main agreements are:

● the 1990 Conventional Armed Forces in Europe (CFE) Treaty, which limits the numbers of heavy weapons in the countries of NATO and the former Warsaw Pact, and includes a verification regime. The CFE Treaty is widely regarded as a linchpin of European security; over 50,000 heavy weapons have been destroyed under the Treaty by its signatories;

- the Vienna Document, developed under the auspices of the OSCE, which is a politically binding agreement by 54 states on the promotion of stability and openness on military matters in Europe; it contains a wide range of confidence- and security-building measures, and verification arrangements; and

- the 1992 Open Skies Treaty, which provides for the overflight and photography of the entire territory of the 27 participating states to monitor their military capabilities and activities. The Treaty, which is being provisionally applied, requires ratification by Russia and Ukraine for entry into force.

The UN Register of Conventional Arms, which came into effect in 1992, is intended to allow greater transparency in international transfers of conventional arms and to help identify excessive arms build-ups in any one country or region. The British Government has pledged to strengthen the Register by encouraging greater disclosure of information on arms exports and arms transfers by all countries.

Landmines

The UK signed the Ottawa Convention banning the use, production, trade, transfer and stockpiling of anti-personnel landmines in 1997. The Convention, which Britain ratified in 1998, entered into force on 1 March 1999 and sets a deadline to destroy stocks of such mines within four years from that date. The UK will have destroyed all its stocks (excepting those to be used for training purposes) by the end of 1999.

The UK has a programme to support humanitarian demining activities, which is focused on helping affected countries develop the capacity to clear landmines and improving the co-ordination of international demining resources.

Export Controls

The UK plays a leading role in all of the international control regimes which govern the export of conventional arms, technology associated with weapons of mass destruction and 'dual-use' goods (those having a legitimate civil use as well as a potential military application).

In 1997 the British Government issued new criteria for assessing licence applications for arms exports, one of the provisions of which is that licences will not be granted if there is a clearly identifiable risk that weapons might be used for internal repression or international aggression. At the same time it banned the export of certain equipment for which there is clear evidence that it has been used for torture or other abuses; it also declared its commitment to preventing British companies from manufacturing, selling or procuring such equipment and to pressing for a global ban.

In 1998 the EU adopted a new code of conduct setting high common standards for arms export licensing in all EU countries.

The UK Government issues an annual report (since 1998) on strategic export controls. The report explains UK policy on arms exports and gives details of physical exports and of what equipment has been licensed for export.

HUMAN RIGHTS

The UK Government has stated its commitment to working for improvements in human rights standards across the world and, in 1999, published its second annual human rights report describing the activities and initiatives pursued during the previous year. The £5 million Human Rights Project Fund, launched in 1998, has supported almost 300 projects worldwide (for example, judicial and legal training in Brazil and China). The UK has also supported the establishment of a strong International Criminal Court to try cases of genocide, crimes against humanity and war crimes. The Government signed the Court's Statute in November 1998 and hopes to be among the first 60 states to ratify it.

International Conventions

United Nations

Universal respect for human rights is an obligation under the UN Charter. Expressions of concern about human rights do not, therefore, constitute interference in the internal affairs of another state.

The UK Government promotes the standards set out in the Universal Declaration of Human Rights, which was adopted by the UN General Assembly in 1948. Since this is not a legally binding document, the General Assembly adopted two international covenants on human rights in 1966, placing legal obligations on those states ratifying or acceding to them. The covenants came into force in 1976, the UK ratifying both in the same year. One covenant deals with economic, social and cultural rights and the other with civil and political rights. States which are parties to the covenants undertake to submit periodic reports detailing compliance with their terms. Each covenant has a treaty-monitoring body which examines these reports. The UK recognises the competence of these bodies to receive and consider state-to-state complaints. Other international instruments to which the UK is a party include those on:

- the elimination of racial discrimination;
- the elimination of all forms of discrimination against women;
- the rights of the child;
- torture and other cruel, inhuman or degrading treatment or punishment;
- the prevention of genocide;
- the abolition of slavery; and
- the status of refugees.

Council of Europe

The UK is also bound by the Council of Europe's Convention for the Protection of Human Rights and Fundamental Freedoms, which covers areas such as:

- the right to life, liberty and a fair trial;
- the right to marry and have a family;
- freedom of thought, conscience and religion;
- freedom of expression, including freedom of the press;
- freedom of peaceful assembly and association;

- the right to have a sentence reviewed by a higher tribunal; and
- the prohibition of torture and inhuman or degrading treatment.

Organisation for Security and Co-operation in Europe

The OSCE's Office for Democratic Institutions and Human Rights (in Warsaw) promotes participating states' adherence to commitments on human rights, democracy and the rule of law, and takes a lead in monitoring elections. The Office shares information and provides a forum for expert exchanges on the building of democratic institutions and the holding of elections in participating states. It also provides expertise and training on constitutional and legal matters, and promotes practical measures to strengthen civil administration.

CRIME AND TERRORISM

The UK plays a major role in international efforts to combat illegal drugs, working with producer and transit countries, especially those where drug production and trafficking represent a direct threat to the UK. Over 50 drug liaison officers are stationed in UK missions in key countries, in co-operation with the host authorities. Working with its EU partners, the UK is helping Latin American, Caribbean and Central Asian states to stem the transit of drugs across their territories. The UK is also actively involved in the United Nations drug control structure, and is one of the largest contributors to the UN International Drug Control Programme. Britain had a co-ordinating role on behalf of the EU at the UN General Assembly's Special Session on Drugs in 1998, where declarations were adopted on reducing the supply of, and demand for, drugs; money laundering; and alternative agricultural development.

The UK and its EU partners are tackling serious and organised international crime through, for example, the establishment of the European Police Office (EUROPOL) to support investigations and operations conducted by national law enforcement agencies. EUROPOL powers and duties are set out in the EUROPOL Convention, which entered into force in October 1998. EU member states also belong to the International Criminal Police Organisation (INTERPOL). British liaison with INTERPOL is provided by the National Criminal Intelligence Service (see p. 217).

The UK Government has stressed its condemnation of all terrorist acts, its opposition to concessions to terrorist demands and its commitment to ensuring that terrorists do not benefit from their acts. It works bilaterally with other like-minded governments, and multilaterally through the UN, EU and G8, to promote closer international co-ordination against terrorism. The UK is party to 11 international counter-terrorism conventions agreed between 1963 and 1991, and in 1998 was one of the first countries to sign the UN Convention on the Suppression of Terrorist Bombings. It is taking an active part in the UN on two new international counter-terrorism conventions on terrorist financing and acts of nuclear terrorism.

The UK contributes to international efforts to counter financial crime, for example through its membership of the Financial Action Task Force against money laundering.

DEVELOPMENT CO-OPERATION

The Department for International Development (DFID) is the UK government department responsible for promoting development and the reduction of poverty internationally. The UK Government is committed to the internationally agreed target to halve the proportion of people living in extreme poverty by 2015, together with associated targets including basic healthcare provision and universal access to primary education by the same date. UK expenditure on development assistance is being increased from £2.06 billion in 1997–98 to £3.04 billion in 2001–02.

Most of DFID's assistance is concentrated in the poorest countries in Asia and sub-Saharan Africa, which will receive 76% of country allocations in 2001–02. DFID also works in middle-income countries and in the

transition countries (former communist states) in Central and Eastern Europe to try to ensure that the widest number of people benefit from the process of change.

Partnerships

The British Government aims to work in partnership with poorer countries which themselves have a commitment, and credible plans, to eliminate their poverty. As well as working with governments, DFID is promoting co-operation with local and private sector interests. Legislation is paving the way for the creation of a Public-Private Partnership (see p. 403) in the Commonwealth Development Corporation—the Government's main instrument for investing in developing countries—to enable it to mobilise more resources for development.

DFID is also seeking a more effective relationship with the international institutions through which around 50% of the development programme is spent.

A key element of the UK approach is a commitment to seek greater coherence on all aspects of government policy affecting developing countries. Policies on issues such as trade, investment and agriculture need to take account of the needs of poor countries and contribute to agreed sustainable development objectives.

Promoting Sustainable Livelihoods

The UK works to promote sound economic management, including well-founded monetary and fiscal policies, in poorer countries. The Government believes that good policies support the strong, broad-based, economic growth which is necessary for poverty reduction. Emphasis is increasingly placed on development assistance at the sector level—for example, in health, education and agriculture. UK support is often targeted at the promotion of employment and small enterprise, restructuring of public expenditure and taxation, and the reversal of environmental degradation. DFID has recently provided such assistance in Ghana, South Africa, Bangladesh and Uganda.

DFID believes that effective government regulation is essential to ensure markets deliver benefits to poor people. It promotes regulation of utilities and financial markets to ensure fair competition and to prevent exploitation of market power. Well-regulated banks, credit co-operatives and stock markets boost domestic savings and promote private sector investment. The UK has taken a lead in improving financial regulation in Asia where instability has led to increased poverty in some areas.

Land tenure arrangements can be a significant determinant of poverty. The UK is encouraging land reform in, for example, India, South Africa and Eastern Europe. It is aiming to improve access to credit and savings; training in business or vocational skills; appropriate technologies; and market information. DFID is investing in basic infrastructure to improve access to markets, for example in rural transport in Nepal.

Good Governance

DFID believes that the quality of governance determines whether poor people achieve their rights and receive basic services. In the past most of its efforts went into improving the efficiency of government through civil service and revenue reform, policing, local government and public enterprise privatisation. DFID now intends to address wider issues. Its new approach will cover a number of strands—democratic accountability, fundamental freedoms, tackling corruption, and access to public services and to justice—which, when brought together, should lead to governance which is representative of, and accountable to, all the people and effective in realising their rights.

Tackling Debt

The UK Government has called for greater efforts by the international community to remove the debt burdens of the poorest, most heavily indebted countries which are committed to eliminating poverty. These calls have been reinforced by the international campaign, led by British agencies and the churches, for the cancellation of unpayable debt.

The UK Government pressed successfully for a comprehensive review of the Highly Indebted Poor Countries (HIPC) initiative to be carried out in 1999, and in March 1999 called for faster and wider debt relief so that HIPC countries have a permanent way out of their debt problems. The G8 summit in Cologne in June 1999 endorsed this call and proposed changes to the HIPC framework. If approved, the proposed revisions to the HIPC initiative will mean that debt relief is delivered more widely and more quickly. The UK Government has also emphasised that the purpose of debt relief is to enable countries to tackle poverty more effectively; it therefore supports the G8 statement that the central objective of debt relief is to release resources for investment in programmes to reduce poverty.

Conflict Prevention and Resolution

Violent conflict disrupts lives and livelihoods, destroys societies and economies, and reduces people's access to basic services. DFID aims to reduce conflict by building the political and social means to enable the resolution of disputes without recourse to violence. This includes promoting economic growth to benefit all sections of society, and ethical trade and investment conditions which are fair to all countries.

DFID also undertakes targeted measures such as addressing small arms proliferation, strengthening international mechanisms for conflict reduction, protecting human rights in conflict situations and supporting post-conflict reconciliation, and working closely with the UN system and in the EU.

Removing Gender Discrimination

Addressing gender inequalities, and supporting specific initiatives for women's advancement, are key elements of UK development policies and programmes. With an estimated 70% of the world's poor being made up of women and girls, greater gender equality is a precondition for the elimination of poverty. A concern for issues of gender equality is incorporated into DFID activities wherever and whenever this is feasible. In 1998–99, about 43% of new bilateral commitments across all sectors (worth almost

£568 million) had gender equality as either a principal or significant objective.

Health

Better health for poor people is a critical component of DFID's overall strategy to reduce by half the numbers in absolute poverty by 2015. DFID proposes to work with others to develop effective international and national policies and systems that promote and safeguard the health of poor people. Priority is being given to supporting:

- strong efficient and effective health systems;
- public health programmes and services which safeguard the right to health:
- a more effective global response to HIV/AIDS;
- a healthier and safer physical and social environment;
- greater utilisation of clean water and sanitation; and
- social sector policies that will affect positively health and fertility.

Education

Helping countries to provide primary education for all their children by 2015 represents a major challenge. Current estimates are that 150 million children do not go to school and many drop out before attaining useful levels of basic education. Almost 900 million adults are illiterate, two-thirds of them women. DFID is working with governments to widen access to school for girls and boys, to improve the quality of education offered, and to keep children in school for the whole primary cycle.

Education plays an essential part in helping people to develop their skills and escape from poverty. In recognition of this, DFID has recently made substantial commitments to the development of education in a number of countries, including £67 million in Uganda, £51 million in Ghana and £34 million in Bangladesh.

Emergency and Humanitarian Needs

The UK's objectives in helping to deal with disasters are not only to save lives, through the provision of financial, material and technical assistance, but also to rebuild communities and livelihoods, and make countries less vulnerable to future hazards. DFID provides humanitarian assistance through governments, UN agencies, the Red Cross, non-governmental organisations and, when necessary, through direct service delivery.

In the last year DFID has responded to a large number of natural disasters including hurricanes in the Caribbean and Central America, floods in Bangladesh and China and, most recently, a severe earthquake in Turkey. Substantial humanitarian assistance has also been provided following more complex crises such as in Kosovo (see p. 89) and Sudan.

Environment

The UK Government believes that poverty elimination can only be achieved through sustainable development, requiring action at local, national, regional and global levels. The UK promotes sustainable livelihoods by community-based approaches to the better management of common property resources, such as forests, grazing land and fresh water. It also aims to improve the access of poor people to energy, water, transport and shelter through infrastructure development and the encouragement of private sector investment.

At a national level the UK is helping countries develop their own national strategies for sustainable development and meet their commitments under the multilateral environmental agreements for climate change, biodiversity, desertification and depletion of the ozone layer.

The Government believes that richer countries should lead in addressing global environmental problems. It also believes that nations and businesses should act responsibly in the handling of new technologies such as genetically modified organisms.

The Global Environment Facility (GEF) and the Multilateral Fund of the Montreal Protocol (MFMP—see p. 338) support developing countries and countries with economies in transition to meet the additional costs of multilateral environmental agreements. In 1998 the GEF was replenished by US$2.75 billion. The MFMP will be replenished in 2000. Since their inception, the UK has contributed £215 million to the GEF and £70 million to the MFMP.

ADMINISTRATION OF FOREIGN POLICY

Foreign & Commonwealth Office

The Foreign & Commonwealth Office (FCO) is in charge of foreign policy. It is headed by the Foreign and Commonwealth Secretary, who is responsible for the work of the FCO and the Diplomatic Service (see p. 61). Diplomatic and consular relations are maintained with 184 countries, and the UK has 220 diplomatic posts worldwide. British diplomatic missions also employ some 7,800 locally engaged staff. Staff overseas deal with political, commercial and economic work; entry clearance to the UK and consular work; aid administration; and information and other activities, such as culture, science and technology.

The FCO's executive agency, Wilton Park International Conference Centre in West Sussex, contributes to the solution of international problems by organising conferences in the UK, attended by politicians, business people, academics and other professionals from all over the world.

An important function of the FCO is to promote understanding of British foreign policies and to project an up-to-date image of the UK worldwide, beyond the reaches of government-to-government diplomacy. Key elements of FCO-funded public communication work include:

- publications, television and radio programmes, the FCO website (see Further Reading), British Satellite News (used regularly by almost 190 television stations worldwide to supplement their news coverage) and various other information initiatives;

- scholarship schemes for overseas students (see p. 143) and programmes for influential foreign visitors;
- the BBC World Service (see p. 275); and
- the British Council (see below).

Other Departments

Several other government departments are closely involved with foreign policy issues. The Department for International Development administers the UK's development aid programmes. The Ministry of Defence maintains military liaison with the UK's NATO and other allies. The Department of Trade and Industry (DTI) has an important influence on international trade policy and commercial relations with other countries, including EU member states. The FCO and DTI work together on export and investment promotion initiatives that focus on the needs of British industry (although the Government has accepted the recommendation of a recent review that trade promotion and development activities of the two departments should be unified in a new joint operation—see p. 423). HM Treasury is involved in British international economic policy and is responsible for the UK's relations with the World Bank and other international financial institutions. British EU policy is co-ordinated through the Cabinet Office European Secretariat.

BRITISH COUNCIL

The British Council is the UK's principal agency for cultural relations overseas. Its purpose is to promote a wider knowledge of the UK and the English language and to encourage cultural, scientific, technological and educational co-operation between the UK and other countries. Its work also supports the FCO's objective of increasing respect and goodwill for the UK. The Council:

- helps people to study, train or make professional contacts in the UK;
- enables British specialists to teach, advise or establish joint projects abroad;
- teaches English and promotes its use;

- provides library and information services;
- promotes scientific and technical training, research collaboration and exchanges; and
- encourages appreciation of British arts and literature.

The Council works in 254 towns and cities in 110 countries. It runs 225 libraries and information centres which have about 370,000 members borrowing over 9 million books, videos and tapes each year. Each year the Council organises over 400 science seminars and 2,000 exchanges of researchers, and administers over 560,000 British professional and academic examinations. In addition, it manages or supports 3,000 events each year with its international partners in the fields of the performing arts, film and television, visual arts, literature and design. The Council is financed partly by a grant from the FCO and partly by income from revenue-earning activities, such as English language teaching, the administration of examinations, and bilateral and international aid contract work. The training and education programmes organised by the Council as part of the British aid programme receive funding from DFID.

Educational Exchanges

The British Council recruits teachers for work overseas, organises short overseas visits by British experts, encourages cultural exchange visits, and organises academic interchange between British universities and colleges and those in other countries.

The British aid programme has helped fund certain Council programmes, such as:

- recruitment of staff for overseas universities;
- secondment of staff from British higher education establishments; and
- organisation of short-term teaching and advisory visits.

The Council's Central Bureau for Educational Visits and Exchanges focuses on education for international understanding through partnerships between educational establishments, curriculum-related exchange programmes, and workshops and conferences related to professional international experience. Information is also provided on work, study and travel opportunities worldwide. The Bureau is government-funded and is the national agency in the UK for many EU education and training programmes.

Further Reading

Foreign & Commonwealth Office Departmental Report 1999: The Government's Expenditure Plans 1999–00 to 2001–02. Cm 4209. The Stationery Office, 1999.

Department for International Development Departmental Report 1999: The Government's Expenditure Plans 1999–00 to 2001–2002. Cm 4210. The Stationery Office, 1999.

Eliminating World Poverty: a Challenge for the 21st Century. Cm 3789. The Stationery Office, 1997.

The British Council: Annual Report 1998-99.

Partnership for Progress and Prosperity: Britain and the Overseas Territories. Cm 4264. The Stationery Office, 1999.

Websites

Foreign & Commonwealth Office: www.fco.gov.uk

Department for International Development: www.dfid.gov.uk

British Council: www.britcoun.org

The Commonwealth: www.thecommonwealth.org

8 Defence

Britain's defence policy supports its wider foreign and security policy, which is to maintain the country's freedom and territorial integrity, and that of its Overseas Territories, as well as its ability to pursue its legitimate interests at home and abroad. As a member of NATO (the North Atlantic Treaty Organisation), the UK makes a significant contribution to efforts to maintain stability throughout Europe.

STRATEGIC DEFENCE REVIEW

In 1998 the Government published a comprehensive Strategic Defence Review, which reassessed the UK's security interests and defence needs, and considered how the roles, missions and capabilities of the armed forces should be adjusted to meet the new strategic realities. The Review concluded that there was no immediate or direct military threat to the UK or its Overseas Territories, but that the end of the Cold War had introduced instability and uncertainty in Europe. There remained the potential threat of the proliferation of nuclear, chemical and biological weapons, terrorism, organised crime and the break-up of existing states with attendant ethnic and religious conflict. In the new security environment, the Review concluded that Britain needed the capability to assist in preventing or containing international crises by rapidly deploying highly trained and well-equipped forces to areas where they were required. The Review therefore set out a range of initiatives to

improve the operational effectiveness of the armed forces (see p. 102). The Government's aim is strong, modern and cost-effective defence, now and for the longer term.

The planned changes outlined in the Review are also designed to reinforce the UK's continuing commitment to international peace and security through NATO and the Western European Union (WEU—see p. 76), and through other international organisations such as the United Nations (UN—see p. 72) and the Organisation for Security and Co-operation in Europe (OSCE—see p. 76).

Defence Missions

The Review redefined the defence missions which underpin the UK's defence planning. These are:

- peacetime security;
- security of the Overseas Territories;
- defence diplomacy;

- support to wider British interests;
- peace support and humanitarian operations;
- responding to regional conflicts both inside and outside the NATO area; and
- responding to strategic attack on NATO.

NORTH ATLANTIC TREATY ORGANISATION

The UK is a founder member of NATO, which celebrated its 50th anniversary in April 1999. UK membership of the organisation is the cornerstone of British defence policy. The Alliance embodies the transatlantic relationship that links North America and Europe in a unique defence and security partnership. The number of members was increased to 19 in March 1999 with the accession of the Czech Republic, Hungary and Poland. Most of the UK's forces are assigned to NATO.

Adaptation of NATO

As part of its continuous post-Cold War evolution, NATO has pursued a number of initiatives, including:

- the establishment of the Euro–Atlantic Partnership Council, which provides the framework for co-operation between NATO and its Partner countries (including former members of the Warsaw Pact);
- the continuing development of the Partnership for Peace initiative, aimed at enhancing practical military co-operation between NATO and Partner states; and
- historic agreements with Russia and Ukraine, and continuing dialogue with other countries wishing to join the Alliance.

NATO is also undergoing a period of internal adaptation with the ongoing development of the European Security and Defence Identity (under which NATO assets and capabilities could be made available for WEU operations), a major review of the military command structure, and the implementation of a Combined Joint Task Force concept. The Alliance summit in Washington in April 1999 approved a new strategic concept for NATO and the launch of an initiative to improve its defence capabilities to ensure the effectiveness of future multinational operations across the full range of Alliance missions. There was also progress at the summit on the UK's initiative to strengthen Europe's military capability (see p. 83).

Kosovo

The refusal of the Federal Republic of Yugoslavia to sign a peace settlement for the Kosovo crisis resulted in NATO members agreeing unanimously in March 1999 to start air operations over that country to bring the repression in Kosovo to an end (see p. 89). Joining forces from 14 other NATO countries, the UK committed Royal Navy vessels and RAF (Royal Air Force) support and strike aircraft; and elements from the Army deployed in Macedonia and Albania as part of a Kosovo Peacekeeping Force and to provide emergency aid to Kosovo Albanians (since a refugee catastrophe could not be averted). The air campaign was successful and a peace agreement is being implemented.

DEFENCE TASKS

The UK and its Overseas Territories

The armed forces are responsible for safeguarding Britain's land territory, airspace and territorial waters. They also provide for the security and reinforcement, as necessary, of the Overseas Territories and, when required, support for the civil authorities in both the UK and the Overseas Territories.

Maritime Defence

The Royal Navy aims to ensure the integrity of British territorial waters and the protection of British rights and interests in the surrounding seas. The maintenance of a 24-hour, year-round presence in British waters is designed to provide reassurance to merchant ships and other mariners. The RAF also contributes to maritime requirements, for instance through the Nimrod force, which provides air surveillance of surface vessels and submarines.

Land Defence

Army units committed to the defence of the UK, its Overseas Territories and the Sovereign Bases in Cyprus include 21 Regular Infantry battalions and seven Home Service battalions. Among their tasks are military support to the machinery of government in war, military aid to the civil power throughout the UK and its Overseas Territories, maintaining the security of the Overseas Territories, and contributing to the security of national and NATO nuclear forces.

Air Defence

Air defence of the UK and the surrounding seas is maintained by a system of layered defences. Continuous radar cover is provided by the Air Surveillance and Control System (ASACS)—formerly the United Kingdom Air Defence Ground Environment—supplemented by the NATO Airborne Early Warning Force, to which the RAF contributes six E-3D aircraft. The RAF also provides five squadrons of all-weather Tornado F3 air defence aircraft, supported by tanker aircraft and, in wartime, an additional F3 squadron. Royal Navy air defence destroyers can be also linked to the ASACS, providing radar and electronic warfare coverage and surface-to-air missiles. Ground-launched Rapier missiles defend the main RAF bases. Naval aircraft also contribute to British air defence.

Overseas Garrisons

The UK maintains garrisons in Gibraltar, the Sovereign Base Areas of Cyprus, the Falkland Islands and Brunei. Gibraltar provides headquarters and communications facilities for NATO in the western Mediterranean, while Cyprus provides strategic communications facilities as well as a base for operations in the eastern Mediterranean and beyond. The garrison on the Falkland Islands is a tangible demonstration of the Government's commitment to uphold the right of the islanders to determine their own future (see p. 77). The garrison in Brunei is maintained at the request of the Brunei Government. In addition, a jungle training support unit is maintained in Belize.

Northern Ireland

The armed forces provide support to the Royal Ulster Constabulary (RUC) in maintaining law and order and countering terrorism. Up to 18 major units are assigned to Northern Ireland, including six Home Service battalions of the Royal Irish Regiment. The number of units deployed to the Province at any one time is dependent on the prevailing security situation. The Royal Navy patrols territorial waters around Northern Ireland and its inland waterways in order to deter and intercept the movement of terrorist weapons. The Royal Marines provide troops to meet Navy and Army commitments, while the RAF provides elements of the RAF Regiment and Chinook, Wessex and Puma helicopters.

Other Tasks

Other tasks include the provision of:

- military assistance to civil ministries, for example in maintaining the essentials of life in the community, providing fishery protection duties and helping in the fight against drugs;
- military aid to the civil community, including during emergencies; and
- military search and rescue.

Britain and its Allies

Maritime Forces

Most Royal Navy ships are committed to NATO and are available for WEU and peacekeeping operations. Permanent contributions are made to NATO's Immediate Reaction and Rapid Reaction Forces in the Atlantic, the English Channel and the Mediterranean. The UK also contributes to NATO's Maritime Augmentation Forces, which are held at the lowest state of readiness and in peacetime comprise ships mainly in routine refit or maintenance.

The main components of the Fleet available to NATO are:

- three aircraft carriers operating Sea Harrier aircraft and Sea King anti-submarine helicopters;

- 32 destroyers and frigates, and 22 mine countermeasure vessels;

- 12 nuclear-powered attack submarines; and

- amphibious forces, including two assault ships and a helicopter carrier.

For information on Britain's independent nuclear deterrent see p. 102.

Land Forces

The multinational Allied Command Europe Rapid Reaction Corps (ARRC) is the key land component of NATO's Rapid Reaction Forces. Capable of deploying up to four NATO divisions, the ARRC is commanded by a British general, and some 55,000 British regular troops are assigned to it, including the UK's contribution of some 60% of the headquarters staff and Corps level combat support and combat service support units. Britain also provides two of the ten divisions available to the Corps—an armoured division of three armoured brigades stationed in Germany, and a division of two mechanised brigades and an airborne brigade based in Britain. An air-mobile brigade, assigned to one of the Corps' two multinational divisions, is also sited in the UK.

Air Forces

The RAF makes a major contribution to NATO's Immediate and Rapid Reaction Forces. Around 100 aircraft and 40 helicopters are allocated to them. Tornado F3, Harrier and Jaguar aircraft, and Rapier surface-to-air missiles form part of the Supreme Allied Commander Europe's Immediate Reaction Force, while Harrier, Jaguar and Tornado GR1/4 aircraft provide offensive support and tactical reconnaissance for the Rapid Reaction Force. Chinook and Puma helicopters supply

troop airlift facilities for the ARRC or other deployed land forces. Modified aircraft provide anti-submarine capabilities for NATO's multinational Maritime Reaction Forces. The RAF provides Nimrod maritime patrol aircraft, and search and rescue helicopters.

The three Tornado GR1/4 squadrons stationed at RAF Bruggen in Germany will be redeployed to the UK by 2002 when the base will be closed. A further Tornado squadron also based at Bruggen was disbanded in early 1999. Two Harrier offensive support squadrons at another German base, RAF Laarbruch, were withdrawn to the UK in early 1999 and that station has closed.

Wider Security Interests

Military tasks to promote the UK's wider security interests may be undertaken by British forces unilaterally or multilaterally under UN, NATO or OSCE auspices. Contingents are deployed in Cyprus, Georgia, Bosnia and Croatia, and on the Iraq/Kuwait border. Over Iraq (see p. 86), Tornado GR1/4s and Jaguars, supported by VC-10s, are policing the no-fly zones to ensure that Iraq does not resume repression of the civilian population and that it does not threaten its neighbours. The Royal Navy is deployed to the Gulf to enforce UN sanctions against Iraq. A substantial British contingent is deployed in Albania and Macedonia to help implement the agreement on Kosovo (see p. 89).

The number of operations against trafficking in illicit drugs has increased in recent years, for example in the Caribbean, where the West Indies Guardship and other Royal Navy ships work closely with the authorities of the United States, the Overseas Territories and the Regional Security System to combat drug trafficking. Although primary responsibility for this work rests with the local law enforcement agencies or other government departments, the armed forces assist where they can do so without detriment to the performance of their other military tasks.

British troops remain ready to participate in operations throughout the world. In the past three years, British troops have taken part in UN and multinational forces in evacuation or humanitarian relief operations in Rwanda, Somalia, Angola, Eritrea, the former Zaire, Sierra Leone and Central America.

About 4,000 overseas students from over 100 countries receive training each year at UK defence establishments. Military assistance is also given through the deployment of service personnel overseas, either on loan or as part of short-term training teams.

NUCLEAR FORCES

Although the Trident submarine force is retained as the ultimate guarantee of national security, the UK and other members of NATO have radically reduced their reliance on nuclear weapons. However, nuclear deterrence still has an important contribution to make in ensuring against the re-emergence of major strategic military threats, in preventing nuclear coercion and in preserving peace and stability in Europe.

The UK is committed to pressing for progress in the negotiations towards mutual, balanced and verifiable reductions in nuclear weapons (see p. 90). When satisfied that verified progress has been made towards the goal of global elimination of nuclear weapons, the Government will ensure that the British nuclear weapons are included in the talks.

Against this background, the Government has undertaken a fundamental re-examination of all aspects of Britain's nuclear capability, and has concluded that fewer than 200 operationally available nuclear warheads are needed—a reduction of one-third. Trident submarines will carry only 48 warheads each, compared with the previous 60 typically deployed. In addition, only one submarine is now on patrol at a time; its missiles are not targeted and it will normally be at several days' 'notice to fire'.

NEW FORCE STRUCTURES AND CAPABILITIES

To achieve its policy objectives, the UK requires forces with a high degree of mobility and effectiveness, at sufficient readiness and with a clear sense of purpose, for combat operations, conflict prevention, crisis management and humanitarian activities.

These forces must be flexible and able to undertake the full range of military tasks.

Measures to increase a joint-service approach to defence were outlined in the Strategic Defence Review, including the creation of:

- Joint Rapid Reaction Forces, a pool of deployable forces from all three Services, able to carry out a range of short-notice missions from war-fighting to peacekeeping operations;

- Joint Force 2000, a joint command of Royal Navy and RAF Harrier aircraft able to operate from aircraft carriers or land bases;

- a new joint helicopter command of some 350 battlefield helicopters—Navy commando helicopters, Army helicopters (including a new attack helicopter when it enters service) and RAF support helicopters;

- a joint Army/RAF ground-based air defence organisation; and

- a joint centre for the development of defence doctrine.

These initiatives aim to further improve the Services' ability to work together efficiently and effectively when required, and to deploy rapidly to potential troublespots and crises. An effective frontline, however, also needs effective logistics, support and equipment. As well as addressing the equipment needs of the Services (see p. 103), the Review sought to improve the way they are supported. Such measures include:

- a Defence Logistics Organisation, covering all three Services;

- the establishment of a second logistic line of communication and two Joint Force Logistic Component Headquarters which will each be able to provide support to an operation of the type conducted in Bosnia and in Kosovo; and

- the restructuring of the management and organisation of the Defence Medical Services, and a commitment to spent an additional £140 million on medical support to deployed forces over the period to March 2002.

Royal Navy

The focus for the Navy will continue to move from large-scale open-ocean warfare to rapid deployment and offshore operations in conjunction with the other Services:

- two large aircraft carriers, capable of operating up to 50 aircraft and helicopters, will replace the existing three aircraft carriers;
- an additional four roll-on, roll-off container ships will strengthen the amphibious force;
- the number of attack submarines will fall from 12 to ten, destroyers and frigates have been reduced from 35 to 32, and mine countermeasure ships will increase to 22 rather than 25 as originally planned; and
- all remaining attack-class submarines will be able to fire Tomahawk land-attack missiles.

Army

Among measures aimed at improving mobility, firepower and the projection of forces are:

- an increase in the number of the armoured or mechanised brigades from five to six through the conversion of the airborne brigade to a mechanised brigade;
- the creation of a new air assault brigade (combining two battalions of the Parachute Regiment), with the new attack helicopter when it enters into service;
- the creation of an additional armoured reconnaissance regiment from an existing armoured regiment, which will be brought back from Germany;
- converting the tank regiments from eight units to six larger ones, each with significantly more personnel and tanks; and
- increasing the operational utility of the Territorial Army (TA—see p. 105).

RAF

The emphasis of the new plans is on the ability to deploy appropriate types of aircraft rapidly to crises. Measures include:

- the procurement of new air-to-air, anti-armour and air-to-surface missiles for Tornado and Eurofighter aircraft;
- developing a new collision warning system for the Tornado GR4;
- improving the capability of the Nimrod reconnaissance aircraft to support both peacekeeping and war-fighting operations; and
- modernising the air transport fleet, in the short term by the acquisition of four C-17 aircraft or their equivalent to provide a strategic airlift capability.

DEFENCE EQUIPMENT

Modern equipment is essential if one of the key aims of Britain's force restructuring programme is to be achieved, namely that of increasing the flexibility and mobility of the armed forces.

Improvements for the *Royal Navy* equipment programme include:

- the introduction of the fourth Trident submarine and the building of the Astute-class attack submarines;
- a modernised destroyer and frigate fleet, including the introduction of a new air defence destroyer which will deploy an anti-air missile system developed with France and Italy;
- the new helicopter carrier, the purchase of additional roll-on, roll-off container ships and the building of two amphibious ships to strengthen the amphibious force; and
- the Merlin anti-submarine helicopter.

The *Army* front line is being enhanced by:

- the introduction of the Challenger 2 battle tank;
- Westland Apache attack helicopters equipped with new anti-tank missiles;

- improved Rapier and new Starstreak air defence missiles;
- new bridging equipment to increase mobility and flexibility; and
- a range of advanced surveillance, target acquisition and reconnaissance equipment.

Improvements for the *RAF* include:

- the Eurofighter from the beginning of the 21st century, to replace Tornado F3 and Jaguar aircraft;
- the upgrading of the Jaguar and Tornado aircraft;
- new Nimrod maritime patrol aircraft;
- orders for new air-launched anti-armour and stand-off missiles; and
- the introduction of EH101 and additional Chinook support helicopters and the introduction of Hercules aircraft.

Defence Procurement

Nearly 45% of the defence budget is spent on military equipment, including the procurement of spares and associated costs. When assessing options, particular consideration is given not just to the initial costs of a project, but also to those necessary to support it throughout its service life. Competition for contracts takes place wherever possible. Measures to improve the procuring of defence equipment, identified by the Strategic Defence Review's 'smart procurement' initiative, include better early planning, an improved through-life approach and joint arrangements with industry. By April 2000, all defence acquisition projects will be run on these 'smart procurement' lines.

International Procurement Collaboration

International collaboration offers military, economic and industrial benefits at a time of rising production costs and reduced defence budgets. The UK plays an active role in NATO's Conference of National Armaments Directors, which promotes equipment collaboration between NATO nations, and in the WEU's Western European Armaments

Group, which is the main European forum for the discussion of armaments matters. The UK is also a founder member of OCCAR, an armament co-operation organisation formed with France, Germany and Italy for managing collaborative procurement activities. Current collaborative programmes in which the UK participates include:

- development of the Eurofighter (with Germany, Italy and Spain);
- anti-tank guided weapons (Belgium, France, Germany and the Netherlands);
- an anti-air missile system (France and Italy);
- a battlefield radar system (France and Germany);
- the EH101 helicopter (Italy);
- a multi-role armoured vehicle (France and Germany); and
- a request for proposals for a future large aircraft (Belgium, France, Germany, Italy, Spain and Turkey).

THE ARMED FORCES

Table 8.1: Strength of Service and Civilian Personnel, 1999

Royal Navy	43,700
Army	109,700
RAF	55,200
Regular reserves	60,900
Volunteer reserves	58,000
Civilians	115,700
UK-based	*100,900*
Locally based	*14,800*

Source: Defence Analytical Services Agency

Commissioned Ranks

Commissions in the armed services, either by promotion from the ranks or by direct entry based on educational and other qualifications, are granted for short, medium and long terms. All three Services have schemes for school, university and college sponsorships.

At the beginning of the 20th century Britain had a Navy second to none. In 1897 over 165 warships were assembled in Spithead to celebrate the Diamond Jubilee of Queen Victoria. This armada included 21 battleships (of a total of 62 battleships in service or being built), 54 cruisers and 20 torpedo boats, all drawn from home waters. The Royal Navy had 112,000 officers and seamen.

The British Army totalled 726,000. The strength of the regular and reserve forces in Britain was 108,000 and 83,000 respectively; a further 120,000 were abroad, including 68,000 in India and 33,000 in other garrisons. Over 415,000 were in auxiliary forces.

When the Boer republics of the Orange Free State and Transvaal in South Africa declared war on Britain in October 1899, the number of British troops in the theatre was no more than 22,000 to defend a 1,000-mile border with the republics. Following 'Black Week' in December 1899, when the British suffered repeated reverses at the hands of the Boer forces, Field-Marshal Lord Roberts, with his Chief of Staff, General Kitchener, took command; the Army was strengthened with regulars, militia, yeomanry and volunteers. At the end of the war in 1902, well over 400,000 troops were in the field against the Boers. To support the Army, over 470,000 horses and 150,000 mules and donkeys were purchased; more than 1,000 ships were brought into service to carry troops and animals; and 1.4 million tons of stores were shipped in.

Commissioned ranks receive initial training at the Britannia Royal Naval College, Dartmouth; the Royal Military Academy, Sandhurst; or the Royal Air Force College, Cranwell. This is followed by specialist training, which may include degree courses at service establishments or universities. Courses of higher training for officers, designed to emphasise the joint approach to the tactical and operational levels of conflict, are provided at a Joint Services Command and Staff College, established in 1997.

Non-commissioned Ranks

Engagements for non-commissioned ranks vary widely in length and terms of service. Subject to a minimum period, entrants may leave at any time, giving 18 months' notice (12 months for certain engagements). Discharge may also be granted on compassionate or medical grounds.

In addition to their basic training, non-commissioned personnel receive supplementary specialist training throughout their careers. Study for educational qualifications is encouraged, and service trade and technical training leads to nationally recognised qualifications. New vocational training and educational initiatives to improve recruitment and retention were announced in the Strategic Defence Review. The Army Foundation College, which opened in 1998, offers a 42-week course combining military training and the opportunity to acquire national qualifications. The course is intended to attract high-quality recruits who will go on to fill senior posts in front-line roles.

Reserve Forces

The Reserve Forces serve alongside the regular forces and are integral to the ability to expand the Services in times of crises. In particular, reserves can provide skills and units not available or required in peacetime. The reserves include former members of the regular armed forces liable for service in an emergency (regular reserve) and volunteer reserves, recruited directly from the civilian community—the Royal Naval Reserve, the Royal Marines Reserve, the TA and the Royal Auxiliary Air Force.

The main contribution of reserves—both individuals and formed units—is to support regular forces in clearly identifiable roles. This requires their full integration into regular formations and ready availability for service, where necessary through selective compulsory call-out during situations short of a direct threat to the UK. Reserves should also be able to serve in peace support operations. Royal Naval and RAF volunteer reserve numbers will increase, and, while the strength of the TA is be reduced from 56,000 to 41,200, it will train as an integral part of the Regular Army, using the same equipment.

Equal Opportunities

The Ministry of Defence and the Services are committed to racial equality programmes and to the elimination of any form of harassment or bullying.

Some 73% of posts in the Royal Navy, 70% of posts in the Army and 96% of posts in the RAF are open to women. The strength of women in the armed forces was 7.7% in April 1999. The Services are also aiming to increase the intake of recruits from the ethnic minorities from 1% to 5% by March 2002.

ADMINISTRATION

The defence budget for 1999–2000 is £22.3 billion. By 2001–02 defence spending will fall from 2.7% to 2.4% of gross domestic product. The current average for NATO European countries is 2.2%.

Defence Management

The Ministry of Defence is both a Department of State and the highest level military headquarters. The Secretary of State for Defence is responsible for the formulation and conduct of defence policy and for the means with which it is carried out. Three junior ministers (one for each Service) and two key officials—the Chief of the Defence Staff (CDS) and the Permanent Under-Secretary (PUS) of State—directly support the Secretary of State in this task.

The CDS is the professional head of the armed forces and the principal military adviser to the Secretary of State and the Government. The three Service Chiefs of Staff report to the CDS and are responsible for their Service's fighting effectiveness, efficiency and morale. The PUS is the Government's principal civilian adviser on defence and has primary responsibility for policy, finance and administration of the Department. The PUS is also personally accountable to Parliament for the expenditure of all public money voted for defence purposes. Both the CDS and the PUS are members of the Defence Council, the highest departmental committee.

A civilian-military central staff support much of the work of Defence Council members, which includes formulating defence policy, resource allocation, defining future equipment requirements and providing the strategic direction for military operations.

Day-to-day activities and management of the armed forces are administered through operational, personnel and logistics commands. The acquisition and support of defence equipment is handled by the Defence Procurement Agency, headed by the Chief of Defence Procurement (CDP), and the new Defence Logistics Organisation (DLO), formed in April 1999 to bring together the three separate service logistics into a single integrated organisation. The DLO is headed by the Chief of Defence Logistics (CDL). The CDP is a member of the Defence Council, as will be the CDL.

Further Reading

The Strategic Defence Review: Modern Forces for the Modern World. Cm 3999. Ministry of Defence. The Stationery Office, 1998.

The Government's Expenditure Plans 1999/2000 to 2001/2002. Departmental Report by the Ministry of Defence. Cm 4208. The Stationery Office, 1999.

Websites
Ministry of Defence: www.mod.uk
NATO: www.nato.int

9   The Social Framework

The population of the UK is increasing and ageing, and living arrangements, relationship formations and lifestyles continue to change. The proportion of lone parent households with dependent children has increased considerably since the 1960s, as has the number of people living alone. There are fewer people marrying, and divorce rates remain high. As living standards rise and technology continues to advance, many more people now have access to home computers and the Internet, satellite and cable television channels, and mobile telephones.

POPULATION PROFILE

The population of the United Kingdom in mid-1998 was estimated to be 59.2 million (see p. 2), the third largest in Europe, and the 18th biggest in the world. The majority of people (about 84%) lived in England, with Northern Ireland having the smallest population of the four countries at 1.7 million (3%). The population density in England is the highest, with about 379 inhabitants per square kilometre.

Since 1961 the population of the UK has increased by 12%, although the four countries have experienced different rates of change. The population of Northern Ireland has increased by 18% over this period, while for England and for Wales the increase has been 14% and 11% respectively. The population of Scotland was actually 1% lower in 1998 than in 1961. Mid-1996 projections suggest that the UK's population will rise to 62.2 million people in 2021. Since the 19th century there has also been a trend for people to move away from congested urban centres into the suburbs. In general, younger people are more likely to live in urban areas and older people in rural areas.

Age and Gender

The UK has an ageing population. The proportion of the population aged 50 and over has nearly doubled in the 20th century, from one in six in 1901 to about one in three in 1998. There has also been a significant increase in the number of people living into their eighties and beyond, and projections indicate that by 2021 there will be 3 million people aged 80 and over, representing almost 5% of the population. Simultaneously, the number of people under the age of 16 has been falling. While about one-quarter of people in the UK were aged under 16 in 1971, this had fallen to just over one-fifth in 1997. Projections indicate that these trends will continue so that by 2021 there will be more people aged 65 and over than children aged under 16 (see chart on p. 108).

UK Population by Selected Age-groups

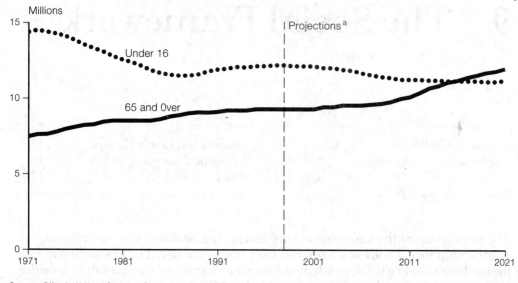

Millions

Projections [a]

Under 16

65 and Over

1971 1981 1991 2001 2011 2021

Sources: Office for National Statistics; Government Actuary's Department; General Register Office for Scotland; Northern Ireland Statistics and Research Agency

[a] 1996 based projections

In 1901 the population of the UK was 38 million. The annual number of deaths was about the same as today, but the population has increased to 59 million.

On average around 1 million babies were born in the UK each year in the early part of the century, although about one child in seven did not live to his or her first birthday. Children were brought up in larger families than now, but by 1900 the decline in family size within marriage, which had first become apparent 30 years earlier, was well established.

Contraception was widely practised by the end of the Victorian era, despite protests from some that it caused spiritual and physical harm to people and society. The majority of births occurred within marriage, and around nine in ten marriages were first marriages. Divorce was very rare, with an average of around 1,000 petitions for divorce filed each year in Great Britain.

The average household in England and Wales consisted of 4.6 people in 1901, partly because of higher fertility rates and larger families, but also because of the presence of resident domestic servants. Contrary to popular belief, there never was a time when 'extended' families were common in Britain.

Between 1901 and 1911 about 800,000 more people emigrated from the UK than migrated into it. Many immigrants were Europeans—especially Irish—seeking work, while some were refugee Jews, also from Europe.

Although more boys are born each year than girls, and men outnumber women in the younger age groups, in 1997 there were about 1 million more women in the UK than men. Around the age of 50 the numbers of men and women are about equal, but above this age women increasingly outnumber men, and in 1997 there were about three women aged 89 to every man of the same age. The male mortality rate is higher than female mortality at most ages.

The size, rate of growth, age and gender structure of the population are dependent upon the influence of birth rates, death rates, and net migration patterns.

Proposals for the next full census of the population were published in March 1999 in the *2001 Census of Population* White Paper. The Government has proposed new questions on the general health of people, the provision of unpaid personal care, and religious affiliation (see p. 240); and revised questions on relationships within the household and ethnic group.

Birth Rates

In 1998 there were about 717,000 live births in the UK, representing 12.2 live births per 1,000 population. This relatively low birth rate reflects a preference for smaller families compared with the past, a trend that began over 100 years ago. Throughout the 1980s and 1990s the total period fertility rate, which indicates average family size, has remained below 2.1, the level needed for long-term natural replacement of the population.

In 1998 almost 38% of all births occurred outside marriage in the UK, around five times the level in 1966. However, a large majority of these births (about eight in ten) in England and Wales in 1998 were jointly registered by both parents, and in most of these cases the parents were living at the same address. The proportion of births outside marriage has consistently been highest for teenagers, and in 1998 about 89% of births to women of this age in England and Wales were outside wedlock. Women under the age of 20 are also the age-group most likely to register their child without details of the father.

Mortality

Since 1971 life expectancy in the UK has been increasing by around two years every decade for men, and around one-and-a-half years for women. At birth the expectation of life is now over 74 years for a man and over 79 years for a woman.

There were about 628,000 deaths in the UK in 1998, a death rate of just under 11 per 1,000 population. There has been a decline in mortality rates at most ages during the 20th century, particularly among children. Rising

standards of living and new developments in medical technology are among the factors that have contributed to improvements in mortality. The infant mortality rate (deaths of infants under one year old per 1,000 live births) was 6.3 for boys and 5.0 for girls in England and Wales in 1998. In general, in all age-groups death rates are higher for men than women, and this helps to explain the gender imbalance among the older population.

The causes of premature death vary by age and gender. In 1994–96 around three in five deaths among men aged between 15 and 30 in England and Wales were due to accidents or violence. Cancer accounts for a higher proportion of deaths among women than men in this age-group. Even so, deaths by external causes still predominate for younger women, although the proportion is smaller than for men. Cancers and circulatory diseases, including heart attacks and strokes, are the most common causes of death among older people. Overall the UK has one of the highest levels of premature death caused by circulatory diseases in the European Union (EU).

HOUSEHOLDS AND FAMILIES

The number of households in Great Britain has risen, from 16.3 million in 1961 to 23.6 million in 1998, at the same time as the average household size has fallen (see Table 9.1). These changes are linked to the rapid increase in the number of one-person households, which now comprise over one-quarter of all households, double the proportion in 1961. The proportion of lone parent households with dependent children has increased threefold since 1961, while over the same period there has been a noticeable decline in the proportion of households consisting of a couple with dependent children. There were 58.3 million people living in private households in the UK in spring 1998. Just over one in ten people lived alone, while seven in ten people were in a household headed by a couple.

Marriage, Divorce and Cohabitation

Slightly over half the population of Great Britain aged 16 and over in 1997 were

Table 9.1: Size of Households in Great Britain			%
	1961	1981	1998
One person	14	22	28
Two people	30	32	35
Three people	23	17	16
Four people	18	18	14
Five people	9	7	5
Six or more people	7	4	2
All households (million)	16.3	20.2	23.6
Average household size (number of people)	3.1	2.7	2.4

Sources: Office for National Statistics and Department of the Environment, Transport and the Regions

married, and about 1 in 12 people were divorced and not remarried. In the same year there were almost four times as many widows as widowers, reflecting the tendency for husbands to be older than their wives, and for women to live longer than men.

In 1997 there were about 310,000 marriages in the United Kingdom, one of the lowest numbers in the 20th century. The increasing prevalence of cohabitation helps to explain this decline. Of the marriages that took place in 1996, about 185,000 were first marriages for both partners, less than half the number in the peak year of 1970. A significant proportion of marriages—about two in five—represent remarriages for one or both partners, and of these the majority were between people who had both been through divorce. There has been a slight decline in the number of religious wedding ceremonies since 1981, and in 1996 they accounted for just under half of all marriage ceremonies in Great Britain. The type of ceremony varies according to the type of marriage. About two in three weddings where both partners were marrying for the first time were conducted by a religious ceremony but for second and subsequent marriages this was less than a fifth.

Although there has been a long-term rise in the number of divorces in the United Kingdom, in recent years the increase appears to have levelled off, with the number granted in 1997—161,100—being below the peak of 1993. The divorce rate for both men and women in England and Wales had fallen to 13

per 1,000 married people in 1997, the lowest rate since 1990. About seven in ten divorces were granted to wives, and the most common reason given by women was the unreasonable behaviour of their husbands. Divorce rates for Scotland and Northern Ireland were lower than the rate in England and Wales.

Cohabitation has become increasingly common in the last two decades, and people in their twenties and early thirties are the most likely to be cohabiting. It is estimated that in 1996 there were nearly 1.6 million cohabiting couples in England and Wales. Of these, around two-thirds were single (never married), and over one-quarter were divorced. Only about 40% of cohabiting men and 30% of cohabiting women were aged over 35.

Family Formation

The proportion of teenagers who became pregnant fell during the 1970s but then rose again in the 1980s, so that in 1990 there were 69 conceptions per 1,000 women under the age of 20 in England and Wales. Since then the teenage conception rate has fallen to just over 62 conceptions per 1,000 in 1997. The under-age conception rate stood at 8.9 conceptions per 1,000 girls aged 13 to 15 in 1997. Just over half of under-age conceptions were terminated by a legal abortion in 1997 (see p. 200).

Generally the fertility rate for older women has increased since 1981, so that women aged 30 to 34 are now more likely to give birth than

110

women in the 20 to 24-year-old age-group. Many women are postponing having children until their late twenties or thirties, having first established themselves in a career. The proportion of women without children has also been increasing. Whereas only about one in nine women born in 1942 were still childless at the age of 45, projections suggest that nearly one in four women born in 1972 will be childless by the time they are aged 45. Meanwhile, technological advances have enabled childless women who wish to conceive to do so. The total number of *in vitro* fertilisation (IVF) treatment cycles has increased considerably since its introduction in 1978, and the success rate has also improved over that time.

In November 1998 the *Supporting Families* Green Paper was published, outlining government proposals for strengthening family life. The welfare of children is at the core of policy, and one of the Government's stated aims is to ensure that all families have access to the advice and support they need. Among proposals to deliver this is a £540 million 'Sure Start' programme aimed at giving families with young children in disadvantaged areas better access to childcare, healthcare, and early education opportunities (see p. 127).

MIGRATION

Population movements occur within the UK as well as internationally. The most mobile age-group within the UK are young adults in their twenties, when many young people leave their parental home to study, work or set up their own home. Over the past two decades there has been a movement of people from north to south, from metropolitan areas to smaller settlements and rural districts, and from inner to outer areas of large cities.

International Migration

In 1997 the total inflow of people intending to stay in the UK for one year or more was 285,000, while the outflow of people leaving to live abroad was 225,000 (see Table 9.2). These figures exclude migration to and from the Irish Republic, and are also likely to exclude people admitted as visitors who were subsequently granted an extension of stay for a year or more. Between 1988 and 1997 net immigration increased the population by about 300,000.

Immigration into the UK is largely governed by the Immigration Act 1971 and the Immigration Rules made under it. The Rules set out the requirements to be met by those who are subject to immigration control and seek entry to, or leave to remain in, the UK. New Immigration Rules came into effect in 1994. British citizens and those Commonwealth citizens who had the right of abode before January 1983 maintain this right and are not subject to immigration control.

Table 9.2: International Migration, 1997

	Inflow	Outflow	Balance
European Union	92,000	70,000	+22,000
Australia, Canada, New Zealand and South Africa	57,000	56,000	+1,000
Other Commonwealth countries	57,000	29,000	+28,000
United States	24,000	25,000	−2,000
Middle East	13,000	11,000	+2,000
Other countries	42,000	34,000	+8,000
All countries	**285,000**	**225,000**	**+60,000**

Source: Office for National Statistics (estimates derived from the *International Passenger Survey*)
Notes: 1. Differences between totals and the sums of their component parts are due to rounding.
2. Figures exclude migration between the UK and the Irish Republic.

With the intention of making the immigration system fairer for marriage partners of British citizens or people already settled in the UK, in 1997 the Government abolished the 'primary purpose' immigration rule introduced in 1980. Under this, an overseas national wishing to settle in the UK with a British citizen or settled spouse could be refused entry to, or leave to remain in, the UK if it was considered that the primary purpose of the marriage was to settle in the UK. In 1997 the Government also introduced a concession to help couples who are by law prohibited from marrying, either because one of the partners cannot remarry or because they are of the same sex. Under the new concession, an applicant may qualify for leave to enter or remain in the UK provided certain criteria are met.

In 1998, some 69,800 people were accepted for settlement, 11,100 more than in 1997. When analysed by nationality there were increases in acceptances particularly from Asia, the Americas and Africa (see Table 9.3). There was little change in the relative importance of each geographical area, however, with the Indian subcontinent and Africa each accounting for almost one-quarter of total acceptances in 1998.

Under the Immigration Rules, nationals of certain specified countries or territorial entities must obtain a visa before they can enter the UK. Other nationals subject to immigration control require entry clearance when coming to work or settle in the UK. Visas and other entry clearances are normally obtained from the nearest or other specified British diplomatic post in a person's home country.

Nationals of the European Economic Area (EEA)—EU member states plus Norway, Iceland and Liechtenstein—are not subject to substantive immigration control. They may work in the UK without restriction. Provided they are working or able to support themselves financially, EEA nationals have a right to reside in the UK.

Asylum

The UK has a tradition of granting protection to those in need, and to this end honours its

Table 9.3: Acceptances for Settlement by Nationality, 1997 and 1998

	1997	1998
Europe	7,740	7,570
of which:		
European Economic Area	110	270
Other Europe	7,640	7,300
Americas	7,790	10,780
Africa	13,200	16,090
Asia	25,610	30,120
of which:		
Indian subcontinent	13,080	16,420
Rest of Asia	12,530	13,700
Oceania	3,100	3,690
Other nationalities[a]	1,280	1,540
All nationalities	**58,720**	**69,790**

Source: Home Office
[a] Includes refugees from South-East Asia.

obligations under the 1951 United Nations Convention, and Protocol, relating to the Status of Refugees. These provide that refugees lawfully resident should enjoy treatment at least as favourable as that accorded to the indigenous population. In recent years there has been a significant change in both the numbers and the motivation of those seeking asylum in the UK, with many asylum seekers apparently motivated by economic rather than political factors. In the late 1980s the total started to rise dramatically from around 4,000 a year during 1985–88 to 44,800 in 1991. Following the introduction of measures in 1991 to deter multiple and other fraudulent applications, numbers fell back in 1992 and 1993. However, applications have increased again, as in many other Western European countries, and reached a record 46,000 in 1998. This was the second largest number in Western Europe, being exceeded only by Germany.

In the United Kingdom an estimated 31,600 asylum decisions were made in 1998, of which around 17% were grants of asylum, an increase from 10% in 1997, reflecting the move to deal swiftly with deserving cases. The main nationalities applying for asylum were people from the Federal Republic of Yugoslavia (16%), Somalia (10%), Sri Lanka (8%), Afghanistan (5%) and Turkey (4%). The majority of Federal Republic of Yugoslavia applications are thought to be from Kosovo, although not all cases have been separately identified. In spring 1999 the Government announced that the UK was willing to admit people from Kosovo whom the United Nations had classified as being vulnerable and in need of evacuation together with their dependants. These people were admitted on an exceptional basis for 12 months and as such are not included in asylum statistics. Under these arrangements, just over 4,300 evacuees from Kosovo arrived in the UK between April and June 1999. Since the end of the conflict some Kosovars have returned to their homeland.

Most failed asylum seekers continued to appeal against their removal from the UK, and nearly 14,500 appeals were lodged in 1998. Of the 25,300 who had their asylum appeals heard before special adjudicators, only 2,350 (9%) were successful.

The Special Immigration Appeals Commission, which began work in 1998, deals with appeals in cases where individuals are liable for deportation on grounds of national security. It was set up in response to criticism by the European Court of Human Rights that such decisions were not subject to judicial supervision.

Immigration and Asylum Bill

The Immigration and Asylum Bill, published in February 1999, will implement key elements of the *Fairer, Faster and Firmer* White Paper published in 1997. Its provisions include:

- modernising the immigration control so that it can be operated with more flexibility. This will help to speed genuine passengers through the control and target resources on potential abuse;
- introducing measures to tackle clandestine entry, including strengthening the

carriers' liability regime and a new civil penalty to tackle clandestine entry in lorries and other vehicles;

- introducing a statutory registration scheme to regulate unscrupulous immigration advisers;
- creating new arrangements to support asylum seekers in genuine need, involving a new national system, separate from the main benefits system, which will relieve the current burden on local authorities. Accommodation will be provided on a 'no choice' basis, with other support generally being provided in kind to reduce the incentive to economic migration; and
- replacing the existing multiple rights of appeal with a single comprehensive right of appeal, and enhancing the role of the Immigration Appeal Tribunal.

NATIONAL AND ETHNIC GROUPS

Citizenship

Under the British Nationality Act 1981 there are three main forms of citizenship:

- British citizenship for people closely connected with the UK;
- British Dependent Territories citizenship for people connected with the dependent territories (now known as 'Overseas Territories'—see p. 77); and
- British Overseas citizenship for those citizens of the United Kingdom and Colonies who did not acquire either of the other citizenships when the 1981 Act came into force.

British citizenship is acquired automatically at birth by a child born in the UK if his or her mother or, if legitimate, father is a British citizen or is settled in the UK. A child adopted in the UK by a British citizen is also a British citizen. A child born abroad to a British citizen born, adopted, naturalised or registered in the UK is generally a British citizen by descent. The Act safeguards the citizenship of a child born abroad to a British citizen in Crown service, certain related services, or in service under an EU institution.

British citizenship may also be acquired:

- by registration for certain children, including those born in the UK who do not automatically acquire such citizenship at birth, or who have been born abroad to a parent who is a citizen by descent;
- by registration for British Dependent Territories citizens, British Overseas citizens, British subjects under the Act, British Nationals (Overseas) and British protected persons after five years' residence in the UK, except for people from Gibraltar, who may be registered without residence;
- by registration for stateless people and those who have previously renounced British nationality; and
- by naturalisation for all other adults aged 18 or over.

Naturalisation is at the Home Secretary's discretion. Requirements include five years' residence, or three years if the applicant's spouse is a British citizen. Those who are not married to a British citizen are also required to have a sufficient knowledge of English, Welsh or Scottish Gaelic; they must in addition intend to have their main home in the UK or be employed by the Crown, or by an international organisation of which the UK is a member, or by a company or association established in the UK.

In 1998, 54,000 people were granted British citizenship in the United Kingdom. Nearly 3,800 applications were refused. Over one in four of all successful applications were from citizens of Indian subcontinent countries, with Africa accounting for almost one in four and the rest of Asia representing about one in five.

Ethnic Profile

For centuries people from overseas have settled in the UK, either to escape political or religious persecution or in search of better economic opportunities. The Irish have long formed a large section of the population. Jewish refugees who came to the UK towards the end of the 19th century and in the 1930s were followed by other European refugees after 1945. Substantial immigration from the Caribbean and Indian subcontinent dates principally from the 1950s and 1960s, while many people of South Asian descent came to this country as refugees from Kenya, Malawi or Uganda in the 1960s and 1970s. In recent years the majority of people have come from the Indian subcontinent, the rest of Asia, and Africa (see Table 9.3).

Analysis of the Labour Force Survey by the Office for National Statistics has found that in 1997 just under 94% of the population of Great Britain belonged to the 'White' group, while about 3.6 million people described themselves as belonging to another ethnic group (see Table 9.4). The Indian group form the largest of the non-White ethnic groups, representing about one in four of the ethnic minority population. In general, these groups tend to have a younger age profile than the White population, and the relatively greater concentration of the ethnic minority population in the fertile age-groups may partly explain the increase in the size of some of these populations in recent years.

The 1991 Census revealed that members of ethnic minority groups were heavily concentrated in the most populous areas of England, with relatively small numbers in Scotland and Wales. Over half lived in the South East of England. The highest concentration was in the London borough of Brent, where nearly 45% of the local population were from non-White groups. There were also variations in the regional concentrations of different ethnic groups. About three-fifths of people from Black ethnic groups lived in London, compared with about two-fifths of Indians and just under one-fifth of Pakistanis. Outside London there were high concentrations of Indians in Leicester, Wolverhampton and Slough, and high concentrations of Pakistanis in Lancashire, Greater Manchester and West Yorkshire.

Alleviating Racial Disadvantage

Although many members of the Black and Asian communities are concentrated in the inner cities, where there are problems of deprivation and social stress, progress has been made over the last 20 years in tackling racial disadvantage in the UK. For example,

Table 9.4: Resident Population by Ethnic Group, 1997, Great Britain[a]

	Number of people (thousands)	%
White	52,936	93.6
All non-White ethnic minority groups	3,599	6.4
of which:		
Black Caribbean	526	0.9
Black African	352	0.6
Black Other (non-mixed)	132	0.2
Black Mixed	175	0.3
Indian	925	1.6
Pakistani	587	1.0
Bangladeshi	209	0.4
Chinese	157	0.3
Other groups	536	0.9
All groups	**56,550**	**100.0**

Source: Office for National Statistics (Labour Force Survey)
[a] Population in private households only

young people from some non-White ethnic groups are leading the way for participation and achievement in education.

Furthermore, many individuals have achieved distinction in their careers and in public life, and the proportion of ethnic minority members occupying professional and managerial positions is increasing. There are at present nine Black and Asian Members of the House of Commons. In May 1999 Keith Vaz MP was appointed Under-Secretary of State in the Lord Chancellor's Department, the first Asian Minister in a British government. Several Asian entrepreneurs are multi-millionaires.

The Government has a Race Equality Unit whose responsibilities include race relations policy and legislation. It also has responsibility for the reception and resettlement of refugees. A Race Relations Forum was established in 1998 to advise the Home Secretary on issues affecting ethnic minority communities. It gives these communities a channel of communication with government, and an input into policy development.

Economic, environmental, educational and health programmes of central government and local authorities exist to combat disadvantage. There are also special allocations which channel extra resources into projects of specific benefit to ethnic minorities, including, for example, the provision of specialist teachers for children needing English language tuition. The Government promotes equal opportunities for ethnic minorities through training programmes, including provision for unemployed people who need training in English as a second language. Cultural and recreational schemes and the health and personal social services also try to take account of the particular needs of ethnic minorities.

Race Relations Legislation

The Race Relations Act 1976, which applies to England, Scotland and Wales, and parallel legislation for Northern Ireland introduced in 1997, make discrimination unlawful on grounds of colour, race, nationality or ethnic or national origin in the provision of goods, facilities and services, in employment, in housing, in education and in advertising. The legislation gives complainants direct access to civil courts and, for employment complaints, to employment tribunals. It is a criminal offence to incite racial hatred under the provisions of the Public Order Act 1986.

In order to protect ethnic minority communities from intimidation, the Crime and Disorder Act 1998 (see p. 214) created new offences of racial harassment and racially motivated violence. It also introduced court orders which prohibit named individuals from harassing the community, including racially motivated harassment.

Commission for Racial Equality

The Commission for Racial Equality (CRE), established by the 1976 Act, is a publicly funded independent organisation working in both the public and private sectors to provide advice to the general public in Great Britain about the Race Relations Act, to tackle racial discrimination and to encourage racial equality. It helps individuals with complaints about racial discrimination; in 1998 about 10,000 people called the CRE for advice on such matters, and 1,657 applications were made for assistance with cases. It has power to investigate unlawful discriminatory practices and to issue non-discrimination notices requiring such practices to cease. It has an important campaigning and educational role, and has issued codes of practice in employment, education, healthcare, maternity services and housing. The CRE can also undertake or fund research. A Commission for Racial Equality for Northern Ireland was established in 1997, with similar powers.

The CRE supports the work of 108 racial equality councils or similar organisations. These are autonomous voluntary bodies set up in most areas to promote equality of opportunity and good relations at the local level. The Commission helps to pay the salaries of officers employed by the racial equality councils, most of which also receive funds from their local authorities. It also gives grants to ethnic minority self-help groups and to other projects run by, or for the benefit of, ethnic minority communities.

Language

English is the main language spoken in the UK, and is also one of the most widely used in the world. Estimates suggest that 310 million people speak it as their first language, with a similar number speaking it as a second language. It is an official language in a large number of overseas countries, and is widely used internationally as the main language for purposes such as air traffic control, international maritime communications and academic gatherings.

Modern English derives primarily from one of the dialects of Old English (or Anglo-Saxon), itself made up of several Western Germanic dialects taken to Britain in the early 5th century. However, it has been very greatly influenced by other languages, particularly Latin and, following the Norman conquest, by French—the language of court, government and the nobility for many years after 1066. The re-emergence of English as the standard language of England was marked by events such as the Statute of Pleading in 1362, which laid down that English was to replace French as the language of law. The 14th century saw

the first major English literature since Anglo-Saxon days, with works such as *Piers Plowman* by William Langland and the *Canterbury Tales* by Geoffrey Chaucer. However, there remained great regional variations in the language, and spellings were not always standardised.

Following the introduction of the printing press to England by William Caxton in the late 15th century, there was a considerable flowering of English literature in the 16th and early 17th centuries. William Shakespeare, Edmund Spenser and Christopher Marlowe produced work that is still famous today, while Cranmer's prayerbook and the Authorised ('King James') Version of the Bible also date from this period. About this time, too, translations of Latin, Italian and other European works into English vastly expanded the English language. The work of early lexicographers, of whom the most famous was Samuel Johnson (1709–84), led to greater standardisation in matters such as spelling.

> Several different languages are spoken in England in addition to English,[1] often within ethnic minority communities. Punjabi is the most commonly spoken South Asian language among British Asians, followed by Urdu and then Hindi. Cantonese is the most commonly spoken language among ethnic Chinese people, while about one in five Caribbeans speak Patois.

ECONOMIC CHANGES

Marked improvements in the UK's standard of living have taken place during the 20th century. The average annual growth of the economy as measured by gross domestic product (GDP) in volume terms was 2.5% between 1951 and 1997. Within the United Kingdom GDP per head varies. In England, for example, it is highest in the regions in the south and east of the country and lowest in the

---

[1] For the Welsh language see p. 30; for Gaelic see p. 26 and for Irish see p. 20.

north and west. Between 1996 and 1997 GDP per head, relative to the UK average, rose in the South West, the North West, Yorkshire and the Humber, and Scotland, with little change in other regions. UK GDP per head in 1997 was around the average for the 15 EU countries.

Income and Wealth

Real household disposable income per head nearly doubled between 1971 and 1997. At the same time the gap between those on high and low incomes grew, especially during the 1980s, although the gap stabilised in the 1990s. Lone parents and pensioners tend to be over-represented among those on low incomes. In 1996–97, 42% of lone parent families were in the bottom fifth of the income distribution.

Wages and salaries remain the main source of household income for most people, although the proportion they contribute has declined, from 61% in 1987 to 56% in 1997. Occupational pensions have become an increasingly important source of income for pensioners while the proportion of income from benefits has fallen, particularly among those who have retired recently. The proportion of recently retired pensioners' income from occupational pensions increased in real terms (after allowing for inflation) from 17% in 1981 to 28% in 1996–97.

The tax and benefit system redistributes income from households on high incomes to those on lower incomes. Households make payments through direct and indirect taxes, and social security contributions, while benefits are received through both cash payments and provision of benefits in-kind, such as the National Health Service. Households with high incomes tend to pay more in taxes than they receive in income, while those on low incomes benefit more than they are taxed. The average original income of the top fifth of households is 19 times the average of the bottom fifth. Taxes and benefits reduce this inequality so that the ratio for final income is four to one. The types of household that tend to be net beneficiaries from the redistribution of taxes and benefits include lone parent families, families with three or more children, and retired households.

Wealth continues to be much more unequally distributed than income, with the most wealthy 10% of the population owning half the total marketable wealth of the household sector in 1995. The value of net wealth held by the household sector in the UK was £3,582 billion in 1997. Investment in life assurance and pension funds accounted for 36% of this total, compared with 24% in 1987. This reflects a greater uptake of personal pension arrangements, with more people making a greater amount of provision, as well as increases in the prices of equities (principally securities and bonds) in which household sector wealth has been invested.

Social Exclusion

Social exclusion is a description of what can happen when individuals or areas suffer from a combination of linked problems, such as unemployment, poor skills, low incomes, poor housing, bad health and family breakdown. The Government has policies for reducing all of these individually, but government programmes have been less effective at tackling the interaction between these problems or preventing them arising in the first place. A Social Exclusion Unit was set up in the Cabinet Office in 1997 to co-ordinate and improve government action to reduce social exclusion in England. The Unit works closely with officials in Wales, Scotland and Northern Ireland. So far the Unit has produced reports on truancy, rough sleeping, the most rundown housing estates and teenage pregnancies.

SOCIAL TRENDS

Eating and Drinking Habits

Since the early 1970s there have been marked changes in the British diet. One feature has been the rise in consumption of poultry while that of red meat (such as beef and veal) has fallen. Fresh fruit is increasingly popular while consumption of fresh green vegetables, including cabbages, peas and beans, was lower in 1998 than in 1970. In addition, the use of convenience food—both frozen and ready meals—has increased. Despite these changes, the British diet is still noticeably different to that in other countries such as those in the Mediterranean, being relatively low in fruit, vegetables and fish. However, there have been important changes within these broad types of food, so that mushrooms and salad vegetables have superseded traditional vegetables, such as swedes and parsnips. Whereas in the early post-war period a typical meal would have been roast beef, roast potatoes and cabbage in the middle of the day, today it is more likely to be microwaved chicken and frozen chips in the evening.

Features of the pattern of consumption in 1998 compared with 1997 included:

- a stabilisation in consumption of carcass beef and veal—this had risen by 9% in 1997 following a fall of 17% in 1996 when consumption had been affected by concern over eating beef; consumption of boned beef joints rose in 1998 to compensate for the ban on beef on the bone introduced in December 1997 (see p. 452);

- consumption of poultry, pork and fish showed little change although, in the case of fish, the increase in recent years in the consumption of fresh fish was again evident;

- a 2% fall in consumption of milk and cream (including yogurts, fromage frais and other dairy desserts)—the fourth slight fall in successive years;

- lower purchases of fresh potatoes (down by 4%) and fresh vegetables (2%) as prices were significantly higher than in 1997; and

- purchases of fruit juice increased by 10%.

Energy intakes from food continued to decline—to an average of 1,850 kilocalories (kcal) in 1998, compared with 1,910 kcal in 1997. Average vitamin intakes were generally above the daily amounts recommended by the Department of Health, although intakes of most essential minerals were slightly under recommended amounts. Health considerations appear to have been influencing some aspects of diet in recent years, for example, in the long-term fall in red meat sales, and the growth in low fat spread consumption.

Pubs retain their popularity, with about 80% of beer being drunk in pubs and clubs, and many have become popular venues for eating out. Three-quarters of adults visit a public house at least once every three months and almost as many have a meal in a non-fast food restaurant. Lager is now estimated to account for nearly 60% of all beer sales. Nowadays 'fast food'

Changing Patterns in Consumption of Foods at Home, Great Britain

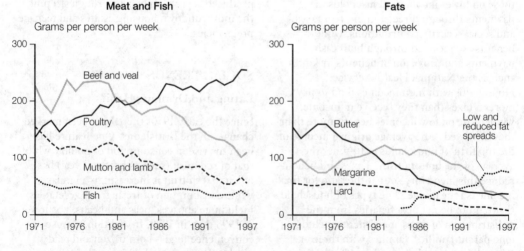

Source: National Food Survey, Ministry of Agriculture, Fisheries and Food

outlets—selling, for example, hamburgers, pizza, chicken and the traditional fish and chips—are widespread in the UK's high streets. In restaurants one can eat food from many other countries—Chinese, Indian, Italian and French are among the most widely available cuisines. Sandwich bars and coffee shops are common, especially in towns and cities.

Women and Men

Employment and Income

The economic and domestic lives of women have changed considerably in the 20th century. Women are taking an increasingly important role in the labour market. In 1971, 91% of men of working age, compared with 57% of women, were economically active in Great Britain. By 1997 women's activity rates had increased to 72% of women of working age, while men's activity rates slowly declined in the 1980s and 1990s to 85% in 1997.

Despite the growth in female employment in recent years, women and men still tend to work in different industries. The main industry group for female full-time employees is public administration, education and health. Although there has been a long-term decline in manufacturing industry since the 1970s, about three in ten full-time working men work in this sector. Women are under-represented in some occupations and at senior levels. For example, even though the proportion of directors who are female has risen since the mid-1970s, fewer than 5% of directors were women in 1998.

The average individual income of men was higher than that of women in all age bands in 1996–97, largely because of their higher levels of earnings, self-employment income and their longer hours of working. The gap between male and female earnings has been closing but the differential remains, with female full-time employees earning around four-fifths of the corresponding male hourly rate. The 'pay gap' increases with age. In addition, men are more likely than women to have certain investments such as pensions.

Public Policy

There are a record 121 women MPs in the Westminster Parliament, representing 18% of the total number of seats. This proportion is close to the EU average of 22%. About two-fifths of the Members of the Scottish Parliament and Welsh Assembly are women. Five women sit in the UK Cabinet, including the Leader of the House of Lords, who is also the Minister for Women. She chairs the Cabinet Sub-committee on Women's Issues. Support is provided by the Women's Unit in the Cabinet Office.

The Government is working to ensure that the perspective of women is automatically taken into account in the development of government policies. It is also seeking to improve communications with women's organisations. Following a review in 1998, action is being taken to make the advisory Women's National Commission more responsive and influential, and better able to represent the views of women's organisations. Its membership is to be increased by 50% to 75 organisations with a view to reaching the smaller groups representing women.

The Government is encouraging the development of 'family-friendly' employment policies and practices. It supports 'Opportunity Now', an employer-led initiative (with around 350 members) to increase the participation of women in the workforce. Action is being taken to enable more women to join or re-enter the labour market and to improve their employment rights. Measures include making it worth their while to work through the national minimum wage (see p. 156), which is expected to benefit more female than male full-time employees, and the New Deal for Partners of Unemployed People (see p. 154), which is intended to help more lone parents (the vast majority of whom are women) and partners of unemployed people to return to work. The Government has issued a National Childcare Strategy, which aims to secure a range of affordable and good-quality childcare for children aged up to 14 in every neighbourhood. There is also a new Childcare Tax Credit, within the Working Families Tax Credit (see p. 178), which will provide help with childcare costs for parents in work; and a review of the pension system to help women provide for their retirement.

Equal Opportunities

The Sex Discrimination Acts 1975 and 1986 make discrimination between men and women unlawful, with certain limited exceptions, in employment, education, training and the provision of housing, goods, facilities and services. Discriminatory job recruitment advertisements are unlawful. Under the Equal Pay Act 1970, as amended in 1984, women in Great Britain are entitled to equal pay with men when doing work that is the same or broadly similar, work which is rated as equivalent, or work which is of equal value. Parallel legislation on sex discrimination and equal pay applies in Northern Ireland.

The Equal Opportunities Commission (EOC), an independent statutory body, has the duties of working towards the elimination of sex discrimination and promoting equality of opportunity. It provides advice to individuals and supports legal actions against discriminatory practices. The EOC runs an 'Equality Exchange', with around 700 members, which enables employers to exchange information on good practice. Further details of the Government's equal opportunities policies may be found in chapter 6, p. 61.

Personal Safety

According to the 1998 British Crime Survey, in 1997 six out of ten incidents of violence in England and Wales were against men, but women were more likely to experience domestic violence than men. Women were the victims of seven in ten violent domestic incidents in 1997, and slightly over two in five (an estimated 582,000) of total violent offences against women were domestic attacks, compared with just over one in ten for men. The Government is developing a programme of measures to prevent violence against women wherever possible, and to protect women and provide justice for them when violence does occur. This will cover England and Wales. Separate strategies are being developed for Scotland and Northern Ireland.

The Voluntary Sector

Across the UK many thousands of voluntary organisations exist, ranging from national bodies to small local groups. Serving the community through volunteering is a long-established tradition in the UK. The voluntary sector employs 485,000 people, has 3 million volunteers, and the economic contribution of the voluntary sector and volunteering is estimated to be just under 2% of GDP. Many volunteers are involved in work which improves the quality of life in their local communities, or give their time to help organise events or groups in areas as diverse as social welfare, education, sport, heritage, the environment and the arts. A large number of older people are involved in a variety of volunteering activities. Indeed, while volunteering rates among the whole population have fallen in the 1990s, an increasing proportion of older people are carrying out a variety of volunteering activities.

The Government greatly values the voluntary sector's contribution to society. For example, voluntary organisations are important providers of government-supported employment and training services for unemployed people. As a result, the Government is keen to encourage productive partnerships between the statutory and voluntary sectors. An Active Community Unit has been established to encourage voluntary and community involvement, to raise the profile of the voluntary sector within government and across society, and co-ordinate the work of government departments in this area.

In order to provide a general framework for enhanced relationships between government and the voluntary sector, 'Compacts' have been drawn up in all four countries of the UK in consultation with the voluntary sector, taking account of the distinct traditions of voluntary activity in each constituent nation. Monitoring the implementation and progress of the Compacts within government has been assigned to a ministerial group. It is intended to encourage other public bodies and local government to adopt or adapt Compacts for use locally.

Charities

The Charity Commission for England and Wales, a non-ministerial government department, is responsible for the registration, monitoring and support of organisations that are charitable in law. At the end of 1998 there were about 188,000 charities registered with the Commission. A review of the Register of Charities is currently taking place to ascertain whether there are any organisations that currently benefit from charitable status which most people would not now regard as charitable, and if there are any bodies not on the register that might be added. Essential characteristics of a charity have been outlined to inform the Review. These define a charity as being an organisation whose aims are for exclusively charitable purposes, and thus providing clear benefit to others in society. This excludes any organisation whose main aim is the pursuit of party or other political aims.

The charitable sector is a major part of the economy. The combined annual income of organisations registered with the Charity Commission for England and Wales in 1998 was just under £20 billion. About 70% of these organisations had a recorded annual income of under £10,000, with the financial wealth of registered charities, measured by annual income, concentrated in a few very large charities such as the National Trust, Oxfam, the Salvation Army and Barnardo's. The Commission gives advice to trustees of charities on their administration, and has a statutory responsibility to ensure that charities make effective use of their resources. Recent legislation has strengthened the Commissioners' powers to investigate and supervise charities. These include new measures to protect charities and donors from bogus fund-raisers and a new framework for charity accounts and reports.

Funding

Voluntary organisations may receive income from several sources, including:

- central and local government grants;
- contributions from individuals, businesses and trusts;
- earnings from commercial activities and investments; and
- fees from central and local government for those services which are provided on a contractual basis.

The introduction of the National Lottery (see below) has given charities and voluntary organisations the opportunity to secure substantial new funding for projects across a range of activities.

CAF (Charities Aid Foundation) is a registered charity that works to increase resources for the voluntary sector in the UK and overseas. As well as providing services that are both charitable and financial, CAF undertakes a comprehensive programme of research and publishing, and is established as a leading source of information on all aspects of the sector.

Another valuable source of revenue for charities is through tax relief and tax exemptions. The Gift Aid scheme provides tax relief on single cash donations of at least £250. Under the Payroll Giving scheme, employees can make tax-free donations to charity from their earnings. In March 1999 Gift Aid 2000 was launched, under which tax relief is available on donations of £100 or more given before the end of the year 2000 to charities working on education or anti-poverty projects in the world's 80 poorest countries. In April 1999 it was announced that the scheme would be extended to include donations to charities helping Kosovan refugees.

Since 1996 a global coalition of charitable and voluntary organisations, referred to as the Jubilee 2000 Coalition, has been campaigning for relief of the debt burden that is borne by many of the world's poorest countries. Jubilee 2000 is being promoted in over 40 countries, including donor countries such as Germany, the US and Britain, as well as developing countries, such as Ghana and Uganda.

National Lottery

National lotteries have existed in Britain intermittently since 1569. Since the National Lottery was launched in 1994 most people have played it and it has become the biggest lottery in the world. In a recent survey, 71% of households reported participating in the Saturday night lottery draw. Those households that played both the Saturday and Wednesday night draws spent an average of £5.37 a week on the lottery.

Ticket sales fell by 5.6% to £5.2 billion in 1998–99. A new game, Thunderball, was launched in June 1999, to revitalise lottery sales. It aims to attract people who want a better chance of winning a prize, even if the amount is smaller. Tickets or scratchcards are available from over 35,000 retail outlets. Camelot Group plc, a private sector consortium, has the franchise to run the Lottery until 2001.

How Each £1 Spent on the National Lottery is Allocated

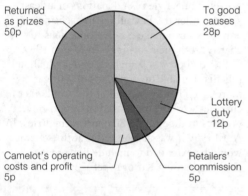

Returned as prizes 50p

To good causes 28p

Lottery duty 12p

Camelot's operating costs and profit 5p

Retailers' commission 5p

Source: National Lottery Commission

Some £7.5 billion had been raised for good causes by the end of May 1999 and over 38,000 awards for £6.7 billion had been distributed. By 2001 this is expected to have reached at least £10.6 billion, around £1.9 billion more than originally forecast. Over half the awards have been for less than £50,000. Lottery money was originally shared equally among five good causes—sport, charities, the arts, heritage and projects to mark the third millennium—but the National Lottery Act 1998 provided for a sixth good cause— education, health and environment projects. The distribution rules have been changed by the Government to shift the emphasis from buildings and capital projects to people.

The Lottery was originally regulated by the Director General of the National Lottery, who headed the Office of the National Lottery. It is now regulated by a five-person National Lottery Commission. Its duties are to protect players' interests, to ensure the Lottery is run with propriety, and—subject to satisfying those two criteria—to maximise the amount raised for good causes. It will also select the next Lottery operator from October 2001 and will be able to appoint a not-for-profit operator if that would provide the best return for good causes.

Leisure Trends

The most common leisure activities are home-based, or social, such as visiting relatives or friends. Television viewing is by far the most popular leisure pastime, with average viewing time exceeding 25 hours a week. Nearly all households have one television set or more, and about 80% of teenagers have a television in their bedroom. In recent years there has been an increase in the number of television channels available (see pp. 269–70). In 1997–98, 13% of households in the UK subscribed to satellite television while 7% subscribed to cable television. Many people also watch videos, either pre-recorded or self-recorded. In 1996–97, 82% of households had a video recorder, double the proportion ten years earlier.

Listening to music is another popular activity. Purchases of compact discs (CDs) have risen very rapidly, although this levelled off in 1997 at nearly 160 million. The proportion of households with a CD player grew from 15% in 1989 to 63% in 1997–98.

Other popular pursuits include reading, do-it-yourself home improvements, gardening and going out for a meal, for a drink or to the cinema. Among adults the most popular daily newspaper remains *The Sun* and the most popular magazine is *Sky TV Guide*.

Technological Change

People in Britain are continually expanding their access to, and use of, modern communication technology for both leisure and business purposes. Two items of technology that have become increasingly common for leisure and business use are mobile telephones (see p. 380) and computers.

In 1997–98 a fifth of households in the United Kingdom owned at least one mobile telephone. The South East was the region with the greatest proportion of mobile telephone owners—three in ten households owned one in 1997–98. The number of households owning home computers in the UK has also increased considerably, from just under one in six households in 1986 to over one in four in 1996–97. Households comprising families with children were more likely than one-person households to own a computer.

The 'information economy'—facilitated through the rapidly growing use of the Internet (see p. 377)—is receiving increasing public policy attention in Britain. In March 1999 the Government announced a £1.7 billion 'computers for all' initiative, with a target of a national network of 1,000 computer learning centres. Another proposal was to try to bring more computers into British homes by enabling employees to borrow computers from their company as a tax-free benefit.

Holidays

In 1997, 57 million holidays of four nights or more were taken by British residents, an increase of 39% since 1971. The number of holidays taken in Great Britain has been broadly stable over the last decade while the number taken abroad has grown. The overall number of holidays taken abroad in 1997 was nearly seven times the number in 1971. Spain remained the most popular holiday destination in 1997, followed by France. The United States was the third most popular destination overall and the most popular non-European destination. Long-haul holidays are growing in popularity—the fastest growing holiday destinations outside Europe are Central and South America, and the Caribbean.

UK residents made 5 million day trips to the continent of Europe in 1997, of which most were to France. About 4.1 million journeys to the continent in 1997 were through the Channel Tunnel.

Further Reading

Ethnic Minorities (2nd edn). Aspects of Britain series. The Stationery Office, 1997.

Population Trends. Office for National Statistics. The Stationery Office.

Social Focus on Families. Office for National Statistics. The Stationery Office, 1997.

Social Focus on Older People. Office for National Statistics. The Stationery Office, 1999.

Social Focus on Women and Men. Office for National Statistics and Equal Opportunities Commission. The Stationery Office, 1998.

The 2001 Census of Population. Cm 4253, The Stationery Office, 1999.

Annual Reports

Annual Abstract of Statistics. Office for National Statistics. The Stationery Office.

British Social Attitudes. Ashgate Publishing.

Family Spending. Office for National Statistics. The Stationery Office.

Living in Britain: Results from the General Household Survey. Office for National Statistics. The Stationery Office.

Social Trends. Office for National Statistics. The Stationery Office.

Travel Trends. Office for National Statistics. The Stationery Office.

Website

Women's Unit: www.womens-unit.gov.uk

10 Education

All children in the United Kingdom are required by law to receive full-time education. After the age of 16, when education is no longer compulsory, young people have a range of choices. Around 70% stay in education, either at school or at further education colleges, and may then go on to higher education institutions. Others go into work, with the remainder being guaranteed a place on the Government's training programmes.

Education is the top priority for the Government, which aims to raise educational standards to levels that compare favourably with the UK's international competitors. New measures have been introduced to reduce infant class sizes, raise standards in schools and local education authorities, enhance the status and quality of the teaching profession, establish a new school framework, promote training for young employees, and reform student support arrangements. The Government is also implementing its plans to encourage lifelong learning, and will establish a University for Industry in 2000.

Government responsibility for education in the UK rests with the Department for Education and Employment (DfEE) in England, the National Assembly for Wales, the Scottish Executive and the Department of Education for Northern Ireland (DENI); the Scottish Executive Education Department is responsible for primary and secondary education in Scotland, while the Scottish Executive Enterprise and Lifelong Learning Department has responsibility for lifelong learning and for further and higher education.

Government helps to set the framework for the education system and works in partnership with other central and local bodies to implement its policies. These are directed towards the continual raising of educational standards and fulfilling the potential of each child in order to:

- promote an efficient and flexible labour market; and

- support economic growth and improve the nation's competitiveness and quality of life.

By the beginning of the 20th century school attendance was compulsory for children throughout the country (although at differing age ranges). Class sizes were much larger than today (numbering around 50 pupils on average), truancy rates were high, and many teachers in schools were not professionally trained. There was much emphasis on learning by rote, and discipline was harsh. A co-ordinated system of education in England and Wales was introduced by the Education Act 1902, under which local government became responsible for state education and for helping to finance existing church-run schools. In Scotland at that time elected school boards were responsible for the provision of education for children between the ages of five and 13 (14 from 1901), although they were subsequently to be replaced by local government authorities in 1918.

INTRODUCTION

The 1944 Education Act (applicable in England and Wales) fixed 11 as the age when children in state-run schools passed from primary to secondary education; many new secondary schools were created and the number of teachers employed doubled over the next 30 years. Pupils aged 11 were required to take a test (the '11-plus'), which determined the type of secondary school they attended. The top 20% of pupils who passed the 11-plus proceeded to grammar schools; the rest went to secondary modern or technical schools.

In the 1960s a new system of comprehensive education, adopted by most local education authorities (LEAs), switched the emphasis to mixed ability teaching with the aim of giving all children equality of opportunity. The 11-plus was scrapped in many areas, and all children within the state school system were taught in comprehensive schools.

In the 1980s, in order to improve standards nationally, the Government sought to establish a more centralised means of monitoring the education system. In England and Wales a National Curriculum (see p. 136), setting out what children were required to learn in a common group of subjects, was drawn up. Levels of attainment were set, and a standardised scale against which to assess children at ages seven, 11 and 14 was established, enabling comparisons to be made between different schools. Publication of the results of the tests has aimed to give parents, children and educationalists more information about how each school is performing. Approved curriculums and the regular assessment of pupils are also required in Scotland and Northern Ireland.

Further changes included allowing individual schools to 'opt out' of local authority control. Schools that took this option were known as grant-maintained (or self-governing) schools and were given more autonomy over their budgets.

Present Arrangements

The policy of opting out has been ended by the present Government. In England and Wales a new structure of foundation, community and voluntary schools is being established (under the provisions of the School Standards and Framework Act 1998) from September 1999. The community category initially accommodates county schools (those formerly owned and funded by LEAs), while the foundation category includes many of the grant-maintained schools. From September 2000 the voluntary category will include those schools with a particular religious ethos. All schools are expected to choose which category best suits their circumstances and aspirations. The arrangements will be phased. There are also two categories of special school under the new framework—community special and foundation special. The legislation aims to give the education system greater flexibility, allowing individual schools at a local level the freedom to develop in their own way; but still providing, at a national level, a framework for ensuring the maintenance and improvement of standards. New codes of practice have been drawn up, outlining the nature of the relationship between individual schools, their governing bodies, LEAs and government. The codes recognise that partnership is essential between the various groups involved in education, and that, wherever possible, schools should be freed from unnecessary bureaucratic interference.

Although all schools in Northern Ireland must be open to pupils of all religions (as elsewhere in the UK), most Roman Catholic students still attend Catholic voluntary-maintained schools, while most Protestant students go to state ('controlled') or non-denominational schools. By September 1999 there were 43 fully 'integrated' schools (out of a total of almost 1,140 schools in the Province) accommodating children from both traditions. Controlled schools in Northern Ireland are run by five education and library boards.

The Scottish education system has a number of distinctive features, including a separate system of examinations and differences in the curriculum. Most education authority schools in Scotland are non-denominational. However, provision is also made for denominational schools.

Major changes have also taken place in higher education. The 1960s saw considerable expansion in new universities. There was also a substantial increase in 1992, when polytechnics and their Scottish equivalents were given their own degree-awarding powers and were allowed to take the university title. At the same time, similar provision was made for higher education colleges which met certain criteria.

GOVERNMENT POLICY ON EDUCATION

The Government believes that investment in education and training is the best way to build a stable, competitive economy with steady growth. New reforms and investment in education aim to:

● ensure National Learning Targets (see p. 127) are achieved;

● reduce class sizes for five to seven year olds;

● tackle social exclusion;

● increase employability; and

● broaden access to further and higher education for an extra 800,000 people by 2002.

Expenditure

Under the Comprehensive Spending Review (see p. 400), an additional £19 billion is being allocated to expenditure on education in the UK over the three years from 1999–2000 to 2001–02, representing an average annual increase in real terms of 5%. This money supplements the extra funds allocated in the Budgets of July 1997 and March 1998 for schools, skills training, childcare and the £3.9 billion for the New Deal (see chapter 11). Total annual expenditure on education in the UK runs at around £40 billion each year.

The Government is aiming to increase the share of gross domestic product (GDP) spent on education from 4.8% in 1990–91 to 5% by 2001–02. A capital investment programme is allocating £1.3 billion over five years (an average of £150 for every pupil in the country) for modernising schools, including £340 million earmarked for school repairs. It is planned that total annual capital investment in schools will more than double between 1997 and 2002. Additional expenditure of £725 million in 1999–2000 and 2000–01 for further education and £776 million for higher education will help to expand both sectors.

Research shows that 20% fewer young people from less well-off households stay on in post-16 education. From September 1999 a new scheme of Education Maintenance Allowances (EMAs) is being piloted, giving a financial incentive to these young people to remain in education.

Pre-school Education

The Government is keen to see an improvement in the provision of pre-school education. Among its current aims are:

● to ensure enough free early education places, at least part-time, for all four year olds in England and Wales whose parents want one; and

● to increase the percentage of three year olds with free nursery education places in England from 34% in January 1997 to 66% by 2002.

In Northern Ireland a phased expansion programme aims to increase the proportion of children experiencing free pre-school education from 45% in 1997–98 to 85% by 2001–02.

The Government requires that LEAs in England and Wales draw up an early years development and childcare plan, incorporating information on how good quality childcare will be made available and how this will be linked to early education. In Northern Ireland pre-school development plans are being drawn up for each education and library board area and childcare plans will be developed for each health and social services board area.

In 1998 the Government announced the establishment of the 'Sure Start' programme to co-ordinate nursery education, childcare, family learning and primary healthcare initiatives for children from birth to the age of three. The programme has funding of £540 million over three years.

The Government is also introducing, from October 1999, a Working Families Tax Credit (applicable throughout the UK—see p. 178), designed to give parents more money to help them meet the heavy costs of childcare.

Class Sizes

The DfEE is aiming to ensure that, from September 1999, fewer than 200,000 children aged five to seven are in infant classes of over 30 pupils (a reduction of 285,000 from January 1998). By 2001, the target is for *no* infant class for those aged five to seven to have more than 30 pupils.

National Learning Targets

In October 1998 the Government announced new National Learning Targets for England (relating to the year 2002) including the following objectives:

- 80% of 11 year olds reaching the expected standard for their age in literacy;
- 75% of 11 year olds reaching the expected standard for their age in numeracy;

- 50% of 16 year olds getting five or more GCSEs (General Certificate of Secondary Education—see p. 129) at grades A to C (out of seven possible grades);
- 85% of 19 year olds reaching NVQ (National Vocational Qualification—see p. 130) Level 2 or equivalent;
- 60% of 21 year olds to reach NVQ Level 3 or equivalent;
- 50% of adults with NVQ Level 3 or equivalent;
- 28% of adults with NVQ Level 4 or equivalent; and
- a 7% reduction in non-learners.

Targets have also been set for large and small organisations to gain Investors in People (IiP) accreditation (see p. 153).

In Wales similar but distinctive targets have been set for 2002.

Literacy and Numeracy

The Government is committed to tackling illiteracy. The report *A Fresh Start: Improving Literacy and Numeracy*, published in 1999, outlines the research of a working group which found that illiteracy levels were at unacceptably high levels among the adult population. Around 20% of those surveyed were unable to give satisfactory responses to basic numeracy and literacy questions. It proposed a new national strategy involving a number of government bodies, including several key recommendations:

- there should be assessment on demand for all adults whose basic skills fall below a certain standard. To ensure progress is maintained at an individual level, the initiative should be linked to the new individual learning accounts (see p. 142);
- the strategy should be linked wherever possible with other initiatives, such as the University for Industry (see p. 141), workplace learning and help for the long-term unemployed; and
- the Basic Skills Agency (concerned with improving literacy, numeracy and related basic abilities in England and Wales)

should monitor the programme and ensure the necessary funding is obtained. Targets proposed by the working group in this area are to double the number of learners from 250,000 a year to 500,000; and to increase further education funding on the project from the current £180 million a year to over £350 million by 2001–02.

Targeting Resources at Areas of Need

Education Action Zones (EAZs) in England are areas where local partnerships between schools and the wider community seek to develop new and imaginative approaches to raising school standards. By the end of January 1999, 25 EAZs had been created. A further 50 zones are being created during the course of 1999. Each EAZ will be allocated substantial additional educational funding.

The Action Plans for Inner Cities scheme, launched in March 1999, makes specific provision for schools in inner city areas in England to develop as Beacon or specialist schools (see p. 137), and sets up schemes where students from disadvantaged homes can make greater use of school facilities outside normal school hours. It also makes it easier, through a loan system, for them to gain access to a home computer.

Another scheme, Excellence in Cities, sets out a three-year programme to improve the education of able inner-city children. The importance of setting children of roughly equal ability to work together in core curriculum subjects is being emphasised and a range of appropriately varied teaching programmes is being developed.

A further initiative is Fresh Start, in which, in exceptional circumstances, under-achieving schools are closed and then re-opened with new management arrangements on the same site.

Promoting Computer Technology

The National Grid for Learning (NGfL), an on-line educational resource created by the Government with the co-operation of the telecommunications industry, is an important means of encouraging and developing computer literacy. Comprising interconnecting learning networks and education services based on the Internet, the Grid will support teaching, learning, training and administration in schools, colleges, universities, libraries, workplaces and homes. By 2002, the Government aims to have all educational establishments connected to the Grid, and has provided funding to ensure all serving teachers achieve at least a basic standard in computer literacy. Its plans for the University for Industry (see p. 141) also include a commitment to promoting computer technology.

OVERVIEW OF THE EDUCATION SYSTEM

Nursery, Primary and Secondary Levels

In Great Britain compulsory schooling starts at the age of five. In England and Wales the Government has guaranteed nursery education places (see also p. 126) for all four year olds whose parents would like them to attend school from this age. Increasingly, nursery school education is provided by primary schools rather than specialised nurseries. Greater provision for pre-school education is also being made in Scotland. Northern Ireland has a lower compulsory school age of four and a single school entry date in September each year.

The emphasis at the early stages of primary school education is on children learning through their own experience, and socialising with their peers. Learning tends to take place through the study of general topics of interest, rather than formal academic subjects. Within their first two years of education, it is expected that most children will have mastered the basics of reading and writing, and will be able to perform simple numerical tasks without the use of a calculator. A small proportion of children do not begin their education in mainstream state schools. Children with disabilities (such as deafness or blindness) can attend 'special' schools where teachers are trained to respond to their particular needs. From the age of seven school life becomes increasingly structured. Children start to study individual subjects (mathematics,

Table 10.1: Number of Pupils by School Type in the UK, 1997–98

Thousands

Type of school	1997–98[a]
State nursery	79
State primary	5,414
State secondary	3,741
Independent schools	615
Special schools	116
Pupil referral units[b]	8
All schools	**9,973**

Source: Department for Education and Employment

[a] Includes 1996–97 data for Wales.

[b] England and Wales only. These units are intended to provide short-term support for children of compulsory school age who are not receiving suitable education, for example because of illness or exclusion from school.

science, English, for example), as well as the earlier topic-based approach to learning.

Secondary Education

The age of 11 (or sometimes 12 in Scotland) is still an important landmark for many children. At this age they progress from primary to secondary education (although some will attend 'middle' schools from around the ages of nine to 13). At secondary schools, children learn subjects in greater depth than in primary schools. New subjects, such as drama, individual sciences and foreign languages, are introduced to the curriculum. Secondary schools tend to be bigger than primary schools, and many have a wider range of resources. There is on average, for instance, one computer for every nine secondary school pupils in Britain, compared with an average of one computer for every 18 primary school pupils.

From 14 onwards children in secondary schools spend time preparing for the public examinations which mark the end of their compulsory academic career. The General Certificate of Secondary Education (GCSE) is the main examination taken by pupils in England, Wales and Northern Ireland at the age of 16. Students in Scotland at that age take the Scottish Certificate of Education at Standard Grade.

Independent Schools

There are approximately 2,500 independent schools in the UK, where parents pay fees to have their children educated. Around 7% of children in Britain attend such schools. Independent schools tend to offer more out-of-school facilities (sporting or musical, for example) to children; they also tend to have smaller classes and often achieve excellent examination results. Some, but not all, independent schools favour a particular religious tradition. Independent primary schools are generally called 'prep schools', and tend to cater for a slightly wider age range (seven to 13) than their counterparts in the state sector. Schools for older pupils from 11, 12 or 13 to 18 or 19 include about 500 which are often referred to as 'public schools'. Fee-paying independent schools providing full-time education for five or more pupils of compulsory school age must register by law with the appropriate government department and are subject to inspection. Many offer academic, music, art and other scholarships, and bursaries to help pupils from poorer families.

Post-compulsory Education

England, Wales and Northern Ireland

From the age of 16 students can stay within the formal education system and spend another two years preparing for a number of advanced level qualifications, such as GCE (General Certificate of Education) AS/A levels and Advanced GNVQs (see p. 130). These qualifications can be studied by students in their existing schools, at a sixth form college (in England and Wales) or in a further education institution.

GCE A levels are internationally recognised, with students taking a number of subjects at this level (usually three), giving them more opportunity to pursue their studies in greater depth. A levels are one of the main routes into higher education and employment and are graded on a scale of A to E.

From September 2000 there will be a number of changes to the post-16 curriculum, to encourage young people to take a wider range of subjects at advanced level. Among them are:

- a new Advanced Subsidiary qualification, representing the first half of a full A level and worth 50% of the marks (to provide better progression from GCSE into advanced level study and to reduce the numbers who drop out with nothing to show for their efforts);

- new A level syllabuses, normally made up of six modules and set at the same standard as current syllabuses, offering candidates the choice of linear (end of course) or modular (staged) assessment;

- a revised GNVQ (General National Vocational Qualification—see below) at Foundation, Intermediate and Advanced levels, aiming to secure consistent standards and more rigorous manageable assessment;

- a new six-unit GNVQ at advanced level, equivalent in size and demand to a single GCE A level and graded on a similar A to E scale; and

- a new Key Skills qualification (see below) to encourage all young people to develop the essential skills of communication, numeracy and information technology (IT) to higher levels.

In addition, students may study Advanced Supplementary (AS) qualifications alongside their A levels. AS qualifications are designed as a means of broadening the curriculum beyond the confines of the three-subject course. They are studied in the same depth as A levels, but in terms of volume of material covered they take up only half the time.

Not everyone wants to remain at school beyond the age of 16. Some young people (around 30%) leave education altogether and start in paid employment. Many attend institutes of further education, which offer a much wider range of courses than schools: students attending them tend to be drawn from a wider age-range than pupils at schools.

General National Vocational Qualifications are an alternative to GCSE/GCE qualifications and job-specific National Vocational Qualifications (NVQs—see below). They are mainly taken by full-time students aged 16 to 19, but can also be taken by adults studying on a part-time basis. GNVQs develop knowledge, skills and understanding in broad vocational areas such as business, health and social care, or tourism. They also include Key Skills of communication, numeracy and IT. GNVQs can be gained in stages and can be mixed and matched with other qualifications. They are available at three levels—Foundation, Intermediate and Advanced.

Further education institutions also offer specific courses directly related to work and leading to NVQs—based on national standards of competence and which can be achieved at Levels 1 to 5—in which practical work skills, such as carpentry, hairdressing, office administration and electrical engineering can be learned. They also offer a wide range of other open learning and day release courses, giving students the flexibility to learn and apply new skills in a package which best suits their individual circumstances.

Broad equivalences of qualifications are as follows:

Advanced GNVQ: two GCE A levels (NVQ Level 3)
Intermediate GNVQ: four GCSEs at grade A*[1]–C (NVQ Level 2)
Foundation GNVQ: four GCSEs at grade D–G (NVQ Level 1).

Innovations in courses offered have increasingly blurred the traditional distinctions between the world of work and the world of learning, for example, the Modern Apprenticeships training scheme (see p. 151). A new vocational qualification, called Part One GNVQ (and equivalent to two

---

[1] Starred A Grade—awarded to candidates showing exceptional ability.

A White Paper, *Learning to Succeed*, published in June 1999, announced proposals for a new Learning and Skills Council for England. The Council will deliver all post-16 education and training (excluding higher education) and assume responsibility for:

- funding colleges from the Further Education Funding Council for England (see p. 135);
- advising the Government on the National Learning Targets;
- funding Modern Apprenticeships, National Traineeships and other government-funded training and workforce development from Training and Enterprise Councils (see chapter 11); and
- developing, in partnership with LEAs, arrangements for adult and community learning.

It is proposed that the Council will be established in April 2001, and will work through a network of up to 50 local councils which will plan and co-ordinate provision locally. Local Learning Partnerships—including, as a core, colleges, Training and Enterprise Councils, local authorities and the careers service, but also, in many instances, employers, the voluntary and community sector, schools, higher education institutions and the Employment Service (see p. 155)—will have a central role in working with education providers to help them address local skills needs.

GCSEs), is being made available to schools and colleges from September 1999, and aims to broaden choices for young people. It is available in seven subject areas: art and design, business, engineering, health and social care, IT, leisure and tourism, and manufacturing.

The Qualifications and Curriculum Authority is responsible for accrediting qualifications and for developing and monitoring the school curriculum in England. Corresponding bodies in Wales and Northern Ireland perform similar functions.

Scotland

In Scotland education for those aged 16 to 18 has been reformed. Traditional, fairly academically orientated 'Highers' (Higher Grade Scottish Certificate of Education) are being replaced by new 'Higher Still' courses and modules, which will offer students greater flexibility and, through a revised assessment system, more opportunities to demonstrate successful educational achievement. It is intended that the new system of Scottish Highers should be fully in place by 2003. A system of Scottish Vocational Qualifications (SVQs)—analogous to NVQs—offers students a more practical, work-related alternative to Highers. The Scottish Qualifications Authority is the national accreditation body and the main awarding organisation.

Higher Education and Beyond

Around a third of young people in England and Wales, 40% in Scotland and 45% in Northern Ireland go to university to study full-time as undergraduates. Students at university usually spend three years researching a subject in-depth and are awarded a Bachelor's degree (for example, Bachelor of Arts, BA; or Bachelor of Science, BSc) on the successful completion of their studies. There are some four-year courses, and medical and veterinary courses normally require five years. All traditional first degree courses in Scotland require a minimum of three years' study (or four years to honours level). Although a university degree can directly prepare students for a professional career in, for example, medicine or law, most degrees offer students broader courses in arts/humanities, science, and many other disciplines.

A number of students go on to do postgraduate studies. These usually lead to an additional formally recognised qualification, such as a Master's degree (for example, Master of Arts, MA; or Master of Science, MSc) or doctorate (PhD).

A growing number of mature students enter the higher education system. The option of mature students staying in work while also studying part-time for a qualification is becoming increasingly popular.

Table 10.2: Numbers of Students in Further and Higher Education (FHE) in the UK, 1997–98[a]

Thousands

	Full-time	Part-time	Total
Further education	864	1,616	2,480
Higher education	1,230	708	1,938
of which postgraduate	*141*	*207*	*347*
All FHE students	**2,094**	**2,324**	**4,418**

Source: Department for Education and Employment
[a] Includes 1996–97 data for Wales.

Table 10.3: Home First Degree Graduates from English Institutions[a]

Thousands

	Academic year			
Subject	1994–95	1995–96	1996–97	1997–98 provisional
Medicine and dentistry	4	4	4	4
Subjects allied to medicine	8	9	10	11
Biological sciences	9	10	11	12
Veterinary, agricultural and related sciences	2	2	2	2
Physical sciences	11	11	11	10
Mathematical sciences	10	10	10	10
Architecture and related studies	15	15	14	13
Engineering and technology	6	6	5	5
Total sciences	**61**	**63**	**64**	**63**
Social sciences	22	24	24	22
Business and financial studies	18	19	19	18
Librarianship and information science	2	2	3	2
Languages and related studies	13	13	13	13
Humanities	8	8	8	8
Creative arts	13	14	15	15
Education	11	12	11	11
Total arts	**86**	**92**	**92**	**89**
Multidisciplinary studies[b]	33	34[c]	33[c]	32[c]
All subjects	**184**	**193**	**194**	**188**

Source: Department for Education and Employment
[a] Includes all home graduates awarded university, CNAA (Council for National Academic Awards), Open University and university-validated degrees.
[b] Includes the Open University.
[c] Includes around 3,000 graduates from further education sector colleges whose subject of degree is not specified.
Note: Differences between totals and the sums of their component parts are due to rounding.

The Chelsea Flower Show—originally the Royal Horticultural Society's Great Spring Show—was first held in the Temple Gardens, Embankment, London in 1888. In 1913 it moved to its present site in the grounds of the Royal Hospital, Chelsea—designed by Sir Christopher Wren and the home of the Chelsea Pensioners. The show has taken place there almost every year since then. In 1999 it was open to the public from 25 to 28 May and attracted 170,000 visitors.

MANAGEMENT

School Admissions

LEAs and school governing bodies responsible for admissions are expected to work with headteachers, the Churches and others in local forums to co-ordinate admissions arrangements, taking account of statutory codes of practice issued in England and Wales in April 1999. In England disagreements are referred to an independent adjudicator on school organisation and admissions (although disputes about religious or denominational criteria are referred to the Secretary of State for Education and Employment for determination). In Wales, the National Assembly decides in all cases of disagreement. Admission authorities of schools with a specialism in certain subjects are able to give priority in admissions to up to 10% of pupils by aptitude for their specialism. Admission authorities are no longer allowed to introduce selection by ability, and where existing partial selection by ability is challenged, the adjudicator decides whether it should continue. Local parents are allowed to petition for a ballot and (if sufficient numbers locally wish it) to vote on whether individual grammar schools should keep selective admission arrangements or (in wholly selective areas) whether the selective system should continue.

Rights and Duties of Parents

Parents in England and Wales must be given general information about a school through a prospectus and the school's annual report or, in Scotland, the school's handbook. They have a statutory right to express a preference for a particular school for their child, and there is an appeal system if their choice is not met.

In England and Wales parents choosing a local secondary school have the right to see:

- national performance tables showing the latest public examination results, vocational qualification results and rates of absence on a school-by-school basis; and

- information in each local school's prospectus on its public examination

results, vocational qualification results, attendance rates and the destinations of school-leavers.

Parents must also be given a written annual school report on their child's achievements containing details about progress on all subjects and activities; attendance record; results of National Curriculum assessments and public examinations; comparative results of pupils of the same age in the school and nationally; and arrangements for discussing pupils' reports with teachers.

Under the School Standards and Framework Act 1998, all schools are required to have home–school agreements setting out clearly what is expected of the school, parents and pupils.

In Scotland information is published for parents on school costs, examination results, pupil attendance and absence, and the destinations of school-leavers. Schools should also provide parents with information about their children's attainment in the various subjects, teachers' comments on their progress, and details about steps to build on success or overcome difficulties. One main school report each year is advised, together with one brief update report.

The Northern Ireland system for reporting to parents is broadly similar to that in England and Wales.

Schools

Increasingly, schools are managed by a closer partnership between the various parties involved—government (see p. 124), LEAs (library and education boards in Northern Ireland), school governors and headteachers.

LEAs. The key duties of an LEA include ensuring schools in its area meet government performance targets. LEAs are required by law to draw up an education development plan (in England—a strategic plan in Wales) saying how targets will be met, and have powers to intervene if a school is shown to be causing concern. Intervention can range from the provision of advice to more drastic measures (for example, closing a school) if more serious problems are encountered. Other LEA duties include:

- maintaining control of capital expenditure within its area;
- establishing an admissions system with the aim of ensuring that problems associated with over- or under-subscribed schools are kept to acceptable levels;
- taking responsibility for assessing children with special educational needs and for ensuring that parents with such children are made aware of all the help that is available to them; and
- assuming responsibility for strategic planning for its area (for example, ensuring an adequate supply of teachers, and implementing initiatives regarding the provision of books and IT).

School governors. The governing body sets, within the framework of legislation, the broad strategy for a school's development and is responsible for the school's budget. It is usually made up of a number of parent, local community, school staff and LEA representatives. In England and Wales the number of elected parent governors is being increased, with at least one elected parent governor serving on each LEA policy-making education committee. The governing bodies of church schools will also include church representatives.

Headteachers. Together with other senior members of staff, the headteacher has responsibility for the leadership, direction and management of the school, within the strategic framework set by the governing body.

Inspection bodies. The Standards and Effectiveness Unit and the Office for Standards in Education (OFSTED) in England, and separate inspection bodies for Scotland, Wales and Northern Ireland, aim to ensure that educational targets are met, and that consistency is maintained through a system of school inspections. All state schools are regularly inspected by a team of independent inspectors containing educationalists and lay people. Reports are published on inspections, and schools must act on their recommendations. Schools in England and Wales are normally inspected every six years, but more often where weaknesses are apparent. Between inspections,

Table 10.4: Number of Schools by Type in the UK, 1997–98

Type of school	1997–98[a]
State nursery	1,685
State primary	23,213
State secondary	4,435
of which grant-maintained	*680*
Independent schools	2,501
of which City Technology Colleges[b]	*15*
Special schools[c]	1,518
Pupil referral units	333
All schools	**33,685**

Source: Department for Education and Employment
[a] Includes 1996–97 schools data for Wales.
[b] For more details on City Technology Colleges see p. 137.
[c] Catering for children with special educational needs (see p. 139). The great majority of special schools are publicly maintained.

school performance is regularly monitored by LEAs, which aim to ensure that the school's improvement plans meet national guidelines set out by the Government.

Recent codes of practice, introduced under the School Standards and Framework Act 1998, set out the principles for the management of schools in England and Wales, for example, management should be about raising standards and there should be zero-tolerance of underperformance. Schools where truancy rates are low and examination success rates are high should be left, as far as practicable, to manage their own affairs; and the resources, specialist advice and management expertise of the LEA should be targeted at those schools in greatest need of help.

Further and Higher Education

Further education institutions in the UK are controlled by autonomous corporations and governing bodies, with substantial representation from business. Public funding to colleges in England, Wales and Scotland is made through Further Education Funding Councils. In Northern Ireland further education colleges are financed by DENI.

Universities and higher education institutions (around 170 in the UK) enjoy academic freedom, appoint their own staff, decide which students to admit and award their own degrees. The number of universities greatly increased in 1992, when polytechnics and their Scottish equivalents were given their own degree-awarding powers and were allowed to take the university title. The oldest universities, Oxford and Cambridge, date from the 13th century.

Government finance for higher education institutions (to help meet the costs of teaching, research and related activities) is distributed by Higher Education Funding Councils in England, Wales and Scotland, and by DENI in Northern Ireland. The private University of Buckingham receives no public grants. As well as teaching students, higher education institutions undertake paid training, research or consultancy for commercial firms. Many establishments have endowments or receive funds from foundations and benefactors.

In 1997 the National Committee of Inquiry into Higher Education, under the chairmanship of Lord Dearing, published its report on the future development and funding of the sector throughout the UK. The report supported a further expansion of up to 40% in higher education over the next 20 years and made 93 recommendations, the majority of which were accepted by the Government when it gave its formal response to the Committee in February 1998.

The Teaching and Higher Education Act 1998, implementing new funding and student support arrangements, was approved by Parliament in July 1998. The Government judged that further improvement or expansion of higher education was unaffordable on the basis of the previous arrangements, and agreed with the Dearing Committee that those who benefit from higher education should contribute more towards its costs. From 1998–99 most full-time students on first degree and other comparable higher education

courses are asked to pay up to £1,000 (depending on their own, and their parents' or spouse's, income) as a contribution towards the costs of their tuition. The balance is paid from public funds, through LEAs.

From 1999–2000 means-tested maintenance grants will be replaced by maintenance loans, part of which will also be means-tested. Loans of at least £1,000 for living costs will be available to make sure that no student or family will have to pay more during the course of studies than they would under the arrangements for existing students.

Student support arrangements in Scotland and Northern Ireland are administered by the Student Awards Agency for Scotland and the Northern Ireland education and library boards respectively.

TEACHERS

England and Wales

New teachers at state primary and secondary schools are required to be graduates. There are currently two main ways of training to become a teacher:

- taking a four-year Bachelor of Education (BEd) degree at a university or college of higher education. This involves combining degree-level study of a specialist subject, with the study of educational theories and basic developmental psychology. Bachelor of Education students are also required to apply their knowledge and develop their classroom management skills in a number of attachments to local schools, where they teach a limited timetable under the supervision of an experienced teacher; or

- taking a first degree (BA or BSc) where students concentrate entirely on a specialist subject, followed by a one-year Postgraduate Certificate in Education (PGCE) covering the theory and practice of education.

Primary school teachers tend to study for a BEd, whereas secondary school teachers, who require more specialist subject knowledge, tend to study for a PGCE.

A consultation document, *Teachers: meeting the challenge of change*, issued by the DfEE at the end of 1998, outlines plans for the development of the teaching profession in England. Key aspects include:

- ensuring that all trainee teachers, including those on employment-based routes, meet the new standards for the award of Qualified Teacher Status before they can qualify to teach;

- establishing a General Teaching Council for England, due in 2000, which will have responsibility for overseeing every aspect of the teaching profession;

- providing more training for headteachers (with mandatory qualifications for new headteachers being introduced by 2002);

- introducing a new pay system for teachers, providing greater opportunities for career progression;

- allocating to teacher training colleges resources to ensure all teachers meet the required standards in numeracy, literacy and computer skills;

- requiring newly qualified teachers taking up their first teaching post to go through a further induction period, enabling them to consolidate their teaching skills; and

- creating a fast-track scheme to attract able graduates to the teaching profession and increasing substantially the number of classroom assistants and support staff.

These arrangements will be tested in the 1999–2000 academic year and will apply from September 2000. Similar reforms to the teaching profession are under consideration in Wales.

Scotland and Northern Ireland

In Scotland all teachers in education authority schools must be registered with the General Teaching Council for Scotland. All entrants to the profession are graduates. New primary teachers qualify either through a four-year BEd or one-year postgraduate course. Secondary school teachers must undertake a one-year postgraduate training course or an undergraduate course combining subject studies, study of education and school

experience. Newly qualified teachers must serve a two-year probationary period at the beginning of their teaching careers.

In Northern Ireland all new entrants to teaching in grant-aided schools are graduates and hold an approved teaching qualification. The principal training courses are BEd Honours (four years) and the one-year Postgraduate Certificate of Education.

THE CURRICULUM

Schools

England and Wales

The subjects taught to children between the ages of five and 16 in state schools are to a large extent determined by the National Curriculum, which has four key stages (see Table 10.5) At each of the four stages the core subjects of English (and in Wales, Welsh), mathematics, science, technology, physical education, and religious education are taught. History, geography, art and music are also compulsory subjects in the earlier stages of the curriculum. A modern foreign language (usually French or German) is added to the curriculum at Key Stages Three and Four. For Key Stage Four the study of history, geography, art and music becomes optional; in Wales a modern foreign language is optional at Key Stage Four. Other subjects, such as drama, dance, and classical languages, remain on the curriculum, but the teaching of them is optional, depending on the resources of individual schools.

Table 10.5: Key Stages of the National Curriculum

	Pupil ages	Year groups
Key Stage One	5–7	1–2
Key Stage Two	7–11	3–6
Key Stage Three	11–14	7–9
Key Stage Four	14–16	10–11

The National Curriculum also contains general requirements for each subject and, for each Key Stage, programmes of study outlining what pupils should be taught, as well as attainment targets setting out expected standards of pupils' performance.

There are varying levels of achievement in each subject which form the basis of the attainment targets for pupils. The National Curriculum outlines by what age the majority of pupils should normally be expected to reach these various targets. The attainment targets are designed to be more challenging as pupils get older.

For the period from September 1998 until 2000 the Government introduced a slimmed-down curriculum for primary schools for foundation subjects. These interim arrangements are designed to give teachers more time to focus on meeting government targets for raising standards in literacy and numeracy. In England national numeracy and literacy strategies have been introduced, requiring all schools to have a literacy and numeracy study hour each day. Less prescriptive literacy and numeracy frameworks are applicable in Wales.

Following a review of the National Curriculum by the Qualifications and Curriculum Authority, decisions on a revised National Curriculum for schools in England, applicable from September 2000, were announced by the DfEE in September 1999. These aim to provide greater coherence in the way schools prepare pupils for their role and responsibility as adults and for their future working lives, and include the creation of citizenship as a new curriculum subject (from 2002) and a non-statutory framework for the teaching of personal, social and health education.

Some categories of school in England are given the chance to build reputations for excellence within specific areas of the curriculum. Pupils attending City Technology Colleges—independent secondary schools created by a partnership of government and business sponsors—follow a course of study meeting all the requirements of the National Curriculum, but use the flexibility given to them to devote more time and resources to the study of science and technology subjects.

'Specialist' schools are state secondary schools specialising in technology, science and mathematics; modern foreign languages; sport; or the arts—in addition to providing the full National Curriculum. A specialist school must have the backing of private sector sponsors. Capital and annual grants are available from public funds to complement business sponsorship. In December 1998 there were 330 designated specialist schools in England, including 227 technology colleges, 58 language colleges, and 26 sports and 19 arts colleges. By 2003 nearly one in four of all secondary schools will be a specialist school.

A further initiative (in England), aiming to give more pupils greater flexibility in the subjects they are expected to study, is the Government's Beacon School programme. This involves existing schools applying for Beacon School status, and being allocated additional funding to act as pioneers of educational innovation. Additional funding is conditional on Beacon Schools giving formal help to other schools in their area.

Scotland and Northern Ireland

In Scotland content and management of the curriculum are not prescribed by statute, responsibility resting with education authorities and headteachers. Government guidelines on the structure and balance of the curriculum for five to 14 year olds have been issued, covering English, mathematics, expressive arts, Latin, Gaelic, modern languages, environmental studies and religious and moral education. For those aged 14 to 16 the curriculum includes study of language and communications, mathematics, science, technology, social studies, creative activities, physical education, and religious and moral education. Provision is made for teaching Gaelic in Gaelic-speaking areas.

The Northern Ireland curriculum, compulsory in all publicly financed schools, consists of religious education (see also p. 239) and six broad areas of study: English, mathematics, science and technology, the environment and society, creative and expressive studies and, in secondary schools and some primary schools, language studies. The common curriculum also has two cross-curricular themes: cultural heritage and education for mutual understanding. A small number of pupils attend Irish-medium schools, where they receive their lessons in Irish.

Careers

All young people in full-time education are entitled to careers information, advice and guidance. All schools have been encouraged to draw up partnership agreements with their local careers service in developing programmes of careers education and guidance. All state secondary schools in England and Wales, and primary and secondary schools in Northern Ireland, provide school-leavers with a Record of Achievement, setting out their school attainments, including public examination and National Curriculum assessment results. In Scotland the National Record of Achievement has been replaced by a Progress File.

Work Experience

The Government is committed to extending the range and quality of vocational and work-related opportunities for pupils in the 14–16 age-group. Since October 1998 the School Standards and Framework Act enables schools in England and Wales to offer more flexible work-related learning choices, by allowing pupils to take up placements at any time in their last two years of compulsory schooling.

Business and Community Links

The Government recognises that school–business links can help raise pupils' levels of achievement and enable them to see the relevance of what they learn at school. It is continuing to support the Education Business Partnership Network. Education Business Partnerships comprise representatives from industry, education and the wider community, and aim to bring about closer links between education and industry in order to ensure that young people develop the necessary skills to help them succeed in the labour market.

The Government has also stated its commitment to increasing the availability to pupils of mentoring initiatives, whereby people experienced in business can help to inspire and motivate groups or individuals.

In Scotland the Education for Work programme has been launched for the ongoing development of business–education links.

Further and Higher Education

After compulsory school age (16) education institutions offer students a wide choice of academic and vocational courses and qualifications. In order to help employers and others with an interest in education interpret the relative merits of the array of educational and training qualifications available, some work has been done in assessing the comparability of the various options available—see p. 130 for the broad equivalences in qualifications.

At universities and institutions of higher education first or higher degrees (see p. 131) in one or two specialist academic subjects remain the cornerstone of study. There is evidence though that universities are becoming more flexible in their approach to learning, with many of them (particularly the former polytechnics) offering term-long placements in work environments to students in addition to their more theoretical courses of study.

ASSESSMENT

Schools

England and Wales

Since September 1998 (September 1999 in Wales) baseline assessment for children aged four to five has become statutory. All children of that age are assessed within seven weeks of first entering primary school on their language skills, mathematical skills, and personal and social skills. Teachers are able to use the information from the assessments to plan their teaching to match children's individual needs.

At the end of Key Stages One, Two and Three of the National Curriculum formal assessment of children is carried out. At Key

Stage One this takes the form of classroom tasks, and at Key Stages Two and Three national tests and tasks. The national tests, which every state-educated child has to sit, assess for each core subject within the National Curriculum. The test and task results help teachers determine, along with their own assessments, which attainment target level their pupils have reached.

National Curriculum assessment performs three main functions:

- to inform the Government whether, at a national level, pupils are developing the skills they will need as adults;

- to assess the performance of schools and teachers in helping children to learn a specific and standardised body of skills and knowledge; and

- to identify directly particular strengths and weaknesses in individual pupils.

Knowledge and skills acquired by pupils throughout the Key Stages of the curriculum are formally tested in the public examinations (GCSEs for most pupils in England and Wales) that they take at the end of their compulsory school career.

Scotland and Northern Ireland

In Scotland there are standardised tests in English and mathematics at five levels within the five to 14 age range. Pupil assessment in Northern Ireland, which is statutory, is broadly in line with practice in England and Wales.

Children with Special Educational Needs

A child is said to have special educational needs (SEN) if he or she has a learning difficulty which needs special provision. A child has learning difficulties if he or she has significantly greater difficulty in learning than most children of the same age or a disability which makes it difficult to use the normal educational facilities in the area. Every child has the right to receive a broad and balanced curriculum. For pupils with SEN planning should take account of each pupil's particular learning and assessment requirements.

England and Wales. Around 1.66 million pupils in England are identified as having special educational needs. The vast majority are educated in mainstream schools, but around 98,000 pupils with more severe and complex needs attend special schools. State schools must try to provide for pupils with SEN and publish information about their SEN policy. LEAs must identify and assess the needs of those children with more severe or complex needs and involve parents in decisions about their child's education. If an LEA believes that it should determine the education for the child, it must draw up a formal statement of the child's special needs and the action it intends to take to meet them. Wherever possible, children with SEN should be taught in mainstream schools. The LEA is required to comply with the parents' choice of school unless this is inappropriate for the child, or incompatible with the efficient education of other children or with the efficient use of resources. Parents have a right of appeal to the Special Educational Needs Tribunal if they disagree with the LEA's decision about their child. The Tribunal's verdict is final and binding on all parties.

A statutory code of practice offers guidance to all LEAs and state schools in England and Wales on identifying and assessing the needs of pupils with SEN.

In November 1998 the Government published *Meeting Special Educational Needs: A programme of action*, setting out its strategy for raising standards for children with SEN in England. The main themes are:

- developing the knowledge and skills of all staff working with children with SEN;

- improving the SEN framework and developing a more inclusive education system; and

- working in partnership with parents and carers.

Under the Schools Access Initiative in England, £100 million will be made available over three years to make mainstream schools more accessible to pupils with disabilities. Further resources have been given to aid the expansion of parent partnership services, and for staff training and development in SEN.

Scotland. The choice of school is a matter for agreement between education authorities and parents. Education authorities must take special educational needs fully into account when making provision for pupils in their areas. There are a small number of pupils (about 2% of the school population) whose needs require the authority to open a record describing the special education necessary to meet them. This process incorporates a right of appeal.

Northern Ireland. Similar arrangements to those in England and Wales, including an appeal system, are in force.

Assessment in Further and Higher Education

Further and higher education courses tend to be assessed by a mixture of coursework and examinations. However, with the shift towards more flexible and practical courses in all educational institutions, the traditional written examination is steadily becoming a less important part of the assessment process. This is particularly so in the case of adult education, through which the Government's commitment to promoting a culture of lifelong learning will be developed (see p. 141).

Educational Achievement

There are variations in educational achievement throughout the UK. In 1998 girls outperformed boys in all National Curriculum teacher assessments and many National Curriculum tests between Key Stages One and Three. At GCSE level girls are much more likely than boys to obtain passes in English, foreign languages and history. At A level choices of subject studied vary for boys and girls, with males making up over three-fifths of mathematics entrants and females making up a similar proportion of English entrants.

In Northern Ireland, 55% of 16 year olds obtained five or more GCSE grade A* to C passes in 1998, while in England and Wales in the same year only 46% achieved the same standard.

Notable variations in educational participation and achievement can be seen across different ethnic groups (see Table 10.6). The Government is investing over £430 million in a new ethnic minority achievement grant over three years from 1999–2000. Under this grant schools are expected to establish policies to help raise the attainment of ethnic minority pupils at risk of underperforming.

English language teaching continues to receive priority for pupils without English as their first language. Schools may also teach the main ethnic minority community languages at secondary level in England and Wales as part of the National Curriculum. They should take account of the ethnic and cultural backgrounds of pupils, and curricula should reflect ethnic and cultural diversity.

ADULT EDUCATION AND LIFELONG LEARNING

Adult Education

Further education for adults is provided by further education institutions, adult education centres and colleges run by LEAs, and voluntary bodies such as the Workers' Educational Association. The duty to secure such education is shared by the Further Education Funding Councils, LEAs and DENI. University departments of continuing education also provide courses for adults.

The Further Education Funding Councils and DENI fund formal academic and vocational programmes, courses leading to access to higher education, and courses in basic literacy and numeracy, including English for speakers of other languages. LEAs are responsible for the less formal leisure and recreational courses. These bodies must take account of adult students with special educational needs.

Adult education has seen substantial changes in the past few years. The Lifelong Learning agenda and the University for Industry (see p. 141) will help to increase access to relevant learning opportunities and enhance employability and performance in the workplace. (More details on training opportunities open to adults can be found in chapter 11.)

Table 10.6: Highest Qualification Held: by Gender and Ethnic Group in Great Britain, 1997–98[a]   %

	Degree or equivalent	Other Higher[b]	A Level or equivalent	GCSE (grades A*–C)	Other	None
Males						
Indian/Pakistani/Bangladeshi	18	5	16	14	25	22
Black	14	6	22	18	24	16
White	14	8	32	18	14	15
Other groups	20	5	17	15	27	15
Females						
Indian/Pakistani/Bangladeshi	9	5	11	18	25	33
Black	9	12	14	27	22	16
White	11	9	16	29	15	20
Other groups	12	8	15	17	33	15

Source: Department for Education and Employment from the Labour Force Survey

[a] Men aged 16 to 64, women aged 16 to 59 for the combined quarters of spring 1997 to winter 1997–98.

[b] Below degree level.

Lifelong Learning

In 1998 the DfEE issued proposals for a major new strategy to encourage the continuous development of everybody's skills, knowledge and understanding, which the Government believes is essential for business competitiveness, individual employability and personal fulfilment. Separate but parallel learning strategies for Wales, Scotland and Northern Ireland were also published. The concept of developing a culture of lifelong learning will underpin all areas of post-16 educational provision.

The Adult and Community Learning Fund, launched in 1998, supports community-based activities, including learning opportunities in familiar relevant surroundings attractive to people who feel excluded from mainstream education. Some £20 million is being made available for the period to March 2002. Over 160 projects have been set up to promote community-based learning through the Fund.

A new Adult Learning Committee will have direct responsibility for advising the Learning and Skills Council (see p. 131) on achieving the National Learning Targets (see p. 127) for adults and for organisations.

The Open University

The Open University is a non-residential university offering degree and other courses for adult students of all ages. Teaching is through a combination of specially produced printed texts, correspondence tuition, television and radio broadcasts, audio/video cassettes and, for some courses, computing and short residential schools. There is a network of study centres for contact with part-time tutors and counsellors, and with fellow students. Students do not need formal academic qualifications to register for most courses.

Its first degrees are the BA (Open) or the BSc (Open), which are general degrees awarded on a system of credits for each course completed. Either degree can be awarded with honours. The OU now offers honours degrees in selected subject areas. There is also an MMath degree for students who have taken an approved combination of courses specialising in mathematics, and an MEng degree for those who have studied an approved combination of courses to achieve the highest professional status of Chartered Engineer. About 200,000 first degrees have been awarded since the University opened in 1970. The OU offers a wide range of postgraduate courses, and of the Masters of Business Administration (MBAs) awarded in the UK 25% are from the OU.

University for Industry (UfI)

The UfI, one of the Government's main innovations for lifelong learning, is intended to bring new learning opportunities to the home, the workplace and the community. It will be launched nationally in autumn 2000, and will cover England, Wales and Northern Ireland. It will work closely with a separate Scottish UfI, which will be tailored to the distinctive Scottish education system, institutions and industrial structure.

Using new technologies and a network of learning centres, the UfI will promote learning ranging from basic skills of literacy and numeracy to specialised technological skills and business management. It is intended to play a key role in improving the nation's competitiveness by raising skill levels and employability.

The Government has allocated £44 million in 1999–2000 for the UfI to take forward its development and implementation plans, and the aim is to set up around 1,000 learning centres by March 2001. The first learning centres should be operational by November 1999.

Individual Learning Accounts (ILAs)

To encourage a culture of lifelong learning, the Government proposes the introduction of individual learning accounts. These will help individuals to save and borrow for investment in their own development. ILAs will be available to everyone, and will be used, at the learner's choice, to pay for learning—whether an evening class or a programme bought through the UfI.

ILAs will act as a vehicle for funding continuous learning where the Government, employers and the individual can all have a part to play. The March 1999 Budget announced a range of new incentives for learning account holders. Any adult with an individual learning account will be able to claim a discount of 20% on learning and a higher discount of 80% for specific courses, including computer literacy. The discounts apply on a course cost limit of £500 per person a year.

LINKS WITH OTHER COUNTRIES

Large numbers of people from other countries come to the UK to study, and many British people work and train overseas. The British aid programme (see chapter 7, p. 93) encourages links between educational institutions in the UK and developing countries.

European Union Schemes

Exchange of students is promoted by the EU's SOCRATES programme through ERASMUS (the European Community Action Scheme for the Mobility of Students), which provides grants to enable university students from the EU and from Norway, Iceland and Liechtenstein to study in other states. The programme covers all academic subjects, and the period of study normally lasts between three and 12 months.

SOCRATES also promotes competence in foreign languages through the LINGUA scheme. Other parts of the programme support partnerships between schools, study visits by senior educationalists and a range of multinational projects including open and distance learning, adult education and education for the children of migrant workers, gypsies and travellers. Around 2,000 UK schools have taken part in transnational SOCRATES partnerships. A new phase of the SOCRATES programme will begin on 1 January 2000.

The LEONARDO DA VINCI programme supports and complements vocational training policies and practices in the EU member states (and in Norway, Iceland and Liechtenstein, ten Central and Eastern European countries and Cyprus), fostering transnational co-operation and innovation in training through pilot projects, exchanges and research projects.

The Youth for Europe programme supports youth exchange projects in EU member states and related activities such as youth leader training. The third phase of the programme, which began in 1995, runs to the end of 1999.

The 15 EU member states, together with the European Commission, work together in funding and running ten European Schools, which provide mother-tongue education for children, aged four to 18, of staff employed at EU institutions. One of the schools is located in the UK, at Culham in Oxfordshire

Overseas Students in the UK

British universities and other higher and further education establishments have built up a strong reputation overseas by offering tuition of the highest standards and maintaining low student-to-staff ratios. About 270,000 overseas students are now studying in the UK at publicly funded higher and further education institutions.

Most overseas students following courses of higher or further education pay fees covering the full cost of their courses. Nationals of other EU member states generally pay the lower level of fees applicable to British home students.

Government Scholarship Schemes

The Government makes considerable provision for foreign students and trainees through its international development programme and other award and scholarship schemes. Some 4,500 overseas students from about 150 countries currently receive awards from scholarship schemes funded in part by the Foreign & Commonwealth Office (FCO) and the Department for International Development (DFID). The two main schemes funded by the FCO and DFID are:

- British Chevening Scholarships, a worldwide programme offering outstanding graduate students and young professionals the opportunity to study at British universities and other academic institutions. An increasing number of these scholarships are jointly funded with British or foreign commercial firms and with academic or other institutions. There are now over 600 such scholarships; and

- the Commonwealth Scholarship and Fellowship Plan, offering scholarships for study in other Commonwealth countries. Under the scheme in the UK scholarships are for postgraduate study or research for one to three years at British higher education institutions.

Other Schemes

Many other public and private scholarships and fellowships are available to students from overseas and to British students who want to study overseas. Among the best known are the British Council Fellowships, the Fulbright Scholarship Scheme, the British Marshall Scholarships, the Rhodes Scholarships, the Churchill Scholarships and the Confederation of British Industry Scholarships. The Overseas Research Students Awards Scheme, funded by the Higher Education Funding Councils, also provides help for overseas full-time postgraduate students with outstanding research potential. Most British universities and colleges offer bursaries and scholarships for which graduates of any nationality are eligible.

THE YOUTH SERVICE

The youth service—a partnership between local government and voluntary organisations—is concerned with the informal personal and social education of young people aged 11 to 25 (five to 25 in Northern Ireland).

Local authorities maintain their own youth centres and clubs and provide most of the public support for local and regional voluntary organisations. In England the service is estimated to reach around 3 million young people, with the voluntary organisations contributing a significant proportion of overall provision.

In England the DfEE supports the youth service through grants to the National Youth Agency, the National Council for Voluntary Youth Services and National Voluntary Youth Organisations. Funded primarily by local government, the National Youth Agency provides support for those working with young people and for information and publishing services.

The Wales Youth Agency is the agent for payment of grant aid to national youth service bodies with headquarters in Wales; it is also responsible for the accreditation of training and staff development for youth workers.

In Scotland the youth service forms part of the community education provision made by local authorities. It is also promoted by Community Learning Scotland. The Scottish Executive gives grants to voluntary youth organisations to help them with their headquarters expenditure and staff training.

In Northern Ireland the education and library boards provide and fund facilities for recreational, social, physical, cultural and youth service activities. They assist with the running costs of registered voluntary youth units, and provide advice and support to youth groups. Boards also help young people visiting the rest of the UK, the Irish Republic and overseas. The Youth Council for Northern Ireland advises the education system on the development of the youth service. It promotes the provision of facilities, encourages cross-community activity and pays grants to the headquarters of voluntary bodies.

Voluntary Youth Organisations

National voluntary youth organisations undertake a significant share of youth activities through local groups, which raise most of their day-to-day expenses by their own efforts. Many receive financial and other help from local authorities, which also make facilities available in many areas. The voluntary organisations vary greatly in character and include the uniformed organisations, such as the Scouts and Girl Guides. Some organisations are church-based. Some also represent Jews and Muslims. In Wales, Urdd Gobaith Cymru (the Welsh League of Youth) provides cultural, sporting and language-based activities for young Welsh speakers and learners.

Thousands of youth clubs encourage their members to take part in sport, cultural and other creative activities. Some youth clubs provide information, counselling and advice.

Many voluntary youth organisations and local authorities provide services for the young unemployed, young people from ethnic minorities, young people in inner cities or rural areas and those in trouble or especially vulnerable. Many authorities have youth committees on which official and voluntary bodies are represented. They employ youth officers to co-ordinate youth work and to arrange in-service training.

Youth Workers

In England and Wales a two-year training course at certain universities and higher education colleges produces qualified youth and community workers; several undergraduate part-time and postgraduate courses are also available. In Scotland one-, two- and three-year courses are provided at teacher education institutions. Students from Northern Ireland attend courses run in universities and colleges in the UK and the Irish Republic.

Other Organisations

Finance is provided by many grant-giving foundations and trusts for activities involving young people. The Prince's Trust and the Royal Jubilee Trust provide grants and practical help to individuals and organisations; areas of concern include urban deprivation, unemployment, homelessness, and young offenders. Efforts are also made to assist ethnic minorities.

The Duke of Edinburgh's Award Scheme challenges young people from the UK and other Commonwealth countries to meet certain standards in activities such as community service, expeditions, social and practical skills, and physical recreation.

Voluntary Service by Young People

Thousands of young people voluntarily undertake community service designed to help those in need, including elderly and disabled people. Many schools also organise community service work as part of the curriculum.

Millennium Volunteers

The Millennium Volunteer programme offers young people aged 16–24 the opportunity to make a contribution to their communities by making a sustained commitment to voluntary activity. Its main aims are the personal development of young people and benefit to the community. Activities may range from helping with reading in schools and hospital visiting to working on projects to improve the environment or sporting and cultural life.

Further Reading

The Government's Expenditure Plans 1999–00 to 2001–02. Department for Education and Employment and Office for Standards in Education. Cm 4202. The Stationery Office, 1999.

The Learning Age: a Renaissance for a new Britain. (Department for Education and Employment paper on lifelong learning.) Cm 3790. The Stationery Office, 1998.

Learning is for Everyone. (Welsh Office paper on lifelong learning.) Cm 3942. The Stationery Office, 1998.

Opportunity Scotland. (The Scottish Office paper on lifelong learning.) Cm 4048. The Stationery Office, 1998.

Learning to Succeed: a new framework for post-16 learning. Department for Education and Employment. Cm 4392. The Stationery Office, 1999.

Websites

Department for Education and Employment: www.dfee.gov.uk

Scottish Executive: www.scotland.gov.uk

National Assembly for Wales: www.wales.gov.uk

Department of Education for Northern Ireland: www.nics.gov.uk/deni

11 The Labour Market

The labour market in the United Kingdom has undergone major changes, with many more women in the workforce, increased levels of part-time working and the continuing move towards employment in service industries, where over three-quarters of employees now work.

The Government provides help, in the form of financial assistance, practical advice and training, for people who find it difficult to find work. It has created a variety of traineeships giving young people the skills and experience they need to enter the labour market and it also encourages those already in work to develop their skills through its lifelong learning initiatives. Legislation gives protection to those in the workplace, in particular the low-paid.

At the beginning of the 20th century, the absence of a formal, state-supported benefit system (most notably, the lack of pensions and child benefit) meant that for many people engaging in some form of paid employment was their only means of supporting themselves. The 1901 Census noted that over 10% of boys aged between ten and 14 (around 140,000) were already 'engaged in occupations'. Nearly 40% of men aged 75 and upwards (around 110,000) were still working. Most women tended to leave paid employment once they got married to devote themselves more fully to their domestic duties. More than half of unmarried women were actively engaged in paid employment, whereas only around 13% (less than 1 million) of married or widowed women were still working.

The range of available jobs was limited by today's standards. Male employees dominated transport and business-related occupations. Manufacturing provided an increasingly large share of the available jobs, and the demand for female and child labour* was particularly high in the textile industries. Affluent private households were another big employer in the labour market: over 40% of women in paid employment at the time worked as maids, cooks or cleaners or were engaged in some other form of domestic service.

PATTERNS OF EMPLOYMENT

Some 29.2 million people aged 16 and over were classed as economically active[1] in the UK in April–June 1999, of whom 27.4 million were in employment: 15.1 million men and 12.3 million women (see Table 11.1). Employment is growing following a decline during the recession of the early 1990s: the Labour Force Survey (LFS), an official measure of labour market activity produced by the Office for National Statistics (ONS), notes that the number of people aged 16 and over in employment rose by 347,000 in the year to April–June 1999. Employment levels are now at their highest ever recorded.

One of the most significant long-term trends in the labour market has been the growth in the number of women in employment. Women now account for around 45% of all those in the labour force in the UK, and economic activity rates for women with children under five have risen from 47% to 57% over the past decade. In most service industries more than half of employees are women, while in manufacturing, construction, agriculture, and transport and communications women account for less than one-third of employees.

Part-time workers over the age of 16 now total 6.8 million. About 44% of women work part-time, compared with 9% of men.

The proportion of employee jobs in service industries has more than doubled in the last 40 years, to around 75% of available jobs. There has also been a gradual move away from manual to non-manual occupations, which are now held by around 60% of those in employment.

The private sector share of employment rose from 71% in 1981 to 82% in mid-1998. The number of employees in the public sector fell from a peak of over 7.4 million in 1979 to ⌐around 5 million in mid-1998, reflecting privatisation of a number of major industries (see p. 386).

Around 1.3 million people have two or more jobs, while roughly 1.7 million (7% of employees) are engaged in temporary jobs (see

Reasons for the greater involvement of women in the workplace are complex:

● more women are putting off having children until their thirties, and when they do have children, they are far more likely to go back to work and make use of the growing number of available childcare options than they were a generation ago;

● many of the new jobs available in the service sector, particularly those involving computers and telephones, are areas where women can compete for jobs with men on equal terms; whereas many of the more traditional jobs, which are declining in number, particularly those in the mining, construction and heavy engineering industries, require a degree of physical strength which puts women at a disadvantage; and

● they are partly the result of legislative change and positive action on the part of employers. One business-led campaign, Opportunity Now, with a membership of over 350 organisations, has encouraged employers to tackle barriers to women's progress and promote an inclusive culture in the workplace.

Table 11.3). Around one in three people work in temporary jobs because they cannot find a permanent one. A similar proportion work in temporary jobs because they prefer to do so.

'Teleworking'—people working from home using information technology (IT)—is becoming more widespread. In spring 1999 some 255,000 people were classed as teleworkers whose main job was primarily in their own home; extending the definition to cover those working in different places using home as a base and those who spent at least one day a week working from home raised the number to 1.32 million.

Around 3.2 million people are self-employed in the UK: 16% of men and 7% of women in employment are self-employed. Agriculture and fishing, and construction have

---

[1] Defined as those who are either in employment (employee, self-employed, unpaid family worker or on a government-supported training programme) or unemployed and actively seeking work.

Table 11.1: Employment in the UK, April–June 1999

Thousands, seasonally adjusted

	Male	Female	Total
All aged 16 and over	22,550	23,675	46,225
Total economically active	16,209	12,946	29,155
of whom:			
In employment	15,118	12,276	27,394
ILO unemployed[a]	1,091	670	1,760
Economic activity rate (%)[b]	84.5	72.5	78.8
Employment rate (%)[b]	78.8	68.7	74.0
ILO unemployment rate (%)[c]	6.7	5.2	6.0

Source: ONS Labour Force Survey
[a] International Labour Organisation definition of unemployment.
[b] For men aged 16 to 64 and women aged 16 to 59.
[c] In May 1999 the ILO unemployment rate for those aged 16 and over was 6.2% in the G7 and 9.4% in the EU.

Table 11.2: Regional Labour Market Structure, April–June 1999

seasonally adjusted

	Economically active (thousands)[a]	Economic activity rate (%)[a]	ILO unemployment rate (%)
England	24,609	79.5	5.8
Wales	1,322	73.8	7.5
Scotland	2,482	77.1	7.2
Northern Ireland[b]	737	71.8	7.6
United Kingdom	**29,155**	**78.8**	**6.0**

Source: ONS: Labour Force Survey
[a] For men aged 16 to 64 and women aged 16 to 59.
[b] Estimates for Northern Ireland are not seasonally adjusted.

Table 11.3: Employment in the UK

Thousands, seasonally adjusted, April–June

	1995	1996	1997	1998	1999
Employees	22,293	22,622	23,156	23,530	23,931
Self-employed	3,354	3,319	3,340	3,246	3,203
Unpaid family workers	144	122	115	99	97
Government-supported training and employment programmes	288	249	225	171	162
Employment	**26,079**	**26,312**	**26,836**	**27,047**	**27,394**
of whom:					
Full-time workers	*19,741*	*19,792*	*20,144*	*20,319*	*20,585*
Part-time workers	*6,334*	*6,519*	*6,687*	*6,721*	*6,803*
Workers with a second job	*1,297*	*1,288*	*1,255*	*1,217*	*1,311*
Temporary employees	*1,631*	*1,668*	*1,808*	*1,730*	*1,690*

Source: ONS: Labour Force Survey.
Note: Differences between totals and the sums of their component parts are due to rounding.

the highest proportions of self-employed people, while relatively few of those engaged in manufacturing and public administration are self-employed.

Employment by Sector

The shift in jobs from manufacturing to service industries has continued in the past decade (see Table 11.4). In the year to March 1999 the number of workforce jobs, a measure of the total number of *jobs*, rather than the number of *employees*, in service industries rose to nearly 21 million. Employment in most service sectors grew.

Transport and communications was one service sector to record a particularly large rise in workforce jobs in the year to March 1999, with the number of jobs up by 4.7% from the previous year to 1.7 million. A contributory factor was the growth in telephone call centres, which are run by several companies, for example in banking, other financial services, retailing and transport. Call centres employ large numbers of people to deal with customer requests, and computer telephonists are one of the fastest growing occupational groups in the UK. The continuing growth in the number of mobile telephones in use in the UK (see p. 378) has also accounted for a large number of new jobs in this sector.

In the last ten years most other sectors have experienced lower levels of employment. Traditional manufacturing industries, such as steel and shipbuilding, have recorded particularly large falls in employment. By March 1999 manufacturing accounted for 17% of employees in employment, compared with 42% in 1955. In March 1999 employee jobs in the main manufacturing sectors included:

- 528,000 jobs in metal and metal products;
- 517,000 in electrical and optical equipment;
- 480,000 in food products, beverages and tobacco;
- 471,000 in paper, pulp, printing, publishing and recording media; and
- 312,000 in clothing, textiles, leather and leather products.

Service sector jobs have continued to rise for a number of reasons:

- technological developments, such as the growth of the Internet, have created a significant demand for new jobs—for example, IT technicians install, maintain,

Table 11.4: Workforce Jobs by Industry, March 1999			*seasonally adjusted*
	Workforce jobs (thousands)	% of workforce jobs	% change over previous year
Agriculture and fishing	526	1.9	−5.2
Energy and water	223	0.8	−0.6
Manufacturing	4,317	15.6	−4.1
Construction	1,805	6.5	0.1
Services	20,806	75.2	1.5
of which:			
Distribution, hotels and restaurants	*6,106*	*22.1*	*0.4*
Transport and communications	*1,661*	*6.0*	*4.7*
Finance and business services	*5,093*	*18.4*	*3.0*
Public administration, education and health	*6,398*	*23.1*	*0.9*
Other services	*1,548*	*5.6*	*−0.3*
All jobs	**27,677**	**100.0**	**0.3**

Source: ONS: employer surveys

and upgrade software packages, while graphic artists design web pages;

- other service sector jobs, most notably financial services, are areas in which the UK continues to enjoy international success, in terms of attracting foreign business and leading the world in the quality of services provided; and

- the growth in jobs in areas such as public relations and marketing reflects the worldwide increase in jobs related to the dissemination of information.

Unemployment

Unemployment in the UK has fallen considerably since the peak at the end of 1992. In April–June 1999, 1.8 million people were unemployed, 6.0% of those in the labour market, compared with 6.3% in the same period of 1998, according to the International Labour Organisation (ILO) definition of unemployment as measured by the Labour Force Survey. Some 501,000 people had been unemployed for more than a year, of whom 301,000 had been out of work for over two years.

Unemployment among 16 to 24 year olds is running at double the overall rate. Reasons for youth unemployment are likely to be associated with their relative lack of skills, qualifications and experience. Unemployment rates tend to fall as the level of qualification increases. In spring 1999, the unemployment rate for those with no qualifications was around four times higher than for those with a higher educational qualification.

Among people with broadly similar educational qualifications, those from ethnic minorities tend to have higher unemployment rates than those from the White group. Unemployment rates are particularly high for young Black people.

Comparing unemployment internationally, the UK rate is similar to that for the major G7 group of nations and substantially lower than that for the EU average.

Areas that used to rely on heavy industries (such as steel, shipbuilding and coal mining) which have since declined are often among those with the highest rates of unemployment. Areas with the lowest levels of unemployment include the South East and East of England, with rates well below the UK average.

LABOUR MARKET POLICY

Key aspects of the Government's labour market policies include promoting job creation and helping people to overcome the barriers preventing them moving from welfare into work. Among the issues which it is tackling are:

- improving the employability of unemployed people;

- removing the barriers in the tax and benefits system which act as a disincentive for people to move from welfare into work (see p. 405 and chapter 12);

- providing minimum legal standards at work, such as on individual employment rights; and

- tackling the social exclusion brought about by long-term unemployment (see chapter 9).

Government policies include the Welfare-to-Work programme (see pp. 154–5), education and training programmes, the national minimum wage (see p. 156) and its employability initiative.

Employability Initiative

'Employability' was an important theme when the UK held the Presidency of the European Union (EU) in 1998 and was also the focus of a special conference of the G8 (group of leading industrialised countries) in the UK in the same year. EU member states have signed up to producing annual 'action plans' which outline how their policies respond to agreed employment guidelines on employability, adaptability (in businesses and their employees), entrepreneurship and equal opportunities between men and women. G8 countries have also produced similar action plans. The UK remains instrumental in shaping both processes. Action on employability is an essential part of the drive to develop a skilled, trained and adaptable labour force and flexible labour market, supported by minimum standards of fairness and decency, including the national minimum wage (see p. 156).

TRAINING AND EDUCATION

Education and training are among the Government's top priorities (see also chapter 10) and are considered essential for ensuring that the UK workforce has the necessary skills to meet the challenges of a rapidly changing world economy. According to the LFS, in spring 1999, 3.7 million employees of working age in the UK had received job-related training in the previous four weeks, 15.9% of such employees. Employees with higher level qualifications are almost six times more likely to have received training than those with no qualifications; younger employees are about two-and-a-half times more likely to have received training than older employees.

Connexions

In June 1999 the Government published the White Paper *Learning to Succeed*, in which it announced its proposals to improve participation and attainment of those aged 16 to 19. The White Paper included measures affecting schools, colleges and work-based training, as well as a new focus for the Careers Service. This strategy is called Connexions, key elements of which include:

● creating a Youth Support Service as a single new source of advice and support for young people;

● providing better learning opportunities by bringing further education and training provision closer together and offering three main alternatives—general academic education, high-quality vocational education, and part-time study while working; and

● offering more unified and improved financial incentives and support, including the extension of Educational Maintenance Allowances (see p. 126) to help young people stay in learning.

Connexions plans to ensure that all young people have access to high-quality education and training, irrespective of whether they opt to take up education in a school sixth form, further education college or work-based training through an apprenticeship, traineeship or other arrangement. In addition, under the Welfare-to-Work programme (see p. 154), all young unemployed people are guaranteed education and training opportunities, while those with poor basic skills have the option of participating in full-time study on an approved course.

National Traineeships are an important part of the Government's strategy. They offer broad and flexible learning programmes, including the key skills of communication, numeracy and IT, and operate to agreed national standards—National Vocational Qualification (NVQ) at Level 2 (see chapter 10) is the primary qualification to be achieved—set by industry and employers in 40 industry sectors. At the end of March 1999, nearly 36,000 young people had started training on National Traineeships, with a government target of 100,000 by March 2000.

Modern Apprenticeships are designed to increase significantly the number of young people trained to technician, supervisory and equivalent levels. The primary achievement of a Modern Apprenticeship is the NVQ at Level 3. Evaluation studies have found that Modern Apprenticeships are of high quality, are very popular and have met the expectations of both employers and young people. At the end of March 1999, around 134,500 young people were on Modern Apprenticeships.

In Scotland the government-funded training programme for young people is Skillseekers; all young people aged 16 and 17 are entitled to Skillseekers training. Its key elements are training leading to a recognised qualification, up to Scottish Vocational Qualification (SVQ) Level 3; an individual training plan; and employer involvement.

Other Training and Support Programmes

In addition to Modern Apprenticeships and National Traineeships, a range of other training opportunities are available:

- The right to time off for study or training for 16 and 17 year olds is coming into effect in Great Britain from September 1999. Under this measure, young people will be entitled to take paid time off to study or train towards a qualification, usually at NVQ Level 2.

- The Improving the Training Market programme covers activities funded by the Department for Education and Employment (DfEE), aimed at encouraging investment by individuals in lifelong learning, and at improving the quality, impact and cost-effectiveness of vocational education and training.

- Career development loans are available to help people pay for vocational education or training in Great Britain. Loans of between £300 and £8,000 are provided through four major banks, and interest payments on the loans during training and for one month after training are funded by DfEE. The loans help to pay for courses lasting up to two years. By the end of March 1999, 117,787 people had received a career development loan, and £384 million had been lent.

- From September 1999 DfEE will introduce the Learning Gateway for 16 and 17 year olds. The Learning Gateway's priority group is those in danger of dropping out of learning because of a lack of the right skills, qualifications or attitudes or who have other personal and social obstacles. Every young person will be assigned a personal adviser, who will help clients improve their self-esteem and motivation, develop their basic and key skills, and sample jobs and courses aimed at assisting them to enter mainstream learning opportunities. The Government has allocated £37 million for the Learning Gateway to TECs (see below) which will be responsible for the delivery of a new 'life-skills' learning option.

- The Small Firms Training Loans programme helps firms with 50 or fewer employees to meet a range of training-related expenses, including training consultancy. Loans of between £500 and £125,000 are available through eight major banks, and repayments can be deferred for up to 12 months.

- The National Training Awards, an annual competition designed to promote good training practice rewards those who have carried out exceptionally effective training. Awards are made each year to around 100 employers, training providers and individuals.

Work-Based Learning for Adults is open to those aged 25 and over who have been unemployed for six months or longer. The aim is to help adults without work move into sustained employment, including self-employment, through work-based learning.

Training Bodies

Training and Enterprise Councils

There are 72 Training and Enterprise Councils/Chambers of Commerce Training and Enterprise (TECs/CCTEs) in England and Wales. These are independent companies with employer-led boards. Their objectives are to foster local economic development and stimulate employer investment in skills. Specifically, they are charged with developing the quality, effectiveness and relevance to the local labour market of government-funded training and business assistance programmes. In 1999–2000 total DfEE funding to TECs/CCTEs is £1.4 billion.

The role of TECs has been subject to review. The White Paper *Learning to Succeed* sets out a new framework for the planning and funding of post-16 learning and skills. The proposals include establishing a national Learning and Skills Council (see p. 131), which will assume responsibility for government-funded training and workforce development from TECs with effect from April 2001.

Local Enterprise Companies

A separate network of 22 Local Enterprise Companies (LECs) exists in Scotland. These have wider-ranging responsibilities than the TECs, covering both economic development and environmental improvement. LECs are also responsible for the delivery of the Government's national training programmes in Scotland but, unlike TECs, have no responsibility for work-related further education. They run under contract to two non-departmental public bodies: Scottish Enterprise and Highlands and Islands Enterprise (see p. 394).

National Training Organisations

National Training Organisations (NTOs) are independent, employer-led sector organisations working strategically with their sectors and with government across education and training throughout the United Kingdom. They aim to ensure that the needs of business are fully taken into account in developing education and training policy.

NTOs draw together wide employment interests, including professional bodies, education, trade unions and trade associations. Their outputs include National Occupational Standards (which provide the basis for NVQs and SVQs), and Modern Apprenticeship and National Traineeship frameworks. They also have a key role in promoting post-16 work-based learning, including, for example, the identification of Modern Apprenticeship places with employers and the use of NVQs and SVQs.

By June 1999 there were 70 NTOs, covering 88% of the workforce. It is expected that by the end of 1999 there will be around 75 NTOs covering more than 95% of the workforce.

Targets and Standards

The National Learning Targets (see p. 127), launched in 1998, focus on the Government's priorities: a globally competitive economy, with successful firms operating in a fair and efficient labour market; and a society where everybody has an equal chance to realise their potential.

A Training Standards Council was established in 1998 to supervise a Training Inspectorate to raise standards of training funded through TECs. The Council has a budget of around £8 million a year.

Investors in People

The Investors in People standard provides a framework for employers to support their investment in education and training. It helps companies to improve their performance by linking the training and development of all employees directly to the achievement of business objectives. By May 1999 nearly 14,500 organisations had achieved recognition as Investors in People, with a further 21,000 committed to achieving the standard. Over 8 million employees work in organisations involved in Investors in People, around 34% of UK employees. Reported benefits include increased productivity, higher profits, lower rates of sickness and absenteeism, and improved morale. The Government is committed to making Investors in People the general standard across all UK employers. It is looking particularly to see many more small businesses work towards the standard, and aims to remove barriers to learning by making Investors in People more accessible to small organisations.

Northern Ireland

The Training and Employment Agency, an executive agency within the Department of Economic Development, aims to promote economic development and help people find work through training and employment services. It has encouraged the formation of a sector training council in each main sector to advise on employers' training needs and develop sectoral training strategies. In addition, the Agency supports company training through its Company Development Programme and encourages management development by providing training programmes and seminars. In 1998 the Agency launched the New Deal initiative under the Welfare-to-Work programme (see p. 154).

Northern Ireland has its own range of training and employment programmes for people seeking work. Its Jobskills programme is designed to raise skill levels—and is linked to the attainment of NVQs—and to enhance the employment prospects of school–leavers and unemployed adults. About 12,000 places are available in 1999–2000. To combat the relatively high level of long-term unemployment in Northern Ireland, the Training and Employment Agency is launching Worktrack, a programme designed to supplement the New Deal in helping the long-term unemployed. The Agency also helps fund Enterprise Ulster (a statutory organisation which provides employment, training and work experience).

RECRUITMENT AND JOB-FINDING

There are a variety of ways in which people look for work. According to the Labour Force Survey in spring 1999, the main job search methods of the unemployed (on the ILO basis) were:

- studying 'situations vacant' notices in newspapers or journals (31%), with a further 8% answering other advertisements;
- visiting a Jobcentre or employment agency office (33%);
- personal contacts (10%); and
- direct approaches to employers (10%).

Welfare-to-Work

The Government's Welfare-to-Work programme is a series of measures designed to tackle youth and long-term unemployment, promote employability and develop skills, and move people from welfare into jobs.

A key aspect is the concept of a 'gateway', which gives all people of working age a single point of access to welfare, and ultimately to work. The Benefits Agency (see p. 172) and the Employment Service (see p. 155) are working together on the gateway process to cut waste and duplication, giving everyone who has the potential to work the help they need to find it. This gateway process is being piloted through a new service called ONE, where each client will have his or her own personal adviser. Pilots for this new service started in June 1999.

The Welfare-to-Work programme is being funded by a windfall tax on the excess profits of the privatised utilities (see p. 407). Some £5.2 billion is being invested in the programme, in a number of 'New Deals' including:

- £2.5 billion for young unemployed people;
- £520 million for the long-term unemployed;
- £190 million for lone parents;
- £195 million for sick and disabled people;
- £60 million for partners of the unemployed;
- £50 million for those aged over 50;
- £40 million for childcare; and
- £1.3 billion for schools.

Young Unemployed

The New Deal for the young unemployed is available to young people aged 18–24 who have been unemployed for more than six months, through four options:

- a job attracting a wage subsidy of £60 a week, payable to employers for up to six months;
- a work placement with a voluntary organisation;
- a six-month work placement with an Environment Task Force (see p. 315); and
- for those without basic qualifications, a place on a full-time education and training course, which might last for up to one year.

All the options include an element of training. For each young person the programme begins with a 'gateway' period of careers advice and intensive help with looking for work, and with training in the skills needed for the world of work. By the end of March 1999, some 137,600 young people were participating in the programme, while 128,700 had completed it, of whom 44% had entered sustained unsubsidised jobs.

Over half of those aged 16 or 17 not staying on in learning are in jobs where there is little opportunity for them to receive any formal training. The Government will contribute to the cost of the young employee's study or training at a current estimated average of £800 per employee per year. Employers may apply to their local TEC for funding support to enable young employees to exercise their right to time off for study or training (see p. 152) if, for whatever reason, mainstream provision such as a National Traineeship is unavailable or inappropriate.

Long-term Unemployed

Under the New Deal for the long-term unemployed, which started in 1998, employers receive a subsidy of £75 a week for six months if they employ anyone who has been unemployed for two years or longer. Since November 1998 a series of pilot schemes has been offering 90,000 opportunities for the long-term unemployed aged 25 and over, with similar arrangements to the New Deal for the young unemployed, including a 'gateway' period of intensive help with looking for, and preparing for, work. Some 30,000 of these new opportunities are available in Northern Ireland, covering all those who have been unemployed for over 18 months.

Other Groups

Since October 1998 the New Deal for Lone Parents has provided job search help, advice and training for lone parents on income support. Pilot schemes to help those who are disabled or on incapacity benefit who want training or work have also started. By April 1999, 250,000 people on incapacity benefits (see chapter 12, p. 180) were covered by such schemes, which are planned to run nationally from April 2000. In the 1998 Budget a New Deal for partners of the unemployed was announced, so that they too will have the option of help needed to return to work. This scheme was established on a nationwide basis in April 1999.

New Deal 50 plus, which is being piloted from October 1999, enables people over 50 who return to full-time work after six months or more on benefits to claim a subsidy of £60 a week for their first year back in work. It is due to be extended nationally in 2000.

Other Initiatives

Prototype Employment Zones were launched in 1998 in five areas of high unemployment: Glasgow, Liverpool, north-west Wales,

Plymouth and south Teesside. From April 2000, new Employment Zones will run in 15 areas of Great Britain. New approaches to tackling unemployment—including the delivery of financial help to individual jobseekers through personal job accounts— will take place in these areas and will be delivered by public, private and voluntary sector organisations which will be selected to run the zones by open competition. About £112 million is available to support this initiative, which aims to help around 48,000 long-term unemployed jobseekers aged 25 and over. In addition, Rapid Response Units have been set up in each Employment Service region, to give advice to any area affected by large-scale redundancies.

Government Employment Services

The Government provides a range of services to jobseekers through the Employment Service, an executive agency of the DfEE. These include:

- a network of local offices, at which people can find details of job opportunities;
- advice and guidance so that people can find the best route back into employment, for example, by training; and
- a range of special programmes, including those for people with disabilities.

The Employment Service has a national network of over 1,000 Jobcentres and a budget in Great Britain of £2,236 million for 1999–2000, of which £1,068 million is connected with the New Deals. In 1998–99 it placed over 1.2 million unemployed people into jobs and conducted nearly 4 million advisory interviews to help people find appropriate work or places on employment and training programmes. The Employment Service also has a key role in the delivery of the Government's Welfare-to-Work measures, particularly in relation to the New Deal programmes and ONE (see p. 154).

Advisory Services

Through the main Jobcentre services, unemployed people have access to vacancies, employment advice and training opportunities. Employment Service advisers see all jobseekers when a claim is made for Jobseeker's Allowance (see p. 175) to assess their eligibility and to provide advice about jobs, training and self-employment opportunities. To receive the allowance, each unemployed person has to complete a Jobseeker's Agreement, which sets out his or her availability for work, the types of job for which he or she is looking, and the steps which, if taken, offer the best chance of securing work. Jobseekers are required to attend a job search review each fortnight and periodic intensive advisory interviews to assess their situation and see what additional help, if any, is needed and, if appropriate, to revise the Jobseeker's Agreement.

With the introduction of the New Deal programmes for the young and long-term unemployed, the range of existing Employment Service programmes is being restructured and brought together into a new package of measures. Programme Centres have been introduced nationally and will gradually replace Jobclubs. These offer flexible and tailored job search help for unemployed jobseekers. Two programmes, Restart and Jobplan, have merged under the name of Jobplan, a mandatory programme to help jobseekers who have been unemployed for 12 months or more develop an action plan to achieve their job goals. This new provision runs parallel with the New Deal, and many New Deal participants will benefit from access to these programmes.

Employment Agencies

There are many private employment agencies, including several large firms with many branches. The total value of the market has been estimated at about £14 billion a year. The law governing employment agencies is less restrictive than in many other EU countries, but agencies must comply with legislation which establishes a framework of minimum standards designed to protect agency users, both workers and hirers. A review of the regulatory framework is planned, and the Department of Trade and Industry (DTI) issued a consultative document in spring 1999, containing proposals for simplifying terms and conditions of employment, and offering new employees greater legal protection.

PAY AND CONDITIONS

Earnings

Average gross weekly earnings of full-time employees on adult rates in Great Britain whose pay was unaffected by absence were £384 in April 1998, according to the ONS New Earnings Survey. Average earnings for men were £427 and for women £310. Earnings were higher for non-manual employees (£425) than for manual employees (£307), with managerial and professional groups the highest paid.

The sectors with the highest average weekly earnings are financial services (£510) and mining and quarrying (£506), while the sectors with the lowest earnings are hotels and restaurants, the manufacture of textiles and textile products, agriculture, hunting and forestry, and the retail trade.

Minimum Wage

The National Minimum Wage Act 1998 set out the regulatory framework for the national minimum wage which was introduced in April 1999, at the following levels:

- £3.60 an hour for those aged 22 or above;
- £3.00 an hour for workers aged 18–21; and
- £3.20 an hour for those aged 22 or over in the first six months of a new job with a new employer, and receiving accredited training.

Workers aged 16 and 17 are exempt from the national minimum wage. Apprentices aged 18 are also exempt. Apprentices aged 19–25 do not need to be paid the national minimum wage for the first 12 months of their apprenticeship.

Nearly 2 million people are estimated to have to benefited from the national minimum wage, including 1.3 million women and

200,000 young people. Other groups who have benefited include lone parents who work, ethnic minority workers and homeworkers. Sectors most affected have been hospitality (hotels and catering), retailing, cleaning, hairdressing, social care, footwear and clothing, and private security.

The rates for the national minimum wage were based on those recommended to the Government in a report by the independent Low Pay Commission, following consultation with employers, employee groups and other interested organisations. The Government has asked the Commission to monitor and evaluate the impact of the introduction of the national minimum wage and report back in December 1999. The Commission will look, among other things, at the effect on pay, employment and competitiveness in low-paying sectors and small firms. It will also review the position of 21 year olds to see if they might be covered by the main £3.60 rate.

Fringe Benefits

Fringe benefits are used by many employers to provide additional rewards to their employees. They include schemes to encourage financial participation by employees in their companies, pension schemes, private medical insurance, subsidised meals, company cars and childcare schemes. About 10.5 million people in Britain are members of occupational pension schemes provided by their employers. Company cars are provided for employees in a wide variety of circumstances. Around 1.7 million people have a company car available for private use and about half of these receive fuel for private motoring in their car.

By the end of March 1999, 11,233 profit-related pay schemes, which link part of pay to changes in a business's profits, were registered with the Inland Revenue, covering around 4.1 million people. Many companies have adopted employee share schemes, where employees receive free shares or options to buy shares at a discount from their employer without paying income tax. A new scheme will be introduced in 2000, allowing employees to buy shares from their pre-tax salary and to receive free shares, with further tax incentives for longer-term shareholding.

Hours of Work

Most full-time employees have a basic working week of between 34 and 40 hours, and work a five-day week. When overtime is taken into account, average weekly hours worked by full-time workers in their main job in the UK in 1999 were 38.3 hours: 40.2 for men and 34.5 for women. For part-time workers the average was 15.4 hours. More men than women work overtime, and those in manual occupations generally work more overtime than employees in non-manual jobs.

Both male and female full-time employees tend to work more hours than in other EU countries. Hours worked tend to be longest in agriculture, construction, and transport and communications, and shortest in most service industries. Self-employed people work, on average, longer hours than those in full-time employment. A significant minority of employees have flexible working hours or are engaged in some sort of shift work.

Holiday entitlements have generally been determined by negotiation. In spring 1999 the average paid holiday entitlement for full-time workers was just under five weeks. However, some employees, such as part-time and temporary employees, may have much less holiday entitlement.

Two EC regulations, on working time and on young workers (in relation to hours of work of adolescents), came into force in the UK in 1998. They apply to full-time, part-time and temporary workers, although workers in certain sectors—including transport, sea fishing, other work at sea, and doctors in training—are currently exempt. They provide for:

- a maximum working week of 48 hours (on average), although individual workers can choose to work longer;
- a minimum of four weeks' annual leave;
- minimum daily and weekly rest periods; and
- a limit for night workers of an average eight hours' work in a 24-hour period.

INDUSTRIAL RELATIONS

Around a third of employees in Great Britain in 1998 were in workplaces covered by collective bargaining, which is generally more prevalent in large establishments and in the public sector. Collective bargaining mainly concerns pay and working conditions. In general, negotiations are now conducted more at a local level, although many large firms retain a degree of central control over the bargaining process. There are relatively few industry-wide agreements; where they do exist, they are often supplemented by local agreements in companies or factories (plant bargaining). The EC's European Works Councils Directive, which requires firms with 1,000 or more employees and which operate in two or more member states to establish European-level information and consultation procedures, will be incorporated into UK legislation by December 1999.

The main findings of the 1998 Workplace Employee Relations Survey, the largest of its kind in the world, were published in September 1999. The Survey was sponsored by the DTI, ACAS (see p. 161), the Economic and Social Research Council and the Policy Studies Institute. Among its key findings were:

- workplace flexibility has increased, with many more workplaces reporting greater use of contracting out, temporary agency workers, fixed-term employees and part-time workers;

- many employers have practices designed to encourage employee commitment and promote high performance—for example, over half of workplaces operated five or more of 16 commonly discussed practices, with teamworking, team briefings and performance appraisals used in over half of workplaces;

- fewer workplaces are recognising trade unions—45%, compared with 53% in 1990;

- over half of employees expressed themselves as satisfied (47%) or very satisfied (7%) with their job—only 19% being dissatisfied (the remaining 27% were neither satisfied nor dissatisfied); and

- harmonious employment relations were widespread, with industrial action being reported in just 2% of workplaces.

Individual Employment Rights

Employment protection legislation provides a number of safeguards for employees. For example, most employees have a right to a written statement setting out details of the main conditions, including pay, hours of work and holidays. Employees with at least two years of continuous employment with their employer are entitled to lump–sum redundancy payments if their jobs cease to exist and their employers cannot offer suitable alternative work.[2]

Minimum periods of notice are laid down for both employers and employees. Most employees who believe they have been unfairly dismissed have the right to complain to an employment tribunal (see p. 160), subject to the general qualifying period. This was reduced from two years' continuous service to one year from June 1999. If the complaint is upheld, the tribunal may make an order for re-employment or award compensation.

Legislation prohibits discrimination on grounds of sex or marital status (see p. 119) or on grounds of colour, race, nationality (including citizenship) or ethnic or national origin (see p. 115), in employment, training and related matters. In Northern Ireland discrimination in employment on grounds of religious belief or political opinion is unlawful. The Equal Pay Act 1970, as amended in 1984, makes it generally unlawful to discriminate between men and women in pay and other terms and conditions of employment. Despite this, there is a continuing pay gender gap.

Under the Disability Discrimination Act 1995, disabled people have the right not to be discriminated against in employment. Employers with 20 or more employees have a duty not to discriminate against disabled employees or applicants.

All pregnant employees have the right to statutory maternity leave with their non-wage contractual benefits maintained, and

---

[2] The statutory redundancy payment is calculated according to a formula based on a person's age, the number of years of continuous service and his or her weekly pay. However, many employers pay more than the statutory amount.

A Disability Rights Commission (see p. 166) was established in April 1999 to protect the rights of all disabled people, both those in work and out of work. It has powers to investigate cases of discrimination at work against people with disabilities, and to ensure employers comply with the appropriate legal regulations.

protection against dismissal because of pregnancy. Statutory maternity pay is payable by an employer for up to 18 weeks to women with at least six months' service with that employer.

New Rights

The Employment Relations Act 1999 is introducing a package of family-friendly employment rights. Key elements are:

- three months' parental leave after one year's service for both women and men, after having a baby or adopting a child;
- extension of the basic right to maternity leave to 18 weeks, in line with maternity pay;
- a reduction to one year of the qualifying period for additional maternity absence;
- continuation of the employment contract throughout parental leave and additional maternity absence;
- a right to take reasonable time off from work to deal with a family emergency, for all employees regardless of length of service; and
- protection against dismissal or detriment for exercising any of the rights in the package.

Collective Requirements

Among the legal requirements governing industrial relations:

- All individuals have the right not to be dismissed or refused employment (or the services of an employment agency)

because of membership or non-membership of a trade union.

- Trade union employees have the right not to have union membership subscriptions deducted from their pay without their authorisation.
- A trade union must elect every member of its governing body, its general secretary and its president. Elections must be held at least every five years and be carried out by a secret postal ballot under independent scrutiny.
- If a trade union wishes to set up a political fund, its members must first agree in a secret ballot a resolution adopting those political objectives as an aim of the union. The union must also ballot its members every ten years to maintain the fund. Union members have a statutory right to opt out of contributing to the fund.
- For a union to have the benefit of statutory immunity when organising industrial action, the action must be wholly or mainly in contemplation or furtherance of a trade dispute between workers and their own employer. Industrial action must not involve workers who have no dispute with their own employer (so-called 'secondary' action) or involve unlawful forms of picketing. Before calling for industrial action, a trade union must obtain the support of its members in a secret postal ballot.

New Provisions

Various changes to industrial relations legislation are being introduced under the Employment Relations Act 1999. For example, there are provisions concerning recognition by employers of trade unions. The new procedures, which apply to firms with over 20 employees, will encourage the parties to reach voluntary agreement where possible, but if this proves impossible a strengthened Central Arbitration Committee (CAC) will decide on the issues concerned. In particular, the CAC will be able to determine the recognition of a union where a ballot of the workers has shown that a majority of those voting and at least 40% of those eligible to vote are in favour of recognition. However, where over half the workforce are already union members, recognition would be automatic, without the need for a ballot. Other provisions include:

- a right for employees dismissed for taking part in lawfully organised official industrial action to complain of unfair dismissal to a tribunal;

- a new legal right for employees to be accompanied by a fellow employee or trade union representative during disciplinary and grievance procedures;

- new arrangements on the provision of information and consultation when redundancies are planned and on the protection of employment when a business is transferred, for example through a merger or acquisition; and

- making up to £5 million available under a new Partnership Fund to contribute to the training of managers and employee representatives in order to assist and develop partnerships at work.

It is expected that these provisions will be implemented, on a phased basis, between 1999 and 2001.

Employment Tribunals

Employment tribunals in Great Britain have jurisdiction over complaints covering a range of employment rights, including unfair dismissal, redundancy pay, equal pay, and sex and race discrimination. They were formerly known as industrial tribunals, but were renamed in 1998 to reflect their new role. This change took effect under the Employment Rights (Dispute Resolution) Act 1998, which streamlined tribunal procedures and encouraged voluntary settlement of disputes on employment rights. The Act also promoted a new voluntary arbitration scheme, developed by ACAS (see p. 161), to settle unfair dismissal claims, and this is planned to be introduced towards the end of 1999. These tribunals received 89,000 applications in 1998–99. Northern Ireland has a separate tribunal system.

Industrial Disputes

In the past 20 years there has been a substantial decline in working days lost through industrial disputes. In 1998 there were 166 stoppages of work arising from industrial disputes, and 282,000 working days were lost as a result. Many of the stoppages were over pay. The United Kingdom has a good record in industrial relations; and the number of days lost per 1,000 employees compares favourably with the EU average.

Trade Unions

Trade unions have members in nearly all occupations. They are widely recognised by employers in the public sector and in large firms and establishments—44 of the UK's 50 largest companies recognise unions. As well as negotiating pay and other terms and conditions of employment with employers, they provide benefits and services such as educational facilities, financial services, legal advice and aid in work-related cases. In recent years many unions have extended their range of services for members.

In 1998 there were 7.1 million trade union members in Great Britain, according to the Labour Force Survey, 20% fewer than in 1989.[3] During this period the proportion of employees who were union members fell from 39% to 30%. The decline in membership was particularly noticeable where it has traditionally been high—among male employees, manual workers and those in production industries. Union membership is now at a similar level among manual and non-manual employees, having fallen much less in the latter group. It is now only slightly higher for men (31%) than for women (28%).

Public administration has the highest density of union members, around 60% of all

---

[3] There are two main sources of information on trade union membership: the ONS Labour Force Survey and data provided by trade unions to the Certification Office. Differences in coverage result in different estimates—for example, the Certification Office's figure for trade union membership at the end of 1997 was 7.8 million, compared with 7.1 million obtained from the Labour Force Survey in autumn 1997.

employees (54% among female employees). Sectors with relatively few union members include agriculture, forestry and fishing, hotels and restaurants, and wholesaling.

Unison, which operates in the public sector and has about 1.3 million members, is the biggest union in Britain. Three other unions have over 500,000 members:

- the Transport and General Workers Union;
- the Amalgamated Engineering and Electrical Union; and
- GMB—a general union with members in a range of public and private sector industries.

At the end of 1998 there were 223 trade unions on the list maintained by the Certification Officer, who, among other duties, is responsible for certifying the independence of trade unions. To be eligible for entry on the list a trade union must show that it consists wholly or mainly of workers and that its principal purposes include the regulation of relations between workers and employers or between workers and employers' associations. A further 19 unions were known to the Certification Officer.

The national body of the trade union movement is the Trades Union Congress (TUC), founded in 1868. Its affiliated membership comprises 77 trade unions, which together represent some 6.7 million people.

The TUC's objectives are to promote the interests of its affiliated organisations and to improve the economic and social conditions of working people. It deals with all general questions concerning trade unions, and provides a forum in which affiliated unions can collectively determine policy. There are six TUC regional councils for England and a Wales Trades Union Council. The annual Congress meets in September to discuss matters of concern to trade unionists. A General Council represents the TUC between annual meetings.

The TUC participates in international trade union activity, through its affiliation to the International Confederation of Free Trade Unions and the European Trade Union Confederation. It also nominates the British workers' delegation to the annual International Labour Conference.

In Scotland there is a separate national central body, the Scottish Trades Union Congress, to which UK unions usually affiliate their Scottish branches. Nearly all trade unions in Northern Ireland are represented by the Northern Ireland Committee of the Irish Congress of Trade Unions (ICTU). Most trade unionists in Northern Ireland are members of unions affiliated to the ICTU, while the majority also belong to unions based in Great Britain, which are affiliated to the TUC.

Employers' Organisations

Many employers in the UK are members of employers' organisations, some of which are wholly concerned with labour matters, although others are also trade associations concerned with commercial matters in general. With the move away from national pay bargaining, many employers' associations are tending to concentrate on areas such as supplying information for bargaining purposes and dealing with specialist issues. As with some of the larger trade unions, a number of employers' associations are increasingly concerned with legislation and other issues relating to Europe.

Employers' organisations are usually established on an industry basis rather than a product basis, for example, the Engineering Employers' Federation. A few are purely local in character or deal with a section of an industry or, for example, with small businesses; most are national and are concerned with the whole of an industry. In some of the main industries there are local or regional organisations combined into national federations. At the end of 1998, 106 listed employers' associations were known to the Certification Officer; a further 101 unlisted associations were in operation.

Most national organisations belong to the Confederation of British Industry (CBI—see p. 399), which represents directly or indirectly around 250,000 businesses.

ACAS

The Advisory, Conciliation and Arbitration Service (ACAS) is an independent statutory body with a general duty of promoting the improvement of industrial relations. ACAS aims to operate through the voluntary co-operation of employers, employees and, where appropriate, their representatives. Its main functions are collective conciliation; provision of arbitration and mediation; advisory mediation services for preventing disputes and improving industrial relations through the joint involvement of employers and employees; and the provision of a public enquiry service. ACAS also conciliates in disputes on individual employment rights, and is developing a new voluntary system for resolving unfair dismissal claims, to be introduced in late 1999.

In Northern Ireland the Labour Relations Agency, an independent statutory body, provides services similar to those provided by ACAS in Great Britain.

HEALTH AND SAFETY AT WORK

There has been a long-term decline in injuries to employees in the UK, partly reflecting a change in industrial structure away from the traditional heavy industries, which tend to have higher risks. In 1997–98 the number of deaths for employees and the self-employed from injuries at work was 274, which represented a fatal injury rate of 1.0 per 100,000 workers. About 6.5 million working days were lost as a result of work-related injuries.

The principal legislation is the Health and Safety at Work etc. Act 1974. It imposes general duties on everyone concerned with work activities, including employers, the self-employed, employees, and manufacturers and suppliers of materials for use at work. Associated Acts and regulations deal with particular hazards and types of work. Employers with five or more staff must prepare a written statement of their health and safety policy and bring it to the attention of their staff.

Health and Safety Commission

The Health and Safety Commission (HSC) has responsibility for developing policy on health and safety at work in Great Britain, including proposals for new or revised regulations and approved codes of practice. Recent work has concentrated on achieving a simpler and more effective system of health and safety regulation.

The HSC has advisory committees covering subjects such as toxic substances, genetic modification and the safety of nuclear installations. There are also several industry advisory committees, each covering a specific sector of industry.

Health and Safety Executive

The Health and Safety Executive (HSE) is the primary instrument for carrying out the HSC's policies and has day-to-day responsibility for enforcing health and safety law, except where other bodies, such as local authorities, are responsible. Its field services and inspections are carried out by the Field Operations Directorate, which includes the Factory, Agricultural and Quarries inspectorates and the regional staff of the Employment Medical Advisory Service.

The HSE's Directorate of Science and Technology provides technical advice on industrial health and safety matters. The Health and Safety Laboratory provides scientific and medical support and testing services, and carries out research.

In premises such as offices, shops, warehouses, restaurants and hotels, health and safety legislation is enforced by inspectors appointed by local authorities, working under guidance from the HSE. Some other official bodies work under agency agreement with the HSE.

Northern Ireland

The general requirements of the Northern Ireland health and safety legislation are broadly similar to those for Great Britain. They are enforced mainly by the Department of Economic Development and the Department of Agriculture through their health and safety inspectorates, although the district councils have an enforcement role similar to that of local authorities in Great Britain. The Health and Safety Agency, roughly corresponding to the HSC but without its policy-making powers, and an Employment Medical Advisory Service were replaced by a new government body, the Health and Safety Executive for Northern Ireland, in April 1999.

Further Reading

Fairness at Work. Cm 3968. Department of Trade and Industry. The Stationery Office, 1998.

The Government's Expenditure Plans 1999–00 to 2001–02. Department for Education and Employment and Office for Standards in Education. Cm 4202. The Stationery Office, 1999.

Labour Market Trends. Office for National Statistics. Monthly.

Learning to Succeed: a new framework for post-16 learning. Department for Education and Employment. Cm 4392. The Stationery Office, 1999.

Social Focus on the Unemployed. Office for National Statistics. The Stationery Office, 1998.

Annual Reports

Advisory, Conciliation and Arbitration Service. ACAS.

Certification Officer. Certification Office for Trade Unions and Employers' Associations.

Health and Safety Commission. HSC.

Websites

Department for Education and Employment: www.dfee.gov.uk

Department of Trade and Industry: www.dti.gov.uk

12 Social Protection

Local authority personal social services and voluntary organisations provide help and advice to many members of the community—elderly, physically disabled and mentally ill people, those with learning disabilities, and children in need of care. The Government has set out its policies for these areas in the White Paper *Modernising Social Services* and the policy statement *Modernising Mental Health Services*. Some of the proposals will need primary legislation which will be introduced as soon as parliamentary time allows.

The Government is also undertaking a far-reaching overhaul of the social security system. This is based on the key objectives of promoting incentives to work, reducing poverty and welfare dependency, and strengthening community and family life. The Welfare Reform and Pensions Bill was introduced in Parliament in February 1999.

Personal Social Services

Personal social services help the elderly, the disabled, children and young people, those with mental illness or learning disabilities, their families and carers. Major services include skilled residential and day care, help for people confined to their homes, and various forms of social work. Services are administered by local authorities but central government is responsible for establishing national policies, issuing guidance and overseeing standards.

The statutory services are provided by local government social services authorities in England and Wales, social work departments in Scotland, and health and social services boards in Northern Ireland. Alongside these providers are the many and varied contributions made by independent private and voluntary bodies.

Much of the care given to elderly and disabled people is provided by families and self-help groups. One in eight adults gives informal care and one in six homes has a carer. There are about 6 million informal carers in the UK; 58% are women and 42% are men. Carers who provide (or intend to provide) substantial care on a regular basis have the right, on request, to an assessment of their own needs.

A National Carers Strategy—*Caring about Carers*—was published in February 1999. This clarifies the Government's objectives for carers and sets out proposals for change. It covers in particular carers' health, breaks from caring, support in the community, and help so that they can stay in work.

Demand for personal social services is rising because of the increasing number of elderly people, who, along with disabled and mentally ill people and those with learning disabilities, have the opportunity to lead more independent lives in the community if they receive suitable support and facilities.

At the end of 1998, the Government published a White Paper—*Modernising Social Services: Promoting Independence, Improving Protection, Raising Standards*—paving the way for radical improvements in the quality, reliability and cost-effectiveness of social services.

Management Reforms

The White Paper signalled the start of reforms in the monitoring of social services performance in England. It set out clear national objectives and priorities together with new systems for monitoring how well services are provided.

The main elements are:

- local authorities to set authority-wide objectives and performance measures;

- local authorities to carry out performance reviews of all their services over a five-year cycle, in consultation with local taxpayers, service users and the wider business community;

- a new performance assessment framework for social services;

- performance plans to identify targets for annual improvements against locally defined indicators;

- Social Service Inspectorate regional offices to carry out annual reviews of the social services aspects of the performance plans; and

- independent inspection to continue to be undertaken by the Social Services Inspectorate, both of individual authorities and on thematic issues across sample authorities.

Elderly People

Older people represent the fastest growing section of the community. The proportion of the population aged 75 and over rose from 4%

Table 12.1: Percentage of People Aged 65 and Over Unable to Manage Certain Tasks on their Own, 1996–97

| | % | |
	Men	Women
Dressing and undressing	3.8	3.7
Getting in and out of bed	1.8	2.6
Getting to the toilet	1.0	1.5
Getting around the house	0.7	1.7
Eating	0.4	0.6

Sources: Office for National Statistics: *General Household Survey*; Northern Ireland Statistics and Research Agency: *Continuous Household Survey*

in 1961 to 7% in 1997. However, the number of elderly people in the population is expected to grow less quickly in the next decade than it has in the previous one.

Services for elderly people are designed to help them live at home whenever possible. These services may include advice and help given by social workers, domestic help, the provision of meals in the home, sitters-in, night attendants and laundry services, as well as day centres, lunch clubs and recreational facilities. Adaptations to the home can overcome a person's difficulties in moving about, and a range of equipment is available for people with poor hearing or eyesight or people with physical disabilities. Alarm systems help elderly people obtain assistance in an emergency. In some areas 'good neighbour' and visiting services are arranged by the local authority or a voluntary organisation. Elderly people who live in residential care homes or nursing homes are subject to means-test charging. Those who cannot afford to pay have their costs met by the State. Local authorities in England, Scotland and Wales may also levy charges for domiciliary services.

The most marked trend in residential care provision over recent years has been the continuing increase in the number of places provided in the private and voluntary sectors and the corresponding fall in the number provided in local authorities' own homes.

As part of their responsibility for social housing, local authorities provide homes designed for elderly people ('sheltered accommodation'); some of these developments have resident wardens. Housing associations and private builders also build such accommodation. Many local authorities provide free or subsidised travel for elderly people within their areas.

A Royal Commission on the funding of long-term care for elderly people in the UK was set up in 1997. The Commission's report—*With Respect to Old Age: Long-Term Care—Rights and Responsibilities*—was published in March 1999. The Government is considering its recommendations, which include splitting the costs of long-term care between living costs, housing costs and personal care, and establishing a National Care Commission.

Disabled People

About 8.6 million disabled adults live in private households. Over the past ten years there has been increasing emphasis on rehabilitation and on the provision of day, domiciliary and respite support services to enable disabled people to live independently in the community wherever possible.

Local authority social services departments help with social rehabilitation and adjustment to disability. They are required to identify the number of disabled people in their area and to publicise services. These may include advice on personal and social problems arising from disability, as well as on occupational, educational, social and recreational facilities, either at day centres or elsewhere. Other services provided may include adaptations to homes (such as ramps for wheelchairs, stairlifts and ground-floor toilets), the delivery of cooked meals, and help with personal care at home. Local authorities and voluntary organisations may provide severely disabled people with residential accommodation or temporary facilities to allow their carers relief from their duties. Special housing may be available for those able to look after themselves.

Some authorities provide free or subsidised travel for disabled people on public transport, and they are encouraged to provide special means of access to public buildings.

The Disability Discrimination Act 1995:

- provides a right for disabled people not to be discriminated against in employment, and places a duty on employers with 15 or more staff to consider reasonable adjustments to the terms on which they offer employment where these would help to overcome the practical effects of a disability; and

- provides a right of access to goods and services which makes it unlawful to refuse to serve a disabled person and may require service providers to make reasonable adjustments to their services to make them more accessible.

The National Disability Council and the Northern Ireland Disability Council advise the Government on eliminating discrimination against disabled people. A new Disability Rights Commission was established under the Disability Rights Commission Act 1999. It is expected to be in place by spring 2000. Its main aims will be to work towards the elimination of discrimination against disabled people; promote equal opportunities for disabled people; encourage good practice; and advise the Government on the operation of the Disability Discrimination Act. In Northern Ireland it is intended that disabled people will have the same rights through the Equality Commission (see p. 18) as disabled people in the rest of the UK.

In 1997 the Government transferred responsibility for disability issues from the Department of Social Security to the Department for Education and Employment. This is intended to signal a move away from treating disabled people merely as recipients of benefits towards a culture which will value their role in society as people willing and able to take advantage of education, training and employment opportunities. The New Deal for Disabled People, part of the Government's Welfare-to-Work programme (see p. 154), is designed to help disabled people find and keep work.

People with Learning Disabilities (Mental Handicap)

The Government encourages the development of local services for people with learning disabilities and their families through co-operation between health authorities, local authorities, education and training services, and voluntary and other organisations.

Local authority social services departments are the leading statutory agency for planning and arranging services for people with learning disabilities. They provide or arrange short-term care, support for families in their own homes, residential accommodation and support for various types of activity outside the home. The main aims are to ensure that as far as possible people with learning disabilities can lead full lives in their communities and are admitted to hospital only when it is necessary on health grounds. People with learning disabilities form the largest group for local authority-funded day centre places and the second largest group in residential care.

The National Health Service (NHS) provides specialist services when the ordinary primary care services cannot meet healthcare needs. Residential care is provided for those with severe or profound disabilities whose needs can only effectively be met by the NHS.

People with a Mental Illness

Government policy aims to ensure that people with mental illnesses should have access to all the services they need as locally as possible. A cornerstone of community care policy for mentally ill people is the Care Programme Approach. Under this, each patient should receive an assessment and a care plan, have a key worker appointed to keep in touch with him or her, and be given regular reviews. The Care Programme Approach is subject to audit, enabling health authorities (health boards in Scotland) to identify any problems with the quality of its implementation. The separate Welsh Mental Health Strategy employs many of the same broad principles in delivering services in Wales. In Scotland, each health board works with its local authority care partners, users of mental health services and their carers to develop local joint strategies to provide local and comprehensive mental health services.

While the total number of places for mentally ill people in the large hospitals has continued to fall, the provision of alternative places has increased in smaller NHS hospitals, local authority accommodation and private and voluntary sector homes.

Arrangements made by social services authorities for providing preventive care and after-care for mentally ill people in the community include day centres, social centres and residential care. Social workers help patients and their families with problems caused by mental illness. In some cases they can apply for a mentally disordered person to be compulsorily admitted to and detained in hospital. In England and Wales the Mental Health Act Commission (in Scotland the Mental Welfare Commission and in Northern Ireland the Mental Health Commission) provides important safeguards for patients to ensure that the law is used appropriately.

A grant of £116.5 million for 1999–2000 to local authorities in England is designed to encourage them to increase the level of social care available to mentally ill patients, including those with dementia who need specialist psychiatric care in the community. Supervision registers for discharged patients most at risk are maintained by the providers of services for mentally ill people and allow hospital staff to keep track of them.

There are many voluntary organisations concerned with those suffering from mental illness (such as MIND, SANE and the Scottish Association for Mental Health), or learning disabilities (such as MENCAP or its Scottish equivalent ENABLE), and they play an important role in providing services for both groups of people. Central Government provides funding to many similar voluntary bodies.

In December 1998 the Government published a policy statement for England and Wales—*Modernising Mental Health Services: Safe, Sound and Supportive*—setting out its new vision for the future delivery of both health and social care for people with mental health problems. One of its primary aims is to reduce nationally the emergency psychiatric readmission of patients discharged from hospital by 2% by 2002 from the 1997–98 level of 14.3%. In Scotland, a committee has been established to undertake a review of mental health legislation. It is due to report in summer 2000.

Help to Families

Local authorities must safeguard the welfare of any child in need, and promote the upbringing of such children by their families, by providing a range and level of services appropriate to those children's needs. These services can include advice, guidance, counselling, help in the home, or family centres, and can be provided for the family of the child in need or any member of the family, if this will safeguard the child's welfare. Local authorities can provide these services directly or arrange for them to be provided by, for example, a voluntary organisation. They are also required to publicise the help available to families in need. Many local authorities or specialist voluntary organisations run refuges for women, often with young children, whose home conditions have become intolerable, through, for example, domestic violence. The refuges provide short-term accommodation and support while attempts are made to relieve the women's problems.

Day Care for Children

Day care facilities are provided for young children by childminders, voluntary agencies, private nurseries and local authorities. In allocating places, where local authorities have their own provision, priority is given to children with special social, learning or health needs. Local authorities currently register and inspect childminders, playgroups and day nurseries but the Government intends to set up a new regulatory body under the Office for Standards in Education (OFSTED) to undertake all nursery education and day care inspections in the future.

Child Protection

Child protection is the joint concern of a number of different agencies and professions. Area child protection committees determine how the different agencies should co-operate to help protect children from abuse and neglect in that area.

Children in Care

Local government authorities must provide accommodation for children who have no parent or guardian, who have been abandoned, or whose parents are unable to provide for them.

In England and Wales a child may be brought before a family proceedings court if he or she is neglected or ill-treated, exposed to moral danger, beyond the control of parents, or not attending school. The court can commit children to the care of a local authority under a care order. Certain pre-conditions have to be satisfied to justify an order. These are that the children are suffering or are likely to suffer significant harm because of a lack of reasonable parental care or because they are beyond parental control. However, an order is made only if the court is also satisfied that this will positively contribute to the children's well-being and be in their best interests. In court proceedings children are entitled to separate legal representation and the right to have a guardian to protect their interests. All courts have to treat the welfare of children as the paramount consideration when reaching any decision about their upbringing. There is a general principle that, wherever possible, children should remain at home with their families.

In Scotland children who have committed offences or are in need of care and protection may be brought before a Children's Hearing, which can impose a supervision requirement on a child if it thinks that compulsory measures are appropriate. Under these requirements most children are allowed to remain at home under the supervision of a social worker, but some may live with foster parents or in a residential establishment while under supervision. Supervision requirements are reviewed at least once a year until ended by a Children's Hearing.

The Government has set up the Quality Protects programme to transform standards of care offered to looked-after children and others needing social services' support. This childcare management strategy is supported by a new special grant of £375 million over the next three years, payments being subject to the preparation and achievement of satisfactory action plans by each local authority.

Fostering and Children's Homes

Local authorities have a duty to ensure that the welfare of children being looked after away from home is properly safeguarded as regards their health, education, contact with their families and general quality of life. When appropriate, children in care are placed with foster parents, who receive payments to cover the child's living costs. Alternatively, the child may be placed in residential care. Children's homes may be provided by local authorities, voluntary organisations or private companies or individuals. Except for small, private, unregistered children's homes accommodating three or fewer children, they are formally inspected.

Parents of children in care retain their parental responsibilities but act as far as possible as partners with the authority. Local authorities are required to produce a plan for the future of each child in their care and to prepare a child for leaving their care and to continue to advise him or her up to the age of 21; they are also required to have a complaints procedure with an independent element to cover children in their care.

In response to a 1997 report (*People Like Us: Review of the Safeguards for Children Living Away from Home*), which was commissioned after several serious cases of abuse of children in care, the Government announced plans for a range of measures to be taken to improve the lives of children living away from home. In addition to the Quality Protects programme (see p. 168), the Government will establish new independent regulatory arrangements for children's homes, fostering agencies and boarding schools. It will also set up a new criminal records agency to improve and widen access to police checks on people intending to work with children and other vulnerable groups.

Recent Trends

The number of children looked after by local authorities in England has declined since 1992 and the proportion of foster placements has gradually risen. The number of children in local authority day care has declined sharply since 1994. In March 1998, 30,000 children in England and Wales were on child protection registers.

Adoption

Local authority social services departments are required by law to provide an adoption service, either directly or by arrangement with approved voluntary adoption societies. Under adoption law it is illegal to receive an unrelated child for adoption through an unapproved third party. The Registrars-General keep confidential registers of adopted children.

Adopted people may be given details of their original birth record on reaching the age of 18 (or 16 if adopted in Scotland), and counselling is provided to help them understand the circumstances of their adoption. An Adoption Contact Register enables adopted adults and their birth parents to be given a safe and confidential way of making contact if that is the wish of both parties. A person's details are entered only if they wish to be contacted. In Scotland a similar service is provided through BirthLink.

The number of children, healthy babies in particular, who are available for adoption is far exceeded by those people wishing to adopt. In recent years fewer than 7,000 children have been adopted annually.

Finance

In 1996-97, gross expenditure in England on personal social services was £9.3 billion. Local authorities' expenditure on services for older people and children accounted for nearly three-quarters of this (see pie chart on p. 170). The largest items of expenditure were for residential care (47%) and day care (38%).

Social Care Workforce

The effective working of social care depends on the skills of the social care workforce of almost 1 million people. Of these, there are about 50,000 professionally qualified social workers who are employed mainly by social services departments of local authorities, including those social workers in the NHS. Most of the workforce are not social workers and are employed in the independent sector.

Action is being taken to raise the training and qualification levels for the whole workforce. The national training organisation for social care will be producing a training strategy for England by the autumn of 1999 analysing workforce and training needs and identifying any skills gaps.

Local Authority Personal Social Services Gross Expenditure by Client Group, England, 1996–97

Total: £9.3 billion

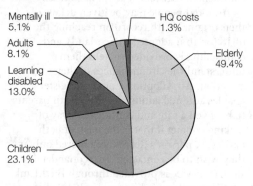

- Mentally ill 5.1%
- HQ costs 1.3%
- Adults 8.1%
- Learning disabled 13.0%
- Elderly 49.4%
- Children 23.1%

Source: *Department of Health. The Government's Expenditure Plans 1999–2000*

The Government is also considering the outcome of a review of professional social work training which has looked at fundamental issues such as the academic level and length of training period, student support and regulation of training. Any programme of development arising from the review will be for the benefit of the General Social Care Council (GSCC) when it is established. The present Central Council for Education and Training in Social Work (CCETSW) will then be abolished. The GSCC will also set and promote standards of conduct and practice for all social care workers.

Social Security

The social security system is designed to secure a basic standard of living for people in financial need by providing income during periods of inability to earn (including periods of unemployment), help for families and assistance with costs arising from disablement.

Social security is the largest single area of government spending. In each year from 1993–94 to 1998–99 spending on social security benefits in Great Britain represented about 30% of total government expenditure.

At the beginning of the 20th century a system of social protection and preventive healthcare in Britain was beginning to emerge, though the level and conditions of care available were generally very poor.

In 1905, the Minority Report of the Royal Commission on the Poor Laws pointed out the differences in standards of healthcare services provided across the country and urged the Government to take action on the matter. It responded with pensions for the elderly and benefits for the unemployed.

The 1908 Old Age Pensions Act granted non-contributory, means-tested pensions—paid from national funds—to people who had reached the age of 70 and whose annual income was under £31. Pensioners received sums ranging from one shilling to five shillings (5p to 25p) a week.

The National Insurance Act 1911 ensured that workers at the bottom end of the wage scale received free treatment from their doctor, but did little to improve the situation for the rest of the population. It was, however, the first step in the Government's recognition that people on low incomes who were sick or without a job needed centrally funded help to improve the quality of their lives. The Act provided insurance for all manual workers between the ages of 16 and 70 earning no more than £160 a year. Other groups such as the self-employed and those who already had health insurance were not covered. The basic weekly sickness benefit was 10 shillings (50p) for men and seven shillings and sixpence (37½p) for women.

At 1998–99 prices, spending grew from £93.2 billion to £95.8 billion over this five-year period, representing a growth rate of about 0.6% a year on average, compared with growth in the economy as a whole of about 3% a year. In 1993–94, benefit expenditure in Great Britain represented nearly 13% of UK gross domestic product (GDP). Since then spending has fallen as a percentage of GDP, and in 1998–99, it accounted for slightly over 11%.

Table 12.2: Planned Benefit Expenditure by Departmental Objective, 1999–2000

	£ million
Support for people of working age	20,470
Support for families and children	8,223
Support for disabled people	25,133
Support for people over working age	47,417
Total planned benefit expenditure	**101,243**

Source: *The Government's Expenditure Plans 1999–2000:* Social Security Departmental Report

There are many reasons for this high level of expenditure, not least the increasing number and range of benefits, as social security has expanded to cover both a wider range of contingencies and the changing shape and expectations of society.

MODERNISING THE SYSTEM

Welfare Reform

The Green Paper *New Ambitions for our Country*, published in 1998, set out the framework for welfare reform, based on eight principles, together with a number of measures of success for each principle, to gauge progress over the next ten to 20 years. The central aim was to replace a cycle of dependency and insecurity with an ethic of work and savings. Following wide consultation, the Government introduced the Welfare Reform and Pensions Bill in February 1999. The main measures in the Bill are:

- a single gateway to the benefit system for those of working age;
- the introduction of the new stakeholder pension schemes (see p. 175);
- pension sharing for divorced couples (see p. 175);
- modernised benefits for widows and widowers; and

- modernising the benefits structure for people with disabilities or long-term illness.

When enacted, the legislation should tackle three key problems: inequality and social exclusion (see p. 117), especially among children and pensioners; barriers to paid work, including financial disincentives; and fraud which is taking money out of the system and away from genuine claimants.

Fighting Fraud

Measures to improve the prevention and detection of fraud in the social security system include:

- The Social Security Administration (Fraud) Act 1997, which has powers to deal with Housing Benefit fraud, including landlord fraud. The Act, among other measures:
  - has created a new criminal offence of obtaining benefit by false representation;
  - permits certain government departments and local authorities to share data with each other;
  - allows local authorities to demand information from certain landlords about their property holdings;
  - enables local authority investigators to gain entry to business premises and to examine business records; and
  - offers people who commit benefit fraud the choice of paying a financial penalty instead of facing prosecution.
- The Benefit Fraud Inspectorate, which came into operation in 1997, examines and reports on standards of performance in the administration of all social security benefits, in particular anti-fraud work, within the Department of Social Security's agencies and local authorities. It also carries out work for the Social Security Agency in Northern Ireland.

The Government recognises the difficulties of measuring a covert activity such as fraud, but latest estimates of benefit fraud in Great Britain indicate that around £2 billion is lost each year through confirmed fraud and a further £3 billion in cases where fraud has probably taken place but no claimant has been proved guilty.

ADMINISTRATION

In April 1999 the Contributions Agency merged with the Inland Revenue (see p. 406) to provide customers with a single point of contact for tax and National Insurance (NI) matters. The remaining executive agencies of the Department of Social Security (DSS) handle the administration of social security in Great Britain, together employing a total of around 77,000 staff:

- the Benefits Agency (BA) administers and pays the majority of benefits;
- the Child Support Agency (CSA) assesses and collects maintenance payments for children (see p. 177);
- the Information Technology Services Agency maintains the computer system which supports the administration of social security; and
- the War Pensions Agency delivers services to war pensioners.

In Great Britain the Housing and Council Tax Benefit schemes are administered by local authorities. In Northern Ireland, social security benefits are administered by the Social Security Agency and the National Insurance Contributions Scheme by the Inland Revenue. The Housing Benefit scheme is administered by the Northern Ireland Housing Executive and the Rate Collection Agency; council tax does not apply in Northern Ireland, where domestic 'rates' are still collected.

Advice about Benefits

The DSS produces a range of leaflets and posters and a website providing general information on entitlement and liability. The leaflets and posters are available in English and a number of other languages. The Benefit Enquiry Line is a confidential telephone service offering general advice on benefits to people with disabilities and their carers. The number is: 0800 88 22 00.

CONTRIBUTIONS

Entitlement to National Insurance (NI) benefits such as Retirement Pension, Incapacity Benefit, contributory Jobseeker's Allowance, Maternity Allowance and Widow's Benefit, is dependent upon the payment of contributions. Major reforms to NI contributions, designed to improve incentives to work, encourage job creation and cut down on bureaucracy, were introduced from April 1999. Among other things, the amount an employee can earn before employer NI contributions are charged is being aligned with the personal allowance for income tax (see p. 405). There are five classes of contributions. **The rates given below are effective from April 1999 to April 2000:**

- Class 1—paid by employees and their employers. Employees with earnings below £66 a week do not pay Class 1 contributions. Contributions on earnings at or above a lower earnings limit of £66 a week in non-contracted out employment are at the rate of 10% up to the upper earnings limit of £500 a week. Employers' contributions at the rate of 12.2% are subject to the same threshold.
- Class 1A—paid by employers who provide their employees with fuel and/or a car for private use. A Class 1A contribution is payable on the cash equivalent of the benefit provided.
- Class 2—paid by self-employed people. Class 2 contributions are at a flat rate of £6.55 a week. The self-employed may claim exemption from Class 2 contributions if their profits are expected to be below £3,770 for the 1999–2000 tax year. Self-employed people are not eligible for unemployment and industrial injuries benefits.
- Class 3—paid voluntarily to safeguard rights to some benefits. Contributions are at a flat rate of £6.45 a week.
- Class 4—paid by the self-employed on their taxable profits over a set lower limit

(£7,530 a year), and up to a set upper limit (£26,000 a year) in addition to their Class 2 contribution. Class 4 contributions are payable at the rate of 6%.

Employees who work after pensionable age (60 for women and 65 for men) do not pay contributions but the employer continues to be liable. Self-employed people over pensionable age do not pay contributions.

BENEFITS

Social security benefits can be grouped into three types:

- **means-tested**, available to people whose income and savings are below certain levels;
- **contributory**, paid to people who have made the required contributions to the National Insurance Fund,[1] from which benefits are paid; and
- **benefits which are neither means-tested nor contributory** (mainly paid to cover extra costs, for example of disability, or paid universally, for example Child Benefit).

General taxation provides over half the income for the social security programme, employers' NI contributions around a quarter and employees' NI contributions about a fifth. Appeals about claims are decided by independent tribunals, but a new system of informing customers of decisions on benefits and handling appeals—the Decision-Making and Appeals (DMA) Programme—is being phased in from June 1999 (see p. 178).

For most contributory benefits there are two conditions. First, before benefit can be paid at all, a certain number of contributions must have been paid. Second, the full rate of benefit cannot be paid unless contributions have been paid or credited to a specific level over a set period. A reduced rate of benefit is payable dependent on the level of

[1] The National Insurance Fund is a statutory fund into which all NI contributions payable by employers, employees and self-employed people are deposited, and from which contributory benefits and their administration costs are paid.

Social Security Expenditure, Great Britain, 1999–2000: benefit expenditure by broad groups of beneficiaries

Total: £101.2 billion

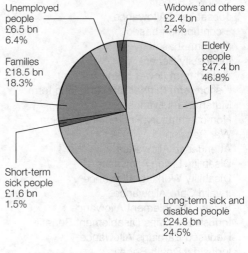

Unemployed people
£6.5 bn
6.4%

Widows and others
£2.4 bn
2.4%

Elderly people
£47.4 bn
46.8%

Families
£18.5 bn
18.3%

Short-term sick people
£1.6 bn
1.5%

Long-term sick and disabled people
£24.8 bn
24.5%

Source: *Social Security Departmental Report: The Government's Expenditure Plans 1999–2000*

contributions paid or credited. For example, a great many of those receiving retirement pensions and widows' benefits receive a percentage-based rate of benefit. Benefits are increased annually in line with percentage increases in retail prices. The main benefits (payable weekly) are summarised on pp. 173–82. **Rates given are those effective from April 1999 until April 2000**.

Retirement

A state **Retirement Pension** is a taxable weekly benefit payable, if the contribution conditions have been met, to women at the age of 60 and men at the age of 65. Legislation was introduced in 1995 to equalise the state pension age for men and women at 65. The change will be phased in over ten years, starting from April 2010. Women born before 6 April 1950 will not be affected; their pension age will remain at 60. The new pension age of 65 will apply to women born on or after 6 April 1955. Pension age for women born between these dates will move up gradually from 60 to 65.

Table 12.3: Estimated Numbers Receiving Benefits in Great Britain 1999–2000 (forecast)[a]

Benefit	Contributory(C) or non-contributory (NC)	Thousands
Retirement Pension	C	10,789
Widow's Benefit	C	258
Jobseeker's Allowance		
contribution-based	C	239
income-based	NC	1,166
Incapacity Benefit	C	
short term (lower rate)		106
short term (higher rate) and long term		1,528
Maternity Allowance	C	14
Non-contributory Retirement Pension	NC	24
War Pension	NC	299
Attendance Allowance	NC	1,290
Disability Living Allowance	NC	2,126
Disability Working Allowance[b]	NC	14
Invalid Care Allowance	NC	376
Severe Disablement Allowance	NC	412
Industrial Injuries Disablement Benefit[c]	NC	295
Reduced Earnings Allowance[c]	NC	151
Industrial Death Benefit	NC	17
Income Support	NC	3,907
Child Benefit	NC	
number of children		12,737
number of families		7,036
One parent benefit/		
Child Benefit (Lone Parent)	NC	935
Family Credit[b]	NC	617
Housing Benefit	NC	
rent rebate		2,565
rent allowance		1,902
Council Tax Benefit	NC	5,268

Source: *The Government's Expenditure Plans 1999–2000:* Social Security Departmental Report
[a] Figures are for beneficiaries at any one time.
[b] From October 1999, Disability Working Allowance (DWA) is being replaced by Disabled Person's Tax Credit (DPTC) and Family Credit is being replaced by Working Families' Tax Credit (WFTC).
[c] Figures refer to the number of pensions being paid, and not to the number of recipients.

The state pension scheme consists of a basic weekly pension of £66.75 for a single person and £106.70 for a married couple, together with an additional earnings-related pension (sometimes called 'SERPS'—state earnings-related pension). Pensioners may have unlimited earnings without affecting their pensions. Those who have put off their retirement during the five years after state pension age may earn extra pension.

A *non-contributory retirement pension* of £39.95 a week is payable to people aged 80 or over who have lived in Britain for at least ten years since reaching the age of 60, and who have not qualified for a contributory pension. People whose pensions do not give them enough to live on may be entitled to Income Support (see p. 176).

Rights to basic pensions are safeguarded for people whose opportunities to work are limited while they are looking after a child or a sick or disabled person. Men and women may receive the same basic pension, provided they have paid full-rate NI contributions when working. The earnings-related pension scheme will eventually be calculated as 20% rather than 25% of earnings, to be phased in over ten years from 1999. However, the pensions of people retiring in the 20th century will be unaffected.

As part of its plan to improve the income of women in retirement, the Government has included provisions in the Welfare Reform and Pensions Bill to enable the courts to divide pension rights equally between divorcing couples. The arrangements are expected to be in force from April 2000.

Occupational and Personal Pensions

Employers may 'contract out' their employees from the state scheme for the additional earnings-related pension and provide their own occupational pension instead. Their pension must be at least as good as the state additional pension. Joining an employer's contracted-out scheme is voluntary: employers are not free to contract out employees from the earnings-related pension scheme without the employees' consent. The State remains responsible for the basic pension.

Occupational pension schemes have over 9 million members. The occupational pension rights of those who change jobs before pensionable age, who are unable or do not want to transfer their pension rights, are now offered some protection against inflation. Workers leaving a scheme have the right to a fair transfer value. The trustees or managers of pension schemes have to provide full information about their schemes. Average weekly income from an occupational pension is around £50 for men and £30 for women.

As an alternative to their employers' scheme or the state additional earnings-related pension scheme, people are entitled to choose a personal pension available from a bank, building society, insurance company or other financial institution. Occupational schemes must provide equal treatment between men and women and make personal pensions flexible and attractive to a broad age range.

The Pensions Ombudsman deals with complaints of maladministration against occupational and personal pension schemes and adjudicates on disputes of fact or law. A pensions registry helps people trace lost benefits.

Pensions Review

In 1997 the Government announced a review of pensions. Its long-term objective is to ensure that everyone has the opportunity to build up an adequate pension to guarantee security in retirement. The review has looked at the central areas of insecurity for elderly people, including all aspects of state provision, and the introduction of a new State Second Pension to replace SERPS from 2002 (see p. 174).

The Government also wants to support and strengthen the framework for occupational pensions. A consultation document was published in 1997 containing proposals on stakeholder pensions for those who do not have access to an employer's occupational pension scheme and for whom a personal pension may not be suitable. Stakeholder pensions will be introduced in April 2001 under the provisions of the Welfare Reform and Pensions Bill currently before Parliament. Plans are also being developed to make the State Second Pension available to carers and others with domestic responsibilities who are unable to contribute to a second pension in their own right.

Unemployment

Jobseeker's Allowance

Jobseeker's Allowance (JSA) is a benefit for people needing financial support because of unemployment. Claimants must be capable of, and available for, work, and actively seeking it. They must normally be aged at least 18 years and under pension age. JSA can be either contribution-based or income-based:

- *Contribution-based JSA*: those who have paid enough NI contributions are entitled to a personal JSA for up to six months (£51.40 a week for a person aged 25 or over), regardless of any savings or partner's income.

- *Income-based JSA*: those on a low income are entitled to an income-based JSA, payable for as long as the jobseeker requires support and continues to satisfy the qualifying conditions. The amount a claimant receives comprises an age-related personal allowance (£51.40 a week for a person aged 25 or over), allowances for dependent children and premium payments for those with extra expenses, for example, disabled children.

Benefit is paid at rates determined by family circumstances on a basis similar to Income Support (see below).

Back to Work Bonus

Recipients of JSA (see above) and people aged under 60 who receive Income Support can benefit from a Back to Work Bonus. This is intended to increase incentives to take up or keep part-time work, and encourage people to move off benefit and into employment. Those who have been unemployed for three months or more and are working part-time may keep the first £5 of their earnings (£10 for couples; £15 for lone parents, disabled people and some people in special occupations) in any week in which they work while still receiving benefit. An amount equal to half of any earnings above that level counts towards the build-up of a bonus amount. When the unemployed person moves off JSA because of an increase in earnings or hours of work, he or she will be able to claim a tax-free lump sum of up to £1,000. The part-time (up to 24 hours a week) earnings of a partner can also contribute towards building up a Back to Work Bonus, which can be paid if the couple leave benefit as a result of an increase in the partner's earnings or hours of work.

Income Support

Income Support is payable to certain people aged 16 or over who are not required to be available for work, and whose income and savings are below certain set levels. They include lone parents, pensioners, carers and long-term sick and disabled people. Income Support is made up of: a personal allowance based on age and on whether the claimant is single, a lone parent or has a partner; age-related allowances for dependent children and additional sums known as premiums; and housing costs. From this total amount other income, including some other social security benefits, is deducted.

Income Support is not payable if savings exceed £8,000. Savings between £3,000 and £8,000 will reduce the amount received. For people living permanently in residential care or a nursing home, the allowance is not payable if savings exceed £16,000; and savings between £10,000 and £16,000 will affect the amount received.

Families

Most pregnant working women receive **Statutory Maternity Pay** directly from their employer. It is paid for a maximum of 18 weeks to any woman who has been working for the same employer for 26 weeks and who earns on average at least £66 a week. She will receive 90% of her average weekly earnings for the first six weeks and a rate of £59.55 a week for the remaining 12 weeks.

Women who are not eligible for Statutory Maternity Pay because, for example, they are self-employed, or have recently changed jobs or left their job, may qualify for a weekly **Maternity Allowance**, which is payable for up to 18 weeks. This amounts to £59.55 a week for employees and £51.70 a week for the self-employed and those not in work. All pregnant employees have the right to take 14 weeks' maternity leave.

An additional payment of £100 from the Social Fund (see p. 179) may be made if the mother or her partner receive Income Support, income-based Jobseeker's Allowance, Family Credit or Disability Working Allowance (Working Families' Tax Credit or Disabled Person's Tax Credit from October 1999—see p. 178). It is also available if a baby is adopted.

The main social security benefit for children is **Child Benefit**. This is a tax-free, non-contributory payment of £14.40 a week for the eldest qualifying child of a couple, and

Table 12.4: Recipients of Benefits for Families, Great Britain

	1991–92	*Thousands* 1996–97
Child Benefit		
Children	12,401	12,752
Families	6,852	7,009
Lone parent families		
One parent benefit only	475	1,011
One parent benefit and Income Support[a]	361	394
Income Support only[a]	584	639
Other benefits		
Maternity Allowance	11	15
Statutory Maternity Pay	85	90
Family Credit	356	734

Source: Department of Social Security

[a] Income Support data includes some income-based Jobseeker's Allowance claimants. Income-based JSA replaced Income Support for the unemployed from October 1996.

£9.60 for each other child. A higher rate of £17.10 is payable for the eldest qualifying child of a person bringing up a child on his or her own, whether the person is the child's parent or not. Child Benefit is payable for children up to the age of 16, and for those up to 19 who continue in full-time non-advanced education. It is generally not payable to people whose entry into the UK is subject to immigration control.

People claiming Child Benefit for an orphaned child they have taken into their family may be entitled to **Guardian's Allowance**. This is a tax-free non-contributory benefit of £7.30 a week for the oldest child and £11.35 for each other child who qualifies. In certain circumstances Guardian's Allowance can be paid when only one parent is dead.

Child Support Agency

An estimated 1 million lone parents in the UK bring up 1.7 million children in households where no one is working. The Child Support Agency (CSA) and its counterpart in Northern Ireland are responsible for assessing child maintenance and, where requested by either parent, collecting and enforcing child maintenance payments from, and for tracing, absent parents.

If any person is living with and caring for a child, and one, or both, of the child's parents are living elsewhere in the UK, he or she may apply to have child support maintenance assessed and collected by the CSA (or its Northern Ireland counterpart). If that person or their present partner claims Income Support, income-based Jobseeker's Allowance, Family Credit or Disability Working Allowance, they may be required to apply for child support maintenance if asked to do so by the CSA (or its Northern Ireland counterpart).

Assessments for child support maintenance are made using a formula which takes into account each parent's income and makes allowance for essential outgoings. (A system of departures from the formula allows the amount of maintenance payable to be varied in a small number of cases.) A child maintenance bonus worth up to £1,000 may be payable to parents living with and caring for a child who have been in receipt of Income Support or income-based Jobseeker's Allowance and in receipt of child maintenance when they leave benefit for work.

The Green Paper *Children First: A New Approach to Child Support* was published in 1998, setting out the Government's proposals for a new local, child support scheme based on a radically simpler method of assessment. It also proposed that parents living with and

Decision-Making and Appeals (DMA) Programme

A new cross-departmental initiative between the Benefits Agency and the Child Support Agency is being introduced in stages from June 1999. Customers of both agencies should benefit through simpler, clearer decisions and improved handling of appeals. The main changes are:

- *A single decision-maker*—BA and CSA customers have their decisions made by one official, rather than several having an interest in only a certain aspect of the case.

- *Clearer notifications*—customers get the information they need on the amount of benefit they are eligible for, or level of child support maintenance payable, in a single notification.

- *Better customer service*—customers are actively encouraged to telephone or visit BA local offices if they do not understand their notification or are unhappy with their decision.

- *Improved dispute resolution*—a more flexible system for resolving disputes enables customers to ask the BA and CSA to look again at their decision, and the agencies have improved powers to correct a decision quickly if it is wrong.

- *Focused appeals submissions*—if, after looking at it again, the decision stands and the customer wishes to appeal, the next stage is a clearly presented appeal which concentrates solely on those issues under dispute.

- *Unified appeal tribunals*—appeals are heard by a unified appeal tribunal, replacing five separate bodies currently specialising in specific areas of BA and CSA work.

- *A new appeals service*—from April 2000, a new executive agency, The Appeals Service (TAS), will be responsible for the administration of appeals across the whole range of DSS business, replacing the Independent Tribunal Service.

caring for a child who are on Income Support should be allowed to keep up to £10 a week of any maintenance paid for their children. Although the new scheme is unlikely to be introduced before 2001, many improvements are already under way or planned. These include: a simpler and more efficient process for making and appealing decisions (see above); and reorganisation of the CSA to centralise processing work and free local staff to concentrate on meeting clients face to face.

Childcare Costs

Families claiming Family Credit, Disability Working Allowance, Housing Benefit and Council Tax Benefit, and who pay for childcare for children aged under 12, can have up to £60 a week in formal childcare costs offset against their earnings when their benefit entitlement is worked out. From October 1999 the maximum childcare disregards will be increased from a maximum of £60 to £100 a week for families where there is one child, and to £150 for families with two or more children.

As part of its Welfare-to-Work programme (see chapter 11), the Government has implemented a national childcare strategy that will help lone mothers to get work instead of being dependent on benefits (see p. 119).

Family Credit/Working Families' Tax Credit

Family Credit, which is being replaced by the new Working Families' Tax Credit (WFTC) from October 1999, is a tax-free benefit payable to low-income working families with children. It is payable to couples or lone parents. One parent must work for at least 16 hours a week. The amount payable depends on a family's net weekly income; the number and ages of the children in the family; the amount of certain childcare charges paid; and the number of hours worked.

A maximum amount of Family Credit (consisting of an adult credit, plus a credit for each child varying with age, and an extra credit if one parent works for at least 30 hours a week), is payable if the family's net weekly income is less than £80.65. If income is more than £80.65, 70 pence of every £1 of the excess is deducted from the maximum payable.

Child Benefit and the first £15 of any child maintenance payment are not counted as income. Certain childcare charges can be offset against earnings before entitlement to Family Credit is calculated. The capital limit for Income Support (see p. 176) also applies to Family Credit.

By introducing a higher income threshold before the new WFTC is withdrawn and withdrawing it at a rate of 55% rather than 70% as with Family Credit, WFTC is designed to improve work incentives and to encourage people to move into and remain in employment. It is central to the Government's major programme of tax and benefit reform, representing a step towards greater integration of the tax and benefits systems. At the same time, a new childcare tax credit, forming part of WFTC, will be introduced. It will be worth 70% of eligible childcare costs up to £100 a week for families with one child and £150 for families with two or more children, thus giving greater help with childcare costs.

Social Fund

Payments, in the form of loans or grants, may be available to people on low incomes to help with expenses which are difficult to pay for out of regular income. There are two kinds. *Discretionary* payments are:

- budgeting loans for important intermittent expenses;

- community care grants to help, for example, people resettle into the community from care, or to remain in the community, to ease exceptional pressure on families, to set up home as part of a planned resettlement programme and to meet certain travel expenses; and

- crisis loans to help people in an emergency or as a result of a disaster where there is serious risk to health or safety. People do not have to be receiving any form of benefit to qualify for this loan.

The Social Fund also provides *regulated* payments (payments that are not cash-limited) to help people awarded certain income-related benefits with the costs of maternity or funerals, or with heating during very cold weather and winter fuel payments.

Widows

Widow's Payment. Widows under the age of 60—or those over 60 whose husbands were not entitled to a state retirement pension when they died—receive a tax-free single payment of £1,000 following the death of their husbands, provided that their husbands have paid a minimum number of NI contributions. Women whose husbands have died of an industrial injury or prescribed disease may also qualify, regardless of whether their husbands have paid NI contributions.

Widowed Mother's Allowance, a taxable benefit of £66.75 a week, is payable to a widowed mother with at least one child for whom she is getting Child Benefit. Additional tax-free amounts of £9.90 for a child for whom the higher rate of Child Benefit is payable, and £11.35 for each subsequent child are available.

Widow's Pension. A taxable, weekly benefit of £66.75 a week is payable to a widow who is 55 years or over when her husband dies or when her entitlement to Widowed Mother's Allowance ends. A percentage of the full rate is payable to widows who are aged between 45 and 54 when their husbands die or when their entitlement to Widowed Mother's Allowance ends. Special rules apply for widows whose husbands died before 11 April 1988. Entitlement continues until the widow remarries or begins drawing retirement pension. Payment ends if she lives with a man as his wife.

A man whose wife dies when both are over pension age inherits his wife's pension rights just as a widow inherits her husband's rights.

Sickness and Disablement

A variety of benefits are available for people unable to work because of sickness or disablement. Employers are responsible for paying **Statutory Sick Pay** to employees from the fourth day of sickness for up to a maximum of 28 weeks. There is a single rate of Statutory Sick Pay for all qualifying employees provided their average gross weekly earnings are at least £66.00 a week. The weekly rate is £59.55.

Incapacity Benefit is for people who become incapable of work while they are employed. Entitlement to Incapacity Benefit begins when entitlement to Statutory Sick Pay ends or, for those who do not qualify for Statutory Sick Pay, from the first day of sickness. There are three types:

- short-term benefit for people under pension age: a lower rate of £50.35 a week for the first 28 weeks; and a higher rate of £59.55 a week between the 29th and 52nd week;

- short-term benefit for people over pension age: lower rate of £64.05; higher rate of £66.75; and

- long-term benefit rate of £66.75 a week (after 52 weeks of incapacity).

Extra benefits may be paid for dependent adults and children. Incapacity Benefit is taxable from the 29th week of incapacity.

The medical test of incapacity for work usually applies after 28 weeks' sickness. It assesses ability to perform a range of work-related activities rather than the ability to perform a specific job.

Severe Disablement Allowance is a tax-free benefit for people who have not been able to work for at least 28 weeks because of illness or disability but who cannot get Incapacity Benefit because they have not paid enough NI contributions. The benefit is £40.35 a week, plus additions of up to £14.05 depending on the person's age when they became incapable of work. Additions for adult dependants and for children may also be paid. Claims may be made by people aged between 16 and 65. Once a person has qualified for the allowance, there is no upper age limit for receipt. New claimants must satisfy the same incapacity test as that used in Incapacity Benefit (see above).

People who become incapable of work after their 20th birthday must also be medically assessed as at least 80% disabled for a minimum of 28 weeks. People already in receipt of certain benefits, such as the higher rate of the Disability Living Allowance care component (see below), will automatically be accepted as 80% disabled.

Other Benefits

Disability Living Allowance is a non-contributory tax-free benefit to help severely disabled people aged under 65 with extra costs incurred as a result of disability. Entitlement is measured in terms of personal care and/or mobility needs. There are two components: a care component which has three weekly rates—£52.95, £35.40 and £14.05; and a mobility component which has two weekly rates—£37.00 and £14.05, payable from age five or older.

Attendance Allowance is a non-contributory tax-free benefit to provide financial help to severely disabled people aged 65 or older with extra costs incurred as a result of disability. It is measured in terms of personal care needs by day and/or night. The two rates are £52.95 and £35.40.

A non-contributory **Invalid Care Allowance** of £39.95 weekly may be payable to people between 16 and 65 who have given up the opportunity of a full-time paid job because they are providing regular and substantial care of at least 35 hours a week, to a severely disabled person in receipt of either Attendance Allowance or the higher or middle care component of Disability Living Allowance. An additional carer's premium may be paid if the recipient is also receiving Income Support, income-related Jobseeker's Allowance, Housing Benefit or Council Tax Benefit.

Disability Working Allowance (DWA, which is being replaced by the Disabled Person's Tax Credit from October 1999, payable under the same rules as those for the new Working Families' Tax Credit—see p. 178) is a tax-free, income-related benefit for people who work at least 16 hours a week but have an illness or disability that limits their earning capacity. Awards are for fixed periods of six months. To claim, a person must be aged 16 or over and have a qualifying benefit, such as Disability Living Allowance, or a comparable benefit. The amount paid depends on whether the person has a partner, and the age and number of children living with them. People with savings over £16,000 cannot get DWA.

Industrial Injuries Disablement Benefit

Various benefits are payable for disablement caused by an accident at work or a prescribed disease caused by a particular type of employment. The main benefit is the tax-free **Industrial Injuries Disablement Benefit**: up to £108.10 a week is usually paid after a qualifying period of 15 weeks if a person is at least 14% or more physically or mentally disabled as a result of an industrial accident or a prescribed disease.

Basic Disablement Benefit can be paid in addition to other NI benefits, such as Incapacity Benefit. It can be paid whether or not the person returns to work and does not depend on earnings. The degree of disablement is assessed by an independent adjudicating medical authority and the amount paid depends on the extent of the disablement and on how long it is expected to last. Except for certain progressive respiratory diseases, disablement of less than 14% does not attract Disablement Benefit. In certain circumstances additional allowances may be payable.

Housing and Council Tax Benefits

Housing Benefit is an income-related, tax-free benefit which helps people on low incomes meet the cost of rented accommodation. The amount paid depends on personal circumstances, income, savings, rent and other people sharing the home. It also normally depends on the general level of rents for properties with the same number of rooms in the locality.

Most single people under 25 years old who are not lone parents and who are renting privately have their Housing Benefit limited to the average cost of a single non-self-contained room (that is, shared use of kitchen and toilet facilities) in the locality.

Council Tax Benefit helps people to meet their council tax payments (the tax set by local councils to help pay for services—see p. 411). The scheme offers help to those claiming Income Support and income-based Jobseeker's Allowance and others with low incomes. It is subject to rules broadly similar to those governing the provision of Housing Benefit (see above). A person who is solely liable for the council tax may also claim benefit for a second adult who is not liable to pay the council tax and who is living in the home on a non-commercial basis.

War Pensions and Related Services

Pensions are payable for disablement as a result of service in the armed forces or for certain injuries received in the merchant navy or civil defence during wartime, or to civilians injured by enemy action. The amount paid depends on the degree of disablement: the pension for 100% disablement for an officer is £5,985 a year; for other ranks it is £114.70 a week.

There are a number of extra allowances. The main ones are for unemployability, restricted mobility, the need for care and attendance, the provision of extra comforts, and as maintenance for a lowered standard of occupation. An age allowance of between £7.65 and £23.60 is payable weekly to war pensioners aged 65 or over whose disablement is assessed at 40% or more.

Pensions are also paid to war widows and other dependants. (The standard rate of pension for a private soldier's widow is £86.60 a week.) War Widow's Pension is also payable to a former war widow who has remarried and then become widowed again, divorced or legally separated.

The War Pensioners' Welfare Service helps and advises war pensioners, war widows and other dependants. It works closely with ex-Service organisations and other voluntary bodies which give financial help and personal support to those disabled or bereaved as a result of war.

Concessions

Other benefits for which unemployed people and those on low incomes may be eligible include exemption from health service charges (see p. 191), grants towards the cost of spectacles (see p. 192), legal aid (see p. 235) and free school meals. People on low incomes, as well as all pensioners, widows and long-term sick people on Incapacity Benefit, receive extra help to meet the cost of VAT (value added tax) on their fuel bills.

Reduced charges are often made to unemployed people, for example, for adult education and exhibitions, and pensioners are usually entitled to reduced transport fares.

Taxation

The general rule is that benefits which replace lost earnings are subject to tax, while those

Table 12.5: Tax Liability of Social Security Benefits

Not taxable	Taxable
Attendance Allowance	Incapacity Benefit (long-term
Child Benefit	or short-term higher rate)
Child's Special Allowance	Industrial Death Benefit Pensions
Council Tax Benefit	Invalid Care Allowance
Disability Living Allowance	Jobseeker's Allowance[a]
Disability Working Allowance[b]	Retirement Pension
Family Credit[c]	Statutory Maternity Pension
Guardian's Allowance	Statutory Sick Pay
Housing Benefit	Widowed Mother's Allowance
Incapacity Benefit (short-term lower rate)	Widow's Pension
Income Support	
Industrial Injuries Disablement Benefit/Reduced Earnings Allowance	
Maternity Allowance	
Severe Disablement Allowance	
War Disablement Pension	
War Widow's Pension	

Source: Inland Revenue

[a] That part of the Jobseeker's Allowance equivalent to the individual or couple rate of personal allowance, as appropriate.

[b] From October 1999 this is being replaced by the Disabled Person's Tax Credit.

[c] From October 1999 this is being replaced by the Working Families' Tax Credit.

intended to meet a specific need are not (see Table 12.5). Various income tax reliefs and exemptions are allowed on account of age or a need to support dependants.

Benefit Controls on People from Abroad

Residence Test

All claimants must be habitually resident in the Common Travel Area (that is, the UK, the Irish Republic, the Channel Isles or the Isle of Man) before a claim for Income Support, income-based Jobseeker's Allowance, Housing Benefit or Council Tax Benefit can be paid. This is in line with most other European countries, which also limit access to their benefit systems to those who have lived in the country for some time.

Asylum Seekers

Generally only people who claim refugee status as soon as they arrive in the UK can claim income-based Jobseeker's Allowance, Income Support, Housing Benefit and

Council Tax Benefit. Their eligibility to receive this will stop if their asylum claim is refused by the Home Office. A new Immigration and Asylum Bill (see p. 113) will, among other things, replace cash benefits for asylum seekers with a voucher system.

ARRANGEMENTS AND COMPARISONS WITH OTHER COUNTRIES

As part of the European Union's efforts to promote the free movement of labour, regulations provide for equality of treatment and the protection of benefit rights for employed and self-employed people who move between member states. The regulations also cover retirement pensioners and other beneficiaries who have been employed, or self-employed, as well as dependants. Benefits covered include Child Benefit and those for sickness and maternity, unemployment, retirement, invalidity, accidents at work and occupational diseases.

The UK has reciprocal social security agreements with a number of other countries which also provide cover for some NI benefits and family benefits.

A comparison of the expenditure on social protection benefits per head for the 12 EU countries for which data are available (Austria, Denmark, Finland, France, Germany, the Irish Republic, Italy, the Netherlands, Portugal, Spain, Sweden and the UK) indicates that, in general, spending is much higher in the more northerly countries than in the south. Denmark spent the most per head in 1996; at just under £5,000 this was three times the amount spent by Portugal, the country which spent the least. The UK spent around £3,000 per head of population.

Further Reading

New Ambitions for Our Country: A New Contract for Welfare. Cm 3805. The Stationery Office, 1998.

Modernising Social Services: Promoting Independence, Improving Protection, Raising Standards. Cm 4169. The Stationery Office, 1998.

Modernising Health and Social Services: National Priorities Guidance 1999/00–2001/02. Department of Health, 1998.

Modernising Mental Health Services: Safe, Sound and Supportive. Department of Health, 1998.

With Respect to Old Age: Long-term Care—Rights and Responsibilities. Cm 4192; vols I–II. Royal Commission on Long-term Care. The Stationery Office, 1999.

Caring about Carers: A National Strategy for Carers. Department of Health, 1999.

A New Contract for Welfare: Partnership in Pensions. Cm 4179. The Stationery Office, 1998.

Children First: A New Approach to Child Support. Cm 3992. The Stationery Office, 1998.

The Government's Expenditure Plans 1999–2000. Social Security Departmental Report. Cm 4214. The Stationery Office, 1999.

The Government's Expenditure Plans 1999–2000. Department of Health Departmental Report. Cm 4203. The Stationery Office, 1999.

Websites

Department of Health: www.doh.gov.uk

Department of Social Security: www.dss.gov.uk

13 Health Services

The Government is implementing its plans to modernise the National Health Service, introducing a new system of integrated care based on partnership and replacing the competitive 'internal market' for healthcare. A new health strategy for England has been set out in a White Paper *Saving Lives: Our Healthier Nation*, published in July 1999, and similar strategies have been published for Scotland, Wales and Northern Ireland. A White Paper tackling smoking as the single biggest preventable cause of poor health was published in December 1998.

The National Health Service (NHS) provides a full range of medical services, available to all residents, regardless of their income. Central government is directly responsible for the NHS, which is administered by health authorities and health boards throughout the UK. The Department of Health (DH) is responsible for national strategic planning in England, and within that department, the NHS Executive, with eight regional offices, is responsible for developing and implementing policies for the provision of health services. The Scottish Executive Health Department, the National Assembly for Wales and the Department of Health and Social Services in Northern Ireland have similar responsibilities. Policies and initiatives for health in Scotland, Wales and Northern Ireland are similar to those for England, but may feature distinctive

approaches which reflect the health variations in the different parts of the UK.

There are 99 health authorities in England and five in Wales, 15 health boards in Scotland and four health and social services boards in Northern Ireland, all of which are responsible for identifying the healthcare needs of the people living in their area. They secure hospital and community health services and arrange for the provision of services by family doctors, dentists, pharmacists and opticians, as well as administering their contracts. The health authorities and boards co-operate closely with local authorities responsible for social work, environmental health, education and other services. There are community health councils (local health councils in Scotland and area health and social services councils in Northern Ireland) covering all parts of the country, representing local opinion on the services provided.

Among the major targets which the Government has set for achievement by the end of this Parliament are:

- to reduce waiting lists in England to 100,000 below (and in Scotland to 10,000 below) the level in May 1997 (see p. 196);
- to begin to reduce inequalities in health, in particular targeting premature deaths from heart disease and stroke, cancer and mental illness; and
- to improve the lives and prospects of children looked after by local authorities.

During the 20th century there have been significant changes in the types of disease that people have suffered from. Certain infectious diseases, such as smallpox and diphtheria, have been eradicated whereas other widespread illnesses such as cancer and heart disease have become more prominent. Life expectancy has also altered dramatically. In 1901 it was 45 years for men and nearly 49 for women. By 1997 this had increased to 74 and 79 years respectively. However, mortality rates have been consistently higher in Northern Ireland and Scotland than in England and Wales.

Although some diseases could be prevented by immunisation at the beginning of the century, specific cures for bacterial diseases were not developed before the 1930s. Advances in surgical techniques and intensive care now save thousands of people each year who previously would have succumbed to accidents, premature birth or fatal weaknesses caused by other conditions. Primary preventive medicine has become more important than cure in the latter part of the century.

Major Policy Developments

PUBLIC HEALTH

In July 1999 the Government published a White Paper, *Saving Lives: Our Healthier Nation (OHN)*, setting out its health strategy for England. Similar strategies have been published for Wales, Scotland and Northern Ireland. The White Paper builds on the work of the Green Paper *Our Healthier Nation*, published in 1998. The two main aims of the new health strategy are:

- to improve the health of the population as a whole by increasing the length of people's lives and the number of years people spend free from illness; and
- to improve the health of the least well-off people in society.

Target Areas

The White Paper sets out action to combat the four major causes of premature death and avoidable ill-health: cancer, coronary heart disease and stroke, accidental injury and mental illness. Targets have been set for 2010 in each priority area:

- *cancer*—to reduce the death rate in people under 75 by at least a fifth;
- *coronary heart disease and stroke*—to reduce the death rate in people under 75 by at least two-fifths;
- *accidents*—to reduce the death rate by at least a fifth and serious injury by one-tenth; and
- *mental health*—to reduce the death rate from suicide and undetermined injury by at least one-fifth.

Implementation

The strategy sets out a three-way partnership in which the Government, communities and individuals work together for better health. Government action includes a range of policies across departments to tackle the underlying causes of ill health and health inequality, such as poverty, unemployment, poor housing and pollution. Policies like Sure Start (see p. 127), Welfare-to-Work (see p. 154) and the New Deal for Communities (see p. 356) all aim to improve health.

There are strategies for other important public health issues, such as sexual health (including teenage conceptions), drugs, alcohol, food safety, water fluoridation and communicable diseases.

Alongside the White Paper, the Government published *Reducing Health Inequalities: an Action Report*. The report details the broad range of government action in the light of the recommendations of the report of the Independent Inquiry into Inequalities in Health, published in November 1998.

At local level *OHN* will be implemented through the mechanisms in place to deliver the White Papers on modernising the National Health Service—*The New NHS: Modern, Dependable*—and *Modernising Local Government* (see p. 188). Often this means joint working between the NHS and local government. Under the Health Act 1999 the NHS and local authorities have a new duty to work together to promote the health and well-being of their local communities and are free to share resources.

OHN encourages individuals to safeguard and improve their own health by quitting smoking, taking regular physical exercise and keeping to a healthy diet. It introduces the Healthy Citizens Programme which builds on *NHS Direct* (see p. 190), a nurse-led 24-hour helpline, and introduces two new main elements: a Health Skills programme to help people to help themselves and others, and an Expert Patients programme to help people manage their own illness.

Healthy Living Centres

The New Opportunities Fund will allocate £300 million from the National Lottery (see p. 121) to fund a series of Healthy Living Centres throughout the UK. Funding will be allocated by 2002. Healthy Living Centres are expected to promote good health in its broadest sense; to target areas and groups that represent the most disadvantaged sectors of the population; and to reduce differences in the quality of health between individuals. In England the Fund has defined specific geographic areas of particular deprivation and some priority will be given to applications within health action zones (see p. 189).

Tobacco Control

Cigarette smoking is the greatest cause of preventable illness and death in the UK. It is associated with around 120,000 premature deaths a year (mainly from cancer and heart and respiratory diseases)—nearly one-fifth of all deaths. Smoking peaked in the 1950s and 1960s and fell steadily in the 1970s and 1980s. However, there is evidence to suggest that the downward trend in smoking may be levelling out (see chart on p. 187). Adult smoking rates rose in 1996 for the first time since 1972. More and more children and young people are starting to smoke and this upward trend is particularly noticeable among girls.

Action to reduce smoking, especially among children and young people, is a government priority. A White Paper—*Smoking Kills*—published in December 1998 set out a number of targets for the UK which included:

- to reduce smoking among children from 13% to 9% or less by 2010, with a fall to 11% by 2005;
- to reduce adult smoking so that the overall rate falls from 28% to 24% or less by 2010, with a fall to 26% by 2005; and
- to reduce the percentage of women who smoke during pregnancy from 23% to 15% by 2010, with a fall to 18% by 2005.

In addition, the Government produced a Public Places Charter in September 1999 which committed signatories to improve the facilities in pubs, bars and restaurants for customers who do not smoke. The Charter sets out how this will be implemented, including a written policy on smoking available to customers and staff and the availability of non-smoking areas with improved ventilation.

Advertising

The Government has published its plans to implement an EC Directive which bans tobacco advertising and sponsorship. Subject to consultation, it is proposed that all general advertising of tobacco products in the UK will end by 10 December 1999; tobacco sponsorship by July 2003; and tobacco sponsorship of exceptional global events, such as Formula 1 racing, by October 2006 (see p. 298).

Adult Cigarette Smoking[1] in Great Britain by Gender

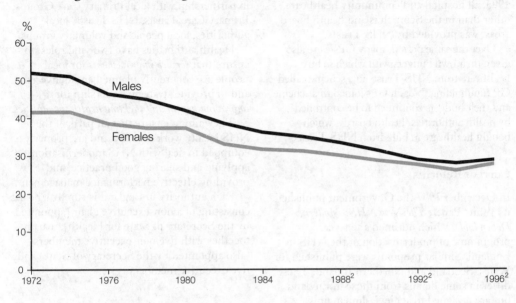

[1] By people aged 16 and over, except for 1972 which included those aged 15. Data are collected every two years.

[2] From 1988 data are for financial years.

Source: General Household Survey, Office for National Statistics

To quit smoking successfully, some smokers need to be strongly motivated and able to deal with the cravings for nicotine. A course in nicotine replacement therapy (NRT) provides the body with nicotine in decreasing doses until the craving is small enough to cope with. Following the White Paper on tobacco, the profile of NRT will be raised to encourage smokers to use it. In addition, for less well-off smokers, the NHS will provide one week's free NRT along with specialist advice and support. Evidence shows that smokers who manage to avoid smoking for a complete week with the help of NRT are more likely to go on to quit for good.

Tax

Research shows that the demand for tobacco products is related to their price: as prices rise, demand falls. High tax levels are therefore one important means of reducing tobacco consumption—tax currently accounts for almost 80% of the price of a packet of cigarettes. The current government commitment is that tobacco duties will be increased on average by at least 5% a year in real terms. The price of a typical packet of 20 cigarettes at the end of 1998 was £3.66, about 55p higher in real terms than at the end of 1996.

REFORMS IN MANAGEMENT

Management reforms introduced under the NHS and Community Care Act 1990 created a form of competition in the running of the NHS—the so-called 'internal market'. This was achieved by making a division between purchasers and providers of healthcare. Under this system, 'purchasers' (health authorities/health boards and some general practitioners —GPs—see p. 194) were given budgets to buy healthcare from 'providers' (acute hospitals; organisations providing care for the mentally ill, people with learning disabilities and the elderly; and ambulance services). To become a provider in the internal market, health organisations became NHS Trusts, independent organisations with their own managements, competing with each other. By 1995, all hospital and community healthcare, other than in the Scottish island health board areas, was provided by NHS Trusts.

Over the same period, many GPs were also given their own budgets with which to buy healthcare from NHS Trusts in a scheme called GP fundholding. Not all GPs joined this scheme and their budgets continued to be controlled by health authorities/health boards, which bought healthcare in bulk from NHS Trusts.

Current Reforms

In December 1997 the Government published its White Paper, *The New NHS: Modern, Dependable*, which outlined a ten-year programme of modernisation of the NHS in England. Similar proposals were published for Wales, Scotland and Northern Ireland. These differ in some details from those in England but are designed to achieve similar aims.

The English White Paper proposed the replacement of the competitive internal market—the present Government considers that the business culture of the internal market is at odds with the ethos of the NHS and its workforce. Instead a new system of integrated care is being introduced to deliver quicker, higher-quality services to patients. This forms the basis for a ten-year programme to renew and improve the NHS through evolutionary change rather than organisational upheaval. The Government has retained the separation between planning and providing services, but is ending competition and replacing it with a new statutory duty for all NHS bodies to work in partnership with each other and with local authorities.

The Government announced its intention to release £1 billion from spending on administration over five years. By the end of 1998–99 it is estimated that around £250 million, which would otherwise have been spent on administrative support, was available for patient care.

Health Authorities

Health authorities provide the strategic leadership for all those working in the local health service. They are responsible for preparing a Health Improvement Programme in partnership with local Primary Care Groups, Primary Care Trusts, NHS Trusts, local authorities, local people and voluntary groups.

Health authorities have two vital roles: to ensure that *service improvements* for local people are coherently planned and delivered; and to provide strategic leadership for *improving health and tackling health inequalities*.

They aim to ensure that all parts of the NHS locally work together and are properly equipped to deal with NHS modernisation, applying and sharing good practice, and providing effective performance management.

Each authority in England is run by a board consisting of a non-executive chair (appointed by the Secretary of State for Health), usually together with five non-executive members (also appointed by the Secretary of State) and five executive members.

Primary Care Groups

GP fundholding will be abolished in October 1999 (except in Northern Ireland where the fundholding scheme will remain in place). Primary Care Groups were introduced in each area, in April 1999, putting GPs and community nurses in charge of shaping services for all patients. The Groups, which are accountable to the local health authority, are responsible for commissioning services for their local communities. GPs and community nurses have a choice about the form their primary care takes. Typically Groups may each serve about 100,000 patients. They have a single unified budget, which gives GPs maximum choice in how patients' needs are met. All Primary Care Groups are expected to work closely with social services to provide properly integrated care.

Primary Care Trusts are larger, more independent Primary Care Groups which involve groups of doctors, nurses and social care professionals—as well as other organisations and agencies—working in partnership to shape local health and social care services. They are free-standing statutory bodies and carry out many functions formerly performed by health authorities. They will also be able to provide a range of community health services directly.

NHS Trusts

NHS Trusts remain responsible for treatment and care, but are also party to the local Health Improvement Programmes. Short-term contracts have ended and NHS Trusts will agree long-term service agreements with Primary Care Groups. These service agreements are generally organised around care groups (such as children) or disease areas (such as heart disease). In this way, hospital clinicians have a greater say in shaping local services for patients. From November 1999 NHS Trusts, for the first time, will have a statutory duty to meet quality standards, and from April 2000 there will be a duty to co-operate with other parts of the NHS. They are required to take part (alongside Primary Care Groups and local authorities) in developing the Health Improvement Programmes under the leadership of the health authority. NHS Trusts are now more accountable to the public and publish details of their performance, including the costs of treatments and services.

Quality Standards

An integral part of the modernisation programme for the NHS set out in 1997 included proposals for new standards of quality and efficiency that will guarantee better services for patients. *National Service Frameworks* (NSFs) will set national standards and describe service models for a defined service or care group. They will put in place programmes to support implementation and establish performance measures against which progress within an agreed timescale will be measured. Building on existing frameworks for cancer and paediatric intensive care, NSFs for coronary heart disease and mental health will be published in 1999, an NSF for older people in spring 2000 and an NSF for diabetes in spring 2001.

The *National Institute for Clinical Excellence (NICE)* was established on 1 April 1999 and intends to develop clear national standards for best practice in clinical care within the NHS. This includes drawing up new guidelines based on clinical and cost effectiveness and ensuring that they reach all parts of the NHS. The Institute's membership is drawn from the health professions, the NHS, academics, health economists and patients. The NICE will become a central point of contact for dissemination of reliable information about health and treatment of ill-health. It brings together the work of the National Prescribing Centre, PRODIGY (a computer-based system for GPs to help them with prescribing medicines), the National Centre for Clinical Audit, the Prescriber's Journal, the National Guidelines Programme, the Professional Audit Programme and Effectiveness Bulletins.

Under the Health Act 1999, an independent *Commission for Health Improvement* will be established to oversee the quality of clinical services at local level, and to tackle shortcomings. Where there are shortfalls in the quality of clinical services, the Commission will have the capacity to identify the source of the problem, and work with the organisation concerned to put these right. It will undertake a systematic review of action taken locally and nationally to monitor progress in the implementation across the NHS of the standards set by the NSFs. The Commission's membership will include those with a wide range of expertise and backgrounds, including clinical, academic and lay experience.

Health Action Zones

In 1998 the first 'health action zones' were set up in 11 areas of England, covering almost 6 million people, and a further 15 zones started in April 1999. Concentrated in areas of deprivation, the zones involve local partnerships between the health service, local councils, voluntary groups and local businesses, and receive government funding. Their job is to make measurable improvements in the health of local people and in the quality of treatment and care. Working closely with the DH, the participants explore ways of breaking through current organisational boundaries to tackle inequalities, and delivering better services and healthcare, building upon and encouraging co-operation across the NHS.

Two health action zones have also been established in Northern Ireland from April 1999 and an initiative to encourage local healthcare partnerships has been launched in Scotland.

NHS Direct, a 24-hour nurse-led helpline, was piloted in three areas in March 1998. The principle is to provide people at home with easier and faster advice and information about health, illness and the NHS so that they are better able to care for themselves and their families.

The three pilot schemes—based in Milton Keynes, Preston and Newcastle upon Tyne—between them covered more than 1.5 million people and up to the end of December 1998 had taken over 60,000 calls. Independent research showed that 97% of users were satisfied with the service provided, which they found prompt, friendly and professional. A range of organisations has been involved in the delivery of the pilot schemes, including the ambulance service, GP co-operatives, the Health Information Service, community trusts and social services. By April 1999 further centres had been opened covering the West Midlands, west London, Essex, Nottinghamshire, Manchester, West Yorkshire, Hampshire, and also Lambeth, Southwark and Lewisham in south London, giving over 20 million people access to the helpline; 60% of the country will have access by December 1999.

In March 1999 it was announced that *NHS Direct Scotland* would be piloted with the support of GP co-operatives. Plans are to establish pilot sites early in 2000.

Electronic Health Records

As part of the Government's information technology (IT) programme in the NHS, organisational records, mainly now in paper form, will become the Electronic Patient Records and in time be part of a lifelong record of each individual's health and healthcare—the Electronic Health Record (EHR). This will mean that healthcare professionals will have access to the relevant elements of patients' histories to enable them to deliver care more effectively. Pilot sites will be selected to test different types of system for building and using records from April 2000.

By 2002 the first generation of EHRs will be in use, followed by 2005 by the first generation of EHRs with 24-hour access.

NHSnet

NHSnet is the short name for a range of voice and data services used by the NHS, covering radio, telephone and computer-based communications. All health authorities and most Trusts are connected to NHSnet, as are a number of major third-party suppliers to the NHS. The White Paper (*The New NHS*—see above) signalled both the expansion and wider exploitation of NHSnet services by the NHS. Regional demonstration sites in England have been established to illustrate direct patient benefits from NHSnet, and targets have been set to ensure that primary care staff can start to use NHSnet for both general and clinical communications. By 2002 a wide range of activities, such as the transfer of laboratory results to GPs, will be carried out electronically. All Scottish GPs are connected to NHSnet. NHSnet will also support the longer-term goal of introducing EHRs to replace the paper-based records. This will enable, for example, secure access by doctors to a patient's records in an emergency when they are away from home. An equivalent scheme, HPSSnet has been set up in Northern Ireland by the Northern Ireland Health and Personal Social Services (HPSS). This is an electronic data network linking HPSS organisations and some other affiliated bodies.

The National Health Service

The NHS is based on the principle that there should be a full range of publicly funded services designed to help the individual stay healthy. The services are intended to provide effective and appropriate treatment and care where necessary while making the best use of available resources. All taxpayers, employers and employees contribute to the cost so that those members of the community who do not require healthcare help to pay for those who do. Most forms of treatment, such as hospital care, are generally provided free, although some may incur a charge.

ADMINISTRATION

Expenditure

The Health and Personal Social Services Programmes consist of:

- NHS Hospital and Community Health Services (HCHS), providing all hospital care and a range of community services;
- NHS Family Health Services (FHS), providing general medical, dental, pharmaceutical and some ophthalmic services, and covering the cost of medicines prescribed by GPs;
- Central Health and Miscellaneous Services (CHMS)—in Scotland, Other Health Services (OHS)—which provide services administered centrally (for example, certain public health functions and support to the voluntary sector);
- provision of social care by local authorities, supported by the DH and the Department of the Environment, Transport and the Regions' programmes in England, and the Scottish Executive in Scotland; and
- the administration of the DH.

Comprehensive Spending Review

The results of the Comprehensive Spending Review were announced by the Chancellor of the Exchequer in 1998 and the White Paper *Modern Public Services for Britain: Investing in Reform* (see p. 400) sets out details of an extra £18 billion for the NHS in England over the three years 1999–2000 to 2001–02, with an extra £1.8 billion for Scotland. This funding includes an 'NHS Modernisation Fund' of at least £5 billion to take forward the Government's modernisation programme covering specific service improvements such as IT and capital investment.

Over £1 billion has been allocated from the Fund for 1999–2000. The key priorities for extra resources are:

- cutting waiting lists;
- modernising hospitals and systems;
- investing in NHS staff;
- ensuring safe and effective mental health care;
- providing better primary care; and
- improving health promotion.

Finance

The NHS is financed mainly through general taxation with an element of National Insurance contributions (see chapter 12), paid by employed people, their employers and self-employed people. The remainder is financed through charges, such as for drugs prescribed by family doctors, receipts from land sales and the proceeds of income generation schemes. In 1998–99, 75% of the NHS was financed through general taxation, with 13% from National Insurance contributions and 12% from charges and other receipts.

Health authorities may raise funds from other sources. For example, some hospitals increase revenue by taking private patients, who pay the full cost of their accommodation and treatment.

Over 510 million prescription items, worth around £4.7 billion, were dispensed in England in 1998, an increase of 32% in real terms since 1993. The proportion of items provided free of charge increased from 82% in 1993 to 85% in 1998. The following groups are exempted from prescription charges: people aged 60 and over; children under 16 and young people aged 16, 17 or 18 in full-time education; women who are pregnant or have given birth in the previous 12 months; and people with certain medical conditions. In addition, people who receive (or whose partners receive) certain social security benefits (see chapter 12) or who otherwise qualify on low income grounds, do not pay prescription charges. In 1998, 50% of all prescription items dispensed by community pharmacies and appliance contractors in England were for elderly people, an increase from around 44% in 1993.

There are charges for most types of NHS dental treatment, including examinations, based on a proportion of the fee paid to the dentist. However, the following people are entitled to free treatment: women who begin a course of treatment while pregnant or within 12 months of having a baby; children under 16; full-time students under 19; and adults on low incomes or receiving the same benefits or tax credits as for free prescriptions.

Health Service Spending in England, 1998–99

Total: £40.2 billion

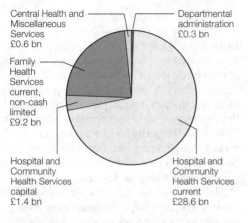

Central Health and Miscellaneous Services £0.6 bn

Departmental administration £0.3 bn

Family Health Services current, non-cash limited £9.2 bn

Hospital and Community Health Services capital £1.4 bn

Hospital and Community Health Services current £28.6 bn

Source: *Department of Health. The Government's Expenditure Plans 1999–2000*

Since 1989 free NHS sight tests have been restricted to children, full-time students under the age of 19, adults on low incomes or receiving the same benefits or tax credits as for free prescriptions, and people who have, or are at particular risk of, eye disease. In April 1999 the Government restored free sight tests to people aged 60 and over.

For the most part, family practitioners (GPs, dentists, optometrists and community pharmacists) are either self-employed or (in the case of pharmacists and optometrists) are employed by independent businesses. They, or the companies they work for, agree to provide services on the NHS's behalf, and are paid by health authorities for doing so. Most GPs are paid by a system of fees and allowances designed to reflect responsibilities, workload and practice expenses. Most dentists are paid by a combination of capitation fees for children registered with the practice, continuing care payments for adults registered, and a prescribed scale of fees for individual treatments. Community pharmacists are paid professional fees for dispensing NHS prescriptions, as well as being reimbursed for the cost of the drugs and appliances concerned. Ophthalmic medical practitioners and optometrists providing general ophthalmic services for the NHS receive approved fees for each sight test carried out.

NHS Workforce

The NHS is one of the largest employers in the world, with a workforce of nearly 1 million people. Staff costs account for approximately 70% of current spending on hospitals and community health services.

Openness in the NHS

The Code of Practice on Openness in the NHS is designed to make NHS organisations more accountable and provide greater public access to information. The Code applies to NHS Trusts, health authorities/boards and local health practitioners such as GPs, dentists and pharmacists. It sets out the information that health authorities/boards and NHS Trusts should publish or otherwise make available.

Table 13.1: Health and Personal Social Services Staff, England, 1986–98

			Whole time equivalents (thousands)		
	1986	**1991**	**1994**	**1997**	**1998**
Directly employed NHS staff:					
Medical and dental	42	46	49	57	59
Non-medical and dental	753	748	706	701	707
All health service staff	**795**	**794**	**756**	**758**	**765**
GPs	24	26	27	27	26
Dentists	14	15	16	17	17
Personal social services	224	237	238	229	224

Source: Department of Health

Note: Differences between totals and the sums of their component parts are due to rounding.

The NHS Code contains, among other things:

- information about services provided, the targets and standards set and results achieved, and the costs and effectiveness of services;
- details of important proposals on health policies or proposed changes in the way the services are delivered; and
- information about how people can have access to their own personal health records.

NHS Complaints System

There is a mechanism for dealing with complaints about all NHS-funded treatments and services. The primary aim of the procedure is to resolve complaints speedily at local level, but where the complainant remains dissatisfied with the local response he or she can request an independent review of the complaint. Where an independent review panel investigation takes place, a report setting out suggestions and recommendations will be produced. Complainants who remain dissatisfied after independent review, or whose request for a panel investigation is turned down, can refer their complaint to the Health Service Commissioner.

In 1997–98 a total of 88,757 written complaints were made about both hospital and community health services and family health services in England, a decline from 92,974 in 1996–97. The main reasons for complaints were aspects of clinical treatment, staff attitudes, communication and information, and appointment delays and cancellations. In Scotland, 9,736 written complaints were made, compared with 10,648 in 1996–97.

Health Service Commissioners

Health Service Commissioners (one each for England, Scotland and Wales) are responsible for investigating complaints directly from members of the public about health service bodies. The three posts are at present held by one person (with a staff of about 250), who is also Parliamentary Commissioner for Administration (Ombudsman—see p. 52). As

Health Service Commissioner, he reports annually to Parliament. In Scotland he reports to the Scottish Parliament. In Northern Ireland complaints about health and social services bodies are investigated by the Commissioner for Complaints (the Ombudsman).

The Health Service Commissioner can investigate complaints that a person has suffered hardship as a result of:

- a failure in a service provided by a health service body;
- a failure to provide a service which the patient was entitled to receive or maladministration by an NHS authority; or
- action by health professionals arising from the exercise of clinical judgment.

Complaints must be sent to the Commissioner in writing, and the health service body concerned should first have been given a reasonable opportunity to respond.

In 1998–99 a total of 2,869 written complaints were received regarding both hospital and community health services and family health services—an increase from 2,660 in 1997–98.

Patient's Charters

Patient's Charters set out the rights of patients and the standards of service they can expect to receive from the NHS. The original Patient's Charter in England came into force in 1992 and an expanded version was issued in 1995, covering dental, optical and pharmaceutical services and the hospital environment. The Patient's Charter sets national standards, which are not legal rights but specific standards of service that the NHS aims to provide. These cover respect for the individual patient; waiting times for ambulances, clinical assessment in Accident and Emergency departments and appointments in out-patient clinics; and cancellation of operations.

Separate though broadly similar Patient's Charters have been developed for Scotland and Wales. In Northern Ireland the Charter for Patients and Clients covers social care services as well as health.

The Government considers that the existing Charter fails to give proper weight to the quality of clinical care and patients' own experiences of how well the service has been delivered. Work is currently under way on a new NHS Charter programme to replace the existing Patient's Charter by April 2000. The new Charter in England will concentrate on the quality and success of treatment, and aim to provide a better balance between the rights of patients and their responsibilities towards the NHS. New Charters are also being developed for Scotland, Wales and Northern Ireland.

FAMILY HEALTH SERVICES

The Family Health Services are those provided to patients by doctors (GPs), dentists, opticians and pharmacists of their own choice. They remain the first point of contact with the NHS for most people. In England there are over 270 million consultations with GPs each year. Often those who visit their GP or dentist need no clinical treatment but healthy lifestyle counselling and preventive healthcare advice instead. The last decade has seen continued growth of the Family Health Services in line with long-standing government policy to build up and extend these services both to improve health and to relieve pressure on the more costly secondary care sector (that is, hospital and specialist services).

GPs provide the first diagnosis in the case of illness, give advice and may prescribe a suitable course of treatment or refer a patient to the more specialised services and hospital consultants. Most GPs in the UK work in partnerships or group practices. Primary healthcare teams also include health visitors and district nurses, midwives, and sometimes social workers and other professional staff employed by the health authorities. Most GPs in Great Britain and about half in Northern Ireland work in health centres. As well as providing medical and nursing services, health centres may have facilities for health education, family planning, speech therapy, chiropody, assessment of hearing, physiotherapy and remedial exercises. Dental, pharmaceutical and ophthalmic services,

hospital out-patient and supporting social work services may also be provided.

There have been substantial increases in primary healthcare staff in recent years. For example, between 1988 and 1998 the number of GPs in England rose steadily at a rate of 0.8% a year, to 29,696 (a whole-time equivalent of 25,831). Between autumn 1997 and autumn 1998, around 300 new GPs started work, which included 100 extra GP trainees. Doctors had about 7% fewer patients on their lists in 1998 than in 1988, with an average list size per GP in 1998 of 1,866. Similarly, the number of general dental practitioners continues to grow, rising to 16,761 in 1998, 2.8% more than in 1997.

New Initiatives in Primary Care

The NHS (Primary Care) Act 1997 is designed to allow flexibility in the delivery of primary healthcare services for patients. It enables GPs, dentists, NHS Trusts and NHS employees to work with health authorities and health boards to develop new ways of delivering primary care under local contracts.

In 1997 the Government launched its Investing in Dentistry scheme in England, to help improve dental care in areas of poor availability and poor oral health. Similar schemes are in operation in Scotland and Wales. Around 300 schemes in England have been approved for funding, giving over 650,000 patients the opportunity to register with an NHS dentist. Assistance includes grants to dentists to help expand or set up new practices in return for long-term commitment to the NHS, and support for newly qualified dentists and women returning from a career break. Up to £19 million was made available between 1997–98 and 1998–99. The Government is working on a new strategy for NHS dentistry in England due to be published later in 1999.

The Department of Health is also preparing a strategy document, to be published in late 1999, on developing the role of community pharmacists within the NHS to make better use of their skills. Current pilot projects involve repeat and instalment dispensing, which has the potential to improve monitoring of treatment and reduce GP paperwork and drug waste; and schemes where pharmacists provide support for patients with medication-related problems, such as complex regimes or difficulties in taking medication effectively.

Midwives, Health Visitors and District Nurses

Midwives provide care and support to women throughout pregnancy, birth and the postnatal period (up to 28 days after the baby is born). Midwives work in both hospital and community settings. Health visitors are responsible for the preventive care and health promotion of families, particularly those with young children. They identify local health needs and work closely with GPs, district nurses and other professions. District nurses give skilled nursing care to people at home or elsewhere outside hospital; they also play an important role in health promotion and education. Practice nurses are based in GP surgeries. They carry out treatments and give advice on health promotion, working closely with GPs, and with other community nurses. Since 1998 district nurses and health visitors and some nurses based in GP practices have been able to prescribe from a limited list of drugs and medical appliances. This has helped to reduce the time patients have to wait for relief of their symptoms.

HOSPITAL AND SPECIALIST SERVICES

District general hospitals offer a broad spectrum of clinical specialities, supported by a range of other services, such as anaesthetics, pathology and radiology. Almost all have facilities for the admission of emergency patients, either through Accident and Emergency departments or as direct referrals from GPs. Treatments are provided for in-patients, day cases, out-patients and patients who attend wards for treatment such as dialysis. Some hospitals also provide specialist services covering more than one region or district, for example, for heart and liver transplants, craniofacial services, and rare eye and bone cancers. There are also specialist hospitals such as the world-famous Hospital for Sick Children at Great Ormond Street, Moorfields Eye Hospital, and the National Hospital for Neurology and Neurosurgery, all in London. These hospitals combine specialist treatment facilities with the training of medical and other students, and international research.

Less than a third of hospitals now pre-date the formation of the NHS in 1948. While much has been done to improve existing hospital buildings, the largest building programme in the history of the NHS is currently in progress, including several major Private Finance Initiative schemes (see p. 196).

Greater Accountability for NHS Trusts

Each NHS Trust (HSS Trust in Northern Ireland) is run by a board of executive and non-executive directors, subject to provisions in the Health Act 1999. Trusts are free to employ their own staff and set their own rates of pay, although staff transferring to Trust employment retain their existing terms and conditions of service. Trusts are also free to carry out research and provide facilities for medical education and other forms of training. The internal market has been replaced with a system of partnership and co-operation (see p. 188). Each health authority is responsible for leading the development of a Health Improvement Programme for its local area. NHS Trusts work with health authorities, local authorities and local people to ensure that the Programme reflects the needs of the local population. Trusts' main contribution remains the provision of hospital and community services to patients. The services they provide will be subject to the new quality standards set by the NICE (see p. 189). If any NHS Trusts fail to meet such standards, then the Commission for Health Improvement (see p. 189) may step in to find ways where improvements can be made.

Since 1998 all Trust board meetings have been required to be open to the public. Measures have also been taken to make boards more representative of the local communities.

Waiting Lists in England

Half of all admissions to hospital are immediate. The other half are placed on a waiting list before

Hospital and Community Health Services Spending by Sector, in England, 1996–97

Total: £22.7 billion

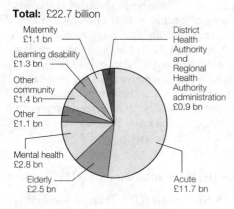

- Maternity £1.1 bn
- Learning disability £1.3 bn
- Other community £1.4 bn
- Other £1.1 bn
- Mental health £2.8 bn
- Elderly £2.5 bn
- District Health Authority and Regional Health Authority administration £0.9 bn
- Acute £11.7 bn

Hospital and Community Health Services Spending by Age, in England, 1996–97

Total: £22.7 billion

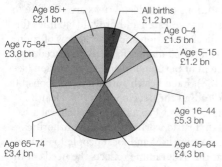

- Age 85 + £2.1 bn
- Age 75–84 £3.8 bn
- Age 65–74 £3.4 bn
- All births £1.2 bn
- Age 0–4 £1.5 bn
- Age 5–15 £1.2 bn
- Age 16–44 £5.3 bn
- Age 45–64 £4.3 bn

Source: *Department of Health. The Government's Expenditure Plans 1999–2000*

the admission takes place. Of patients admitted from waiting lists, half are admitted within six weeks, and around two-thirds within three months. In May 1997 there were just under 1.2 million patients waiting for NHS treatment in England and this figure had been increasing, while in-patient and out-patient waiting times had been getting longer.

The Government is aiming to reduce the level of NHS waiting lists and times by 100,000 by the end of the present Parliament. At the end of 1998–99, the number of patients waiting for NHS treatment had fallen to just under 1.1 million. The Government has also said that no patient should have to wait longer than 18 months for admission and this was achieved for the first time in March 1998. It has made a commitment that no woman should wait longer than two weeks for an out-patient appointment if referred urgently with suspected breast cancer. By 2000 this standard will apply to all cancers.

The Government made £417 million available to reduce waiting lists in England in 1998–99 and will invest a further £320 million in 1999–2000. Under a new *National Booked Admissions Programme*, patients will be able to pre-book their appointments for a time convenient to them.

Private Finance Initiative

The Private Finance Initiative (PFI) was launched in 1992 to promote partnership between the public and private sectors on a commercial basis (see chapter 24). In the health service it involves the use of private finance in NHS capital projects for the design, construction and operation of buildings and support services. The Government introduced legislation in 1997 to reinvigorate the system by clarifying powers of NHS Trusts to sign PFI agreements, and, following a review of PFI hospital building schemes in England, announced a major new hospital building programme. Under this, 25 major hospital schemes in England—with a capital value of around £2.2 billion—have been approved to proceed. Eleven major PFI schemes in Scotland worth £408 million are also proceeding. In Wales, 15 PFI schemes with a capital value of around £35 million have been concluded, including a community hospital, day surgery and endoscopy facilities, sterile services and staff residences, while further schemes are planned including a major general hospital.

The hospitals will be designed, built, maintained and owned by the private sector, which will lease the completed facilities back to the NHS. Clinical services will continue to be provided by NHS staff, and the NHS will remain in control of the key planning and clinical decisions. On current plans the PFI will provide over £600 million worth of capital investment in 1999–2000.

Haughmond Abbey: near Shrewsbury in Shropshire.
The earliest records date from 1135 and refer to 'Prior Fulk
and his brethren'. Early in the 12th century it attracted the
patronage of the FitzAlan family, who supported Queen Matilda
in the Civil Wars of King Stephen's reign and were well rewarded
when her son came to the throne as Henry II in 1154.
Haughmond was richly endowed and gained the status,
unusual for an Augustinian house, of an abbey.

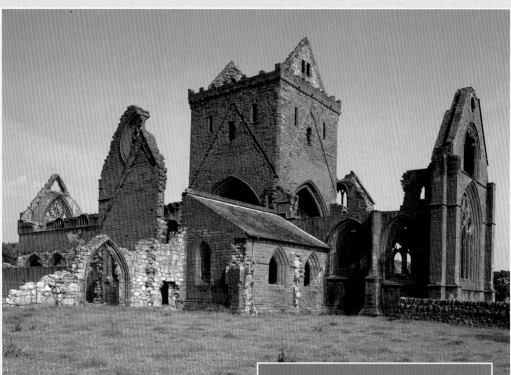

Sweetheart: founded in 1273 by Devorguilla de Balliol. When her husband died, Devorguilla had his heart embalmed and put in an ivory and silver casket, which she always carried with her, and the abbey became known as Dulce Cor, or Sweetheart. She also founded Balliol College in Oxford and named it after her husband. The abbey is situated at New Abbey, 8 miles south of Dumfries.

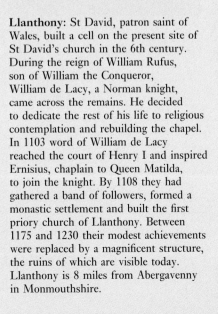

Llanthony: St David, patron saint of Wales, built a cell on the present site of St David's church in the 6th century. During the reign of William Rufus, son of William the Conqueror, William de Lacy, a Norman knight, came across the remains. He decided to dedicate the rest of his life to religious contemplation and rebuilding the chapel. In 1103 word of William de Lacy reached the court of Henry I and inspired Ernisius, chaplain to Queen Matilda, to join the knight. By 1108 they had gathered a band of followers, formed a monastic settlement and built the first priory church of Llanthony. Between 1175 and 1230 their modest achievements were replaced by a magnificent structure, the ruins of which are visible today. Llanthony is 8 miles from Abergavenny in Monmouthshire.

Grey Abbey: founded in 1193 by
Affreca, daughter of the King of
Man and wife of John de Courcy,
as a thanksgiving for a safe sea
journey during a ferocious storm.
It is unusual, showing early Gothic
features, at a time when late
Romanesque work was common
elsewhere in Ireland. This Cistercian
abbey, 10 miles east of Belfast on
the Ards peninsula, County Down,
was used for worship as late as the
18th century.

Organ Transplants

The United Kingdom Transplant Support Service Authority (a special health authority of the NHS) provides a 24-hour support service to all transplant units in the UK for the matching and allocation of organs for transplant. During 1998, 1,593 kidney transplants were performed. (There were also 23 kidney/pancreas transplants.) A similar service exists for corneas and, in 1998, over 2,200 were transplanted.

There are seven designated thoracic transplant centres in England, and one in Scotland. In 1998, 281 heart, 88 lung, and 52 heart/lung transplants were performed. There are six designated liver transplant units in England and one in Scotland. In 1998, 693 liver transplants were performed.

A voluntary organ donor card system enables people to indicate their willingness to become organ donors in the event of their death. The NHS Organ Donor Register is a computer database of those willing to be organ donors. By June 1999 it contained 7.6 million names. Commercial dealing in organs for transplant is illegal in the UK.

Blood Transfusion Services

Blood transfusion services are run by the National Blood Authority in England, the Scottish National Blood Transfusion Service, the Welsh Blood Service and the Northern Ireland Blood Transfusion Agency. The UK is self-sufficient in blood components.

In the UK around 3 million donations are given each year by voluntary unpaid donors. These are made into many different life-saving products for patients. Red cells, platelets and other components with a limited 'shelf life' are prepared at blood centres, whereas the production of plasma products is undertaken at the Bio Products Laboratory in Elstree (Hertfordshire) and the Protein Fractionation Centre in Edinburgh.

Each of the four national blood services co-ordinates programmes for donor recruitment, retention and education, and donor sessions are organised regionally, in towns, villages and workplaces. Donors are normally aged between 17 and 70. Blood centres are responsible for blood collection, screening, processing and supplying hospital blood banks. They also provide laboratory, clinical, research, teaching and specialist advisory services and facilities. These blood centres are subject to nationally co-ordinated quality audit programmes, through the Medicines Control Agency.

Ambulance and Patient Transport Services

NHS emergency ambulances are available free to the public through the 999 telephone call system for cases of sudden illness or collapse and for accidents. They are also available for doctors' urgent calls. Rapid response services, in which paramedics use cars and motorcycles to reach emergency cases, have been introduced in a number of areas, particularly London and other major cities with areas of high traffic density. Helicopter ambulances, provided through local charities, serve many parts of the country and an integrated NHS-funded air ambulance service is available throughout Scotland. Between 1997–98 and 1998–99 the number of emergency calls rose by 8% to 3.8 million and the number of emergency patient journeys grew by 2%.

Non-emergency patient transport services are free to NHS patients considered by their doctor (or dentist or midwife) to be medically unfit to travel by other means. In many areas the ambulance service organises volunteer drivers to provide a hospital car service for non-urgent patients. Patients on low incomes may be eligible for reimbursement of costs of travelling to hospital.

Rehabilitation

NHS and social services undertake rehabilitation work for large numbers of people of all ages to restore and maintain their independence and social participation. Rehabilitation plays an important role in improving the quality of life of people, enabling them to return to, or remain in, employment or education and preventing inappropriate admissions to hospital or long-term care.

Health and social services are encouraged to develop a range of rehabilitative options and to be flexible in meeting people's needs. A new Partnership Grant, announced in the *Modernising Social Services* White Paper (see p. 165) and totalling nearly £650 million over three years, has a particular emphasis on improving rehabilitation services and avoiding unnecessary admissions to hospital and other institutional care. The Health Act 1999 has also introduced new operational flexibilities for the NHS and local government in connection with developing innovative rehabilitation services.

Hospices

Hospice or palliative care is a special type of care for people whose illness may no longer be curable; it enables them to achieve the best possible quality of life during the final stages. The care may be provided in a variety of settings: at home (with support from specially trained staff), in a hospice or palliative care unit, in hospital or at a hospice day centre.

Hospice or palliative care focuses on controlling pain and other distressing symptoms and providing psychological support to patients, their families and friends, both during the patient's illness and into bereavement.

Palliative care was first developed in the UK in 1967 by the voluntary hospices and continues to be provided by them in many areas, but is now also provided within NHS palliative care units, hospitals and community services.

Hospices and palliative care services mostly help people with cancer, although patients with other life-threatening illnesses, such as AIDS, are also cared for. Several hospices provide respite care for children from birth to 16 years of age.

The National Council for Hospices and Specialist Palliative Care Services is an umbrella organisation which brings together both voluntary and health service providers in order to provide a co-ordinated view of the service; it covers England, Wales and Northern Ireland. Its Scottish counterpart is the Scottish Partnership Agency for Palliative and Cancer Care.

Private Medical Treatment

Some NHS hospitals share expensive equipment with private hospitals, and NHS patients are sometimes treated (at public expense) in the private sector when it represents value for money. The scale of private practice in relation to the NHS is, however, relatively small.

It has been estimated that about three-quarters of those receiving acute treatment in private hospitals or NHS hospital pay beds are funded by health insurance schemes, which make provision for private healthcare in return for annual subscriptions. According to the Consumers' Association, 12.7% of people in the UK subscribe to such schemes, compared with fewer than 2% in the 1950s. Around 60% of these are covered by group schemes, some arranged by firms on behalf of employees.

Many overseas patients come to the UK for treatment in private hospitals and clinics. Harley Street in London is an internationally recognised centre for medical consultancy.

Parents and Children

Special preventive services are provided under the NHS to safeguard the health of pregnant women and of mothers with young children. Services include free dental treatment; health education; and vaccination and immunisation of children against certain infectious diseases (see p. 203).

A woman is entitled to care throughout her pregnancy, the birth and the postnatal period. Care may be provided by a midwife, a community-based GP, a hospital-based obstetrician, or a combination of these. The birth may take place in a hospital maternity unit, a midwife/GP-led unit, or at home. After the birth, a midwife will visit until the baby is at least ten days old and after that a health visitor's services are available. Throughout her pregnancy and for the first year of her baby's life, a woman is entitled to free prescriptions and dental care. Prescriptions for children, including older children (up to the age of 19 when in full-time education), are free of charge.

A comprehensive programme of health surveillance, provided for pre-school children (under five years of age), is run by community health trusts and GPs who receive an annual payment for every child registered on the programme. This enables doctors, dentists and health visitors to oversee the health and development of pre-school children so that any health problems are picked up and appropriate intervention arranged as early and as quickly as possible. The Health Education Authority produces a child development book *Birth to Five,* which is a complete guide to the early stages of development, nutrition, weaning and common childhood ailments; it is made available to all first-time mothers free of charge.

There is a welfare food scheme for mothers on low income, where distribution of formula feed and vitamins is free of charge. This is often undertaken at the child health clinic. New mothers also receive a Personal Child Health Record for their child. This is based on a model record produced by the Royal College of Paediatrics and Child Health. It enables and prompts parents to keep an easy access record of immunisation, tests, birth details and health checks. Children of school age attending a state-maintained school have access to the school health service, as well as usually being registered with a GP and local dentist. In addition to providing health advice to children and young people, the school health service assists teachers with pupils having medical needs. This is supplemented by guidance produced by the Department for Education and Employment, in collaboration with DH. Work has been undertaken to build up the 'Wired for Health' Internet website as an additional resource in the promotion of good health and well-being for schoolchildren.

Child guidance and child psychiatric services provide help and advice to families and children with psychological or emotional problems. In recent years special efforts have been made to improve co-operation between the community-based child health services and local authority education and social services for children. This is particularly important in the prevention of child abuse and for the health and welfare of children in care (see p. 168).

Human Fertilisation and Embryology

The world's first 'test-tube baby' was born in the UK in 1978, as a result of the technique of *in vitro* fertilisation. This opened up new horizons for helping with problems of infertility and for the science of embryology. The social, ethical and legal implications were examined by a committee of inquiry under Baroness Warnock (1984) and led eventually to the passage of the Human Fertilisation and Embryology Act 1990, one of the most comprehensive pieces of legislation on assisted reproduction and embryo research in the world.

The Human Fertilisation and Embryology Authority (HFEA) licenses and controls centres providing certain infertility treatments, undertaking human embryo research or storing gametes or embryos. The HFEA maintains a code of practice giving guidance to licensed centres and reports annually to Parliament.

The law prohibits surrogacy arrangements made on a commercial basis and prohibits any advertising concerning surrogacy. An independent review of aspects of surrogacy law was set up in 1997 to consider whether payments, including expenses, to surrogate mothers should continue to be allowed and, if so, on what basis; to examine whether there is a case for regulating surrogacy arrangements through a recognised body; and to advise whether changes are needed to the present legislation. Following the publication of the review team's report in October 1998, its recommendations are under consideration.

Family Planning

The Government's public health strategy aims to ensure the provision of effective family planning services. Free family planning advice and treatment is available from GPs or from family planning clinics. Clinics are also able to provide condoms and other contraceptives free of charge.

Teenage Pregnancies

DH is working closely with the Government's Social Exclusion Unit (see p. 117) to develop a strategy on teenage pregnancy. Live birth rates to women under 20 in England and Wales are the highest in Western Europe. In

1997, the conception rate for girls under the age of 16 was 8.9 per 1,000 women; the majority of these conceptions were to girls aged 15.

The Social Exclusion Unit was asked to build on work already done by DH, and make recommendations aimed at cutting the rates of teenage parenthood—particularly under-age parenthood—to the European average and to propose better solutions to combat the risk of social exclusion for vulnerable teenagers and their children. The Unit's report was published in June 1999 and sets out a national programme with two goals: to halve by 2010 the rate of conceptions in England among those aged under 18 and to lessen the risks of young parents suffering the consequences of social exclusion by getting more teenage parents back into education, training or employment. A £60 million package of measures includes:

- a new task force of ministers, led by the Minister for Public Health, to co-ordinate the policy across government, supported by an implementation unit in DH;
- a national publicity campaign to reinforce the report's key messages;
- improved access to contraceptive and sexual health services for teenagers;
- new guidance on sex and relationships education in school; and
- special action targeted on prevention for the most vulnerable groups, including children looked after by a local authority, those excluded from school and young offenders.

The Minister for Public Health is developing an action programme on sexual and reproductive health for all health authorities and local authorities in England. It will bring together current initiatives in sexual health, including the HIV/AIDS strategy (see p. 204), work on chlamydia, and the Social Exclusion Unit report.

Abortion

Under the Abortion Act 1967, as amended, a time limit of 24 weeks applies to the largest category of abortion—risk to the physical or mental health of the pregnant woman—and also to abortion because of a similar risk to any existing children of her family. There are three categories in which no time limit applies: to prevent grave permanent injury to the physical or mental health of the woman; where there is a substantial risk of serious foetal handicap; or where continuing the pregnancy would involve a risk to the life of the pregnant woman greater than if the pregnancy were terminated. The Act does not apply in Northern Ireland.

Between 1997 and 1998:

- the number of legal abortions on women resident in England and Wales increased by 4.2% to 177,332;
- abortions rose by 11% in the under 20 age-group, by 6% in the over 30 age-group, but by only 1% in the 20 to 29 age-group;
- abortions carried out under the NHS increased by 6% to 131,372, while non-NHS abortions decreased by 1% to 45,960. NHS abortions represented 74% of legal abortions on women resident in England and Wales; and
- the overall abortion rate for women resident in England and Wales rose to 13.8 abortions for every 1,000 women aged 14 to 49, compared with a rate of 13.3 in 1997, while in Scotland it grew to 11.4 abortions for every 1,000 women residents aged 15 to 44.

Substance Misuse

Drug Misuse

The misuse of drugs, such as heroin, cocaine and amphetamines, is a serious social and health problem, and the Government is making the fight against such misuse a priority. It has reviewed its anti-drugs work and has drawn up a new drugs strategy for the UK (see p. 215). The health departments are contributing to the new strategy through their responsibilities for treatment, policy and publicising public health messages on prevention and reducing harm. Wales, Scotland and Northern Ireland have their own distinctive strategies; these too have been under review. In Scotland where the review is complete, the enhanced drugs strategy *Tackling Drugs in Scotland: Action in Partnership* sets out a comprehensive programme of action covering all service areas, with specific objectives and action priorities. In Wales the National Assembly will refocus the existing Drug and Alcohol Strategy *Forward Together*.

Research on various aspects of drug misuse is funded by several government departments. The Government is advised on matters relating to drug misuse and connected social problems by the Advisory Council on the Misuse of Drugs (in Scotland the Scottish Advisory Committee on Drug Misuse and in Wales the Substance Misuse Advisory Panel).

Prevention

As part of the Government's anti-drugs strategy, a new Drugs Prevention Advisory Service (DPAS) was set up in April 1999 (see p. 216). This replaced the Home Office Drugs Prevention Initiative which had provided funding for local drugs prevention teams in 12 areas of England.

The new DPAS works with Drug Action Teams in England to encourage good drugs prevention practice, based on available evidence, and to assist in developing appropriate demonstration programmes. There are nine regional teams, covering the whole of England.

In Wales a Strategic Prevention Action Plan on Drugs and Alcohol has been published and is currently being evaluated. The Welsh Drug and Alcohol Unit will monitor the implementation of the Plan.

The Government makes funds available through local education authorities in England and Wales to provide in-service training for teachers involved in drugs prevention work in schools. As part of the National Curriculum in England and Wales (see chapter 10), children in primary and secondary schools receive education on the dangers of drug misuse. In Scotland, education authorities are encouraged to address health education including drug education within a comprehensive programme of personal and social education.

Government publicity campaigns have been run since 1985 to persuade young people not to take drugs, and to advise parents, teachers and other professionals on how to recognise and combat the problem. A wide range of materials are used, including targeted press and radio advertising and drug educational literature. In Wales the Welsh Drug and Alcohol Unit has developed a media strategy in consultation with national broadcasters and press.

UK National Drugs Helpline

A national drugs and solvents telephone helpline provides 24-hour free confidential advice, counselling and information throughout the UK to anyone concerned about the health implications of drugs or solvent misuse. The telephone number is 0800 77 66 00.

Treatment and Rehabilitation

Treatment for drug dependence includes: specialist in-patient and residential detoxification and rehabilitation; substitute prescribing services; community drug dependency services; needle and syringe exchange schemes to combat the spread of HIV/AIDS and other blood-borne infections; advice and counselling; and after-care and support services. An increasing number of GPs treat drug misusers, but only a limited number of doctors are licensed to prescribe certain controlled drugs to them, such as heroin and cocaine. However, any doctor may prescribe methadone as a substitute drug for drug misusers. All doctors must notify the authorities of any patient they consider to be addicted to certain controlled drugs.

A number of non-statutory agencies work with, and complement, health service provision. Advice and rehabilitation services, including residential facilities, for example, are provided by many voluntary organisations.

The total amount available to health authorities in England for drug treatment services in 1999–2000 is £53.2 million. In addition, a grant is payable each year to local authorities to enable them to support voluntary organisations providing services to drug and alcohol misusers. In Scotland, £11.3 million is being made available to health boards in 1999–2000 for the support of drug treatment services. Additional funding has also been made available to fund alternatives to prosecution and imprisonment for drug misusing offenders.

Solvent Misuse

Government policy aims to prevent solvent misuse through educating young people, parents and professionals about the dangers and signs of misuse, and, where practicable, restricting the sales of solvent-based liquefied gas and aerosol products to young people.

In England, Wales and Northern Ireland it is an offence to supply such substances to children under 18 if the supplier knows or has reason to believe they are to be used to induce intoxication. In Scotland proceedings can be taken under the common law. From October 1999 it will be an offence in the UK to sell butane lighter refills to people under 18; these refills are implicated in more than 50% of deaths from solvent abuse.

The DH funds a hospital-based unit in London to collect and publish annual mortality statistics associated with solvent misuse. The latest available statistics show that the number of deaths has risen from 69 in 1995 to 73 in 1997, when solvent misuse accounted for one in 50 of all deaths among teenagers between the ages of 15 and 19.

Alcohol Misuse

Alcohol is consumed by over 90% of the adult population. While the vast majority drink sensibly and safely, alcohol misuse does cause preventable illness and social problems, and is a factor in many accidents.

The most widely accepted estimate of the cost of alcohol misuse in England and Wales is £2.7 billion a year. Between 9 and 15 million working days each year are thought to be lost through alcohol-related absence, while up to 40,000 deaths a year are estimated to be alcohol-related.

The Government seeks to tackle alcohol-related problems through a co-ordinated programme of action across government

---

The Government is preparing a new strategy to tackle alcohol misuse in England. Its broad aims are:

- to encourage people who drink to do so sensibly in line with guidance, so as to avoid alcohol-related problems;
- to protect individuals and communities from anti-social and criminal behaviour related to alcohol misuse; and
- to provide services of proven effectiveness that enable people to overcome their alcohol misuse problems.

The Government intends to publish the strategy, after public consultation, early in the year 2000.

New strategies are also envisaged in Wales, where there is a combined Drug and Alcohol Strategy, and in Scotland, where developing the strategy will be the responsibility of the Scottish Advisory Committee on Alcohol Misuse.

---

departments, and involving health and local authorities, the voluntary and private sectors, employers, the police and criminal justice system, and the alcohol industry.

Part of the funds allocated to the Health Education Authority (see p. 205) is for promoting sensible drinking in England, and equivalent bodies are similarly funded in other parts of Britain. 'Drinkline' provides confidential telephone advice about alcohol problems and services in England and Wales.

Treatment and rehabilitation within the NHS includes in-patient and out-patient services in general and psychiatric hospitals and some specialised alcohol treatment units. Primary care teams and voluntary organisations providing treatment and rehabilitation in hostels, day centres and advisory services also play an important role.

There is close co-operation between statutory and voluntary organisations. In England, Alcohol Concern plays a prominent role in improving services for problem drinkers and their families; increasing public awareness of alcohol misuse; and improving training for professional and voluntary workers. The Scottish Council on Alcohol has a similar role in Scotland.

A report, *Reducing Alcohol Related Harm in Northern Ireland,* was published in June 1999 and is being considered by the Department of Health and Social Services (NI), with a view to formulating a strategy for the Province.

Communicable Diseases

Health authorities/health boards have a key responsibility for prevention and control of outbreaks of infectious disease, liasing closely with colleagues in environmental health departments of local authorities. They are assisted by the Public Health Laboratory Service, which aims to protect the population from infection through the detection, diagnosis, surveillance, prevention and control of communicable diseases in England and Wales. Similar facilities are provided in Scotland by the Scottish Centre for Infection and Environmental Health and, in Northern Ireland, by the Communicable Disease Surveillance Centre, the Northern Ireland Public Health Laboratory and other hospital microbiology laboratories.

Immunisation

Health authorities/health boards carry out programmes of immunisation against diphtheria, measles, mumps, rubella, poliomyelitis, tetanus, tuberculosis, whooping cough and haemophilus influenzae type B infection ('Hib'). Immunisation is not compulsory. Parents are provided with information about the safety and efficacy of vaccines and are encouraged to have their children immunised. Immunisations are mainly given by GPs and their practice nurses.

Annual immunisation rates are now at their highest ever levels—for example, the uptake of diphtheria, tetanus and polio immunisation by the age of two in 1997–98 was 96%. The incidence of such childhood diseases is at its lowest ever level. Since the introduction of the Hib vaccine in 1992, Hib meningitis has been almost completely eliminated in young children. A new vaccine to protect against meningococcaal Group C has been developed, with DH funding, and is to be introduced into the immunisation programme from autumn 1999. The UK will be the first country in the world to use this vaccine.

HIV/AIDS

The latest figures from the Public Health Laboratory Service show that to the end of December 1998 there were a total of 16,028 cases of AIDS and 33,764 cases of HIV reported in the UK. Of these, 90% were from England with HIV infection rates remaining higher in London than elsewhere in the UK. Although the UK has a relatively low prevalence of HIV/AIDS as a result of sustained public education and health campaigns, about 3,000 new infections continue to be reported each year. The use of combination drug therapy is delaying progression of the disease, and mortality in 1998 had fallen to almost a quarter of that in 1995–96. As a consequence, the number of individuals within the population infected with HIV is increasing. During 1998 there were 16,891 people with HIV in contact with the statutory health services.

Those most vulnerable to HIV infection remain homosexual/bisexual men, injecting drug users and people from high prevalence communities, currently those from sub-Saharan Africa. Although the UK has not seen a large-scale spread of HIV to the heterosexual population, the rate in pregnant women giving birth in London remains relatively high at one in 500. The Government has introduced a range of initiatives to inform pregnant women about having an HIV test as an integral part of their antenatal care. Most HIV-infected pregnant women accept measures to decrease the risk of passing the infection to their babies. Health authorities are aiming to achieve a reduction in the number of children with HIV by around 80% by 2002.

In England NHS funding in 1999–2000 for HIV/AIDS treatment and care to health authorities amounts to £234 million, with a further £53.4 million for HIV prevention. A consultation paper on a proposed new government strategy for HIV/AIDS is expected by spring 2000.

Some £15.5 million has been made available in 1999–2000 to local authorities as a contribution towards the cost of community care services for people with severe HIV and AIDS. In addition, over £1.6 million has been made available to voluntary organisations who provide care information and support services to people infected or affected by HIV/AIDS.

Strategies by the Government to prevent transmission include:

- placing contracts for national health HIV/AIDS health promotion work for both the general population and groups at risk;
- providing information on antenatal HIV testing which helps pregnant women to reach an informed decision; and
- the National AIDS Helpline, which provides confidential information and advice on all aspects of HIV and AIDS.

A concerted approach is being maintained, spanning government, the NHS, local authorities and the voluntary sector (including women's groups, religious communities and organisations working with ethnic minorities).

Tuberculosis

The UK has an excellent record of tuberculosis (TB) control. Notifications of TB are at the relatively low level of around 6,500 cases a year, compared with nearly 50,000 in 1950. These levels have been achieved and maintained through an immunisation programme, treatment of identified cases and screening of their close contacts, screening and treatment for immigrants from countries with a high prevalence of TB and active surveillance. However, there has been a worldwide resurgence in TB that is having a small but important impact on trends in the UK, although small increases in the annual number of cases between 1987 and 1993 have since levelled out. The Government has taken steps to strengthen the surveillance, prevention and control of TB, including drug-resistant TB, within the UK. A detailed survey of notifications is in progress and is expected to provide important information on trends in incidence.

Cancer Care

Care and treatment of cancer forms a significant part of the NHS's work, consuming nearly 7% of its total budget. A framework for the future development of cancer services, announced in 1995, recommended that services should be organised at three levels, with *primary care* seen as the initial focus of care; *cancer units* created in many local hospitals of a sufficient size to support a multidisciplinary team with the expertise and facilities to treat commoner cancers; and *cancer centres* situated in larger hospitals to treat less common cancers and to support smaller cancer units by providing services not available in all local hospitals. Health authorities/health boards are now planning to implement these changes.

The Government is committed to improving the provision and availability of high-quality cancer services and is directing savings achieved from cuts in the cost of the NHS internal market (see p. 188) into patient care.

Cancer Screening

Breast cancer is recognised as a major health problem in the UK: some 14,000 women die from it each year; and one in ten women will develop it. The UK was the first country in the European Union to introduce a nationwide breast screening programme, under which women aged between 50 and 64 are invited for mammography (breast X-ray) every three years by computerised call and recall systems. Women aged 65 and over are entitled to request screening. In 1997–98 in England:

- 64% of women aged 50 to 64 invited for screening were screened;
- 1.2 million women of *all ages* were screened within the programme; and
- 6,914 cases of cancer were diagnosed among women screened.

The nationwide cervical screening programme aims to reduce death from cancer of the cervix by inviting women aged between 20 and 64 (20 and 60 in Scotland) to take a smear test at least once every five years.

Special payments are made to GPs who achieve targets of 50% and 80% for the uptake of smear tests. The Government estimates that almost all GPs now receive these payments for meeting cervical screening targets. In England over 85% of women invited to attend were screened over the last five years. In 1997–98 in Scotland 87% of women invited to attend were screened over the last 5½ years.

Deaths from cervical cancer in England and Wales have fallen since the programme began, dropping from 1,942 in 1988 to 1,155 in 1998, and in Scotland from 191 in 1988 to 145 in 1998.

Health Education

In England, Scotland and Northern Ireland responsibility for health education lies with separate health education authorities, which work alongside the national health departments. These authorities are part of the NHS. They are the Health Education Authority; the Health Education Board for Scotland; and the Health Promotion Agency for Northern Ireland. Their aims are:

- to provide information and advice about health directly to members of the public;
- to support other organisations and health professionals who provide health education to members of the public; and
- to advise the Government and other policy makers on health education and promotion.

In Wales a new health promotion division has been established in the National Assembly for Wales, with responsibility for health promotion policy and strategy, and the development and delivery of national programmes and initiatives to promote health and well-being.

The health education authorities and the National Assembly for Wales health promotion division undertake a range of programmes and initiatives, which focus on improving health and inequality. These include initiatives on: coronary heart disease, stroke, cancer, smoking, diet, accidents, drug abuse, alcohol misuse, physical activity, sexual health and HIV/AIDS, mental health and tackling inequalities in health.

Almost all NHS health authorities/health boards have their own health education service, which works closely with health professionals, health visitors, community groups, local employers and others to determine the most suitable local programmes.

Nutrition

Despite the growing public awareness in recent years of the importance of a healthy diet, the proportion of adults who are obese or overweight has increased. In 1997, 20% of women and 17% of men aged 16 and over in England were classified as obese, compared with 8% and 6% respectively in 1980 in Great Britain.

Medical research has shown that a diet which is low in fats, especially saturates, and rich in fruit, vegetables and starchy foods contributes to good health and can reduce the risk of certain serious illnesses, such as coronary heart disease, stroke, and some cancers.

The Committee on the Medical Aspects of Food and Nutrition Policy published its report *Nutritional Aspects of the Development of Cancer* in 1998. It noted that research suggests that diet might contribute to about one-third of all cancers. Its main recommendations are consistent with the Government's healthy eating advice to the effect that a healthy and balanced diet is one which is varied and rich in fruit and vegetables and dietary fibre. The report also underlined the importance of maintaining a healthy body weight throughout adult life.

The major supermarket groups and most food manufacturers have introduced voluntary labelling schemes indicating the energy, fat, protein and carbohydrate content of food. Nutrition labelling is compulsory on products for which a nutritional claim is made.

ENVIRONMENTAL HEALTH

Environmental health provides public health protection through control of the physical environment—atmospheric pollution and noise; contaminated land, food and water; waste management; housing; occupational health and safety; communicable diseases; and statutory nuisances. In the UK no single government department is responsible for environmental health as a whole, although the DH advises other government departments on the health implications of their policies. Environmental health services are provided by local government.

Professionally trained environmental health officers are employed principally by local authorities. They are concerned with inspection, health promotion and regulation.

The Institute for Environment and Health, established by the Medical Research Council (see p. 436), is concerned mainly with research and management of research into the hazards to which people may be exposed through the environment. In Scotland the Scottish Centre for Infection and Environmental Health provides surveillance and advisory services on environmental health matters.

DH, the National Assembly for Wales, the Scottish Executive and the Northern Ireland Department of Health and Social Services have established National Focus, a unit based in Cardiff, to co-ordinate work on responses to chemical incidents and surveillance of health effects of environmental chemicals. A major research programme to find out more about the health effects of chemical pollutants in the environment was announced in 1998.

Accidents

The Department of Trade and Industry records home and leisure accidents needing hospital treatment. Data for 1997 show that every five hours, one older person dies from an accidental fall in the home. Altogether around 1.2 million people in the UK go to a hospital casualty department each year as a result of an accidental fall. Around 43,000 people experience falls from ladders each year, and burns from barbecues are thought to affect about 500 people.

Food Safety

Under the Food Safety Act 1990, it is illegal to sell or supply food that is unfit for human consumption or falsely or misleadingly labelled. The Act covers a broad range of commercial activities related to food production, to the sources from which it is derived, such as crops and animals, and to articles which come into contact with food. There are also more detailed regulations which apply to all types of food and drink and their ingredients. Local authorities are responsible for enforcing food law in two main areas: trading standards officers deal with the labelling of food, its composition and most cases of chemical contamination; environmental health officers deal with hygiene, with cases of microbiological contamination of foods, and with any food which for any reason is unfit for human consumption. See p. 451 for details of the proposed new independent Food Standards Agency.

CJD and Public Health

CJD (Creutzfeldt-Jakob disease) is a rare transmissible spongiform encephalopathy in humans. In 1996 the Government announced that the National CJD Surveillance Unit in Edinburgh had identified a previously unrecognised form of the disease, variant CJD (vCJD).[1] The Spongiform Encephalopathy Advisory Committee (SEAC) concluded that the most likely explanation, in the absence of any credible alternative, was that these cases were linked to exposure to BSE (see p. 451) before the introduction of the specified bovine offals ban in 1989. Since 1996 SEAC has continued to review emerging scientific findings. In 1997 SEAC considered the results of two separate experiments and concluded that they provided convincing evidence that the agent that causes BSE is the same as that which causes vCJD. However, these results did not provide information about the route of infection. In light of the increased number of cases of vCJD, the Committee has concluded that vCJD is an acquired prion disease caused by exposure to a BSE-like agent.

The direct connection of BSE as the cause of vCJD is not absolutely proved scientifically, but to safeguard public health the Government is providing substantial additional funding for research into CJD and BSE, including the work carried out at the National CJD Surveillance Unit, which monitors the incidence of the disease.

An independent public inquiry was set up in 1998 to establish and review the history of the

---

[1] Sometimes referred to as new variant CJD (nvCJD).

emergence and identification of BSE and vCJD in the UK; it is due to report by 31 March 2000. (See chapter 27 for details of government measures to control the spread of BSE.)

Safety of Medicines

Only medicines that have been granted a marketing authorisation issued by the European Medicines Evaluation Agency or the Medicines Control Agency may be sold or supplied to the public. Marketing authorisations are issued following scientific assessment on the basis of safety, quality and efficacy.

THE HEALTH PROFESSIONS

Doctors and Dentists

Only people on the medical or dentists' registers may practise as doctors or dentists in the NHS. University medical and dental schools are responsible for undergraduate teaching; the NHS provides hospital and community facilities for training. Full registration as a doctor requires five or six years' training in a medical school and hospital, and the community, with a further year's experience in a hospital. For a dentist, five years' training at a dental school is required plus satisfactory completion of one year's mandatory vocational training before working as a principal in the General Dental Services of the NHS is permitted.

Following a review of specialist medical training, the Government has introduced a new specialist registrar grade, which reduces from three to two the number of specialist training grades, and will increasingly allow doctors to complete their training at an earlier age. This change, together with other policies to increase consultant numbers and reduce junior doctors' hours, are expected to increase the amount of service provided to NHS patients by consultants.

The regulating body for the medical profession is the General Medical Council and, for dentists, the General Dental Council. The main professional associations are the British Medical Association and the British Dental Association.

Nurses, Midwives and Health Visitors

Nursing students undertake the pre-registration Diploma in Higher Education (Project 2000) programme, which emphasises health promotion as well as care of the sick and enables students to work either in hospitals or in the community. The programme lasts three years and consists of periods of college study combined with practical experience in hospital and in the community.

Midwifery education programmes for registered general/adult nurses take 18 months, but the direct entry programme lasts three years. Health visitors are registered adult nurses who have a further specialist qualification in health visiting. District nurses are registered adult nurses who have a further specialist qualification in district nursing and care for clients in the community.

The United Kingdom Central Council for Nursing, Midwifery and Health Visiting is responsible for regulating and registering these professions. Four National Boards—for England, Wales, Scotland and Northern Ireland—are responsible for ensuring that training courses meet Central Council requirements as to their type, content and standard. The Government intends to bring forward proposals for legislation to replace the existing structure with a single regulatory body. The main professional associations are the Royal College of Nursing, the Royal College of Midwives and the Community Practitioners and Health Visitors Association.

Pharmacists

Only people on the register of pharmaceutical chemists may practise as pharmacists. Registration requires four years' training in a school of pharmacy, followed by one year's practical experience in a community or hospital pharmacy approved for training by regulatory bodies for the profession—the Royal Pharmaceutical Society of Great Britain or the Pharmaceutical Society of Northern Ireland.

Optometrists (Opthalmic Opticians)

The General Optical Council regulates the professions of ophthalmic optician and dispensing optician. Only registered ophthalmic opticians (or registered ophthalmic medical practitioners) may test sight; training for the former takes four years, including a year of practical experience under supervision. Dispensing opticians take a two-year full-time course with a year's practical experience, or follow a part-time day-release course while employed with an optician.

Other Health Professions

The Council for Professions Supplementary to Medicine and its professional boards regulate the initial training and subsequent practice of nine health professions: chiropodists; radiographers; orthoptists; physiotherapists; occupational therapists; dietitians; medical laboratory scientific officers; prosthetists and orthotists; and arts therapists (art, drama and music therapists).

The boards are responsible for promoting high standards of professional education and conduct among members, approving training institutions, qualifications and courses, and maintaining registers of those who have qualified for state registration—state registration in these professions is mandatory for employment in health authorities, Trusts and local authority social services. These criteria will shortly apply to prosthetists and orthotists, and to arts therapists. Measures to extend state registration to the professions of speech and language therapists, clinical scientists and paramedics came into force in June 1999.

The Government also intends to bring forward proposals for legislation to reform the Professions Supplementary to Medicine Act 1960 to improve protection to the public through the statutory regulation of key groups of health professions.

Dental therapists and dental hygienists are almost exclusively recruited from certified dental nurses who have taken at least one year's training. Dental therapists then take a two-to-three-year training course and dental hygienists take a course lasting two years; both carry out specified dental work under the supervision of a registered dentist.

National and Scottish Vocational Qualifications (NVQs and SVQs—see p. 130) have been developed for healthcare support workers, ambulance personnel, operating department practitioners, physiological measurement technicians, and administrative and clerical staff.

Complementary Medicine

Complementary medicine (or complementary therapies) can cover a range of therapies and practices, the best known being osteopathy, chiropractic, homoeopathy, acupuncture and herbalism. With the exception of homoeopathy, complementary medicine is usually available only outside the NHS. There is a wide variety of regulatory and professional arrangements ranging from statutory regulation to little or no regulation at all. The Government is providing funding to encourage professional self-regulation.

HEALTH ARRANGEMENTS WITH OTHER COUNTRIES

The member states of the European Economic Area (EEA—see p. 81) have special health arrangements under which EEA nationals resident in a member state are entitled to receive emergency treatment, either free or at a reduced cost, during visits to other EEA countries. Treatment is provided, in most cases, on production of a valid Form E111 which, in the UK, people normally obtain from a post office before travelling. There are also arrangements for people who go to another EEA country specifically for medical care, or who require continuing treatment for a pre-existing condition. Unless falling into an exempt category (for example, foreign students) or covered by an appropriate EC form, visitors to the UK are generally expected to pay for routine, non-emergency treatment, or if the purpose of their visit is to seek specific medical treatment. The UK also has a number of separate bilateral agreements with certain other countries, including Australia and New Zealand.

Further Reading

Department of Health Annual Report 1999. The Government's Expenditure Plans 1999–2000. Cm 4203. The Stationery Office, 1999.

Better Health Better Wales. Cm 3922. The Stationery Office, 1998.

Designed to Care: Renewing the National Health Service in Scotland. Cm 3811. The Stationery Office, 1998.

Fit for the Future (consultation paper on the future of the Health and Personal Social Services in Northern Ireland). The Stationery Office, 1998.

The New NHS: Modern, Dependable. Cm 3807. The Stationery Office, 1997.

NHS Wales—Putting Patients First. Cm 3841. The Stationery Office, 1998.

Our Healthier Nation: A Contract for Health. Cm 3852. The Stationery Office, 1998.

Reducing Health Inequalities: an Action Report. The Stationery Office, 1998.

A Regional Strategy for Health and Social Wellbeing. Northern Ireland Department of Health and Social Services, 1997.

Report of the Independent Inquiry into Inequalities in Health, Sir Donald Acheson. The Stationery Office, 1998.

Saving Lives: Our Healthier Nation. Cm 4386. The Stationery Office, 1999.

Smoking Kills. Cm 4177. The Stationery Office, 1998.

Working Together for a Healthier Scotland. Cm 3584. The Stationery Office, 1998.

Annuals

Health and Personal Social Services Statistics for England. The Stationery Office.

Health in Scotland Annual Report. Scottish Executive.

Health Statistics Wales.

On the State of the Public Health. The Annual Report of the Chief Medical Officer of the Department of Health. The Stationery Office.

Scottish Health Statistics. Information and Statistics Division, National Health Service in Scotland.

Welsh Health: Annual Report of the Chief Medical Officer. National Assembly for Wales.

Website

Department of Health: www.doh.gov.uk

14 Criminal and Civil Justice

The first phase of reform of the civil justice system in England and Wales was implemented in April 1999. The Access to Justice Act 1999, which received Royal Assent in July, contains radical reforms to legal aid and the provision of legal services. The Youth Justice and Criminal Evidence Act 1999, also enacted in July, includes new measures to ensure that young people take greater responsibility for their behaviour and to provide better protection for vulnerable witnesses in criminal trials.

Introduction

The United Kingdom does not have a single legal system. Instead, England and Wales, Scotland and Northern Ireland have their own systems, with considerable differences in law, judicial procedure and court structure. There is, however, substantial similarity on many points and a large volume of modern legislation applies throughout the UK. In all three systems there is a common distinction between criminal law and civil law.

Criminal and Civil Law

Laws can be classified as either criminal or civil. Criminal law deals with wrongs affecting the community for which a prosecution may be brought in the criminal courts. Civil law is about deciding disputes between two or more parties—individuals, companies or other organisations—and for providing a means of

legal scrutiny of the actions of public bodies. The purpose of civil proceedings is not to punish, but to obtain compensation or some other appropriate remedy, although in England and Wales the payment of damages may sometimes have a punitive element.

The distinction between civil and criminal matters is imprecise. Courts may be classified as criminal courts and civil courts, but in England and Wales and Northern Ireland magistrates' courts have both a civil and a criminal jurisdiction as have the sheriff courts in Scotland. Conduct may amount to both a civil and a criminal wrong. However, the court of trial and the rules of procedure and evidence will usually differ in civil and criminal cases.

Increasingly, civil remedies and the criminal process are being used together to deal with social problems. The Crime and Disorder Act 1998 has introduced an anti-social behaviour order, which is a civil order designed to prevent continued criminal and sub-criminal anti-social acts. Breach of this civil order constitutes a criminal offence. Other recent examples of this overlap are orders relating to protection from harassment, and sex offender orders, designed to prevent behaviour by sex offenders that poses a serious risk to the public.

Sources of Law

Statutes passed by Parliament are the ultimate source of law. There are no legal limits on what may be done by Act of Parliament, although a legal duty exists to comply with European Community (EC) law. A statute may also confer power on a minister, local authority or other executive body to make delegated legislation. Provided that the person exercising the power keeps within what Parliament intended, delegated legislation is equivalent to statute. A court cannot declare a statute to be invalid (but see the European Convention on Human Rights—below), and a statute may reverse a decision by the courts with which Parliament disagrees. Parliament can repeal an Act, wholly or partly, replacing it with new provisions. Sometimes this will follow recommendations for law reform from an official committee, or from the Law Commission, a statutory body established to examine and report on law reform matters. Some Acts create new law, while others consolidate the law by drawing together existing law on a given topic.

Modern statutes are usually brought into effect by an Order made by a minister of the Crown. This allows provisions to be brought into effect when it is practical to do so. The operation of a statutory provision may be tested by the use of a pilot scheme. Occasionally, if circumstances or policies change, provisions are not brought into effect, and may be repealed.

Many key areas of law have, over the centuries, developed through the decisions of the courts. This is known as *common law*. The doctrine of binding precedent means that decisions of higher courts bind those courts lower down in the court hierarchy. This ensures consistency of judicial approach. Judges give reasons for their decisions, and principles of law are stated, developed and modified. The common law can develop new rules, or modify existing ones, but judges generally take great care not to develop the common law in ways involving policy choices best left to Parliament. When the legality of government action is being tested, a court will try to ensure that it is not overstepping its proper role; it should avoid examining the merits of the particular action or policy being challenged.

European Sources

EC law, which applies in the UK by virtue of its membership of the European Union (see p. 69), derives from the EC treaties, from the Community legislation adopted under them, and from the decisions of the European Court of Justice. That court has the ultimate authority, under the Treaty of Rome, to decide points of Community law. Where a point arises before the UK court, it may refer the point of law to the Court of Justice for it to decide. Sometimes a court is obliged to make a reference to the European Court.

The decisions of the Court of Justice do not directly bind British courts, but the UK is under treaty obligations to uphold Community law. Consequently, British courts are obliged to apply European law, even at the expense of not applying the provision of an Act of Parliament. If a rule of statute or common law is incompatible with Community law, it is Community law that will be applied by a UK court.

European Convention on Human Rights

The European Convention on Human Rights is an international treaty containing a statement of some basic human rights, such as right to life, prohibition of torture, right to a fair trial, respect for private and family life, and freedom of expression and assembly. These rights have to be balanced against competing rights and public interests (for example public health, public safety and security).

Although the Convention was ratified by the UK in 1951, it is not part of UK domestic law. However, the judgments of the European Court of Human Rights are binding in international law on the UK, and successive governments have responded to adverse findings by amending domestic law or practice where necessary.

The Human Rights Act 1998, which will be brought fully into effect in October 2000, requires all public authorities, including courts of law, to act in accordance with the Convention rights. It enables individuals to rely on those rights in any legal proceedings and to bring a claim against a public authority which has acted incompatibly with those rights. The Act requires a court to give effect to legislation, as far as possible, in a way which is compatible with Convention rights. A court cannot declare invalid an Act of Parliament which is incompatible with the Convention, but the higher courts may make a declaration of incompatibility, which will trigger a special procedure enabling a minister to change the legislation in question quickly to make it compatible with Convention rights.

Under the Scotland Act 1998, the Scottish Parliament and Executive may not exercise their powers in a way which is incompatible with any of the Convention rights.

Personnel of the Law

The law is enforced by judicial officers, ranging from judges in the House of Lords and the superior courts to stipendiary and lay justices who, together with juries in certain cases, are responsible for deciding disputed cases. The law also depends on officers of the court who have general or specialised functions of an administrative, and sometimes of a judicial, nature in the courts to which they are attached.

Courts are presided over by judges and magistrates. Judges are legally qualified, being appointed from the ranks of practising barristers and advocates or solicitors. They have independence of office, and can be removed only in rare and limited circumstances involving misconduct or incapacity. They are not subject to ministerial control or direction.

Lay magistrates in England and Wales, and justices of the peace in Scotland, are trained in order to give them sufficient knowledge of the law, including the rules of evidence, and of the nature and purpose of sentencing. In Northern Ireland members of a lay panel who serve in juvenile courts undertake training courses. Lay magistrates are advised on the law by magistrates' clerks. The Lord Chancellor appoints lay magistrates from names submitted by local advisory committees; district court justices in Scotland are appointed by the First Minister on the recommendation of local justices of the peace advisory committees. Some courts have one or more full-time, legally qualified magistrates (stipendiaries). In Northern Ireland, resident magistrates, drawn from practising solicitors or barristers, have powers similar to those of stipendiary magistrates. There are over 30,000 lay magistrates and 90 stipendiary magistrates in England and Wales, and 4,000 justices of the peace in Scotland. In Northern Ireland there are 17 resident magistrates and 23 deputy (part-time) magistrates.

Although people are free to conduct their own cases if they so wish, barristers—or advocates in Scotland—and solicitors generally represent the interests of parties to a dispute, and it is rare for an accused person in a criminal case to be unrepresented. There are over 9,000 practising barristers in England and Wales and around 71,640 practising solicitors. Scotland has about 400 practising advocates and some 8,250 solicitors; in Northern Ireland there are about 450 barristers. Barristers practise as individuals, but join a group of other barristers, in Chambers. Advocates practise as individuals and do not operate from Chambers as barristers do. Solicitors usually operate in partnership with other solicitors. Large firms of solicitors will comprise not only qualified staff, but also legal executives and support staff. Certain legal functions may be performed by non-lawyers—licensed conveyancers can act in conveyancing matters (the transfer of interests in land).

Traditionally, rights of audience in the higher courts—the Judicial Committee of the Privy Council, House of Lords, Court of Appeal, High Court and Crown Court, High Court of Justiciary (Scotland) and Court of Session (Scotland)—have mostly been limited to barristers and advocates, who are regarded as specialist court pleaders. The power to extend those rights of audience has existed since 1990, including in some circumstances the power to extend them to persons beside solicitors, barristers and advocates (such as non-qualified legal staff known as legal executives). In 1998 the Government proposed that all qualified barristers, advocates and solicitors should have rights of audience in the higher courts, provided they meet relevant experience and training requirements. This would include solicitors directly employed by government departments, the Crown Prosecution Service (CPS) and local authorities. These proposals will be implemented under the Access to Justice Act 1999.

The two branches of the profession have separate professional bodies: the Bar Council for barristers (in Scotland, the Faculty of Advocates); and the Law Society (or the Law Society of Scotland) for solicitors. The profession is self-regulating, with the professional bodies exercising disciplinary control over their members.

The Legal Services Ombudsman for England and Wales conducts investigations into the way professional bodies handle complaints against barristers, solicitors and licensed conveyancers. The Scottish Legal Services Ombudsman performs a similar task.

Measures against Crime

Crime Statistics

There are two main measures of the scale of crime in the UK—the recording of crimes by the police, and periodic surveys which ask representative samples of the population about their experiences of crime.

Recorded Crime

In 1997, in England and Wales:

- overall recorded crime totalled almost 4.6 million offences (see Table 14.1), a decrease of 8.7% compared to 1996;

- the overall clear-up rate was 28%;

- about 91% of offences recorded by the police were against property, while 8% involved violence; and

- vehicle crime accounted for about 24% of all recorded crimes.

In 1998 the Government amended the way notifiable offences are recorded in England

Table 14.1: Notifiable Crimes Recorded by the Police in England and Wales, 1997 *thousands*	
Offence Group	**1997**
Violence against the person	250.8
Sexual offences	33.2
Burglary	1,015.0
Robbery	63.1
Theft and handling stolen goods	2,165.0
Fraud and forgery	134.4
Criminal damage	877.0
Other	59.8
Total	**4,598.3**

Source: Home Office

and Wales, changing the counting rules so that the number of crimes corresponds more closely to the number of victims. The first figures under the new rules will be for the period April 1998 to March 1999 and should be published in October 1999. The 1997 figures reproduced above, using the previous recording method, represented the fifth consecutive yearly fall in overall crime.

In Scotland figures show that there were 432,000 crimes recorded by the police in the 1998 calendar year. This represents a 3% increase on the 1997 figure and is the first rise in recorded crime in Scotland in seven years. The overall crime clear-up rate rose to 41%.

Recorded crime in Northern Ireland in 1997 totalled over 62,200 offences, representing a fall of 9% on the 1996 level. About 78% of recorded offences were against property. The overall clear-up rate was 31%.

Crime Surveys

The British Crime Survey (BCS) is a large household survey first conducted in 1982, which has a sample representative of people aged 16 and over and of private households in England and Wales. The BCS asks respondents whether they have experienced certain personal and household crimes in the preceding year, regardless of whether or not they reported the incident to the police. The survey therefore provides a measure of those crimes not reported to, or recorded by, the

The following figures relating to 1900, for indictable offences known to the police, are from the official *Judicial Statistics, England and Wales*. While they cannot be compared directly with current statistics, given the changes in recording practices and in population levels, they still give an illustration of the extent, and type, of crime at that time.

Offences against the person	3,490
Offences against property, with violence	7,764
Offences against property, without violence	63,604
Malicious injury to property (for example, arson, criminal damage)	444
Forgery and counterfeiting	486
Other offences	2,146
Total	**77,934**

police. It also provides a measure of the underlying trend in crime that is not affected by changes in the public's willingness to report incidents to the police. The survey can also show the types of people most at risk of victimisation of particular types of crime, and what people think of the police and judiciary, and about issues such as fear of crime. The 1998 BCS estimated that there were 16.4 million crimes in 1997 (an overall fall of 14% since the last survey which covered crime in 1995). There was a 7% decrease in burglaries and a 19% fall in vehicle theft between 1995 and 1997; the number of violent crimes also fell by 17%.

The 1996 Scottish Crime Survey estimated that just under 1 million crimes were committed against individuals and private households in Scotland during 1995. This was 8% fewer than the number estimated in the 1993 survey.

Crime Reduction

Reducing crime, particularly youth crime, is central to the Government's criminal justice policy. Within the Home Office, the Crime Reduction Unit aims to encourage and develop strategies and tactics to this end. The unit supports the police crime reduction effort through its Crime Prevention College (in North Yorkshire), which is the national centre for training police officers in prevention skills.

Significant crime reduction initiatives include:

- a £250 million Crime Reduction Programme, announced by the Home Secretary in 1998, which focuses on reducing burglary and promoting targeted policing;

- a £150 million investment in closed-circuit television (CCTV) surveillance systems in public areas such as housing estates, shopping centres, railway stations and car parks;

- Neighbourhood Watch schemes, in which residents look out for suspicious activity in their area and inform the police;

- crime prevention panels, which meet regularly to examine crime problems in their area and to suggest practical solutions;

- youth action groups, encouraging young people to tackle problems relevant to them—for example bullying, vandalism or drug misuse; and

- partnerships set up under the Crime and Disorder Act 1998, which bring together the police, local authorities and other relevant agencies to develop strategies for dealing with local crime problems.

There is a Crime Prevention Council in Scotland and a Crime Prevention Panel in Northern Ireland.

Crime and Disorder Act 1998

The Crime and Disorder Act 1998 creates a framework designed to keep individuals, particularly young offenders, out of the criminal justice system, and to ensure timely action to prevent reoffending. Particular emphasis is placed on preventing offending behaviour by persons under 18 (see p. 225).

The Act requires police services and local authorities in England and Wales to develop statutory partnerships for crime prevention and the promotion of community safety. The partnerships must examine local levels of crime and disorder, consult local people and then set targets for tackling the problems that have been identified. The statutory provisions do not, however, apply to Scotland, where police forces and local authorities already enter into such partnerships.

Prohibitive anti-social behaviour orders may be applied to individuals or groups whose threatening and disruptive conduct harasses the local community. Anyone in breach of such an order is guilty of a criminal offence. The Act also empowers the courts to grant an order against convicted sex offenders, prohibiting behaviour which causes concern for public safety (for example, loitering near schools). Anti-social behaviour orders and sex offender orders are applicable throughout the UK.

Control of Weapons

The UK has strict legislative controls on firearms. The police license the possession of firearms and have powers to regulate their safekeeping and movement. A ban on the private ownership of machine guns, high-powered self-loading rifles and burst-fire weapons has been extended to include all handguns. It is illegal to manufacture, sell or import certain weapons such as knuckledusters. Penalties relating to the carrying of knives have been increased.

Helping Victims and Witnesses

In England and Wales a government-funded organisation, Victim Support, provides practical help and emotional support to victims of crime with the help of 16,000 volunteers. It also runs the Witness Service, which advises victims and other witnesses attending Crown Court centres (and is developing similar services in magistrates' courts). Broadly similar support schemes operate in Scotland and Northern Ireland.

In 1998 the Government published a report (*Speaking up for Justice*) on improving the treatment of witnesses (including children) who become involved in the criminal justice system in England and Wales. The report made 78 recommendations to give greater protection to vulnerable witnesses and those subject to intimidation, from the initial crime investigation stage through to the trial and beyond. These included:

- a ban on cross-examination of victims of rape and serious sexual assault by defendants who are unrepresented in court;

- live CCTV links and screens for witnesses likely to be distressed by being in court and facing defendants;

- video-recorded evidence for vulnerable adults and recorded pre-trial cross-examination for witnesses suffering from mental or physical disabilities; and

- measures to help child witnesses give evidence and understand questioning in court.

Twenty-six of the report's recommendations required statutory force and have been included in the Youth Justice and Criminal Evidence Act 1999.

Blameless victims of violent crime in England, Wales and Scotland may be eligible for compensation from public funds under the Criminal Injuries Compensation Scheme. In Northern Ireland there are separate statutory arrangements for compensation for criminal injuries, and for malicious damage to property.

Tackling Drug Misuse

The problem of drug misuse remains formidable. Levels of drug seizures reveal the increasing threat of a widening range of trafficking routes to the UK against a background of expanding global production.

In 1998 the Government's UK Anti-Drugs Co-ordinator assumed responsibility for co-ordinating the fight against illegal drugs in the UK and drew up a ten-year national strategy (*Tackling Drugs to Build a Better Britain*). This cross-government strategy—focusing mainly on England, but reflecting the UK and international dimension of the problem—has four main elements:

- helping young people resist drug misuse in order to achieve their full potential in society;

- protecting communities from drug-related anti-social and criminal behaviour;
- enabling people to overcome drug problems through treatment; and
- stifling the availability of illegal drugs on the streets.

As part of the strategy, action is being taken to:

- channel seized assets from drug dealers into anti-drug work;
- provide appropriate drug education to all children aged from 5–16;
- pilot drug treatment and testing orders for offenders;[1] and
- shift resources to preventing, rather than reacting to, the problem.

The UK Anti-Drugs Co-ordinator's first annual report and action plan was published in May 1999.

The Drugs Prevention Advisory Service (DPAS) was launched in April 1999 (replacing the previous Drugs Prevention Initiative) to promote community-based drugs prevention at local, regional and national level in line with the objectives of the Government's national strategy. In particular, the DPAS provides information, advice and support to local Drug Action Teams (the bodies charged with local implementation of the national strategy) to encourage good drugs prevention practice based on available and emerging evidence, and promotes consistent and coherent prevention policy across Government. DPAS teams have been established in each of the nine Government Regions in England (see p. 10).

Countering Terrorism

In the light of serious terrorist attacks that have taken place in the UK, it is the Government's view that the ordinary criminal law is not sufficient to deal with terrorism

effectively. The law has been supplemented by the Prevention of Terrorism (Temporary Provisions) Act 1989 (PTA) and successive Northern Ireland (Emergency Provisions) Acts (EPA), and most recently amended and reinforced by the Criminal Justice (Terrorism and Conspiracy) Act 1998 (see below).

The PTA has a UK-wide application while the EPA applies only in Northern Ireland. Both Acts are temporary and must be renewed by Parliament each year. They are intended to strike a balance between providing powers that are necessary to protect the public and safeguarding the rights of individuals. They give the security forces wider powers to question and arrest people suspected of involvement in terrorism and to search property, including vehicles.

The Criminal Justice (Terrorism and Conspiracy) Act 1998 aims to underpin the Good Friday Agreement in Northern Ireland (see p. 16) by making it easier to secure the conviction of members of proscribed organisations which are not observing a complete and unequivocal ceasefire. It also makes it an offence to conspire in the UK to commit terrorist or other serious offences in another country.

The Government intends to rationalise and modernise the temporary arrangements and, in December 1998, published proposals for permanent UK-wide counter-terrorism legislation, including:

- the adoption of a new definition of terrorism which will extend to domestic as well as Irish and international terrorism;
- the abolition of exclusion order powers;
- stronger powers for dealing with terrorist fund-raising;
- a new judicial authority to consider applications for extensions of detention of terrorist suspects; and
- a review of the provisions of the Criminal Justice (Terrorism and Conspiracy) Act 1998.

Public consultation on these proposals ended in March 1999, and the Government intends to introduce legislation as soon as parliamentary time allows.

---

[1] The Crime and Disorder Act 1998 is introducing drug treatment and testing orders throughout the UK for drug-misusing offenders aged 16 and over. An order will include a requirement that the offender submits to drug treatment and testing under appropriate supervision.

Police Service

Government ministers, together with police authorities and chief constables, are responsible for providing an effective and efficient police service in the UK.

Organisation

There are 52 police forces, organised on a local basis—43 in England and Wales, eight in Scotland and one (the Royal Ulster Constabulary—RUC)[2] in Northern Ireland. The Metropolitan Police Service and the City of London force are responsible for policing London.

Police strength in England and Wales is about 127,000 (of which the Metropolitan Police numbers around 26,000). There are some 14,800 officers in Scotland and 8,500 in the RUC. Each force in Great Britain has volunteer special constables who perform police duties in their spare time, without pay, acting in support of regular officers. They number about 20,000 in all.

Police forces are maintained in England and Wales by local police authorities. In the 41 police areas outside London, they normally have 17 members—nine locally elected councillors, three magistrates and five independent members. The Home Secretary is currently the police authority for the Metropolitan Police District. However, the Greater London Authority (GLA) Bill (see p. 9) will, subject to parliamentary approval, create a new Metropolitan Police Authority (MPA) from July 2000, the majority of whose 23 members would be elected representatives. For the City of London Police Area, the authority is the Common Council of the Corporation of London. Police authorities, in consultation with the chief constables and local community, set local policing objectives, while the Government sets key objectives for the police as a whole. The police authorities in Scotland are composed of elected councillors. In Northern Ireland the Secretary of State appoints the Police Authority.

Provincial police forces are headed by chief constables (appointed by their police authorities, with government approval), who are responsible for the direction and control of their forces and for the appointment, promotion and discipline of all ranks below assistant chief constable. On matters of efficiency they are generally answerable to their police authorities. The Commissioner of the Metropolitan Police is appointed on the recommendation of the Home Secretary.

Independent inspectors of constabulary report on the efficiency and effectiveness of police forces.

National Crime Bodies

The National Criminal Intelligence Service (NCIS), which was put on an independent statutory footing in 1998, has the leading role in collecting and analysing criminal intelligence for use by police forces and other law enforcement agencies in the UK. It has a headquarters and south-east regional office in London, five other regional offices in England and offices in Scotland and Northern Ireland. NCIS co-ordinates the activities of the Security Services in support of the law enforcement agencies against organised crime, and liaises with the International Criminal Police Organisation (INTERPOL), which promotes international co-operation between police forces. It also provides the channel for communication between the UK and EUROPOL (see p. 92).

In 1998 a National Crime Squad, with 1,400 officers, replaced six regional crime squads in England and Wales. Its role is to prevent and detect organised and serious crime across police force and national boundaries and to support provincial forces in their investigation of serious crime. The Scottish Crime Squad performs the same function in Scotland.

Information Systems

The Police Information Technology Organisation is responsible for specifying and procuring the delivery of national information

---

[2] Legislation passed in 1998 provides for the continuance of the RUC as the body of constables in Northern Ireland, but introduces the concept of the Northern Ireland Police Service to include all those staff under the day-to-day management of the chief constable. Under the terms of the Good Friday Agreement, an independent commission has inquired into policing in Northern Ireland and its report was published in September 1999 (see p. 18).

technology systems (such as the Police National Computer) for the police service, and for promoting the National Strategy for Police Information Systems, which develops common information technology applications at force level.

The Police National Computer provides all police forces in the UK with rapid 24-hour-a-day access to operationally essential information, particularly vehicle information. Phoenix, the Criminal Justice Record Service, gives the police direct on-line access to national records of arrests, cautions, bail decisions and convictions. In England and Wales a national automated fingerprint identification system, linked to the Police National Computer, will be available to all forces by the year 2001. In Scotland the Scottish Criminal Records Office provides a fully automated criminal and fingerprint records service, and a project for the integration of Scottish criminal justice information systems is in progress.

Forensic Science Service

The Forensic Science Service (FSS) is a Home Office executive agency, providing scientific support in the investigation of crime and expert evidence to the courts. Its customers include the police, the CPS, Customs and Excise, coroners and defence solicitors. The FSS serves all police forces in England and Wales through six regional laboratories. It also operates the national DNA database, which provides intelligence information to police forces by matching DNA profiles taken from suspects to profiles from samples left at the scenes of crime. In addition, it provides support to law enforcement agencies overseas.

In Scotland forensic science services are provided by forces' own laboratories. Northern Ireland has its own laboratory.

Powers and Procedures

England and Wales

Police powers and procedures are defined by legislation and accompanying codes of practice. Evidence obtained in breach of the codes may be ruled inadmissible in court. The codes must be readily accessible in all police stations.

- *Stop and search*—Police officers can stop and search people and vehicles if they reasonably suspect that they will find stolen goods, offensive weapons or implements that could be used for burglary and other offences. An officer must record the grounds for the search, and anything found, and the person stopped is entitled to a copy. Senior police officers can authorise broader stop and search operations in specified localities if they believe that serious incidents of violence may take place, or to prevent acts of terrorism.

- *Arrest*—The police may arrest a suspect on a warrant issued by a court, but can arrest without warrant for *arrestable* offences (for which the sentence is fixed by law or for which the term of imprisonment is five years or more). This category includes *serious arrestable* offences such as murder and rape. There is a general power of arrest for all other offences if it is inappropriate to proceed by way of a court summons, or if an officer believes a suspect may injure someone else or damage property.

- *Detention and questioning*—Suspects must be cautioned before the police can ask any questions about an offence. They must be told that they do not have to say anything, but that anything they do say may be given in evidence in court, and that it may be harmful to their defence if they fail to mention something during questioning which they later rely on in court. For *arrestable* offences, a suspect can be detained in police custody without charge for up to 24 hours. Someone suspected of a *serious arrestable* offence can be held for up to 96 hours, but not beyond 36 hours unless a warrant is obtained from a magistrates' court.

Interviews with suspects at police stations are generally tape-recorded when the police are investigating indictable offences and in certain other cases. Suspects are entitled to a copy of the recording if charged or told that they will be prosecuted.

If someone thinks that his or her detention is unlawful, he or she may apply to the High Court for a writ of *habeas corpus* against the person responsible, requiring them to appear before the court to justify the detention. *Habeas corpus* proceedings take precedence over others.

- *Charging*—Once there is sufficient evidence, the police have to decide whether a detained person should be charged with an offence. If the police institute criminal proceedings against a suspect, the CPS (see p. 221) then takes control of the case.

Scotland and Northern Ireland

The police in Scotland can arrest someone without a warrant, under wide common law powers, if they are seen or reported as committing a crime or are a danger to themselves or others. They also have specific statutory powers of arrest for some offences. In other cases they may apply to a justice of the peace for a warrant. As in England and Wales, Scottish police have powers to enter a building without a warrant if they are pursuing someone who has committed, or attempted to commit, a serious crime. A court can grant the police a warrant to search premises for stated items in connection with a crime, again as in England and Wales. The police may search anyone suspected of carrying an offensive weapon. Someone suspected of an imprisonable offence may be held for police questioning without being arrested, but for no more than six hours without being charged. If arrested, suspects must be charged and cautioned. The case is then referred to the procurator fiscal (see p. 228). Tape recording of interviews with suspects is common practice.

The law in Northern Ireland relating to police powers in the investigation of crime and to evidence in criminal proceedings is similar to that in force in England and Wales.

Firearms

The policy in Great Britain is that the police should not generally be armed but that there should be specialist firearms officers, deployed on the authority of a senior officer where an operational need arises. Most forces operate armed response vehicles that can be deployed quickly to contain firearms incidents. In Northern Ireland police officers are issued with firearms for their personal protection.

Police Discipline

A police officer may be prosecuted if suspected of a criminal offence. Officers are also subject to a code of conduct. If found guilty of breaching the code, an officer can be dismissed.

New conduct and efficiency arrangements came into effect in April 1999. The main changes include introducing the civil standard of proof at disciplinary hearings; a fast-track procedure to deal swiftly with officers caught committing serious criminal offences; and separate formal procedures (for the first time) for dealing with unsatisfactory performance.

Complaints

Members of the public can make complaints against the police if they feel that they have been treated unfairly or improperly. In England and Wales the investigation of such complaints by the force concerned is overseen, or in more serious cases supervised, by the Police Complaints Authority. In Scotland complaints against police officers involving allegations of criminal conduct are referred to the procurator fiscal for investigation. The Scottish Inspectorate of Constabulary considers representations from complainants dissatisfied with the way the police have handled their complaints. In Northern Ireland the Independent Commission for Police Complaints is being superseded by a Police Ombudsman.

Community Relations

Within every police authority there are police/community liaison consultative arrangements, involving representatives from the police, local government and community groups. Home Office and police service initiatives have sought to ensure that racist crime[3] is treated as a police priority (despite the shortcomings that came to light in the Stephen Lawrence case—see below). HM Inspectorate of Constabulary collects statistics on the number of racist incidents recorded by forces.

The need to recruit more members of the ethnic minorities to the police service, and retain them, has been recognised. In England and Wales there are about 2,200 officers from ethnic minorities. The corresponding figure for Scotland is about 50. In April 1999 the Government set new targets for the number of ethnic minority officers in all areas of the country (with the basic aim of achieving a similar proportion of ethnic minority officers to that of the population in a particular police force area).

The Stephen Lawrence Inquiry

In April 1993 a young black student, Stephen Lawrence, was murdered in a racist attack in south-east London. Concerns about inadequacies in the investigation of the case by the Metropolitan Police Service led ultimately to an official inquiry, which reported in February 1999. The report was critical, with some exceptions, of police conduct, claiming there was a combination of professional incompetence, institutional racism and a failure of leadership by senior officers. Among its 70 recommendations to improve trust and confidence in policing, the report proposed:

- a review of racism awareness training throughout the police service;

- an inspection of the Metropolitan Police Service by the Inspectorate of Constabulary;

- greater accountability of the Metropolitan Police Service to the communities that it serves (a concern which should be addressed by the

---

[3] New racially aggravated offences have been created under the Crime and Disorder Act 1998.

pending creation of a new police authority for London—see p. 217);

- the establishment of a fully independent police complaints system;

- the promotion of cultural diversity and prevention of racism in schools;

- the extension of the Race Relations Act 1976 (see p. 115) to the police service (a proposal that the Government intends to apply to all public services); and

- revisions to police disciplinary procedures (see p. 219).

The report was welcomed by the Government, which announced an action plan in March to take forward the recommendations (most of which should be implemented by the end of 1999; the remainder should be in place within three years). The Home Secretary has taken personal responsibility for the delivery of the programme set out in the inquiry report.

Legal System of England and Wales

Responsibility for the administration and management of the English legal system is divided between various government departments and agencies.

The *Lord Chancellor* is the head of the judiciary and sits as a member of the judicial committee of the House of Lords. He also presides over the House of Lords in its legislative capacity, and is a senior cabinet minister heading a government department, the Lord Chancellor's Department, which has overall responsibility for the court system, including the Supreme Court (comprising the Court of Appeal, High Court and Crown Court) and the county courts in England and Wales. That responsibility is exercised through the Court Service. He has overall responsibility for magistrates' courts. He advises the Crown on the appointment of most members of the higher judiciary, and appoints most magistrates. He has responsibility for the civil justice process, for promoting general reforms of the civil law and for the legal aid schemes.

The *Home Secretary* has overall responsibility for criminal law, the police service, the prison system and the probation service, and for advising the Crown on the exercise of the royal prerogative of mercy.

The *Attorney General* and the *Solicitor General* are the Government's principal legal advisers, providing advice on a range of legal matters, including proposed legislation. They may represent the Crown in appropriate domestic and international cases of difficulty or public importance, although they do not always do so. As well as exercising various civil law functions, the Attorney General has final responsibility for enforcing the criminal law. The Solicitor General is the Attorney's deputy.

The Crown Prosecution Service is headed by the *Director of Public Prosecutions (DPP)*, who is independent, but superintended by the Attorney General. Other prosecuting authorities include the Serious Fraud Office, which answers to the Attorney General, and bodies such as the Inland Revenue, Customs and Excise Commissioners, local authorities and trading standards departments which prosecute cases within their own sphere of activity. Private prosecutions by individuals are permitted in respect of most crimes, but some require the consent of the Attorney General and they may be taken over by the DPP. They are few in number.

Some administrative functions are performed by senior members of the judiciary: the Lord Chief Justice,[4] for example, has some responsibilities for the organisation and work of the criminal courts. Other functions are performed by statutory committees. The Civil Procedure Rules Committee, created by the Civil Procedure Act 1997, is responsible for the making of rules that govern the civil justice process, and comprises members of the judiciary, members of the legal profession and lay representatives.

Responsibility for the management of functions often lies with executive bodies or agencies. Examples include the Prison Service, Forensic Science Service, the Legal Aid Board, and the Youth Justice Board, which started work in 1998.

The Government is advised by a range of bodies of a statutory and non-statutory nature. These include the police inspectorates, the magistrates' courts service, the probation service, the Audit Commission, the Criminal Justice Consultative Committee, law reform bodies such as the Law Commission and *ad hoc* Royal Commissions and departmental committees.

PROSECUTION AND THE CRIMINAL COURTS

Prosecution Arrangements

Crown Prosecution Service

The CPS is the government department responsible for prosecuting people in England and Wales who have been charged with a criminal offence. It works closely with the police, but is an independent body. Every year the CPS deals with more than 1.3 million cases in magistrates' courts and about 120,000 in the Crown Court. With headquarters in London and York, the Service operates under a structure (introduced in April 1999) of 42 geographical Areas in England and Wales. The Areas correspond to the 43 police forces in England and Wales, with the CPS London Area covering the operational boundaries of both City of London and Metropolitan Police Forces. Each Area is headed by a Chief Crown Prosecutor, who is responsible for prosecutions within the Area, supported by an Area Business Manager.

The CPS:

- advises the police on possible prosecutions;
- reviews prosecutions started by the police to ensure that the right defendants are prosecuted on the right charges before the appropriate court;
- prepares cases for court; and
- prosecutes cases at magistrates' courts and instructs counsel to prosecute cases in the Crown Court and higher courts.[5]

---

[4] The Lord Chief Justice is head of the Queen's Bench Division of the High Court, and ranks second only to the Lord Chancellor in the judicial hierarchy.

[5] Under a change in legal rules, a number of CPS lawyers are now qualified to appear in some cases in the Crown Court and other higher courts.

Structure of the Courts in England and Wales

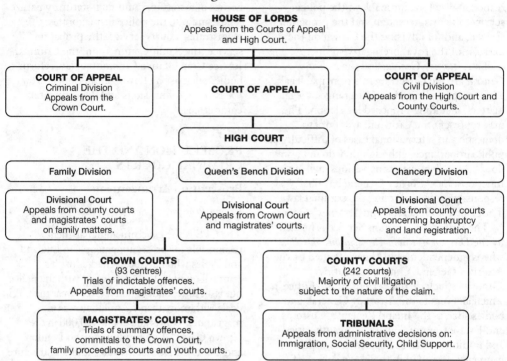

The decision by the CPS on whether or not to go ahead with a case is based on two criteria. Crown Prosecutors must be satisfied that there is enough evidence to provide a realistic prospect of conviction against each defendant on each charge. There may also be instances where an analysis of the public interest will lead to a decision not to prosecute, although these must clearly outweigh any other factors which point in the opposite direction.

Serious Fraud Office

Cases of serious or complex fraud are prosecuted by the Serious Fraud Office. Investigations are conducted by teams of lawyers, accountants, police officers and other specialists. The Office has wide powers that go beyond those normally available to the police and prosecuting authorities.

Initial Stages

For minor offences, the police may decide to caution the offender rather than prosecute. A caution does not amount to a conviction, and will not take place unless the person admits the offence. Under the Crime and Disorder Act 1998, cautioning for young offenders is being replaced with the final warning scheme (see p. 225).

If the police decide to charge a person, that person may be released on bail to attend a magistrates' court. If not granted police bail, the defendant must be brought before a magistrates' court (or, if under 18, a youth court) as soon as possible. There is a general right to bail, but magistrates may withhold bail if there are substantial grounds for believing that an accused person would abscond, commit an offence, or otherwise obstruct justice.

If bail is refused, an accused has the right to apply again, subject to certain limitations, to the Crown Court or to a High Court judge in chambers. He or she must be told of this right. In certain circumstances, the prosecution may appeal to a Crown Court judge against the granting of bail by magistrates.

Once a person has been charged, it is for the CPS to decide whether the case should proceed.

Criminal Courts

Criminal offences are divided into: *summary* offences, which are the least serious and are triable only in a magistrates' court; and *indictable* ones, which are subdivided into 'indictable-only' offences (such as murder, manslaughter or robbery) which must be tried on indictment[6] at the Crown Court by judge and jury, and *either-way* offences, which may be tried either summarily or on indictment. Either-way offences, such as theft and burglary, can vary greatly in seriousness. A magistrates' court decides whether an either-way case is serious enough to warrant trial in the Crown Court, but if the magistrates decide in favour of summary trial, the accused person can elect to have trial by jury in the Crown Court (although this right would be abolished under government proposals announced in May 1999).

Magistrates' courts deal with about 97% of criminal offence prosecutions in England and Wales.

Where a case is to be tried on indictment, the magistrates' court must be satisfied that there is a case to answer. In most cases this is accepted by the defence and the magistrates do not need to consider the evidence. If the defence challenges the case, the magistrates consider the documentary evidence: no witnesses are called to give evidence. If there is a case to be answered, the accused is committed for trial.

A magistrates' court usually comprises three lay magistrates (see also p. 212), known as justices of the peace (JPs), who sit with a court clerk to advise them on law and procedure. The court clerk will be qualified to act as such, although not always a qualified lawyer.[7] In some areas a stipendiary (paid professional) magistrate sits instead of the JPs. Stipendiary magistrates are becoming increasingly common, although most cases are still dealt with by lay magistrates.

---

[6] An indictment is a written accusation against a person, charging him or her with serious crime triable by jury.

[7] New rules came into force in January 1999 to provide for all new court clerks to be professionally qualified as a barrister or solicitor.

Responsibility for running the magistrates' courts service locally rests with magistrates' courts committees (MCCs), made up of lay magistrates selected by their colleagues. The number of MCCs is being reduced, and their areas increased, to improve efficiency and to bring their boundaries to closer alignment with those of other criminal justice agencies, such as the police and the CPS.

Youth courts are specialist magistrates' courts, which sit separately from those dealing with adults. They deal with all but the most serious charges against people aged at least ten (the age of criminal responsibility) and under 18. JPs who have been specially trained sit in youth courts. Proceedings are held in private.

The Crown Court sits at about 90 venues, in six regional areas called circuits, and is presided over by High Court judges, circuit judges and part-time recorders. The type of judge who will preside over a case, with a jury of 12 members of the public, will depend on which Crown Court the case is being heard in: not all Crown Courts deal with cases of the same level of seriousness.

Trial

Criminal trials have two parties: the prosecution and the defence. The law presumes the innocence of an accused person until guilt has been proved beyond reasonable doubt by the prosecution.

Pre-trial Procedure

Accused people have a right at all stages to remain silent; however, an adverse inference may be drawn from their failure to mention facts when questioned which they later rely upon in their defence. The prosecution discloses to the defence the material which it proposes to rely on at the trial. In addition, the law requires the prosecution to disclose to the defence material in its possession that it does not intend to use in the trial:

Primary disclosure—The prosecution must disclose material which might undermine the prosecution case.

Defence disclosure—In Crown Court cases the defence must give a statement outlining in general terms the nature of the defence, including details of any alibis. This statement is voluntary in cases tried in magistrates' courts.

Secondary disclosure—The prosecution must disclose any unused material not previously disclosed which might reasonably be expected to assist the defence as disclosed in the defence statement.

The prosecution may apply for sensitive material not to be disclosed; the defence may apply for disclosure where it considers that material which should have been disclosed has not been provided by the prosecution.

In a case to be tried on indictment, a judge may hold a preliminary hearing, where pleas of guilty or not guilty are taken. If the defendant pleads guilty the judge will proceed to sentence. In contested cases, the prosecution and defence are expected to assist the judge in identifying key issues, and to provide any additional information required for the proper and efficient trial of the case.

Trial Procedure

Criminal trials normally take place in open court. The burden of proof is on the prosecution, and strict rules of evidence govern how matters may be proved. Certain types of evidence may be excluded because of their prejudicial effect, or because of their unreliability. Documentary statements by witnesses are allowed with the consent of the other party or in limited circumstances at the discretion of the court. Otherwise evidence is taken from witnesses testifying orally on oath. Child witnesses may testify without taking the oath and their evidence must be received by the court unless the child is incapable of giving intelligible testimony. A child in some circumstances can testify through a live TV link, and the court may consider a video-recorded interview as the evidence of the child, subject to the defence having the right to question the child in cross-examination. Further measures to help both child witnesses and adult vulnerable or intimidated witnesses to give their best evidence in court are being introduced under the Youth and Criminal Evidence Act 1999 (see p. 224).

The Jury

In jury trials the judge decides questions of law, sums up the case to the jury, and discharges or sentences the accused. The jury is responsible for deciding questions of fact. The jury verdict may be 'guilty' or 'not guilty', the latter resulting in acquittal. Juries may, subject to certain conditions, reach a verdict by a majority of at least 10 to 2.

If an accused is acquitted, there is no right of prosecution appeal, and the accused cannot be tried again for that same offence. However, an acquittal may be set aside and a retrial ordered if the acquittal has been tainted by a conviction for interfering with or intimidating a juror.

A jury is independent of the judiciary and any attempt to interfere with its members is a criminal offence. People aged between 18 and 70 whose names appear on the electoral register are, with certain exceptions, liable for jury service; their names are chosen at random.

Sentencing

The court will sentence the offender after considering all the relevant information, which may include a pre-sentence report and any other necessary specialist report, and a plea in mitigation by a defence advocate. The powers of the magistrates' court in respect of sentence are limited to a maximum period of 12 months' imprisonment. The offender may be sent to the Crown Court for sentence if the magistrates feel their powers of sentence are insufficient.

A custodial sentence can be imposed only where the offence is so serious that a custodial sentence alone is justified. A term of up to two years' imprisonment may be suspended. A second serious violent or sexual offence requires a court to impose a life sentence unless there are exceptional circumstances. Life imprisonment is the mandatory sentence for murder, and is available for certain other serious offences.

For offences not so serious as to require a custodial sentence, community sentences may be imposed. These can include probation orders (involving supervision in the

In January 1999 the Government announced the introduction of three-year minimum sentences for those convicted of a third offence of domestic burglary. This will take effect from December 1999.

community—see p. 235), community service (work within the community), combination orders (a mixture of probation and community service), and curfew orders (requiring the offender to remain at a specified place for specified periods, monitored by electronic tagging). A fine is the most common punishment, with most offenders fined for summary offences. A court may also impose compensation orders, which require the offender to pay compensation for personal injury, loss or damage resulting from an offence; or impose a conditional discharge, whereby the offender may be resentenced for the original offence if the discharge is broken by reoffending.

Young Offenders

Offenders aged 10 to 17 years come within the jurisdiction of youth courts, but may also be tried in an adult magistrates' court or in a Crown Court, depending on the nature of the offence. Existing non-custodial penalties include: conditional discharge; fines and compensation orders (where the parents of offenders may be ordered to pay); supervision orders (where the offender would have to comply with certain requirements, which might possibly include a stay in local authority accommodation); and attendance centre orders; 16- and 17-year-olds may also be given the same probation, community service, combination and curfew orders as older offenders.

Custodial sentences are available to the courts where no alternative is considered appropriate. The main custodial sentence for those aged 15 and over is currently detention in a young offender institution. Remission of part of the sentence for good behaviour, release on parole and supervision on release are available. A secure training order may be given to those persistent offenders aged 12 to 14 who fulfil certain strict criteria.

A number of measures have been taken under the Crime and Disorder Act 1998 to prevent offending and reoffending by young people. Local authorities are required to produce annual youth justice plans detailing how youth justice services in their areas will be provided and funded. They are also having to establish one or more youth offending teams whose membership will be drawn from the police, social services, the probation service, health and education authorities and, if considered appropriate locally, the voluntary sector. As well as supervising existing community sentences, these teams will provide and supervise a range of new orders and powers under the Act (see below).

The Act introduces a statutory final warning scheme to replace the practice of repeat cautioning by the police. The scheme is intended to provide a swift response to early incidences of criminal behaviour, and a final warning will also trigger referral to a youth offending team to draw up a rehabilitation programme to address the factors which led the young person into offending.

New orders include: a *reparation order*, which will require young offenders to make non-financial reparation to the victim(s) of their offence or to the community which they have harmed; and an *action plan order*, which will require them to comply with an individually tailored action plan intended to address their offending behaviour. These new orders, together with the final warning scheme, are being piloted in certain specified areas for 18 months from the end of September 1998. There will also be a *detention and training order*, which will combine custody and community supervision; this is to be implemented in April 2000.

The new criminal orders will be complemented by a range of other powers. These include *parenting orders*, which will require a parent or guardian to attend counselling and guidance sessions, and may direct them to comply with specified requirements; and *child safety orders*, which place a child under ten who is at risk of becoming involved in crime or is behaving in an anti-social manner under the supervision of a specified, responsible officer.

The Youth Justice Board for England and Wales, established under the Crime and

Disorder Act 1998, began operation in September 1998 to monitor the youth justice system, promote good practice and advise the Home Secretary on the operation of the system and the setting of national standards.

> A new sentence of referral to a youth offender panel is being introduced under the Youth Justice and Criminal Evidence Act 1999. It will be available for young people pleading guilty who are convicted for a first time, and its primary aim is to prevent reoffending. The panel will work to establish a programme of behaviour for the young offender. This will include making restoration to the victim, taking responsibility for the consequences of his or her actions, and achieving reintegration into the law-abiding community.

Appeals

A person convicted by a magistrates' court may appeal to the High Court, on points of law, and to the Crown Court, by way of re-hearing. Appeals from the Crown Court go to the Court of Appeal (Criminal Division). A further appeal can be made to the House of Lords on points of law of public importance. A prosecutor cannot appeal against an acquittal, but mechanisms exist to review over-lenient sentences and rulings of law. Alleged miscarriages of justice in England, Wales and Northern Ireland are reviewed by the Criminal Cases Review Commission, which is independent of both government and the courts. Referral of a case requires some new argument or evidence not previously raised at the trial or on appeal.

Coroners' Courts

The coroner (usually a senior lawyer or doctor) must hold an inquest if the deceased died violently, unnaturally, suddenly, if the cause is unknown, in prison or in certain specified circumstances. The coroner's court establishes how, when and where the deceased died. A coroner may sit alone or, in certain circumstances, with a jury.

CIVIL JUSTICE SYSTEM

Jurisdiction in civil matters is split between the High Court and the county courts. Some 90% of all cases are dealt with by the county courts, but most civil disputes do not go to court at all. Many are dealt with through statutory or voluntary complaints mechanisms, or through mediation and negotiation. Arbitration is a common form of adjudication in commercial and building disputes. Ombudsmen have the power to determine complaints in the public sector, and, on a voluntary basis, in some private sector activities (for example, banking, insurance and pensions).

A large number of tribunals exist to determine disputes. About 80 different types of tribunal are supervised by a statutory supervisory body, the Council on Tribunals, and deal with disputes such as liability for tax (Commissioners for Income Tax), eligibility for social benefit (Social Security Appeals Tribunals) and the compulsory treatment of an individual for mental health problems (Mental Health Review Tribunals).

Courts

The High Court is divided into three Divisions (see chart on p. 222).

- The Queen's Bench Division deals with disputes relating to contracts, general commercial matters (in a specialist Commercial Court), and liability in tort (general civil wrongs, such as accidents caused by negligence, or defamation of character). A Queen's Bench Divisional Court has special responsibility for dealing with applications for judicial review of the actions of public bodies, and has the power to declare the action of a public individual, department or body unlawful.

- The Chancery Division deals with disputes relating to land, wills, companies and insolvency.

- The Family Division deals with matters relating to divorce and the welfare of children.

The county courts deal with claims in contract and in tort, with family matters (including divorce and the welfare of children) and a wide range of statutory matters. Magistrates' courts have limited civil jurisdiction, in family matters (when they sit as a Family Proceedings Court) and in miscellaneous civil orders.

Appeals in civil cases in the county courts or High Court generally go to the Court of Appeal (Civil Division). Appeals from magistrates' courts in civil matters go to the High Court, on matters of law, or to the Crown Court, if the case is to be re-heard. A further appeal on points of law of public importance goes to the House of Lords. The Access to Justice Act 1999 will reform the jurisdiction of the courts to hear appeals in civil and family cases, and the constitution of the Civil Division of the Court of Appeal (see below).

Reform of the Civil Justice System

The Government has stated its intention to modernise and simplify court procedures wherever possible, and reduce delay. Following a thorough review of the civil justice system, the first phase of reform was implemented in April 1999. The key elements are the introduction of:

- a unified code of procedural rules, written in plain English, and replacing separate sets of High Court and county court rules. The main objective of the new rules is to enable the courts to deal with cases more appropriately. This includes the court taking a more active case management role than before, to ensure that cases are dealt with in a way which is proportionate to their value, complexity and importance;

- pre-action protocols (for clinical negligence and personal injury cases) setting standards and timetables for the conduct of cases before court proceedings are started. This will require more exchange of information and fuller investigation of claims at an earlier stage. People should therefore be in a better position to make a realistic assessment of the merits of a case far earlier than before, encouraging them to settle

disputes without recourse to litigation. Where litigation is unavoidable, cases coming to court should be better prepared than before. Judges are expected to apply the protocols strictly, and impose sanctions on those breaching them; and

- a system of three tracks to which disputed claims will be assigned by a judge according to the value and complexity of the case. These are:

    —the small claims track, which will deal with cases worth less than £5,000 at an informal hearing by a district judge;

    —the fast track, which will deal with cases worth from £5,000 to £15,000 and set a fixed timetable from allocation to trial; and

    —the multi-track, for cases worth over £15,000 or of unusual complexity, which will be supervised by a judge and given timetables tailored to each case.

The great majority of civil cases, other than small claims, will be run under the fast track procedure. Judges have a key role in ensuring that the new procedures deliver the objectives of reducing cost, delay and complexity, by managing cases to ensure that litigants and their representatives keep to the timetable, and undertake only necessary work. As part of the reform programme, the Court Service is introducing further information technology to support the work of judges and staff in civil courts.

The Access to Justice Act 1999 will reform the workings of the appeals system according to the principles of proportionality and efficiency that underpin the civil justice reforms generally. The objectives of proportionality and efficiency will be achieved by:

- diverting from the Court of Appeal those cases which, by their nature, do not require the attention of the most senior judges; and

- making various changes to the working methods and constitution of the Court, which will enable it to deploy its resources more effectively.

The Civil Justice Council has been established to oversee the working of the civil justice system, and to make proposals for its improvement.

Legal System of Scotland

Scots law belongs to a small group of 'mixed' legal systems which have legal principles, rules and concepts modelled on both Roman and English law. The main sources of Scots law are judge-made law, certain legal treatises having 'institutional' authority, legislation, and EC law. The first two sources are sometimes referred to as the common law of Scotland. Legislation, as in the rest of the UK, consists of statutes (Acts of Parliament) or subordinate legislation authorised by Parliament.

PROSECUTION AND THE CRIMINAL COURTS

Awaiting Trial

When arrested, an accused person in Scotland may be released by the police to await summons, on an undertaking to appear at court at a specified time, or be held in custody to appear at court on the next working day. Following that appearance, the accused person may be remanded in custody until trial or released by the court on bail. If released on bail, the accused person must undertake to appear at trial when required, not to commit an offence while on bail, and not to interfere with witnesses or obstruct justice. The court may impose additional conditions on the accused (for example, to keep away from certain people or locations). There is a right of appeal to the High Court by an accused person against the refusal of bail, or by the prosecutor against the granting of bail, or by either against the conditions imposed.

Bail will not be granted where an accused person is charged with murder, culpable homicide, rape or attempted rape, and has any previous conviction for such a crime (in the case of culpable homicide, involving a prison sentence).

Prosecution Arrangements

The Lord Advocate is responsible for prosecutions in the High Court, sheriff courts and district courts. In contrast to England, the police in Scotland cannot initiate criminal proceedings, and private prosecutions are extremely rare. The Lord Advocate discharges his responsibility for criminal prosecution through the Crown Office, which is staffed by legally qualified civil servants and run by the Crown Agent, who is head of the Procurator Fiscal Service. Procurators fiscal are the Lord Advocate's local representatives, with one for each sheriff court. They are lawyers and full-time civil servants subject to the direction of the Crown Office. They must be either advocates or solicitors, but are usually solicitors.

Prosecutions in the High Court are prepared by procurators fiscal and Crown Office officials, and are conducted by the Lord Advocate and the Solicitor General for Scotland; they in turn delegate the bulk of their work to advocates depute, collectively known as Crown Counsel, of whom there are 13. In all other criminal courts the decision to prosecute is made, and prosecution carried out, by procurators fiscal.

The police report gives details of alleged crimes to the local procurator fiscal who has discretion whether or not to prosecute. He or she may receive instructions from the Crown Council on behalf of the Lord Advocate.

The office of coroner does not exist in Scotland. Instead the local procurator fiscal inquires privately into sudden or suspicious deaths and may report the findings to the Crown Office. When appropriate, a fatal accident inquiry may be held before the sheriff; this is mandatory in cases of death resulting from industrial accidents and deaths in custody.

Criminal Courts

There are three criminal courts in Scotland: the High Court of Justiciary, the sheriff court and the district court. Cases are heard under one of two types of criminal procedure:

- In *solemn procedure* in both the High Court of Justiciary and the sheriff court, an accused person's trial takes place before a judge sitting with a jury of 15 lay people. As in England and Wales, the alleged offence is set out in a document called an indictment. The judge decides questions of law and the jury decide questions of fact and may reach a decision by a simple majority. They may decide to find the accused 'guilty', 'not guilty' or 'not proven'; the last two are acquittals and have the effect that the accused cannot be tried again for the same offence.

- In *summary procedure* in sheriff and district courts, the judge sits without a jury and decides questions of both fact and law. The offence charged is set out in a document called a summary complaint.

In Scotland the court in summary cases is required to fix an additional hearing (intermediate diet) at some time between the court appearance and the trial to establish the state of readiness of both the defence and the prosecution. Solemn procedure in the sheriff court also requires a hearing to find out whether the case is ready to go for trial. The prosecution in solemn cases must give the defence advance notice of the witnesses it intends to call and of the documents and other items on which it will rely.

The *High Court of Justiciary* is the Supreme Criminal Court in Scotland, based in Edinburgh and sitting in Glasgow and other major towns and cities. It tries the most serious crimes and has exclusive jurisdiction in cases involving murder, treason and rape.

The 49 *sheriff courts* deal mainly with less serious offences committed within the sheriff court district over which they have jurisdiction. These courts are organised in six sheriffdoms, and at the head of the judiciary of each sheriffdom is the sheriff principal. There are over 100 permanent sheriffs, most of whom are appointed to particular courts. Fifteen are 'floating' sheriffs who may take cases in any court. In addition, there is a panel of temporary sheriffs who may undertake duties in any sheriffdom.

The sheriff has jurisdiction in both summary and solemn criminal cases. In the summary court, the sheriff may impose prison sentences of up to three months, or in some cases 12 months, or a fine not exceeding the 'prescribed sum', that is, up to £5,000 for a common law offence. Under solemn procedure, the sheriff may impose imprisonment for up to three years and unlimited financial penalties, and has an additional power of remit to the High Court of Justiciary if he or she thinks a heavier sentence should be imposed. The sheriff also has available a range of non-custodial sentences, principally community service and probation.

District courts, which deal with minor offences, are the administrative responsibility of the local authority. The longest prison sentence which can be imposed is generally 60 days and the maximum fine is £2,500. The bench of a district court will usually be made up of one or more lay justices of the peace. A local authority may also appoint a stipendiary magistrate, who must be a professional lawyer of at least five years' standing, and who has the same summary criminal jurisdiction and powers as a sheriff. At present, only Glasgow has stipendiary magistrates sitting in the district court.

Sentencing

In Scotland a court must obtain a social enquiry report before imposing a custodial sentence if the accused is aged under 21 or has not previously served a custodial sentence. A report is also required before making a probation or community service order, or in cases involving people already subject to supervision.

Non-custodial sentences

Non-custodial sentences available to the courts include fines, and community service orders, for which the minimum number of hours is 80 and the maximum, under solemn procedure, 300. Restriction of liberty orders, restricting an offender's movements for up to 12 months, are being piloted in three areas. Compliance is monitored by electronic tags. Offenders must be aged 16 or over. Supervised attendance orders provide an alternative to imprisonment for fine default, and incorporate aspects of work and training.

Appeals

The High Court of Justiciary also sits (in a court of at least two judges) as the Scottish Court of Criminal Appeal. In both solemn and summary procedure, a convicted person may appeal against conviction, or sentence, or both. The Court may authorise a retrial if it sets aside a conviction. There is no appeal from this court in criminal cases.

In April 1999 the Scottish Criminal Cases Review Commission—a new, independent, non-departmental public body—assumed responsibility from the Secretary of State for considering alleged miscarriages of justice in Scotland and referring cases meeting the relevant criteria to the Court of Appeal for review.

CIVIL COURTS

The main civil courts are the Court of Session (the supreme court, subject to appeal only to the House of Lords in London) and the sheriff court (the principal local court).

The *Court of Session* sits in Edinburgh, and may hear cases at first instance as well as those transferred to it and appealed from sheriff courts and from tribunals. A leading principle of the court is that cases originating in it are both prepared for decision, and decided, by judges sitting singly whose decisions are subject to review by several judges. The total number of judges is 27, of whom 19, called Lords Ordinary, mainly decide cases in the first instance. This branch of the court is called the Outer House. The other eight judges are divided into two divisions of four judges each, forming the Inner House. The First Division is presided over by the Lord President of the Court of Session and the Second Division by the Lord Justice-Clerk. The main business of each division is to review the decisions of the Lords Ordinary or inferior courts which have been appealed to it.

In addition to its criminal jurisdiction, the *sheriff court* deals with most civil litigation in Scotland. Its jurisdiction is very wide. The value of the subject matter with which the court can deal has, with very few exceptions, no upper limit, and a broad range of remedies can be granted. Cases dealt with include, among other things, debts, contract, reparation, rent restrictions, actions affecting the use of property, or affecting leases and tenancies, and actions in relation to children. It also deals with actions between husband and wife, and can vary Court of Session decrees dealing with parental rights and responsibilities or awards of custody or financial provision. The sheriff court has concurrent jurisdiction with the Court of Session in actions for divorce. There is a right of appeal in some cases from the sheriff to the Sheriff Principal and thence, in some cases, to the Court of Session.

Civil Proceedings

The formal proceedings in the Court of Session are initiated by serving the defender with a summons or, in sheriff court cases in ordinary actions, an initial writ. A defender who intends to contest the action must inform the court; if he or she fails to do so, the court normally grants a decree in absence in favour of the pursuer. Where a case is contested, both parties must prepare written pleadings. Time is allowed for either party to adjust their pleadings in the light of what the other has said. At the end of this period a hearing will normally be arranged.

In summary actions involving sums between £750 and £1,500 in the sheriff court, a statement of claim is incorporated in a summons. The procedure is designed to enable most actions to be settled without the parties having to appear in court. Normally, they, or their representatives, need appear only when an action is defended.

In cases below £750 a special small claim procedure enables those who do not have legal advice to raise claims themselves. The procedures are similar to, but less formal than, the summary procedure. In addition to the courts, there is a wide range of tribunals which administer justice in special types of case. Many of these are common to the rest of Great Britain; others, such as the Land Court, the Lands Tribunal and the

Children's Hearings, are peculiar to Scotland.

Children

Criminal proceedings may be brought against any child aged eight years or over, but the instructions of the Lord Advocate are necessary before anyone under 16 years of age is prosecuted.

Most children under 16 who have committed an offence or are considered to be in need of care and protection may be brought before a Children's Hearing. The hearing, consisting of three lay people, determines in an informal setting, often with the child and his or her parents, whether compulsory measures of care are required and, if so, the form they should take. An official known as the reporter to the Children's Hearing decides whether the child should come before a hearing. If the grounds for referral for a hearing are not accepted by the child or parent, the case goes to the sheriff for proof to establish the grounds. If the sheriff finds the grounds established, he or she sends the case back to the reporter to arrange a Children's Hearing. The sheriff also hears appeals against a hearing's decision.

Young people aged between 16 and 21 serve custodial sentences in young offender institutions. Remission of part of the sentence for good behaviour, release on parole and supervision on release are available.

ADMINISTRATION OF THE SCOTTISH LEGAL SYSTEM

The Scottish Executive Justice Department, under the Minister for Justice, is a new Department bringing together the Scottish Office Home Department and the Scottish Courts Administration. Since devolution, it is responsible for civil law and criminal justice, including criminal justice social work services, police, prisons, courts administration, legal aid, and liaison with the legal profession in Scotland. There are two agencies in the Department—the Scottish Prison Service (see p. 233) and the Scottish Court Service, which deals with the work of the Supreme Courts and the sheriff courts.

The Lord Advocate and the Solicitor General for Scotland serve as the Law Officers of the Scottish Executive, providing it with advice on legal matters and representing its interests in the courts. Both officers have ceased to be members of the UK Government. Advice to the UK Government on Scots law is now provided by the Advocate General for Scotland.

The role of the new Scottish Parliament is to make laws in relation to devolved matters in Scotland. In these areas, it is able to amend or repeal existing Acts of the UK Parliament and to pass new legislation of its own in relation to devolved matters. It is also able to consider and pass private legislation, promoted by individuals or bodies (for example, local authorities) in relation to devolved matters.

The Court of Session and the High Court of Justiciary enact the rules regulating their own procedure and the procedures of the sheriff courts and the lay summary courts. The Court of Session and Criminal Courts Rules Councils, and the Sheriffs Courts Rules Council, consisting of judges and legal practitioners, advise the courts about amending the rules.

Legal System of Northern Ireland

Northern Ireland's legal system is similar to that in England and Wales. Jury trials have the same place in the system, except in the case of offences involving acts of terrorism (see **below**). In addition, the course of litigation is the same and the legal profession has the same two branches.

Superior Courts

The Supreme Court of Judicature comprises the Court of Appeal, the High Court and the Crown Court. All matters relating to these courts are under the jurisdiction of the UK Parliament. Judges are appointed by the Crown.

The *Court of Appeal* comprises the Lord Chief Justice (as President) and two Lords Justices of Appeal. The High Court comprises the Lord Chief Justice and five other judges. The practice and procedure of the Court of Appeal and the High Court are virtually the same as in the corresponding courts in England and Wales. Both courts sit in the Royal Courts of Justice in Belfast.

The Court of Appeal has power to review the civil law decisions of the High Court and the criminal law decisions of the Crown Court, and may in certain cases review the decisions of county courts and magistrates' courts. Subject to certain restrictions, an appeal from a judgment of the Court of Appeal can go to the House of Lords.

The *High Court* is divided into a Queen's Bench Division, dealing with most civil law matters; a Chancery Division, dealing with, for instance, trusts and estates, title to land, mortgages and charges, wills and company matters; and a Family Division, dealing principally with matrimonial cases, adoption, wardship, patients' affairs and undisputed probate matters.

The *Crown Court* deals with all serious criminal cases.

Inferior Courts

The inferior courts are the county courts and the magistrates' courts, both of which differ in a number of ways from their counterparts in England and Wales.

County courts are primarily civil law courts. They are presided over by one of 14 county court judges, two of whom—in Belfast and Londonderry—have the title of recorder. Appeals go from the county courts to the High Court. The county courts also deal with appeals from the magistrates' courts in both criminal and civil matters. In civil matters, the county courts handle most actions in which the amount or the value of specific articles claimed is below a certain value. The courts also deal with actions involving title to, or the recovery of, land; equity matters such as trusts and estates; mortgages; and the sale of land and partnerships.

The day-to-day work of dealing summarily with minor local criminal cases is carried out in *magistrates' courts* presided over by a full-time, legally qualified resident magistrate. The magistrates' courts also exercise jurisdiction in certain family law cases and have a very limited jurisdiction in other civil cases.

Terrorist Offences

People accused of offences specified under emergency legislation (see p. 216) are tried in the Crown Court without jury. The onus remains on the prosecution to prove guilt beyond reasonable doubt and the defendant has the right to be represented by a lawyer of his or her choice. The judge must set out in a written statement the reasons for convicting and there is an automatic right of appeal to the Court of Appeal against conviction and/or sentence on points of fact as well as of law.

Administration of the Law

Court administration is the responsibility of the Lord Chancellor, while the Northern Ireland Office, under the Secretary of State, deals with policy and legislation concerning criminal law, the police and the penal system. The Lord Chancellor has general responsibility for legal aid, advice and assistance.

The Director of Public Prosecutions for Northern Ireland, who is responsible to the Attorney General, prosecutes all offences tried on indictment, and may do so in other (summary) cases. Most summary offences are prosecuted by the police.

Following the Good Friday Agreement of 1998 (see p. 16), the Government launched a review of criminal justice in Northern Ireland. (This excludes policing and emergency legislation, which are being considered separately.) The review is addressing the structure, management and resourcing of publicly funded elements of the criminal justice system, covering issues such as:

- appointments to the judiciary and magistracy;
- the organisation and supervision of the prosecution process;
- the responsiveness and accountability of the system;

- law reform;
- scope for co-operation between agencies in Northern Ireland and the Irish Republic; and
- the structure and organisation of criminal justice functions that might be devolved to a Northern Ireland Assembly.

Prison Service

The Prison Service in England and Wales, the Scottish Prison Service and the Northern Ireland Prison Service are all executive agencies. There are currently 136 prison establishments in England and Wales (seven of which are run by private contractors), 22 in Scotland and four in Northern Ireland.

Prison accommodation ranges from open prisons to high security establishments. Sentenced prisoners are classified into different risk-level groups for security purposes. Women prisoners are held in separate prisons or in separate accommodation in mixed prisons. There are no open prisons in Northern Ireland.

In recent years the prison population as a whole has been growing steadily in Great Britain, but falling in Northern Ireland (see Table 14.2).

Table 14.2: Average Daily Prison Population, 1993–98

	1993	1995	1998
England and Wales	44,566	51,047	65,298
Scotland	5,637	5,626	6,017 [a]
Northern Ireland	1,933	1,762	1,402 [b]

Sources: Home Office, the Scottish Executive and Northern Ireland Office
[a] Provisional.
[b] 1998–99 figure.

Independent Oversight of the Prison System

Every prison establishment in England, Wales and Northern Ireland has a board of visitors, comprising volunteers drawn from the local community appointed by the Home Secretary or Secretary of State for Northern Ireland. Boards, which are independent, monitor complaints by prisoners and concerns of staff, and report as necessary to ministers. In Scotland, visiting committees to prisons are appointed by local authorities.

Independent Prisons Inspectorates report on the treatment of prisoners and prison conditions, and submit annual reports to Parliament. Each prison establishment is visited about once every three years.

In England and Wales prisoners who fail to get satisfaction from the Prison Service's internal request and complaints system may complain to the Prisons Ombudsman, who is independent of the Prison Service. In Scotland, prisoners who exhaust the internal grievance procedure may apply to the independent Scottish Prisons Complaints Commission.

Privileges and Discipline

Prisoners in the UK may write and receive letters, be visited by relatives and friends, and make telephone calls. Privileges include a personal radio; books, magazines and newspapers; watching television; and the opportunity to buy goods from the prison shop with money earned in prison. Offences against prison discipline are dealt with by prison governors, who act as adjudicators. In England, Wales and Scotland measures to counter drug misuse in prisons include mandatory drug testing. Voluntary testing has been piloted in Northern Ireland but there is no mandatory programme. People awaiting trial in custody have certain rights and privileges not granted to convicted prisoners.

Prison Industries

Prison industries aim to give inmates work experience which will help with their resettlement into the community on release and to secure a return which will reduce the cost of the prison system. The main industries are clothing and textile manufacture, engineering, woodwork, laundry and horticulture. A small number of prisoners are employed outside prison, some in community-based service projects.

Prison Education

Education is compulsory for young people in custody below school-leaving age; otherwise it is voluntary. There are many facilities available for prisoners to gain vocational qualifications, and some prisoners study for public examinations, including those of the Open University (see p. 141).

Physical education is compulsory for young offenders, but otherwise voluntary. Opportunities are given for inmates to obtain sporting proficiency awards. Inmates also compete against teams from the local community.

Early Release of Prisoners

Prisoners in England and Wales sentenced to less than four years are released once they have served half of their term. Those sentenced to four years or more may be considered for early release after serving half of their sentence; if found unsuitable at that stage for parole, they are released automatically at the two-thirds point. The Parole Board has the final decision on the early release of prisoners sentenced to four years or more, but less than seven years. In other cases it makes a recommendation to the Home Secretary about a prisoner's suitability for parole. Prisoners sentenced to a year or more are released on licence to be supervised until the three-quarters point of the sentence; they can be recalled to prison if they present an unacceptable risk to the public during that time. If convicted of another offence punishable with imprisonment and committed before the end of the original sentence, a released prisoner may have to serve all or part of the original sentence outstanding at the time the fresh offence was committed.

In Scotland similar arrangements apply except that the Parole Board has the power to release prisoners serving between four and ten years from halfway through their sentence. The release of prisoners serving more than ten years needs the consent of the First Minister. All prisoners sentenced to four years or more are supervised from release until the end of their sentence.

The Crime and Disorder Act 1998 provides for:

- the release of selected short-term prisoners in England and Wales on a home detention curfew licence (from the end of January 1999), enforced by electronic monitoring, up to two months before the normal date of release;

- the imposition of a court sentence on a sexual or violent offender which includes an extended period of post-release supervision (also applicable in Scotland); and

- supervision of recalled and returned short-term prisoners following their second release from detention.

In Northern Ireland prisoners serving terms of more than five days are eligible for remission of half their sentence. Following the enactment of the Northern Ireland (Sentences) Act 1998 (realising a commitment made in the Good Friday Agreement—see p. 16), prisoners serving sentences of five years or more may make application for early release from custody. Their eligibility for release rests with the Sentence Review Commission, whose members have been approved by the Secretary of State for Northern Ireland.

Life Sentence Prisoners

The release on licence of prisoners serving mandatory life sentences for murder may only be authorised in England and Wales by the Home Secretary on the recommendation of the Parole Board. The Home Secretary is required to release prisoners serving life sentences for offences other than murder after an initial period set by the trial judge if so directed by the Parole Board. Similar procedures apply in Scotland. In Northern Ireland the Secretary of State reviews life sentence cases on the recommendation of an internal review body.

On release, life sentence prisoners remain on licence for the rest of their lives and are subject to recall if their behaviour suggests that they might again be a danger to the public.

Preparation for Release

Prisoners may be released on temporary licence for short periods, but they are subject to a rigorous risk assessment and are released only for precisely defined and specific activities which cannot be provided in prison establishments.

Pre-release schemes in England and Wales and in Scotland enable selected long-term prisoners to spend some time before release in certain units or prisons in order to help them readapt to society and renew ties with their families. Prisoners in such units work in paid employment in the community and return to the unit each evening. In Northern Ireland there is also a pre-release system and, for long-term prisoners, extended Christmas and summer home leave. Professional support is given to offenders after release.

Probation

The Probation Service in England and Wales supervises offenders in the community under direct court orders and after release from custody. It also advises offenders in custody. All young offenders and all prisoners in England and Wales sentenced to 12 months' imprisonment and over are supervised on release by the Probation Service, or, in the case of certain young offenders, by local authority social services departments or youth justice teams.

A court probation order requires offenders to maintain regular contact with their probation officer, who is expected to supervise them. The purpose of supervision under a probation order is to secure the rehabilitation of the offender, to protect the public and to prevent the offender from committing further offences. A probation order can last from six months to three years; an offender who fails to comply with any of the requirements can be brought before the court again. The Probation Service also administers some supervision orders and supervises those subject to community service orders and those released from prison on parole.

HM Inspectorate of Probation has both an inspection and an advisory role, and also monitors any work that the Probation Service carries out in conjunction with the voluntary and private sectors.

In Scotland local authority social work departments supervise offenders on probation, community service and other community disposals, and offenders subject to supervision on release from custody.

In Northern Ireland the probation service is administered by the government-funded Probation Board, whose membership is representative of the community.

Legal Aid

Someone who needs legal advice, assistance or representation may be able to get help with legal costs from the legal aid scheme. People who qualify for help may have all their legal costs paid for, or may be asked to make a contribution towards them, depending on their means and, in civil cases, the outcome of the case. Legally aided mediation is also available on a means-tested basis for certain family matters.

Legal Advice and Assistance

Legal advice is available under the Legal Advice and Assistance ('Green Form') Scheme in England and Wales. Those whose income and capital are within certain limits are entitled to free advice from a solicitor on most legal matters. The scheme provides initially for up to three hours' work for matrimonial cases where a petition is drafted, and two hours for other work. Similar schemes operate in Northern Ireland and Scotland.

Plans for a unified Probation Service to replace the 54 autonomous, individual services currently covering England and Wales were announced by the Government in April 1999. Under the proposed new structure, the Service will comprise 42 local operational areas, matching police force boundaries, and be led by a director who will be accountable to the Home Secretary. Chief Probation Officers, employed by the Home Office, will manage each area.

Legal Aid in Civil Proceedings

At present civil legal aid may be available for most civil proceedings to those who satisfy the financial eligibility conditions and have reasonable grounds for taking, defending or being a party to proceedings. It may be refused if, in the circumstances of the case, it is considered unreasonable to grant it. Payments to lawyers are made through the Legal Aid Fund, administered by the Legal Aid Board. Scotland has a separate Legal Aid Fund, administered by the Scottish Legal Aid Board. In Northern Ireland legal aid is administered by the Law Society for Northern Ireland.

An assisted person has some protection against orders for costs being made against him or her, and in certain limited circumstances the successful unassisted opponent of a legally aided party may recover costs from the Legal Aid Fund. Where the assisted person recovers or preserves money or property in the proceedings, the Legal Aid Fund will usually have a first call on that money or property to recover money spent on the assisted person's behalf (the 'statutory charge').

Legal Aid in Criminal Proceedings

England, Wales and Northern Ireland

In criminal proceedings legal aid may be granted by the court if it appears to be in the interests of justice and if a defendant is considered to require financial assistance. A contribution towards the costs may be payable.

The Legal Aid Board makes arrangements for duty solicitors to assist unrepresented defendants in the magistrates' courts. Solicitors are also available, on a 24-hour basis, to give advice and assistance to those being questioned by the police. These services are not means-tested and are free.

Where legal aid is granted for criminal cases in Northern Ireland it is free. There is a voluntary duty solicitor scheme at the main magistrates' court in Belfast.

Scotland

A duty solicitor is available to represent people in custody on their first appearance in the sheriff courts and the district courts without enquiry into the person's means. In other cases, a person seeking legal aid in summary criminal proceedings must apply to the Scottish Legal Aid Board, which must be satisfied that the expenses of the case cannot be met by the applicant without undue hardship, and that it is in the interests of justice that legal aid is awarded. In solemn proceedings the court decides on the availability of legal aid and must be satisfied that the accused cannot meet the expenses of the case without undue hardship. Where legal aid is granted to the accused in criminal proceedings, he or she is not required to pay any contribution towards expenses.

Administrative Reform

England and Wales

The Access to Justice Act 1999 is reforming the legal aid scheme and the provision of legal services. In the year 2000 the Legal Aid Board will be replaced by the Legal Services Commission, which will run the scheme. The Government also plans to establish a Criminal Defence Service, which will replace criminal legal aid. This will aim to ensure that people accused of crime are properly defended, while securing value for money and remaining sensitive to the needs of victims and witnesses and the public interest in the speedy administration of justice. There will also be a number of other changes:

- From January 2000 only franchised organisations which have a contract with the Legal Aid Board will be able to give civil advice and assistance. This will also apply to civil legal aid cases for family matters.

- It is likely that legal aid will no longer be available for most personal injury cases (except clinical negligence). Most personal injury cases will be brought under 'no win, no fee' agreements between solicitors and clients.

- The Community Legal Service will be set up throughout England and Wales. The Legal Services Commission will work with local government authorities and others to make sure people have access to the legal services that they need.

Scotland

Since October 1998 all solicitors providing criminal legal assistance must register with the Scottish Legal Aid Board and conform to the Board's code of practice; a pilot scheme for public defence solicitors employed by the Board has been introduced to test alternative ways of providing publicly funded legal representation. Fixed payments for solicitors providing legal aid in summary cases were introduced in April 1999.

In 1998, the Government issued a consultation paper (*Access to Justice—Beyond the Year 2000*) on reforming civil legal assistance, reflecting its aim of ensuring that legal aid is properly targeted and cost-effective. Responses to the consultation are under consideration.

Other Legal Advice

In some urban areas law centres provide free legal advice and representation. They may employ a salaried lawyer and many have community workers. Much of their time is devoted to housing, employment, social security and immigration problems.

Advice is also available in Citizens Advice Bureaux, consumer and housing advice centres, and from voluntary organisations. The Legal Aid Board has entered into contracts with some of these agencies to fund the provision of legal aid and assistance.

Further Reading

The Lord Chancellor's Departments: Departmental Report—The Government's Expenditure Plans 1999–2000 to 2001–2002. Cm 4206. The Stationery Office, 1999.

Home Office Annual Report 1999: The Government's Expenditure Plans 1999–2000 to 2001–2002. Cm 4205. The Stationery Office, 1999.

Modernising Justice. Cm 4155. The Stationery Office, 1998.

Tackling Drugs to Build a Better Britain: A Ten-Year Strategy for Tackling Drug Misuse. Cm 3945. The Stationery Office, 1998.

The Criminal Justice System—Strategic Plan 1999–2002 and Business Plan 1999–2000. Home Office, Lord Chancellor's Department and Attorney General's Office, 1999.

Access to Justice—Beyond the Year 2000. The Scottish Office, 1998.

Websites

Lord Chancellor's Department: www.open.gov.uk/lcd

Home Office: www.homeoffice.gov.uk

Scottish Executive: www.scotland.gov.uk

15 Religion

Everyone in the United Kingdom has the right to religious freedom. Religious organisations and groups may conduct their rites and ceremonies, promote their beliefs within the limits of the law, own property and run schools. There is no religious bar to the holding of public office.

INTRODUCTION

Christianity is the predominant religious tradition in the UK in terms of the size of its following, but there are also large Muslim, Hindu, Jewish and Sikh communities, and smaller communities of Baha'is, Buddhists, Jains and Zoroastrians. Although members within each community share many beliefs and practices, there may be significant differences of tradition, organisation, language and ethnicity. There has been a significant development of other forms of religious expression, with the growth of a range of independent churches and other groups often referred to as 'cults' or 'sects' which have now become known collectively as 'new religious movements'. Another recent trend has been the rise in 'New Age' spirituality, drawn from a variety of spiritual traditions and practices, and characterised by a concern for ecology and personal development. The UK also has a large proportion of people who may actively involve themselves in religious life only at times of crisis or significant events such as birth, marriage and death. Organisations such as the British Humanist Association and the National Secular Society offer non-religious alternatives.

Table 15.1: Church Membership[a] in the United Kingdom, 1970–95 *Thousands*

	1970	1980	1990	1995
Christian (Trinitarian[b])	9,122	7,554	6,693	6,361
Non-Trinitarian	285	353	459	522
Hindu	80	120	140	155
Jewish	120	111	101	94
Muslim	130	306	495	580
Sikh	100	150	250	350
Others	21	53	87	116

Source: Christian Research

[a] Active adult members.

[b] Trinitarian means acceptance of the historic formulary of the Godhead as three eternal persons.

Relations with the State

There are two churches legally recognised as official churches of the State, or established churches, in the UK: in England the Anglican *Church of England*, and in Scotland the Presbyterian *Church of Scotland*. There is no longer an established Church in Wales or Northern Ireland. Ministers of the established churches, as well as clergy belonging to other religious groups, work in services run by the State, such as the armed forces, national hospitals and prisons, and may be paid a state salary for such services.

Religious Education

In England and Wales all state schools must provide religious education, each local education authority being responsible for producing a locally agreed syllabus. Syllabuses must reflect Christianity, while taking account of the teaching and practices of the other principal religions represented in the UK. State schools must provide a daily act of collective worship. Parents may withdraw their children from religious education.

There are similar requirements in Scotland, where education authorities must ensure that schools practise religious observance and give pupils religious instruction. The law does not specify the form of such education but it is recommended that pupils be provided with a broad-based curriculum which gives a central place to Christianity, encouraging tolerance and respect of other religions.

In Northern Ireland a core syllabus for religious education has been approved by the main churches and this must be taught in all state schools. Integrated education is encouraged and all schools must be open to pupils of all religions, although in practice most Catholic pupils attend Catholic maintained or Catholic voluntary grammar schools, and most Protestant children are enrolled at controlled schools or non-denominational voluntary grammar schools.

Church Maintenance

The State does not contribute to the general expenses of church maintenance although some state aid does help repair historic churches. In 1998–99, the joint scheme of English Heritage and the Heritage Lottery Fund offered grants to churches totalling £12.2 million. Assistance is also given to meet some of the costs of repairing cathedrals, with £2.6 million made available in 1998–99. Funding is not restricted to Church of England buildings.

The Historic Chapels Trust was established to take into ownership redundant chapels and other places of worship in England of outstanding architectural and historic interest. Buildings of all denominations and faiths are taken into care, including Nonconformist chapels, Roman Catholic churches, synagogues and private Anglican chapels.

The Churches Conservation Trust (formerly the Redundant Churches Fund) of the Church of England preserves Anglican churches of particular cultural importance that are no longer used as regular places of worship. At present 317 churches are being maintained in this way.

Social Involvement

The Church of England's Church Urban Fund is an independent charity which raises money to enable those living in the most disadvantaged urban areas to set up local projects to help alleviate the effects of poverty on their lives. These projects help support a wide range of community-based programmes concerned with issues such as education, employment, young people and poverty. Although rooted in the Christian faith, the Fund does not restrict its grants on the basis of religious belief. By 1999 it had made grants totalling £33 million to nearly 2,000 different projects. In 1998, £3.6 million was awarded to 298 projects; 168 projects received grants of between £2,000 and £50,000, and 130 projects received between £200 and £2,000.

The General Assembly of the Church of Scotland debates annual reports from its Committee on Church and Nation, on social, economic and political matters; and, through its Board of Social Responsibility, it is the largest voluntary social work agency in Scotland. The Board currently runs and manages more than 80 projects offering care and support to over 4,000 people every day.

The Inner Cities Religious Council, based in the Department of the Environment, Transport and the Regions, provides a forum in which the Government and the faith communities work together on issues relating to urban regeneration in England. Chaired by a government minister, the Council comprises senior leaders of the Christian, Hindu, Jewish, Muslim and Sikh faiths.

The Census and Religious Affiliation

Questions are not normally asked about religious beliefs in censuses or for other official purposes, except in Northern Ireland. However, the Government White Paper *The 2001 Census of Population* (see p. 109), published in March 1999, proposes that the next census should include a question on religion for England and Wales, subject to a change in the Census Act 1920. It will be for the Scottish Parliament to approve separate legislation for Scotland if it chooses to do so.

The Sacred Land Project

The Sacred Land Project, a five-year programme launched in 1997, is promoting the environmental improvement of sacred sites in the UK. It brings together religious, conservation and heritage groups to undertake specific projects, such as reopening historic pilgrimage routes, and restoring or developing sacred sites. The project has the support of the major Christian denominations, other faith traditions and environmental groups, and is backed by the World Wide Fund for Nature–UK and the Alliance of Religions and Conservation.

THE CHRISTIAN COMMUNITY

Church of England

The Church of England became the established church during the Reformation in the 16th century. Conflicts between Church and State culminated in the Act of Supremacy in 1534, which repudiated papal supremacy and declared Henry VIII to be the Supreme Head of the Church of England. The title was altered to 'Supreme Governor' by Elizabeth I when she acceded to the throne in 1558. The Church of England's form of worship was set out in successive versions of the Book of Common Prayer from 1549 onwards. The Church's relationship with the State is one of mutual obligation, since the Church's privileges are balanced by certain duties it must fulfil.

The Monarch is the 'Supreme Governor' of the Church of England and must always be a member of the Church, and promise to uphold it. The Church can regulate its own worship. Church of England archbishops, bishops and deans of cathedrals are appointed by the Monarch on the advice of the Prime Minister, although the Crown Appointments Commission, which includes lay and clergy representatives, plays a key role in the selection of archbishops and diocesan bishops. All clergy swear allegiance to the Crown. Clergy of the Church, together with those of the Church of Scotland, the Church of Ireland and the Roman Catholic Church, may not sit in the House of Commons. The two archbishops (of Canterbury and York), the bishops of London, Durham and Winchester, and 21 other senior bishops sit in the House of Lords. The Government does not propose any change in the transitional House of Lords (see p. 41) in the representation of the Church of England within the House.

The Church of England is divided into two provinces: Canterbury, comprising 30 dioceses, including the Diocese in Europe; and York, with 14 dioceses. The dioceses are divided into archdeaconries and deaneries, which are in turn divided into about 13,000 parishes, although in practice many of these are grouped together. Altogether, there are about 13,000 Church of England clergy, excluding those in mainland Europe. In 1997, 189,000 people were baptised in the Church in the two provinces, excluding the Diocese in Europe; of these, 141,000 were under one year old, representing 23% of live births. In the same year there were 43,000 confirmations. In 1997, 80,000 marriages were solemnised in the Church of England. These accounted for 66% of all marriages with religious ceremonies, and 30% of all marriages in England.

In 1998 the General Synod, the central governing and legislative body, approved proposals to overhaul the central organisation and structure of the Church. The number of Church Commissioners (see below) was reduced by two-thirds and some of their powers transferred to an Archbishops' Council which became the Church's central co-ordinating body. The Council, chaired by the Archbishops of Canterbury and York, started work in early 1999 and comprises bishops, clergy and lay members. It is the centre of an administrative system dealing with inter-church relations, inter-faith relations, social questions, recruitment and training for the ministry, and missionary work. It also covers the care of church buildings, church schools (which are largely maintained from public funds), colleges and institutes of higher education, voluntary and parish education, and other church work in the UK and overseas.

The Church Commissioners are responsible for managing the greater part of the Church of England's assets. The Prime Minister appoints an MP to the unpaid post of Second Church Estates Commissioner to represent the Commissioners in Parliament. Apart from the Church Commissioners' investment income, most of the remainder of the Church's income is provided by local voluntary donations. The average annual stipend of a Church of England priest is about £15,760; additional benefits include free housing (valued at £7,820) and a non-contributory pension.

The Church of England reported an increase in the ordination of new clergy between 1997 and 1998 (from 410 to 476), and in the number of people in training for ordination. There are at present over 1,400 people in training.

The first women priests were ordained in 1994 and by 1998 they numbered 1,900. Women priests cannot, however, be appointed bishop or archbishop.

Other Anglican Churches

The Church of England is part of a worldwide Communion of Anglican churches. These are similar in organisation and worship to the Church of England and originated from it. There are four distinct Anglican Churches in the British Isles: the Church of England, the Church in Wales, the Episcopal Church in Scotland, and the Church of Ireland (which operates in both Northern Ireland and the Irish Republic). Each is governed separately by its own institutions.

The Anglican Communion comprises 38 autonomous Churches in the UK and abroad, and three regional councils overseas, with a total membership of about 70 million. Links between the components of the Anglican Communion are maintained by the Lambeth Conference of Anglican bishops, which is held in Canterbury every ten years, the last conference having taken place in 1998. Presided over by the Archbishop of Canterbury, the Conference has no executive authority, but enjoys considerable influence. Issues debated at the 1998 Conference included Third World debt, sexuality, human rights, and relationships with other faiths.

The Anglican Consultative Council, an assembly of lay people and clergy as well as bishops, meets every two or three years to allow consultation with the Anglican Communion. The Primates Meeting brings together the senior bishops from each Church at similar intervals.

Church of Scotland

The Church of Scotland became the national church following the Scottish Reformation in the late 16th century and legislation enacted by the Scottish Parliament. The Church's status was then consolidated in the Treaty of Union of 1707 and by the Church of Scotland Act 1921, the latter confirming its complete freedom in all spiritual matters. The Church appoints its own office bearers, and its affairs are not subject to any civil authority.

The adult communicant membership is over 660,000; and there are 1,167 ministers serving in parishes. Both men and women may join the ministry. The Church of Scotland has a Presbyterian form of government, that is, government by church courts or councils, composed of ministers, elders (presbyters), all of whom are ordained to office, and deacons. The 1,300 churches are governed locally by courts known as Kirk Sessions, consisting of ministers and elders. The next court is the Presbytery, responsible for a geographical area made up of a number of parishes; and finally there is the General Assembly, the supreme court, consisting of elected ministers, elders and deacons. The General Assembly meets annually under the chairmanship of an elected moderator, who serves for one year. The Monarch is normally represented by the Lord High Commissioner at the General Assembly.

There are also a number of independent Scottish Presbyterian churches, largely descended from groups which broke away from the Church of Scotland. They are very active in the Highlands and Islands.

Free Churches

The term 'Free Churches' is often used to describe those Protestant churches in the UK which, unlike the Church of England and the Church of Scotland, are not established churches. Free Churches have existed in various forms since the Reformation, developing their own traditions over the years. Their members have also been known as dissenters or nonconformists. Although this historical experience has given these churches a certain sense of shared identity, they otherwise vary greatly in doctrine, worship and church government. All the major Free Churches—Methodist, Baptist, Presbyterian, United Reformed and Salvation Army—have ministers of both sexes.

The Methodist Church, the largest of the Free Churches, originated in the 18th century following the Evangelical Revival under John Wesley (1703–91). It has 353,330 adult full members and a community of more than 1.2 million. The present church is based on the 1932 union of most of the separate Methodist Churches. It has 3,727 ministers and student ministers and 6,452 places of worship.

MAYC, the youth service of the Methodist Church, serves over 50,000 young people between the ages of 13 and 25. Each year MAYC organises a national youth event which is one of the largest in Europe, bringing together dance, drama, rock music and worship.

The Baptists first achieved an organised form in Britain in the 17th century. Today they are mainly organised in groups of churches, most of which belong to the Baptist Union of Great Britain (re-formed in 1812) with about 147,100 members, 1,780 ministers and 2,100 places of worship. There are also separate Baptist Unions for Scotland, Wales and Ireland, and other independent Baptist Churches.

The third largest of the Free Churches is the United Reformed Church, with some 92,000 members, 950 serving ministers and 1,740 places of worship. It was formed in 1972 upon the merger of the Congregational Church in England and Wales (the oldest Protestant minority in the UK, whose origins can be traced back to the Puritans of the 16th century) with the Presbyterian Church of England (a church closely related in doctrine and worship to the Church of Scotland). In 1981 there was a further merger with the Reformed Association of the Churches of Christ.

The Salvation Army was founded in the East End of London in 1865 by William Booth (1829–1912). Within the UK it is second only to the Government as a provider of social services. It is the largest provider of hostel accommodation, offering almost 4,000 beds every night. Other services include work with alcoholics, prison chaplaincy and a family tracing service which receives 5,000 enquiries each year. The Salvation Army in the UK is served by 1,600 officers (ordained ministers) and runs over 800 worship centres.

The Religious Society of Friends (Quakers), with about 17,000 adult members and 9,500 attenders in the UK and 490 places of worship, was founded in the middle of the 17th century under the leadership of George Fox (1624–91). It has no ordained ministers and no formal liturgy or sacraments. Silent worship is central to its life as a religious organisation and emphasis is also placed on social concern and peacemaking.

Among the other Free Churches are: the Presbyterian Church in Ireland, the largest Protestant church in Northern Ireland, where it has around 300,000 members; the Presbyterian (or Calvinistic Methodist) Church of Wales, with 49,750 members and the largest of the Free Churches in Wales; and the Union of Welsh Independents with 40,750 members.

Pentecostalist Organisations and Charismatic Groupings

A recent development has been the rise of Pentecostalism and the charismatic movement. A number of Pentecostalist bodies were formed in the UK at the turn of the century. The two main Pentecostalist organisations in the UK today are the Assemblies of God, with approximately 54,000 members, over 900 ministers and over 650 places of worship; and the Elim Pentecostal Church. Since the Second World War immigration from the Caribbean has led to a significant number of Black majority Pentecostalist churches.

In the early 1960s a Pentecostalist charismatic movement began to influence some followers in the Church of England, the Roman Catholic Church and the historic Free Churches. The Christian 'house church' movement (or 'new churches') began in the 1970s when some of the charismatics began to establish their own congregations. Services were originally held in private houses although many congregations have now acquired their own buildings. The movement, whose growth within the UK has been most marked in England, is characterised by lay leadership and is organised into a number of loose fellowships, usually on a regional basis, such as the Ichthus Fellowship in south-east London.

Roman Catholic Church

The formal structure of the Roman Catholic Church in England and Wales, which was suppressed after the Reformation, was restored in 1850, and that of the Scottish Roman Catholic Church, suppressed in the early 17th century, in 1878. There are now seven Roman Catholic provinces in Great Britain, each under an archbishop; and 30 dioceses each under a bishop—22 in England and Wales and eight in Scotland. There are 2,843 parish churches in England and Wales and 828 other churches and chapels open to the public. Scotland has 463 parish churches.

The Catholic Church in Ireland is organised as a unit covering the whole island. There are 1,329 parishes, and, as many parishes have more than one church, 2,646 churches. Northern Ireland is covered by seven dioceses, some of which also have territory in the Irish Republic.

There are approximately 12,000 members of religious orders in England, Scotland and Wales. These orders undertake teaching and chaplaincy, and social work such as nursing, childcare and running homes for the elderly.

Other Churches

Other Protestant Churches include the Unitarians and Free Christians, whose origins go back to the Reformation. The Christian Brethren are a Protestant body organised by J.N. Darby (1800–82). There are two branches: the Open Brethren and the Closed or Exclusive Brethren.

Many Christian communities founded by migrant communities, including the Orthodox, Lutheran and Reformed Churches of various European countries, the Coptic Orthodox Church and the Armenian Church, have established their own centres of worship, particularly in London. All these churches operate in a variety of languages. The largest is probably the Greek Orthodox Church, many of whose members are of Cypriot origin.

There are also several other religious groups in the UK which were founded in the United States in the last century. These include the Church of Jesus Christ of the Latter-Day Saints (the Mormon Church, with about 180,000 members), the Jehovah's Witnesses (146,000 members), the Christadelphians, the Christian Scientists, and the Seventh-Day Adventists. The Spiritualists have about 36,000 members, over 500 churches and nearly 300 ministers.

Co-operation among the Churches

Churches Together in Britain and Ireland is the main co-ordinating body for the Christian churches in the UK. The Council co-ordinates the work of its 32 member churches and associations of churches, in the areas of social responsibility, international affairs, church life, world mission, racial justice and inter-faith relations. The Council's member churches are also grouped in separate ecumenical bodies, according to country: Churches Together in England, Action of Churches Together in Scotland, Churches Together in Wales, and the Irish Council of Churches.

The Free Churches' Council, with 19 member denominations, includes most of the Free Churches of England and Wales. It promotes co-operation among the Free Churches (especially in hospital chaplaincy and in education matters).

The Evangelical Alliance, with a membership of individuals, churches or societies drawn from 20 denominations, represents over 1 million evangelical Christians.

Inter-church discussions about the search for Christian unity take place internationally, as well as within the UK, and the main participants are the Anglican, Baptist, Lutheran, Methodist, Orthodox, Reformed and Roman Catholic Churches. In 1999 the Church of England and the Methodist Church began formal discussions on a move towards unity. The Baptist Union, the Moravian Church, the Roman Catholic Church and the United Reformed Church had participating observers at the discussions. Informal trilateral contact between the Church of England, the Methodist Church and the United Reformed Church also began in 1999.

OTHER FAITH COMMUNITIES

The Buddhist Community

The Buddhist community in the UK has followers both of British or Western origin, and of South Asian and Asian background. In 1907, a Buddhist Society of Great Britain and Ireland was formed but did not become firmly established. In 1924 Christmas Humphreys (1901–83) founded the Buddhist Centre of the Theosophical Society from what remained of the earlier society. This became the Buddhist Lodge of the Theosophical Society in 1926, and was constituted as a new and independent organisation—the Buddhist Society—in 1943. The Society promotes the principles, but does not adhere to any particular school, of Buddhism. The Network of Buddhist Organisations represents many of the various Buddhist educational, cultural, charitable and teaching organisations.

Although religious buildings are not as central to Buddhist life as to that of some other religious traditions, there are well over 500 Buddhist groups and centres, including some 50 monasteries and temples in the UK.

The Hindu Community

The Hindu community in the UK originates largely from India, although others have come from countries to which earlier generations had previously migrated, such as Kenya, Tanzania, Uganda, Zambia and Malawi. Migrants have also come from Fiji and from Trinidad and other Caribbean islands. It is estimated that the number of members is around 400,000 to 550,000, although some community representatives suggest a considerably higher figure (of close to 1 million). They are predominantly Gujaratis (between 65% and 70%) and Punjabis (between 15% and 20%). Most of the remainder have their ancestral roots in other parts of India such as Uttar Pradesh, West Bengal, and the Southern states, as well as other countries such as Sri Lanka.

The first Hindu temple, or mandir, was opened in London in the 1950s and there are now over 120 mandirs in the UK; many are affiliated to the National Council of Hindu Temples (UK). Other national bodies serving the Hindu community include the Hindu Council (UK) and Vishwa Hindu Parishad.

The Swaminarayan Hindu Temple, in north London, is the first purpose-built Hindu temple in Europe, having a large cultural complex with provision for conferences, exhibitions, marriages, sports and health clinics.

The Jewish Community

Jews first settled in England at the time of the Norman Conquest. They were banished by royal decree in 1290, but readmitted following the English Civil War (1642–51). Sephardi Jews, who originally came from Spain and Portugal, have been present in the UK since the mid-17th century. The majority of Jews in the UK today are Ashkenazi Jews, of Central and East European origin, who fled persecution in the Russian Empire between 1881 and 1914, and Nazi persecution in Germany and other European countries from 1933 onwards.

The Jewish community in the UK numbers about 285,000, and about 70% are affiliated to synagogues. Of these, most Ashkenazi Jews (60%) acknowledge the authority of the Chief Rabbi, while the more strictly observant (7%) have their own spiritual leaders, as do the Sephardim. The Reform movement (founded in 1840), the Liberal and Progressive movement (founded in 1901) and the recently established Masorti movement, account for most of the remaining 30% of synagogue members.

Jewish congregations in the UK number about 365. The Board of Deputies of British Jews is the officially recognised representative body for these groups. Founded in 1760, it is elected mainly by synagogues, but a growing number of communal organisations are also represented. The Board serves as the voice of the community to both government and the wider non-Jewish community.

Roughly two in every five Jewish children aged 5 to 17 attend Jewish day schools, some of which are supported by public funds. Over 100 agencies provide welfare services throughout the community.

The Muslim Community

A significant Muslim community has existed in the UK since Muslim seamen and traders, from the Middle East and the Indian subcontinent, settled around the major ports in the early 19th century. There was further settlement from those demobilised from military service in the British army after the First World War, and of workers seeking, or recruited for, employment in the mills and factories in the 1950s and 1960s because of a shortage of labour following the Second World War. The 1970s saw the arrival of large numbers of Muslims of Asian origin from Kenya and Uganda. There are also well-established Turkish Cypriot and Iranian Muslim communities, while more recently Muslims from Somalia, Iraq, Bosnia and Kosovo have sought refuge in the UK. It is estimated that there are between 1.5 million and 2 million Muslims in the UK and estimates from within the community suggest that the proportion of young people in demographic terms is significantly higher than the national average.

There are over 600 mosques and numerous community Muslim centres throughout the UK. Mosques are not only places of worship; they also offer instruction in the Muslim way of life and facilities for education and welfare. The first mosque in the UK was established at Woking, Surrey, in 1890. Mosques now range from converted houses in many towns to the Central Mosque in Regent's Park, London, and its associated Islamic Cultural Centre, one of the most important Muslim institutions in the western world. The Central Mosque has the largest congregation in the UK, and during festivals it may number over 30,000. The main conurbations in the Midlands, North West and North East of England and in Scotland also have their own central mosques with a range of community facilities.

Sunni and Shi'a are the two principal traditions within Islam and both are represented among the Muslim community in the UK. Sufism, the mystical aspect of Islam, can be found in both traditions, and members of some of the major Sufi traditions have also developed branches in British cities.

The Muslim Council of Britain, founded in 1997, is a representative body of established national and regional Muslim bodies as well as local mosques, organisations and specialist institutions. The Council aims to promote co-operation, consensus and unity on Muslim affairs in the UK.

The Sikh Community

Most of the Sikh community in the UK are of Punjabi ethnic origin. A significant minority came from East Africa and other former British colonies to which members of their family had migrated, but the vast majority have come to the UK directly from the Punjab. It is estimated that there are between 400,000 and 500,000 members, making it the largest Sikh community outside the Indian subcontinent.

The first gurdwara, or temple, in the UK was opened in Shepherd's Bush, London, in 1911. The largest is situated in Southall, Middlesex. Gurdwaras cater for the religious, educational, social welfare and cultural needs of their community. A granthi is usually employed to take care of the building and to conduct prayers. There are over 200 gurdwaras in the UK, the vast majority being in England and Wales.

Other Faiths

Jainism is an ancient religion brought to the UK by immigrants mainly from the Gujarat and Rajasthan areas of India. It is estimated that there are between 25,000 and 30,000 members in the UK. The Zoroastrian religion, or Mazdaism, is mainly represented in the UK by the Parsi community, whose ancestors left Iran in the 9th century and settled in north-west India. Founders of the UK community originally settled in the 19th century and it is estimated there are between 5,000 and 10,000 members. The Baha'i movement originated in Persia in the 19th century. The UK community has around 6,000 members connected to 200 local groups and 180 local spiritual assemblies. Rastafarianism, with its roots in the return-to-Africa movement, emerged in the West Indies early in the 20th century. It arrived in the UK with immigration from Jamaica in the 1950s.

New Religious Movements

A number of new religious movements, established since the Second World War and often with overseas origins, are active in the UK. Examples include the Church of Scientology, the Transcendental Meditation movement, the Unification Church and various New Age groups. INFORM (Information Network Focus on Religious Movements), which is supported by the main Churches, carries out research and seeks to provide objective information about new religious movements.

CO-OPERATION BETWEEN FAITHS

The Inter Faith Network for the United Kingdom links a wide range of organisations with an interest in inter-faith relations, including the representative bodies of the Baha'i, Buddhist, Christian, Hindu, Jain, Jewish, Muslim, Sikh and Zoroastrian communities. The Network promotes good relations between faiths in the UK and runs a public advice and information service on inter-faith issues. The Council of Christians and Jews works for better understanding among members of the two religions and deals with educational and social issues. Churches Together in Britain and Ireland (see p. 243) has a Commission on Inter Faith Relations. There are now many organisations in the UK dealing wholly, or in part, with inter-faith issues. Many towns and cities now have inter-faith councils or groups whose focus is working for good inter-faith relations locally.

Faith and the Year 2000

In the UK many national and civic millennium celebrations will have a specifically Christian framework. However, the Government wants to ensure that the celebrations are relevant and accessible to people of all faiths. *Marking the Millennium in a Multi-Faith Context*, published by the Department for Culture, Media and Sport in association with the Inter Faith Network, gives guidance to events organisers on how to make the millennium celebrations inclusive of both Christians and followers of other faiths. Many local congregations are planning activities and events under three themes: 'a new start with God', 'a new start at home' and 'a new start for the world's poor'. Local churches will be distributing a special millennium candle pack to every household in December 1999.

Further Reading

UK Christian Handbook 1998–99, ed. Peter Brierly and Heather Wraight. OM Publishing.

UK Christian Handbook—Religious Trends No. 1, 1998–99, ed. Peter Brierly. Paternoster Publishing.

Religions in the UK: A Multi-Faith Directory, ed. Paul Weller, University of Derby and The Inter Faith Network for the United Kingdom, 1997.

16 Culture

The biggest ever reform of cultural funding and organisation is encouraging wider access to, and excellence and innovation in, the arts, to improve the quality of people's lives. It involves extra grants of £290 million among cultural institutions in England during 1999–2002, while the Arts Council of England will allot 15% more funding in 1999–2000 than in 1998–99. Thirteen out of 24 Academy Awards in 1999 went to artists working on films shot largely in the UK. The new Museum of Scotland in Edinburgh is the first national museum to be built in Britain for 120 years.

The UK's cultural life flourished in 1998–99, with more opera, music of all kinds, dance, drama, art and film than ever before. The newly restored Royal Opera House in London is on target to reopen in November 1999. Opera audiences in the UK are steadily increasing, with 3 million adults claiming to be attenders. Enthusiasm for British pop, rock and jazz shows no sign of diminishing. British ballet companies have programmes at home and overseas. Some of the UK's most favourably reviewed theatrical productions have been exported with success, while leading US performers have been applauded in the UK. London has been host to outstanding art exhibitions, one of them giving rise to the UK's first 24-hour art show. There has also been unprecedented praise, and awards, for recent films, either UK-funded or made in Britain, with British players, directors, writers and technicians.

In November 1998 the Creative Industries Task Force (CITF—see p. 248) reported that

The fascination of Shakespeare for audiences and readers is undiminished. His enduring and growing appeal, it was said, transcended cultural, social, historical and linguistic boundaries. A BBC Radio 4 poll named him 'personality of the millennium' and critics held him to have had greater influence on European literature than any other writer.

UK creative industries (including music, television and radio, software, theatre, film, publishing, design, architecture, fashion, crafts and antiques), with a current annual growth rate of 5%, generate £60 billion of revenue a year and employ over 1.4 million people, with potential to create 50,000 new jobs over the next three years. The export market in creative goods and services is about £7.5 billion a year. Britain's share of international exports in the cultural sector, at just over 16%, is three times greater than its share of world trade overall. British talent is behind two out of every five successful computer games in the world; British publishing firms are worth £16.3 billion, design £12 billion, and television and radio £6.4 billion.

Government Policy

The Department for Culture, Media and Sport (DCMS) determines government policy and administers expenditure on national museums and art galleries in England, the Arts Council of England (see below), the British Library and other national arts and heritage bodies. Other responsibilities include the regulation of the film and music industries, broadcasting and the press, the National Lottery and the export licensing of antiques.

The National Assembly for Wales, the Scottish Parliament and the Northern Ireland Assembly have taken over responsibility for the arts in their countries, including museums, galleries and libraries, and their respective Arts Councils (see below).

Government funds are distributed to arts organisations indirectly, through bodies such as the Arts Councils, the British Film Institute (*bfi*) and Scottish Screen. In the most wide-ranging reform of UK cultural institutions for decades, the DCMS budget of £912 million is to be raised to £1,038 million by 2001–02, with an extra £290 million to be spent on the arts, media and sport, a rise in real terms of 5.5%. From this extra funding, £99 million is to go to museums and galleries, with provision for the removal of all entry charges for national collections sponsored by the DCMS by 2001, and £125 million to the performing and visual arts. (An additional £31 million has been made available for the arts in Scotland during 1999–2002.)

The reform includes:

- new arrangements to support the crafts at national level while safeguarding the work that the Crafts Council currently does;

- creation of a national body to champion architecture, taking on the Royal Fine Art Commission's design review role and the Arts Councils' awards programmes;

- a single Film Council to develop film culture and the film industry;

- a Museums, Libraries and Archives Council to replace the Museums & Galleries Commission (see p. 261) and the Library and Information Commission;

- DCMS representation in the Government Offices for the Regions (see p. 9);

- three-year funding agreements with most sponsored bodies, coupled with responsibilities to fulfil their targets; and

- establishment of a Quality, Efficiency and Standards Team (QUEST) to monitor financial management across DCMS sectors.

The CITF identifies key issues vital to the economic health of the creative industries. Among its present priorities are developing skills among the creative workforce; improving access to funding for their businesses; maximising exports; ensuring copyright protection of intellectual property; and focusing on more regional activity.

Arts Councils

The independent Arts Councils of England, Scotland, Wales and Northern Ireland are the main channels for the distribution of government grants and lottery funding to the visual, performing, community arts and literature. The Arts Councils give financial assistance and advice not only to the major performing arts organisations, but also to small touring theatre companies, experimental performance groups and literary organisations. They provide funds for training arts administrators and help to develop sponsorship and local authority support. They also promote education and public access to, and participation in, performing and visual arts and literature.

The Arts Council of England (ACE) is the authority for the arts in England and acts as their 'champion'. It rewards quality through its annual award allocations and through its stabilisation programme, which helps arts organisations manage long-term change. The

ACE's Recovery Programme is designed to provide rapid, shorter-term help to arts organisations with pressing financial difficulties.

The ACE is delegating funding decisions for many arts companies to the ten *Regional Arts Boards* (RABs), which assumed extended responsibilities from April 1999 and deal with an average 19% increase in allocation for 1999–2000. Other sources of money for the RABs are the *bfi* and local authorities. The ACE will continue to decide awards to the Royal Opera, the Royal Ballet, the Birmingham Royal Ballet, English National Opera, the Royal Shakespeare Company (RSC), the Royal National Theatre and the South Bank Centre; and to the main touring companies, such as Opera North and English National Ballet.

The Arts Council of Wales's Collectorplan Scheme (established in 1987 and the largest such scheme in the UK) has handled some 13,400 loans valued at over £4.3 million, enabling the public to buy about 16,000 works of art.

Finance

In England planned central government expenditure through the DCMS in 1999–2000 amounts to £219.7 million for museums and galleries; £228 million for the visual and performing arts; £103.7 million for broadcasting and the media (including film); and £89.7 million for libraries. Funding for the arts is channelled mainly through the ACE, which has a grant of £227.3 million in 1999–2000 (an increase of £37.9 million on 1998–99), including the Pairing Scheme for the Arts (see p. 250) and funding for Crafts. In addition, all four Arts Councils distribute National Lottery proceeds, amounting to about £265 million a year (£227.8 million for the ACE).

Planned 1999–2000 expenditure by the Arts Councils for Scotland, Wales and Northern Ireland is respectively £28.4 million, £14.8 million and £6.9 million, between 3% and 4% up on 1998–99. The Scottish Executive is also providing £42 million for Scotland's National Galleries and Museums, National Library and film industry, while the National Assembly for Wales is giving some £35 million for Wales's National Museum, National Library and other

arts. Planned spending by the Department of Education for Northern Ireland on the National Museums (see p. 263) and arts amounts to £7.5 million in 1999–2000.

National Lottery

By December 1998, Lottery awards of some £1.3 billion had been announced by the Arts Councils for arts projects. Grants for the acquisition of works of art from the Heritage Lottery Fund (HLF—see p. 328) to museums, galleries and other organisations between June 1995 and April 1999 amounted to £49.7 million. The Lottery's New Opportunities Fund, launched in January 1999, is developing a network of community centres, linked to libraries and the National Grid for Learning (see p. 128), to open up access to information. Millennium Festival Awards for All, allowing community organisations to apply for grants of up to £5,000, has been available throughout Great Britain from April 1999. Larger one-off Lottery awards, for example to Chester's Gateway Theatre (£23,200) and to Ilkley's Literature Festival (£20,000), support millennium arts projects. Among substantial awards in Scotland are £1.4 million to the Pitlochry Festival Society for upgrading facilities. The Millennium Theatre in Londonderry, which has received £2.5 million, will open at the end of 2000.

NESTA

The National Endowment for Science, Technology and the Arts has initial finance of £200 million from the National Lottery. It aims to help talented individuals or groups to develop their full potential; to turn creativity into products and services that are effectively exploited with rights effectively protected; and to contribute to public knowledge and appreciation of science, technology and the arts. It launched its first programmes in summer 1999.

Local Authorities

Local authorities maintain about 1,000 local museums and art galleries, and a network of public libraries (see p. 265). They also provide grant aid for professional and amateur orchestras, theatres, and opera and dance companies. In England total expenditure on museums, galleries and libraries for 1998–99 was £941 million. Fourteen authorities are to pilot Local Cultural Strategies, a DCMS scheme to bring cultural issues into the heart of local government planning in 1999–2000.

The Corporation of London, the local authority for the City of London, is one of the largest sponsors of the arts in the UK, with a budget of £46 million in 1998–99 from various funds. The Corporation owns, funds and manages the Barbican Centre (Europe's largest multi-arts and conference centre), which has the London Symphony Orchestra and RSC as residents; owns, funds and manages the Guildhall School of Music and Drama; and jointly funds and manages the Museum of London with the DCMS.

Business and Other Sponsorship

Total UK business investment in the arts rose by 20% in 1997–98, to a record £115 million. London attracted most of the investment—£48.8 million—followed by Scotland and the West Midlands. Theatre, and museums and galleries, received £20 million each; music £11 million; and opera £8 million. Sponsorship in kind increased by over 20%, to £9.2 million. As one example, EDS, the US IT services company, is investing £2 million in the £6 million Lowry Centre at Manchester.

Sponsorship from charitable trusts has also been notable. The Weston Foundation, for example, has contributed £20 million towards the £97.9 million needed to complete the freeing and covering of the British Museum's Great Court. From the Jerwood Foundation some £3 million has gone towards the renewal of the Royal Court theatre in London, and a further £500,000 to the UK's third sculpture park, at Witley Court (Worcestershire). The Helen Hamlyn Foundation has given £1 million to finance a design centre at the Royal College of Art to work out design solutions to the social problems of the future. In 1998, the first year of a three-year scheme, the Paul Hamlyn Foundation awarded prizes of

£30,000 each to five young British exponents of visual art.

Arts & Business (formerly ABSA) exists to promote and encourage partnerships between business and the arts. It has over 350 business members and manages the Pairing Scheme on behalf of the ACE and DCMS. Under the scheme, government funding of between £500 and £25,000 is awarded to arts organisations to match or part match sponsorship that they have secured from businesses. The scheme awards 50% match funding for first-time sponsors, 100% match funding for projects which give exceptional access to the arts and 100% for the first year of projects supported by first-time sponsors who commit to a three-year contract. In 1998–99 the scheme attracted £8.5 million from business and since 1984 has contributed over £145 million (including £47 million from the Government) to the arts.

First prize of £100,000, out of 400 nominations, in the Arts & Business first Creative Britons awards in 1999 went to Mary Ward for her Chicken Shed theatre for children (able-bodied and disabled), which, among other productions, organised 1,000 young people from 22 London boroughs in a Caribbean musical at the Royal Albert Hall. With a Lottery award she is opening a purpose-built theatre at Southgate in north London, providing performance space for a 650-strong company.

Some £4 million from the Foundation for Sport and the Arts, run by the Pools Promoters Association, was used to help the arts in 1998 in the form of awards. Many arts organisations also benefit from the fund-raising activities of Friends groups and from private individuals' financial support.

Cultural Diversity

The Arts Councils promote cultural diversity in the arts. The Scottish Arts Council (SAC), for example, is funding the Sikh festival Vaisakhi da Mela in Glasgow and the African and Caribbean Resource Centre in Scotland. CAMDAD, funded by the Arts Council of

Wales, runs a cultural diversity training programme for artists and arts organisations. Measures to foster cultural diversity in Northern Ireland include funding for arts in both the Irish language and Ulster Scots. The Councils encourage the growth of Caribbean carnival across the UK, of which the most famous is the annual Notting Hill Carnival, the largest street festival in Europe, now sponsored by Western Union. In recent years the Belfast Carnival has attracted an international audience. The Mu-len Theatre Company has launched its own British-Oriental youth drama group, thought to be the first of its type in the UK.

The Arts and Disability

The National Disability Arts Forum and other similar national agencies are funded by the ACE, as are creative organisations, such as Candoco, a company of disabled and non-disabled dancers. The ACE also supports an apprenticeship scheme for disabled people in major arts organisations, such as the RSC, which is part of an initiative aimed at increasing employment opportunities for disabled people in the arts; and projects involving disabled artists in schools. The SAC supports Art Link and Project Ability, which help the disabled to develop their creativity.

Provision of access for disabled people to arts buildings is a criterion for all grants made from the National Lottery (see p. 121).

Arts Centres

Over 200 arts centres in the UK give people the chance of seeing a range of specialist art and of taking part in activities, especially educational projects. Nearly all the centres are professionally managed, while using the services of volunteers. They are assisted mainly by the Arts Councils, RABs and local authorities, while the ACE currently funds two national centres, the South Bank Centre and the Institute of Contemporary Arts (ICA), both in London. ARC, at Stockton on Tees, with a 600-seat auditorium, two theatres, a cinema, rehearsal spaces and a digital arts suite, opened in January 1999. Chapter Arts Centre in Cardiff helps to promote international artists and collaborations.

The British Council

The British Council (see p. 96) promotes international understanding of British creativity internationally in the arts, literature and design, and highlights Britain's cultural diversity. In 1998 it supported nearly 3,000 cultural events overseas. It works with a range of artists, including Rastafarian poet Benjamin Zephaniah, the RSC, painter Gary Hume and author A.S. Byatt. The Visiting Arts Office of Great Britain and Northern Ireland is a joint venture of the British Council with the Foreign & Commonwealth Office, the Arts Councils and the Crafts Council. It encourages the inward flow to the UK of arts from other countries

Broadcasting

Arts programmes broadcast by BBC radio and television and the independent companies (see chapter 17) have won many international awards, such as at the Prix Italia and Montreux International Television Festivals. Independent television companies also give grants for arts promotion in their regions. Broadcasting has created its own art forms—nothing like the arts documentary or drama series exists in any other medium. For example, in an arts documentary in April 1999, Gwyneth Jones talked on BBC Radio 3 about her career as a leading Wagnerian soprano and the techniques and training needed to sustain such demanding roles.

In 1998 Channel 4's *Granton Star Cause* (from a story by Irvine Welsh) won the Prix Italia for single drama, and British television productions won half the major titles in the international Emmy awards, which honour the best shows made outside the United States. Among these successes were BBC1's *The Vicar of Dibley* (with Dawn French) and the children's series *Blabbermouth and Sticky Beak* (also Channel 4). For her role in *Waiting for the Telegram*, one of Alan Bennett's *Talking Heads* monologues (BBC2), the 87-year-old Thora Hird won the 1998 Royal Television Society's Actress of the Year award and the BAFTA television award for Best Actress. Other BAFTA awards went to Tom Courtenay for Best Actor in *A Rather English*

Marriage (BBC2), which also won the prize for Best Single Drama. BBC2's adaptation of Dickens's *Our Mutual Friend* won the award for Best Drama Serial.

The BBC has five orchestras, which employ many of Britain's full-time professional musicians. Each week it broadcasts about 100 hours of classical and other music (both live and recorded) on Radio 3 (see p. 274). BBC Radio 1 broadcasts rock and pop music, and much of the output of BBC Radio 2 is popular and light music. Of the two national commercial radio stations which broadcast music, Classic FM offers mainly classical and Virgin Radio plays rock. Much of the output of the UK's local radio stations is popular and light music.

For its 1999 Promenade Concerts (the 'Proms'), the world's largest music festival, the BBC commissioned seven works from five British and two overseas composers, including a Flute Concerto by Richard Rodney Bennett and *Inside Story* (for violin, viola and orchestra) by Piers Hellawell. The Proms opened with Tippett's *The Mask of Time*. The 20th Prom was devoted to 100 Years of Film Music, the 43rd was a centenary celebration of the jazz legend Duke Ellington, and the 66th and 67th featured the Vienna Philharmonic under Simon Rattle. The second half of the 72nd (Last Night) was relayed on a giant screen to 35,000 people in Hyde Park and to similar events in Swansea and Birmingham.

Festivals

Some 500 professional arts festivals take place in the UK each year. Cinemagic, the first international children's film festival, established in Belfast in 1990, has become a national resource, touring seven UK cities in 1998. The 1999 Edinburgh International Festival featured 167 performances of music, theatre, opera and dance, opening with Handel's oratorio *Saul*, under Charles Mackerras (with soprano Joan Rodgers, tenor Ian Bostridge and baritone Bryn Terfel, three major British singers, among the soloists, the Scottish Chamber Orchestra and the Festival Chorus). Three performances by Sweden's Cullberg Ballet were arranged by their radical choreographer Mats Ek. The Edinburgh Festival Fringe, with programmes (including street events) to suit all tastes and persuasions, takes place alongside the main events. In 1999 there were over 15,000 performances by 600 different companies. Other Edinburgh events include the International Film and Television Festivals and the annual Book Festival.

In 1999 the 52nd Aldeburgh Festival began with the opera by its artistic director, Thomas Adès, *Powder Her Face*, which has been performed worldwide since its 1995 première. Alfred Brendel played Haydn, Mozart and Schubert, and also read from his own poems.

For a calendar of the main arts events in the UK in 2000, see Appendix 5, p. 547.

Arts 2000

Arts 2000 is an Arts Council initiative which celebrates the approach of the millennium. Since 1992, one city, town or region in the UK has been nominated, through competition, to celebrate a particular art form, with the help of Arts Council and matching funds. Glasgow was the City of Architecture and Design for 1999. The year 2000 will be Year of the Artist, covered by a *national* programme.

DRAMA

At the turn of the century, audiences in London were enjoying a wide range of high-quality cultural performances. In 1901 Sir Henry Irving opened his season with Shakespeare's *Coriolanus*, and Sarah Bernhardt was in London to play in Rostand's *L'Aiglon* and *Cyrano de Bergerac*. In 1902, at His Majesty's Theatre, Sir Herbert Beerbohm Tree produced Shakespeare's *The Merry Wives of Windsor*, with Ellen Terry and Madge Kendal; in 1903 Mrs Patrick Campbell starred in a revival of Pinero's *The Second Mrs Tanqueray*; in 1904 J.M. Barrie's *Peter Pan* at the Duke of York's (with Gerald Du Maurier as Captain Hook and Nina Boucicault as Peter) brought 'the very spirit of childhood on to the stage'; and 1905 saw the opening of Shaw's *Man and Superman* at the Court Theatre.

Repertory, whereby a group of actors takes part in more than one play during a given period, and initiatives to revive interest in regional theatre were features of 1998–99. Trevor Nunn at the Royal National Theatre (RNT), for example, has formed a repertory company to perform four plays together, and Ian McKellen spent six months in repertory at the West Yorkshire Playhouse in Leeds. In 1998 'See it Live—Barclays Theatre Week' at more than 100 theatres outside London aimed to persuade first-time, infrequent and lapsed theatregoers to see that week's local or touring production through special ticket offers. The ACE and RABs are spending more than £50 million to support drama, including regional theatre, in 1999–2000—27% of the ACE's total grant. In Scotland, Dundee Repertory Theatre received a £2.3 million Lottery award in 1999 for building improvements to expand its range of work.

Highlights of the UK theatrical year included the unveiling of the restored neo-baroque ceiling of Liverpool's Empire Theatre, at a cost of £10.5 million, of which £7.5 million came from the National Lottery. Manchester's Royal Exchange Theatre, severely damaged in 1996 by a bomb, reopened in December 1998 (a £2.3 million Lottery award helping towards its restoration) with the play whose run had been halted (Stanley Houghton's *Hindle Wakes*). Belfast's Grand Opera House, a 1,000-seat Victorian theatre which presents opera, drama, ballet and musicals, won the Barclays award for Most Welcoming Theatre. In London the remains of the Rose (1587–1606), the theatre of Christopher Marlowe and the young Shakespeare, were saved for permanent exhibition and, it is hoped, further excavation.

At the end of 1998 Glasgow Citizens Theatre staged a triptych of plays to great acclaim: Seneca's *Medea* (in modern dress), Harold Pinter's *The Homecoming*, and David Mamet's *Oleanna*. At the same time, Clwyd Theatr, Cymru (based at Mold in Flintshire), 'the national theatre of Wales', enhanced its reputation with Terry Hands's direction of Alan Ayckbourn's trilogy *The Norman Conquests*. John Wood's performance as A.E. Housman in Tom Stoppard's *The Invention of Love*, which moved from the RNT to the

In 1998–99 London's two small, off-centre theatres, the Almeida and the Donmar, continued to excel, and to attract big-name actors willing to work for nominal wages. Almeida productions showed in the West End: Diana Rigg, Toby Stephens and Barbara Jefford in Ted Hughes's and Robert David MacDonald's versions of Racine's tragedies *Britannicus* and *Phèdre*, and Cate Blanchett in David Hare's *Plenty*. At the Donmar two leading ladies from the United States enjoyed admiring notices: Nicole Kidman joined Iain Glen in Hare's *The Blue Room* and Elizabeth McGovern played opposite Colin Firth in Richard Greenberg's *Three Days of Rain*. *The Blue Room* and the Almeida production of Eugene O'Neill's *The Iceman Cometh*, with Kevin Spacey and Tim Pigott-Smith, moved successfully to New York, as did Patrick Marber's *Closer*, for which Rupert Graves, Ciaran Hinds, Anna Friel, and Marber took the 1999 Theatre World awards for most outstanding new performances (with *Closer* best foreign play), and Hare's *Amy's View*, another triumph for Judi Dench, for which advance ticket sales reached £3 million.

The Iceman Cometh took two 1999 Olivier awards: for Best Actor (Kevin Spacey) and for Best Director (Howard Davies); Eileen Atkins won Best Actress for Yasmina Reza's *The Unexpected Man*; the RNT's *Cleo, Camping, Emmanuelle and Dick*, by Terry Johnson, was Best Comedy, while its production of *Oklahoma!* won four awards, among them Outstanding Musical Production.

West End, was described by one critic as 'the greatest piece of acting to be seen in London'. Stoppard became the first living foreign playwright to have his work performed at the Comédie Française in Paris when his *Arcadia* opened there in November 1998. Success in France had also been won by Declan Donnellan, whose direction of Corneille's *Le Cid* was regarded as the hit of the Avignon festival the previous summer. At a ceremony at the Bolshoi in Moscow in April 1999 he won Russia's Golden Mask award for his direction of Shakespeare's *The Winter's Tale* (designed by Nick Ormerod) with Maly Drama Theatre in St Petersburg, a production which moved to the UK. Among notable RSC offerings have been *Richard III*, with Robert Lindsay in the title role; *A Midsummer Night's Dream*, with Josette Simon as Titania and Hippolyta; and Biyi Bandele's adaptation of Aphra Behn's novel *Oroonoko* (1688), the trials of an African prince made slave. The RNT's programme in 1999 included Hanif Kureshi's first play for it, *Sleep with Me*, and a revival of Noel Coward's *Private Lives* (1930—with Juliet Stevenson). A return to all-male Shakespeare productions was a feature of the third Globe season; artistic director Mark Rylance playing the Egyptian queen in *Antony and Cleopatra*. Praise for its 'dreamlike beauty' was typical of the notices won by *The Street of Crocodiles*, a production of Theatre de Complicite, a British enterprise funded by the ACE and London Arts Board, and supported by the British Council, which has toured in 41 countries and won 25 international awards under its artistic director, Simon McBurney.

Some of the UK's 300 professional theatres are privately owned, but most belong to local authorities or to non-profit-making organisations. The tiny Mull Theatre in the Hebrides has 43 seats; its company tours the Highlands and Islands and runs an education programme.

London

London's 100 or so theatres include:

- the RNT, which stages modern and classical plays in its three auditoriums on the South Bank;
- the Barbican Centre, which has two auditoriums, is home for half the year to the RSC, with a varied drama programme for the other half, including the Barbican International Theatre Event; and
- the Royal Court Theatre in Sloane Square, home to the English Stage Company, which specialises in new work and reopened in 1999.

In 1998 the average West End attendance for each performance increased to 744. Total West End takings were up £11.8 million to just over £257.9 million.

Table 16.1: West End Theatres, 1988 and 1998

	1988	1998
Attendances	10.9 m	11.9 m
Increase/decrease on previous year	+0.2%	+4.0%
Average number of theatres open during year	43	41
Number of performances	16,970	16,018
Number of productions	228	207

Source: *The Society of London Theatre Box Office Data Report 1998*
Note: The 51 theatres which are members of the Society include grant-aided and commercial ones.

Theatre for Young People

The annual National Connections youth programme is sponsored by BT (£600,000): some 150 groups chosen from schools and youth theatre clubs performed new plays by 12 writers in 1999, under the guidance of the RNT and the writers themselves, who included Alan Ayckbourn. The National Youth Theatre in London, the peripatetic National Youth Theatre of Wales and the Scottish Youth Theatre in Glasgow offer early acting opportunities to the young. The ACE supports several national touring companies that produce plays for children, including Pop-Up, Quicksilver and Theatre Centre.

Training

In December 1998 the DCMS and the Department for Education and Employment (DFEE) announced that £19 million a year would replace the previous discretionary grants for drama and dance students, thus alleviating their problems in obtaining funds for tuition and maintenance. From autumn 1999 over 800 students a year will be able to cover their tuition fees on the same basis as other higher and further education pupils. All training must be at accredited institutions and towards recognised qualifications, with annual evaluation by the

DCMS and DFEE to ensure that standards are maintained. Among drama schools which train actors, directors, technicians and stage managers are the Royal Academy of Dramatic Art (RADA), the Central School of Speech and Drama, the London Academy of Music and Dramatic Art (LAMDA), and the Drama Centre (all in London); the Bristol Old Vic School, the Royal Scottish Academy of Music and Drama (Glasgow) and the Welsh College of Music and Drama (Cardiff). Competition to enter the School of Performing Arts at Stratford-upon-Avon College is keen.

Pantomime

Pantomine, a quintessentially British art form, originated in England in the harlequinade afterpieces of early 18th-century plays. In Victorian times its themes shifted to fairy tales, with juggling and acrobatics, as wholesome entertainment for children. After the mid-19th century, performances became limited to an extended Christmas season. By tradition a young actress (or nowadays a pop singer) takes the part of the hero (principal boy) and a comic actor plays an old woman, or dame. Pantomimes such as *Cinderella*, *Aladdin* and *Dick Whittington*, with favourite singers, comedians, and television and sporting personalities as additional draws, play to packed houses which hiss the villains and cheer the heroes.

MUSIC

In 1998 more than 200 million music albums and 80 million singles were sold in the UK, while turnover increased by over 5% on the previous year. Gross overseas earnings by the UK music industry were £1.3 billion, of which more than half came from the sales of recordings, and the net surplus on overseas trade was over £500 million. The industry employs about 130,500 people. In 1998–99 the Government's Music Industry Forum addressed trade barriers and CD piracy, and the provision of venues for live music.

Orchestral and Choral Music

During 1998–99 the London Symphony Orchestra (LSO) took its Elgar series to New York in January, before returning to London and performances under Myung-Whun Chung, Lorin Maazel and Bernard Haitink (Barbican Centre) and at the Proms under Colin Davis. The Philharmonia played German Romantic music, as well as an Elgar series. The London Philharmonic performed under Haitink and under the young British conductor Daniel Harding. The Royal Philharmonic gave Brahms and Berg at the Barbican, and the second half of a Mahler cycle at the Royal Albert Hall. The City of Birmingham Symphony toured Europe under Simon Rattle, after his official farewell in 1998 as its principal conductor (954 concerts in 18 years). In Glasgow, the Royal Scottish National Orchestra's Discovery series continued with works by Tippett and Korndorf. At the Huddersfield Contemporary Music Festival, helped by a £2.4 million EC grant and directed by Richard Steinitz, 60 events (and works by 60 composers) took place in 11 days. In June 1999 Truro inaugurated the Cornish Sinfonia, to go with its recently opened Hall for Cornwall.

The Bournemouth, Birmingham and London Symphony Orchestras and the Royal Liverpool Philharmonic will see their ACE awards rise by 10% or more during 1999–2000.

Anthony Payne's completion of Elgar's Third Symphony won widespread praise, and the vote of the critic of the *Financial Times* as one of the six best recordings of the year—by the BBC Symphony Orchestra under Andrew Davis. In March 1999 a festival in Helsinki celebrated Thomas Adès (see p. 252). The 1999 Kathleen Ferrier prize (worth £10,000 and awarded to a young singer on the threshold of a career, in memory of the great English contralto—1912–53) was won by the 23-year-old soprano Sally Matthews.

Almost all the leading orchestras maintain their own choral societies, which sing, especially in oratorio, at the leading music festivals. British performers also show their expertise in this medium abroad, as at the Halle Festival in Germany in 1999, in Handel's *Samson*. The English tradition of ecclesiastical choral singing is exemplified by choirs such as those of King's College Chapel, Cambridge, and Christ Church Cathedral,

Oxford. The choir at Westminster Cathedral, which went on a United States tour in 1998, is known for its more astringent tone (based on that of the Sistine Chapel at Rome). Male-voice choirs are an essential part of the Welsh tradition.

Two celebrated events in the musical calendar are the Leeds International Pianoforte Competition for young pianists and the biennial Cardiff Singer of the World Competition, which attracts outstanding young singers from all countries.

Pop and Rock Music

In 1998–99 British pop groups and singers continued to win praise for their creativity. Some fuse traditional music, of increasing significance in Wales, Scotland and Northern Ireland, into their work. The Welsh contribution is especially strong: Manic Street Preachers won a 1998 Q award for Best Band in the World Today and a 1999 Brit award for Best Group. Another Q award went to Catatonia for Best Single ('Road Rage'); their singer Cerys Matthews was called 'the finest set of Welsh tonsils since Tom Jones and she's not afraid to use them'. The Stereophonics and Super Furry Animals, who regularly record in Welsh, also reflect the vibrant Welsh entertainment scene. The Q award for Best New Band went to the Merseyside band Gomez, who also won the Technics Mercury Music Prize for their debut album *Bring It On*. Robbie Williams won three Brit awards for Best British Solo Artist, and for his single 'Angels' and video *Millennium*. Des'Ree was Best British Female Solo Artist. The Eurythmics (Annie Lennox and Dave Stewart) received the Brit award for Outstanding Contribution to British Music. In 1998 the Spice Girls (who have sold over 9 million albums in the United States alone), with 'Goodbye', became the second group (after the Beatles) to top the Christmas singles chart for three consecutive years. Black Star Liner and Joi are the latest bands to emerge from what is known as the British Asian Underground, while Bradford rockers Terrorvision, with their hit album *Tequila*, fused funk, jazz and rap into their own brand of heavy metal.

In a poll conducted for BBC Radio 2 in 1999 on the top 100 songs of the 20th century, the number one song was the Beatles' *Yesterday*.

March 1999 saw the opening of the National Centre for Popular Music in Sheffield; £11 million of the total cost of £15 million was provided by a Lottery award. Its four sections explain the genre's context and derivation, while computers, instruments, mixing desks and edit suites encourage visitor participation.

Jazz

The Brecon, Cheltenham, London Oris jazz festivals, and Edinburgh International Jazz and Blues Festival, and venues such as Ronnie Scott's in London's Soho, have helped win new audiences for jazz in the UK and showed how it can evolve when exposed to other musical influences, such as pop and Brazilian rhythms. Claire Martin, described by a critic as 'the most accomplished jazz singer Britain has produced in a long while', explored pop territory in her 1999 album *Take My Heart*, while Nucleus, regarded as the most influential jazz-rock fusion band in Britain, made a Contemporary Music Network tour of the UK. Julian Joseph, a leading young British jazz pianist and composer, synthesises West Indian and British folk influences, traditional jazz and classical music, while the violinist Nigel Kennedy has continued to mix the jazz and classical genres.

Training

Professional training in music is given at universities and conservatoires. The leading London conservatoires are the Royal Academy of Music, the Royal College of Music, the Guildhall School of Music and Drama, and Trinity College of Music. Outside London are the Royal Scottish Academy of Music and Drama (RSAMD) in Glasgow, the Royal Northern College of Music in Manchester, the Welsh College of Music and Drama in Cardiff, and the Birmingham Conservatoire.

With the help of grants from the European Regional Development Fund, Glasgow Development Agency, the Foundation for Sport and the Arts and £2.5 million from the SAC's Lottery Fund, the Alexander Gibson Opera School opened at the RSAMD in December 1998.

Other Educational Schemes

The National Foundation for Youth Music (formerly Youth Music Trust), set up in 1999, aims to improve opportunities for young people to get involved in music-making, with £10 million a year from ACE Lottery funds and donations from other sources, including British Phonographic Industry. In addition, some £150 million from the DFEE's standards fund will be used over three years to help buy musical instruments for schools, restore free tuition and provide extra training for teachers. The LSO won a £3.7 million ACE Lottery award towards a £15 million music education centre at St Luke's, a disused church in east London which is to be transformed into recording studios, rehearsal rooms and classrooms.

The national youth orchestras of Great Britain, Scotland, Ulster and Wales, and other youth orchestras have established high standards. Nearly a third of the players in the European Community Youth Orchestra come from the UK. There is also a National Youth Jazz Orchestra and a network of other youth jazz orchestras and wind bands.

OPERA

London's Royal Opera House at Covent Garden is due to reopen in November 1999 after a £214 million restoration and redevelopment, which includes the reconstruction of E.M.Barry's dome of 1858, 80 extra places and improved access for audiences 'in the gods'. It plans to broaden the appeal of opera and ballet. There will also be a studio theatre for educational work and improved access for the public, including free lunchtime concerts and exhibitions in the foyer areas.

UK opera companies staged acclaimed performances during 1998–99. Joan Rodgers headed the cast, with the veteran soprano

Elizabeth Vaughan, in the 1999 English National Opera (ENO) production of Poulenc's *The Carmelites*, conducted by her husband, Paul Daniel. Another ENO triumph in 1999 was Robert Carsen's staging of Handel's *Semele*, for which the soprano Rosemary Joshua, the mezzos Sarah Connolly and Susan Bickley, and the tenor John Mark Ainsley received rapturous reviews.

Sadlers Wells in London, rebuilt and reopening to record audiences and box office receipts, received £4.2 million of ACE Lottery funding to help complete the theatre. It was host to a revival of Britten's 'American' opera *Paul Bunyan* (1941). Among Welsh National Opera successes at home and on tour were Janáček's *Jenufa* and Britten's *Peter Grimes* (the latter with Janice Watson and John Daszak under Carlo Rizzi). Critics had high praise for Opera North's autumn 1998 production of Verdi's *Don Carlos*, singling out Julian Gavin in the title role, Alastair Miles as Philip and the US soprano Lori Phillips as Elisabeth. Among Scottish Opera's achievements in 1999 were Donald McVicar's staging of Strauss's *Der Rosenkavalier* (under Richard Armstrong), and a revival of James MacMillan's *Inés de Castro*, with the admired contralto Anne Collins in the cast.

DANCE

The Royal Ballet, with an unrivalled repertory, has been called one of the greatest artistic achievements in Britain in the 20th century, has produced masterpieces by some of the world's finest creators and has nurtured dancers of international fame. In April and May 1999 it toured the Far East, visiting Japan and China; in July, at Sadlers Wells it performed new work by William Tuckett and revived Frederick Ashton's *Ondine*. Birmingham Royal Ballet, at Sadlers Wells in February, gave David Bintley's *Edward II* and revived Ninette de Valois' *The Prospect before Us* (to the music of Boyce arranged by Constant Lambert). English National Ballet was at the Coliseum at Christmas and at the Royal Albert Hall for a summer season (with *Swan Lake*). Scottish Ballet toured Scotland in spring 1999 with *La Sylphide* and a modern triple bill (three short pieces in one performance). Northern Ballet Theatre staged a new *Carmen* in Leeds in February, while the Rambert Dance Company visited Austria and Italy in the spring and did a Sadlers Wells season in May, including new work by the US choreographer Twyla Tharp.

London's annual festival, Dance Umbrella, a showcase for the most innovative in present-day world choreography, celebrated its 20th anniversary in September 1998. British performers included Michael Clark and the Siobhan Davies Dance Company. Her first full-length work for nearly 30 years, *Wild Air*, had its première in Oxford in May 1999.

Training

Professional training for dancers and choreographers is provided mainly by specialist schools, which include the Royal Ballet School, the Central School of Ballet, the Northern School of Contemporary Dance (Leeds) and the London Contemporary Dance School.

All government-funded dance companies provide dance workshops and education activities. Phoenix Dance Company and English National Ballet, for example, have won awards for their projects. Ludus Dance Company, in Lancaster, works mainly with young people. The National Youth Dance Company gives a chance for young people to work with professionals.

FILMS

Across the European Union (EU) there are some 54 aid schemes which distribute about £470 million a year to the audio-visual industries: France provides 39% of this figure, Germany 20% and the UK and Italy both 6%. Films made in the UK, with British makers, actors and technicians, excited intense interest in 1998–99, but the UK audience for British films declined from 23% of the total UK box office receipts in 1997 to 14% in 1998. Total investment in feature films production in the UK fell by 15% to £578 million, compared with a peak of £676 million in 1997. The number of US productions shot in Britain costing more than £10 million fell from six to four, and their combined budgets

from £233 million to £139 million. During 1996–99 US film-makers have contributed 54% of the money spent making films in the UK, for example the highly acclaimed *Saving Private Ryan* and *Shakespeare in Love*. However, order books for the main UK studios were fuller in 1999 than in the productive 1950s and Britain is ahead in the digital technologies of film-making, which gives it importance as a centre in the final stages of production. Furthermore, the turnover of its rapidly expanding computer-generated special effects industry was more than £31 million in 1998.

Among government initiatives in 1998–99 to boost the UK film industry were:

- Film Export UK, an industry body to help exports of British films worldwide;

- Film Finance Forum, to generate more British and European investment in film and to improve links between the City of London (see p. 506) and the industry;

- establishment of a British Film Office in Los Angeles to provide a focus for contact between the UK and US industries;

- reforming the rules under which British films can qualify for tax and other benefits, thus helping to attract increased investment; and

- establishment of a Film Education Working Group, under the auspices of the British Film Institute, to draw up a strategy for creating a more 'cineliterate' population.

The Government also proposes to set up, by April 2000, the Film Council, a body to develop film culture and the film industry, and to be the Lottery distributor—of at least £27 million a year—to the industry.

In 1998, approximately 96 films were shot in the UK by British or foreign companies or by British companies shooting abroad. Of these 78 were wholly or partly produced by British companies. Total box office takings in 1998 topped £332 million, with total admissions of 135.2 million, a decrease of nearly 3% on 1997.

Government support for the film industry allows a 100% tax write-off on the production

The Full Monty (1997) and *Four Weddings and a Funeral* (1994), which cost £1.6 million and £2 million to make, are the highest-earning British films of all time, earning £161 million and £155 million worldwide respectively. In third place is *Bean: the Ultimate Disaster Movie* (1997; £146 million), followed by *Trainspotting* (1996; £44 million) and *Sliding Doors* (1998; £42 million). In March 1999 the main British Academy Award success was *Shakespeare in Love* (US-financed but made in Britain, mostly with British talent), winning the award for Best Picture, and awards for Gwyneth Paltrow (Best Actress), Judi Dench (Best Supporting Actress), Mark Norman and Tom Stoppard (Best Screenplay), Martin Childs and Jill Quertier (Best Art Direction), Stephen Warbeck (Best Musical Score) and Sandy Powell (Best Costume). The British film *Elizabeth* won an Academy Award for Jenny Shircore (Best Make-up), who gained the BAFTA award as well. The BAFTA Best Actress was Australian Cate Blanchett in *Elizabeth*. *Shakespeare in Love* also won the BAFTA awards for Best Film, Best Supporting Actress (Judi Dench) and Best Supporting Actor for Australian Geoffrey Rush. The Alexander Korda award for Outstanding British Film went to *Elizabeth*.

Among the many other international awards to British talent were two for Kate Winslet (People's Choice European Actress of the Year—from the European Film Academy in Berlin—and *Empire* magazine award for Best Actress in *Titanic*). Among the London *Evening Standard* awards were Michael Caine and director Ken Loach (Special Achievement), Julie Christie (Best Actress—*Afterglow*), Derek Jacobi (Best Actor—*Love is the Devil*), and Eileen Atkins (Best Screenplay—*Mrs Dalloway*); Best Film was John Boorman's *The General* and Most Promising Newcomer Guy Ritchie, director of *Lock, Stock and Two Smoking Barrels*, which also won an Orange Audience Award. Two British films by first-time directors won plaudits at the Cannes film festival in May 1999: Damien O'Donnell's *East is East* and Lynne Ramsay's *Ratcatcher*.

and acquisition costs for British movies with budgets of up to £15 million.

Animation

The BAFTA award in 1999 for Best Short Animated Film went to the BBC's *The Canterbury Tales*, a collaboration by seven directors from England, Wales and Russia. A total of £1.37 million in National Lottery film production awards has been made since 1995 to animated film (£517,000 in 1998). In addition, the ACE contributes £50,000 a year to a scheme for experimental animation, in conjunction with Channel 4. *Midnight Dance*, a Nerve Centre production from Northern Ireland, won Best Animation award at the 1998 International Short Film Festival at Palm Springs in the United States.

Government Support

The Government supports a number of organisations which promote the film industry. The largest public source of finance is the ACE's Lottery Film Programme. Since 1995 the ACE has awarded £67 million to 79 feature films. A further £1.4 million in awards has helped production of 49 short films. The Government's largest grants go to the *bfi* (see p. 260), to *Scottish Screen*, which promotes film-making in Scotland, and to the *Northern Ireland Film Commission* (NIFC), which has a similar remit in the Province.

The British Film Commission (BFC) markets the UK film and television production service industry to overseas producers, to attract inward investment. The BFC works alongside the UK Film Commission Network, which comprises 24 area or city offices.

British Screen Finance (BSF), a private sector company, provides loans to enable feature films involving new British talent to be produced. It also helps finance short films and the cost of developing screenplays and setting up film projects. Total commitment since 1986 is £48.8 million. Among successful recent films supported by BSF are *Hilary and Jackie* and *Beautiful People*.

The European Co-Production Fund, a UK initiative, offers loans of up to 30% of a film's budget, enabling British producers to collaborate in the making of films with other European producers. It has committed £16 million to about 50 feature movies, with a total value of some £140 million. Recent award-winning pictures made with help from the Fund include *Ma Vie en Rose* (Golden Globe award for Best Foreign Film in 1998) and *On Connaît la Chanson* (winner of seven César awards).

British Film Institute (*bfi*)

The development of film, video and television as art forms is promoted by the *bfi*, and by Scottish Screen and the NIFC.

The *bfi* maintains the National Film and Television Archive, which contains over 350,000 titles dating from 1894, together with extensive collections of stills, posters and designs. The *bfi* National Library forms the world's largest collection of film-related books, periodicals, scripts and other written materials.

On the South Bank *bfi* activities include running the National Film Theatre, which screens over 2,000 films and television programmes each year, and the *bfi* London IMAX, Britain's largest screen. The *bfi* also runs the annual London Film Festival, now in its 43rd year, and supports newer festivals in the UK.

A network of independent cinemas across the UK also receives *bfi* support. Its educational activities include courses, conferences and other events, and helping to formulate national film education policy.

Training in Film Production

The National Film and Television School is financed jointly by the Government and by the film, video and television industries. It offers postgraduate and short course training for directors, editors, camera operators, animators and other specialists. The School enrols 50–60 full-time students a year and about 850 on short course programmes. The London International Film School, the Royal College of Art, and some universities and

other institutions of higher education, also offer courses in production. In May 1999 the Government announced a Skills Investment Fund, worth £1.5 million, to boost UK film production training.

Cinema Licensing and Film Classification

Public cinemas must be licensed by local authorities, which have a legal duty to prohibit the admission of children to unsuitable films, and may prevent the showing of any picture. In assessing films the authorities normally rely on the judgment of an independent non-statutory body, the British Board of Film Classification (BBFC), to which all items must be submitted. It does not use any written code of censorship, but can require cuts to be made before granting a certificate; on rare occasions, it refuses a certificate.

Films passed by the BBFC are put into one of the following categories:

- U (universal), suitable for all;
- PG (parental guidance), in which some scenes may be unsuitable for young children;
- 12, 15 and 18, for people of not less than those ages; and
- Restricted 18, for restricted showing only at premises to which no one under 18 is admitted, for example, licensed cinema clubs.

Videos

The BBFC is also legally responsible for classifying videos under a system similar to that for films. It is an offence to supply commercially a video which has not been classified or to supply it in contravention of its designation.

MUSEUMS AND GALLERIES

Some 81 million visits were made in 1998–99 to the UK's 2,500 or so museums and galleries open to the public, which include the major national collections, about 1,000 independent museums, and 800 receiving support from

A Design Council initiative which aims to identify and promote products and services created in Britain. Millennium Products are selected because they are pioneering in their field, challenge existing conventions, and are innovative and creative.

Wannabe a Pop Star: a CD-ROM enabling non-musical teenagers to create songs.

OptiMusic: music 'played' by interrupting light beams.

Nautilus: high performance speakers.

Barless Grand Piano: grand piano constructed without cross-tension bars to enhance sound quality.

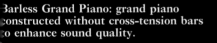

Lotus Elise:
high performance, lightweight sportscar.

Eurostar: frequent rail sevices now provide
direct links between London and Paris/Brussels.

TX1 London Taxi:
new London taxi designed
to give maximum comfort
for driver and passengers.

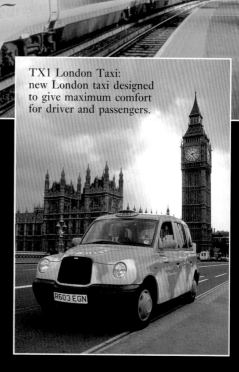

**Europa XS: an economical light aircraft which
can be stored on a trailer and in a garage.**

Aerorig Production Series:
free-standing rig system
for sailing yachts of all sizes.

**Severn Class Lifeboat: the RNLI's
most advanced all-weather lifeboat.**

Lorry powered by liquid natural gas.

Land Rover Freelander: four-wheel drive vehicle with hill descent control.

Teletruk: fork-lift vehicle with a telescopic arm.

Marin-ARK: inflatable life raft with telescopic chute giving direct access to evacuees from ship to raft.

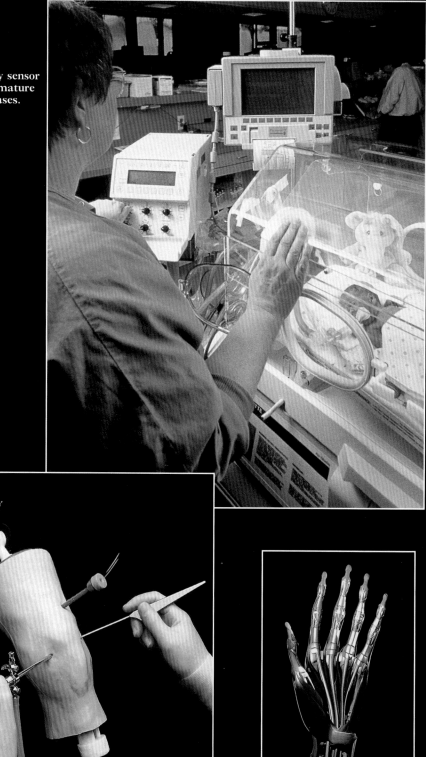

Neotrend: a tiny sensor to measure premature babies' blood gases.

Hillway Knee: artificial knee for practising keyhole surgery.

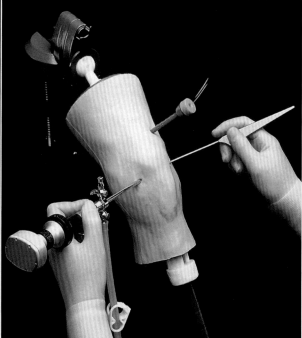

Interactive Hand: a complete 3-D anatomy of the human hand.

Biogel Reveal: the world's first
puncture-indicating
surgical gloves.

Blatchford's IP+:
the first computer-controlled prosthetic limb
which adapts to the user's walking pattern.

LarvE: sterile larvae for the treatment of wounds.

Oxfam Stackable Water Carrier: hygienic and lightweight stackable water carrier for emergency relief.

Waterbeds for quadrupeds: waterbeds for dairy cows which provide comfort and eliminate injury, and are more hygienic than conventional bedding.

Enercon E-66 Wind Energy Converter.

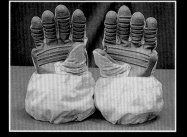
Gorix: a versatile fabric which can be heated evenly across its entire surface.

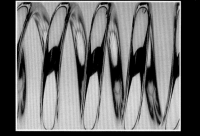
Hot Springs: cost-effective coiled spring radiators which can be placed in small areas.

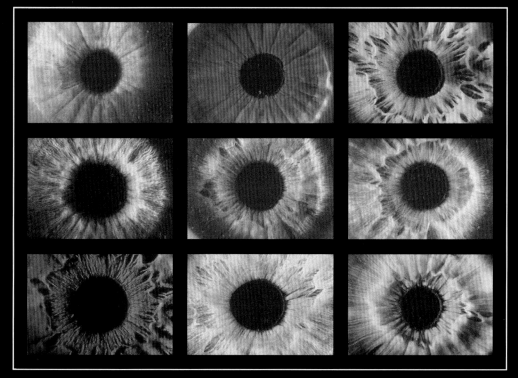
Iris Recognition: computer software to identify people by their unique iris pattern.

The Remarkable Recycled Pencil: one plastic cup makes one recycled pencil.

Psion Series 5: a hand-held computer which is the size of a cheque book.

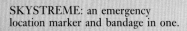
SKYSTREME: an emergency location marker and bandage in one.

SpinGrip Outsole: a football boot with a unique injury-reducing sole.

Gecko Marine Safety Helmet: the first safety helmet designed specifically for marine use.

local authorities. About a third of international visitors come to the UK because of its museums. Some 40,000 staff are employed in this sector. Among government initiatives in 1999 to ensure that the country's 'hidden treasures' are opened up to as wide an audience as possible are:

- 24-Hour Museum, on the Internet (www.24hourmuseum.org.uk), which provides a gazetteer of all UK museums and galleries, a magazine, search facilities and educational resources;

- Museums for the Many, a set of standards to encourage all major museums and galleries to offer the widest possible access to their collections; and

- a £15 million challenge fund to increase access to collections held by 43 'designated museums' or museum services in England, such as Harewood House in Yorkshire.

Museums and galleries in the UK receive about £500 million a year in public expenditure. National museums are financed chiefly from government funds; some charge for entry to their permanent collections and special exhibitions, although the Government wishes admission charges to be phased out (see p. 248); from spring 1999, all children have been allowed free access to those sponsored by the DCMS. All national museums in England and Scotland are managed by independent trustees.

Museums and galleries maintained by local authorities, universities and independent or privately funded bodies may receive help in building up their collections through grants administered by the Museums & Galleries Commission (MGC) and the Area Museum Councils throughout the UK. Support to national and regional public and independent museums and galleries is also given by the Arts Councils and by trusts, voluntary bodies, the Heritage Lottery Fund and the National Art Collections Fund.

Much of the MGC's work is in helping museums maintain, preserve and develop their collections. It also provides funds to the seven English Area Museum Councils, which supply services and their own small grants to individual museums, and to the Cultural

Heritage National Training Organisation and the Museum Documentation Association.

The MGC advises the Secretary of State on the Acceptance in Lieu scheme, whereby pre-eminent works of art may be accepted by the Government in settlement of tax and allocated to public galleries. Items accepted in 1998–99 include: a Pre-Raphaelite painting by Millais (Tate Gallery) and the Sherborne Missal (British Library).

By April 1999 UK museums were estimated to have benefited from £529 million of National Lottery money. In addition to £24 million to the National Museums & Galleries on Merseyside and £15 million to the Victoria and Albert (V&A) Museum, in 1998–99 £18.75 million was allocated to the Tate Gallery of British Art on Millbank, due for completion in 2000, and £3.75 million for an extension to London's Geffrye Museum, which illustrates the domestic lives of ordinary people.

Among noted exhibitions in 1998–99 the Tate at Liverpool presented the only European showing of works (mostly 1930s) by Salvador Dalí, and at St Ives 'Partnerships and Practice' focused on schools and artists associated with west Cornwall from the 1930s to the 1960s. In London, Patrick Caulfield, regarded as one of the best painters to emerge from the British Pop-Art movement, had a retrospective at the Hayward; the National Portrait Gallery mounted 'British Sporting Heroes'; the Design Museum opened 'Modern Britain', which tracked the influence of Art Deco in British design; and the Canon Photography Gallery at the V&A presented a photographic record, 'Studies from Life, 1857–64 by Clementina Lady Hawarden'.

In November 1998 the Museum and Art Gallery at Birmingham celebrated the native symbolist painter Edward Burne-Jones. In spring 1999 the 'Glasgow 1999' project 'Vertigo' looked at ten major architectural schemes around the world, while Edinburgh drew praise for 'The Draughtsman's Art', master drawings from the National Gallery of Scotland, and 'O Caledonia!', which focused on Scotland's Romantic past as fostered by Walter Scott.

After eight years of restoration the Royal Armouries at the Tower of London

Two events in London in early 1999 were devoted to French painters. The Royal Academy's 'Monet in the 20th century' sold 100,000 advance tickets, saw an average 8,470 visitors a day, took a total of £3.9 million at the box office, and stayed open for 24 hours to give art lovers a last chance to catch it. The National Gallery's 'Portraits by Ingres: image of an epoch', the largest show (40 portraits and 50 portrait drawings) ever devoted to this artist, saw long queues for admission.

The beginning of the world's first great work of literature, the 4,000-year-old Mesopotamian *Epic of Gilgamesh*, was rediscovered in 1998 on clay tablets in a storeroom of the British Museum (BM). It is only one of dozens of archaeological treasures which resurface every year inside the BM. Only 1% of the objects are on view; the rest, kept in store, constitute the world's largest archaeological research collection.

The Dean Gallery of 20th-century Art, opened in Edinburgh in 1999, contains the UK's most significant modern collection after the Tate Gallery and is its most important centre for the study of Dada and Surrealism.

redisplayed its impressive collection of arms and armour, including the suits of armour made for Henry VIII, Charles I and James II. At a cost of £33 million, the Great Court of the British Museum, unseen for 150 years, has been restored to its original 2-acre expanse.

The Turner Prize (worth £20,000), awarded annually at the Tate Gallery to a British artist under 50 years of age for an outstanding exhibition or other presentation of their work, was won in 1998 by the painter Chris Ofili (for 'the originality and energy of his painting and his dynamic use of colour').

National Collections

The national museums and art galleries contain some of the world's most comprehensive exhibits of objects of artistic, archaeological, scientific, historical and general interest. The English national museums are:

- the British Museum;
- the Natural History Museum;
- the V&A (fine and decorative arts);
- the National Museum of Science & Industry, including the Science Museum and its two regional institutes, the National Railway Museum (York) and

Table 16.2: Visits to National Museums and Galleries in England, 1998–99

	Number of visits *million*	% increase/decrease over 1997–98
British Museum[a]	5.5	−10
Imperial War Museum	1.4	+2
National Gallery[a]	4.8	−2
National Maritime Museum	0.5	0
National Museums & Galleries on Merseyside	0.7	+11
National Portrait Gallery[a]	1.2	+21
Natural History Museum	1.9	+6
National Museum of Science & Industry	2.2	−8
Tate Gallery[a,b]	3.0	+43
Victoria and Albert Museum	1.5	+3
Wallace Collection	0.2	+6
Royal Armouries	0.4	−7

Source: Department for Culture, Media and Sport

[a] Free admission. The DCMS allocated £2 million to the National Galleries of England in 1998–99 to maintain free admission.

[b] Tate Gallery Liverpool temporarily closed in 1997–98.

the National Museum of Photography, Film and Television (Bradford);

- the National Gallery (western painting from about 1260 to 1900);

- the Tate Gallery, with collections in London (British painting and modern art), Liverpool and St Ives (St Ives School and modern art);

- the National Portrait Gallery;

- the Imperial War Museum, which has three sites in London and one at Duxford (which includes the American Air Museum) in Cambridgeshire;

- the Royal Armouries, Britain's oldest museum, which has exhibits in the Tower of London (relating to the Tower's history), Leeds (arms and armour) and Fort Nelson, near Portsmouth (artillery);

- the National Army Museum;

- the Royal Air Force Museum;

- the National Maritime Museum;

- the Wallace Collection (paintings, furniture, arms and armour, and *objets d'art*); and

- the National Museums & Galleries on Merseyside.

In Scotland the national collections are held by the National Museums of Scotland and the National Galleries of Scotland. The former include the Royal Scottish Museum, the Museum of Scotland, the Scottish United Services Museum and the Scottish Agricultural Museum, in Edinburgh; the Museum of Flight, near North Berwick; and the Museum of Costume at Shambellie House near Dumfries. The arrangements of the new Museum of Scotland, built at a cost of £52 million and devoted to Scottish history, have been praised by a critic for their 'unabashed Scottishness' and imagination.

The National Galleries of Scotland comprise the National Gallery of Scotland, the Scottish National Portrait Gallery, the Scottish National Gallery of Modern Art, and the Dean Gallery of 20th-century Art (see p. 262). The National Galleries also have deposits at Paxton House near Berwick and Duff House in Banff. In 1998–99 the National

Museums of Scotland attracted 632,400 visitors, and the National Galleries of Scotland 842,000.

The National Museum of Wales in Cardiff has a number of branches, including the Museum of Welsh Life at St Fagans, the Slate Museum at Llanberis and the Industrial and Maritime Museum in the Cardiff Bay development. The Centre for Visual Arts in Cardiff (with galleries for permanent and temporary exhibitions), which has benefited from a £7.5 million Lottery award, opened in 1999.

Northern Ireland's three major museums—the Ulster Museum in Belfast, the Ulster Folk and Transport Museum in County Down, and the Ulster-American Folk Park in County Tyrone—merged in 1998 to form the National Museums and Galleries of Northern Ireland.

Other Collections

Other important collections in London include the Museum of London (whose 'London Bodies' exhibition in 1998 shed light on the medical condition of Londoners of the past); the Courtauld Institute Galleries (masterpieces of 14th–20th-century European painting); and the London Transport Museum.

Museums outside London include the Shoe Museum at Street in Somerset, which shows footwear since Roman times, and museums associated with universities, such as the Ashmolean in Oxford, the Fitzwilliam at Cambridge and the Hunterian in Glasgow. Newly opened to the public is the Henry Moore open-air museum of sculpture at Perry Green in Hertfordshire.

The Government has indicated that owners of works of art who do not have to pay inheritance tax (see p. 409) because they have promised public access will have to advertise their opening hours nationally.

Among a number of national art exhibiting institutions is the Royal Academy of Arts, at Burlington House in London, which holds an annual Summer Exhibition and other important ones during the year. The Summer Exhibition is the world's largest open present-day art display and combines work by established artists and by others showing for the first time. The Royal Scottish Academy holds annual exhibitions in Edinburgh. There are also children's shows, including the National Exhibition of Children's Art.

Open-air museums depict the life of an area or preserve early industrial remains, such as the Weald and Downland Museum in West Sussex, the Ironbridge Gorge Museum in Shropshire and the North of England Open Air Museum at Beamish in County Durham. Skills of the past are revived in a number of 'living' museums, such as the Gladstone Pottery Museum near Stoke-on-Trent and the Quarry Bank Mill at Styal in Cheshire.

Training in Art and Design

Most practical education in art and design is provided in the art colleges and fine and applied art departments of universities (these include the Slade School of Art and Goldsmith's College of Art, London), which have absorbed the former independent art schools, and in further education colleges and private art schools. Some of these institutions award degrees at postgraduate level. The Royal College of Art in London is the only postgraduate school of art and design in the world. Art is also taught at an advanced level at the four Scottish Art Schools.

University courses concentrate largely on academic disciplines, such as the history of art. The Courtauld and Warburg Institutes of the University of London and the Department of Classical Art and Archaeology at University College London are leading institutions. Art is a foundation subject in the National Curriculum (see p. 136). The Society for Education through Art, among other activities, encourages schools to buy original works by organising an annual Pictures for Schools exhibition.

The UK's first big prize, awarded by the Jerwood Foundation, to help young designers to establish themselves in the fashion industry, and worth £125,000 in cash and other benefits, was won in 1999 by Shelley Fox.

Export Control of Works of Art

The UK market is second only to that of the United States. The UK sales industry directly employs 40,000 and has an annual turnover of £2.2 billion (about 50% of the EU market). Auctions of works of art take place in the main auction houses (two of the longest established being Sotheby's and Christie's), and through private dealers.

A licence is required before certain items can be exported, and if a DCMS Expert Adviser objects to the granting of a licence, the matter is referred to the Reviewing Committee on the Export of Works of Art. If the Committee considers a work to be of national importance, it can recommend to the Government that a decision be deferred on the licence application for a specified time to give a chance for an offer to be made to buy it at or above the recommended fair market price.

The UK opposes an EU proposal to impose artists' resale rights, whereby the price of any work of art sold during an artist's lifetime, or for 70 years after his or her death, would include a tax payable to the artist or heirs. The Government is working with its EU partners to devise a solution which would not increase the cost of selling in London and drive dealers and collectors elsewhere.

LITERATURE AND LIBRARIES

Over 200 literary prizes are awarded yearly in the UK, ranging in value from £30 to £30,000, and for many different categories of work. The winner of the 1998 Booker Prize for Fiction (worth £20,000; UK and Commonwealth citizens eligible) was the British writer Ian McEwan, for *Amsterdam*, while the Whitbread awards (valued at £2,000 each with £21,000 extra for Book of the Year; for British subjects), announced in January 1999, were distributed as follows:

- Book of the Year and Poetry award: the late Ted Hughes, who died in 1998, *Birthday Letters*;

- Novel award: Justin Cartwright, *Leading the Cheers*;

- First Novel award: Giles Foden, *The Last King of Scotland*;

- Biography award: Amanda Foreman, *Georgiana, Duchess of Devonshire*; and

- Children's Book of the Year (£10,000): David Almond, *Skellig*.

Birthday Letters also won Ted Hughes the 1998 T.S. Eliot award (worth £5,000) and *Amsterdam* won Ian McEwan the 1999 Hamburg Shakespeare prize, worth £15,000. William Trevor won the fourth David Cohen British Literature Prize, worth £30,000. The world's largest fiction prize (£100,000), the International Impac Dublin literary award, went for the first time to a British novelist, Andrew Miller, for *Ingenious Pain*.

In 1999 Andrew Motion succeeded Ted Hughes as Poet Laureate, who receives a stipend as an officer of the Royal Household and whose role is, for the first time, limited to ten years.[1]

Authors' Copyright and Performers' Protection

Original literary works (including computer programs and databases), and dramatic, musical or artistic works, films, sound recordings, cable programmes and broadcasts, are automatically protected by copyright in the UK. This protection is also given to works from EU member states, or from countries party to international copyright conventions, the World Trade Organisation or reciprocal agreements. The copyright owner has rights against unauthorised reproduction, public performance, broadcasting, rental and lending, and issue to the public of his or her work; and against dealing in unauthorised copies. In most cases the author is the first owner of the copyright, and the term of copyright in literary, dramatic, musical and artistic works is generally the life of the author and a period of 70 years from the end of the year in which he or she dies. For films the term is 70 years from the end of the calendar year in which the death occurs of the last to die of the following: principal director, authors of the screenplay and dialogue, or composer of music for the film. Sound recordings are protected for 50 years from the end of the year of making or release, and broadcasts for 50 years from the end of the year of broadcast.

Performers are also given automatic protection against unauthorised

communication to the public or recording of live performances, reproduction of recordings, and issue to the public or rental or lending of copies of a recording. This lasts for 50 years from the year of performance or release of a recording of it. They also have a right to equitable remuneration for the playing in public, or inclusion in a broadcast or cable programme service, of a commercially published sound recording of their performance. A right against the extraction and re-utilisation of the contents of a database ('database rights') was introduced from January 1998, where there has been substantial investment in obtaining, verifying or presenting the contents of the database.

Literary and Philological Societies

Societies to promote literature include the English Association, the Royal Society of Literature and the Welsh Academy (Yr Academi Gymreig). The leading society for studies in the humanities is the British Academy for the Promotion of Historical, Philosophical and Philological Studies (the British Academy).

Other specialist societies are the Early English Text Society, the Bibliographical Society and several devoted to particular authors, such as Jane Austen and Charles Dickens. The Poetry Society sponsors poetry readings and recitals. London's South Bank Centre runs a programme of literary events.

Public Libraries

Local authorities in Great Britain and education and library boards in Northern Ireland have a duty to provide a free lending and reference library service. There are almost 5,000 public libraries in the UK. In Great Britain over 60% of adults are members of their local library and about half of these borrow at least once a month. About 483 million books and 37 million audio-visual items were borrowed from UK public libraries in 1997–98. Adult fiction accounted for 51%, adult non-fiction for 25% and children's books for 23%.

Many libraries have collections of compact discs, records, audio- and video-cassettes, and musical scores for loan to the public, while a

---

[1] The first appointment to the office was John Dryden, confirmed by King Charles II in 1670.

number also lend from collections of works of art, which may be originals or reproductions. Most libraries hold documents on local history, and all provide services for children, while reference and information sections, and art, music, commercial and technical departments, meet a growing demand. The information role is important for all libraries: online public access catalogues, library management systems, personal computers for public use, Internet access, CD-ROMs and reference databases figure prominently. A government initiative under the New Opportunities Fund of the Lottery (see p. 121) is providing £20 million for information and communications technology training of library staff and £50 million for enabling library material to be stored and accessed in digitised form.

The Government is advised (until April 2000—see p. 248) by the Library and Information Commission, a forum for policy on library and information provision in general. It is committed to networking all public libraries and connecting them to the National Grid for Learning by 2002.

Public Lending Right Scheme

The Public Lending Right Scheme gives registered authors royalties from a central fund (totalling £5 million in 1998–99) for the loans made of their books from public libraries in the UK. Payment is made according to the number of times an author's books are lent out. The maximum yearly payment an author can receive is £6,000.

In 1997–98 the most borrowed popular author from UK public libraries was Catherine Cookson, with 12 out of the top 20 fiction titles; the most borrowed children's author was R.L. Stine, with 15 out of the top 20 children's titles.

The Library Association

The Library Association is the principal professional organisation for those engaged in library and information management. Founded in 1877, the Association has some 25,000 members. It maintains a Register of Chartered Members and is the designated

---

In 1900 the deaths occurred of John Ruskin, R.D. Blackmore (*Lorna Doone*) and Oscar Wilde, and Joseph Conrad's *Lord Jim* was published. Two years later Samuel Butler (*Erewhon*) died, as did G.A. Henty, prolific writer of adventure books for boys. The same year saw the publication of Rudyard Kipling's collection of poems *The Five Nations* (including 'White Man's Burden' and 'Recessional'; his novel Kim appeared in 1901), Beatrix Potter's *Peter Rabbit*, Conan Doyle's Sherlock Holmes thriller *The Hound of the Baskervilles* and Arnold Bennett's *Anna of the Five Towns*.

Table 16.3: Most Borrowed Classic Authors, July 1997 to June 1998

1 Beatrix Potter
2 Daphne Du Maurier
3 A.A. Milne
4 Jane Austen
5 William Shakespeare
6 J.R.R. Tolkien
7 Charles Dickens
8 Thomas Hardy
9 Anthony Trollope
10 E.M. Forster
11 George Orwell
12 Rudyard Kipling
13 D.H. Lawrence
14 Arthur Conan Doyle
15 Louisa M. Alcott
16 George Eliot
17 Virginia Woolf
18 John Buchan
19 C.S. Forester
20 Wilkie Collins

Source: Registrar of Public Lending Right

---

authority for the recognition of qualifications gained in other EU member states.

The British Library and National Libraries

The British Library (BL), the national library of the UK, is custodian of the most important research collection in the world. It is also the largest UK publicly funded building constructed in the 20th century. The total floor space is approximately 100,000 sq metres. The basements, the deepest in London, have 300 km of shelving for 12 million books. There are 11 reading areas, three exhibition galleries and a conference centre with a 255-seat auditorium. British publishers are legally obliged to deposit a copy of their publications at the BL. The National Libraries of Scotland and Wales, the Bodleian at Oxford and the Cambridge University Library (and the Library of Trinity College, Dublin) can also claim copies of all new British publications under legal deposit.

Treasures on display in the BL's John Ritblat Gallery include the *Lindisfarne Gospels* (c. 700), *Magna Carta* (1215) and Shakespeare's First Folio (1623), together with musical, historical and literary pieces in the handwriting of Handel, Nelson and Jane Austen, and many others. Some 475,000 reader visits are made to the BL each year. The reading rooms are open to those who need to see material (for example, manuscripts, newspapers, journals, stamps and maps, as well as books) not readily available elsewhere or whose work or studies require the facilities of the national library.

The BL's Document Supply Centre at Boston Spa (West Yorkshire) is the national centre for inter-library lending within the UK and between the UK and other countries. It dispatches over 4 million documents a year.

Other Libraries

As well as public and national libraries there are nearly 700 libraries in higher and further education, about 5,600 in schools and 2,220 specialised libraries within other public and private sector organisations (such as commercial companies, research councils and government departments).

The university book collections of Oxford and Cambridge, with over 7 million and more than 6 million items held by their respective university libraries, are unmatched by those of other foundations. However, the combined stores of the colleges and institutions of the University of London total 9 million volumes,

the John Rylands University Library of Manchester contains 3.5 million volumes, Edinburgh 2.5 million, Leeds 2.3 million, and Durham, Glasgow, Liverpool and Aberdeen each have over 1 million volumes. Many universities have vital research collections in special subjects—the Barnes Medical Library at Birmingham and the British Library of Political and Economic Science at the London School of Economics, for example.

Besides a number of private collections, such as that of the London Library (for private subscribers), there are the collections of such learned societies as the Royal Institute of International Affairs, the Royal Geographical Society and the Royal Academy of Music. The Poetry Library in the South Bank Centre, owned by the ACE, is a collection of 20th-century poetry written in or translated into English; it has about 60,000 volumes.

The Public Record Office (PRO) in London and in Kew (Surrey) houses the records of the superior courts of law of England and Wales and of most government departments, as well as millions of historical documents, such as *Domesday Book* (1086) and autograph letters and documents of the sovereigns of England. Public records, with a few exceptions, are available for inspection by everyone 30 years after the end of the year in which they were created. The Scottish Record Office in Edinburgh and the PRO of Northern Ireland in Belfast serve the same purpose.

Books

In 1998 British publishers issued over 104,600 separate titles (including new editions). The UK book industry exported books worth over £1.1 billion in 1998, 30% up on 1997. A recent trend has been the success of narrative non-fiction, tracing an arcane or scientific subject through history. London's first international festival of literature took place in March 1999. In May 1999 the illustrator Quentin Blake was appointed first Children's Laureate (a roving ambassador of books for the young—with a prize of £10,000). A children's author named (by *The Times*) one of the top five bedtime favourites for grown-ups in 1999 was J.K. Rowling, for her Harry Potter books.

Among the leading trade organisations are the Publishers Association (PA), which has 200 members; and the Booksellers Association, with about 3,300 members. The PA, through its International Division, promotes the export of British books. The Welsh Book Council and the Gaelic Books Council support the publication of books in Welsh and in Gaelic. The Book Trust encourages reading and the promotion of books through an information service and a children's library.

Historical Manuscripts

The Royal Commission on Historical Manuscripts locates, reports on, and gives information and advice about historical papers outside the public records. It also advises private owners, grant-awarding bodies, record offices, local authorities and the Government on the acquisition and maintenance of manuscripts. The Commission maintains the National Register of Archives (the central collecting point for information about British historical manuscripts) and the Manorial Documents Register, which are available to researchers.

CRAFTS

The crafts in the UK have an annual turnover estimated at £400 million. Government aid amounted to £3.2 million in 1998–99. Policy and funding for the crafts in England are, since April 1999, the responsibility of the ACE, which is required to allocate at least £3.4 million, £3.6 million and £3.8 million for crafts for the years 1999–2000, 2000–01 and 2001–02 respectively, with a further £750,000 for development. The Crafts Council runs the National Centre for Crafts in London, organises the annual Chelsea Crafts Fair (which generated sales of £2.1 million for the trade in 1998), and co-ordinates British groups at international fairs. Five Crafts Council exhibitions took place at its London gallery in 1998 and 201,000 people visited these shows in London and on tour. Craft Forum Wales has a membership of 600 craft business groups in Wales; they had a turnover of over £30 million in 1998. Craftworks, an independent company, is the development agency for Northern Ireland. The Arts Council of Northern Ireland also funds crafts promotion, while the SAC has a Crafts Department, which promotes crafts and helps craftworkers in Scotland.

Further Reading

Department for Culture, Media and Sport: Annual report 1999. Cm 4213. The Stationery Office, 1999.

Creative Industries Mapping Document. Creative Industries Task Force. DCMS, 1998.

Website

Department for Culture, Media and Sport: www.culture.gov.uk

17 The Media

The United Kingdom is at the forefront of the digital broadcasting age. New digital terrestrial and satellite television services have been launched since late 1998 and cable and commercial digital radio services are getting under way during 1999. Newspapers throughout the UK—despite a gradual decline in hard-copy circulations for some national titles—continue to serve a wide readership. The Internet is providing, increasingly, an additional medium for information, entertainment and communication.

Television and Radio

Broadcasting in the UK, while traditionally viewed as a public service accountable to the people, also embraces the principles of competition and choice. Three public authorities have the main responsibility for television and radio services. They work to broad requirements and objectives defined or endorsed by Parliament, but are otherwise independent in their day-to-day conduct of business. The authorities are:

- the BBC (British Broadcasting Corporation), which broadcasts television and radio programmes;
- the ITC (Independent Television Commission), which licenses and regulates commercial television services including cable, satellite and independent teletext services; and

- the Radio Authority, which licenses and regulates commercial radio services, including cable and satellite.

The Department for Culture, Media and Sport is responsible for government policy towards broadcasting.

On average, people in the UK spend over 25 hours a week watching the television. There are five established terrestrial analogue channels, offering a mixture of drama, light entertainment, films, sport, educational, children's and religious programmes, news and current affairs, and documentaries. These comprise two national BBC networks, financed almost wholly by a licence fee, and the commercial ITV (Channel 3), Channel 4 and Channel 5 services, which are funded by advertising and sponsorship. In Wales, S4C—Sianel Pedwar Cymru—broadcasts programmes on the fourth channel.

Satellite television and cable services are mainly funded by subscription income. The largest satellite programmer is BSkyB (British Sky Broadcasting—see also p. 278) which, with around 7 million subscribers, dominates subscription-based television in the UK.

The UK's first digital satellite and terrestrial television services[1] were launched in autumn 1998, providing the existing analogue programmes in a digital format, together with free-to-air and subscription and pay-per-view services. Digital cable services are beginning from 1999.

There are three national commercial radio stations. About 225 independent local radio (ILR) services are also in operation (a record number of 23 new licences having been awarded in 1998). Stations supply local news and information, sport, music and other entertainment, education and consumer advice.

A considerable expansion of local and national radio will be made possible by digital audio broadcasting. BBC digital radio broadcasts began in 1995. The first commercial digital radio services are starting in 1999.

Television Audience Share Figures April 1998–March 1999

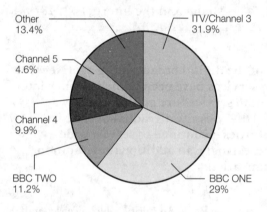

- Other 13.4%
- ITV/Channel 3 31.9%
- Channel 5 4.6%
- Channel 4 9.9%
- BBC TWO 11.2%
- BBC ONE 29%

Source: Independent Television Commission

The BBC has five national radio networks, which together transmit all types of music, news, current affairs, drama, education, sport and a range of features programmes. There are also 39 BBC local radio stations serving England and the Channel Islands, and national radio services in Scotland, Wales and Northern Ireland, including Welsh and Gaelic language stations. BBC radio services currently attract about 50% of listeners.

---

[1] Digital broadcasting is a new, more effective way of transmitting television (and radio) services. It allows much more information than before to be transmitted, and can offer many more channels, extra services, interactivity, and higher quality picture and sound to viewers and listeners willing to invest in new receiving equipment.

The UK television industry has a worldwide reputation for innovation and quality programmes. In 1997 British television exports were worth some £470 million. However, the UK runs a significant balance of trade deficit in television owing to the increasing number of imported television programmes on UK cable and satellite channels. In April 1999, following the publication of an independent research report, the Government announced an inquiry into the television programming market to see how UK television exports can be improved and their value increased.

CHANGES IN REGULATION

Broadcasting in the UK is undergoing radical change. The availability of more radio frequencies, together with satellite, cable and microwave transmissions, has already made a greater number of local, national and international services possible. The transition from analogue to digital transmission technology has the potential to expand this capacity enormously.

Legislation

In recognition of this potential, legislation was passed in 1996 setting out a flexible regulatory framework for the introduction of digital terrestrial broadcasting and paving the way for more broadly based competitive media groups. There were four key governmental objectives:

- to safeguard plurality of media ownership and diversity of viewpoint;
- to preserve the UK's tradition of public service broadcasting;
- to support the competitiveness of the British broadcasting industry and give the UK the opportunity to lead the world in exploiting digital technology; and
- to ensure broadcasters maintain appropriate standards of impartiality, taste and decency.

Digital Terrestrial Broadcasting

The 1996 Broadcasting Act provided for:

- the licensing of up to 36 national digital terrestrial television channels, transmitted on six frequency channels or 'multiplexes',[2] and serving, in the medium term, from 70% to over 90% of the population; and
- the licensing of at least 12 digital radio services on two national multiplexes, with at least one multiplex available for local services in most areas of the UK, and an additional multiplex for extra local services in areas of greatest demand.

The legislation guaranteed capacity on three of the six digital television multiplexes and on one national radio multiplex for the existing public service broadcasters. It also stipulated that the ITC and Radio Authority award national multiplex licences[3] to those applicants whose plans best promote the development of digital broadcasting—by installing the new transmission network as quickly as possible, making consumer receiver equipment as affordable as possible,[4] and broadening consumer choice of programming.

Many of the new services on digital television will be available on a subscription or pay-per-view basis. Any broadcaster wishing to offer pay-television needs to use a 'conditional access' system (covering encryption, scrambling and subscription management services) to ensure that only those who have paid for a particular service receive it. Since any dominant provider of such systems would have the power to determine who can, or cannot, enter the pay-television market, it is important that providers are subject to effective regulation. The Government has implemented European Union regulations to ensure that all broadcasters can gain access on 'fair, reasonable and non-discriminatory terms' to any digital set-top boxes which can receive their signal. OFTEL (see p. 378), in consultation with the ITC, has powers to intervene over anti-competitive behaviour.

Media Ownership

Legislation in 1990 laid down rules enabling the ITC and Radio Authority to keep ownership of the broadcasting media widely spread and to prevent undue concentrations of single and cross-media ownership, in the wider public interest. The 1996 Broadcasting Act relaxed those rules, both within and across different media sectors, to reflect the needs and aspirations of the industry against the background of accelerating technological change:

- allowing for greater cross-ownership between newspaper groups, television companies and radio stations, at both national and regional levels; and

---

[2] Through the process known as multiplexing, the signals of several broadcasters are combined into a single stream on a single-frequency channel. There is therefore no longer a direct one-to-one relationship between a television service and a frequency.

[3] The multiplex, or carriage and delivery system, is licensed separately from the programme and additional services which are carried on the multiplexes. Licences to operate commercial digital terrestrial television (DTT) multiplexes were awarded by the ITC in 1997, and all DTT multiplexes started broadcasting in November 1998. The Radio Authority awarded the national commercial radio multiplex licence in October 1998 (with services expected to begin in October 1999) and has started advertising local commercial multiplex licences to provide local digital services to most of the main population centres across the UK over the next two to three years.

[4] Digital television services can be received through an existing television aerial, a cable connection or a satellite dish. However, viewers who choose to receive digital television by any of these methods need a special set-top box decoder which enables digital television pictures to be reassembled on screen. In time, television sets with a built-in decoder will increasingly be available. Radio listeners also need to invest in new sets to hear digital radio.

- introducing 'public interest' criteria by which the regulatory authorities can assess and approve (or disallow) mergers or acquisitions between newspapers and television and radio companies.

The 1996 Act overturned the rule that no one company could own more than two of the ITV (Channel 3) licences; instead, a new limit was set whereby no company could control franchises covering more than 15% of the total television audience. Local newspapers with more than a 50% share of their market may own a local radio station, providing at least one other independent local radio station is operating in that area.

In January 1999 the Government announced its intention to relax restrictions on digital radio ownership to encourage greater investment.

Recent Developments

Existing analogue transmissions will continue for some time, but the Government wants to announce a switch-off date for analogue services as soon as is practicable. In 1998, it published a consultation paper on the transition from analogue to digital broadcasting, and in September 1999 said that the switchover could start to happen as early as 2006 and be completed by 2010.

The Government has also reviewed the future regulation of broadcasting and telecommunications, taking account of the implications of the increasing convergence between the two sectors. A Green Paper published in 1998 noted that rapid technological advances were having a significant impact on communications, acknowledged that developments would challenge the existing approach to both economic and content regulation, and sought views on what regulatory structures might be more appropriate in the longer term. In a follow-up report published in June 1999 (*Regulating Communications: the Way Ahead*), the Government announced that its preferred evolutionary and flexible approach to reforming communications regulation had received widespread support in responses to the Green Paper.

THE BBC

A Royal Charter and Agreement govern the constitution, finances and obligations of the BBC. The Corporation's Board of Governors, including the Chairman, Vice-Chairman and a National Governor each for Scotland, Wales and Northern Ireland, is appointed by the Queen on the advice of the Government. The Board of Governors is ultimately responsible for all aspects of broadcasting by the BBC. The Governors appoint the Director-General, the Corporation's chief executive officer, who heads the Executive Committee and Board of Management—the bodies in charge of the daily running of the Corporation.

The BBC has a regional structure throughout the UK. The English regions, BBC Scotland, BBC Wales and BBC Northern Ireland make television and radio programmes for their local audiences as well as contributing to the national network.

The National Broadcasting Councils for Scotland, Wales and Northern Ireland advise on the content of television and radio programmes intended mainly for reception in their areas. Ten Regional Councils in England advise the Board of Governors on the needs and concerns of their audiences.

BBC Charter and Agreement

In 1996 a new Royal Charter came into effect, enabling the BBC to continue as the UK's main public service broadcaster until 2006. The Agreement between the BBC and the Secretary of State for Culture, Media and Sport, which runs concurrently with the Charter, formally establishes the Corporation's editorial independence in all matters of programme content, scheduling and management. It also provides for the licence fee (see p. 273) to remain the chief source of finance for the BBC's public service activities until at least 2002.

The Charter and Agreement maintain the BBC's essential characteristics as a public corporation; preserve its main objectives of providing broadcasting services of information, education and entertainment; and reinforce the duties placed on the Governors to maintain programme standards and to ensure the Corporation's accountability to its audiences. They also allow for the development of the BBC's commercial activities, in partnership with the private sector, in the UK and abroad (although these must be funded, operated and accounted for separately from its licence-fee-funded services).

Organisation

The structure of the BBC comprises:

- BBC Broadcast, which schedules channels and commissions services for audiences in the UK and abroad;
- BBC Production, which develops the BBC's in-house radio and television production capability across all genres and media;
- BBC News, which is responsible for an integrated national and international news operation across the full range of BBC services;
- BBC Worldwide (see p. 275);
- BBC World Service (see p. 275);
- BBC Resources, a wholly owned subsidiary which provides support facilities and expertise to BBC programme-makers and broadcasters; and
- the Corporate Centre, which provides strategic services to the BBC as a whole.

Finance

The domestic services of the BBC are financed predominantly by a licence fee. All households or premises with a television set must buy an annual licence (costing £101 for colour and £33.50 for black and white in 1999–2000).

Licence income (which totalled £2.155 billion in 1998–99) is supplemented by profits from BBC Worldwide commercial activities, such as television programme exports, sales of recordings, publications and other merchandise connected with BBC programmes, film library sales, and exhibitions based on programmes. The BBC World Service's radio broadcasting operations are financed by a grant-in-aid from the Foreign & Commonwealth Office, while BBC Worldwide Television is self-financing.

In October 1998 the Government announced an independent review of the future of the BBC licence fee after 2002, aimed at ensuring the Corporation's continuing ability to meet its public service obligations and its need to operate effectively in a competitive market. The review panel published its report in August 1999, its main recommendations including:

- a digital licence supplement, on top of the existing licence fee, to be introduced from April 2000;
- no introduction of advertising and sponsorship on the BBC's public services;
- partial privatisation of BBC Worldwide and BBC Resources; and
- reviews of BBC fair trading arrangements and financial reporting by the Office of Fair Trading and the National Audit Office.

BBC Television

The BBC, which launched the world's first regular television service in 1936, broadcasts 20,000 hours of television each year on its two domestic channels to national and regional audiences:

- BBC ONE is the channel of diverse appeal. In 1998–99 it broadcast some 1,265 hours of features, documentaries and current affairs programmes, around 1,100 hours of drama and light entertainment, just over 600 hours of sport and nearly 500 hours of children's programmes.

- BBC TWO aims for innovation and originality, with a variety of programmes including drama, documentaries, arts, comedy, and leisure and lifestyle shows.

Programmes are made at, or acquired through, Television Centre in London and six major bases throughout the UK (Glasgow in Scotland, Cardiff in Wales, Belfast in Northern Ireland, and Birmingham, Bristol and Manchester in England); or they are commissioned from independent producers—the BBC must ensure that at least 25% of its original programming comes from the independent sector.

The Corporation is providing a range of digital channels to all licence-fee payers, including:

- an extended BBC ONE and BBC TWO in widescreen;
- BBC News 24 (see below);
- BBC Choice, a supplementary service to complement and enhance the network schedules, which began in September 1998;
- BBC Parliament (coverage of proceedings in the House of Commons, House of Lords, the new Parliament in Scotland and the new assemblies in Wales and Northern Ireland);
- BBC Knowledge (the UK's first fully integrated public service multimedia learning service), launched in June 1999; and
- BBC Text, a new graphically enhanced text and information service.

Education is a central component of the BBC's public service commitment on its domestic channels. A wide range of educational programmes is broadcast for primary and secondary schools (over 90% of which use BBC schools television), further education colleges and the Open University (see p. 141), while programmes for adults cover numeracy, literacy, language learning, health, work and vocational training. Books, pamphlets, computer software, and audio and video cassettes are produced to supplement the programmes.

BBC News 24, the Corporation's 24-hour news channel, began broadcasting in 1997 on cable services and during the night on BBC ONE. In 1997 the BBC also launched its Online channel on the Internet (see p. 287), with constantly updated news, sport, finance, travel and other information. As with BBC News 24, this is funded by the licence fee and free to users.

BBC Network Radio

BBC Network Radio, broadcasting to the whole of the UK, transmits over 42,000 hours of programmes each year on its five networks (broadcasting 24 hours a day):

- BBC Radio 1 (broadcasting on 97–99 FM) is a leading contemporary music station, serving a target audience of 15- to 24-year-olds. It plays top-selling, new and specialist music, covers live performances and social action campaigns, and broadcasts features and news programmes relevant to a young audience.
- BBC Radio 2 (88–90.2 FM), which attracts more listeners than any other national network, offers a broad range of music (including pop, rock and roll, rhythm and blues, folk, jazz, country, brass band and gospel), light entertainment, documentaries, public service broadcasting and popular culture.
- BBC Radio 3 (90.2–92.4 FM) offers a wide repertoire of classical music and jazz, more than half of which is performed live or is specially recorded, together with drama, documentaries and discussion.
- BBC Radio 4 (broadcast with some differences on 92.4–94.6 FM and 198 Long Wave) has a backbone of authoritative news and current affairs coverage, complemented by drama, science, the arts, religion, natural history, medicine, finance and gardening; it also carries parliamentary coverage and cricket in season on Long Wave, and BBC World Service (see p. 275) overnight.
- Radio 5 Live (693 and 909 MW) offers news, current affairs and extensive sports coverage.

The BBC has been transmitting digital radio since 1995 and currently reaches 60% of the UK on its own multiplex, which offers Radios 1, 2, 3, 4, and 5 Live as well as coverage of Parliament and additional live sports events.

BBC Worldwide

In 1994 the international and commercial interests of the BBC were brought together in BBC Worldwide, to enable the Corporation to develop its role in the fast-expanding broadcast and media world. With responsibility for the BBC's commercial activity, BBC Worldwide is a major international broadcaster and a leading distributor and co-producer of BBC programmes.

BBC Worldwide works closely with BBC production departments, independent producers and its own network of international offices to determine commercial strategies for key programmes with international licensing potential. It is also developing premium channels to compete in the international marketplace. Its core service is BBC World, an advertiser-funded, 24-hour international news and information channel. The channel provides news bulletins, in-depth analysis and reports, and is available to around 135 million homes around the world. BBC Prime, an entertainment and drama channel for Europe and Africa, has over 7 million subscribers.

In its first commercial broadcasting venture in the UK, the BBC began themed subscription services in 1997, in partnership with Flextech plc, under the brand name UKTV. These services are not funded by the licence fee.

In 1998 BBC Worldwide signed an agreement with a US media company, Discovery Communications Inc., creating a BBC-branded network (BBC America) in the United States and jointly developing quality channels for pay-television around the world. The agreement is intended to increase investment in BBC factual programme-making and strengthen the international standing of the Corporation.

BBC Worldwide is the third largest publishing house in the UK. Its operations cover magazines, books, videos, audio sales, CD-ROMs and a commercial on-line service.

BBC World Service

BBC World Service broadcasts by radio in English and 42 other languages worldwide. It has an estimated global weekly audience of over 140 million listeners. This excludes any estimate for listeners in countries where it is difficult to survey audiences. The core programming of news, current affairs, business and sports reports is complemented by a wide range of cultural programmes, including drama, literature and music. The World Service announced in February 1999 that, while maintaining short wave broadcasts for mass audiences, it plans to make programmes more widely available on FM frequencies and to deliver services in major languages through digital broadcasting and on the Internet.

BBC World Service programmes in English and many other languages are made available by satellite for rebroadcasting by agreement with local or national radio stations, networks and cable operators. The BBC's Radio International sells recorded programmes to other broadcasters in over 100 countries.

BBC Monitoring, the international media monitoring arm, provides transcripts of radio and television broadcasts from over 140 countries. As well as providing a vital source of information to the BBC, this service is used by other media organisations, government departments, the commercial sector and academic institutions.

INDEPENDENT BROADCASTING

Independent Television Commission

The ITC is responsible for licensing and regulating commercial television services (including BBC commercial services) operating in, or from, the United Kingdom. It does not make, broadcast or transmit programmes itself.

The ITC must ensure that a wide range of commercial television services is available throughout the UK and that they are of a high quality and appeal to a variety of tastes and interests. It must also ensure fair and effective competition in the provision of these services, and adherence to the rules on media ownership.

The Commission regulates the various television services through licence conditions, codes and guidelines. The codes cover programme content, advertising, sponsorship and technical standards. If a licensee does not comply with the conditions of its licence or the codes, the ITC can impose penalties. These range from a formal warning or a requirement to broadcast an apology or correction, to a fine. In extreme circumstances, a company's licence may be shortened or revoked.

ITC staff regularly monitor programmes, and take into account comments from viewers and audience research. They are also advised by 12 Viewer Consultative Councils (nine in England, and one each in Wales, Scotland and Northern Ireland), and by specialist committees on educational and religious broadcasting and advertising.

ITV (Channel 3)

The first regular ITV programmes began in London in 1955. ITV is made up of 15 regionally based television companies which are licensed to supply programmes in the 14 independent television geographical regions. There are two licences for London, one for weekdays and the other for the weekend. An additional ITC licensee provides a national breakfast-time service, transmitted on the ITV network.

The ITV licences for Channel 3 are awarded for a ten-year period by competitive tender to the highest bidder (who has to have passed a quality threshold). Licensees must provide a diverse programme service designed to appeal to a wide range of viewers' tastes and interests. They have a statutory duty to present programmes made in, and about, their region, and there is also a requirement for district and regional programming to be aimed at different areas within regions.

Each company plans the content of the programmes to be broadcast in its area. These are produced by the company itself, by other programme companies, or are bought from elsewhere. As with the BBC, at least 25% of original programming must come from the independent sector. About one-third of the output is made up of informative programmes—news, documentaries, and coverage of current affairs, education and religion—while the remainder covers drama, entertainment, sport, arts and children's

programmes. Programmes are broadcast 24 hours a day throughout the country. A common national and international news service is provided by Independent Television News (ITN).

Channel 3 companies are obliged to operate a national programme network. The ITV Network Centre, which is owned by the companies, independently commissions and schedules programmes.

Operating on a commercial basis, licensees derive most of their income from selling advertising time. Their financial resources and programme production vary considerably, depending largely on the population of the areas in which they operate. Newspaper groups can acquire a controlling interest in Channel 3 companies, although safeguards exist to ensure against any undue concentrations of media ownership (see p. 271).

Granada and Carlton, two of the largest regional ITV (Channel 3) television companies, jointly own ONdigital, which occupies three of the six multiplexes licensed for digital terrestrial television. ONdigital services were launched in November 1998.

Channel 4 and S4C

Channel 4 provides a national 24-hour television service throughout the UK, except in Wales, which has a corresponding service— S4C (Sianel Pedwar Cymru). Channel 4 is a statutory corporation, licensed and regulated by the ITC, and funded by selling its own advertising time.

Channel 4's remit is to provide programmes with a distinctive character and to appeal to tastes and interests not generally catered for by Channel 3. It must present a suitable proportion of educational programmes and encourage innovation and experiment. Channel 4 commissions programmes from the ITV companies and independent producers, and buys programmes from overseas.

The fourth channel in Wales is allocated to S4C, which is regulated by the Welsh Fourth Channel Authority. Members of the Welsh Authority are appointed by the Government. S4C must ensure that a significant proportion of programming—and the majority between

18.30 and 22.00 hours—is in the Welsh language. At other times it transmits national Channel 4 programmes. In November 1998 S4C launched a new digital service incorporating current analogue Welsh programmes and additional material. Roughly 15% of S4C's income comes from advertising, programme sales, publicity and merchandising; the remainder comes from a government grant, the level of which is fixed by statute.

Channel 5

The UK's newest national terrestrial channel went on air in March 1997, its ten-year licence having been awarded by competitive tender to Channel 5 Broadcasting Limited. Channel 5 serves about 70% of the population and is supported by advertising revenue.

Like Channel 3, the service is subject to positive programming requirements. It must show programmes of quality and diversity, with a wide range of original productions and commissions from independent producers.

Gaelic Broadcasting

The Gaelic Broadcasting Committee is an independent body committed to ensuring that a wide range of quality television and radio programmes is broadcast in Gaelic for reception in Scotland. Its members are appointed by the ITC, in consultation with the Radio Authority. The Committee distributes government money to programme makers through the Gaelic Broadcasting Fund.

The Radio Authority

The Radio Authority's licensing and regulatory remit covers all independent radio services, including national, local, cable and satellite services. Its three main tasks are to plan frequencies, appoint licensees with a view to broadening listener choice, and regulate programming and advertising.

Like the ITC, the Radio Authority has to make sure that licensed services are of a high quality, and offer programmes which will appeal to many different tastes and interests. It has published codes covering engineering,

programmes, news and current affairs, and advertising and sponsorship, to which licensees must adhere.

Independent National Radio (INR)

There are currently three independent national radio services, whose licences were awarded by the Radio Authority through competitive tender, and which broadcast 24 hours a day:

- Classic FM (100–102 FM), which broadcasts mainly classical music, together with news and information;
- Virgin 1215 (105.8 FM and 1215 MW), which plays broad-based rock music (and is supplemented by a separate Virgin station which operates under a local London licence); and
- Talk Radio UK (1053 and 1089 MW), which is a speech-based service.

The three stations have guaranteed places on the new national commercial digital multiplex.

Independent Local Radio (ILR)

Independent local radio stations have been broadcasting in the UK since 1973. ILR stations broadcast a wide variety of programmes and news of local interest, as well as music and entertainment, traffic reports and advertising. There are also stations serving ethnic minority communities. The Radio Authority awards independent local licences, although not by competitive tender; the success of licence applications is in part determined by the extent to which applicants widen choice and meet the needs and interests of the people living in the area and in part by whether they have the necessary financial resources to sustain programme plans for the eight-year licence period. Local radio stations do not have guaranteed slots on digital local radio multiplexes.

The Radio Authority also issues restricted service licences (RSLs)—short-term RSLs, generally for periods of up to 28 days, for special events or trial services, and long-term RSLs, primarily for student and hospital stations, to broadcast to specific establishments.

TELETEXT, CABLE AND SATELLITE SERVICES

Teletext Services

Teletext is written copy broadcast on television sets. There are several teletext services; one is operated by the BBC and others by independent television. They offer constantly updated information on a variety of subjects, including news, sport, travel, weather conditions and entertainment. The teletext system allows the television signal to carry additional information which can be selected and displayed as 'pages' of text and graphics on receivers equipped with the necessary decoders. About 16 million homes have sets with teletext decoders. The BBC and Channels 3, 4 and 5 increasingly provide subtitling for people with hearing difficulties.

The ITC awards teletext licences for the capacity on Channels 3, 4, and 5 by competitive tender for a period of ten years. Applicants have to satisfy certain statutory requirements before their cash bid can be considered.

Cable Services

Cable services are delivered to consumers through underground cables and are paid for by subscription. The franchising of cable systems and the regulation of cable television services are carried out by the ITC, while the Radio Authority issues cable radio licences.

'Broadband cable' systems can carry between 30 and 65 television channels using analogue technology (including terrestrial broadcasts, satellite television and channels delivered to cable operators by landline or videotape), as well as a full range of telecommunications services. Digital technology is being introduced which will support up to 500 television channels. Cable also has the capacity for computer-based interactive services such as video-on-demand, home shopping, home banking, security and alarm services, electronic mail and high-speed Internet access (see p. 287). It can additionally supply television services tailored for local communities; cable operators are testing programming concepts to find out what works best at the local level.

Cable franchises have been granted covering areas which include 83% of all homes and nearly all urban areas in the UK. Regulation is as light as possible to encourage the development of a wide range of services, and flexible enough to adapt to new technology. In April 1999 there were 12.1 million homes able to receive broadband cable services and 3 million subscribing homes (representing a TV penetration of 24.5%).

ITC licences are required for systems capable of serving more than 1,000 homes. Systems extending beyond a single building and up to 1,000 homes require only an individual licence regulated by OFTEL.

There are no specific quality controls on cable services. However, if cable operators also provide their own programme content as opposed to just conveying services, they require a programme services licence from the ITC, which includes consumer protection requirements.

Direct Broadcasting by Satellite

Direct broadcasting by satellite (DBS), by which television is transmitted directly by satellite into people's homes, has been available throughout the UK since 1989. The signals from satellite broadcasting are received through specially designed aerials or 'dishes'. Most services are paid for by subscription. Some offer general entertainment, while others concentrate on specific areas of interest, such as sport, music, children's programmes and feature films.

All satellite television services provided by broadcasters established in the UK are licensed and regulated by the ITC. Around 200 satellite television service licences were in force in January 1999. Many of these are foreign language services, some of them designed for ethnic minorities within the UK and others aimed primarily at audiences in other countries. Viewers in the UK may also receive a variety of television services from other European countries. Satellite services must comply with the ITC's programmes, advertising and sponsorship codes, but they are not subject to any positive programming obligations.

BSkyB, the UK's largest satellite programmer, launched its digital satellite service (SkyDigital) in October 1998 (carrying more than 140 channels). It plans to launch new interactive services in autumn 1999.

Satellite radio services must be licensed by the Radio Authority if they are transmitted from the UK for general reception within the country, or if they are transmitted from outside the UK but are managed editorially from within it.

OTHER ASPECTS

Advertising and Sponsorship

The BBC may not raise revenue from broadcasting advertisements or from commercial sponsorship of programmes on its public service channels. Its policy is to avoid giving publicity to any firm or organised interest except when this is necessary in providing effective and informative programmes. It does, however, cover sponsored sporting and artistic events. Advertising and sponsorship are allowed on commercial television and radio services, subject to controls. The ITC and the Radio Authority operate codes governing advertising standards and programme sponsorship, and can impose penalties on broadcasters failing to comply with them.

Advertisements on independent television and radio are broadcast in breaks during programmes as well as between programmes. Advertisers are not allowed to influence programme content. Advertisements must be distinct and separate from programmes. Advertising on terrestrial television is limited to an average of seven minutes an hour during the day and seven-and-a-half minutes in the peak evening viewing period. Advertising is prohibited in broadcasts of religious services and in broadcasts to schools. Political advertising and advertisements for betting (other than the National Lottery, the football pools and bingo) are prohibited. All tobacco advertising is banned on television and cigarette advertisements are banned on radio. Religious advertisements may be broadcast on commercial radio and television, provided they comply with the guidelines issued by the ITC and the Radio Authority.

Sponsorship in Independent Broadcasting

In the UK sponsorship is a relatively new way of helping to finance commercial broadcasting, although the practice has long been established in other countries. In return for their financial contribution, sponsors receive a credit associating them with a particular programme. The ITC's Code of Programme Sponsorship and the Radio Authority's Advertising and Sponsorship Code aim to ensure that sponsors do not exert influence on the editorial content of programmes and that sponsorships are made clear to viewers and listeners. News and current affairs programmes may not be sponsored. Potential sponsors for other categories of programme may be debarred if their involvement could constrain the editorial independence of the programme maker in any way. References to sponsors or their products must be confined to the beginning and end of a programme and around commercial breaks; they must not appear in the programme itself. All commercial radio programmes other than news bulletins may be sponsored.

Since September 1998 the ITC has permitted masthead programming (programmes with the same title as a magazine and made or funded by its publishers) on all UK commercial television services (Channels 3, 4, and 5 having previously been excluded).

Government Publicity

Government publicity material to support non-political campaigns may be broadcast on independent television and radio. This is paid for on a normal commercial basis. Short public service items, concerning health, safety and welfare, are transmitted free by the BBC and independent television and radio. All government advertisements and public service information films are subtitled to help people with hearing difficulties.

Broadcasting Standards

The independence enjoyed by the broadcasting authorities carries with it certain obligations over programme content. Broadcasters must display, as far as possible, a proper balance and wide range of subject matter, impartiality in matters of controversy and accuracy in news coverage, and must not offend against good taste. Broadcasters must also comply with legislation relating to obscenity and incitement to racial hatred.

The BBC, the ITC and the Radio Authority apply codes providing rules on impartiality, the portrayal of violence and standards of taste and decency in programmes, particularly during hours when children are likely to be viewing or listening. Television programmes broadcast before 21.00 hours (or 20.00 hours on certain cable and satellite services) are required to be suitable for a general audience, including children.

Broadcasting Standards Commission (BSC)

The BSC acts as a forum for public concern about fairness and taste and decency on television and radio. It decides on complaints received from the public about taste and decency, and adjudicates on claims of unfair or unjust treatment in broadcast programmes and of unwarranted infringement of privacy in programmes or in their preparation. It also undertakes and commissions research and the monitoring of public attitudes, and has drawn up a code of practice on both broadcasting standards and fairness which the broadcasters and regulators are required to reflect in their own programme guidelines. In 1998–99 the Commission received 139 fairness complaints which were within its remit; 94 fairness adjudications were completed, of which 63% were upheld in full or in part. It also received 3,564 complaints about standards (an increase of 42% on 1997–98); of those adjudicated upon, 31% were upheld in full or in part (up from 19% in 1997–98).

Parliamentary Broadcasting

The proceedings of both Houses of Parliament may be broadcast on television and radio, either live or, more usually, in recorded and edited form on news and current affairs programmes. The BBC has a specific obligation to transmit on radio an impartial account day by day of the proceedings in both Houses of Parliament. In October 1998 the Corporation launched a new seven-day-a-week parliamentary television service (initially on analogue cable), additional to, and independent of, its existing coverage of Parliament. The proceedings of the Scottish Parliament and the assemblies for Wales and Northern Ireland are also broadcast live on occasions and in recorded and edited form on a regular basis by the BBC.

Party Political Broadcasts

In the absence of paid political advertising in the UK, there is a long-standing practice that broadcasters make time available for party political and election broadcasts on television and radio. Recent reforms to the system have been introduced by broadcasters to reflect the increased number of elections in the UK following devolution and to re-focus broadcasts between elections at key times in the political calendar (for example, the Budget, the Queen's Speech and party conferences). The content of these broadcasts is the responsibility of the parties, although they have to comply with ground rules laid down by the broadcasters. In addition, the Government may make ministerial broadcasts on radio and television, with opposition parties also being allotted broadcast time.

Audience Research

Both the BBC and the commercial sector are required to keep themselves informed on the state of public opinion about the programmes and advertising that they broadcast. This is done through the continuous measurement of the size and composition of audiences and their opinions of programmes. For television, this work is undertaken through BARB (the Broadcasters' Audience Research Board). Joint research is undertaken for BBC radio and for commercial radio by RAJAR (Radio Joint Audience Research).

The BBC, the commercial sector and the BSC conduct regular surveys of audience opinion on television and radio services. Public opinion is further assessed by the BBC and ITC through the work of their advisory committees, councils and panels.

INTERNATIONAL CO-OPERATION

European Agreements

The UK has implemented two important European agreements on cross-border broadcasting—the European Community Broadcasting Directive (which was revised in 1997) and the Council of Europe Convention on Transfrontier Television. These aim to ensure the free flow of television programmes and services throughout participating countries, setting minimum standards on advertising, sponsorship, taste and decency, and the portrayal of sex and violence. If a broadcast meets these standards then no participating country may prevent reception in its territory.

Audiovisual Eureka (AVE), which has a membership of 33 European countries including the UK, aims to help improve aspects of the European audiovisual industry through practical measures to enhance training, development and distribution. It concentrates its work on the countries of Central and Eastern Europe.

The UK participates in the European Community MEDIA programme, which is aimed at enhancing the strength of member states' national audiovisual industries by encouraging greater collaboration between them, and wider distribution of their products.

European Broadcasting Union

The BBC and the Radio Authority are members of the European Broadcasting Union, which manages Eurovision, the international network of television news and programme exchange. The Union is responsible for co-ordinating the exchange of programmes and news over the Eurovision network and intercontinental satellite links. It provides a forum linking the major public services and national broadcasters of Western Europe and other parts of the world, and co-ordinates joint operations in radio and television.

The Press

On an average weekday it is estimated that well over half of people aged 15 and over in the UK read a national morning newspaper (61% of men and 52% of women in 1997–98); nearly 65% read a Sunday newspaper. Over 85% of people read a regional or local newspaper. National papers have an average total circulation of 13 million on weekdays and about 14 million on Sundays, although the total readership is considerably greater.

There are about 1,350 regional and local newspaper titles and over 7,000 periodical publications.

Several newspapers have had very long and distinguished histories. *The Observer*, for example, first published in 1791, is the oldest national Sunday newspaper in the world, and *The Times*, Britain's oldest daily national newspaper, began publication in 1785.

The press caters for a range of political views, interests and levels of education. Newspapers are almost always financially independent of any political party. Where they express pronounced views and show obvious political leanings in their editorial comments, these may derive from proprietorial and other

'In the early days of newspapers the difficulty was to find news enough to fill the tiny and intermittent sheets that then appeared. Nowadays the principal function of a large editorial staff is to squeeze into the space available the huge volume of intelligence with which day by day every newspaper is overwhelmed. In the first place, there are the claims of the advertisements, which must always be the life-blood of any self-supporting and competitive press . . . The matter which fills the columns not devoted to advertisements may be divided into . . . editorial comments, official announcements, special articles and correspondence, foreign news, political news (. . . which includes the debates in Parliament), law and police reports, city news (. . . a review of the state of the money market and the tendencies of the stock exchange), sporting intelligence and general home news . . . Many of the great newspapers in London and the country have their own special correspondents in the important capitals of the world.'

This is a description of the substance of the British press by the *Harmsworth Encylopaedia* published at the beginning of the 20th century—not a great deal seems to have changed.

non-party influences. Nevertheless, during General Election campaigns many newspapers recommend their readers to vote for a particular political party. Even newspapers which adopt strong political views in their editorial columns sometimes include feature and other types of articles by authors of different political persuasions.

In order to preserve their character and traditions, some newspapers and periodicals are governed by trustee-type arrangements. Others have management arrangements that try to ensure their editors' authority and independence.

Newsprint, more than half of which is imported, forms about a quarter of average national newspaper costs; labour represents over half. In addition to sales revenue, newspapers and periodicals earn considerable amounts from their advertising. Indeed, the press (newspapers, magazines and directories) is the largest advertising medium in the UK. Unlike most of its European counterparts, the British press receives no subsidies and relatively few tax and postal concessions.

NATIONAL AND REGIONAL TITLES

Ownership of the national, London and many regional daily newspapers lies in the hands of a number of large corporations, most of which are involved in the whole field of publishing and communications.

The National Press

The national press consists of ten morning daily papers and ten Sunday papers (see Table 17.1). At one time London's Fleet Street was the centre of the newspaper industry, but now all the national papers have moved their editorial and printing facilities to other parts of London or away from the capital altogether. Editions of several papers, for example the *Financial Times* and *The Guardian*, are also printed in other countries.

National newspapers are often described as 'quality', 'mid-market' or 'popular' papers on the basis of differences in style and content. Five dailies and four Sundays are usually described as 'quality' newspapers, which are

directed at readers who want full information on a wide range of public matters. Popular newspapers appeal to people wanting news of a more entertaining character, presented more concisely. 'Mid-market' publications cover the intermediate market. Quality papers are normally broadsheet (large-sheet) in format and mid-market and popular papers tabloid (small-sheet).

Many newspapers are printed in colour and most produce supplements as part of the Saturday or Sunday paper, with articles on travel, food and wine, and other leisure topics.

Regional Newspapers

Most towns and cities throughout the UK have their own regional or local newspaper. These range from morning and evening dailies to Sunday papers and others which are published just once a week. They mainly include stories of regional or local attraction, but the dailies also cover national and international news, often looked at from a local viewpoint. They provide a valuable medium for local advertising.

London has one paid-for evening paper, the *Evening Standard*. Its publisher (Associated Newspapers) also produces a free newspaper, *London Metro*, launched in March 1999. There are local weekly papers for every district in Greater London; these are often different local editions of one centrally published paper.

The *Daily Record* has the highest circulation of the Scottish papers. A new Scottish broadsheet, the *Sunday Herald*, was launched in February 1999. The weekly press in Wales includes Welsh-language and bilingual papers. Welsh community newspapers receive an annual grant as part of the Government's wider financial support for the Welsh language. Newspapers from the Irish Republic, as well as the British national press, are widely read in Northern Ireland.

Several hundred free distribution newspapers, mostly weekly and financed by advertising, are published in the UK. They have enjoyed rapid growth in recent years.

Table 17.2 lists the average net circulations of the leading regional daily, Sunday and paid-for weekly newspapers across the UK.

Table 17.1: National Newspapers

Title and foundation date	Controlled by	Circulation average (January–June)			
		1969	1979	1989	1999
Dailies					
Populars					
Mirror (1903)	Mirror Group	4,924,157	3,623,039	3,199,103	2,313,063
Daily Star (1978)	United News & Media	n.a.	n.a.	912,372	615,038
The Sun (1964)	News International	951,132	3,793,007	4,173,267	3,730,466
Mid-market					
Daily Mail (1896)	Daily Mail & General Trust	1,992,591	1,943,793	1,750,303	2,350,241
Express (1900)	United News & Media	3,731,673	2,405,609	1,589,306	1,095,716
Qualities					
Financial Times (1888)	Pearson	172,347	206,360	199,275	385,025
Daily Telegraph (1855)	Telegraph Group	1,380,367	1,476,887	1,113,033	1,044,740
The Guardian (1821)	Guardian Media Group	292,602	379,429	438,732	398,721
The Independent (1986)	Irish Independent Newspapers	n.a.	n.a.	405,423	223,304
The Times (1785)	News International	437,278	293,989[a]	441,342	740,883
Sundays					
Populars					
News of the World (1843)	News International	6,227,684	4,708,575	5,294,317	4,209,173
Sunday Mirror (1963)	Mirror Group	5,008,731	3,888,631	3,012,143	1,981,059
The People (1881)	Mirror Group	5,455,372	3,930,849	2,660,177	1,643,310
Mid-market					
The Mail on Sunday (1982)	Daily Mail & General Trust	n.a.	n.a.	1,961,506	2,279,430
Express on Sunday (1918)	United News & Media	4,235,326	3,257,728	1,943,089	1,003,287
Qualities					
Sunday Telegraph (1961)	Telegraph Group	753,441	1,278,894	656,120	816,653
The Independent on Sunday (1990)	Irish Independent Newspapers	n.a.	n.a.	n.a.	250,034
The Observer (1791)	Guardian Media Group	879,024	1,124,018	693,939	404,859
The Sunday Times (1822)	News International	1,454,079	1,409,296[a]	1,317,865	1,374,436
Sunday Business (1998)	European Press	n.a.	n.a.	n.a.	55,494

Source: Audit Bureau of Circulations (consisting of publishers, advertisers and advertising agencies)

[a] January–June 1978 (publication suspended from November 1978–November 1979).

n.a. = not applicable.

Ethnic Minority Publications

Many newpapers and magazines in the UK are produced by members of ethnic minorities. Most are published weekly, fortnightly or monthly. A Chinese newspaper, *Sing Tao*, the Urdu *Daily Jang* and the Arabic *Al-Arab*, however, are dailies.

Afro-Caribbean newspapers include *The Gleaner*, *The Voice* and *Caribbean Times*, which are all weeklies. The *Asian Times* is an English language weekly for people of Asian descent. Ethnic language publications appear in Bengali, Gujarati, Hindi and Punjabi. The fortnightly *Asian Trader* and *Asian Business* are both successful ethnic business publications, while *Cineblitz International* targets those interested in the Asian film industry.

Muslim News, a free newspaper distributed weekly across the UK, claims a readership of over 60,000.

Many provincial papers print special editions for their local ethnic minority populations.

THE PERIODICAL PRESS

There are over 7,000 separate periodical publications which carry advertising. They are generally defined as either 'consumer' titles, providing readers with leisure-time information and entertainment, or 'business and professional' titles, which provide people with material of relevance to their working lives. Within the former category, there are general consumer titles, which have a wide appeal, and consumer specialist titles, aimed specifically at groups of people with particular interests, such as motoring or classical music. A range of literary and political journals, appearing monthly or quarterly, caters for a more academic readership. There are also many in-house and customer magazines produced by businesses or public services for their employees and/or clients.

The weekly periodicals with the highest sales are those which carry full details of the forthcoming week's television and radio programmes, including satellite schedules. *Sky TV Guide* circulates over 3 million copies, while *What's on TV* and *Radio Times* have

Table 17.2: Top Regional Newspaper Circulations, (July–December 1998 average)

	Circulation
Regional daily newspapers	
Daily Record (Scotland)	676,411
Evening Standard (London)	450,089
Evening Mail (Birmingham)	187,598
Express & Star (West Midlands)	186,969
Manchester Evening News	173,446
Liverpool Echo	157,999
Belfast Telegraph	124,530
Glasgow Evening Times	116,486
Evening Chronicle (Newcastle upon Tyne)	109,685
Leicester Mercury	108,478
Regional Sunday newspapers	
Sunday Mail (Glasgow)	810,353
Sunday Post (Dundee)	738,848
Sunday Mercury (Birmingham)	149,639
Scotland on Sunday (Edinburgh)	125,124
Sunday Sun (Newcastle upon Tyne)	112,918
Sunday Life (Belfast)	101,210
Sunday World (Northern Ireland edition)	72,725
Wales on Sunday (Cardiff)	62,286
Regional weekly newspapers	
West Briton (Cornwall)	50,603
Essex Chronicle	49,683
Surrey Advertiser	45,492[a]
Kent Messenger	45,383
Chester Chronicle	44,322
Western Gazette (Somerset)	44,077
Derbyshire Times	41,950
Kent & Sussex Courier	40,751

[a] January–December 1998.
Source: Audit Bureau of Circulations/Newspaper Society

sales well in excess of 1 million. *Reader's Digest*, which covers a wide range of topics, has the highest circulation (1.3 million) among monthly magazines.

Women's magazines traditionally enjoy large readerships, while several men's general interest titles have reached high levels of circulation in the 1990s (see Table 17.3).

Children are well served with an array of comics and papers, while magazines like *Smash Hits* and *It's Bliss*, with their coverage of the pop scene and features of interest to young people, are very popular with teenagers.

Leading journals of opinion include the *Economist*, an independent commentator on national and international affairs, finance and business, and science and technology; *New Statesman*, which reviews social issues, politics, literature and the arts from an independent socialist point of view; and the *Spectator*, which covers similar subjects from a more conservative standpoint. A rather more irreverent approach to public affairs is taken by *Private Eye*, a satirical fortnightly.

Weekly listings' magazines like *Time Out* provide details of cultural and other events in London and other large cities.

There are more than 4,500 business and professional titles, with the highest concentrations in medicine, business management, sciences, architecture and building, social sciences, and computers. Controlled (free) circulation titles represent about two-thirds of the business and professional magazine market. Around 95% of business and professional people regularly read the publications relevant to their sector.

Table 17.3: Top Women's and Men's Titles

	Average net circulation (end-1998)
Women's titles	
Take a Break	1,273,820
Woman	711,133
Woman's Own	654,473
Bella	610,843
Woman's Weekly	594,680
Men's general interest titles	
FHM	751,493
Loaded	457,318
Maxim	321,947
Men's Health	283,359

Source: Audit Bureau of Circulations/Periodical Publishers Association

PRESS INSTITUTIONS

Trade associations include the Newspaper Publishers Association, whose members publish national newspapers, and the Newspaper Society, which represents British regional and local newspapers (and is believed to be the oldest publishers' association in the world). The Scottish Daily Newspaper Society represents the interests of daily and Sunday newspapers in Scotland; the Scottish Newspaper Publishers Association acts on behalf of the owners of weekly newspapers in Scotland; and Associated Northern Ireland Newspapers is made up of proprietors of weekly newspapers in Northern Ireland. The membership of the Periodical Publishers Association includes most independent publishers of business, professional and consumer journals.

The Society of Editors is the officially recognised professional body for newspaper editors and their equivalents in radio and television. It exists to defend press freedom and to promote high editorial standards. The British Association of Industrial Editors is the professional organisation for editors of house journals. Organisations representing journalists are the National Union of Journalists and the Chartered Institute of Journalists. The main printing union is the Graphical, Paper and Media Union. The Foreign Press Association was formed in 1888 to help the correspondents of overseas newspapers in their work by arranging press conferences, tours, briefings, and other services and facilities.

News Agencies

The top international news agencies operating in the UK are Reuters, Associated Press and United Press International. The main agency which gathers news inside the UK is the Press Association (PA), which provides comprehensive coverage to the national and regional print, broadcast and electronic media. A number of other British and foreign agencies and news services have offices in London (for example, Agence France Presse), and there are smaller agencies based in other British cities. Most regional agencies are members of the National Association of Press Agencies.

PRESS CONDUCT AND LAW

The Press Complaints Commission

In a free society, there is a delicate and sometimes difficult balance in the relationship between the responsibilities of the press and the rights of the public. The Press Complaints Commission, a non-statutory body, was set up in 1991 by the newspaper and periodical industry in response to growing criticism of press standards, with allegations of unjustified invasion of privacy and inaccurate and biased reporting. A policy of self-regulation under the Commission, rather than statutory control or a law of privacy, has since been pursued.

The 16-member Commission is drawn from both the public and the press and has a lay majority. It deals with complaints about the content and conduct of newspapers and magazines, and operates a Code of Practice agreed by editors covering inaccuracy, invasion of privacy, harassment and discrimination by the press. The Commission's jurisdiction also extends to publications on the Internet placed there by publishers who already subscribe to the Code. In 1998 the Commission dealt with 2,601 complaints, resolving about 87% of cases pursued under the Code.

Significant revisions to the Code, which came into effect in 1998, include:

- a recognition of everyone's entitlement to respect for their private lives;
- stipulations against the taking of pictures of people in 'private places' (defined as public or private property where there is reasonable expectation of privacy);
- a ban on the publication of pictures obtained as a result of harassment or 'persistent pursuit'; and
- a requirement that young people should be free to complete their time at school without unnecessary press intrusion.

The Press and the Law

There is no state control or censorship of the newspaper and periodical press, and newspaper proprietors, editors and journalists are subject to the law in the same way as any other citizen. However, certain statutes include sections which apply to the press.

There are laws governing:

- the extent of newspaper ownership in television and radio companies (see p. 271);
- the transfer of newspaper assets; and
- the right of press representatives to be supplied with agendas and reports of meetings of local authorities, and reasonable facilities for taking notes and telephoning reports.

There is a legal requirement to reproduce the printer's imprint (the printer's name and address) on all publications, including newspapers. Publishers are legally obliged to deposit copies of newspapers and other publications at the British Library (see p. 266).

Publication of advertisements is governed by wide-ranging legislation, including public health, copyright, financial services and fraud legislation. Legal restrictions are imposed on certain types of prize competition.

Laws on contempt of court, official secrets and defamation are also relevant to the press. A newspaper may not publish comments on the conduct of judicial proceedings which are likely to prejudice the reputation of the courts for fairness before or during the actual proceedings; nor may it publish before or during a trial anything which might influence the result. The unauthorised acquisition and publication of official information in such areas as defence and international relations, where such unauthorised disclosure would be harmful, are offences under the Official Secrets Acts 1911 to 1989. However, these are restrictions on publication generally, not just through the printed press.

Most legal proceedings against the press are libel actions brought by private individuals.

Defence Advisory Notices

Government officials and representatives of the media form the Defence, Press and Broadcasting Advisory Committee, which has agreed that in some circumstances the publication of certain categories of information might endanger national security. Details of these categories are contained in Defence Advisory Notices (DA Notices) circulated to the media, whose members are asked to seek advice from the Secretary of the Committee, a retired senior military officer, before publishing information in these areas. Compliance with any advice offered by the Secretary is expected but there is no legal force behind it and the final decision on whether to publish rests with the editor, producer or publisher concerned.

Advertising Practice

Advertising in all non-broadcast media, such as newspapers, magazines, posters, sales promotions, cinema, direct mail, and electronic media such as CD-ROM and the Internet is regulated by the Advertising Standards Authority (ASA). The ASA is an independent body whose role is to ensure that everyone who prepares and publishes advertisements conforms to the British Codes of Advertising and Sales Promotion. The Codes are written and enforced by the advertising industry through the Committee of Advertising Practice. They require that advertisements and promotions:

- are legal, decent, honest and truthful;
- are prepared with a sense of responsibility to the consumer and society; and
- respect the principles of fair competition generally accepted in business.

The ASA monitors advertisements to ensure their compliance with the Codes and investigates any complaints received. Pre-publication advice is available to publishers, agencies and advertisers. If an advertisement is found to be misleading or offensive, the ASA can ask the advertiser to change or remove it. Failure to do so can result in damaging adverse publicity in the ASA's monthly report of its judgments, the refusal of advertising space by publishers, and the loss of trading privileges. In the rare cases of deliberate or persistent offending, the ASA can also refer misleading advertisements to the Director General of Fair Trading (see p. 396), who has the power to seek an injunction to prevent their publication.

The Media and the Internet

The Internet plays an increasingly important role in the provision and dissemination of information and entertainment. Broadly, it is a loose collection of computer networks around the world—it links thousands of academic, government, military and public computer systems, giving millions of people access to a wealth of stored information and other resources. No one owns it—there is no centralised controlling or regulating body. Access to the Internet usually requires a computer with the necessary software, a telephone and a modem (allowing computers to talk to each other over a telephone line), although television-based Internet services are being developed.

The system dates from the 1960s, when it began life in the military and academic communities in the United States, but it has only assumed widespread significance in commercial and consumer terms during the 1990s. It is the World Wide Web (WWW or Web) which has given the Internet its user appeal and accessibility. The Web consists of many thousands of pages or 'sites' on the Internet, which can be viewed by a browser (a programme that provides a window in a computer screen on which the pages are displayed). Users can move from page to page in search of whatever information or service they are after.

It has been estimated that the number of pages on the Web is doubling every three months. Many newspapers and publishing groups have set up their own websites, for example the *Daily Mail*, *The Times*, *The Guardian*, *The Daily Telegraph*, *Financial Times* and the Press Association—and also prominent magazine publishers, like EMAP and IPC. There are over 200 regional newspaper websites, offering a range of editorial, directory and advertising services. Broadcasters and regulators, including the BBC, the ITV companies, Channel 4, Channel 5, Sky and the ITC, are similarly represented. BBC Online is the most visited Internet content site in the UK.

Further Reading

Department for Culture, Media and Sport Annual Report 1999: The Government's Expenditure Plans 1999–2000. Cm 4213. The Stationery Office, 1999.

Regulating Communications: the Way Ahead. Department for Culture, Media and Sport and Department of Trade and Industry, 1999.

Media Ownership Regulation: an explanatory guide to the provisions in the Broadcasting Acts 1990 and 1996. Department of National Heritage, 1996.

Digital Terrestrial Broadcasting: an explanatory guide to the provisions introduced by the Broadcasting Act 1996. Department of National Heritage, 1996.

The BBC Beyond 2000. BBC, 1998.

The Future Funding of the BBC (Independent Panel Review), 1999.

Websites

Department for Culture, Media and Sport: www.culture.gov.uk

British Broadcasting Corporation (BBC): www.bbc.co.uk

Independent Television Commission (ITC): www.itc.org.uk

18 Sport and Active Recreation

UK sportsmen and sportswomen hold world titles in a variety of sports, such as athletics, rowing, professional boxing, snooker and motorcycle sports. The Government is working on a new national sports strategy which will embrace all sections of the community. The United Kingdom Sports Institute is being set up, with its headquarters in London, as a network of centres of excellence for UK sport. Funding from the National Lottery is making a substantial contribution towards financing sport, from grass roots to the highest level.

The most popular participation sports or activities in the UK are walking (including rambling and hiking), swimming, snooker/pool/billiards, keep fit/yoga, cycling and football. In 1996–97, 71% of men and 57% of women took part in at least one sporting activity in the four-week period before they were interviewed for the General Household Survey in Great Britain and the Continuous Household Survey in Northern Ireland. Walking and cycling are becoming more popular (see Table 18.1).

Many important sporting events take place each year in the UK, including the Wimbledon lawn tennis championships, the Open Golf championship and the Grand National steeplechase. In 1999 the Cricket World Cup was staged mostly in the UK, in May and June, while the Rugby World Cup will be held in October and November. The Rugby League World Cup will be staged mostly in the UK in 2000 and the Commonwealth Games will take place in Manchester in 2002.

SPORTS POLICY

A 'Sports Cabinet' was established in 1998 to identify strategic priorities for sport. It is headed by the Secretary of State for Culture, Media and Sport and includes the ministers responsible for sport in England, Wales, Scotland and Northern Ireland. The Government intends to publish early in 2000 a new national sports strategy, which will be based on:

- improving access to facilities and to better coaching;
- achieving better health through participation in sport and active recreation;
- improving sporting performance at all levels; and
- maximising the potential of sport for creating wealth and employment.

Extending Sporting Opportunities

The Government wishes to ensure that sporting opportunities are widely available to

Table 18.1: Trends in Participation in the Most Popular Sports and Physical Activities in Great Britain, 1987–96

% participation by those aged 16 and over in the previous four weeks

	1987	1990	1993	1996
Men				
Walking	41	44	45	49
Snooker/pool/billiards	27	24	21	20
Cycling	10	12	14	15
Indoor swimming	10	11	12	11
Soccer	10	10	9	10
Women				
Walking	35	38	37	41
Keep fit/yoga	12	16	17	17
Indoor swimming	11	13	14	15
Cycling	7	7	7	8
Snooker/pool/billiards	5	5	5	4

Source: *General Household Survey: Trends in Adult Participation in Sport in Great Britain 1987–96* (Sport England/UK Sport)

The year 1900 saw the second of the modern-day Olympics, which were held in Paris. They were on a relatively small scale, with just over 100 participants in the athletics events. On the athletics track UK winners included Alfred Tysoe in the 800 metres and Charles Bennett in the 1,500 metres, two events in which Britain has been strong throughout most of the 20th century. Some sports—such as cricket—already had established international competitions, but these were relatively limited. Among the UK winners in 1900 was one of the nation's most successful golfers, Harry Vardon, who was the first non–US winner of the US Open. In tennis Reginald Doherty won the men's singles at Wimbledon, while he and his brother Lawrence took the men's doubles; the two dominated the men's singles at Wimbledon during 1897–1906, winning in all but one of those years,[1] and were an integral part of the British team which won the Davis Cup between 1903 and 1906.

The previous year, 1899, had seen a notable feat in cricket when J. T. Hearne had taken a hat-trick in the Test against Australia at Headingley (Leeds). This feat was not to be repeated by an England bowler in Tests against Australia until Darren Gough took a hat-trick in the Sydney Test in January 1999—only the 23rd hat-trick in the history of Test cricket.

the entire community, irrespective of age, gender, social background, location or ability. Its national sports strategy will be concerned with how best to target the provision of sporting facilities on those groups with below-average participation, including women, ethnic minorities and the most vulnerable and disadvantaged groups.

A number of initiatives are in progress to promote access at all levels of sport. In March 1999 the Government announced a 'green spaces initiative', involving expenditure of £125 million from the Lottery's New Opportunities Fund over the next three years. This will allow schools, local authorities and

---

[1] Before 1922 the Wimbledon champion was the winner of the 'challenge round', in which the winner of the previous year's tournament faced the winner from among the current year's competitors.

Table 18.2: Selected Domestic Sporting Champions 1998–99

Basketball
Budweiser Championship—London Towers

Cricket
PPP Healthcare County Championship
—Surrey
NatWest Trophy—Gloucestershire
Benson & Hedges Super Cup
—Gloucestershire
CGU National Cricket League
—Lancashire

Football
FA Carling Premiership—Manchester
United
AXA-sponsored FA Cup—Manchester
United
Worthington Cup—Tottenham Hotspur
Scottish Premier League—Glasgow
Rangers
Tennents Scottish Cup—Glasgow Rangers

Hockey
Premier Division (Men)—Cannock
Premier Division (Women)—Slough

Ice Hockey
Sekonda Superleague—Manchester Storm
Sekonda Superleague play-off final
—Cardiff Devils
Benson & Hedges Cup (1998)
—Nottingham Panthers

Rugby League
Super League Grand Final—St Helens
Silk Cut Challenge Cup—Leeds Rhinos

Rugby Union
Five Nations Championship—Scotland
Allied Dunbar Premiership—Leicester
Tetley's Bitter Cup—Wasps
National League (Wales)—Llanelli
SWALEC Cup—Swansea

Tennis (1998)
National Champion (men)—Danny
Sapsford
National Champion (women)—Julie Pullin

Note: This table gives a list of champions from selected sports. For details of major international sporting achievements, see the section on Popular Sports, pp. 299–310.

other organisations to apply for grants to improve their local environment for projects such as creating playing fields, parks and green areas from derelict 'brownfield' sites. Tighter planning controls have been introduced to minimise the loss of playing fields to development.

There are several initiatives designed to increase sporting opportunities for young people, including:

- specialist Sports Colleges, providing high-quality facilities and training to support the most talented and promising pupils, and preparing them for careers in professional sport, coaching and teaching;

- a Sportsmark scheme to recognise secondary and special schools that have effective policies for promoting sport and a proposed Active Primary School Award, to help schools with the

development of their physical activity programmes—in Wales a Sportsmarc Cymru scheme is open to all schools;

- an Active Schools Programme in England, designed to encourage sporting participation and to develop children's sports skills;

- in Scotland, Team Sport Scotland (which has helped 180,000 young people and 12,000 coaches and teachers since its inception in 1991), a youth sport strategy, and a programme to increase levels of physical activity among young children; and

- in Wales, the Sports Council for Wales has introduced two schemes: Dragon Sport, to increase the profile of sport for children of primary school age, and Clwb Cymru, which aims to help children (mainly between 11 and 16) to progress to the club structures provided within the community.

A number of leading sportsmen and sportswomen have agreed to become Sporting Ambassadors under a scheme in which they visit schools to pass on their experiences to pupils and teachers and to promote the benefits of a healthy sporting lifestyle. In England about 230 sportsmen and sportswomen from over 30 sports are involved in the scheme. Ambassadors in England include Steven Redgrave (rowing) and Kelly Holmes (athletics).

Promoting Sporting Excellence

Funding of around £20.5 million a year from the National Lottery Sports Fund is being earmarked for two main schemes designed to promote sporting excellence:

- *The World Class Performance Programme* provides support to the UK's most talented athletes to enable them to improve their performance and win medals in major international competitions. Since April 1997 grants totalling nearly £65 million have been committed to more than 30 sports in the Programme, and 2,100 athletes have received support. Funding is already beginning to have a positive effect on UK performers' ability to compete at the highest level in international competitions, reflected in the performance, for example, at the World Rowing Championships (see p. 307) and the World Short Course Swimming Championships (see p. 309).

- *The World Class Events Programme* aims to ensure that major international events can be staged successfully in the UK. About £3 million a year is available to support funding of up to 35% of the cost of bidding for and staging events. By mid-1999, £4.6 million had been awarded to assist with the bidding for and staging of 13 international events, with the largest award being for £3

million to assist with the bidding for the UK to host the football World Cup in 2006.

Lottery funding will also make an important contribution towards the funding of the new United Kingdom Sports Institute (see p. 295).

Ground Safety

The Football Trust is providing grant aid to help football clubs to complete the safety work required by the Government in response to the Taylor Report following the Hillsborough stadium disaster in 1989, when 96 spectators died. In England and Wales, licences issued by the Football Licensing Authority (FLA) require all clubs in the Premier League and those in the First Division of the Football League to have all-seater grounds. In addition, from August 1999, licences require clubs in the second and third divisions of the Football League to ensure that any terracing retained complies with the highest safety standards, as outlined in guidance from the FLA. The FLA will be succeeded by a new Sports Ground Safety Authority (SGSA), which will have a wider role in advising other sports on outdoor ground safety; the SGSA is expected to be in operation by April 2001. In a related development, some £65 million will be spent in England alone over the next four years to improve standards at cricket, football, rugby league and rugby union grounds.

In Scotland the all-seating policy is being implemented through a voluntary agreement under the direction of the Scottish football authorities.

Sport on Television and Radio

Major sporting events receive extensive television and radio coverage and are watched or heard by millions of people. Football matches attract very high ratings, especially when the UK's national teams are involved in the final stages of international tournaments— 23.7 million people watched the 1998 World Cup match between England and Argentina, the highest ever ratings figure in the UK for a sports event. A range of other sports,

Manchester United—one of the UK's best-known football teams—achieved major success in the 1990s, with Sir Alex Ferguson as manager. In a ten-day period in May 1999, they won three championships. After finishing top of the FA Premier League and beating Newcastle United 2–0 in the FA Cup Final, they overcame Bayern Munich 2–1 in the final of the European Champions League.

Colin Jackson, after his gold medal run in the 110 metres hurdles at the World Athletics Championships in Seville in August 1999. He regained the title which he had first won in 1993.

Paula Radcliffe, leading at the half-way mark in the 10,000 metres at the World Athletics Championships on her way to winning the silver medal in a new British and Commonwealth record time. Earlier in the year she achieved a bronze medal in the world cross-country championships in Belfast.

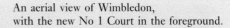

An aerial view of Wimbledon,
with the new No 1 Court in the foreground.

In a dramatic finish to the 1999 Open Golf
Championship at Carnoustie, Paul Lawrie
(who started the final day ten shots behind the
leader) shot a fourth-round 67 and eventually
won a three-way play-off to take the title.

Stephen Hendry on his way to
winning the Embassy World
Professional Championship for
a seventh time. He defeated
Mark Williams 18 frames to 11
in the final in May 1999.

Carl Fogarty celebrating his victory in the first race of the 1999 World Superbike Championships. He dominated the 1999 series, to take the title for the fourth time.

Denise Lewis won a silver medal in the heptathlon at the 1999 World Athletics Championships.

Peter Nicol, winning the Hong Kong Squash Open in August 1999. In September 1999 he became world champion, with a win in straight sets in the final of the World Open in Cairo.

including rugby, horse racing, cricket and athletics, also achieve high ratings figures.

For several years, many satellite and cable channels have concentrated on sport. Live coverage of a number of major events and competitions is now shown exclusively by subscription broadcasters. In the Government's view, there are a small number of sporting occasions to which everyone should have access. These events are included on a protected list and cannot be shown on subscription channels unless they have first been offered to the UK's universally available free-to-air broadcasters (the BBC, the ITV network and Channel 4). In 1998 the list was revised and extended, and it now protects secondary coverage of certain events. Live coverage of these Group B events may be shown by satellite and cable channels on the condition that an acceptable level of secondary coverage is made available to the universally available, free-to-air channels. The revised list is as follows:

Group A Events (with full live coverage protected)
Olympic Games
FIFA World Cup football finals tournament
European Football Championship finals tournament
FA Cup Final
Scottish FA Cup Final (in Scotland)
the Grand National
the Derby
Wimbledon Tennis Championships finals
Rugby League Challenge Cup Final
Rugby World Cup Final

Group B Events (with secondary coverage protected)
Cricket Test matches played in England
Wimbledon Tennis Championships (other than the finals)
Rugby World Cup Finals tournament (other than the Final)
Six Nations Rugby Union matches involving home countries
Commonwealth Games
World Athletics Championship
Cricket World Cup—Final, semi-finals and matches involving home nations' teams
Ryder Cup
Open Golf Championship

ORGANISATION AND ADMINISTRATION

Sports Councils

Government responsibilities in sport and recreation are largely channelled through five Sports Councils:

- the United Kingdom Sports Council, operating as UK Sport;
- the English Sports Council, operating as Sport England;
- the Sports Council for Wales;
- the Scottish Sports Council, operating as **sport**scotland; and
- the Sports Council for Northern Ireland.

UK Sport takes the lead on all aspects of sport and physical recreation which require strategic planning, administration, co-ordination or representation for the UK as a whole, including the United Kingdom Sports Institute. It works alongside the Sports Cabinet in undertaking its main functions, which include:

- co-ordinating support to sports in which the UK competes internationally (as opposed to the four home countries separately);
- tackling drug misuse;
- co-ordinating policy for bringing major international sports events to the UK; and
- representing British sporting interests overseas and increasing influence at international level.

All the Sports Councils distribute Exchequer and Lottery funds. UK Sport focuses on elite athletes, while the home country Sports Councils are more concerned with the development of sport at the community level by promoting participation by all sections of the community, giving support and guidance to facility providers, and supporting the development of talented sportsmen and women, including people with disabilities. They also manage the National Sports Centres (see pp. 295–6).

Sports Governing Bodies

Individual sports are run by over 410 independent governing bodies. Some have a UK or Great Britain structure, while others are constituted on a home country basis. Their functions include drawing up rules, holding events, regulating membership, and selecting and training national teams. Governing bodies receiving funding from the Sports Councils are required to produce development plans, from the grass roots to the highest competitive levels. In order to have access to Lottery revenue funds for their top athletes, they need to prepare 'world-class performance' plans, with specific performance targets. There are also organisations representing people who take part in more informal physical recreation, such as walking. Most sports clubs in the UK belong to, or are affiliated to, an appropriate governing body.

Other Sports Organisations

The main sports associations in the UK include:

- The Central Council of Physical Recreation (CCPR), the largest sport and recreation federation in the world, comprises 245 UK bodies and 61 English associations, most of which are governing bodies of sport. The Scottish Sports Association, the Welsh Sports Association and the Northern Ireland Sports Forum are equivalent associations. Their primary aim is to represent the interests of their members to the appropriate national and local authorities, including the Sports Councils, from which they may receive some funding.

- The British Olympic Association (BOA), comprising representatives of the 35 national governing bodies of Olympic sports, organises the participation of British teams in the Olympic Games, determines the size of British Olympic teams, sets standards for selection and raises funds. It is supported by sponsorship and by donations from the private sector and the general public.

The BOA makes important contributions to the preparation of competitors in the period between Games, such as arranging training camps. The BOA also works through its steering groups to deliver programmes to national governing bodies and their athletes in areas such as acclimitisation, psychology and physiology. Its British Olympic Medical Centre at Northwick Park Hospital in Harrow provides medical services for competitors before and during the Olympics. Over 300 competitors represented the UK in the 1996 Olympics winning 15 medals: one gold, eight silver and six bronze.

- The Women's Sports Foundation promotes the interests of women and girls in sport and active recreation. It encourages the establishment of women's sports groups throughout the UK and organises events and activities. It runs both the Sportswomen of the Year Awards and an annual nationwide awards scheme for girls and young women between the ages of 11 and 19.

Sport for Disabled People

The governing bodies of sport are increasingly taking on responsibility for sport for people with disabilities. As well as those concerned with individual disabilities and single sports, the key organisations are:

- Disability Sport England, which organises regional and national championships in many sports and also runs training courses. Scottish Disability Sport, the Federation of Sports Associations for the Disabled (Wales) and Disability Sports NI have similar co-ordinating roles. In England, Sport England and disability organisations have co-operated in the formation in April 1999 of the English Federation of Disability Sport, which aims to integrate disability sport into mainstream sporting activities as much as possible;

- the United Kingdom Sports Association for People with Learning Disability (UKSAPLD), a co-ordinating body with a membership of over 20 national organisations, which promotes and develops opportunities in sport and recreation for people with learning disability; and

- the British Paralympic Association (BPA), which organises participation by British athletes in the summer and winter Paralympics. The BPA is responsible for the core preparation and management of the Paralympic team. In 1996, 244 British competitors participated in the Paralympics and won 122 medals: 39 gold, 42 silver and 41 bronze.

UK Sport is undertaking a strategic review of disability sport, with a key objective being the organisational integration of able-bodied and disabled sport across a range of sports.

All distributing bodies of Lottery funding are required to ensure that applicants incorporate access and availability for people with disabilities—Sport England has provided funds of nearly £26 million for 200 projects which specifically target disabled people. The Government also wishes to see better facilities for disabled spectators. New facilities at football grounds will include a minimum number of wheelchair spaces offering an unobstructed view of the pitch, and funding from the Football Trust (see p. 292) for new facilities will only be given on condition that football clubs consult disabled people before work begins.

SPORTS FACILITIES

The UK has a range of world-class sporting facilities including 13 National Sports Centres, operated by the home country Sports Councils. Manchester will host the Commonwealth Games in 2002. Funds of £90 million will be provided for a new 50,000-seat sports stadium and £22 million for an Olympic-sized swimming complex.

United Kingdom Sports Institute

The United Kingdom Sports Institute (UKSI) is being set up under the strategic

Wembley Stadium in London is to be redeveloped, creating a new 90,000 capacity all-seater national stadium for football, rugby league and athletics. It will cost around £475 million, of which £120 million will be provided from Lottery funding. Wembley National Stadium Ltd, the Football Association's development company, is responsible for building the new stadium and for its future operation. The new stadium will be the foundation of the bid to host the 2006 football World Cup and to stage other major international sporting events.

direction of UK Sport and in partnership with the home country Sports Councils. The aim is to provide facilities and integrated support services to potential and elite athletes and teams. All sports will have access to the UKSI's services, although it will concentrate on Olympic sports and those minority sports lacking a commercial element. The headquarters will be in London, and there will be a network of regional centres in England, Scotland, Wales and Northern Ireland. The UKSI's funds will come mainly from the National Lottery.

The first UKSI support services are being launched in 1999. They will include the Athlete Career Education (ACE UK) programme, designed to enhance athletes' personal development and sporting performance; a High Performance Coaching Programme; and sports science and medicine services. The organisation and delivery of sports medicine, sports science and coaching services (see p. 297) are expected to change significantly as a result of the development of the UKSI.

UKSI Regional Network

England

In England the UKSI network, co-ordinated by Sport England, will consist of ten centres, of which four will be based around National Sports Centres:

- Crystal Palace in London, which is a leading competition venue for a wide range of sports and a major training centre, and has Olympic-size swimming and diving pools, and a sports injury centre;

- Bisham Abbey in Berkshire, which caters for a number of sports, including tennis, football, hockey, weightlifting, squash, rugby union and golf;

- Lilleshall National Sports Centre in Shropshire, which is used by a variety of national teams and has extensive playing fields for football and hockey, together with facilities for archery and gymnastics; and

- the National Water Sports Centre at Holme Pierrepont in Nottinghamshire, which is one of the most comprehensive water sports centres in the world, with facilities for rowing (including a 2,000-metre regatta course), canoeing, water-skiing, powerboating, ski-racing, angling and sailing—the East Midlands Network Centre will be jointly based here and around Loughborough University.

The six other network centres will be based around the Don Valley Stadium in Sheffield, Gateshead International Stadium, Manchester Sportcity, Southampton University, the University of Bath and Bedford Network Centre.

Wales

The centre of the UKSI network in Wales is the Welsh Institute of Sport in Cardiff, run by the Sports Council for Wales, which is the premier venue in Wales for top-level training and for competition in many sports. The Institute has close links with other specialist facilities, including the National Watersports Centre at Plas Menai in north Wales, which is a centre of excellence for sailing and canoeing; the national indoor athletics centre at University of Wales Institute Cardiff; and the cricketing school of excellence at Sophia Gardens, Cardiff.

Plas y Brenin National Mountain Centre, in Snowdonia National Park in north Wales, is run by Sport England. It offers courses in rock climbing, mountaineering, canoeing, orienteering, skiing and most other mountain-based activities, and is the UK's leading training institution for the development of mountain instructors.

Scotland

A new Scottish Institute of Sport was set up by the Scottish Sports Council in 1998. It will receive Lottery funding of £20 million over the next five years. Initially it is catering for seven sports—athletics, badminton, curling, football, hockey, rugby and swimming—and there will be six area centres. The Scottish Sports Council runs three National Sports Centres:

- Glenmore Lodge near Aviemore, which caters for a range of activities, including hill walking, rock climbing, mountaineering, skiing, kayaking and canoeing;

- Inverclyde in Largs, which has many indoor and outdoor facilities, including a gymnastics hall, golf training, and sports medicine and sports science facilities of an international standard; and

- the Scottish National Water Sports Centre—Cumbrae—on the island of Great Cumbrae in the Firth of Clyde.

Northern Ireland

The Sports Council for Northern Ireland has announced a partnership with the University of Ulster for the development of a Northern Ireland network centre of the UKSI. This will involve creating high-quality training facilities and support services, primarily at the University's Jordanstown campus, with the establishment of links with nearby facilities. It is envisaged that the centre will include the development of an indoor training centre, athletics training track, sports medicine facilities, a 50-metre training pool and outdoor pitches, with support services such as sports science and coaching.

The Tollymore Mountain Centre in County Down, run by the Sports Council for Northern Ireland, offers courses in mountaineering, rock climbing, canoeing and outdoor adventure. Leadership and instructor courses leading to nationally recognised qualifications are also available.

Local Facilities

Local authorities are the main providers of basic sport and recreation facilities for the local community. In England they manage over 1,500 indoor sports centres. Other facilities include parks, lakes, playing fields, playgrounds, tennis courts, artificial pitches, golf courses and swimming/leisure pools.

Over 150,000 voluntary sports clubs are affiliated to the national governing bodies of sport. Some local clubs cater for indoor recreation, but more common are those which provide sports grounds, particularly for cricket, football, rugby, hockey, tennis and golf. Many clubs linked to businesses and other employers cater for sporting activities. Commercial facilities include fitness centres, tenpin bowling centres, ice and roller-skating rinks, squash courts, golf courses and driving ranges, riding stables and marinas.

SUPPORT SERVICES

Sports Medicine

The National Sports Medicine Institute (NSMI), funded by UK Sport and Sport England, is responsible for the co-ordination of sports medicine services. Based at the medical college of St Bartholomew's Hospital, London, its facilities include a physiology laboratory, library and information centre.

In Scotland a network of 26 accredited sports medicine centres provides specialist help with sports injuries. Wales has 11 sports medicine centres, accredited by the NSMI, which are linked closely with the UKSI network in Wales. The Northern Ireland Sports Medicine Centre is a partnership between the Sports Council for Northern Ireland and a local healthcare trust.

Sports Science

The development of sports science support services for the national governing bodies of sport is being promoted by the Sports Councils, in collaboration with the British

Olympic Association and the National Coaching Foundation, in an effort to raise the standards of performance of national squads. The type of support provided may cover biomechanical (human movement), physiological or psychological factors.

Coaching

The National Coaching Foundation (NCF) works closely with sports governing bodies, local authorities, and higher and further education institutions. Supported by the Sports Councils, it provides a comprehensive range of services for coaches in all sports. Since 1983 the NCF has provided educational and development opportunities for 115,000 coaches. In 1998, 15,000 coaches and 12,000 schoolteachers participated in NCF programmes.

DRUG MISUSE

UK Sport aims to prevent doping and achieve a commitment to drug-free sport and ethical sporting practices. Its Ethics and Anti-Doping Directorate co-ordinates a drugs-testing programme and conducts a comprehensive education programme aimed at changing attitudes to drug misuse. Samples are analysed at a laboratory accredited by the International Olympic Committee, at King's College, University of London; UK Sport is responsible for reporting the results to the appropriate governing body. In 1998–99 the drugs-testing programme involved nearly 60 national governing bodies and 22 international sporting federations from 38 sports. A total of 5,147 tests were conducted—3,141 in competition and 2,006 out of competition—and 98.5% were negative. UK Sport provides a Drug Information Line to allow athletes to check whether a licensed medication is permitted or banned under their governing body's regulations, and issues a comprehensive guide on drugs and sport for competitors and officials. The UK is at the forefront of work to establish a new International Anti-Doping Agency.

SPONSORSHIP AND OTHER FUNDING

Sport is a major industry in the UK. In addition to professional sportsmen and sportswomen, around 400,000 people are employed in the provision of sports clothing, publicity, ground and club maintenance and other activities connected with sport. A joint Department of Trade and Industry/Sports Industries Federation competitiveness analysis, published in July 1999, found that the UK sports industry is worth almost £5 billion a year. The private sector makes a substantial investment in sport, with more than 2,000 UK companies involved. The sports sponsorship market was estimated to be worth £353 million in 1998.

Recent examples of sponsorship include:
- the 1999 Cricket World Cup, which had four official sponsors—Emirates Airlines, National Westminster Bank, Pepsi and Vodafone;
- the England football team, which is being sponsored by the Nationwide Building Society in a deal worth £15 million over four years; and
- the Millennium Youth Games, for which airport operator BAA is the lead sponsor—this is a series of events over three years in which more than 300,000 people are expected to participate, with a Grand Final in Southampton just before the Sydney Olympics.

Sponsorship may take the form of financing specific events or championships, such as horse races or cricket leagues, or grants to sports organisations or individual performers. Motor sport and football receive the largest amounts of private sponsorship, which is encouraged by a number of bodies, including:

- the Institute of Sports Sponsorship (ISS), which comprises some 100 UK companies involved in sponsoring sport; and
- the Sports Sponsorship Advisory Service, administered jointly by the CCPR (see p. 294) and the ISS, and funded by Sport England, and similar advisory services of the Scottish Sports Council and the Sports Council for Wales.

Under the EC's Tobacco Advertising Directive (see p. 186), the Government intends to ban tobacco sponsorship of sport from 2003 in most cases and from 2006 for certain exceptional global events. It has set up a task force of business and sponsorship experts to help the sports affected. Seven sports have sought assistance to make the transition—rugby league, clay pigeon shooting, billiards and snooker, pool, darts, ice hockey and angling.

Sportsmatch

Sportsmatch aims to increase the amount of business sponsorship going into grass roots sport and physical recreation. It offers matching funding for new sponsorships and for the extension of existing ones. Priority is given to projects involving disabled people, the young and ethnic minorities and to projects in deprived areas.

In England the ISS runs the scheme on behalf of Sport England. Since 1992 Sportsmatch has approved 2,492 awards in England, totalling £19.6 million and covering about 70 different sports. Football, rugby union, cricket, tennis and basketball have received most awards.

In Scotland and Wales the scheme is managed by the appropriate Sports Council's Sponsorship Advisory Service.

National Lottery Awards

Sport is one of the main recipients of funds raised by the National Lottery. By June 1999 awards totalling over £1 billion had been made to nearly 3,000 projects in the UK. Around 60 sports have received Lottery funding, with projects ranging from the provision of small items of equipment to the building of major sports venues.

Some of the funds from the Millennium Commission (see p. ix) are also for sporting and recreational developments. Major schemes include £46 million for the Millennium Stadium in Cardiff (see p. 308), and £42.5 million for a new national cycle network (see p. 366).

SportsAid

SportsAid (the Sports Aid Foundation) raises funds to help talented young British sportspeople meet their personal training expenses and realise their sporting potential. Assistance is given to those needing financial help and is concentrated on individuals who do not qualify for awards from the National Lottery Sports Fund. SportsAid raises its funds by commercial sponsorship and by donations from companies, local authorities, voluntary organisations and members of the public. Scottish SportsAid, SportsAid Wales and the Ulster Sports and Recreation Trust have similar functions.

Foundation for Sport and the Arts

The Foundation for Sport and the Arts, set up by the football pools promoters in 1991, funds small-scale projects in sport and the arts. This initiative followed the 1991 Budget, in which pools betting duty was reduced by 2.5%, provided that the money forgone by the Government was paid into the new Foundation; a further cut in duty announced in the 1999 Budget will ensure that funding continues until at least 2002. The Foundation has made awards to schemes benefiting over 100 sports.

Betting and Gaming

Most betting in Great Britain continues to be on horse racing and greyhound racing, although betting on other sporting events, such as football, is becoming more popular. Bets may be placed with on-course bookmakers at racecourses and greyhound tracks, or off-course through over 8,000 licensed betting offices. In addition, telephone and Internet betting has grown steadily. A form of pool betting—totalisator betting—is organised on racecourses by the Horserace Totalisator Board (the Tote), which also has a credit betting operation and a chain of off-course betting offices. In May 1999 the Government announced its intention to introduce legislation to sell the Tote.

A proportion of horserace betting turnover by bookmakers and the Tote is returned to the racing industry through an annual levy. The levy is based on a scheme agreed each year between the Bookmakers' Committee and the Horserace Betting Levy Board. If agreement cannot be reached, it is determined by the Home Secretary. The Levy Board distributes the levy to promote the improvement of horse breeds, and for the advancement of veterinary science and the improvement of horse racing.

Gross expenditure on all forms of gambling, including the National Lottery, is estimated at approximately £40 billion a year. New opportunities for the betting and gaming industry and the consumer have arisen through, for example, a relaxation on membership conditions and advertising of casinos (of which there are 119 in the UK), and on broadcast advertising of commercial bingo.

POPULAR SPORTS

Some of the major sports in the UK, many of which were invented by the British, are described below.

Angling

Angling is one of the most popular sports, with an estimated 3 million anglers in the UK. In England and Wales the most widely practised form of angling is for coarse fish (freshwater fish other than salmon or trout). The rivers and lochs of Scotland and in Wales are the main areas for salmon and trout fishing. Separate organisations represent game, coarse and sea fishing clubs in England, Wales, Scotland and Northern Ireland, and there are separate competitions in each of the three angling disciplines.

The UK has several world champion anglers. In 1998 Alan Scotthorne won the world freshwater fishing championships for the third year running, and England took the men's team title. Jimmy Jones won the world shore championships and Scotland took the men's team title.

Athletics

In the UK athletics incorporates many activities, including track and field events, cross country and road running, race walking, and fell and hill running. The governing body for the sport is UK Athletics, which was set up in February 1999.

One of the major developments has been the significant growth in mass participation events, notably marathons and half marathons. The largest UK marathon is the London Marathon each April, with a record 31,600 runners taking part in the 1999 event. The Great North Run, a half marathon, takes place between Newcastle upon Tyne and South Shields, and in October 1998 attracted 40,000 runners. In these and other similar events, many runners are sponsored, raising considerable amounts for charities and other good causes.

British athletes held world records in two events in mid-1999: Jonathan Edwards in the triple jump, achieved in 1995 when he became the first man to jump beyond 18 metres; and Colin Jackson in the 110 metre hurdles (achieved in 1991). British athletes won six medals in the 1996 Olympics in Atlanta, with silver medals for Jonathan Edwards and for Roger Black (400 metres), Steve Backley (javelin) and the men's 4 x 400 metres relay team; and bronze medals for Denise Lewis (heptathlon) and Steve Smith (high jump). In the 1999 World Athletics Championships in Seville (Spain) British athletes won seven medals: a gold medal for Colin Jackson (110 metres hurdles), four silver medals—Denise Lewis (heptathlon), Dean Macey (decathlon), Paula Radcliffe (10,000 metres) and the men's 4 x 100 metres relay team—and two bronze medals, for Dwain Chambers (100 metres) and Jonathan Edwards (triple jump). Earlier in 1999, at the world indoor championships, Colin Jackson won a gold medal in the 60 metres hurdles, while two other UK athletes were gold medallists: Jamie Baulch (400 metres) and Ashia Hansen (triple jump).

Badminton

Badminton takes its name from the Duke of Beaufort's country home, Badminton House, where the sport was first played in the 19th century. The game is organised by the Badminton Association of England and the Scottish, Welsh and Irish (Ulster branch) Badminton Unions. According to the latest research, around 2 million people play badminton regularly. The Badminton Association of England has a coach education system to develop coaches for players of all levels and a development department with a network of part-time county development officers.

The All England Badminton Championships, staged at the National Indoor Arena in Birmingham, is one of the world's leading tournaments. At the World Championships in May 1999 in Copenhagen, Simon Archer and Joanne Goode were runners-up in the mixed doubles, and Simon Archer and Nathan Robertson reached the semi-finals of the men's doubles, while Kelly Morgan (who won a gold medal at the 1998 Commonwealth Games) achieved a win over the then world champion in the women's singles where she reached the quarter-finals.

Basketball

Over 3 million people participate in basketball in the UK. The English Basketball Association is the governing body in England, with similar associations in Wales, Scotland and Ireland (Ulster Branch). All the associations are represented in the British and Irish Basketball Federation, which acts as the co-ordinating body for the UK and the Irish Republic.

The leading clubs play in the National Basketball Leagues, which cover four divisions for men and two for women, while there are also leagues for younger players. Mini-basketball has been developed for players under the age of 13. Wheelchair basketball is played under the same rules, with a few basic adaptations, and on the same court as the running game.

The English Basketball Association runs various development schemes for young people which aim to increase participation and improve the quality of basketball. With support from National Lottery funds, some 6,000 outdoor basketball goals have been installed in parks and play areas in England under a scheme to encourage recreational participation in the sport, and a further 4,000 will be installed in 1999–2000.

Bowls

The two main forms of bowls are lawn (flat green and crown green) and indoor bowls. About 6,000 flat green lawn bowling clubs are affiliated to the English, Scottish, Welsh and Irish Bowling Associations, which, together with Women's Bowling Associations for the four countries, play to the laws of the World Bowls Board. Crown green bowls and indoor bowls have their own separate associations. The World Bowls Tour now organises bowls at the professional level. Proposals for a single world governing body are under discussion.

British bowlers have achieved considerable success in international championships. At the world outdoor championships (held every four years) the winners at the most recent event, held in Adelaide in 1996, included Tony Allcock, who became the first man to defend the singles title successfully, and Scotland, winners of the team title. At the 1999 world indoor championships, held in Hopton-on-Sea (Norfolk), Alex Marshall won the singles event, while Steve Rees and John Price won the pairs title.

Boxing

Boxing in its modern form is based on the rules established by the Marquess of Queensberry in 1865. In the UK boxing is both amateur and professional, and in both strict medical regulations are observed.

All amateur boxing in England is controlled by the Amateur Boxing Association of England. There are separate associations in Scotland and Wales, and boxing in Northern Ireland is controlled by the Irish Amateur Boxing Association. The associations organise amateur boxing championships as well as training courses for referees and coaches. Headguards must be used in all UK amateur competitions. The first residential boxing academy, with places for up to 30 16- to 18-year-olds, will begin operating in September 1999 at the Peterlee sports site of East Durham Houghall Community College.

Professional boxing in the UK is controlled by the British Boxing Board of Control. The Board appoints referees, timekeepers, inspectors, medical officers and representatives to ensure that regulations are observed, and that contests take place under carefully regulated conditions. Medical controls and safety measures must be in place at all licensed tournaments, to minimise the risk to boxers. The Board nominates challengers for British championships and represents the interests of British licensed boxers in the international championship bodies of which it is a member.

Lennox Lewis is the World Boxing Council (WBC) heavyweight champion, and in March 1999 he drew his title fight with Evander Holyfield of the United States (who holds two other versions of the heavyweight title). The UK currently has five other world champions (as recognised by organisations of which the British Boxing Board of Control is a member): Naseem Hamed, who holds the World Boxing Organisation (WBO) featherweight title; super-middleweights Joe Calzaghe (WBO) and Richie Woodhall (WBC); Johnny Nelson (WBO cruiserweight); and Jason Matthews (WBO middleweight).

> The first licensed women's professional boxing match in the UK took place in London in November 1998 when Jane Couch from the UK (world welterweight champion) beat a German opponent.

Chess

There are local chess clubs and leagues throughout the UK, and chess is also played widely in schools and other educational establishments. Domestic competitions include the British Championships, the National Club Championships and the County Championships. The Hastings Chess Congress, which started in 1895, is the world's longest running annual international chess tournament.

The governing bodies are the British Chess Federation (responsible for England and for co-ordinating activity among the home nations), the Scottish Chess Association and the Welsh and Ulster Chess Unions.

England won the European Team Championship for the first time in 1997. A number of UK chess players feature among the world's best, including Michael Adams and Nigel Short.

Chess is not currently recognised as a sport, but the Government has announced plans to make it so by introducing legislation in Parliament.

Cricket

The rules of cricket became the responsibility, in the 18th century, of the Marylebone Cricket Club (MCC), based at Lord's cricket ground in north London, and it still frames the laws today. The England and Wales Cricket Board (ECB) administers men's and women's cricket in England and Wales. The Scottish Cricket Union administers cricket in Scotland.

Cricket is played in schools, colleges and universities, and amateur teams play weekly games in cities, towns and villages. There is a network of first-class cricket, minor counties and club games with a variety of leagues. The professional cricket competitions are in the process of being restructured. The main competition is the PPP Healthcare County Championship, played by 18 first-class county teams in four-day matches. From 2000 it will be played in two divisions. Three main one-day competitions were held in 1999: the NatWest Trophy, the Benson & Hedges Super Cup and the CGU National Cricket League, which was split into two divisions for the first time.

England hosted the 1999 World Cup, involving 12 countries. Around 476,800 spectators watched the matches, and the worldwide television audience was estimated at 2 billion. The final at Lord's was won by Australia, who beat Pakistan by 8 wickets.

Every year there is a series of five-day Cornhill Insurance Test matches played between England and one or more touring teams from Australia, India, New Zealand (who toured England in 1999), Pakistan, South Africa, Sri Lanka, the West Indies or Zimbabwe. A team representing England usually tours one or more of these countries in the UK winter.

Cycling

Cycling includes road and track racing, time-trialling, cyclo-cross (cross country racing), touring and bicycle moto-cross (BMX). All-terrain or mountain bikes are increasingly popular.

The British Cycling Federation has 14,000 members and is the internationally recognised governing body for British cycling as a sport. The Road Time Trials Council controls road time trials and has more than 1,000 member clubs. In 1998 over 100,000 rides were completed in open time trials in England and Wales. The CTC (Cyclists' Touring Club), with 65,000 members and affiliates, is the governing body for recreational (including off-road) and urban cycling, and holds the CTC rally each year in York. CTC Scotland represents cyclists in Scotland, Wales has its own Cycling Union and Northern Ireland also has separate federations for competitive cycling.

Chris Boardman is the UK's most successful current cyclist. He won the 4,000 metres pursuit title at the World Cycling Championships in 1996 and was one of two UK bronze medallists in cycling—along with Max Sciandri—at the Atlanta Olympics.

Equestrianism

Leading horse trials, comprising dressage, cross-country and show jumping, are held at a number of locations. The Badminton Horse Trials, sponsored by Mitsubishi Motors, is one of the UK's largest sporting events, attracting around 250,000 spectators. The major show jumping events include the Horse of the Year Show at Wembley in London and the Hickstead Derby in West Sussex.

The British Equestrian Federation (BEF) acts as the international secretariat on behalf of its members, which include the British Show Jumping Association, the British Horse Trials Association, British Dressage, British Horse Driving Trials Association, British Endurance

Riding Association and British Equestrian Vaulting. These associations act as the governing bodies of the different sporting disciplines in the UK and oversee the organisation of the major national and international events. The British Horse Society, which includes British Riding Clubs, is responsible for promoting training, road safety, rights of way and the welfare of horses, while the Pony Club provides training for children.

At the 1998 World Equestrian Games in Rome, the British team won a bronze medal in show jumping, through the team of Geoff Billington, Di Lampard, Nick Skelton and John Whitaker. In September 1999 the three-day event team—consisting of Jeanette Brakewell, Pippa Funnell, Tina Gifford and Ian Stark—won the European Championships a Luhmuhlen (Germany), and Pippa Funnell won the individual title.

Exercise and Fitness

Exercise and fitness is a term covering a variety of activities—such as exercise to music, aqua exercise, weight training and circuit training—which aim to improve health and fitness. Exercise England is the national governing body in England for exercise and fitness, and aims to promote a positive approach to sport and health. It maintains the English Exercise and Fitness Register, which lists qualified teachers/instructors, and is designed to protect the public by raising standards and promoting codes of practice. The Keep Fit Association (KFA), which has 1,500 teachers and a membership of 12,000, promotes fitness through movement, exercise and dance for people of all ages and abilities. Its national certificated training scheme for KFA teachers is recognised by local education authorities throughout the UK. Autonomous associations serve Scotland, Wales and Northern Ireland.

Field Sports

Field sports in the UK include hunting, shooting, stalking and hare coursing. Fox hunting with a pack of hounds is the most popular hunting sport. There are over 300 recognised packs of quarry hounds in the UK, of which more than 180 are foxhound packs recognised by the Masters of Fox Hounds Association. A number of hunts organise 'point-to-point' race meetings (see p. 305). The Countryside Alliance promotes the interests of field sports.

A private member's Bill seeking to ban hunting with hounds received a second reading in the House of Commons in 1997, with a substantial majority in favour, but did not become law owing to a lack of parliamentary time.

Football

Association football is controlled by separate football associations in England, Wales, Scotland and Northern Ireland. In England 340 clubs are affiliated to the Football Association (FA) and more than 42,000 clubs to regional or district associations. The FA, founded in 1863, and the Football League, founded in 1888, were both the first of their kind in the world. In Scotland there are 78 full and associate clubs and nearly 6,000 registered clubs under the jurisdiction of the Scottish Football Association.

In England the FA Premier League comprises 20 clubs. A further 72 full-time professional clubs play in three main divisions run by the Football League. Over 2,000 English League matches are played during the season, from August to May. A £40 million scheme has been introduced to establish new centres of excellence for coaching and developing young players, with a contribution of £20 million from the FA Premier League being matched by £20 million from Sport England's Lottery Fund.

Three Welsh clubs play in the Football League, while the National League of Wales contains 20 semi-professional clubs. In Scotland a new Scottish Premier League, with ten clubs, held its first fixtures in 1998. A further 30 clubs play in the Scottish Football League, equally divided into three divisions. In Northern Ireland, 16 semi-professional clubs play in the Irish Football League.

The major annual knock-out competitions are the FA Cup (sponsored by AXA) and the League Cup (the Worthington Cup) in England, the Tennents Scottish Cup, the

Scottish League Cup, the Irish Cup and the Welsh FA Cup.

The Football Task Force was established in 1997 to advise on a range of issues affecting football. It has issued reports on disabled access, racism and community involvement. The Government has taken steps to implement the recommendations which are its concern, and has asked the other bodies named in the report to implement the recommendations concerning them. The Task Force's final report, on the commercial aspects of the game, is due to be produced later in 1999.

Football has seen an influx of money, particularly into the top British clubs (such as Arsenal, Manchester United, Chelsea, Rangers and Celtic), and a number of the leading clubs are quoted on the London Stock Exchange. Many leading footballers from other countries are now playing in the top divisions in the UK. Footballers feature strongly among the UK's highest paid sports performers, with several receiving over £1 million a year (including their earnings from sponsorship).

Following the success in staging the European Championship finals in 1996, the FA has submitted a bid to host the World Cup in 2006. Both England and Scotland played in the final stage of the 1998 World Cup in France.

Manchester United won the European Cup (the final of the European Champions League) in May 1999 when they beat Bayern Munich in Barcelona. This followed winning the FA Premier League and the FA Cup in 1998–99, the first English club to win all three events in the same season.

Gaelic Games

Gaelic Games, increasingly popular in Northern Ireland, cover the sports of Gaelic football, handball, hurling, camogie (women's hurling) and rounders. There are over 700 clubs in Northern Ireland affiliated to the Gaelic Athletic Association and the Camogie Council, the official governing bodies responsible for Gaelic Games.

Golf

Golf originated in Scotland and since 1897 the rules have been administered worldwide (excluding the United States) by the Royal and Ancient Golf Club (R & A), which is situated at St Andrews. The Golfing Union of Ireland and parallel unions in Wales, Scotland and England are the national governing bodies for men's amateur golf. These bodies are affiliated to the R & A and are represented on the Council of National Golf Unions, which is the UK co-ordinating body responsible for handicapping and organising home international matches. Women's amateur golf in Great Britain is governed by the Ladies' Golf Union. Club professional golf is governed by the Professional Golfers' Association (PGA) and tournament golf by the European PGA Tour and the European Ladies Professional Golfers' Association. Women's golf in the home countries is governed by the English Ladies Golf Association, the Welsh Ladies Golf Union, Scottish Ladies Golf Association and the Irish Ladies Golf Union.

The main tournament of the British golfing year is the Open Championship, one of the world's four 'major' events. Other important competitions include the World Matchplay Championship at Wentworth; the Walker Cup and Curtis Cup matches for amateurs, played between Great Britain and Ireland and the United States; and the Ryder Cup and Solheim Cup matches for men and women professionals respectively, played every two years between Europe and the United States.

There are over 2,000 golf courses in the UK. Some of the most famous include St Andrews, Royal Lytham and St Anne's, Royal Birkdale, and Carnoustie.

The 1999 British Open Championship, held at Carnoustie, was won by Paul Lawrie after a three-way play-off. Both Lee Westwood (the winner of several tournaments recently) and Colin Montgomerie (who headed the European list of money winners in 1998 for the sixth year running) are ranked in the world's top ten. In the women's game Alison Nicholas won the US Women's Open in 1997 and Laura Davies has recorded several recent wins.

Greyhound Racing

Greyhound racing is one of the UK's most popular spectator sports, with about 5 million spectators a year. The rules for the sport are drawn up by the National Greyhound Racing Club (NGRC), the sport's judicial and administrative body. The representative body is the British Greyhound Racing Board.

Meetings are usually held three times a week at each track, with at least ten races a meeting. The main event of the year is the Greyhound Derby, run in June at Wimbledon Stadium, London. Tracks are licensed by local authorities. There are 33 major tracks that operate under the rules of the NGRC and around 45 smaller tracks.

Gymnastics

Gymnastics is divided into seven main disciplines: artistic (or Olympic) gymnastics, rhythmic gymnastics, sports acrobatics, general gymnastics, sports aerobics, trampolining and gymnastics and movement for people with disabilities.

The governing body for the sport is British Gymnastics, to which 800 clubs are affiliated. It is estimated that between 3 and 4 million schoolchildren take part in some form of gymnastics every day.

Highland Games

Scottish Highland Games cover a wide range of athletic competitions, including running, cycling and dancing. The heavyweight events are the most popular and include throwing the hammer, tossing the caber and putting the shot. Over 70 events of various kinds take place throughout Scotland, the most famous being the annual Braemar Gathering.

The Scottish Games Association is the official governing body responsible for athletic sports and games at Highland and Border events in Scotland.

Hockey

The modern game of hockey was founded in England in 1886. A single association—the England Hockey Association—now governs men's and women's hockey in England; there are similar single associations in Scotland and Wales. Cup competitions and leagues exist at national, divisional or district, club and school levels, both indoors (six-a-side) and outdoors, and there are regular international matches and tournaments. The National Hockey Stadium in Milton Keynes, opened in 1996, is the venue for all major hockey matches in England.

Horse Racing

Horse racing takes two main forms—flat racing and National Hunt (steeplechasing and hurdle) racing. The turf flat race season lasts from late March to early November, but all-weather flat racing and National Hunt racing take place throughout the year. The UK has 59 racecourses and about 12,000 horses currently in training. Point-to-point racing, restricted to amateur riders on horses which are qualified by going hunting, takes place between January and June, and is growing in popularity.

The Derby, run at Epsom, is the outstanding event in the flat racing calendar. Other classic races are: the 2,000 Guineas and the 1,000 Guineas, both held at Newmarket; the Oaks (Epsom); and the St Leger (Doncaster). The meeting at Royal Ascot in June is another significant flat racing event. The most important National Hunt meeting is the National Hunt Festival held at Cheltenham in March, which features the Gold Cup and the Champion Hurdle. The Grand National, run at Aintree, near Liverpool, since the 1830s, is the world's best-known steeplechase.

In April 1999 Richard Dunwoody became the most successful National Hunt jockey in the UK, when he rode his 1,679th winner, overtaking the previous record held by Peter Scudamore.

As the governing authority for racing, the British Horseracing Board (BHB) is responsible for the fixture list, race programmes, relations with the Government and the betting industry, and central marketing. The Jockey Club, as the regulatory authority, is responsible for licensing, discipline and security.

Ice Hockey

Ice hockey is a significant indoor spectator sport, with over 2 million spectators each season and attendances growing. Eight teams contest the British Superleague, and 16 the Benson & Hedges Cup. A further eight teams take part in the British National League, run by the British Ice Hockey Association, while ten teams are involved in the English Premier League. There are around 7,500 players in the UK.

Ice Skating

Ice skating has four main disciplines: ice figure (single and pairs), ice dance, speed skating and synchronised skating. Participation in ice skating is concentrated among the under-25s, and is one of the few sports that attracts more female than male participants. The governing body is the National Ice Skating Association of UK Ltd, to which 75 clubs are affiliated. There are over 70 rinks in the UK. A new rink has opened at the Deeside Leisure Centre in north Wales, and plans are in hand for other new rinks, including two double ice rink facilities at Nottingham and Sheffield, both of which will receive funding from the National Lottery Sports Fund.

Judo

Judo is popular not only as a competitive sport and self-defence technique, but also as a means of general fitness training. An internationally recognised grading system is in operation through the sport's governing body, the British Judo Association. Birmingham will stage the world championships in October 1999. At the previous championships in 1997 Kate Howey won the middleweight title. Karina Bryant has won the world junior heavyweight title and was European champion in 1998, while Debbie Allan won the featherweight title at the 1999 European Championships.

Martial Arts

Various martial arts, mainly derived from the Far East, are practised in the UK. There are recognised governing bodies for karate, ju-jitsu, aikido, Chinese martial arts, kendo, taekwondo and tang soo do. The most popular martial art is karate, with over 100,000 participants.

Motor-car Sports

The main four-wheeled motor sports include motor racing, autocross, rallycross, rallying and karting. In motor racing the Formula 1 Grand Prix World Championship is the major form of the sport. The British Grand Prix is held at Silverstone (Northamptonshire) each July.

The governing body for four-wheeled motor sport in the UK is The Royal Automobile Club Motor Sports Association, which issues licences for a variety of competitions. It also organises the Rally of Great Britain, an event in the World Rally Championship, and the British Grand Prix.

The UK has had more Formula 1 world champions than any other country. The most recent is Damon Hill (son of Graham Hill, a previous world champion), who won the 1996 World Championship and has won 22 Grand Prix. Three other British drivers, all of whom are Grand Prix winners, are currently in Formula 1: David Coulthard, Johnny Herbert and Eddie Irvine; Eddie Irvine was in second place in the World Championship in September 1999.

UK car constructors, including McLaren and Williams, have enjoyed outstanding success in Grand Prix and many other forms of racing. Most of the cars in Formula 1 have been designed, developed and built in the UK. The UK motor sport industry is estimated to generate an annual turnover of over £1.3 billion (of which exports account for 60%) and to employ more than 50,000 people.

Colin McRae won the World Rally Championship in 1995, and finished second in 1996 and 1997, and third in 1998.

Motorcycle Sports

Motorcycle sports include road racing, moto-cross, grass track, speedway, trials, drag racing, enduro (endurance off-road racing) and sprint. There are between 40,000 and 50,000 competitive motorcyclists in the UK.

The governing bodies of the sport are the Auto-Cycle Union in England and Wales, the

Scottish Auto-Cycle Union and the Motor Cycle Union of Ireland (in Northern Ireland). The major events of the year include the Isle of Man TT races and the British Road Race Grand Prix. The Auto-Cycle Union also provides off-road training by approved instructors for riders of all ages.

Carl Fogarty has been by far the most successful rider in the World Superbike Championships since they began in 1988. In 1999 he won the event for the fourth time, following successes in 1994, 1995 and 1998. In 1999 he recorded his 50th individual victory.

Mountaineering

The representative body is the British Mountaineering Council (BMC), which works closely with the Mountaineering Councils of Scotland and Ireland. The main areas of work include access and conservation. The BMC estimates that the number of active climbers is around 150,000, not including the many hill walkers. There are over 300 mountaineering and climbing clubs in the UK, and three National Centres for mountaineering activities run by the Sports Councils (see pp. 296–7).

UK mountaineers have been prominent among the explorers of the world's great mountain ranges. The best-known is Sir Chris Bonington, who has climbed Everest and led many other expeditions.

Netball

More than 60,000 adults play netball regularly in England and a further 1 million young people play in schools. The sport is played almost exclusively by women and girls.

The All England Netball Association is the governing body in England, with Scotland, Wales and Northern Ireland having their own separate organisations. National competitions are staged annually for all age-groups, and England plays a series of international matches against other countries, both in England and overseas.

Rowing

Rowing takes place in many schools, universities and rowing clubs throughout the

UK. The main types of boats are single, pairs and double sculls, fours and eights. The governing body in England is the Amateur Rowing Association; similar bodies regulate the sport in Scotland, Wales and Ireland (Ulster Branch).

The University Boat Race, between eight-oared crews from Oxford and Cambridge, has been rowed on the Thames almost every spring since 1836. The Head of the River Race, also on the Thames, is the largest assembly of racing craft in the world, with more than 420 eights racing in procession. At the Henley Regatta in Oxfordshire crews from all over the world compete each July in various kinds of race over a straight course of 1 mile 550 yards (about 2.1 km).

Steven Redgrave has won four successive Olympic gold medals, a feat achieved by only a very few people in Olympic history. He and Matthew Pinsent won the gold medal in the coxless pairs in both the 1992 and 1996 Olympics. Together with Ed Coode and James Cracknell, they won a gold medal in the coxless four event in the world championships in Ontario in 1999, and the coxless four is expected to be a strong medal contender in the Olympic Games in Sydney in 2000. At the 1999 world championships the UK also won four silver medals.

Rugby League

Rugby league (a 13-a-side game) originated in 1895 following the breakaway from rugby union (see p. 308) of 22 clubs in the north of England, where the sport is still concentrated. In the UK there are 32 professional clubs, with about 1,000 professional players, and some 400 amateur clubs with a total of around 40,000 players.

The governing body of the professional game is the Rugby Football League, while the amateur game is governed by the British Amateur Rugby League Association. The major domestic club match of the season is the Challenge Cup Final.

The main leagues now take place in the summer rather than the winter. The JJB Super League consists of 14 clubs: 13 from the north of England and one from London. In 1999 the other two divisions merged, forming the Northern Ford Premiership with 18 clubs.

Sixteen nations are expected to contest the World Cup in 2000, which will be staged in England, Wales, Scotland, Ireland and France.

Rugby Union

Rugby union football (a 15-a-side game) is thought to have originated at Rugby School in the first half of the 19th century. The sport is played under the auspices of the Rugby Football Union in England and parallel bodies in Wales, Scotland and Ireland (Ulster Branch). Each of the four countries has separate national league and knock-out competitions for its domestic clubs.

The last Five Nations Championship, contested by England, Scotland, Wales, Ireland (a team from the Irish Republic and Northern Ireland) and France, was held in 1999 (and won by Scotland). This will be succeeded in 2000 by the Six Nations Championship when Italy joins the competition. Overseas tours are undertaken by the national sides and by the British or Irish Lions, a team representing Great Britain and Ireland. Tours to the UK are made by teams representing the major rugby-playing nations.

The 1999 Rugby World Cup is taking place in Wales, England, Scotland, Ireland and France. Twenty teams will contest the event. The final will be in November at the Millennium Stadium in Cardiff, which has been rebuilt. It now has a capacity of 72,500 and is the world's biggest stadium with a retractable roof.

Ulster succeeded Bath as European club champions when they won the European Cup in January 1999, beating Colomiers of France in the final.

Skiing and Other Winter Sports

Skiing takes place in Scotland from December to May and also at several English locations when there is sufficient snow. The five established winter sports areas in Scotland are Cairngorm, Glencoe, Glenshee, the Lecht and Nevis Range. All have a full range of ski-lifts, prepared ski-runs and professional instructors.

There are over 115 artificial or dry ski-slopes throughout the UK, and 1.5 million people take part in the sport. The British Ski and Snowboard Federation is the representative body for international competitive skiing and snowboarding. The four home country ski councils are responsible for the development of the sport, mainly through coaching, race training and arranging competitions.

The four-man bobsleigh team of Sean Olsson, Dean Ward, Paul Attwood and Courtney Rumbolt won a bronze medal at the 1998 Winter Olympics in Nagano in Japan.

Snooker and Billiards

Snooker was invented by the British in India in 1875 and is played by approximately 7 million people in the UK. British players have an outstanding record and have dominated the major professional championships. The main tournament is the annual Embassy World Professional Championship, held in Sheffield. In 1999 Stephen Hendry regained the title to register his seventh victory, a record number of wins since the event has been staged at Sheffield.

The controlling body for the non-professional game in England is the English Association for Snooker and Billiards. Scotland, Wales and Northern Ireland have separate associations. The World Professional Billiards and Snooker Association organises all world-ranking professional events and holds the copyright for the rules. The representative body for women is the World Ladies' Billiards and Snooker Association.

Squash

Squash derives from the game of rackets, which was invented at Harrow School in the 1850s. The governing body for squash in England is the Squash Rackets Association; there are separate governing bodies in Wales, Scotland and Northern Ireland. The British Open Championships is one of the major world events in the sport.

The number of players in the UK is estimated at over 2 million, of whom more than 500,000 compete regularly in inter-club league competitions. There are nearly 9,000 squash courts in England, provided mainly by squash clubs, commercial organisations and local authorities.

In September 1999 Peter Nicol won the World Championships in Cairo, regaining the position of world number one; in 1998 he had finished runner-up in the World Championships and had been the first UK winner of the British Open for 25 years. Suzanne Horner and Sue Wright both reached the semi-finals of the 1998 World Open Championships in Stuttgart. In early 1999 the UK had eight men and nine women in the respective top 20 world rankings.

Swimming

Swimming is a popular sport and form of exercise for people from all age-groups. Competitive swimming is governed by the Amateur Swimming Association (ASA) in England and by similar associations in Scotland and Wales. Together these three associations form the Amateur Swimming Federation of Great Britain, which co-ordinates the selection of Great Britain teams and organises international competitions. Instruction and coaching are provided by qualified teachers and coaches who hold certificates awarded mainly by the ASA.

In the 1996 Olympics Paul Palmer gained a silver medal in the 400 metres freestyle and Graeme Smith a bronze medal in the 1,500 metres freestyle. At the World Short Course Championships in Hong Kong in April 1999 the British team won four gold medals: Mark Foster (50 metres freestyle and 50 metres butterfly), James Hickman (who retained his 200 metres butterfly title) and the women's 4 x 100 metres freestyle relay team. At the European Championships in Istanbul in July 1999, Paul Palmer (in the 400 metres freestyle) and Sue Rolph (100 metres freestyle) won gold medals, while Tony Ali took gold in the 3 metre diving event.

Table Tennis

Table tennis originated in England in the 1880s and was particularly popular at the beginning of the 20th century. Today it is played by all age-groups and social groups,

and in a variety of venues, ranging from small halls to specialist, multi-table centres. It is also a major recreational and competitive activity for people with disabilities. The governing body in England is the English Table Tennis Association. There is also an English Schools Association and separate associations in Scotland, Wales and Northern Ireland.

Tennis

The modern game of tennis originated in England in 1873 and the first championships were played at Wimbledon in 1877. The governing body for tennis in Great Britain is the Lawn Tennis Association (LTA), to which Tennis Wales and the Scottish LTA are affiliated. Tennis in Northern Ireland is governed by Tennis Ireland (Ulster Branch).

The Wimbledon Championships, held within the grounds of the All England Club, are one of the four tennis 'Grand Slam' tournaments. They attracted a record 457,000 spectators in 1999 and generated £33 million for British tennis in 1998. Prize money totalled £7.6 million in 1999.

The two leading British players—Tim Henman and Greg Rusedski—are both ranked in the world's top ten. Tim Henman reached the semi-finals in the 1998 and 1999 Wimbledon Championships, while Greg Rusedski was runner-up in the 1997 US Open. In the 1996 Olympics Neil Broad and Tim Henman were runners-up in the men's doubles.

About 5 million people play tennis in the UK. There are national and county championships, while national competitions are organised for schools. Short tennis has been introduced for children aged five and over.

The LTA has a five-year plan for developing tennis in Great Britain, with the aim of expanding participation, encouraging regular competition and producing more world-class tennis players. Tennis facilities are being improved, and about £40 million will be provided by the LTA towards more indoor tennis centres, clay courts and floodlit courts. Over 50 community tennis partnerships have been established between local authorities, schools and tennis clubs, creating almost 300 club-school links involving over 2,000 schools.

Yachting

Yachting/boating comprises yacht and dinghy racing and cruising, powerboat racing, motor cruising and windsurfing, on inland and offshore waters. The Royal Yachting Association (RYA) is the national governing body for boating in the UK and aims to make boating in all its forms as accessible as possible; it also includes RYA Sailability, the charity for disabled sailors. About 4.75 million people participate in the sport. Among well-known yachting events in the UK are the Admiral's Cup, Cowes Week and the Fastnet Race.

At the 1996 Olympics, silver medals were won by Ben Ainslie in the Laser class and by John Merricks and Ian Walker in the 470 double-handed dinghy class. Ben Ainslie won the Laser class world championship in Melbourne in January 1999. Jonathan Jones is a world powerboating champion, having won the World Formula One title in December 1998. Nik Baker is currently the World Indoor Windsurfing Champion on the Professional Windsurfing Association World Tour.

Further Reading

BBC Radio 5 Live Sports Yearbook (annual). Oddball Publishing.

Investing for Our Sporting Future: Sport England Lottery Fund Strategy 1999–2009. Sport England, 1999.

Websites

Department for Culture, Media and Sport: www.culture.gov.uk

UK Sport: www.uksport.gov.uk

Sport England: www.english.sports.gov.uk

19 Sustainable Development

Sustainable development is becoming increasingly recognised and promoted, both in the UK and internationally. A widely used international definition is 'development that meets the needs of the present without compromising the ability of future generations to meet their own needs', or as the Government has explained it: 'ensuring a better quality of life for everyone, now and for generations to come'. The Government has recently adopted a new strategy for sustainable development on the UK, including 14 'headline indicators' against which progress will be monitored. A new Sustainable Development Commission will be set up in 2000 to help monitor progress.

Introduction

The UK's first strategy on sustainable development was published in 1994, following the Rio de Janeiro 'Earth Summit' in 1992 (the United Nations Conference on Environment and Development). In May 1999 the Government published a revised strategy—*A Better Quality of Life: A Strategy for Sustainable Development for the UK*. This differs from its predecessor by emphasising the importance of considering social progress alongside the more familiar issues of the economy, environment and resource use. It stresses the importance of integrated policies in meeting four broad objectives at the same time, in the UK and the world as a whole:

- social progress which meets the needs of everyone;
- effective protection of the environment;
- prudent use of natural resources; and
- maintenance of high and stable levels of economic growth and employment.

The establishment in 1999 of the Scottish Parliament and the National Assembly for Wales means that, where matters are devolved, the new administrations will decide how to proceed in the light of their country's particular circumstances. Thus while some of the policies described in this strategy apply to the UK as a whole, others are exclusive to England: some publications of the devolved administrations are listed in the Further Reading section.

Sustainable development requires international co-operation on matters such as trade, the relief of global poverty and environmental problems. For the UK, the European Union (EU) is especially influential. Changes to the Treaty of Rome, agreed in the Treaty of Amsterdam (see p. 80), give sustainable development a much greater prominence in Europe, by making it a requirement for environmental protection concerns to be integrated into EU policies. The Treaty states that the particular objective of this requirement is to promote sustainable development.

In working towards these broad objectives, government policy will take account of ten guiding principles and approaches:

- putting people at the centre of concerns for sustainable development;
- taking a long-term perspective;
- taking account of costs and benefits;
- creating an open and supportive economic system;
- combating poverty and social exclusion;
- respecting environmental limits;
- the precautionary principle—it is no longer acceptable to say, 'we can't be sure that serious damage will happen, so we'll do nothing to prevent it';
- using scientific knowledge;
- transparency, information, participation and access to justice; and
- making the polluter pay.

Indicators of Sustainable Development

The most widely used measure of the economic progress of the nation is Gross Domestic Product (GDP, see p. 382), but the limitations of this single measure in the context of sustainable development are well known. In 1998, the Office for National Statistics produced a first set of Environmental Accounts for the UK—linking environmental statistics with GDP and national accounts. The Government would like to see the use of a wider range of 'headline indicators' of sustainable development, covering social and environmental issues alongside such well-established economic measures as GDP, inflation and unemployment.

The UK published a set of approximately 120 indicators of sustainable development in 1996. The new UK strategy includes a revised and expanded set of about 150 indicators, including 14 'headline indicators'. This will enable the Government to monitor and report on progress (or otherwise) towards targets, and give a broad overview of whether a 'better quality of life for everyone, now and for

generations to come' is being achieved. The 14 headline indicators, covering economic, social and environmental concerns, are:

- total output of the economy (GDP);
- investment in public, business and private assets;
- the proportion of people of working age who are in work;
- qualifications at age 19;
- expected years of healthy life;
- the number of homes judged unfit to live in;
- the level of recorded crime;
- emissions of greenhouse gases;
- days when air pollution is moderate or high;
- the amount of road traffic;
- rivers of good or fair quality;
- populations of wild birds;
- new homes built on previously developed land; and
- the amount of waste and its management.

A core series of indicators, linked to the national ones, is also being developed specifically for local authorities to use.

Government Role

The Government is committed, as part of its strategy for sustainable development, to integrating environmental considerations into its decision-making at all levels, and in every sphere of its activity—the Greening Government Initiative.

A *Green Minister* has been appointed in each main Whitehall department. Individually, they act as advocates for sustainable development and the environment within their own departments and their associated agencies and non-departmental public bodies (NDPBs). Collectively, they meet regularly under the chairmanship of the Environment Minister, in the Department of the Environment, Transport and the Regions (DETR), to share best practice and to ensure that systems are in place across the public sector to bring the environment into policy-making and the running of buildings and facilities.

Some Indicators of the Quality of Surroundings, England

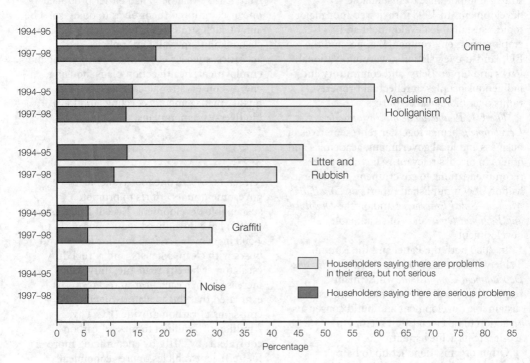

Source: Department of the Environment, Transport and the Regions

Green Ministers focus particularly on ensuring that there is an effective system for environmental appraisals of policy and, in terms of greening operations, on energy efficiency, waste management, staff travel and procurement. They have also taken action to introduce Environmental Management Systems to help departments better manage their environmental impacts.

Green Ministers report to the *Cabinet Committee on the Environment,* which has responsibility, at the strategic level, for ensuring that environmental considerations are fully integrated into all areas of policy, to help achieve sustainable development. The Committee is chaired by the Deputy Prime Minister.

The Government has also created the parliamentary *Environmental Audit Committee* to scrutinise how far the policies and programmes of government departments, agencies and NDPBs contribute to environmental protection and sustainable

development. In doing so, the Committee undertakes a range of inquiries, including regular investigations of progress on the Greening Government Initiative.

A *Sustainable Development Unit* was set up within the DETR in 1997 as a focal point for government policy, strategy and planning on sustainable development. It works closely with other departments and is able to offer advice on how best sustainable development can be taken into account in managing policy and operations. One of the Unit's activities is promoting freedom of access to information on the environment. The UK intends to ratify the 1998 (UN Economic Commission for Europe) Aarhus Convention on Access to Information, Public Participation in Decision-Making and Access to Justice in Environmental Matters. New legislation is required first, however, and has been proposed in the draft Freedom of Information Bill (see p. 58).

The British Government Panel on Sustainable Development is an independent body which advises government on issues of major strategic importance to sustainable development. In 1998 it reviewed four major topics: sustainable development and employment; environmental issues and the EU; land-use legislation governing National Parks and Green Belts; and community and indigenous peoples' intellectual property rights over biological resources.

The UK Round Table on Sustainable Development brings together representatives of business and local government, academics and others to discuss relevant issues, and makes recommendations to government. In the first half of 1999 it published reports on *Small and Medium-Sized Enterprises* and on the *Devolved and Regional Dimensions* of sustainable development.

In 2000 both the Panel and the Round Table will be absorbed into a new *Sustainable Development Commission*, whose main responsibility will be to monitor progress on sustainable development and build consensus on action to be taken by all sectors to accelerate its achievement.

Other organisations set up to help formulate, or implement, policy in this area are the Advisory Committee on Business and the Environment (see p. 316), the Trade Unions and Sustainable Development Advisory Committee, and *Going for Green*, which seeks to persuade individuals and groups to commit themselves to sustainable development (in Scotland, this role is taken by *Forward Scotland*).

Local Agenda 21

At the Rio de Janeiro 'Earth Summit' in 1992, an 'Agenda for the 21st Century' was adopted by the international community. It set out a framework of objectives and activities for governments and major groups of civil society, including business, on sustainable development necessary for the 21st century. Two-thirds of the actions in Agenda 21 require the full involvement of local authorities, and Chapter 28 of the Agenda encouraged them to adopt a 'Local Agenda 21' by 1996.

The Government wants all UK local authorities to have adopted a Local Agenda 21 strategy by the year 2000, and reported in March 1999 that 88% had either produced one or committed themselves to doing so. The aim of such strategies is to integrate sustainability into all local policies and activities, such as: economic development and employment; health action plans; housing; energy conservation; local transport; air quality management; recycling; and local biodiversity action plans.

Taxes

'Green taxes' are one tool available to government in its efforts to promote sustainable development. Recent Budgets (see p. 406) have introduced reductions of up to £500 in Vehicle Excise Duty for lorries and buses with clean exhausts, and a 'fuel duty escalator', whereby road-fuel duty will increase by 6% each year in real terms. It is estimated that the escalator will cut UK emissions of carbon dioxide (CO_2) by 2 million to 5 million tonnes (of carbon equivalent) by 2010, by encouraging more fuel-efficient vehicles, more economical driving styles and less vehicle use.

One tax measure in 1998 increased the difference in duty between ultra low sulphur diesel (ULSD) and standard diesel from 1 to 3 pence a litre over two years, in order to reduce emissions of particulates and nitrogen oxides. By February 1999 the proportion of ULSD sold was 43% and a further increase in the duty differential in the March 1999 Budget increased this percentage to 96% by August and is expected to convert the whole diesel market to ULSD by the end of the year.

Since June 1999, 1.8 million small cars with an engine size of 1,100 cc or less have benefited from a reduced annual rate of Vehicle Excise Duty from £155 to £100. From autumn 2000 owners of all *new* cars will pay duty according to their car's rate of CO_2 emissions. Another measure announced in the 1999 Budget is the reform of the company car tax regime from 2002. This will encourage the use of more fuel-efficient cars.

Perhaps the most radical tax reform is the proposed 'climate change levy' (see p. 488) on the use of energy in business and the public sector from 2001, to reduce emissions of CO_2, the principal greenhouse gas (see p. 337). The overall tax burden on the non-domestic sectors will not increase, however, nor will their competitiveness be damaged, since the levy will be offset by a corresponding cut in the level of employers' National Insurance contributions, and by other financial incentives to promote energy efficiency and the use of renewable sources of energy.

Other recent Budget measures include a reduction in value added tax (VAT) on the installation of energy-saving materials, so that more low-income households can afford to insulate their homes; further increases in the landfill tax (for waste disposal—see p. 331) in an attempt to encourage recycling and increases in tax credits for voluntary financial contributions by landfill operators to environmental bodies. The Government is also considering the introduction of taxes or charges on the quarrying of aggregates (sand, gravel and crushed rock), if the industry cannot agree to a system of voluntary environmental improvements, and on pesticides.

Education and Training

In 1998 the Government set up an expert panel (for England) to consider the provision of education for sustainable development in schools, youth services, further and higher education, at work and at home. In April 1999 the panel published proposals for a ten-year programme, which included the recommendation, for schools, that all children should be entitled to education for sustainable development. This entitlement would be delivered through the National Curriculum (see p. 136), backed up by appropriate initial and in-service teacher training, and monitored by the school inspection framework.

In Scotland, education for sustainable development has been led by a group of experts, associated with the Advisory Group on Sustainable Development, since 1995, and is now well integrated into the Scottish curriculum. The Environmental Education Council for Wales has developed a Welsh educational strategy, and launched the first phase of its Environment Network Centres in 1998.

The Environment Task Force (ETF), one of four options available to 18–24 year olds under the New Deal for the Young Unemployed (see p. 154), was launched in 1998. The ETF aims to improve long-term employment prospects through a combination of high-quality work experience and training. It consists of projects which deliver benefits in line with the Government's sustainable development policies and objectives.

Business and the Consumer

The Government has launched a number of initiatives to help business improve its environmental awareness and consumers to make environmental choices about what they buy and from whom. For example, households are being encouraged not only to recycle their waste, but also to buy products that contain recycled material.

Sectoral sustainability strategies provide the framework for addressing the 'triple bottom line'—integrating action and setting priorities to improve business performance on economic, environmental and social aspects. The Government is encouraging trade associations and other representative bodies to develop and implement strategies within at least six business sectors by the end of 2000, building on existing initiatives and best practice.

In March 1999 the Government published a strategy for 'sustainable distribution' (see p. 366). As well as improving the efficiency of distribution, its main aims are to reduce the number of accidents, injuries and cases of ill health, noise and disturbance associated with freight movements, and to minimise congestion and pollution. This will involve better use of the transport infrastructure and land-use planning framework, and will help to deliver fair and open markets for UK producers, consignors and operators of freight transport services.

The Environmental Technology Best Practice Programme (ETBPP), launched in 1994, is an eight-year programme which promotes the use of better environmental practices that reduce business costs for industry and commerce. It provides information and advice on environmental technologies and techniques by means of publications, events, and a freephone UK helpline. By 1999 the ETBPP had stimulated savings for businesses of £70 million a year as a result of their adopting better environmental practices and cleaner technology. The ETBPP works in partnership with the Energy Efficiency Best Practice Programme (EEBPP, see p. 489) which supports energy efficiency measures. In April 1999 the Government launched the *Sustainable Technologies Initiative (STI)*, to build on the ETBPP and the EEBPP. The STI will provide £7.8 million of support over the next three years for the development of new technologies that will help businesses to be more efficient in their use of resources, and produce less waste and pollution.

The environmental industries sector— including companies that specialise in producing cleaner technology, clean-up technology and environmental monitoring systems—is a growth area of the British economy. In 1997 the sector achieved an annual turnover of about £7.5 billion, of which exports accounted for £0.7 billion or 4.4% of the global market.

The Queen's Awards for Environmental Achievement are presented in recognition of products, technology or processes developed by British industry which offer major environmental benefits compared with the existing competition. Awards are granted only for products, technology or processes which have achieved commercial success. In 1999, there were five awards, including for:

- the Jesse Brough Metals Group of Hixon in Staffordshire, for recycling of furnace waste;
- Exotherm Products Ltd of Cardiff, for energy-efficient electric heaters ('Insulwatt'); and
- Synetix of Billingham in Cleveland, for fixed-bed catalytic destruction technology for waste sodium hypochlorite.

The Advisory Committee on Business and the Environment (ACBE) consists of business leaders appointed by the Government and serving in a personal capacity. It gives advice to government on environmental issues of concern to business; provides a link with international business initiatives on the environment; and helps to mobilise the business community through demonstrating good environmental practice. In October 1998, ACBE published its eighth progress report, which contained 50 recommendations on how businesses can act on issues ranging from climate change and transport policy to sustainable consumption and the use of water resources.

Many leading companies now address environmental issues in their annual reports, and several publish separate environmental performance reports. The Government is encouraging the top 350 UK businesses to measure, reduce and report on their emissions of CO_2 and other greenhouse gases. For example, the Royal Mail has reported a CO_2 reduction of almost 12% between 1990 and 1997 for each letter delivered.

Environmental Management Systems

In 1996, the International Organisation for Standardisation (ISO) published ISO 14001, a standard which allows organisations to evaluate how their activities, products and services affect the environment, and gives them a systematic approach to improving their overall environmental performance. Certification is achieved only after an audit of the organisation's environmental management system by an independent body, such as the British Standards Institution (see p. 392). Accreditation of certification bodies in the UK is carried out by the United Kingdom Accreditation Service (UKAS). By April 1999, 899 organisations in the UK had UKAS-accredited ISO 14001 certification, out of a global figure of 2,892 UKAS-accredited certificates.

The Government will sponsor work on development of a 'sustainability management system' to help integrate sustainable development into the plans and operations of companies.

The Eco-Management and Audit Scheme (EMAS), developed by the European Commission, is a voluntary scheme applicable to industry, although it has been extended in the UK to local government as well. In Britain, registrations to EMAS are lodged with the Institute of Environmental Assessment. The environmental management system element of EMAS corresponds to ISO 14001. However, EMAS also requires a published environmental statement, which provides the public with independently validated information on the organisation's environmental performance. By June 1999 over 70 industrial sites in the UK and four local authorities had registered under the scheme.

Environmental Labelling

Consumers are increasingly making environmental choices in the goods they buy and often rely on the information given in product labels. To help them, the Government is keen to promote accurate and relevant environmental labelling, as part of an integrated approach to reducing the environmental impact of consumer products. In 1998, the Government launched a voluntary Green Claims Code which sets out guidance for businesses making environmental claims about their products. This code has been endorsed by the Confederation of British Industry, the British Retail Consortium and the Local Authority Co-ordinating Body on Food and Trading Standards. The principles have been developed further in a new international standard on environmental labelling—ISO 14021—which was adopted in 1999.

The Government has established the Market Transformation Programme to encourage more energy-efficient domestic appliances, including a graded Energy Label to permit the easy comparison of products. Following a consultation process, the Government has wound up the UK Ecolabelling Board and has taken over the running in the UK of the voluntary EU Ecolabelling scheme. The Government is also considering options for possible new labelling initiatives and has set up the Advisory Committee on Consumer Products and the Environment to assist the development of a comprehensive approach to consumer product

policy and strategic environmental labelling issues.

In May 1999 the Government embarked on a £25 million *'Are You Doing Your Bit'* publicity campaign to communicate the key elements of its new Sustainable Development Strategy to the general public in England over the next three years. The campaign will reinforce and complement the activities of Going for Green, local authorities and other organisations, and will draw attention to the simple everyday actions everyone can take to save money and reduce waste.

In 1999–2000, the Environmental Action Fund, which supports voluntary programmes to encourage more sustainable lifestyles, is giving funding of £4 million to some 165 initiatives.

Biodiversity

Another outcome of the 1992 'Earth Summit' was the Convention on Biological Diversity. Among its many obligations, the Convention required its 170 signatory countries (including the UK) to develop national strategies for the conservation and sustainable use of biological diversity, and in particular to protect the world's growing number of endangered species. The UK was one of the first countries to publish a national strategy and action plan (in 1994) and to carry out pioneering work in developing costed targets for individual species and habitats. The partnership engaged in carrying this work forward has involved government departments and their agencies; local authorities; industry; academic institutions and scientific collections; farming; land management; and voluntary sector conservation organisations.

In 1995, the UK Biodiversity Steering Group published a report which included, for the first time, fully costed action plans for the conservation of 116 species and 14 habitats, and recommendations for programmes to improve biological recording and monitoring, and public awareness. By autumn 1999 action plans for 391 species and 45 habitat action plans will be in place. Over 100 local biodiversity action plans are at various stages of implementation. The targets and programmes contained in these plans will form a basis for nature conservation in the UK in the 21st century.

Since the 1992 'Earth Summit' the UK has committed £160 million in support of biodiversity programmes (such as the management of ecosystems, research, training and education) in 53 developing countries. It has also committed £215 million to the Global Environment Facility, which supports the Convention on Biological Diversity. The UK continues to participate in international efforts to implement the Convention and intends to play a key role at the next meeting of the Conference of the Parties to the Convention, to be held in Nairobi in May 2000. The UK is keen to reconvene the Extraordinary Meeting of the Conference of the Parties to discuss and conclude negotiations on a Biosafety Protocol, which would regulate the transboundary movement of living modified organisms. The aim of the Protocol is to secure protection for the global environment while avoiding the creation of unnecessary barriers to trade.

Further Reading

A Better Quality of Life: A Strategy for Sustainable Development for the United Kingdom. Cm 4345. DETR. The Stationery Office, 1999.

Government Panel on Sustainable Development, *Fifth Annual Report.* DETR, 1999.

UK Round Table on Sustainable Development, *Small and Medium-Sized Enterprises; Sustainable Development—Devolved and Regional Dimensions.* DETR, 1999.

Down to Earth: A Scottish Perspective on Sustainable Development. Scottish Executive, 1999.

A report of the Welsh Office Conference is available from the National Assembly for Wales.

Shaping our Future. Towards a Strategy for the Development of the Region. Draft Regional Strategic Framework. Department of the Environment (NI), December 1998. Available from The Stationery Office.

Convention on Biological Diversity: The United Kingdom's First National Report. DETR. 1997.

Biodiversity: The UK Steering Group Report. Volumes I and II. DETR. The Stationery Office, 1995.

Biodiversity: The UK Action Plan. DETR. The Stationery Office, 1994

UK Environmental Accounts 1998. Office for National Statistics. The Stationery Office, 1998.

Websites

Department of the Environment, Transport and the Regions: www.environment.detr.gov.uk

UK Biodiversity Group: www.jncc.gov.uk/ukbg

20 Environmental Protection

Environmental matters affect the formulation of policy in all areas. An integrated Environment White Paper is planned before the end of the current Parliament, together with a Rural White Paper and major policy documents on chemicals and waste. Government funding for countryside and wildlife programmes in England and Wales will rise from £122 million in 1999–2000 to £150 million in 2001–02.

Conservation

The Department of the Environment, Transport and the Regions (DETR) is responsible for countryside policy and environmental protection in England. The Department for Culture, Media and Sport (DCMS) has responsibility for archaeology and the identification, recording and protection of the built heritage in England. The Scottish and Welsh Offices had broadly equivalent responsibilities until mid-1999, when they passed to the newly created Scottish Executive and National Assembly for Wales. The Northern Ireland Office also has broadly equivalent responsibilities. All these bodies delegate many of their conservation functions to the agencies described below. In addition, local authorities and many voluntary organisations are actively involved in environmental conservation and protection.

The Countryside and Wildlife

Countryside and Wildlife Agencies

The Countryside Agency has a duty both to promote the conservation and enhancement of the English countryside and to increase the opportunities for the public to enjoy it and promote economic and social development of rural areas. It was created in April 1999 by a merger of the Countryside Commission and part of the Rural Development Commission (founded by Lloyd George with his 'People's Budget' of 1909). It has a budget of nearly £50 million for 1999–2000. The Agency works with a range of partners in central and local government, and with the private and voluntary sectors. It will publish its long-term strategy and priorities in summer 2000, taking account of the Government's proposed Rural White Paper.

Various dates are put forward for the founding of the modern conservation movement in the UK. The years 1970-71 were undoubtedly an important milestone: in 1970 the word 'environment' first achieved government departmental status with the creation of the Department of the Environment, and in 1971 the voluntary organisations Friends of the Earth and Greenpeace were founded. However, the environment was already a matter of concern around the end of the 19th century—even if not the issue of social, economic and political importance that it is today. For example, the formation in 1877 of the Society for the Protection of Ancient Buildings was followed in 1889 by the founding of the Royal Society for the Protection of Birds, originally to protest against the wholesale killing of birds for their plumage. In 1895 the National Trust was formed to preserve places of historic interest and natural beauty, while 1908 saw the establishment of the Royal Commissions on historic monuments for England, Scotland and Wales, and in 1912 the Society for the Promotion of Nature Reserves was formed.

Scottish Natural Heritage (SNH) and the Countryside Council for Wales (CCW) have responsibilities in Scotland and Wales for landscape conservation and countryside recreation similar to those of the Countryside Agency in England and also for nature conservation. In Northern Ireland, the Environment and Heritage Service (EHS) protects and manages landscapes, habitats and species, and also has an environmental protection role.

English Nature, the CCW and SNH are responsible for providing advice to the Government and public information on nature conservation; for notifying land of special interest for its wildlife, geological and natural features; and for establishing National Nature Reserves. These three agencies operate through the Joint Nature Conservation Committee (JNCC) to fulfil their responsibilities for Great Britain as a whole and for international conservation matters. All of these agencies support and conduct their own environmental research.

The 'Countryside Survey 2000', which first began in 1978, has been developing a national audit of habitats and landscape features in Great Britain to mark the millennium; a similar survey has been undertaken in Northern Ireland. The results will show how the British countryside has changed over the past ten years and will be used to help assess whether policies for a sustainable countryside are working.

National Parks, Areas of Outstanding Natural Beauty and National Scenic Areas

The Countryside Agency and the CCW can designate National Parks and Areas of Outstanding Natural Beauty (AONBs), subject to confirmation by the Secretary of State for the Environment, Transport and the Regions and the National Assembly for Wales in their respective countries.

Ten National Parks have been established in England and Wales (see map at the beginning of the book). Their aims are to conserve and enhance their natural beauty, wildlife and cultural heritage, and to promote opportunities for the understanding and enjoyment by the public of the areas they cover. They are 'national' in the sense that they are of special value to the nation as a whole. However, most of the land remains in private hands. Each Park is administered by an independent National Park Authority.

The Norfolk and Suffolk Broads are also administered by their own independent authority and enjoy protection equivalent to that of a National Park. Since 1994 the planning policies that apply to the National Parks have applied also to the New Forest Heritage Area in Hampshire. (For general planning policy see chapter 21.)

A total of 41 AONBs have been designated in England and Wales. They comprise areas of national landscape quality, but the promotion of recreation is not an objective of their designation. The Government is considering advice from the Countryside Agency on strengthening the arrangements for managing

Table 20.1: National Parks and Other Designated Areas, 1998

	National Parks area (sq km)[a]	% of total area	Areas of Outstanding Natural Beauty (sq km)[b]	% of total area
England	9,934[c]	8[c]	20,393	16
Wales	4,129	20	832	4
Scotland	-	-	10,018	13
Northern Ireland	-	-	2,849	20

Sources: Countryside Agency, Countryside Council for Wales, Scottish Natural Heritage, Environment and Heritage Service (NI)
[a] One square kilometre = just over a third of a square mile.
[b] National Scenic Areas in Scotland.
[c] Including the Norfolk Broads.

and protecting AONBs, the South Downs and the New Forest.

In Scotland there are four regional parks and 40 National Scenic Areas (NSAs), together covering some 11,000 sq km (4,250 sq miles). In NSAs certain developments are subject to consultation with SNH and, in the event of a disagreement, with the Scottish Executive. Two areas of outstanding natural importance—the Cairngorms, and Loch Lomond and the Trossachs—will shortly become National Parks, subject to legislation by the Scottish Parliament (see p. 24).

In Northern Ireland the Council for Nature Conservation and the Countryside advises the Government on the preservation of amenities and the designation of AONBs. Nine such areas have been designated and two more (Erne Lakeland and Fermanagh Caveland) have been proposed for designation.

Forest and Country Parks

There are 17 forest parks in Great Britain, covering nearly 3,000 sq km (1,150 sq miles), which are administered by the Forestry Commission (see pp. 464–5). Northern Ireland has eight Forest Parks, three Forest Drives and over 40 minor forest sites, all administered by the Forest Service of the Department of Agriculture.

The Countryside Agency recognises over 200 country parks and more than 250 picnic sites in England. A further 35 country parks in Wales are recognised by the CCW, and there are also 36 country parks in Scotland.

Public Rights of Way and Open Country

County, metropolitan and unitary councils in England and Wales (see p. 62) are responsible for keeping public rights of way signposted and free from obstruction. Public paths are usually maintained by these 'highway authorities', which also supervise landowners' duties to repair stiles and gates. In Scotland planning authorities are responsible for asserting and protecting rights of way. Subject to public consultation, and, if necessary, a public inquiry, local authorities in Great Britain can create paths, close paths no longer needed for public use, and divert paths to meet the needs of either the public or landowners. Farmers in England and Wales are required by law to restore any cross-field public paths damaged or erased by agricultural operations. England has about 169,000 km (106,000 miles) of rights of way and Wales about 40,000 km (25,000 miles). In 1998 the Isle of Wight became the first local authority in England to achieve the National Target for rights of way, set in 1987, which required authorities to have all their public rights of way legally defined, properly maintained and well publicised before the millennium.

There are 13 approved National Trails open in England, stretching more than 3,000 km (nearly 2,000 miles), two in Wales covering about 510 km (320 miles), and three Long Distance Routes in Scotland, covering about 550 km (340 miles). The Cotswold Way was approved as a National Trail in 1998. A new National Trail following the route of Hadrian's Wall will be ready in 2002. In

Wales, Glyndŵr's Way (a roughly circular route in Powys), and in Scotland a new Great Glen Way, are at an advanced stage of planning.

Horseriding and cycling in the countryside are also encouraged, for example on the Pennine Bridleway (currently being extended) and the National Cycle Network (see p. 366). About 22% of the rights of way in England may be lawfully used by horseriders and cyclists.

In May 1999 the Ministry of Agriculture, Fisheries and Food (MAFF) published a series of new guides giving details of more than 1,500 farmland walks for the public created under its agri-environment schemes (see p. 455). The walks are listed in county-by-county registers, which are available free of charge from MAFF, libraries and tourist information offices; and on the Internet as a regularly updated Conservation Walks Register (www.countrywalks.org.uk).

Common land totals more than 550,000 hectares (1.4 million acres) in England and Wales. Only one-fifth of common land has a right of public access, although the open character of commons has made them popular for informal recreation. Four-fifths of common land is privately owned, but people other than the owner may have rights over it, for example, as pasture land. Commons are protected by law and ministerial consent is usually required to undertake works on them. There is no common land in Scotland or Northern Ireland.

There is currently no automatic right of public access to open country in England and Wales, where local authorities can secure access by means of agreements with landowners. If agreements cannot be reached, authorities may acquire land or make orders for public access. Similar powers cover Scotland and Northern Ireland; in Northern Ireland, the primary responsibility lies with district councils. In Scotland, there is a tradition of freedom to roam, based on tolerance between landowners and those seeking reasonable recreational access to the hills.

In March 1999, the Government announced its intention to introduce laws, as soon as parliamentary time allows, to give walkers a new right to explore the open countryside. The new statutory right of access would apply to mountain, moor, heath, down and registered common land (about 1.6 million hectares or 4 million acres), and may be extended to other types of open country such as some woodland. It would not apply to any developed land or agricultural land except that used for rough grazing. The right would be coupled with clear responsibilities for walkers to respect the rights of landowners and managers. New local access forums would bring together farmers, landowners and conservationists, to agree how improved access should be managed. The provisions for access to enclosed farmland under some agri-environment schemes, such as Environmentally Sensitive Areas (see p. 455), are also under review.

In Scotland, legislation is to be introduced into the first session of the Scottish Parliament to establish a statutory right of access, exercised responsibly, to all land and inland water for the purposes of informal recreation and passage.

The Countryside Agency is completing a programme to establish at least 250 new Millennium Greens in and on the edge of cities, towns, villages and hamlets across England to mark the year 2000. The programme has been aided by a £10 million Lottery grant from the Millennium Commission. By September 1999, 251 communities had been offered grants to help them prepare their plans, acquire their land and begin to create their local Millennium Green.

The Coast

Local planning authorities are responsible for planning land use at the coast; they also aim to safeguard and enhance the coast's natural attractions and preserve areas of scientific interest. The policy for the protection of the coastline against erosion and flooding is

Table 20.2: Areas in the UK Protected for their Wildlife, March 1999

Type of site[a]	Number of sites	Area (sq km)[b]
National Nature Reserves	376	2,184
Local Nature Reserves (Great Britain only)	689	428
Sites of Special Scientific Interest (SSSIs)(Great Britain only)	6,461	21,788
Areas of Special Scientific Interest (ASSIs)(Northern Ireland)	158	835
Statutory Marine Nature Reserves	3	194
Areas protected by international agreements		
Candidate Special Areas of Conservation (SACs)[c]	333	16,879
Special Protection Areas (SPAs)[c]	199	9,329
Ramsar sites[c]	137	6,491

Source: Joint Nature Conservation Committee
[a] Some sites may be included in more than one category.
[b] One square kilometre = 100 hectares (247 acres), or just over a third of a square mile.
[c] See p. 326.

administered by MAFF (for England), the National Assembly for Wales, the Scottish Executive and the Department of Agriculture for Northern Ireland. Operational responsibility lies with local authorities and the Environment Agency (see p. 330).

Certain stretches of undeveloped coast of particular beauty in England and Wales are defined as Heritage Coast. Jointly with local authorities, the countryside agencies have designated 45 Heritage Coasts, protecting 1,540 km (960 miles), about 35% of the total length of coastline.

The National Trust (see p. 329), through its Neptune Coastline Campaign, raises funds to acquire and protect stretches of coastline of great natural beauty and recreational value. About £32 million has been raised since 1965 and the Trust now protects around 940 km (600 miles) of coastline in England, Wales and Northern Ireland. The National Trust for Scotland owns large parts of the Scottish coastline and protects others through conservation agreements.

English Nature has supported 13 groups in developing and managing a variety of marine conservation initiatives. So far, 36 estuary management plans have been completed or are in preparation, covering 39 estuaries or 85% of England's total estuaries by area. (The Dee and Severn estuary plans were jointly funded with the CCW.) There are also 29 informal

marine consultation areas in Scotland. In addition, SNH has established the Focus on Firths initiative to co-ordinate management of the main Scottish estuaries. In Wales the CCW provides grant-in-aid to the Arfordir (or Coastal) Group, which is concerned with the sustainable management of the whole coast of Wales. Altogether there are 163 estuaries in the UK, representing about 30% of the North Sea and Atlantic seaboard of Western Europe. The UK also has about 75% of the European chalk coast.

Wildlife Protection

The UK has about 96,000 separate species, out of a global total of nearly 1.8 million. The principal legislation protecting wildlife in Great Britain is the Wildlife and Countryside Act 1981 (as amended). This extended the list of protected species; restricted the introduction into the countryside of animals not normally found in the wild in the UK; afforded greater protection for SSSIs (see p. 324) than previously; and made provision for Marine Nature Reserves.

The list of protected species is reviewed by the three statutory nature conservation agencies, acting jointly through the JNCC, every five years, when recommended changes can be submitted to the Government. In 1998

Population of Wild Birds, UK

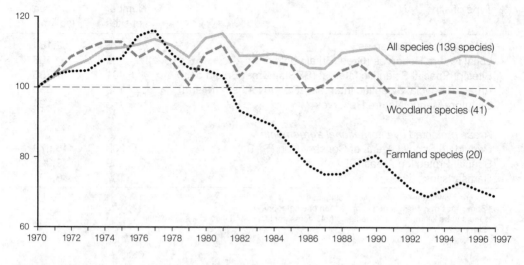

Source: Royal Society for the Protection of Birds, British Trust for Ornithology and Department of the Environment, Transport and the Regions

Note: Index: 1970 = 100

a further 28 species of flora and fauna were added to the list of protected species.

Farming practices are an important factor in environmental considerations, as agriculture dominates land use in Britain. Some of the UK's schemes which encourage environmentally beneficial farming practices are described in chapter 27 (pp. 455–6). MAFF is also developing a group of indicators of 'sustainable agriculture', in order to help monitor the impact of farming on the environment and the rural economy.

Sites of Special Scientific Interest (SSSIs)

By the end of July 1999, 6,474 SSSIs had been notified in Great Britain for their (often rare) plant, animal, geological or physiographical features. Some are of international importance and have been designated for protection under the European Commission (EC) Birds and Habitats Directives or the Ramsar Convention on Wetlands of International Importance. Most are privately owned.

English Nature, the CCW and SNH have powers to enter into land management agreements with owners and occupiers of SSSI land, where this is necessary, to safeguard the sites from damaging operations, and to support the management of their

natural features. The Northern Ireland Council for Nature Conservation and the Countryside advises the Government on nature conservation matters, including the establishment and management of land and marine nature reserves and the declaration of Areas of Special Scientific Interest.

Following public concern that the current legislation and practice affecting SSSIs does not provide adequate safeguards against neglect and damage (including damaging development), the Government is proposing to introduce reforms that would give them greater protection and improve their management. These reforms would include an obligation to take full consideration of environmental effects in planning policy, changing the rules for new road schemes, and employing more conservation officers to develop relationships with owners/occupiers of SSSIs and improve site management. Proposed legislation would also provide greater powers to prevent damage and counter neglect.

Wildlife Trusts (based on conurbations, counties or regions), the Royal Society for the Protection of Birds (RSPB) and the Scottish Wildlife Trust play an important part in protecting wildlife throughout the UK, and between them have established over 2,000 reserves. The Trusts are affiliated to a parent

Habitats: Recent Developments

- Hedgerows, which are vitally important corridors for wildlife on farmland, have been declining at the rate of about 4% a year, largely through removal. In March 1999 the Government announced that, as part of its drive to protect field boundaries, walls and hedges—of a length sufficient to surround the British Isles—are being built, renovated, replanted and maintained under the Countryside Stewardship scheme (see p. 455).

- World Wetlands Day, on 2 February 1999, marked the 28th anniversary of the Ramsar Convention on Wetlands of International Importance, especially as habitats for waterfowl. The UK had established 137 Ramsar sites covering 649,000 hectares (1.6 million acres) by early 1999.

- Between 1992 and 1997, over 4% of England's ancient meadows and grasslands were lost to development and changes in agricultural practices. The Meadowlands Partnership, which manages meadowland sites from Cornwall to the Isle of Arran, is supplying seed gathered from its meadows to farmers and developers to re-create grassland in areas under conservation or agri-environment schemes, and around roadsides and new developments.

- Ordnance Survey maps of 1880 recorded about 800,000 ponds— bigger than about 20 feet across—in England and Wales. Three-quarters of these have now disappeared, together with the wildlife that relies on them. In March 1999 the Ponds Conservation Trust, which has the backing of English Nature and the Environment Agency among others, launched an initiative to restore 2,000 sites in the next four years.

organisation, 'RSNC The Wildlife Trusts'. The RSPB is the largest voluntary wildlife conservation body in Europe, with just over 1 million members.

The Partnership for Action Against Wildlife Crime includes representatives of many statutory and voluntary bodies involved in enforcing wildlife controls. It provides a strategic overview of wildlife law enforcement issues. Wildlife crime takes many forms and has been increasing in recent years: for example, theft of eggs from birds of prey, illegal shooting, trapping, poisoning, digging up of wild plants, and the illicit trade in endangered species. DNA testing is playing an increasing role in combating crime of this kind, and there are now specialist wildlife officers in almost every police force in the UK.

The UK is a party to the Convention on International Trade in Endangered Species of Wild Fauna and Flora (CITES), which strictly regulates trade in endangered species by means of a permit system. The UK continues to play a leading role in CITES and since 1997 has been the Chair of the Standing Committee.

Species Recovery and Reintroduction

Extensive research and management are carried out, principally by the three nature conservation agencies, to encourage the recovery of populations of species threatened with extinction in the UK. Species recovery programmes form part of the UK's Biodiversity Action Plan (see p. 317). Individual Action Plans cover a large number of plants and animals in need of conservation action, including some which are close to extinction.

While some well-known species, such as the skylark and red squirrel, are still declining, others like the otter and red kite are recovering. In the past year, the rarest frog in the UK, the European pool frog, has been found in a suburban garden; the glutinous snail, believed to be extinct, has turned up in north Wales; and a rare fish, the allis shad, has been caught in the river Tamar, 121 years after it was last recorded in Cornwall.

The Royal Botanic Gardens at Kew (see p. 441) has been successful for many years with reintroduction projects. Its new Millennium Seed Bank will hold seeds of all 1,442 native UK wildflowers, plants and trees by the end of 1999, together with 10% of flowering plants from the arid regions of the world by 2010, and 25% by 2025. The Royal Botanic Garden in Edinburgh (see p. 441) promotes conservation programmes for rare plants in Scotland and for coniferous trees worldwide, maintaining genetically diverse populations in cultivation at many sites as pools for eventual reintroduction to the wild.

Tree Preservation and Planting

Tree Preservation Orders enable local authorities to protect trees and woodlands. Once a tree is protected, it is, in general, an offence to cut down or reshape it without permission. Courts can impose substantial fines for breaches of such orders. Where protected trees are felled in contravention of an order or are removed because they are dying, dead or dangerous, replacement trees must be planted. Local authorities have powers to enforce this.

Tree planting is encouraged through various grant schemes, including the Forestry Commission's Woodland Grant Scheme, and the planting of broadleaved trees has greatly increased since the 1980s. Major afforestation projects involving the DETR and the Countryside Agency include the creation of 12 Community Forests in and around major cities, covering 450,000 hectares (1.1 million acres). The aim of these forests is to increase woodland cover near the cities from 6.5% to about 30%; restore areas scarred by industrial dereliction; create sites for recreation, sport and environmental education; and form new habitats for wildlife. A separate National Forest is taking shape in the English Midlands (see p. 465), and the Central Scotland Forest is also being developed. In Wales the Amman Gwendraeth initiative is creating new woodlands in the Welsh valleys.

The Woodland Trust is a voluntary body which protects existing woods, and plants new areas of woodland. It owns woods across the UK covering about 17,000 hectares (42,000 acres) and, since it was founded in 1972, has planted over 2 million trees. It acquires woods at the rate of about one a week, and gained ownership of its 1,000th wood by the end of May 1999.

International Action

The UK's international obligations to conserve wildlife include membership of the World Conservation Union and of several international Conventions. Under the EC Habitats Directive, 333 sites in Britain have been put forward as candidate Special Areas of Conservation (SACs). Together with Special Protection Areas (SPAs), classified under the EC Wild Birds Directive, SACs will form a network of protected sites across the European Union (EU) known as Natura 2000. In March 1999 an area of Lewis in the Outer Hebrides, attractive to the threatened corncrake, became the 100th site in Scotland to be classified as an SPA.

The UK is party to the Ramsar Convention, whose objectives are to stem the progressive encroachment on, and loss of, wetlands, and to promote their wise use. In addition to the 137 Ramsar sites in the UK itself, there are ten sites in the British Overseas Territories: seven in Bermuda and one each in the British Virgin Islands, the Cayman Islands and the Turks and Caicos Islands. A further 30 sites have been identified as candidate Ramsar sites in the British Overseas Territories and two in the Crown Dependencies.

The Darwin Initiative forms part of the measures announced by the UK at the 1992 'Earth Summit' (see p. 311). It makes British experience, expertise and financial support available to developing countries with important biological resources, to help them with the conservation and sustainable use of their species. A committee of experts advises the Government on the Initiative, which receives funding of £3 million a year. Nearly 200 projects have been funded so far, and the latest round of 26 projects, announced in March 1999, includes: a research project to conserve western lowland gorillas in Gabon; a study of the conservation of coastal vegetation in Lebanon; and a pilot project to maintain a sustainable waste management plan for a hotel and village on a coral reef in Fiji.

Among other international projects supported financially by the UK in 1998–99 were:

- the 21st Century Tiger Initiative;
- the Global Tiger Forum;
- measures to conserve the African elephant;
- the Regional Seas Trust Fund to help protect the world's oceans;
- conservation of coral reefs in South Asia; and
- research into seahorse conservation.

The Environmental Know How Fund, an aim of which is to help the countries of Central and Eastern Europe improve their environment, has approved over 350 projects since 1992, with funding of £13 million. A further £8 million is planned for 1999–2000.

Buildings and Monuments

In England lists of buildings of special architectural or historic interest are compiled by DCMS with the advice of English Heritage.[1] In Scotland and Wales buildings are listed by Historic Scotland and Cadw: Welsh Historic Monuments. It is against the law to demolish, extend or alter the character of any 'listed' building without prior consent from the local planning authority or the appropriate Secretary of State, Scottish minister or National Assembly secretary in Wales. A local planning authority can issue a 'building preservation notice' to protect for six months an unlisted building which it considers to be of special architectural or historic interest and is at risk, while a decision is taken on whether it should be listed. In Northern Ireland historic buildings are listed by the Department of the Environment (DOENI) on the recommendation of the EHS

---

[1] In April 1999 English Heritage and the Royal Commission on Historical Monuments of England were administratively merged to form a single new organisation, called English Heritage, with lead responsibility for the built heritage in England.

following consultation with the advisory Historic Buildings Council (HBC).

Ancient monuments are protected through a system of scheduling. English Heritage is assessing all known archaeological sites in England, in order to identify which (out of some 600,000 sites) should be afforded statutory protection. Similar efforts are being made to identify buildings and ancient and historic monuments eligible for statutory protection in Scotland, Wales and Northern Ireland.

In England details of all listed buildings are contained in about 2,000 volumes which can be inspected at the English Heritage offices in Swindon (National Monuments Record Centre) and London. The lists for particular areas are also held by the relevant local planning authorities, where they are available for inspection, and at some public libraries. EHS's Monuments and Buildings Record in Belfast holds information on all historic monuments and buildings in Northern Ireland.

Photographs of all the historic listed buildings of England are to be put on the National Monuments Record's Images of England Internet website (www.imagesofengland.org.uk), with the help of a £3.1 million Millennium Festival grant. The website, which will be the largest free on-line picture library in the world, is due for completion in 2002. Among England's more unusual listed sites are 52 garden sheds, 499 pigsties, 277 lavatories, 2,221 telephone boxes, eight skating rinks and one racing pigeon loft.

English Heritage is responsible for the maintenance, repair and presentation of 409 historic properties in public ownership or guardianship, and gives grants for the repair of ancient monuments and historic buildings in England. Most of its properties are open to the public, and there were nearly 5.8 million visitors to its staffed properties alone in 1998–99. Government funding for English Heritage is £115 million in 1999–2000.

In Scotland and Wales, Historic Scotland, which cares for over 330 monuments, and

Table 20.3: Scheduled Monuments and Listed Buildings, Spring 1999

	Listed buildings	Scheduled monuments
England	368,321[a]	18,063[b]
Wales	22,308	3,155
Scotland	44,401	6,989
Northern Ireland	8,430	1,365

Sources: Department for Culture, Media and Sport, National Assembly for Wales, Scottish Executive, Environment and Heritage Service (NI).

[a] This is the number of list entries, some of which include more than one building. There are about 450,000 listed buildings in England.

[b] This is the number of scheduled entries, some of which cover more than one site. There are approximately 30,105 individual sites in England.

Cadw, with 130, perform similar functions. There were 3 million visitors to Historic Scotland's staffed properties in 1998–99. An Ancient Monuments Board and an HBC advise the Scottish Ministers. The DOENI has 182 historic monuments in its care, managed by the EHS (another 1,365 are scheduled). It is also advised by a Historic Monuments Council.

Local planning authorities have designated more than 9,000 'conservation areas' of special architectural or historic interest in England; there are 482 in Wales, 602 in Scotland and 53 in Northern Ireland. These areas receive additional protection through the planning system, particularly over the proposed demolition of unlisted buildings.

The National Heritage Memorial Fund helps towards the cost of acquiring, maintaining or preserving land, buildings, works of art and other items of outstanding interest which are of importance to the national heritage. The Fund is also used for distributing the heritage share of the proceeds from the National Lottery (see p. 121). By June 1999, over £1.3 billion had been awarded from the Heritage Lottery Fund for 2,834 projects.

Many of the royal palaces and parks are open to the public; their maintenance is the responsibility of the Secretary of State for Culture, Media and Sport, and Historic Scotland. Historic Royal Palaces and the Royal Parks Agency carry out this function on behalf of the Secretary of State in England.

In summer 1999 a Commission for Architecture and the Built Environment came into being. Its main remit is to promote the importance, benefit and understanding of high-quality architecture and urban design in villages, towns and cities, and to act as a 'national champion' for architecture.

Industrial, Transport and Maritime Heritage

As the first country in the world to industrialise on a large scale, the UK has a rich industrial heritage, including such sites as the Ironbridge Gorge, where Abraham Darby (1677–1717) first smelted iron using coke instead of charcoal (now a World Heritage Site—see p. 329). Many other museums devoted to the preservation of industrial buildings and equipment have been set up, such as the National Coal Mining Museum at the former Caphouse Colliery near Wakefield and the Carrickfergus Gasworks Museum.

Several industrial monuments in Scotland are in the care of the First Minister, including Bonawe Iron Furnace, the most complete charcoal-fuelled ironworks surviving in Britain; the working New Abbey Corn Mill; and Dallas Dhu Malt Whisky Distillery.

The UK pioneered railways, and has a fine heritage of railway buildings and structures. A large number of disused railway lines have been bought by railway preservation societies, and several railway museums have been established.

Reminders of the UK's maritime past are also preserved. Portsmouth is home to HMS *Victory* (Admiral Nelson's flagship), HMS *Warrior* (the world's first iron battleship, launched in 1860), and the remains of King Henry VIII's *Mary Rose*, the world's only surviving 16th-century warship.

A voluntary body, the Maritime Trust, preserves vessels and other maritime items of historic or technical interest. The Trust's vessels include the clipper *Cutty Sark* (launched in 1869) at Greenwich, in London. In all, about 400 historic ships are preserved in the UK, mostly in private hands.

World Heritage Sites

The UK has 17 sites in the World Heritage List, which was established under the 1972 World Heritage Convention to identify and secure lasting protection for sites of outstanding universal value:

- Canterbury Cathedral (begun in 1070), with St Augustine's Abbey and St Martin's Church, in Kent;
- Durham Cathedral (begun in 1093) and Castle;
- Studley Royal Gardens (18th century) and Fountains Abbey (founded in 1132), in North Yorkshire;
- Ironbridge Gorge, with the world's first iron bridge (1779) and other early industrial sites, in Shropshire;
- the prehistoric stone circles at Stonehenge and Avebury, in Wiltshire;
- Blenheim Palace (early 18th century), in Oxfordshire;
- the Palladian city of Bath, in north-east Somerset;
- Hadrian's Wall, the former Roman frontier in northern England;
- the Tower of London (begun in the 11th century);
- the Palace of Westminster, Westminster Abbey and St Margaret's, Westminster;
- Maritime Greenwich, also in London;
- the islands of St Kilda, in Scotland;
- Edinburgh Old and New Towns;
- the castles and town walls of King Edward I (1272–1307), in north Wales;
- the Giant's Causeway and Causeway Coast, in Northern Ireland; and
- two natural sites in the UK's Overseas Territories (see p. 77)—Gough Island (part of Tristan da Cunha) in the South Atlantic, and Henderson Island in the South Pacific.

The UK, which is seeking election in 1999 to become one of the 21 members of the World Heritage Committee, has nominated 25 new sites for World Heritage status, including two that will be formally nominated in 1999: Bleanavon Industrial Landscape in south Wales and the town of St George in Bermuda.

The Voluntary Sector

Voluntary organisations are well represented in conservation work (over 2,000 are involved with natural history and nature conservation alone). Although they are funded largely by subscription, private donations and entrance fees, many receive government support and grants, sometimes in recognition of statutory responsibilities that they perform.

The National Trust (for Places of Historic Interest or Natural Beauty), a charity with about 2.6 million members, owns and protects over 300 properties open to the public, in addition to 270,000 hectares (667,000 acres) of land in England, Wales and Northern Ireland. It looks after historic houses and gardens, ancient monuments and archaeological remains, forests, woods, fens, farmland, downs, moorland, islands, nature reserves and villages. The separate National Trust for Scotland owns 125 properties and 75,000 hectares (185,000 acres) of countryside.

Pollution Control

Administration

Executive responsibility for pollution control is divided between local authorities and central government agencies. The central administration makes policy, promotes legislation and advises pollution control authorities on policy implementation. In England, the Secretary of State for the Environment, Transport and the Regions has general responsibility for co-ordinating the work of the Government on pollution control. Similar responsibilities are exercised in Scotland by the Minister for Transport and the Environment, in Wales by the National Assembly Environment Secretary and in Northern Ireland by the DOENI.

Local authorities also have important duties and powers. They are responsible for:

- collection and disposal of domestic wastes;
- keeping the streets clear of litter;
- control of air pollution from domestic premises and, in England and Wales, from many industrial premises;
- review, assessment and management of local air quality; and
- noise and general nuisance abatement.

The Environment Agency for England and Wales and the Scottish Environment Protection Agency (SEPA) regulate the major pollution risks to air, water and land, and waste. In Northern Ireland, the EHS exercises similar functions.

There is an extensive framework of national and EC legislation on the manufacture, distribution, use and disposal of hazardous chemicals. New and existing chemicals placed on the market are subject to notification and assessment procedures under EC legislation. Pesticides, biocides and veterinary medicines are subject to mandatory approval procedures. International controls on the movement of hazardous waste were further strengthened under the Basel Convention in November 1998.

An independent standing body, the Royal Commission on Environmental Pollution, advises the Government. It has produced 21 reports so far on a variety of topics; the next, on energy and the environment, is due for completion by the end of 1999.

In 1999 the Environment Agency published league tables of the companies which had received the largest aggregate fines for pollution in the previous year. In all, the Agency conducted 744 prosecutions during 1998, but the largest fine so far—for £4.8 million (including legal costs)—was imposed in January 1999 on the Milford Haven Port Authority, following the Sea Empress oil spill in 1996 that temporarily devastated fishing, wildlife and tourism in west Wales.

Industrial Pollution Control

The Environmental Protection Act 1990 established two pollution control systems for Great Britain: Local Air Pollution Control (LAPC) and Integrated Pollution Control (IPC), which both take account of releases to air, land and water.

In England and Wales LAPC is operated by local authorities and IPC by the Environment Agency. In Scotland SEPA operates both IPC and LAPC. In Northern Ireland the EHS exercises broadly similar controls, and a system similar to IPC was introduced in 1998.

A new, but similar, Pollution Prevention and Control (PPC) regime, implementing an EC Directive on Integrated Pollution Prevention and Control (IPPC), is to be phased in during 2000–07, to succeed IPC and LAPC. Regulators will be required, by prior authorisation, to ensure minimum pollution from industry through use of best available techniques, subject to assessment of costs and benefits. Both systems require regulators to take account of the special characteristics of an installation and its local environment.

Under PPC, integrated authorisations will apply to a larger number of industrial activities. These include, for example, animal rendering, currently regulated under LAPC, as well as some, such as food and drink and intensive livestock, which hitherto have not been controlled. Regulators will also be required to take a wider range of environmental impacts (including noise, energy efficiency and site restoration) into account when issuing integrated permits. Those LAPC installations not covered by the IPPC Directive will continue to have emissions to air only regulated under PPC.

Installations will be phased into the new system on a sectoral basis. Regulators will, with some exceptions, continue to be responsible for those installations they currently regulate under IPC and LAPC.

Local authorities will therefore be responsible for some integrated permits. In Scotland SEPA will continue to regulate all installations falling within the regime.

In May 1999 the Environment Agency launched a Pollution Inventory, which provides details of emissions to air, water and land from processes regulated under IPC, and their contributions to national emission levels. An advisory committee, with representatives from industry, government, and non-governmental organisations such as Friends of the Earth, has been set up to help the Agency in the Inventory's development, including information about other processes it regulates, such as landfill and sewage treatment works.

Land, Waste and Litter

Soil quality in the UK is relatively good, but with some localised erosion and loss of soil, and areas of contamination, natural and man-made. The Government is preparing a draft soil strategy for England, to promote the sustainable use of soil and to raise public awareness of the importance of this. The UK's legacy of contaminated land results from an industrial age that generated wealth but also caused much pollution.

In most cases redevelopment is considered the best solution for contaminated land, which can be brought back into safe and beneficial use for new buildings and open spaces. Where current use causes a problem, local authorities and the Environment Agency have powers to take action. A new, strengthened, regulatory regime for dealing with contaminated land is to come into force in England early in 2000.

Local authorities in England and Wales are responsible for the collection and disposal of all household waste and some commercial waste. In two-tier areas district councils are responsible for waste collection and county councils for waste disposal, while in unitary areas the council has both roles. In Scotland local authorities carry out both roles and waste regulation rests with SEPA, while in Northern Ireland responsibility for waste regulation is being transferred from district councils to the DOENI.

The Environmental Protection Act 1990 and the Waste Management Licensing Regulations 1994 regulate waste management. Anyone who deposits, recovers or disposes of controlled waste must comply with the conditions of a waste management licence (or with the terms of an exemption from licensing), in a way that does not pollute the environment or harm human health. 'Controlled waste' means household, commercial or industrial waste, and those who produce, import, carry, keep, treat or dispose of it have a duty of care to ensure that it is properly managed, recovered and disposed of safely, and is transferred only to those authorised to receive it. 'Special' (hazardous) wastes are subject to additional controls related to their transport and movement. Policies on waste shipment into and out of the UK are under review.

Final disposal, generally through landfill, makes little practical use of waste. The Government is committed to reducing reliance on landfill and in 1999 increased the standard rate of landfill tax from £7 to £10 a tonne, with a further rise of £1 a tonne a year until at least 2004, to encourage less waste and more recycling. An EC Directive, which introduces progressive targets to reduce the amount of biodegradable municipal waste going to landfill and tightens EC landfill regulations, has been agreed.

In late 1999 the Government plans to publish a Waste Strategy for England and Wales, to show how waste will be managed during the next 20 years; the Scottish National Waste Strategy will also be published. Northern Ireland will have a separate strategy.

Recycling and Materials Reclamation

The reclamation and recycling of waste materials are encouraged whenever these are the best practicable environmental option. Local authorities are obliged to make plans for the recycling of waste. However, just 8% of municipal waste in England and Wales was recycled in 1997–98. The Government recognises that substantial increases in recycling, composting and energy recovery from waste (by incineration) are needed, and this will be incorporated in the new waste strategy for England and Wales.

Under the EC Directive on packaging and packaging waste, at least 50% of the UK's packaging waste must be recovered and at least 25% recycled by the year 2001. New regulations that came into force in 1998 in Great Britain and in 1999 in Northern Ireland stipulate that all packaging must be 'recoverable' through at least one of the following: recycling; incineration with energy recovery; or composting or biodegradation.

The general public can deposit used glass containers in bottle banks for recycling. In 1998 there were some 22,000 bottle bank sites in the UK and over 5,000 steel can banks. In 1996 there were over 9,000 can banks accepting aluminium cans and 700 cash-for-cans centres. A variety of other materials, such as textiles, paper and plastics, are also recycled. One of the Government's waste goals is for a third of household waste to be recycled by 2015. Another is that 30% of household waste should be recycled or composted by 2010.

Litter and Dog Fouling

It is a criminal offence to leave litter in any public place in the open air or to dump rubbish except in designated places. The maximum fine upon successful prosecution is £2,500. The optional litter fixed penalty fine, which discharges a person's liability to prosecution, is £25.

Local authorities have a duty to keep their public land free of litter and refuse, including dog faeces, as far as is practicable. Members of the public have powers to take action against authorities which fail to comply with their responsibilities. In England, Wales and Northern Ireland local authorities also have powers to make it an offence not to clear up after one's dog in specified places, and may issue a fixed penalty fine of £25 under the Dogs (Fouling of Land) Act 1996. In Scotland it is an offence to allow a dog to foul in specified places.

The Tidy Britain Group is the national agency for tackling litter, in collaboration with local authorities and the private sector. Its 1999 month-long National Spring Clean campaign involved 2.9 million people who collected 14,500 tonnes of litter.

The environment agencies, local authorities, police and the Tidy Britain Group have been monitoring the incidence of 'fly tipping' (illegal dumping of waste) since the introduction of the landfill tax (see p. 331). There has been an increase since 1994–95, but not as great as originally feared. The maximum penalty for fly tipping (and other offences relating to waste) is up to five years' imprisonment and/or an unlimited fine. The Environment Agency and SEPA provide a free 24-hour hotline in the UK (0800 807060) which the public can use to report incidents.

Water

In the UK 96% of the population live in properties connected to a sewer, and sewage treatment works serve over 80%. In England and Wales the water industry is planning an investment programme of some £7 billion during the period 2000 to 2005 for improvements to water quality. Progressively higher treatment standards for industrial waste effluents and new measures to combat pollution from agriculture are expected to bring further improvements in water quality.

In Scotland responsibility for the provision of all water and sewerage services lies with three Water Authorities, covering the north, east and west of the country. For details on the water supply industry and the Drinking Water Inspectorate, see pp. 503–5.

All discharges to water in the UK require the consent of the appropriate regulatory authority. In England and Wales the Environment Agency's principal method of controlling water pollution is through the regulation of all effluent discharges, including sewage, into controlled waters (groundwaters, inland and coastal waters). The Agency maintains public registers containing information about water quality, discharge consents, authorisations and monitoring. Applicants for consents to discharge have the right of appeal if they are dissatisfied with the Agency's decision; most of these appeals are dealt with by the Planning Inspectorate, an executive agency of the DETR. In Scotland control is the responsibility of SEPA, and

Rivers of good or fair quality, UK

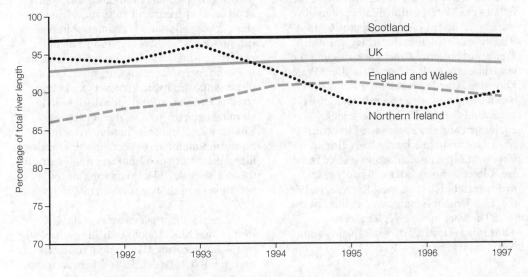

Source: Environment Agency, Scottish Environment Protection Agency, Environment and Heritage Service

appeals are dealt with by the Scottish Executive. In Northern Ireland the EHS is responsible for controlling water pollution.

The Environment Agency reported 17,863 substantiated water pollution incidents in 1998, of which 3,600 were industrial. The biggest polluter was the construction industry, with 625 incidents.

In 1997 and 1998 the Government introduced statutory Environmental Quality Standards for 33 substances in the aquatic environment, further implementing the EC Dangerous Substances Directive. The new regulations give legal force for the first time to environmental quality standards for certain dangerous substances under the Directive, including arsenic, atrazine and simazine. Among other chemicals causing concern are 'endocrine disrupters', which mimic hormones, and persistent organic pollutants (including some insecticides), on which the UK is playing a leading role to secure a global treaty by 2001. The Government intends to publish a White Paper on the control of chemicals in 1999.

There are 68 designated Nitrate Vulnerable Zones (NVZs) in England and Wales covering about 600,000 hectares (1.5 million acres), one in Scotland and three in Northern Ireland.

Their aim is to protect water against pollution caused by nitrates used in fertilisers for agriculture. Nitrates are essential for the normal functioning of a healthy ecosystem, but become pollutants if they are overabundant; they are now the most widespread pollutants in the western world. Since December 1998 (June 1999 in Northern Ireland) farmers in NVZs have been required to keep formal records of their use of fertilisers and organic manures so that the restrictions on nitrates leaching into rivers and groundwater can be monitored.

Bathing Waters and Coastal Sewage Discharges

The quality of UK bathing waters improved slightly during 1998, with 89% of waters meeting EC mandatory coliform bacteria standards, compared with 88% in 1997 and 66% in 1988. The water industry is investing around £2 billion to provide treatment of coastal sewage discharges and improve the quality of the UK's bathing waters. There are 117 schemes, covering 198 bathing zones, to improve sewage outfalls and overflow arrangements, of which 102 were ready for the 1999 bathing season.

A record 45 beaches in the UK were awarded Europe's 'Blue Flag' in 1998. This fell to 41 in 1999, but the number of marinas gaining the award rose from six to 26.[2] Blue Flag awards recognise the achievement of a number of objectives, including meeting the guideline standards of the EC Bathing Waters Directive as well as excellent water quality, beach cleanliness, dog control, wheelchair access and the provision of life-saving equipment and other facilities. However, according to surveys by the Tidy Britain Group and Beachwatch, many seaside resorts are still let down by litter and badly maintained beach lavatories. Even so, in 1999 the Tidy Britain Group gave Seaside Awards to 260 beaches in the UK, for meeting demanding standards of water quality and beach management.

Marine Environment

The Second London Oceans Workshop, in December 1998, emphasised that the two greatest problems facing the oceans are unsustainable exploitation of fisheries and land-based sources of marine pollution. The 1998 Ministerial Meeting of the OSPAR (Oslo-Paris) Convention—which covers inputs and discharges of harmful substances, from both land and sea, into the north-east Atlantic—reached agreement on several issues, including:

- the adoption of long-term strategies to protect ecosystems and biodiversity, and to guide work on hazardous substances, radioactive substances and eutrophication;[3]

- the end of the potential opt-out for France and the UK on the dumping of radioactive waste at sea; and

- a total ban on the dumping at sea of all steel installations (see p. 492).

---

[2] Out of a total of 1,822 beaches and 618 marinas in Europe as a whole.

[3] In which aquatic life in a nutrient-rich environment is killed by being deprived of oxygen as a result of the decomposition of a dense plant population.

The Maritime and Coastguard Agency (see p. 373) is responsible for dealing with spillages of oil or other hazardous substances from ships at sea. The various counter-pollution facilities for which it is responsible include: remote-sensing surveillance aircraft; aerial and seaborne spraying equipment; stocks of oil dispersants; mechanical recovery and cargo transfer equipment; and specialised beach cleaning equipment. The Agency has an Enforcement Unit at its headquarters in Southampton for apprehending ships making illegal discharges of oil and other pollutants off the British coast. The maximum fine for pollution from ships was raised to £250,000 in 1997.

Decisions about which areas of the UK Continental Shelf should be made available for petroleum licensing take account of advice from the JNCC (see p. 320). Where areas are made available for exploration and development, special conditions may be imposed on the licence holders to minimise or avoid any impact on the marine environment. These conditions are agreed with the JNCC.

The UK does not permit any deposit of waste in the sea where there is a safe land-based alternative unless it can be demonstrated that disposal at sea is the best practicable option. Under the OSPAR Convention, the Government is working towards achieving substantial reductions of radioactive discharges to near background values for naturally occurring substances and close to zero for artificial substances. Disposal of sewage sludge at sea ceased at the end of 1998. From 1999 the only types of waste that will routinely be considered for deposit in the sea will be dredged material from ports and harbours, and small quantities of fish waste.

Air

Air quality in the UK has improved in the past 40 years. However, although the dense smoke-laden fogs, or 'smogs', that afflicted London and other major cities in the 1950s and 1960s have entirely disappeared, new concerns have arisen, especially over emissions from the growing number of motor vehicles, which periodically produce 'summertime smogs' and 'wintertime smogs'. These can consist of elevated levels of sulphur dioxide (SO_2), nitrogen dioxide, ground-level ozone, airborne particles (particulate matter—PM_{10}) and other pollutants. Measures have consequently been adopted to reduce emissions from road vehicles (see below). Emissions of all the main air pollutants continued to decline in 1997.

Industrial processes with the greatest potential for producing harmful emissions are subject to IPC (see p. 330). Processes with a significant but lesser potential for air pollution require approval, in England and Wales from local authorities, in Scotland from SEPA and in Northern Ireland from the EHS. Local authorities also control emissions of black smoke from commercial and industrial premises, and implement smoke control areas to deal with emissions from domestic properties.

The UK National Air Quality Strategy, the first of its kind in Europe, was published in 1997 and sets out air quality objectives for the pollutants of main concern: nitrogen dioxide, PM_{10}, ground-level ozone, SO_2, carbon monoxide, lead, benzene and 1,3-butadiene. The target date for achieving the objectives is 2005. However, a rolling review is continually reassessing the Strategy in the light of new scientific evidence. The Government has indicated that some of the objectives will be made tougher and target dates brought forward. Local authorities have a duty to review and assess air quality in their areas and, if the Strategy's air quality objectives are unlikely to be achieved by 2005 with the measures they already have in place, to designate Air Quality Management Areas and produce remedial action plans.

The UK has an automatic air quality monitoring network with sites covering much of the country, in both urban and rural areas. In recent years, this network has undergone a rapid expansion, and it now has 108 sites. Daily Air Quality Bulletins make air pollution data from the monitoring network available to the public. These give the concentrations of the main pollutants, together with an air pollution forecast. The information features in television and radio weather reports, and appears in many national and local newspapers. Information, updated hourly

PM_{10} is among the most difficult pollutants to control. Day-to-day changes in PM_{10} concentrations have been associated with increases in hospital admissions and deaths brought forward, especially among the elderly and those with advanced heart and lung disease. The main sources of PM_{10} in the UK are road traffic, other air pollutants such as SO_2 and nitrogen dioxide, and suspended soils, dusts and sea salt.

from the automatic monitoring sites, is also available directly on a free telephone number (0800 556677), on videotext systems and on the Internet on the UK's National Air Quality Archive website (www.environment.detr.gov.uk/airq.aqinfo.htm).

Vehicle Emissions

All new petrol-engined passenger cars in the UK must be fitted with catalytic converters, which typically reduce emissions by over 75%. Three EC Directives agreed during the UK Presidency in 1998, and which will come into force from January 2000, will further improve emissions from passenger cars and light commercial vehicles. The European Commission has set further standards for both car emissions and fuel quality, to be introduced in 2005.

In December 1998 European environment ministers reached agreement to cut pollution from lorries and buses by 60%. As well as reductions in oxides of nitrogen, hydrocarbons and carbon monoxide, this involves cutting emissions of particulate matter by 30% by 2000 and by 86% by 2005. Lorries and buses are responsible for 55% of particulate transport emissions (and 39% of oxides of nitrogen). The use of new 'particulate traps' will remove most of the smallest particles, which pose the greatest health risk.

Compulsory tests of emissions from vehicles in use are a key element in the UK's strategy for improving air quality. Metered emission tests and smoke checks feature in the

Emissions of Air Pollutants, UK, 1970–97

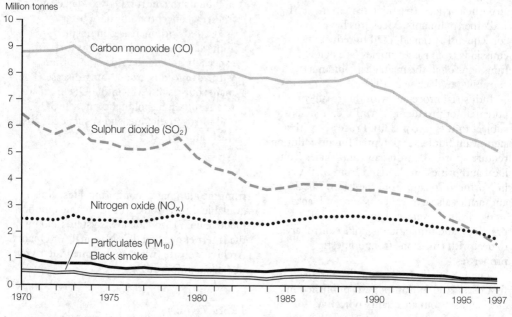

Million tonnes

Source: National Environmental Technology Centre (NETCEN)

annual 'MoT' roadworthiness test (see p. 364). Enforcement checks carried out at the roadside or in operators' premises also include a check for excessive smoke. The Vehicle Inspectorate (see p. 364) carried out 96,342 roadside emissions checks in 1998–99 (on cars, coaches, lorries, buses and taxis) and 149,641 roadworthiness checks. Under a trial scheme introduced in 1997, seven local authorities were given powers to enforce vehicle exhaust emissions standards by random testing at the roadside, with a £60 fixed penalty fine for offenders causing avoidable pollution.

The Cleaner Vehicles Task Force is creating a partnership between government and the private sector to promote the development and marketing of environmentally friendly vehicles (and fuels). At the same time, the Government's Foresight Vehicle programme is promoting R&D in cleaner vehicle technology (such as electric, hybrid and fuel cell technologies), while its Powershift programme aims to establish a market for vehicles that use alternative fuels, such as compressed natural gas and liquefied petroleum gas. By December 1998 Powershift

had helped to secure over £20 million worth of orders for alternatively powered vehicles, including 64 electric ones. For tax incentives to encourage the use of cleaner fuels and smaller cars, see p. 410.

Sales of unleaded petrol have risen from virtually nothing in the mid-1980s to almost 79% of all petrol sold in 1998. In line with an EC Directive, leaded petrol in the UK will be withdrawn from general sale on 1 January 2000. Urban levels of lead have already fallen to 0.2 micrograms per cubic metre at most—that is, below the maximum level recommended for health reasons.

Climate Change

Several gases naturally present in the atmosphere keep the Earth at a temperature suitable for life by trapping energy from the sun—the 'greenhouse' effect. Emissions from human activities are increasing the atmospheric concentrations of several important greenhouse gases, which in turn are increasing the greenhouse effect and leading to global warming and climate change. Easily the most significant greenhouse gas in the UK is

Carbon Dioxide Emissions by End User, UK

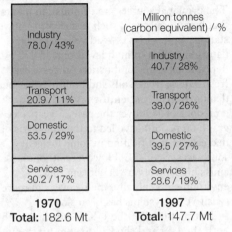

Million tonnes (carbon equivalent) / %

1970
Total: 182.6 Mt

Million tonnes (carbon equivalent) / %

1997
Total: 147.7 Mt

Source: National Environmental Technology Centre

Note: Emissions of carbon dioxide (CO_2) from transport have doubled in the past 30 years, while there has been a marked decline in industrial emissions over the same period.

carbon dioxide (CO_2—see charts above), followed by methane and nitrous oxide. Some other greenhouse gases, such as hydrofluorocarbons (HFCs), have high global warming potential but comparatively low levels of emission, although these have been rising.

Globally, 1998 was the hottest year since instrument records began in 1860, and six out of the last ten years have been the hottest on record. Research at the Hadley Centre, part of the Meteorological Office, is focused on improving climate predictions and investigating the cause of recent climate change. Results from its latest climate model suggest that, with current levels of increase in greenhouse gases, the global mean sea level will rise about 20 cm by the 2050s, and there will be a rise in average global temperature of up to 3°C over the next 100 years.

It is becoming increasingly important to understand and predict the possible *impacts* of climate change on the natural environment and society, so that adaptation measures can be planned. The Government has set up the UK Climate Impacts Programme to allow detailed assessments of the impacts to be made, both at UK and regional levels. In

Britain there may be more droughts in the south and east, more flooding in the north and west, more damage as a result of storm surges, threats to the coast and low-lying agricultural land, and changes in wildlife and habitats.

International action on climate change dates from the 'Earth Summit' in Rio in 1992 (see p. 312), where the Framework Convention on Climate Change called for the stabilisation of greenhouse gas concentrations in the atmosphere at a level which would prevent dangerous man-made interference with the climate system. The UK is on course to meet its Convention commitment to return greenhouse gas emissions to 1990 levels by the year 2000. Emissions of CO_2 fell by 8%, and the 'basket' of six gases by 9%, between 1990 and 1997. This achievement is the result of the UK's first Climate Change Programme, published in 1994.

At the third Conference of the Parties to the Framework Convention, held in Kyoto (Japan) in 1997, developed countries agreed legally binding targets to reduce emissions of the six main greenhouse gases: CO_2, methane, nitrous oxide, HFCs, perfluorocarbons (PFCs) and sulphur hexafluoride. The Protocol committed developed nations to a 5.2% reduction in greenhouse gas emissions below 1990 levels by 2008–12. The EU agreed to a collective reduction target of 8%.

In 1998 the EU decided how its 8% should be shared out among member states. The individual country targets range from a reduction of 28% for Luxembourg to a permitted increase of 27% for Portugal. The UK's target is a reduction of 12.5%, but the Government is committed to moving beyond that towards a domestic goal of reducing CO_2 emissions to 20% below 1990 levels by the year 2010.

Having consulted widely on the policy options for meeting Britain's Kyoto target and moving towards the domestic goal, the Government aims to publish a draft Climate Change Programme in late 1999 for further consultation, and a new programme in 2000.

Stratospheric Ozone Layer

Stratospheric ozone forms a layer of gas about 10 km to 50 km (6 to 30 miles) above the

Earth's surface, protecting it from the more harmful effects of solar radiation. British scientists first discovered ozone losses over much of the globe, including a 'hole' in the ozone layer over Antarctica, in 1985. Ozone depletion is caused by man-made chemicals containing chlorine or bromine, such as chlorofluorocarbons (CFCs) or halons, which have been used in aerosol sprays, refrigerators and fire extinguishers.

The 1987 Montreal Protocol deals with the protection of the stratospheric ozone layer and has been signed by over 160 countries. The parties to the Protocol meet annually, and major reviews every two to three years progressively tighten the controls on ozone-depleting substances. The UK is meeting its obligations under both the Montreal Protocol and subsequent EC Regulations which go beyond the Protocol. For example, consumption of CFCs was phased out in the UK and EU by the end of 1994, one year ahead of the Protocol, although it is still allowed for a small number of essential uses, such as asthma inhalers.

Developing countries have until 2010 to phase out CFC consumption. A multilateral fund has been established to help them comply with controls on ozone-depleting substances; the UK contributes towards this.

The Protocol has also placed controls on hydrochlorofluorocarbons (HCFCs), which are transitional substances with much lower ozone-depleting potential than CFCs. They are needed in a number of areas to allow industry to stop using CFCs more quickly, but are to be phased out by 2030 in developed countries. The EU has introduced even tighter controls on HCFCs, requiring their consumption to be phased out by 2015. Methyl bromide, a pesticide, is also covered by the Protocol; its production and consumption must be phased out by 2005 in developed countries and by 2015 in developing countries.

The growing amount of ozone-depleting substances in the stratosphere is still cause for concern. However, provided that all countries meet their obligations under the Montreal Protocol, the ozone layer, though continuing to suffer damage over the next few years, is expected to recover gradually.

Emissions of Sulphur Dioxide and Oxides of Nitrogen

SO_2 and oxides of nitrogen (NO_x) are the main gases whose emissions lead to acid rain. The principal sources are combustion plants that burn fossil fuels, such as coal-fired power stations and, for NO_x, road vehicles. The damaging effect of high levels of acid depositions from combustion processes on freshwaters, trees, soils and buildings has been demonstrated by scientific research. Lower emissions of SO_2 over the past 25 years (see graph on p. 336) have led to the first signs of a decrease in acidification in some lochs in south-west Scotland. However, although emission controls are benefiting the environment generally, the recovery of more sensitive ecosystems has been slow.

Internationally, the UK is working with both the UN and the EU to step up the fight against acid rain. Britain's ratification of the Second Sulphur Protocol of the UN's Convention on Long Range Transboundary Pollution commits it to an 80% reduction of its 1980 sulphur emissions by 2010. (By the end of 1997 it was 16% ahead of the intermediate target of a 50% reduction by 2000.) The UK is currently involved in the development of further international agreements aimed at combating acidification, eutrophication and ground-level ozone. The proposed EC National Emission Ceilings Directive and the UN Multi-Pollutant Multi-Effect Protocol aim to set national emission ceilings for 2010 for SO_2, NO_x, ammonia and volatile organic compounds.

Noise

Local authorities have a duty to inspect their areas for 'statutory nuisances', including noise nuisance from premises and vehicles, machinery or equipment in the street. They must take reasonable steps to investigate complaints, and serve a noise abatement notice where it is judged to be a statutory nuisance. They can also designate noise abatement zones, within which registered levels of noise from certain premises may not be increased without their permission. There are specific provisions in law to control noise from construction and demolition sites; to control the use of loudspeakers in the streets; and to enable individuals to take independent action through the courts against noise nuisance.

The Noise Act 1996 has strengthened the law in England, Wales and Northern Ireland on action that can be taken against noisy neighbours. For example, it clarifies the procedures under which local authorities can confiscate noise-making equipment, and provides powers to make night noise treatable as a separate offence. In addition, the Housing Act 1996 has given local authorities new powers to deal with anti-social behaviour by tenants, including noise.

Compensation may be payable for loss in property values caused by physical factors, including noise from new or improved public works such as roads, railways and airports. Highway authorities are required to make grants available for the insulation of homes when they are subject to specified levels of increased noise caused by new or improved roads. Equivalent regulations exist for railways.

In England and Wales new noise mitigation measures for trunk roads were introduced in March 1999, including quieter surfaces for new roads, an annual £5 million budget to address problems on particularly noisy existing trunk roads, and maintenance resurfacing using new materials. A £700,000 research programme funded by the DETR and supported by industry is aimed at reducing the noise generated by vehicle tyres in rolling over the road surface. (One use for old vehicle tyres, which are themselves difficult to dispose of satisfactorily, is to recycle them in granulated form for road and playground surfaces.)

Under international agreements, noisier subsonic jet aircraft are due to be phased out by 2002. Already around 85% of UK-registered jets are the quieter 'Chapter 3' types. Various operational restrictions, including at night, aim to reduce noise disturbance at the UK's major airports. The Government has commissioned research on the non-auditory health effects of aircraft noise.

Every city in the EU with more than 250,000 inhabitants may be required to draw up a 'noise map' of its streets by 2002, in response to a forthcoming European Commission proposal for a Directive on limiting pollution. According to the Commission, about 80 million people in the EU currently 'suffer unacceptable levels of continuous outdoor transport noise'.

Radioactivity

Man-made radiation represents about 15% of what the population is exposed to; most occurs naturally. A large proportion of the exposure to man-made radiation comes from medical uses, such as X-rays. This and other man-made radiation is subject to stringent control. Users of radioactive materials must be registered by the Environment Agency in England and Wales and its equivalents in Scotland and Northern Ireland. Authorisation is also required for the accumulation and disposal of radioactive waste. The Health and Safety Executive (HSE—see p. 162) is responsible for regulating safety at civil nuclear installations. No such installation may be constructed or operated without a licence granted by the HSE.

International Commitments

Having already signed it, the UK is preparing to ratify and implement the International Joint Convention on the Safety of Spent Fuel Management and on the Safety of Radioactive Waste Management. In 1998 members of the OSPAR Convention, including the UK, agreed to reduce radioactive discharges by 2000 to levels whereby the additional concentrations of radioactive substances in the marine environment are close to zero (see p. 334).

Radon

In 1987 the first measures were announced to deal with the problem, in certain parts of the country, of radon, a naturally occurring radioactive gas which can accumulate in houses and which accounts for half of the total average population radiation dose. Long-term exposure to the gas can increase the risk of lung cancer. In 1998–99 the Government completed its programme of offering free measurement of radon to all households in Radon Affected Areas, and is now working with local authorities to encourage building works that reduce radon levels in homes.

Radioactive Waste Disposal

Currently all radioactive waste in the UK is either disposed of safely in suitable facilities on land or stored pending such disposal. The UK has not disposed of any solid radioactive waste at sea since 1982.

The disposal of such waste is regulated by law. Radioactive wastes vary widely in nature and level of activity, and the methods of disposal reflect this. Most solid *low-level waste*, material of low radioactivity, is disposed of at the shallow disposal facility at Drigg in Cumbria. Some small quantities of very low-level waste are disposed of at authorised landfill sites. *Intermediate-level waste* is stored at nuclear licensed sites, usually those sites where it is generated. Most of the UK's inventory is at Sellafield in Cumbria. *High-level or heat-generating waste* is stored in either raw (liquid) or vitrified (glasslike) form. Once vitrified it will be stored for at least 50 years to allow it to cool to a safe temperature for disposal.

In spring 1999 the House of Lords Select Committee on Science and Technology published a report on the management of nuclear waste. It recommended that underground disposal facilities for solid radioactive waste sites should be built in geologically stable areas of the UK, but that waste should be retrievable if necessary. The Committee also recommended that an authoritative Commission should be set up to oversee implementation of policy and to co-ordinate research, and that a disposal company should be set up to design, construct, operate, and monitor and eventually close underground repositories. The roles of Nirex—the company set up by the nuclear industry with agreement of government to dispose of intermediate and some low-level waste—should be subsumed by the new organisations, and the Government's Radioactive Waste Management Advisory Committee should be disbanded when the Commission is set up. A two-year study to identify the research strategy needed to make progress with the disposal of high-level waste and spent fuel is due to publish its findings. The Government plans to publish a consultation paper early in 2000 on the options for the future management of radioactive waste.

Environmental Research

Several government departments—such as the DETR, MAFF, the Department of Health and the Scottish Executive—have substantial environmental research programmes. In 1999–2000 the DETR will commission about 140 research contracts with a total value of £19 million. An increasingly important area is research into the environmental effects of genetically modified crops and micro-organisms (see pp. 438 and 450).

Among the other organisations that carry out environmental research are the Meteorological Office (including the Hadley Centre); the Environment Agency, whose R&D grant-in-aid for 1999–2000 is £10.6 million; the Natural Resources Institute of the University of Greenwich at Chatham (Kent); and the Climatic Research Unit at the University of East Anglia. Nearly 100 British universities and colleges run courses on environmental studies or natural resource management; many also carry out research. In addition to research funded directly by SEPA and the EHS, the Scottish and Northern Ireland Forum for Environmental Research also commissions research.

Most of the government-funded Research Councils (see pp. 436–9) have a role in environmental science research, but the Natural Environment Research Council (NERC) is particularly important. It has a Science Budget allocation of £176 million for 1999–2000, and about £44 million from other sources. The NERC undertakes and supports research and monitoring in the environmental sciences (both life science and physical science) and funds postgraduate training. Its programmes cover five main issues: biodiversity; environmental risks and hazards; global change; natural resource management; and pollution and waste.

British zoos play an important part in the conservation of endangered species and the promotion of biodiversity through public education, research and breeding programmes.

Further Reading

DETR Annual Report 1999: The Government's Expenditure Plans 1999–2000 to 2001–02. The Stationery Office, 1999.

Digest of Environmental Statistics, No. 20. Annual report. The Stationery Office, 1998. (The 1999 edition will be available only on DETR's website.)

The Scottish Environment Statistics, No. 6, 1998. The Stationery Office, 1998

Websites

Department of the Environment, Transport and the Regions: www.environment.detr.gov.uk

Countryside Agency: www.countryside.gov.uk

Countryside Council for Wales: www.ccw.gov.uk

English Nature: www.english–nature.org.uk

Environment Agency for England and Wales: www.environment-agency.gov.uk

Scottish Environment Protection Agency: www.sepa.org.uk

Scottish Natural Heritage: www.snh.org.uk

21 Planning, Housing and Regeneration

As the United Kingdom is a relatively densely populated country, there are considerable pressures on the use of land to accommodate the rising population and the demands of a growing economy. The Government aims to create a fair and efficient land-use planning system that respects regional differences and promotes sustainable, high-quality development.

The number of dwellings in the UK was estimated at 24.9 million in 1998. Preliminary projections suggest that the number of households in England will rise from 20.2 million in 1996 to 24.0 million in 2021. The Government is seeking to encourage the use of brownfield sites, particularly in inner cities, to promote urban regeneration, thereby minimising the use of greenfield land for housing development and preserving the countryside as far as possible.

PLANNING

Land-use planning is the direct responsibility of local authorities in Great Britain. The Secretary of State for the Environment, Transport and the Regions has overall responsibility for the operation of the system in England. In Wales, since 1 July 1999, it has come under the control of the National Assembly for Wales, while in Scotland, planning was wholly devolved to the Scottish Parliament from the same date. In Northern Ireland, the Planning Service, an executive agency within the Department of the Environment (DOENI), is responsible for the implementation of the Government's policies for town and country planning in consultation with district councils.

In England the Department of the Environment, Transport and the Regions (DETR) issues national planning policy guidance on housing, transport, retail development, sport and recreation facilities, minerals and waste, and across planning as a whole. Working with the Government Offices for the Regions (GOs), it ensures that regional planning guidance and local authorities' development plans and decisions on planning applications are consistent with national policies. The Planning Inspectorate, an

executive agency acting on behalf of the
Secretary of State for the Environment,
Transport and the Regions in England and the
National Assembly for Wales, is responsible
for determining, and in some cases reporting
on, all planning and enforcement appeals and
holding inquiries into development plans. It
also deals with planning-related casework,
compulsory purchase orders and cases arising
from the Environmental Protection and Water
Acts. In 1998–99, 13,200 planning appeal cases
were determined. Regional planning guidance
(RPG) in England encourages individual local
authorities to co-operate regionally on issues
such as housing, transport, air quality, energy
and waste. It also complements the economic
strategies of the Regional Development
Agencies (see p. 11). A new planning policy
guidance note will introduce arrangements
bringing greater openness to the preparation of
RPG and increasing regional responsibility of
both the issues and their resolution. In general,
the responsibility for regional planning is
shifting from central government to local and
regional bodies.

In Wales, local planning authorities are
responsible for the day-to-day operation of the
planning system, including the determination
of planning applications and the preparation of
development plans. The National Assembly
for Wales works with, regulates and guides
local planning authorities in undertaking their
functions so as to achieve a proper balance
between the needs of conservation and
development, in a way which is consistent
with the principle of sustainable development.
Similar planning procedures operate in
Scotland. In Northern Ireland the Planning
Service is responsible for issuing planning
policy guidance across planning as a whole,
the determination of planning applications and
the preparation of development plans.

Development Plans

Development plans have a central role in
shaping patterns of change in an area, as
planning decisions must be made in
accordance with the development plan unless
'material considerations' indicate otherwise.

All local planning authorities in England
must prepare development plans in line with

Tough new planning guidance on opencast
coal mining in England came into force
from April 1999. This will ensure that
planning permission for new opencast coal
mining is only given where it is
environmentally acceptable or provides
overriding local benefits.

the Town and Country Planning Act 1990.
Structure plans, produced by county councils
and unitary authorities (often on a joint basis),
set out broad strategic policies for the
development and use of land, and are in place
in all areas where they are required. Unitary
development plans (produced in the main by
London boroughs and metropolitan districts)
and area-wide local plans (produced by
districts and most unitary authorities) set out
more detailed land-use policies. At the end of
1998, 67% of these plans were in place, with a
target of 83% in place by the end of 1999 and
100% coverage being reached after 2000. The
DETR scrutinises all plans, with the aim of
ensuring that local plans do not conflict with
national policies and regional guidance, unless
justified by local circumstances, and that they
contain clear and effective policies. The plans
provide the main means of reconciling the
need to make adequate provision for
development with the need to protect the
environment.

In Wales, the National Assembly for Wales
requires local planning authorities to prepare
and maintain up-to-date and relevant
development plans. Authorities should have
unitary development plans in place by the end
of the year 2000. In Scotland, land-use planning
has been wholly devolved to the Scottish
Parliament. In the meantime, the emphasis is on
modernising the planning system: the Planning
Audit Unit has been examining how authorities
handle planning applications with a view to
improving performance and disseminating good
practice advice. In Northern Ireland, a
Development Plan Programme was put in place
in 1998 by the Planning Service. This
programme is reviewed and rolled forward
annually, and is designed to meet the
development planning needs of all districts.

Brownfield Land

Local councils in England will in future have to consider reusing brownfield (that is, previously developed) land as the first option for housing development. A revised version of the Government's *Planning Policy Guidance note 3: Housing*, published in March 1999, emphasises the importance of making the best use of previously developed urban land and existing buildings, in order to achieve a national target to raise the percentage of new homes built on previously developed land to 60%. This will minimise the use of greenfield sites, encourage urban regeneration and help create more sustainable patterns of development. The Guidance advises developers and local authorities to place the needs of people before cars in designing the layout of residential developments. If redeveloping sites is not possible, the next most sustainable option is to extend urban areas, making use of existing infrastructure and public transport links.

New statistics of changes in land use in England were published in December 1998. These show that, in 1996, 53% of new dwellings were built on previously developed land, compared with 49% in 1994. The Government has established the framework of a National Land Use Database which will provide a consistent assessment of vacant previously developed land that may be available for housing or other developments. Preliminary results from the database, published in May 1999, show an estimate of 33,000 hectares of previously developed vacant and derelict land in total. Some 4,800 hectares of this land was allocated in local plans or had planning permission for housing, about 4,500 hectares for mixed use and around 13,400 hectares for other uses. In total, just over 12,000 hectares of vacant and derelict land either had planning permission, were allocated in the local plan for housing or were judged suitable for housing.

Not all greenfield development will be rejected; some will be necessary to accommodate housing growth. Where this is so, the Government again prefers extending existing urban areas—and redrawing Green Belts (see below) in exceptional circumstances—to new settlements, such as those proposed at Grazeley in Berkshire, Micheldever in Hampshire and Broadclyst in Devon. Builders will no longer be allowed to develop homes at very low densities of up to 20 or 25 dwellings per hectare, as in some of the recent large-scale developments, for example, Milton Keynes. However, the Guidance says that there will be no return to the tower blocks built in the 1960s and 1970s, and instead suggests a preference for terraced houses with gardens, and town houses that use communal open space, with a new maximum standard for car parking, possibly 1½ to 2 spaces per dwelling.

Green Belts

Green Belts are areas of land intended to be left open and protected from inappropriate development. They aim to check the sprawl of large built-up areas, safeguard surrounding countryside from encroachment, prevent neighbouring towns from merging, preserve the special character of historic towns, and assist in urban regeneration by encouraging the reuse of derelict and other urban land. The first major Green Belt established was around the fringes of Greater London, under the London and Home Counties Green Belt Act 1938.

Green Belts have been established around other major cities and conurbations, including Glasgow, Edinburgh, Aberdeen, Greater Manchester, Merseyside, and the West Midlands, as well as several smaller towns. In England, some 1.5 million hectares (3.8 million acres) have been designated as Green Belt, while in Scotland there are six Green Belt areas, totalling 156,600 hectares. There are no Green Belts at present in Wales, but creation of some is under consideration. Great importance is attached to the protection of Green Belts, and development on them is only allowed in exceptional circumstances.

Development Control

Most development requires specific planning permission. Applications are dealt with on the basis of development plans and other relevant planning considerations. In 1997–98, in England, there were some 462,000 district planning authority applications determined out of a total of 505,000 applications received, of which 62% were decided within eight weeks (the target being 80%). In Scotland, around 42,000 applications are received each year, of which about 65% are determined within two months. There is a target of 80% of cases called in to be decided within two months, and the remainder within three months. In Northern Ireland, some 20,000 planning applications were received in 1998–99 and 18,500 decisions made. Targets set are for 70% of minor and major applications to be taken to district council consultation within eight weeks.

Applicants have a right of appeal to the Secretary of State in England, the National Assembly for Wales and Scottish ministers in Scotland if a local authority refuses planning permission, grants it with conditions attached, or fails to decide an application within eight weeks or, in Scotland, two months. Occasionally the appropriate minister can 'call in' an application for their own determination. A small number of cases end up as public inquiries. Some categories of planning application have to be notified to the appropriate ministerial authority in certain circumstances; for example, those involving a significant departure from the approved development plan. In Scotland, the determination of the majority of planning appeals is delegated to the Scottish Executive Inquiry Reporters Unit, which is responsible for organising public local inquiries into planning proposals and related matters. In Northern Ireland, appeals are determined by the Planning Appeals Commission, which is also responsible for holding public local inquiries.

Unnecessarily long planning inquiries that last for months or even years, such as that for the fifth terminal at London's Heathrow Airport, could end under government proposals put forward in a consultation paper issued in May 1999. The purpose of the proposals is to achieve significant improvements in the time taken to handle major projects, while continuing to ensure that adequate opportunity is given for people to have a say, test the evidence and reach a sound decision. The package of proposals is designed to deliver significant savings by streamlining the procedures for handling major projects and speeding the decision-making process, so reducing delay, costs and uncertainty for those involved and securing more quickly the benefits of approved projects.

Planning applications for certain types of development must be accompanied by an 'environmental statement', which should describe the likely environmental effects and measures to minimise any adverse ones. Planning authorities must consider the environmental statement, and any representations received, before granting planning permission.

The Architects Registration Board, together with the architects' professional bodies, exercises control over standards in architectural training, and encourages high standards in the profession. The Royal Town Planning Institute carries out similar functions for the planning profession.

HOUSING

The Government's objective for housing is to offer everyone the opportunity of a decent home and so promote social cohesion, well-being and self-dependence. The Government is making available nearly £5 billion extra for investment in housing over the life of this Parliament. In England and Northern Ireland it is the responsibility of the Secretaries of State for the Environment, Transport and the Regions and for Northern Ireland to determine housing policy and supervise the housing programme. Responsibility for housing in Wales and Scotland has now passed, respectively, to the new National Assembly for Wales and to the Scottish Parliament. In Great Britain, the Government works closely with local authorities (which are responsible for preparing local housing strategies) and with the private and voluntary sectors. In England, the DETR also works with the Housing Corporation, which regulates registered social landlords (RSLs—see p. 351) and provides financial support to help them supply affordable housing. In Northern Ireland, the DOENI has overall responsibility for housing policy and works closely with the Northern Ireland Housing Executive (NIHE) on its implementation in the public sector. The NIHE is the single housing authority in the Province.

A new initiative to help raise the quality of homes in England was launched in February 1999. Housing Quality Indicators will allow designers to 'score' housing schemes in aspects such as internal and external layout, space standards, construction and energy efficiency. After construction the ratings can be checked. The Indicators will initially be used to evaluate new publicly funded housing schemes, and the Housing Corporation has recommended that all RSLs use them. The DETR will carry out trials on new and existing stock in both the public and private sectors, to assess the Indicators' potential for use across the whole of the housing sector.

Housing Stock and Housebuilding

At the end of 1998 there was a stock of 20.8 million dwellings in England, 1.26 million in Wales and 596,000 in Northern Ireland. In Scotland, there were estimated to be 2.27 million dwellings in 1997. Estimated housing completions in Great Britain during 1998 at 168,900 were 7% lower than in 1997. Around 86% of new dwellings are constructed by the private sector for sale to owner-occupiers. Owner-occupied homes represented about 67% of all dwellings at the end of 1997; rented homes from local authorities and New Town development corporations 17%; those rented privately or with a job or business 11%; and those rented from registered social landlords 5%.

The number of households in England is projected to increase from 20.2 million in 1996 to 24.0 million in 2021, a slightly lower increase than in the previous forecast. Although the numbers of households in all regions are projected to grow, the size of the increase varies across England. It ranges from around 25% in the South East, East of England and the South West to under 10% in the North East.

In England there were an estimated 753,200 vacant dwellings at 1 April 1998:

- 623,200 were in the private sector, many of which represent transitional vacancies (properties lying vacant for a short period as part of the normal buying and selling process);
- 81,700 were council homes, 49,500 of which were properties available for letting immediately, or after minor repairs;
- 29,400 were in the RSL sector; and
- 19,000 were elsewhere within the public sector, the majority of these being owned by central government (Ministry of Defence and other departments).

In Scotland, the Empty Homes Initiative received a £15 million boost in November 1998, bringing total investment to £24 million from 1997–98 to 2001–02. The extra money will help councils develop vacant homes as affordable housing for those who need it most.

Home Ownership

At the end of 1997, the number of owner-occupied dwellings in the UK was 16.7 million, 67% of all dwellings. In England, the highest areas of owner occupation at the end of 1998 were in the South East at 74.7%, followed by the South West at 72.8%, while the East Midlands at 54.9% and Greater London at 56.1% were the lowest. The percentage of owner occupation for Wales and Northern Ireland were 71.5% and 71.4% respectively. In Scotland, where owner occupation has traditionally been lower, the figure reached 60.2% by the end of 1997. Owner-occupiers may own their properties outright, but many are in the process of paying off a mortgage loan to a bank or building society.

'Right to buy' (see p. 348)—introduced in 1980—has been the main route into owner-occupation for former public sector tenants. By the end of 1998, some 2.3 million council, housing association and New Town development corporation houses had been sold into owner-occupation in Great Britain, and sales are currently around 60,000 a year.

Tenure Change in England, 1914–96

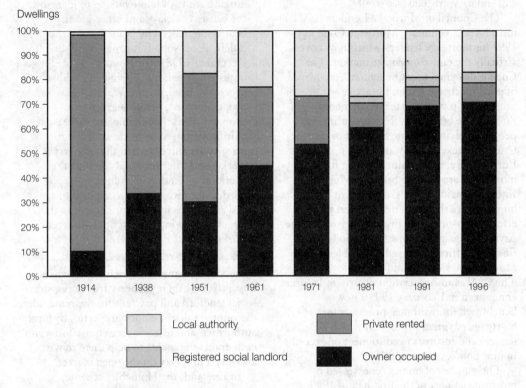

Dwellings

Local authority

Private rented

Registered social landlord

Owner occupied

Source: *English House Condition Survey, 1996*

Mortgage Loans

A feature of home ownership in the UK is the relatively high proportion of homes owned with a mortgage. Most people buy their homes with a mortgage loan, using the property as security. These are obtained mainly through banks and building societies, as well as from insurance companies, other financial institutions and local authorities. Some companies offer low-interest loans to their employees.

There are two main types of mortgage: a repayment mortgage, where the borrower's monthly payment covers the interest repayment and a contribution towards repaying the capital, so that the loan will be paid off at the end of the mortgage period; and an interest-only mortgage, under which the payment covers the interest charge and a contribution towards a fund which builds up with the aim of achieving a lump sum

sufficient to repay the loan in full at the end of the mortgage period. Most funds are endowments, linked to an insurance policy, but a growing number of funds go into other investments, such as a personal pension or ISAs (individual savings accounts), which succeeded PEPs from April 1999 (see p. 518).

In the second quarter of 1999, interest-only mortgages accounted for 52.5% of new mortgages taken out in the UK, and repayment mortgages 46%, according to the Council of Mortgage Lenders. Endowment mortgages have recently become less popular with borrowers because of falling interest rates and the possibility that policies may not grow fast enough to repay the capital borrowed.

The amount that mortgage lenders are prepared to advance to potential house purchasers is usually calculated as a multiple of their annual income, typically up to three times their earnings, usually over a term of 25 years. Owner-occupiers have been able to claim tax relief on interest payments on the first £30,000 of their mortgages on their main home, but this will end in April 2000 (see p. 407).

The Council of Mortgage Lenders (CML) introduced a voluntary Mortgage Code in 1997 for mortgage lenders which now covers virtually the entire mortgage market. The Code is designed to set benchmark standards of good mortgage lending practice. At present, help with mortgage payments through the benefits system is confined to people receiving Income Support or income-based Jobseeker's Allowance (see p. 175). Furthermore, most claimants wait for nine months before Income Support Mortgage Interest is paid. In the Government's view, home buyers therefore need better, more effective, insurance to protect their mortgage payments against unforeseen periods of financial difficulty caused by problems such as accidents, sickness and unemployment. The CML and Association of British Insurers announced in February 1999 a new benchmark for insurance products for mortgage payment protection which all lenders and insurers need to meet or exceed in new policies from July 1999.

The number of homes repossessed by mortgage lenders in the first half of 1999, according to the CML, was 16,410, 5% lower than in the same period a year earlier.

Right to Buy and Low-cost Ownership

With few exceptions, public tenants across the UK with secure tenancies (see p. 352) of at least two years' standing are entitled to buy their house or flat at a discount, dependent upon the length of their tenancy, under the Right to Buy scheme. New regional discount limits on the sale of property under this scheme were introduced in England in February 1999. They are based on 70% of the average local authority prices in each region (65% in London, where pressure on social housing is currently greatest), rounded up to the nearest £2,000. The limits range from £22,000 in the North East to £38,000 in London and the South East. These limits replaced the previous discount of up to £50,000 across the country.

Other schemes which aim to increase low-cost home ownership include shared

> The Government has carried out a wide-ranging study of home buying to identify the causes of delays and other problems being experienced by home buyers and sellers. A consultation paper was issued in December 1998 setting out proposals for improving the home buying and selling process in England and Wales. A key proposal is that, before marketing a property, the seller should assemble a pack of information to be made available to prospective buyers when the property is marketed. Other proposals include the adoption by lenders of voluntary targets for dealing with mortgage applications, and adherence by local authorities to the target of replying to searches within ten working days.

ownership schemes, in which homeowners buy a share of their property from a registered social landlord and pay rent for the remainder, discounted sales of empty properties by local authorities, and interest-free equity loans and cash grants to tenants to help them move out and buy a property on the open market.

In England, the Homebuy scheme, introduced in April 1999, helps tenants of RSLs and local authorities, or those selected from the council waiting list, living in areas with a shortage of social housing to buy a home on the open market. Homebuy offers qualifying tenants an interest-free equity loan to meet 25% of the cost of buying a home of their own. Local authorities may continue to fund the Do-it-Yourself Shared Ownership scheme (DIYSO) for at least another two years where this makes a useful contribution to their housing strategies. DIYSO allows local authority and RSL tenants living in areas with a shortage of social housing to buy a home on the open market on shared ownership terms with an RSL. Local authorities can also offer grants to local authority tenants to assist them to move out and buy a home. The level of grant varies between local authorities.

In Wales, local authorities and housing associations operate a low-cost home ownership scheme allowing purchasers to buy a home for 70% of its value, the balance being

Average House Prices, UK, 1985–98

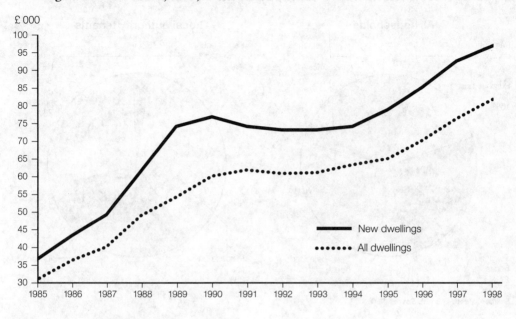

£ 000

Source: *Housing and Construction Statistics*

secured as a charge on the property. Scottish Homes (see p. 351) operates a scheme to encourage private developers to build for owner-occupation in areas they would not normally consider. The Northern Ireland Co-ownership Housing Association administers the 'buy half-rent half' (shared ownership) scheme operating in the Province.

Rented Sector

At the end of 1997, over 21% of all homes were rented to tenants by the public sector and non-profit-making bodies (such as housing associations). The highest level was in Scotland, with 33% of homes. Together with the Irish Republic and the Netherlands, the UK has one of the smallest privately rented sectors in the European Union (10.4% of homes), with Greater London at 17.3% at the end of 1997 the highest in the UK.

Privately Rented Housing

The Government wants to see a healthy private rented sector. Assured and assured-shorthold tenancies enable landlords to charge a reasonable market rent and recover possession of their property when they need to. The Housing Act 1996 introduced measures to encourage small landlords in England and Wales to let property, by reducing paperwork for letting on an assured-shorthold tenancy and by speeding up action on rent arrears. A 'Rent a Room' scheme enables homeowners to let rooms to lodgers without having to pay tax on rents up to a level of about £80 a week.

From 1 February 1999, increases in fair rents in England were limited by linking them to the Retail Prices Index. This is expected to bring relief to thousands of tenants, many of them elderly and on fixed incomes, with regulated tenancies starting before January 1989. Some of these tenants had been facing excessive increases as a result of recent court cases.

Plans have also been announced by the Government to tackle the problems of some private tenants in getting back their rent deposits at the end of their tenancies. Organisations representing landlords and tenants have been invited to set up a voluntary self-financing scheme to ensure that tenants' deposits are held safely and also to provide an

Type of Accommodation Occupied, Great Britain, 1996

All households

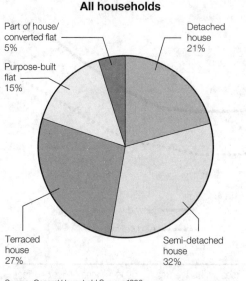

Part of house/converted flat 5%

Detached house 21%

Purpose-built flat 15%

Terraced house 27%

Semi-detached house 32%

Local authority tenants

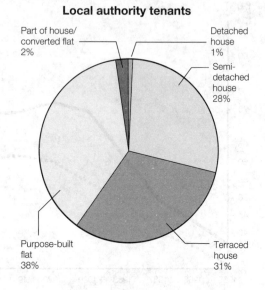

Part of house/converted flat 2%

Detached house 1%

Semi-detached house 28%

Purpose-built flat 38%

Terraced house 31%

Source: *General Household Survey, 1996*

There are about 900,000 leaseholders of houses in England and Wales and more than 1 million leaseholders of flats. The Government wishes to improve security of tenure and other conditions for leaseholders. Proposals, contained in a consultation paper issued in 1998, include making it easier for leaseholders of flats to join together to buy the freehold; a new right to manage their block of flats for people who do not want to buy; a range of options for improving management standards and controlling the activities of property managers; and options to tackle landlords who use the threat of forfeiture proceedings to intimidate leaseholders into paying unreasonable charges. The Government also plans to introduce a new form of tenure for flats—commonhold— which enables individual flat owners in a block to own and manage the whole building collectively from the outset.

independent arbitration scheme to deal with disputes.

A consultation paper on proposals for a national Houses in Multiple Occupation (HMO) licensing scheme was issued in February 1999. This, with related legislative changes, will strengthen local authorities' powers to ensure acceptable standards in HMOs, where the worst housing conditions are often found.

Social Housing

The Government supports partnership between the public sector, RSLs, such as housing associations, and the private sector as providers of good quality social housing— housing provided at rents affordable to people on low incomes, usually below market prices and with rent rises tending to be in line with inflation.

Public Housing

Most social housing in Great Britain is provided by local housing authorities—the structure of local authorities is outlined on pp. 62–4. Public housing in Scotland is also provided by Scottish Homes, which currently has a stock of 15,000 homes. However, it is in the process of transferring its houses to alternative landlords, such as housing associations. In Northern Ireland, the NIHE is responsible for the assessment of the need for, and arranging for the supply of, social housing and, in 1998–99, it managed just over 134,000 houses. Since 1996 an increasing amount of social housing has been provided by Registered Housing Associations.

Public housing authorities in England own about 4.5 million houses and flats. Around 90 authorities have transferred all or part of their stock to RSLs, involving the transfer of more than 360,000 properties by mid-1999 and raising over £6 billion in private finance.

Local authorities meet the capital costs of modernising their housing stock from central government grants, their own resources, including receipts, and from borrowing. Local authorities commonly borrow from the Public Works Loan Board—an independent statutory body—and private sector financial bodies.

Local authorities in England have been allocated £1.4 billion in 1999–2000 to help meet housing and housing-related regeneration needs through the Housing Investment Programme (£838 million) and the Capital Receipts Initiative (£570 million). This money provides additional resources to improve existing council houses, to fund private sector renovation grants and to support the building or acquisition of homes by RSLs. Local authorities in Wales and Scotland are receiving net capital allocations (including the Capital Receipts Initiative) for 1999–2000 amounting to £201 million and £155 million respectively. The NIHE's capital programme is financed mainly by borrowing from government and receipts from house sales; in 1999–2000 borrowing will total £16 million. Revenue expenditure is funded from rental income and by a government grant, which in 1999–2000 is about £159 million.

Housing revenue accounts are kept separate from other council funds. The Government grants English and Welsh local authorities Housing Revenue Account Subsidy, planned at £3.5 billion in England and £172 million in Wales in 1999–2000. In Scotland, Housing

Support Grant of £13 million and £274 million grant-in-aid to Scottish Homes are planned for 1999–2000.

In Scotland, the Government has committed a further £278 million to its New Housing partnerships initiative. This, together with private sector investment, is expected to provide 5,000 new homes, improve 2,500 more and support around 9,000 jobs. Forty-five new partnership projects will receive assistance, including development, regeneration and transfer partnerships. The latter could result in 25% of council houses transferring to community ownership by 2002, leading to increased investment in improvement and repairs programmes.

Registered Social Landlords

Registered Social Landlords are the major providers of new subsidised homes for those in housing need. They own and manage 1.135 million self-contained units in England, including 169,000 units of sheltered accommodation and 29,000 units of supported housing. They are diverse bodies, ranging from small almshouses to very large housing associations managing many thousands of homes. They also include large-scale voluntary transfer and local housing companies, set up to own and manage council houses transferred out of the local authority sector.

RSLs are non-profit-making bodies run by voluntary committees and over 2,200 are registered with the Housing Corporation, a non-departmental public body responsible for funding and regulating RSLs in England. The Corporation ensures RSLs provide their tenants with substantial rights and a good quality of service. It provides public funding to help RSLs supply affordable homes for rent and for sale, and to support the management and service costs of schemes for tenants with special needs (for example, for frail older people and tenants with learning difficulties).

Since 1988, 92 local authorities in England have transferred all or part of their housing stock to new RSLs, with the support of the tenants and the approval of the Secretary of State for the Environment, Transport and the Regions. The transfers, involving over

350,000 dwellings, have generated more than £3 billion in capital receipts, and raised over £6 billion of private finance to spend on improvements. In 1999–2000 over 130,000 local authority dwellings are expected to be transferred to new landlords.

The Government has extended the permissible powers of RSLs in England and Wales to allow them to play a full part in bringing new life to their communities. They will still focus the majority of their work on providing housing to tenants, but they are now able to provide services and amenities to people who are not resident in RSL property, as long as some of their tenants benefit. They can also engage in wider social regeneration activities such as the New Deal for Communities (see p. 356).

Similar arrangements apply in Wales with the National Assembly's Housing Department, in Scotland with Scottish Homes and in Northern Ireland with housing associations under the strategic direction of the NIHE. RSL schemes can also be funded by local authority resources.

Northern Ireland's 40 Registered Housing Associations which build for rent, plan to start 2,200 new homes in 1999–2000 and to spend £70 million which includes £3.6 million on the Northern Ireland Co-Ownership Housing Association. Housing association schemes are expected to attract some £40 million in private finance in 1999–2000.

Tenants' Rights

Local authority tenants in England, Wales and Scotland have security of tenure and other statutory rights, which are set out in the Council Tenant's Charter. In addition to the right to buy, these include the right to have certain urgent repairs done quickly at no cost to themselves and the right to be reimbursed for any improvements which they have financed should they move home. Tenants must be kept closely involved in the process of letting tenders to manage council estates. They also have the right to take over their estates through tenant management organisations. Some 150 are operational and another 100 are in the process of development. Tenants of RSLs enjoy similar rights to those of local authority tenants. These are set out in the Secure Tenant's Charter and the Assured Tenant's Charter, produced by the Housing Corporation.

A government consultation paper, published in January 1999, proposes to give council tenants in England and Wales a central role in the planning, management and delivery of housing services through new Tenant Participation Compacts. Under these proposals, local housing authorities will have to negotiate by April 2000 council-wide and neighbourhood-level agreements with their tenants. The Compacts will set out clearly how tenants will be involved collectively in shaping local decisions on housing issues. Councils will also have to provide training and support for tenants, so that they can fully take up their role. The Compacts will be based on a national framework which, for the first time, sets national core standards for tenant participation. A similar consultation exercise has already been carried out in Scotland and a National Strategy on Tenant Participation was launched in March 1999.

Housing for Older People

Sheltered housing provides specialised facilities for older people, such as common and laundry rooms, alarm systems and resident or non-resident warden support. Increased emphasis is being placed on schemes to help the elderly continue to live in their own homes by, for example, adapting their present homes to meet particular needs. In England, 184 home improvement agencies assist elderly and disabled people and those on low incomes to carry out repairs and improvements to their properties. Government funding for this work has been raised to £6.6 million for 1999–2000 to 2001–02. Under the three-year matched funding scheme, local authorities are required to give similar financial support. Similar schemes operate in Scotland and Wales.

In the longer term, support services for older people, such as those provided in sheltered housing and by home improvement agencies, will be funded through new arrangements for local housing and social services authorities to jointly commission support services. The proposals for these arrangements were set out in a consultation document in December 1998.

Rural Housing

If a clear need exists for low-cost housing in rural areas, local authorities can permit housing in localities where development would normally not be allowed, as long as the new housing can be reserved to meet that need. The Housing Corporation finances a special rural programme to build houses in villages with a population of 3,000 or less; funding for the building of 16,000 such homes has been approved since 1989–90. The National Assembly for Wales Housing Department has an extensive programme devoted to rural areas, and in Scotland considerable progress is being made through a range of initiatives as part of the Scottish Homes Rural Strategy. A rural strategy is also operated by the NIHE.

Improving Existing Housing

Slum clearance and large-scale redevelopment used to be major features of housing policy in urban areas of the UK. Recently there has been a trend towards the modernisation and conversion of sub-standard homes in order to help maintain existing communities. Housing conditions have improved considerably, but problems remain in some areas where there are concentrations of dwellings requiring substantial repairs. In some cases, however, clearance may still be the most satisfactory course of action. To help overcome objections to clearance, local authorities can pay a discretionary relocation grant to those displaced to enable them to buy at least a part share in a new home in the same area. In Great Britain, about 6,300 dwellings were demolished or closed in 1997.

Social Housing

Rundown estates are being improved through the Single Regeneration Budget Challenge Fund (see p. 355), which encourages local partnerships in England to tackle social and economic problems, including housing improvements. The Estates Renewal Challenge Fund, set up in 1995 with the aim of regenerating some of the remaining big, rundown local authority estates by facilitating their transfer to RSLs, enables private finance to be raised to help meet some of the costs. In all, £525 million is being spent by 24 local authorities on 39 transfer schemes involving over 44,000 homes. The third, and final, round of funding was announced in 1998.

Housing Action Trusts (HATs), non-departmental public bodies, took over some of the worst local authority housing estates between 1991 and 1994, in London (Stonebridge, Tower Hamlets and Waltham Forest), Birmingham (Castle Vale), Liverpool and North Hull. With £650 million of public expenditure to date, they have provided more than 2,400 new and 2,500 renovated homes, trained over 8,000 residents and helped over 5,000 people into jobs. The North Hull eight-year programme was completed in March 1999. A further £445 million is planned to be spent on the remaining HATs programme.

In Wales, Estate Partnership was set up to assist local authorities in tackling the worst problems on local authority housing estates by co-ordinating efforts to raise the quality of the housing stock, along with social and environmental improvements. Options include transferring ownership to the private sector. A total of £6.5 million is forecast to be spent in 1999–2000 by central government, to supplement local authority and private sector contributions.

Private Housing

The Government offers assistance through house renovation grants to owners of private housing who are on low incomes and unable to afford necessary repairs and improvements. Specific help is available to disabled people needing adaptations to their homes. Grants may provide up to 100% support to the poorest homeowners for essential repairs and improvements. In addition, in Scotland there is a grant scheme called the Warm Deal to improve home energy efficiency, under which grants of £500 are available to eligible households for measures to reduce fuel bills or provide more warmth for the same cost. Scottish local authorities award grants for improvement and repair. Scottish Homes also has the power to provide grants to complement the role of local authorities in private house renewal. In Northern Ireland, funding is allocated through the house renovation grants scheme, administered by the NIHE, on a similar basis to that in England and Wales. In rural areas, financial assistance to replace isolated dwellings which cannot be restored is also on offer.

Homelessness

Local authorities have legal duties to provide housing assistance for families and vulnerable people who are eligible for assistance, unintentionally homeless and in priority need. The priority need group includes households with dependent children or containing a pregnant woman; people who are vulnerable as a result of old age, mental or physical illness or disability or other special reason; and people who are homeless in an emergency. The Government introduced new regulations in 1997 to ensure that people assisted under homelessness legislation will receive reasonable preference in the allocation of social tenancies from the local authority housing register. In Scotland, a new code of guidance on homelessness was issued in 1997. Northern Ireland policy on homelessness broadly follows that in England and Wales and is reviewed taking account of any changes to policies or legislation there.

In 1998–99, local authorities in England made a total of 245,480 decisions on applications for housing from households eligible under the homelessness provisions of the 1985 and 1996 Housing Acts. They accepted more than 105,470 households as meeting the conditions of eligibility for assistance. Of these acceptances, 27% arose because parents, relatives or friends were no longer able, or willing, to accommodate the household, and 24% were because of the breakdown of a relationship with a partner. In 1997–98 it is estimated that some 43,118 households were assessed as homeless or potentially homeless in Scotland, of which over a quarter (12,665) were in Glasgow. In 1998–99, 4,997 households were accepted by the NIHE as being in need of priority housing.

The Government aims to reduce the number of people sleeping rough on the streets in England by two-thirds between 1999

and 2002. Funding is now through the Homelessness Action Programme, which replaced the original Rough Sleepers Initiative[1] in April 1999.

In London, the London Rough Sleepers Unit, established in April 1999, has a budget of £145 million over the three years to March 2002. Almost £39 million of capital and associated revenue funding has been allocated to 26 housing associations. This will provide almost 500 units of move-on accommodation, new hostel places and the refurbishment or replacement of more than 200 places in existing hostels. The funding will also provide support services to ensure that former rough sleepers do not subsequently lose their accommodation. Outside London, a total of £34 million has been allocated to voluntary organisations over three years from April 1999 to help tackle and prevent rough sleeping. From September 1999, responsibility for reducing rough sleeping across England has been integrated within the Rough Sleepers Unit.

A scheme, Safe in the City, to prevent youth homelessness, is operating in eight London boroughs. The total cost of the project is £11.8 million, partly funded by a £6 million Single Regeneration Budget grant, and partly by private sector sponsorship. The Index of Homelessness Risk, published by Safe in the City in March 1999, has been developed as a method for identifying young people likely to become homeless, so they can be helped at an early stage.

In Wales, £1.1 million has been allocated in 1999–2000 to support voluntary organisations, of which £785,000, in partnership with local authorities, will help alleviate rough sleeping. Provision in Scottish Executive expenditure on homeless initiatives over a three-year period from 1997–98 to 1999–2000 was £16 million under the Rough Sleepers Initiative, and £804,000 under grants to voluntary bodies.

Under the Housing Act 1996, local authorities have a duty to secure the provision

---

[1] Originally established in 1990 in Central London, where the problem of sleeping rough on the streets has been especially acute; the Initiative was later extended to 27 other areas.

of advice to prevent homelessness. Housing associations and other voluntary bodies supply such advice and undertake a number of other roles, for example advising people about their rights under housing law or encouraging energy efficiency in the home.

REGENERATION

The main objective of regeneration policy is to enhance economic development and social cohesion by effective regional action and integrated local regeneration programmes. These programmes work through partnership between the public and private sectors and involve a substantial contribution from the latter. They support and complement other programmes tackling social and economic decline, and initiatives such as Welfare-to-Work (see p. 154), health action zones (see p. 189), employment zones (see p. 155) and the work of the Cabinet Office Social Exclusion Unit (see p. 117).

The Government is adopting a more coherent approach to regional economic development and planning, and intends to improve regional accountability. Devolution has taken place in Scotland and Wales from July 1999 (see chapters 4 and 5) and eight Regional Development Agencies (RDAs) in the English regions outside London were established in 1999, with a ninth planned for London in 2000. The RDAs have taken over rural regeneration programmes from the Rural Development Commission, regional regeneration programmes from English Partnerships, and the administration of the Single Regeneration Budget (formerly SRB Challenge Fund) from the Government Offices for the Regions (GOs—see p. 9). They will also be responsible for co-ordinating inward investment in their own regions. The nine GOs work in partnership with local people to maximise competitiveness, prosperity and quality of life in each region.

Rundown areas in the UK benefit from EU Structural Funds (see p. 395), notably the European Regional Development Fund (ERDF), which assists a wide variety of projects in the least prosperous urban and rural areas of the European Union. Its objectives include promoting the development of regions lagging behind the rest of the EU (*Objective 1*), and redeveloping regions that are seriously affected by industrial decline (*Objective 2*).

England

The Secretary of State for the Environment, Transport and the Regions has overall responsibility for the Single Regeneration Budget (SRB) and the New Deal for Communities (NDC).

The SRB provides resources to support regeneration initiatives in England carried out by local regeneration partnerships. It is an important instrument in the Government's drive to tackle social exclusion and promote equality. In 1998 the Government announced resources of £2.4 billion for SRB over the three years 1999–2000 to 2001–02. Around 80% of additional resources of £770 million will be targeted on the most deprived local authority areas of England, with the balance being used to tackle pockets of deprivation elsewhere, including rural areas and former coalfield areas. Since 1 April 1999, SRB has been administered by RDAs in all regions except London, where the Government Office will continue to administer until the transfer to the Greater London Authority in April 2000, subject to legislation.

Regeneration partnerships, consisting of key local organisations including the voluntary sector, can bid for SRB resources to support regeneration. There have been five annual 'bidding rounds'. In July 1999, the Government announced details of successful bids under the fifth round; 163 schemes were approved worth over £1 billion in SRB support over their lifetime of up to seven years. These aim to attract over £2.4 billion in other public and private investment. This is on top of over 600 schemes under the first four rounds which already stand to receive over £3.4 billion of SRB money over the lifetime of up to seven years.

Key outputs forecast for the fifth SRB round include 156,000 people trained; jobs for over 65,000 target area residents; and over 1.3 million people to benefit from community safety initiatives. This is in addition to projected results from the first four rounds, which envisage the creation or safeguarding of 670,000 jobs, with over 650,000 people trained and obtaining qualifications; over 83,000 business start-ups; 330,000 dwellings built or improved; and 53,000 voluntary groups supported.

> About £800 million is planned to be spent by the private sector on redeveloping the Birmingham city centre Bull Ring shopping area and so revitalising the eastern side of the city centre. The eight-year plan should create an additional 5,000 retailing jobs and will be the biggest retail regeneration project in Europe. Alongside the shops will be an indoor market, restaurants and leisure facilities. It will be twice the size of the Lakeside out-of-town shopping centre in Essex.

Some of the country's poorest neighbourhoods will get help through the NDC. Over the next three years £800 million will be available to help tackle the problems of multiple deprivation and social exclusion faced by people in these neighbourhoods. Key objectives of the NDC include tackling the problems of worklessness, high levels of crime, poor health and educational underachievement. Initially 17 areas in England are eligible for NDC funding.

English Partnerships

The regional roles, functions, staff and assets of English Partnerships, a non-departmental public body, were taken over by RDAs from 1 April 1999 and its central core merged with the Commission for New Towns; in London the transfer will take place in 2000. English Partnerships has promoted job creation, inward investment and environmental improvement, through the reclamation of vacant, derelict or contaminated land in areas of need throughout England, within a framework of sustainable development. It has been funded through grant-in-aid and through its own activities. Direct expenditure in 1999–2000 is planned to be £76 million, which includes spending on the Greenwich Millennium site (see p. ix). A further £155

million is also available and includes investment under the Partnership Investment Programme. It has also attracted complementary funding from the ERDF and the private sector.

Coalfields Regeneration

In a report in June 1998, the Coalfields task force made a number of recommendations for revitalising the former coalfields communities affected by pit closures. In December 1998 the Government announced a ten-year programme to regenerate coalfield communities with an investment package of £354 million over three years. This comprised £196 million under an English Partnerships Coalfields programme, extra resources of £70 million from the SRB, £45 million for a new Coalfields Regeneration Trust, £28 million for housing and £15 million for a new Coalfield Enterprise Fund.

Groundwork

Groundwork comprises a national co-ordinating body, the Groundwork Foundation, 43 trusts and a subsidiary company, the National Urban Forestry Unit. In 1998–99, funding of £7.5 million, together with £11.5 million from the private sector, supported project activities in 38 local English Trusts. These trusts develop partnerships at local level between the public, private and voluntary sectors to carry out environmental regeneration projects. In 1998–99, Groundwork upgraded an estimated 1,560 hectares of land, planted 669,000 trees, helped 653 businesses improve their environmental performance and involved 80,612 volunteers.

Urban Policy

The Urban Task Force was set up in 1998 to find out the causes of urban decline in England and to recommend practical solutions to make cities, towns and neighbourhoods more attractive places in which to live. Its report, launched in June 1999, sets out a broad range of recommendations. The report will inform the Government in preparing its

An occasional festival, celebrating Britain's seafaring heritage and sharing it with the worldwide maritime community.

The cutter *Renard* passing in front of the world's largest tallship, the four masted sail training ship *Sedov*.

A P&O cross-Channel ferry passes
behind the gaff Schooner *Antares*
and other classic sailing boats.

Three Thames sailing barges.

Grand Turk, a 45m reconstruction
of an 18th century Royal Naval Frigate
launched in 1997 in Marmaris and used
as Hornblower's frigate *Indefatigable*
in a recent television series.

Archer class patrol boats
HMS Tracker 274,
HMS Dasher 280 and
HMS Puncher 291
with *HMS Invincible*
in the background.

NATIONAL GLASS CENTRE

The National Glass Centre in Sunderland, Tyne and Wear,
brings together a wide range of activities
related to glass: artistic, craft and industrial production,
education, research and public enjoyment.
There is no comparable centre in the world.

The National Glass Centre
forms the centre-piece of
Sunderland's new waterfront.

Examples of work produced by
Bridget Jones to illustrate the
history of glassmaking displayed
in the 'Sunderland Room'.

A demonstration of glass blowing by studio manager Barry Clark.

planned White Paper on Urban Policy, due to be issued by the end of 1999, which will look at education and training, jobs, health, crime and safety, cultural and leisure activities, housing, regeneration, planning, transport, local government and environmental issues. It will complement work being carried out by the Social Exclusion Unit on deprived neighbourhoods.

Rural Development

Although most problems arising from dereliction and unemployment occur in urban areas, some rural areas have also been affected as employment in traditional sectors, such as agriculture, mining and rurally based defence establishments, has declined. Low wages and a decline in local public transport and other services have caused problems for some rural residents. The movement of people into the countryside from towns has increased pressure on housing and this is likely to continue. However, some rural areas have been successful in recent years in attracting high-technology industries, while the spread of modern telecommunications facilities and information technology has made it much easier for people to work from home.

The Rural Development Commission (RDC), which used to act as the Government's statutory adviser on the economic and social development of rural areas of England, and promoted regeneration through a variety of programmes, merged with the Countryside Commission to form the new Countryside Agency in April 1999 (see p. 319). The Countryside Agency retains responsibilities for innovative and pilot projects, while the RDC's rural regeneration programmes have been transferred to the new RDAs.

Rural areas benefit from resources directed through the SRB. The Rural Challenge Fund[2] has been incorporated into the SRB and bids covering rural areas will be eligible for SRB support. In addition, the RDAs' rural regeneration programmes are supporting a variety of projects in designated rural development areas. The Government will be

setting out its policies for rural England in a White Paper to be published in 2000.

Wales

Parts of Wales have been adversely affected by the decline in traditional industries, especially the coal industry. In particular, the South Wales valleys have some of the most economically disadvantaged communities. The Valleys Forum, launched in 1998, is committed to increasing economic prosperity and the quality of life for all the people of the South Wales valleys. Regeneration will be taken forward within the framework of the National Development Strategy being prepared for consultation by the European Structural Funds Task Force.

Work in progress in Wales to a great extent mirrors that being addressed in England. It embraces a broad span of responsibilities, including social inclusion, competitiveness, housing, delivery of public services, regional development, planning, transport, community involvement, voluntary sector issues, sustainable development, education, training and crime prevention. The National Assembly for Wales will take forward policies aimed at improving the lives of those living in Wales' urban communities.

The main economic regeneration scheme operated directly by the National Assembly has been the Welsh Capital Challenge, which supports an integrated approach to capital expenditure and promotes sustainable regeneration or development and benefits disadvantaged areas, with particular emphasis on those in the South Wales valleys, west Wales and the most deprived rural areas. Approved local authority regeneration projects, on which expenditure of £31 million is planned in 1999–2000, are expected to lead to the creation of 2,300 jobs as a direct result, with a further 2,200 projected for the longer term if the private sector funding of £50 million for site development and other industrial and commercial development is secured.

Coalfields communities in Wales are included in the remit of the Coalfields Regeneration Trust, (see p. 356). The work of the Trust will substantially boost the efforts being made to

---

[2] Rural Challenge was initiated in 1994 as a means of encouraging innovation and partnership in rural areas.

secure economic, social and environmental regeneration throughout the former coalfields, in both north and south Wales. The National Assembly for Wales will be making a contribution of £3.5 million over three years.

Four Groundwork Trusts operate in Wales, covering five local authority areas. Groundwork Wales has recently been set up to ensure the development and future co-ordination of Groundwork in Wales. In 1997 the 'Changing Places' Millennium projects were launched in Wales. Funding of over £7 million was awarded by the Millennium Commission, to be matched by the Groundwork Foundation, resulting in projects worth over £13 million. The bid aims to improve the environment in celebration of the new Millennium and will create new community facilities on derelict land in the three valley areas of Bridgend, Caerphilly and Merthyr Tydfil. In 1998–99 Groundwork worked with over 4,500 volunteers, planted over 1,000 trees and shrubs and advised over 200 businesses on environmental issues.

The Rural Partnership for Wales is an advisory body that brings together representatives of the National Assembly, the Welsh Development Agency, the Welsh Local Government Association, the farming unions and other key interested parties with an interest in the countryside. One of its key tasks is the development of a statement on rural Wales for consideration by the National Assembly.

The Cardiff Bay Development Corporation was set up in 1987 to regenerate almost 1,100 hectares of South Cardiff. Its main priority is the £197 million Barrage project, construction of which will be completed in late 1999. Work is under way to provide a 375-hectare bird reserve on the Gwent Levels, south of Newport, to compensate for the loss of the Cardiff Bay habitat from impoundment of the Bay by the Barrage. The Corporation will be wound up on 31 March 2000, when it is expected to have achieved over 70% of its main targets including 29,000 jobs created or safeguarded in the Bay area and £1.4 billion of private sector investment attracted.

Under the Government of Wales Act 1998, the Welsh Development Agency (WDA) merged with the Development Board for Rural Wales and the Land Authority for Wales. The enlarged WDA now has broader functions and powers and is better placed to contribute to economic regeneration across the whole of Wales. It runs four main programmes covering urban and rural regeneration. Two of the programmes are 'Business Infrastructure', which includes a programme of land reclamation, the development of strategic sites for development and environmental improvements; and Community Regeneration, which includes provision for Urban Investment Grants, Town Improvement Grants and individual initiatives such as those in the slate valleys in north Wales and market towns in mid-Wales.

Scotland

In 1999–2000 some £68 million is earmarked for the area regeneration programme. In particular, the Government seeks to help excluded communities and people through Social Inclusion Partnerships (SIPs). SIPs will focus on the most needy members of society, co-ordinate and fill gaps between existing programmes to promote inclusion, and seek to prevent people becoming socially excluded. Support is also provided to city-wide partnerships.

The Urban Programme has been the means by which grants are paid to councils in order to meet social needs in deprived areas. It has supported individual projects approved under previous policy arrangements, and partnerships in Priority Partnership Areas and Regeneration Programme areas designated in 1996. A review was undertaken in 1998 to ensure that this funding mechanism could effectively support the new SIPs and that regeneration money could be spent to achieve a lasting impact. The Programme became the Social Inclusion Partnership Fund from April 1999, and 26 new SIPs began their work then. A total of £48 million has so far been allocated on supporting the new SIPs in the three years to 2002.

Funding will also be provided through the Working for Communities and Listening to Communities programmes to test and develop new models for delivering integrated local services in deprived areas, and developing the capacity of excluded communities to influence decisions that affect their lives.

Northern Ireland

Urban Regeneration programmes in Northern Ireland are designed to reverse and ameliorate urban decline and decay by improving the infrastructure, environment, economy, and the social and community fabric of disadvantaged areas. The programmes are managed by the Urban Regeneration Group (URG) of the Department of the Environment (NI). URG may operate directly or with other government and public sector bodies, as well as through grants to the private sector or voluntary and community groups. Many of the initiatives employed are geared towards encouraging investment. URG's annual gross programme expenditure is £42 million, aside from other resources which are realised through participation in European Union and International Fund for Ireland programmes.

The regeneration effort is focused on Belfast and Londonderry and on major towns and villages in the rest of the Province. URG also administers the Belfast and Londonderry sub-programmes of the European Union's Urban Initiative and the relevant parts of the EU Special Support Programme for Peace and Reconciliation throughout Northern Ireland. Under the EU's District Partnership scheme, for example, 26 partnerships have been established, one in each district council area, which are composed of one-third elected representatives, one-third from the community and voluntary sector and one-third from the business, trade union and statutory agency sector. Overall over 600

people are involved in these Partnerships. By June 1999 the District Partnerships, which started in 1996, had spent £23 million on 2,624 projects across Northern Ireland.

Urban Development Grant (UDG) is the principal urban regeneration measure in Northern Ireland and is aimed at the most rundown parts of Belfast and Londonderry (some £4 million is planned to be spent in 1999–2000). In Belfast, UDG of £76 million has, since 1983, generated £62 million of private sector investment, while in Londonderry, UDG of £34 million has generated some £125 million of private sector investment.

Making Belfast Work was launched in 1988 to advance efforts being made by community interests, the private sector and the Government to address problems facing residents in the most disadvantaged areas of Belfast; £234 million had been allocated to this initiative by March 1999. The Londonderry Initiative was also launched in 1988 to address urban decline and to target resources at the most disadvantaged parts of the city. By March 1999 over £28 million had been allocated to the Initiative.

The Laganside Corporation is charged with regenerating the once derelict area around Belfast docks and the city's waterfront. To date, cumulative public spending inclusive of EU funds has been £90 million, attracting £219 million of private sector and other investment with a further £52 million on the fringes of Laganside. It is estimated that 3,866 permanent jobs located in Laganside have been created.

Further Reading

Housing and Construction Statistics. Annual Report. The Stationery Office.

DETR Annual Report 1999: The Government's Expenditure Plans 1999–2000. The Stationery Office, 1999.

The Housing Corporation: Annual Report. The Housing Corporation.

Websites

Department of the Environment, Transport and the Regions: www.environment.detr.gov.uk

National Assembly for Wales: www.wales.gov.uk

Northern Ireland Office: www.nio.gov.uk

Scottish Executive: www.scotland.gov.uk

22 Transport and Communications

The Government is beginning to implement its integrated transport policy, which is designed to make better use of existing facilities and infrastructure. A higher priority is being given to more environmentally sustainable forms of transport, such as walking and cycling. Public expenditure on transport will be significantly higher in real terms in 2001–02 than in 1998–99, with additional expenditure being provided over the three years to 2001–02 for modernising local and public transport. Telecommunications services are expanding rapidly, helped by substantial growth in demand for mobile telephones (there are now some 16 million users) and for services over the Internet.

Transport

TRAVEL TRENDS

Passenger travel was 716 billion passenger-kilometres in 1998 (see Table 22.1). Travel by car, van and taxi has doubled in the past 25 years, and air travel has also grown substantially. Travel by bus has experienced a steady decline since the 1950s, but recently bus patronage appears to have stabilised. Motorcycling, walking and cycling have declined in the last ten years. Rail travel has recently been growing strongly again after a period of decline in the first half of the 1990s, and travel on the various light rail/supertram systems is also rising.

Travel by car remains by far the most popular mode of passenger travel, accounting for 86% of passenger mileage within Great Britain in 1998, compared with 44% in 1958. Most freight is carried by road, which accounts for 81% of goods by tonnage and 65% in terms of tonne-kilometres.[1]

At the end of 1998 there were 27.5 million vehicles licensed for use on the roads of Great Britain, according to the Driver and Vehicle Licensing Agency, which maintains official records of drivers and vehicles in Great Britain. There were 22.1 million cars (of which 2.3 million were company-owned); 2.4 million light goods vehicles; 412,000 other goods vehicles; 684,000 motorcycles, scooters and mopeds; and 80,000 public transport vehicles with nine or more seats.

---

[1] A tonne-kilometre is equivalent to 1 tonne transported for 1 kilometre.

Table 22.1: Passenger Transport in Great Britain by Mode   *Billion kilometres*

	1988	1993	1996	1997	1998
Buses and coaches	46	44	44	44	43
Cars, vans and taxis	536	584	606	614	616
Motorcycles, mopeds and scooters	6	5	4	4	4
Pedal cycles	5	4	4	4	4
All road	**594**	**637**	**658**	**666**	**667**
Rail[a]	41	36	38	41	42
Air[b]	5	5	6	7	7
All modes[c]	**640**	**678**	**703**	**714**	**716**

Source: *Transport Statistics Great Britain*
[a] Financial years.
[b] Excludes air taxi services, private flying and passengers paying less than 25% of the full fare. Includes Northern Ireland and the Channel Islands.
[c] Excluding travel by water within the UK.
Note: Differences between totals and the sums of their component parts are due to rounding.

The 20th century has seen a huge expansion in motor vehicle usage. The first British car was given its initial trial in 1896. By 1950 there were around 2 million cars, but 86% of households did not have access to one. By 1998 there were about 22 million cars; in 1996-97, 70% of households in the UK owned one or more cars, 21.5% two or more cars and 4.5% three or more cars. Most of the rail network had been built by 1900, and the railways in the UK (including the whole of Ireland) carried 1,142 million passengers and 425 million tonnes of freight in that year. Tramways were continuing to expand, and by the end of 1900 there were 1,177 miles of tramway in the UK (including Ireland); they carried 1,065 million passengers in 1900. At the turn of the century the UK was the world's leading maritime nation, and in 1914 its merchant fleet of 18.9 million gross tons represented 42% of world shipping.

TRANSPORT POLICY

In 1998 the Government issued a White Paper, *A New Deal for Transport: Better for Everyone*, setting out its policy for creating an integrated transport system to tackle the growing problems of congestion and pollution.

Its main proposals include:

- better integration between different types of transport, to improve connections, and better co-ordination of transport policy with other policies, such as on the environment and land-use planning;

- new sources of funding for local authorities, including charges for driving into town centres and for workplace parking, which will enable them to tackle congestion and boost public transport;

- better local bus services, through upgraded 'quality partnerships' between local authorities and bus operators, and in England and Wales minimum concessionary bus fares for pensioners;

- a new Strategic Rail Authority;

- better information for travellers, including a national public transport information system to be introduced by the year 2000;

- improved motoring conditions, with greater resources for road maintenance and better traffic information and management;

- a review of safety arrangements across all transport modes; and

- development of regional ports and airports, so that they play their full part in meeting local demand.

> Local transport plans (local transport strategies in Scotland) will be a key element in developing an integrated transport system. The first plans are to be produced by local authorities by July 2000. The Government envisages that the plans will favour public transport, walking and cycling.

Following the White Paper, a series of policy documents has been issued, including papers on trunk roads, traffic congestion, sustainable distribution, bus services and shipping. Legislation will be required to implement some of the proposals, for example, to enable local authorities to charge for driving into town centres and for parking at workplaces. Public-Private Partnerships (see p. 403) will have an increasingly important role in transport, notably for the Channel Tunnel Rail Link, the London Underground and air traffic control.

A new Commission for Integrated Transport has been set up to provide independent advice to the UK Government on implementing the integrated transport policy, review progress towards meeting government objectives, and identify best practice on transport issues from the UK and overseas. It will advise on setting targets for road traffic and public transport, on lorry weights and the development of rail freight, the review of transport safety arrangements, and progress on adopting 'green transport' plans (see p. 365).

The White Paper's approach covers the whole of the UK. Separate but complementary White Papers/policy documents have also been issued for Scotland, Wales and Northern Ireland. A selection of the main points is given below.

Wales

The integrated approach to transport policy in Wales, now being taken forward by the National Assembly for Wales, envisages improved public transport in both urban and rural areas—grants of £5 million are available in 1999–2000 to support non-commercial bus services and £250,000 is available for community transport schemes in rural areas. To lessen congestion, the Assembly will be encouraging the introduction of car-sharing arrangements and the adoption of traffic management measures. It is also encouraging all major employers to prepare green transport plans—the National Assembly for Wales already has its own plan. It is working with rail and air operators to improve existing services between north and south Wales, and to introduce new ones. A new core network of trunk roads, comprising east-west links in north and south Wales, and important north-south roads, will be the starting-point for future trunk road investment priorities.

The Welsh Transport Advisory Group, which included representatives of most organisations with an interest in transport issues in Wales, produced its final report in March 1999, *Developments in Transport Policy in Wales*, which will be taken forward by the Assembly.

Scotland

The future strategy for transport in Scotland was set out in the White Paper *Travel Choices for Scotland*. New integrated local transport strategies will be supported by a Public Transport Fund, which is providing £90 million over the three years to 2001–02 to support developments such as new railway stations, 'park-and-ride' facilities, and bus priority schemes. The Scottish Executive is consulting on how to improve transport co-ordination at the regional level.

A review of trunk roads is expected to be completed later in 1999. Some £186 million is being spent on motorways and trunk roads in 1999–2000. New schemes include the completion of the final stage of the A74(M), a key route to England.

For many remote communities in rural Scotland, the car will remain the main form of transport. The Scottish Executive is providing £4.5 million a year to support rural transport provision, including £3.5 million for public transport services and £600,000 for community transport projects. Substantial additional support has been made available for essential services to the Scottish Islands, including £20 million for two new ferries in the Hebrides and a new £9 million terminal, opened in 1999, at Inverness Airport.

Developments in transport policy in Scotland will be taken forward by the Scottish Parliament and Executive (see chapter 4).

Northern Ireland

A key feature of the measures outlined in the policy document for transport in Northern Ireland, *Moving Forward*, is development of a new Regional Transport Plan, initially covering the five years from 2001–02. Meanwhile, proposed improvements are being taken forward in an interim plan, including:

- expenditure of £87 million on road improvements, including upgrading strategic routes and completion of by-passes for five towns and villages;

- investment of £16 million in new buses—trials of electric buses are in progress in Ballymena;

- reopening of the railway line from Antrim to Bleach Green and upgrading of railway track throughout the Province;

- more bus priority measures, including a pilot 'quality bus corridor' in Belfast, which would involve modern buses running with greater frequency along a series of bus lanes; and

- better facilities for cyclists and walkers, and the establishment of strategies to increase cycling and walking.

Transport is one of the functions to be assumed by the new Northern Ireland Assembly (see p. 18).

ROADS

The total road network in Great Britain in 1998 was 371,600 kilometres (231,000 miles). Trunk motorways[2] accounted for 3,300 kilometres (2,050 miles) of this, less than 1%, and other trunk roads for over 12,200

---

[2] That is, those motorways that are the direct responsibility of the central administration rather than the local authority.

kilometres (7,580 miles), or 3.3%. However, motorways carry 18% of all traffic, and trunk roads another 16%. Combined, they carry over half of all goods vehicle traffic in Great Britain. In Northern Ireland the road network is over 24,000 kilometres (15,000 miles), of which 111 kilometres (69 miles) are motorways.

Motor traffic in Great Britain was 1.7% higher in 1998 than in 1997, rising to an estimated 459.4 billion vehicle-kilometres (see Table 22.2). Traffic on motorways is growing much faster than on any other type of road, rising by 27% between 1993 and 1998 to 81.1 billion vehicle-kilometres.

The central administration meets most of the costs of construction and maintenance of trunk roads, while local authorities are responsible for non-trunk roads.

Road Traffic in Great Britain by Vehicle Type, 1998

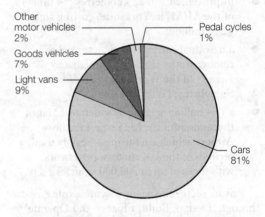

Source: Department of the Environment, Transport and the Regions

Note: Light vans = goods vehicles under 3.5 tonnes gross weight.
Goods vehicles = goods vehicles over 3.5 tonnes gross weight.
Other motor vehicles include two-wheel motor vehicles and large buses and coaches.

Road Programme

The Highways Agency—an executive agency of the Department of the Environment, Transport and the Regions (DETR)—is improving the condition of the national road network in England to minimise long-term costs and disruption to the public. The Agency is responsible for about 70% of the motorway and trunk road network in England, with the other 30% being the responsibility of

Table 22.2: Motor Vehicle Traffic in Great Britain			Billion vehicle-kilometres		
	1988	1993	1996	1997	1998
Motorways	54.5	63.9	73.7	77.9	81.1
Trunk roads	62.4	68.7	72.6	74.1	75.6
Principal roads	115.5	127.5	134.2	134.6	136.2
Minor roads	143.3	152.2	161.9	166.0	166.6
All roads	**375.7**	**412.2**	**442.5**	**452.5**	**459.4**

Source: *Transport Statistics Great Britain*
Note: Differences between totals and the sums of their component parts are due to rounding.

local authorities. Its budget for 1999–2000 is £1.5 billion. This is allocated in accordance with the Agency's new priorities, with the emphasis being to make better use of existing roads rather than building new roads. The greatest allocation is to maintenance, which is receiving £765 million.

The Agency's seven-year programme of road improvements has 37 schemes, costing a total of £1.4 billion. Among the schemes are:

- improvements to 22 kilometres (14 miles) of the A1(M) in Yorkshire, costing some £210 million;

- a new dual carriageway in a tunnel to remove traffic from the immediate vicinity of the World Heritage Site at Stonehenge (Wiltshire); and

- a £94 million scheme to widen to 12 lanes the sections of the M25 near Heathrow Airport, which are the most heavily used sections of the UK motorway network, with flows of up to 200,000 vehicles a day.

Private sector finance is playing a role through 'Design, Build, Finance and Operate' (DBFO) contracts, under which the private sector provides the funding for construction and maintenance, and receives government payments linked to usage and performance. Ten DBFO roads are now open to traffic in England and five of the Agency's 37 projects are part of the DBFO scheme.

Standards

Minimum ages for driving are:

- 16 for riders of mopeds, drivers of small tractors, and disabled people receiving a mobility allowance;

- 17 for drivers of cars and other passenger vehicles with nine or fewer seats (including that of the driver), motorcycles and goods vehicles not over 3.5 tonnes maximum weight;

- 18 for goods vehicles weighing over 3.5, but not over 7.5, tonnes; and

- 21 for passenger vehicles with more than nine seats and goods vehicles over 7.5 tonnes.

New drivers of motor vehicles must pass both the practical driving test and a separate written theory test in order to acquire a full driving licence. In May 1999 the practical driving test was lengthened and made tougher, with the aim of improving the testing of candidates' ability to drive in modern traffic conditions. In 1998, 1.22 million driving tests were conducted in Great Britain by the Driving Standards Agency (DSA), the national driver testing authority. Some 46% of drivers passed the test, raising the number of holders of a car full driving licence to about 31 million. The DSA also supervises professional driving instructors and the compulsory basic training scheme for learner motorcyclists.

Before most new cars and goods vehicles are allowed on the roads, they must meet safety and environmental requirements, based primarily on standards drawn up by the European Union (EU). The Vehicle Certification Agency is responsible for ensuring these requirements are met through a process known as 'type approval'.

The Vehicle Inspectorate is responsible for ensuring the roadworthiness of vehicles, through their annual testing. It also uses roadside and other enforcement checks to ensure that drivers and vehicle operators comply with legislation. In Northern Ireland the Driver and Vehicle Testing Agency is responsible for testing drivers and vehicles under statutory schemes broadly similar to those in Great Britain.

Road Safety

Although Great Britain has one of the highest densities of road traffic in the world, it has a good record on road safety, with the lowest road accident death rate for adults in the EU. In 1998, 3,421 deaths occurred in road accidents in Great Britain, while there were 40,800 serious injuries and nearly 281,000 slight injuries.

Since 1981–85 there has been a significant decline in deaths and serious casualties, by 39% and 45% respectively, while road traffic has risen by 55% in this period. Developments in vehicle safety standards, better roads, traffic-calming measures (such as road humps), legislation on seat-belt wearing, and local safety initiatives (such as 20 mph—32 km/h—zones) have contributed to this long-term decline. However, slight injuries have risen, so that the total of 325,200 casualties in 1998 was 1% more than the yearly average for 1981–85.

The Government intends to issue a new road safety strategy in autumn 1999. It wishes to improve safety for all road users and will set a target for reducing casualties by 2010. A review of vehicle speed policy is being undertaken and is expected to be completed at about the same time as the new strategy is published.

Congestion

Traffic congestion in the UK is a serious problem in many towns and cities in the main morning and evening peak periods and for much of the day in inner and central London. An estimated 1.6 billion hours were lost in 1996 by drivers and passengers on the roads of Great Britain as a result of congestion, of which 80% occurred in urban areas.

Traffic management schemes in many urban areas aim to reduce congestion through measures such as traffic-free shopping precincts, bus priority measures (such as bus lanes and traffic light priority signalling), and controls on on-street parking. In London a 512-km (318-mile) network of priority 'red routes', with special stopping controls designed to improve traffic flow, is expected to be fully operational by 2000.

> In June 1999 the first bus lane on a major motorway in England was opened, a lane reserved for buses, taxis and coaches on the London-bound section of the M4 near Heston.

In 1998 the Government issued a consultation document, *Breaking the Logjam*, setting out its proposals for legislation to allow local authorities in England and Wales to introduce charging schemes for road users and to levy a charge on workplace parking, where these measures would help to reduce congestion or traffic growth or achieve other objectives contained in their local transport plans. A key feature is that local authorities would be able to retain all the net revenue generated from the charges for at least ten years, provided that these were used to fund local transport improvements. A similar consultation document covering Scotland was published in 1999. The Government is supporting companies which have adopted 'green transport' plans to encourage fewer staff to travel to work by car and more to use public transport, cycling, walking, or car-sharing arrangements. Leeds and Edinburgh will host the first full-scale demonstrations of electronic road user charging equipment in the UK, starting around the end of 2000.

Traffic Information

The Government is working with interested parties to ensure that accurate and relevant traffic information is widely available, both for pre-trip planning and in-trip purposes. Traffic information is already provided throughout Great Britain by a variety of means, such as the media, roadside signs and in-vehicle systems. Information originates from a range of sources, such as roadside sensors, the traffic police and highway authorities. It is collated by motoring organisations, such as the Automobile Association (AA) and the Royal Automobile Club (RAC), and by information service providers, such as Integrated Traffic Information Services (ITIS), Metro Networks and Trafficmaster. Local traffic control centres across Great Britain help to manage traffic and provide information about traffic conditions. Centres covering wider areas exist in Scotland and Wales, and are planned for England.

Cycling and Walking

Cycling has been declining over a long period, with mileage travelled now around a fifth of that in the early 1950s. A National Cycling Strategy, launched in 1996, aims to double the number of cycling journeys by 2002 and to double the level again by 2012. The National Cycling Forum is co-ordinating its implementation and the strategy has been endorsed by the Government. Local authorities are being encouraged to give greater priority to cycling and to improve conditions for cyclists by, for example, providing designated cycle routes.

The Government is supporting the National Cycle Network, a linked series of traffic-free paths and roads with traffic-calming features, which is being developed by the transport charity Sustrans to open up new opportunities for commuter, tourist and recreational cycling. The first routes, covering 3,500 miles (5,600 kilometres), will be opened in June 2000, with the network reaching 8,000 miles (12,800 kilometres) by 2005.

People in the UK are walking significantly less than in the past, with fewer journeys on foot and many more by car. The Government wishes to reverse this trend, and is expecting local authorities to give more priority to walking by providing, for example, wider pavements, pedestrianisation schemes, more direct, safe and convenient routes for walking, and more pedestrian crossings. The DETR and the devolved administrations are monitoring the effectiveness of 'home zones', residential streets which have been designed so that they are primarily places for the local community to walk and meet, rather than

routes for motor vehicles. Nine such schemes are being monitored until 2002.

Road Haulage

There are about 113,000 holders of an operator's licence (which is required for operating goods vehicles over 3.5 tonnes gross weight) in the UK, and 427,000 heavy goods vehicles. About 88% of operators have fleets of five or fewer vehicles. Road haulage traffic by heavy goods vehicles amounted to 152,000 million tonne-kilometres in Great Britain in 1998. Road hauliers have faced greater competition, especially from hauliers on the continent of Europe, and are taking steps to improve efficiency, such as using larger and more efficient vehicles carrying heavier loads—85% of the traffic, in terms of tonne-kilometres, is now carried by vehicles of over 25 tonnes gross weight. Journey lengths are increasing, with the average haul now being 93 kilometres (58 miles), 37% longer than in 1980. Hauliers licensed to transport other firms' goods account for 75% of freight carried in terms of tonne-kilometres.

International road haulage has grown rapidly and in 1998 about 2.1 million road goods vehicles were ferried to mainland Europe, of which 544,000 were powered vehicles registered in the UK. In 1998 UK vehicles carried 15.5 million tonnes internationally, and about 96% of this traffic was with the EU.

In March 1999 the Government issued a UK strategy on the sustainable distribution of goods and services (see p. 315). It will investigate with the road haulage industry how to maximise the efficiency of freight movements and to promote the integration of transport (such as greater use of freight interchanges) and the consolidation of loads.

The general maximum weight in the UK for articulated vehicles with five or more axles rose from 38 tonnes to 40 tonnes in January 1999 to conform with EU requirements. At the same time, as an incentive to hauliers to purchase vehicles causing less road damage, the Government allowed 41-tonne lorries with six axles, which cause less wear to roads and bridges than 40-tonne, five-axle vehicles. The Government has asked the Commission for

Integrated Transport to consider the case for a general increase in the maximum weight for six-axle lorries to 44 tonnes.

Bus Services

In 1997–98 some 4,337 million passenger journeys were made on local bus services in Great Britain, similar to the level in 1996–97 but 18% fewer than in 1987–88. Usage has been declining in nearly all areas, although in London (which accounts for nearly a third of bus journeys in Great Britain) bus patronage has risen. There are around 76,200 buses and coaches in Great Britain, of which 32% are minibuses or midibuses (which are becoming more widespread) and 22% double-deckers (which have fallen in number). Operators are increasing investment, which is now about £270 million a year, involving the purchase of around 7,300 new buses. A number of these are low-floor with easy access, which helps groups such as shoppers, the elderly and people in wheelchairs.

Most local bus services are provided commercially, with 85% of bus mileage outside London operated on this basis. Local authorities may subsidise services which are not commercially viable but are considered socially necessary. Support for bus travel in Great Britain is almost £1 billion a year, including over £440 million on concessionary fares (such as for the elderly) and £220 million on the purchase of additional non-commercial bus services.

Operators

Almost all bus services in Great Britain are provided by companies in the private sector, apart from 17 bus companies owned by local authorities. London Transport (LT), a statutory corporation, is responsible for providing or procuring public transport in London. It oversees about 700 bus routes run by private sector companies under contract.

Following a series of mergers and takeovers, five main groups now operate bus services: Arriva, FirstGroup, Go-Ahead Group, National Express and Stagecoach. These have become substantial undertakings—for example, FirstGroup has over 20 separate bus operations, with a fleet of 9,000 vehicles. Most of these groups have diversified into running other transport services, such as rail services and airports, while some have also expanded into transport services in other countries. For example, National Express has become the third largest operator of school bus services in the United States, and Stagecoach is to buy Coach USA, the largest US charter and tour coach operator.

In Northern Ireland almost all road passenger services are operated by subsidiaries of the publicly owned Northern Ireland Transport Holding Company (NITHC), collectively known as 'Translink'. Citybus Ltd operates services in Belfast, and Ulsterbus Ltd runs most of the services in the rest of Northern Ireland, carrying respectively 22 million and 50 million passengers a year.

Future Developments

In March 1999 the Government issued a strategy for supporting the development of bus services in Great Britain, which will feature prominently in the new local transport plans and strategies (see p. 362). The Government will be providing statutory backing for 'quality partnerships', which will be developed by local authorities and bus operators in the context of these plans. Partnerships have been developed in over 30 towns and cities, including Aberdeen, Birmingham, Edinburgh, Leeds, Oxford and Swansea. These have led to better services with higher-quality buses, with examples of increased patronage of 10% to 20%.

Partnerships have also been successful in rural areas, such as around Pwllheli in north Wales, where, as a result, bus patronage has risen by 22% in two years. Extra funding of around £170 million over three years is being provided to rural bus services in the UK, and a 'rural bus challenge' has been held in England to stimulate the development of innovative services in rural areas.

Other features of the Government's strategy include:

- measures to promote stability in services, for example by reducing frequent timetable changes;

- improving information for bus passengers and giving local authorities a statutory duty to ensure bus information is available in their areas;
- improved ticketing arrangements, such as tickets covering both buses and trains;
- minimum standards for concessionary fares; and
- new powers for local authorities to arrange the provision of extra services.

A new £50 million 'guided' busway (with buses travelling on segregated track) is to be built in Edinburgh to link the airport to the city centre. The project is being undertaken by a consortium involving FirstGroup and the construction group Balfour Beatty.

Coaches

Coaches account for much of the non-local mileage operated by public service vehicles—this rose by about 4% in 1997–98 to 1,559 million vehicle-kilometres. Organised coach tours and holiday journeys account for about 60% of coach travel in Great Britain. High-frequency scheduled services, run by private sector operators, link many towns and cities. About 20,000 people use coaches to commute into and out of London each weekday, and commuter services also operate into some other major centres. The biggest coach operator, National Express, has a national network of routes and in 1998 carried 17 million passengers on its UK express coach and airport coach services linking 1,200 destinations.

Taxis

There are about 55,300 licensed taxis in England and Wales, mainly in urban areas, around 8,500 in Scotland, and about 7,000 in Northern Ireland. In London (which has around 19,400 taxis) and several other major cities, taxis must be purpose-built to conform to strict requirements. In many districts, taxi drivers have to pass a test of their knowledge of the area.

Private hire vehicles with drivers ('minicabs') may be booked only through the operator and not hired on the street. In most areas outside London, private hire vehicles are licensed; there are about 66,000 in England and Wales outside the capital. It is estimated that at least 60,000 minicabs operate in the London area. The Private Hire Vehicles (London) Act 1998 provides the basis for regulating minicab operators, drivers and vehicles. In May 1999 the Government issued a consultation paper on the details for operator licensing in London, while further consultation papers are planned on driver and vehicle licensing.

RAILWAYS

Railways were pioneered in Britain: the Stockton and Darlington Railway, opened in 1825, was the first public passenger railway in the world to be worked by steam power. Privatisation of railway services in Great Britain was completed in 1997. The main system now involves Railtrack, which is responsible for operating all track and infrastructure; three rolling stock companies, which lease locomotives and passenger carriages; 25 passenger train operating companies; four freight service providers; and a number of infrastructure maintenance companies.

Rail Regulation

The Government wishes to see tighter regulation of the railway industry. It has therefore introduced into Parliament the Railways Bill, which will establish a Strategic Rail Authority (SRA) to support the Government's integrated transport policy. The Authority would subsume OPRAF (the Office of Passenger Rail Franchising) and the British Railways Board. The two bodies are currently operating as the Shadow Strategic Rail Authority (SSRA)—until the Bill is enacted—and are developing a strategic plan for the railways, covering both passenger and freight services.

The SSRA is also responsible for negotiating, awarding and monitoring the franchises for operating rail services. Most franchises last seven years, but some are for up to 15 years in return for increased investment commitments. Each agreement specifies provisions governing the contractual level of passenger services to be provided by the operator, for example, on the frequency of trains and stations served, and, in general, provides for gradually reducing subsidies to the franchisee. Support for passenger rail services amounted to £1.2 billion in 1998–99.

There is also the Office of the Rail Regulator, which licenses the railway operators, deals with agreements governing access by operators to track and stations, and promotes rail users' interests. It sponsors a network of statutory rail users' consultative committees which represent the interests of passengers. These committees and the Regulator's role in promoting rail users' interests, will transfer to the SRA. In addition, the Office of the International Rail Regulator has responsibilities for licensing the operation of certain international rail services in the European Economic Area, and for access to the railway infrastructure in Great Britain for the operation of such services.

In February 1999 a National Rail Summit was held, with representatives from government, the rail industry and passengers. A package of measures was agreed to improve the quality of rail services and tackle some of the problems affecting the railways (such as late-running services and overcrowding), including:

- the acquisition of 2,300 new vehicles, so that by 2002 half the passenger rolling stock will be new or refurbished;

- investment of £39 million in improving passenger information systems in stations; and

- measures to improve passenger security.

In addition, the Government announced plans for tougher performance measures, and a new National Passenger Survey later in 1999. It also indicated that it would be prepared to consider renegotiation of franchises if operators guaranteed to deliver improved services.

Railtrack

Railtrack owns and manages the rail infrastructure in Great Britain. Assets include 32,000 kilometres (20,000 miles) of track; 40,000 bridges, tunnels and viaducts; 2,500 stations; and connections to over 1,000 freight terminals. Apart from 14 major stations operated directly by the company, nearly all stations and depots are leased to the train operating companies. Turnover in 1998–99 totalled £2.6 billion, of which 92% represented payments by passenger and freight train operators for access to the rail network.

Railtrack plans to invest £27 billion in the rail network in the ten years from 1999: £16.4 billion on renewing and maintaining existing infrastructure and £10.7 billion on schemes to enhance the network. Major projects include modernising the West Coast and East Coast main lines, the Thameslink 2000 project to increase the capacity of north-south services through London, and improved rail links to airports (such as Heathrow and Stansted).

Passenger Services

The passenger network (see map facing inside back cover) comprises a fast inter-city network, linking the main centres of Great Britain; local stopping services; and commuter services in and around the large conurbations, especially London and the South East. About 18,000 scheduled services operate each day. Some 890 million passenger journeys were made on the rail network in 1998–99, 5% more than in 1997–98.

Passenger services (other than Eurostar services—see pp. 370–1—and the Heathrow Express) are run under franchise by 25 train operating companies. Bus and coach operator National Express has the largest number of franchises—five. Other main operators include Connex (which is French-owned and has two franchises running commuter services in the South East), Virgin, Prism and Stagecoach. The companies lease their rolling stock from the three rolling stock companies: Angel Train Contracts, Forward Trust and Porterbrook Leasing (a subsidiary of Stagecoach). BAA (see p. 376) runs the

Heathrow Express, between Heathrow Airport and Paddington in central London.

Investment

Train operating companies are placing substantial orders for new or refurbished passenger trains. Virgin Rail has ordered 55 new high-speed tilting trains to run at speeds of up to 140 miles per hour (225 km/h) on the West Coast main line between London and Glasgow, the first of which will enter service in 2001, and 74 high-speed diesel trains for its cross-country routes. Many other companies have placed substantial orders for new trains.

The Government has made available from April 1999 two new investment funds:

- the Rail Passenger Partnership scheme, which is designed to encourage innovative rail services at local and regional levels; and
- the Infrastructure Investment Fund, which is supporting projects to tackle bottlenecks in the rail network.

Freight

Rail freight traffic is relatively constant following a long-term decline. In 1998–99 traffic totalled 102 million tonnes. Over 80% of traffic by volume is of bulk commodities, mainly coal, coke, iron and steel, building materials and petroleum. The two largest operators are English, Welsh & Scottish Railway (EWS), which also runs trains through the Channel Tunnel to the continent of Europe; and Freightliner, which operates container services between major ports and inland terminals.

The Government is keen to encourage more freight to be moved by rail, to relieve pressure on the road network and to bring environmental benefits; grants are available to encourage companies to move goods by rail or water rather than by road. It has endorsed the expansion targets of the main operators. The freight operators are investing £600 million in the next four years in new locomotives and freight wagons. In 1998 EWS opened the first commercial 'piggyback' service in the UK,

carrying lorry trailers on specially designed rail wagons between Mossend (near Glasgow) and Willesden in London. Other investment plans include a £15 million Freightliner terminal at Westloog, near Cardiff, and a £200 million scheme for a railfreight terminal, the London International Freight Exchange, which has been proposed for a site near Heathrow Airport.

Northern Ireland

In Northern Ireland, the Northern Ireland Railways Company Ltd, a subsidiary of the NITHC (see p. 367), operates the railway service on about 336 kilometres (211 miles) of track and handled 6 million passenger journeys in 1998–99. The Belfast to Dublin service has been upgraded, with new track and rolling stock, and a major track upgrade programme is planned for the rest of the rail network in the Province.

Channel Tunnel

The Channel Tunnel, the largest civil engineering project in Europe financed by the private sector, was opened to traffic in 1994. It cost about £10 billion and was undertaken by Eurotunnel, a British-French group, under an operating concession from the British and French governments.

Eurotunnel Services

Eurotunnel operates a drive-on, drive-off shuttle train service, with separate shuttles for passenger and freight vehicles, between terminals near Folkestone and Calais. At peak periods there are up to four passenger shuttles and up to four freight shuttles an hour in each direction. In 1998 the service took 52% of car traffic, 39% of coach traffic and 37% of freight traffic on the Dover/Folkestone–Calais route.

Eurostar Passenger Services

Eurostar high-speed train services are operated jointly by Eurostar (UK) Ltd,

French Railways and Belgian Railways. Up to 32 Eurostar services run daily in each direction through the Channel Tunnel between London (Waterloo) and Paris or Brussels, taking less than 3 hours and 2 hours 40 minutes respectively. Trains also serve Ashford (Kent), Calais, Lille, Disneyland Paris and, during the winter months, Bourg St Maurice in the French Alps. Eurostar handled 6.3 million passengers in 1998.

Construction work has started on the first stage of the high-speed Channel Tunnel Rail Link, costing some £4.2 billion, following the completion of a Public-Private Partnership refinancing deal agreed between the Government, London & Continental Railways (LCR—the consortium selected to design, build and operate the Link) and Railtrack. As a result, Railtrack and Bechtel (of the United States) will manage the construction on LCR's behalf. Railtrack will purchase the first stage, from the Channel Tunnel to Fawkham Junction in north-west Kent, when it is completed in 2003. A government guarantee now underpins bond finance for the project, while LCR's concession has been reduced, so that the railway, including Eurostar, will revert to public ownership in 2086, at around the same time as the Eurotunnel concession. Initial preparatory work has begun on the second stage, from Fawkham Junction to St Pancras (London), which is due for completion by 2007.

Other Railways in London

London Underground Ltd, a subsidiary of LT, operates services on 391 kilometres (243 miles) of railway, of which about 171 kilometres (106 miles) are underground. The system, the oldest in the world, has 268 stations, with 489 trains running in the peak period. Around 866 million passenger journeys were made on London Underground trains in 1998–99. In May 1999 the first stage of the £3.2 billion extension of the Jubilee Line was opened, and the remaining stages of the extension, which will provide a fast link from central London to Stratford (east London) via Docklands and the Millennium Dome site at North Greenwich, are due to open by the end of 1999.

The Government has announced plans for a new Public-Private Partnership for the Underground, under which the private sector will be invited to undertake a £7 billion investment programme. Railtrack will enter into negotiations to take over the sub-surface lines and will possibly work with London Underground on a proposal to link these lines to the national rail network. Two other private sector contracts will be awarded to maintain and modernise the rest of the Underground's infrastructure and rolling stock. London Underground will continue to operate the services as a public sector body.

The Docklands Light Railway (DLR) connects Docklands with the City of London, Beckton and Stratford. It is operated under franchise by Docklands Railway Management Ltd, owned by Serco Group plc. A £200 million extension to Greenwich and Lewisham is due to open by January 2000, which will extend the network to 26 kilometres (16 miles) with 36 stations. A link to London City Airport is to be opened by 2004, and an extension to North Woolwich is under consideration.

The Croydon Tramlink, a 28-km (18-mile) light rail network in south London, running partly along existing and disued railway track and partly along or beside roads, is due to open by the end of 1999. Tramtrack Croydon Ltd (a private sector consortium) is building and will operate the network, as a joint undertaking with LT.

Other Railways and Tramways

Four other light rail systems are in operation: the Tyne and Wear Metro, Manchester Metrolink, South Yorkshire Supertram and the Midland Metro. The first stage of the Midland Metro, between Birmingham and Wolverhampton, was opened in May 1999, and two extensions are under consideration. More light rail schemes have been proposed, but the Government has indicated that light rail is likely to be a cost-effective option in only a few places, as in the case of the 13-km (8-mile) Nottingham Express Transit system which will link Hucknall to the centre of Nottingham from 2002.

The Glasgow Underground, a heavy rapid transit system, operates on a 10-km (6-mile) loop in central Glasgow. Traditional trams still operate in Blackpool and Llandudno.

Over 100 other passenger-carrying railways, many concerned with the preservation of steam locomotives, are to be found throughout Great Britain. Most are operated on a voluntary basis and provide limited services for tourists and railway enthusiasts. They generally run on former branch lines, but there are also several narrow-gauge lines, mainly in north Wales.

INLAND WATERWAYS

Inland waterways are popular for leisure boating and general recreation, as well as playing a significant role nationally as a focus for regeneration, in land drainage and water supply, and for freight-carrying. Most waterways are now used primarily for leisure. Research indicates that the canals are visited by 10 million people a year, representing 160 million visits, of which 90% are by sightseers and walkers.

British Waterways, a public corporation sponsored by the DETR, manages 3,200 kilometres (2,000 miles) of waterways, making up the greater part of the canal and navigable river system in Great Britain.

The Government is keen to see greater use of waterways. In February 1999 it announced a series of measures to help British Waterways further develop the canals. These included:

- an increase in grant, by £8 million to nearly £59 million a year, to enable British Waterways to deal with a backlog of maintenance work;

- proposals for British Waterways to collaborate with the private sector on developing Public-Private Partnerships in its property, water transfer and maintenance operations, and to collaborate with local authorities and other public sector partners on local canal improvements; and

- plans for British Waterways to consult on a membership scheme linked to a charitable trust.

The DETR is encouraging more passenger and freight transport on the inland waterways, including the development of river services to the millennium celebrations at Greenwich (see p. ix) as a means of revitalising passenger transport on the Thames. Two operators will run river transport services and invest £6 million in new vessels, while £15 million is being invested in new and upgraded piers.

Several stretches of canal are being restored. One example is the £78 million Millennium Link project (see p. xii) to connect again Glasgow and Edinburgh by canal; British Waterways is working in a partnership consortium of public sector and voluntary bodies.

SHIPPING

The UK accounts for 6% of world merchant shipping; the shipping industry is a major service-sector exporter and supports a wide range of shore-based, maritime-related facilities in the City of London and elsewhere in the UK. About 95% by weight (75% by value) of the UK's foreign trade is carried by sea. The UK shipping fleet contains a number of world-leading operations in sectors such as cruising, container services, tanker and dry bulk carriers, offshore support and other specialist activities. Nevertheless, the UK fleet has declined considerably in tonnage terms in the last 25 years. This reflects changing trade patterns, removal of grants, and greater competition, both from overseas shipping lines and from ships operating under 'flags of convenience' (open shipping registers which have no effective national link between the flag state and the ships on its register, and which often have less rigorous controls on matters such as safety standards).

At the end of 1998 there were 616 UK-owned merchant trading ships of 100 gross tonnes or more, with a total tonnage of 9.8 million deadweight tonnes. There were 159 vessels totalling 4.4 million deadweight tonnes used as oil, chemical or gas carriers, and 457 vessels totalling 5.3 million deadweight tonnes employed as dry-bulk carriers, container ships or other types of cargo ship. In all, 72% of UK-owned vessels (68% by tonnage) are registered in the UK or British Overseas Territories such as Bermuda.

In December 1998 the Government announced a series of measures for reviving the shipping industry and reversing the downward trend in the UK fleet. The implementation of these measures, announced in August 1999, includes:

- a new, more attractive fiscal regime, under which shipping would be taxed on the basis of tonnage, as has been adopted by a number of other countries;

- more training and career opportunities for seafarers, and a new 'minimum training obligation', involving a formal commitment by shipping companies to train seafarers as a condition of owners' eligibility for the new tax on tonnage; and

- a new role for the Maritime and Coastguard Agency (see below) in promoting the use of the British flag alongside its existing role of maintaining the high standards of the UK register.

Cargo Services

International revenue earned by the UK shipping industry in 1998 was £3.5 billion: £2.8 billion from freight—£2.3 billion on dry cargo and passenger vessels and £531 million on tankers and liquefied gas carriers—£179 million from charter receipts and £462 million from passenger revenue.

Nearly all scheduled cargo-liner services from the UK are containerised. British tonnage serving these trades is dominated by a relatively small number of companies. P&O Nedlloyd (owned by P&O and Royal Nedlloyd of the Netherlands) is among the three largest container carriers in the world. Besides the carriage of freight by liner and bulk services between the UK and the rest of Europe, many roll-on, roll-off services carry cars, passengers and commercial vehicles.

Passenger Services

Around 53 million passenger journeys a year take place on international and domestic ferry services linking the UK with Ireland and with mainland Europe. Domestic passenger and freight ferry services run to many of Britain's offshore islands, such as the Isle of Wight, Orkney and Shetland, and the islands off the west coast of Scotland. Traffic from southern and south-eastern ports accounts for a large proportion of traffic to the continent.

P&O European Ferries is the largest ferry operator in north-west Europe, with a fleet of 51 ships operating on 22 routes around the UK. Two 60,600-tonne ferries, the largest in the world, have been ordered for the Hull to Rotterdam route from 2001. Cross-Channel services are operated by roll-on, roll-off ferries, hovercraft (run by Hoverspeed), high-speed catamarans and high-speed monohulls. Capacity has been reduced following the merger in 1998 of P&O's cross-Channel operations with those of Stena Line to form P&O Stena Line.

P&O Cruises Ltd is one of the three leading cruise operators in the world. In 1998 P&O's US cruise subsidiary, Princess Cruises, handled 4.4 million passengers and took delivery of the then world's largest cruise ship, the 109,000-tonne *Grand Princess*.

Maritime Safety

The DETR's policies for improving marine safety and pollution control are implemented by the Maritime and Coastguard Agency, which inspects UK ships and foreign ships using UK ports to ensure that they comply with international safety, pollution prevention and operational standards. In 1998, 169 overseas-registered ships were detained in UK ports.

In 1998 HM Coastguard co-ordinated action in 11,553 incidents (including cliff rescues), in which 14,366 people were helped. In an emergency it co-ordinates facilities, such as its own helicopters; cliff rescue companies; lifeboats of the Royal National Lifeboat Institution (a voluntary body); aircraft, helicopters and ships from the armed forces; and merchant shipping and commercial aircraft.

Some locations around the UK are potentially hazardous for shipping. Measures to reduce the risk of collision include the separation of ships into internationally agreed shipping lanes, as applies in the Dover Strait, one of the world's busiest seaways, which is monitored by radar from the Channel Navigation Information Service near Dover. There are over 1,000 marine aids to navigation around the UK coast and responsibility for these rests with the general lighthouse authorities: Trinity House Lighthouse Service (for England and Wales), the Northern Lighthouse Board (for Scotland and the Isle of Man) and the Commissioners of Irish Lights (which covers the whole of Ireland).

In 1998 a new EC directive was agreed requiring roll-on, roll-off ferries to undergo safety checks before entering service and to carry voyage data recorders ('black boxes').

PORTS

There are about 80 ports of commercial significance in Great Britain, while several hundred small harbours cater for local cargo, fishing vessels, island ferries or recreation. There are three broad types of port: over 90 trust ports owned and run by boards constituted as trusts; those owned by local authorities (predominantly small ports, but including a few larger ones, such as Sullom Voe and Portsmouth); and company-owned facilities. Major ports controlled by trusts include Aberdeen, Dover, Milford Haven and Tyne.

Associated British Ports (ABP) is the UK's largest port owner and operates 23 ports, including Cardiff, Grimsby and Immingham,

Hull, Ipswich, Newport, Southampton and Swansea. Altogether they handled 122 million tonnes of cargo in 1998, when ABP invested £46 million in its ports and transport business. Other major facilities owned by private sector companies include Felixstowe, Harwich and Thamesport (all owned by the Hong Kong group Hutchison Whampoa), Clyde, Forth, Liverpool, Medway and Manchester.

The Government intends to issue a paper on UK ports policy, which will involve a greater role for ports in the promotion of environmentally sustainable transport and the regeneration of local communities, and reflect its view that all ports should be publicly accountable for their statutory powers and duties. Responses to a separate consultation paper on trust ports are under consideration.

Port Traffic

In 1998 traffic through major UK ports (those handling over 2 million tonnes a year) amounted to 530 million tonnes: 173 million tonnes of exports, 198 million tonnes of imports and 159 million tonnes of domestic traffic (which included offshore traffic and landings of sea-dredged aggregates). Minor ports handled an additional 38 million tonnes.

The UK's main ports, in terms of total tonnage handled, are shown in Table 22.3. Forth, Milford Haven and Sullom Voe (Shetland) mostly handle oil, while the principal destinations for non-fuel traffic are

Table 22.3: Traffic through the Principal Ports of Great Britain					*million tonnes*
	1994	1995	1996	1997	1998
London	51.8	51.4	52.9	55.7	57.3
Tees and Hartlepool	43.0	46.1	44.6	51.2	51.4
Grimsby and Immingham	42.9	46.8	46.8	48.0	48.4
Forth	44.4	47.1	45.6	43.1	44.4
Southampton	31.5	32.4	34.2	33.1	34.3
Sullom Voe	38.6	38.3	38.2	32.1	31.1
Liverpool	29.5	30.0	34.1	30.8	30.4
Felixstowe	22.1	24.0	25.8	28.9	30.0
Milford Haven	34.3	32.5	36.6	34.5	28.8
Dover	14.1	12.7	13.2	19.1	17.7

Source: DETR

London, Felixstowe, Grimsby and Immingham, Tees and Hartlepool, and Liverpool.

Container and roll-on, roll-off traffic in the UK was 133 million tonnes in 1998 and now accounts for 71% of non-bulk traffic. By far the most important port for container traffic is Felixstowe (which handles 42%), followed by London (11%) and Southampton (9%). Dover is the leading port for roll-on, roll-off traffic. It is also the major arrival and departure point, handling around half of international sea passenger movements to and from the UK.

Northern Ireland has four main ports, at Belfast, Larne, Londonderry and Warrenpoint. Belfast handles over 60% of Northern Ireland's seaborne trade.

CIVIL AVIATION

UK airlines are entirely in the private sector, as are many of the major airports. Air traffic is continuing to grow rapidly. In 1998 UK airlines flew a record 1.3 billion aircraft kilometres, 71% higher than in 1988: 886 million kilometres on scheduled services and 410 million kilometres on non-scheduled flights. They carried 62 million passengers on scheduled services and 31 million on charter flights. Passenger seat occupancy was 77%, being much higher on charter flights (90%) than on scheduled services (71%). It is also higher for international flights (78%) than internal services (62%).

The Government wishes to achieve further liberalisation of international air services in bilateral negotiations with other countries. A new policy on airports, covering the next 30 years, is being prepared. Meanwhile, a series of studies on regional airports is in progress.

Day-to-day responsibility for the regulation of civil aviation rests with the Civil Aviation Authority (CAA).

Airlines

British Airways

British Airways is the world's eighth largest carrier in terms of passengers carried, and the largest international airline. During 1998–99 its turnover from airline operations was £8.9

billion, and the British Airways group, which employs over 55,000 people worldwide, carried 45 million passengers.

The airline's scheduled route network serves 168 destinations in 87 countries and its main operating base is London's Heathrow Airport. British Airways has recently formed the 'Oneworld' alliance (the world's largest airline alliance, handling over 200 million passengers a year) with American Airlines, Canadian International Airlines, Cathay Pacific and Qantas; three other airlines have agreed to join the alliance. The British Airways group has a fleet of 281 aircraft, including seven Concordes, 59 Boeing 737s, 79 Boeing 747s, 53 Boeing 757s, 28 Boeing 767s and 26 Boeing 777s. It is acquiring 39 Airbus A319s, the first of which will be delivered in October 1999. British Airways has adopted a new fleet strategy, concentrating on profitable business while reducing capacity on less profitable services.

Other UK Airlines

British Midland is the second largest scheduled carrier and operates an extensive network of scheduled services with 37 aircraft, which carried 6 million passengers in 1998. Britannia Airways is the world's biggest charter airline and carried 8.2 million passengers in 1998 on its 36 aircraft. Virgin Atlantic operates scheduled services to 15 overseas destinations with 25 aircraft, and in May 1999 launched a new service to Shanghai. Low-fare, 'no-frills' airlines are expanding their services; operators in the UK include EasyJet and the British Airways subsidiary Go.

Airports

Of over 150 licensed civil aerodromes in the UK, nearly one-quarter handle more than 100,000 passengers a year each. In 1998 the UK's civil airports handled a total of 143.4 million passengers (142.2 million terminal passengers and nearly 1.3 million in transit), and 2.0 million tonnes of freight.

Heathrow is the world's busiest airport for international travellers and is the UK's most important for passengers and air freight,

Table 22.4: Passenger Traffic at the UK's Main Airports[a]				*million passengers*
	1988	1993	1996	1997	1998
London Heathrow	37.5	47.6	55.7	57.8	60.4
London Gatwick	20.7	20.1	24.1	26.8	29.0
Manchester	9.5	12.8	14.5	15.7	17.2
London Stansted	1.0	2.7	4.8	5.4	6.8
Birmingham	2.8	4.0	5.4	5.9	6.6
Glasgow	3.6	5.0	5.5	6.0	6.5
Edinburgh	2.1	2.7	3.8	4.2	4.5
Luton	2.8	1.8	2.4	3.2	4.1
Newcastle	1.4	2.1	2.4	2.6	2.9
Aberdeen	1.6	2.3	2.4	2.6	2.7
Belfast International	2.2	2.2	2.4	2.5	2.6
East Midlands	1.3	1.4	1.8	1.9	2.1

Source: Civil Aviation Authority
[a] Terminal passengers, excluding those in transit.

handling 60.4 million passengers (excluding those in transit) and 1.2 million tonnes of freight in 1998. Gatwick is also one of the world's busiest international airports and has the world's busiest single runway.

Ownership and Control

BAA plc is the world's largest commercial operator of airports. In the UK it owns and operates seven airports—Heathrow, Gatwick, Stansted and Southampton in southern England, and Glasgow, Edinburgh and Aberdeen in Scotland—which handled 112.5 million passengers in 1998–99. Overseas, BAA manages all or part of eight airports: four in the United States, Naples Airport in Italy, Melbourne and Launceston airports in Australia, and Mauritius. It also manages commercial facilities at its airports, and is a major international duty-free retailer.

The UK's second largest operator is TBI, which controls Belfast International and Cardiff. In May 1999 it acquired Airport Group International, so that it now has an interest in 29 airports worldwide. Manchester and Newcastle airports are among those owned by local authorities.

All UK airports used for public transport and training flights must be licensed by the CAA for reasons of safety. Stringent requirements, such as adequate fire-fighting,

medical and rescue services, have to be satisfied before a licence is granted. Strict security measures are in force at UK terminals; these were tightened in May 1999 following a review of airport security. Regulations require airlines to account for, and authorise for carriage, every item of hold baggage placed on board international flights originating in the UK.

Airport Development

At Heathrow, BAA has put forward plans for a fifth terminal, which could eventually cater for 30 million passengers a year. A planning inquiry into the proposals was concluded in spring 1999. If approval is granted, the new terminal could be operational by 2006. Connections to Heathrow have been improved following the opening in 1998 of the £450 million Heathrow Express rail link to central London. BAA is planning to invest over £200 million at Stansted in the next five years to increase its capacity to around 15 million passengers a year, and £100 million a year over the next ten years at Gatwick, mainly to expand terminal facilities and raise annual capacity to around 40 million passengers. Full-scale redevelopment of the passenger terminal at Edinburgh Airport is in progress. Among other large-scale improvements at UK airports are:

- a second runway at Manchester Airport, the first full-length runway to be built in the UK for 20 years, which is expected to open in 2000;
- a £37 million investment programme to provide a new terminal at Bristol Airport; and
- a £30 million expansion scheme at Belfast City Airport.

Air Traffic Control

Civil and military air traffic control over the UK and the surrounding seas, including much of the North Atlantic, is undertaken by National Air Traffic Services Ltd (NATS, a subsidiary of the CAA), working in collaboration with military controllers. Air traffic control facilities are expanding to meet the continuing growth in air traffic. All civil and military *en route* air traffic control operations in the UK will eventually be concentrated at two sites:

- a new air traffic control centre, at Swanwick (Hampshire), which will handle traffic over England and Wales and is expected to open in 2002; and
- a new Scottish centre at Prestwick, which will handle traffic over Scotland and Northern Ireland and replace the existing Prestwick centre in 2005–06.

The Government has announced a new Public-Private Partnership for NATS, involving the sale of 51% to the private sector, to help finance further investment and improve passenger safety. Air safety regulation, however, will remain with the CAA.

Air Safety

The CAA imposes very high safety standards on UK airlines. It certifies aircraft and air crews, licenses air operators and air travel organisers, and approves certain air fares and airport charges. To qualify for a first professional licence, a pilot must undertake a full-time course of instruction approved by the CAA—or have acceptable military or civilian flying experience—and pass ground examinations and flight tests. Every company operating aircraft used for commercial air transport purposes must possess an Air Operator's Certificate, which the CAA grants when it is satisfied that the company is competent to operate its aircraft safely. All aircraft registered in the UK must be granted a certificate of airworthiness by the CAA before being flown.

The CAA works closely with the Joint Aviation Authorities (JAA), a European grouping of aviation safety regulation authorities. The Government and the CAA support the concept of a new European Aviation Safety Authority, which would build on the work of the JAA.

The DETR's Air Accidents Investigation Branch investigates accidents and serious incidents occurring in UK airspace and those that happen overseas to aircraft registered or manufactured in the UK.

Communications

Telecommunications is one of the most rapidly expanding sectors of the UK economy. Growth has been particularly strong in new services, such as those provided over the Internet—there are an estimated 7 million users in the UK. A report for the Department of Trade and Industry found that business use of the Internet grew by 27% in 1998; 51% of UK companies have their own website; 72% use electronic mail; and usage of e-mail rose by 24% in 1998. Postal services remain important, and the volume of conventional mail continues to increase.

TELECOMMUNICATIONS

The UK was one of the first countries to introduce competition in its telecommunications network, when British Telecom (BT) became a private sector company in 1984. Britain now has one of the world's most open telecommunications markets, with nearly 400 licences issued to more than 300 different providers.

Services

Effective competition exists in most large urban areas of the UK, as new fixed link operators have extended their networks, resulting in a wider choice of supplier for users and lower prices. Competitors to BT have increased their share of the market, especially the business market (see Table 22.5). Cable companies now have 21% of the business market in international calls and other companies 42%, with BT's share 37%.

Telephone traffic has been rising quickly, with calls from fixed links growing by 14% a year, stimulated by price cuts and greater marketing by operators. Calls to mobile telephones in particular are growing rapidly, by over 50% a year. Exchange lines are continuing to increase, with business exchange lines rising at a faster rate than residential lines. BT still has a relatively high proportion of exchange lines—85% of residential lines and nearly 90% of business lines. However, cable operators are gaining customers in the residential market and among small businesses. There are around 16 million mobile telephone users, about 70% more than in 1998.

Office of Telecommunications (OFTEL)

OFTEL, a non-ministerial government department, is the independent regulatory body for the telecommunications industry. It is headed by the Director General of Telecommunications, whose functions include:

- ensuring that licensees comply with the conditions of their licences;

- promoting effective competition in the telecommunications industry;

- providing advice to the Secretary of State for Trade and Industry on telecommunications matters; and

- investigating complaints against public telecommunications operators.

Rapid developments in the sector are changing the emphasis of OFTEL's work. It is moving away from detailed regulation in basic domestic telecommunications services and looking to ensure that competition applies in

Table 22.5: Telecommunications Statistics

	BT	Kingston	Cable & Wireless Communications	Other cable	Others	Total
Call minutes 1998 (million)[a]	126,668	1,497	15,423	13,855	12,327	169,769
of which:						
Residential customers	85,505	n.a.	7,691	10,268	715	104,179
Business customers	40,544	n.a.	7,732	2,368	11,395	62,039
% of call revenue						
(4th quarter 1998)	71.2	0.4	11.6	6.4	10.5	100
of which:						
Residential market	81.6	n.a.	7.0	9.4	2.0	100
Business market	58.9	n.a.	17.4	3.7	20.0	100
Exchange lines at end of 1998						
(thousand)	27,945	209	1,519	2,784	169	32,626
of which:						
Residential lines	20,093	163	1,044	2,453	7	23,761
Business lines	7,852	46	474	331	161	8,864

Source: OFTEL Market Information Update, August 1999
[a] Services from fixed links—excludes mobile telephone calls. Figures may include a small amount of double counting, as in some instances calls supplied by an operator to a reseller may be counted by both operator and reseller. In some cases, business and residential statistics may not add up to the total figure.
n.a. = not available.
Note: Differences between totals and the sums of their component parts may also be due to rounding.

international and mobile services, and to considering the effects of the convergence of the telecommunications and broadcasting sectors.

Service Providers

BT

BT is currently the UK's biggest telecommunications company, with a turnover in 1998–99 of £18.2 billion. It runs one of the world's largest public telecommunications networks, including over 20 million residential lines and 8 million business lines (see Table 22.5). It has 7,500 local telephone exchanges, 69 main switching units, and over 142,000 public payphones, and employs 124,700 people. Originally BT handled mainly fixed-voice telephone calls, but its traffic in data communications—including e-mail, the Internet and electronic commerce—is growing by over 30% a year and now exceeds voice traffic on its network. BT is planning investment of £5 billion in data and multimedia services.

BT has extensive international interests through its 'Concert' operation. Concert Communications Services has over 4,700 major corporate customers in 52 countries. In 1998 BT and AT&T (one of the largest telecommunications companies in the United States) announced their intention to create a joint venture combining their international assets, network and traffic (including the Concert services), which would serve 237 countries and territories. The new venture is expected to begin operating later in 1999 if regulatory approval is received.

Cable & Wireless

Cable and Wireless plc has operations in 50 countries and employs over 50,000 people. Turnover in 1998–99 (excluding associated companies and joint ventures) was £7.9 billion, of which 32% came from its interests in Hong Kong. Around 73% of its revenue comes from business customers, and in 1999 the company adopted a new strategy to concentrate on the business sector, especially

in data, Internet and other advanced services; revenue from these services is growing by 30% a year. It has recently acquired the Internet assets of the US telecommunications company MCI, giving it a leading position in the US Internet market, as well as acquiring the Japanese international communications company IDC. It has also sold its submarine cable laying and maintenance business, and has agreed to sell its interest in the One 2 One mobile telephone operator. It has announced additional capital expenditure, including £610 million over three years to build a fully integrated voice and data network linking over 40 cities in Europe and £410 million on developing its US Internet network.

In the UK, Cable and Wireless plc has a 53% stake in Cable & Wireless Communications, currently the largest provider of integrated communications and television services in the UK. Under a deal reached with NTL in July 1999, the operations of Cable & Wireless Communications will be split probably early in 2000, with Cable and Wireless plc acquiring full ownership of business services operations; currently Cable & Wireless Communications provides services to over 150,000 business customers, while 1.1 million residential homes take direct telephony or cable television from the company. NTL will acquire the residential business of Cable & Wireless Communications.

Vodafone AirTouch

Vodafone AirTouch is the UK's biggest mobile telephone operator, with over a third of the market. It was formed in 1999 following a takeover by Vodafone of the US mobile telephone group AirTouch. The new company, with over 23 million subscribers in 23 countries, has become the largest mobile telecommunications company in the world.

Other Operators

Other public telecommunications operators include:

- COLT Telecom, which has high-capacity optical fibre networks in 19 major European cities in nine countries;

- Energis, which is concentrating on enhanced voice and advanced data services, with a network of over 6,500 kilometres (4,040 miles) across the National Grid electricity transmission infrastructure;
- Kingston Communications, the long-established network operator for the Kingston upon Hull area—it was floated on the London Stock Exchange in July 1999, with the local council retaining a minority stake; and
- ScottishTelecom, a division of ScottishPower.

Following a substantial consolidation among the cable operators, the three main companies are currently Cable & Wireless Communications (see p. 379), Telewest and NTL. By the end of 1998 cable operators had installed around 4.3 million telephone lines in the UK, and 12 million homes were able to receive broadband cable services.

Mobile Communications

Around a quarter of people in the UK have a mobile telephone. Mobile telephone usage is continuing to grow strongly, helped recently by rising sales of pre-paid schemes, under which customers pay for their calls in advance by purchasing vouchers. Vodafone AirTouch and BT Cellnet are the two largest operators, with 6 million and 4.8 million subscribers respectively.

The UK was the first country to offer personal communications network (PCN) digital services. The two PCN operators are Orange, with 2.8 million customers, and One 2 One (which, it was announced in August 1999, is to be acquired by Deutsche Telekom from Cable and Wireless and MediaOne of the US), with 2.5 million subscribers. Early in 2000 the Government will offer for sale by auction licences to run the third generation of mobile telephones, which will provide high-speed access to a large number of entertainment and information services. Five licences will be auctioned, with one reserved for a new entrant to the market.

Dolphin Telecommunications is due to launch later in 1999 the first mobile telephone network using the TETRA technology, which enhances the variety and quality of available services, including advanced speech and data facilities, and greater security.

Other licences awarded include four to operate national paging networks and four to run mobile data networks.

Internet Service Providers

There are around 300 Internet service providers (ISPs) in the UK offering access to the Internet. Internet use has recently been stimulated by the arrival in the market of ISPs offering free access to the Internet. The biggest ISP is Freeserve, which was launched by the retailer Dixons in 1998 and has some 1.3 million users.

POSTAL SERVICES

The Post Office, founded in 1635, pioneered postal services and was the first to issue adhesive postage stamps as proof of advance payment for mail. Today, its Royal Mail service delivers to 26 million addresses in the UK, handling 77 million letters each working day. In 1998–99 it processed 18.1 billion inland letters and 873 million outgoing international letters. Mail is collected from 112,000 posting boxes, and from post offices and large postal users. The Post Office employs 201,000 people.

The postal market is undergoing rapid change. In a White Paper (see Further Reading), issued in July 1999, the Government set out its plans to transform the Post Office and the postal market in the UK. The measures give the Post Office greater commercial freedom to operate at arm's length from the Government and to invest in new business opportunities. The new freedoms are part of a package of measures which also includes the introduction of greater competition and tough new regulation to promote the interests of consumers and ensure fair competition. The new regulator—the Postal Services Commission—will take up its duties on 1 April 2000. One of its first tasks will be to consider the effects of a reduction in the Post Office's current monopoly on letters and packets costing less than £1 or weighing less than 350g, and to make recommendations to the Government on an appropriate threshold.

Royal Mail has invested substantially in the latest mail-sorting technology. High-speed mail-handling machinery—the Integrated Mail Processor—should enable automatic handling of 90% of letter mail by 2000. Automatic sorting utilises the information contained in the postcode; the UK postcode system is one of the most sophisticated in the world, allowing mechanised sorting down to part of a street on a postman's round and, in some cases, to an individual address (see map opposite p. 5).

International Services, part of the Post Office, has its own mail-handling centre at Heathrow, which handles about four-fifths of outward airmail. It uses 1,400 flights a week to send mail direct to over 300 destinations worldwide. Taking advantage of its new commercial freedoms, the Post Office is already expanding overseas, through the acquisition earlier in 1999 of German Parcel, the third largest private carrier in Germany.

Post Office Counters Ltd handles a wide range of transactions, with a total value of £154 billion in 1998–99. It acts as an agent for Royal Mail and Parcelforce Worldwide, government departments, local authorities and Alliance & Leicester Giro banking services. There are about 19,000 post offices in the UK, of which around 600 are operated directly by the Post Office. The remainder are franchise offices or are operated on an agency basis by sub-postmasters.

Post Office Specialist Services

The Post Office offers a variety of specialist services. Parcelforce Worldwide provides a door-to-door overnight delivery service throughout the UK and an international service to over 240 countries and territories. It handles 138 million items a year. 'Datapost Sameday' provides a rapid delivery within or between major UK cities. The Philatelic Bureau in Edinburgh is an important outlet for the Post Office's philatelic (postage stamp) business, including sales to overseas collectors or dealers.

Private Courier and Express Services

Private sector couriers and express operators are allowed to handle time-sensitive door-to-door deliveries, subject to a minimum fee, currently of £1. The courier/express service industry has grown rapidly and the annual revenue earned by the carriage of these items is estimated at about £2 billion. The UK is a major provider of monitored express deliveries in Europe, with London one of the main centres for air courier/express traffic.

Further Reading

Moving Forward. Northern Ireland Transport Policy Statement. Department of the Environment for Northern Ireland, 1998.

A New Deal for Transport: Better for Everyone. Cm 3950. The Stationery Office, 1998.

A New Deal for Trunk Roads in England. DETR, 1998.

Post Office Reform: A world class service for the 21st century. Department of Trade and Industry. Cm 4340. The Stationery Office, 1999.

Transporting Wales into the Future. Welsh Office, 1998.

Transport Statistics Great Britain, annual report. The Stationery Office.

Travel Choices for Scotland. Cm 4010. The Stationery Office, 1998.

Website

Department of the Environment, Transport and the Regions: www.detr.gov.uk

23 The Economy

The UK economy has been affected by the downturn in the global economy, with a slowing in the rate of economic growth. However, employment has been rising and inflation is running at a historically low level. Interest rates are lower than in 1998, and there are indications of a revival of confidence among business and consumers.

The Government's economic policies are directed towards the achievement of high and stable levels of growth and employment, with the aim of enabling everyone to share in higher living standards and greater job opportunities. It is working to increase UK competitiveness through promoting enterprise and innovation, creating strong and competitive markets, and developing an effective legal and regulatory framework for business.

STRUCTURE AND PERFORMANCE

The value of all goods and services produced for final consumption in the economy is measured by gross domestic product. In 1998 GDP at current market prices totalled £843.7 billion. Between 1995 and 1998 GDP at constant prices increased by 8.5% (see Table 23.1). Values for two of the main economic indicators are shown in the charts on p. 383.

Output

Long-term economic growth in the UK has averaged around 2.25% a year. The recession of the early 1990s was followed by a recovery in output. GDP grew by 3.5% in 1997, but by 2.2% in 1998, reflecting a slower rise in domestic demand—under the influence of tighter monetary and fiscal policy—and a negative contribution to overall growth from

net trade as a result of the strengthening in sterling and the slowdown in the global economy. Slower growth is expected in 1999, mainly as a result of weaker growth in UK export markets, and GDP is forecast by HM Treasury (in the 1999 Budget forecast) to rise by 1% to $1^{1}/2\%$. However, growth is expected to be stronger in 2000.

Recent decades have generally seen the fastest growth in the services sector (see chapter 30), and this pattern has continued during the 1990s. In 1998 service industries' output increased by 3.7%, with particularly strong growth in transport, storage and communications (6.5%) and business services and finance (5.3%). Manufacturing (see chapter 28) now contributes less than a quarter of GDP, compared with over a third in 1950. Manufacturing growth has been well below that of services, and in 1998 as a whole manufacturing output rose by 0.4%, with

RPI Inflation, 1975–98 (All Items)

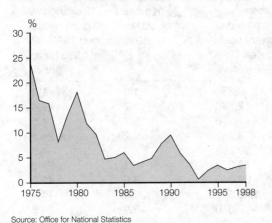

Source: Office for National Statistics

Percentage Change in GDP at 1995 Market Prices, 1975–98

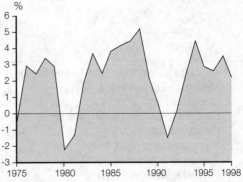

Source: Office for National Statistics

Table 23.1: Gross Domestic Product and Gross National Income					£ million
	1988	1993	1996	1997	1998
Final consumption expenditure	383,285	542,963	631,529	664,805	698,688
Gross capital formation	100,458	101,550	127,261	138,580	151,823
Exports of goods and services	107,434	162,078	220,303	229,326	224,202
less Imports of goods and services	−124,657	−168,774	−224,492	−228,822	−232,714
Statistical discrepancy	—	—	—	—	1,726
GDP at current market prices	466,520	637,817	754,601	803,889	843,725
Gross national income at current market prices	464,661	633,992	758,824	812,461	855,462
GDP at 1995 market prices	640,587	664,018	730,767	756,430	773,380
GDP index at 1995 market prices (1995 = 100)	89.9	93.2	102.6	106.2	108.5

Source: *United Kingdom National Accounts 1999—the Blue Book*

output falling back in the second half of the year.

Over the past 25 years the UK has experienced lower economic growth than its major competitors. In terms of purchasing power, income per head in 1998 was below that of the other G7 countries. Productivity is also lower than in many other industrialised countries, partly reflecting earlier low levels of investment (see below). Data from the Organisation for Economic Co-operation and Development (OECD) shows the UK's

productivity gap with the United States, France and Germany is substantial—up to a third.

Investment

In recent decades the UK's capital investment has accounted for a smaller share of GDP than other industrialised countries—around 17% of GDP, compared with the OECD average of 21%. This has left a legacy of low capital stock per worker. In November 1998 a survey for the Department of Trade and Industry of

Table 23.2: Output by Industry

	Gross value added at current basic prices 1998 (£ million)	% of gross value added 1998	% change in gross value added 1990–98 at 1995 basic prices
Agriculture, hunting, forestry and fishing	9,656	1.3	1.9
Mining and quarrying	12,748	1.7	42.4
Manufacturing	147,306	19.7	4.5
Electricity, gas and water supply	16,737	2.2	24.3
Construction	39,262	5.3	−4.8
Wholesale and retail trade	113,070	15.1	24.0
Transport and communications	63,340	8.5	42.0
Financial intermediation	206,347	27.6	14.9
Adjustment for financial services	−29,370	−3.9	24.5
Public administration and defence	40,495	5.4	−7.4
Education, health and social work	89,041	11.9	28.2
Other services	38,912	5.2	37.7
Total gross value added	747,544	100.0	18.0
Intermediate consumption at purchasers' prices	851,795		
Total output at basic prices	1,599,339		

Source: *United Kingdom National Accounts 1999—the Blue Book*

Table 23.3: Gross Fixed Capital Formation at Constant 1995 Prices   £ million

	1993	1996	1997	1998
New dwellings, excluding land	21,491	22,154	22,669	23,798
Other buildings and structures	32,414	30,764	32,590	35,616
Transport equipment	10,589	11,777	12,982	14,266
Other machinery and equipment and cultivated assets	36,958	49,124	54,241	61,616
Intangible fixed assets	3,677	4,162	4,103	4,575
Costs associated with the transfer of ownership of non-produced assets	3,857	4,061	4,661	4,313
Gross fixed capital formation	**109,127**	**122,042**	**131,246**	**144,184[a]**

Source: *United Kingdom National Accounts 1999—the Blue Book*
[a] Of which business investment accounted for £104,602 million, general government £10,483 million, public corporations £1,597 million and other private sector £27,502 million.

capital expenditure of 500 of the top UK companies found that as a whole UK firms appeared to be investing less than their main international competitors. In certain sectors though—notably oil, pharmaceuticals, water supply, telecommunications and food retailers—UK firms were investing at levels at, or above, the international average. The largest UK investors were Shell, BT, BP, Cable & Wireless, and British Airways.

Following growth of around 4% a year in the 1980s, investment in the UK declined during the recession of the early 1990s. However, in 1998 investment (gross fixed capital formation) at constant 1995 prices increased by 9.9% to £144 billion (see Table 23.3), representing £148 billion at current prices.

Business investment has been rising strongly since 1995, and in 1998 was up by 12.5% at constant prices, the highest rate of growth since 1988. The rise was heavily concentrated in private sector services, where investment rose by 18.8%, while manufacturing investment increased by only 3.8%.

General government investment has declined in recent years. However, it rose by 8.2% in 1998 and is forecast to rise substantially over the next three years (see p. 402).

Business Structure

The UK has around 3.7 million businesses. They include many big companies—of the top 500 European companies recorded by the *Financial Times* in 1998, around 150 were UK-based. About 3,000 UK businesses employ over 500 people and account for 38% of total employment by UK businesses and a similar proportion of turnover. In some sectors a small number of large companies and their subsidiaries are responsible for a substantial

Expenditure on acquisitions overseas by UK companies reached a record £54 billion in 1998, when the UK overtook the United States to become the largest buyer of overseas firms in that year. This primarily reflected the merger between British Petroleum (BP) and Amoco of the US to form BP Amoco. Other recent large-scale cross-border mergers and acquisitions involving UK companies include the merger between Zeneca and Astra of Sweden in April 1999 to form AstraZeneca (one of the world's largest pharmaceuticals companies) and the takeover by Vodafone of AirTouch of the US to form Vodafone AirTouch. The UK has also attracted large-scale inward investment, including acquisitions by overseas companies. The cumulative value of inward investment in the UK is now almost £200 billion, while inward direct investment totalled £38 billion in 1998.

proportion of total production, for instance in chemicals, pharmaceuticals, motor vehicle assembly and aerospace. The growing importance of financial and other services is illustrated in the composition of the top 20 UK companies by market capitalisation, where six are in the retail banking sector, two in insurance/life assurance and three in telecommunications (see Table 23.4).

Table 23.4: Top UK Companies by Market Capitalisation,[a] December 1998

Company/ business sector	Market capitalisation (£ million)[b]
BP Amoco/oil and gas	87,734
Glaxo Wellcome/ pharmaceuticals	74,852
BT/telecommunications	58,501
SmithKline Beecham/ pharmaceuticals	46,863
Lloyds TSB/retail banking	46,461
HSBC/retail banking	41,995
Shell Transport & Trading/ oil and gas	36,707
Vodafone[c]/telecommunications	30,195
Zeneca[c]/pharmaceuticals	24,855
Diageo/alcoholic beverages	24,492
Unilever/food producers	21,978
Halifax/retail banking	20,816
National Westminster Bank/retail banking	19,664
Barclays/retail banking	19,469
Abbey National/retail banking	18,201
Cable & Wireless/ telecommunications	17,772
Prudential/life assurance	17,640
BG/gas distribution	15,101
General Electric/electronic and electrical equipment	14,504
Allied Zurich/insurance	14,081

Source: London Stock Exchange *Fact File 1999*
[a] According to the FT 500 Survey, the top ten companies by turnover in 1998 were Shell Transport & Trading, British Petroleum, Unilever, Tesco, BT, J. Sainsbury, Diageo, ICI, British Airways, and Marks & Spencer.
[b] Market capitalisation = the number of shares issued multiplied by their market price.
[c] Now Vodafone AirTouch and AstraZeneca respectively (see panel).

Small firms play an important part in the UK economy: around 45% of the workforce work for companies employing fewer than 50 people. Around 2.3 million businesses are sole traders or partners without employees, while a further 900,000 businesses employ one to four people. Together these 3.2 million enterprises account for 89% of the number of businesses, 24% of business employment and 16% of turnover.

Private sector firms predominate in the economy. The public sector has become much less significant following the privatisation since 1979 of some 100 public sector businesses, including gas, electricity supply, coal and telecommunications. The remaining major nationalised industries are the Post Office, London Transport, BNFL (British Nuclear Fuels) and the Civil Aviation Authority.

Household Income and Expenditure

Total resources of the household sector (including non-profit institutions serving households) rose by 4.5% in 1998 to nearly £825 billion. Gross disposable income—after deductions, including taxes and social contributions—totalled £566 billion. In real terms, households' disposable income in 1998 was similar to that in 1997. Household net financial wealth continues to grow strongly, and in 1998 amounted to £2,072 billion. Wages and salaries accounted for nearly 60% of household primary income in 1998 and rose by almost 7% during the year.

In 1998, 94% of after-tax household income was spent and 6% saved. The household saving ratio fell from 9.3% in 1997 to 6.4% in 1998. This fall, to what is a more normal level, reflected households using savings to support their spending during a period of temporarily slower income growth.

Households' final consumption expenditure accounted for 75% of total final consumption expenditure in 1998, and amounted to £525 billion at current market prices. In terms of constant prices, it grew by 3.3% in 1998, although there was an underlying slowing in consumer demand through the year. Expenditure on services, however, remained relatively strong, rising by 4.4% in real terms in 1998. Expenditure on durable goods was 6.5% higher than in 1997.

Table 23.5 shows the changing pattern of households' final consumption expenditure. Over the longer term, as incomes rise, people tend to spend increasing proportions of their disposable income on durable goods and certain services. Spending on leisure pursuits and tourism, communications, health and financial services have all shown significant growth in recent years. Declining proportions are being spent on food and alcoholic drink, tobacco, and fuel and power.

Inflation

The two main measures of retail price inflation used in the UK are:

- the Retail Prices Index (RPI), which records the price of goods and services purchased by households in the UK and is used to calculate what is often referred to as 'headline' inflation; and

- the RPI excluding mortgage interest payments (RPIX), which is used to calculate 'underlying' inflation and is the target measure used by the Government (see p. 388).

The Office for National Statistics is engaged in a three-year programme to examine the RPI series and potential ways of improving its relevance to the UK economy.

Underlying annual inflation in the last 20 years has fluctuated considerably, with a peak of 20.8% in the year to May 1980. However, it has been much lower in the 1990s, and since 1993 it has been in a relatively narrow range, from 2%–3.5%. In 1998 it averaged 2.6%—the RPI was 3.4%—and it has been close to the government target in recent months. Sharp falls in import prices—reflecting the appreciation in sterling since summer 1996 and relatively low world commodity prices—have contributed to the low level of inflation. The impact of these factors is also evident in the data on producer prices. Input prices for materials and fuel purchased by manufacturing industry fell by 17.3% in the two years to December 1998. The index has fluctuated since then, but remains below the levels recorded as far back as 1992. Output price inflation has also remained low, with prices of manufactured products in the UK rising by just 1.3% in the year to August 1999.

Table 23.5: Household Final Consumption Expenditure[a]

	Expenditure in 1990 (£ million)[b]	Expenditure in 1998 (£ million)[b]	% of expenditure in 1998[b]	% growth in expenditure at 1995 market prices 1990–98
Food and non-alcoholic beverages	41,817	54,113	10.3	10.4
Alcoholic beverages and tobacco	30,009	41,577	7.9	–12.7
Clothing and footwear	21,934	32,479	6.2	41.6
Housing, water and fuels	56,729	94,341	18.0	9.6
Furnishings, household equipment and house maintenance	19,882	31,999	6.1	35.3
Health	3,559	6,186	1.2	21.8
Transport	51,767	78,806	15.1	10.5
Communications	6,485	10,835	2.1	72.8
Recreation and culture	35,733	58,485	11.2	34.0
Education	3,221	8,492	1.6	41.0
Restaurants and hotels	24,762	39,910	7.6	12.0
Other goods and services	40,166	66,149	12.6	17.3
Total	**336,064**	**523,372**	**100.0**	**16.2**
of which:				
Durable goods	34,517	52,627	10.1	34.0
Non-durable goods	155,119	222,464	42.5	13.6
Services	146,428	248,281	47.4	14.4

Source: *United Kingdom National Accounts 1999—the Blue Book*
[a] Expenditure by households and non-profit institutions serving households.
[b] At current market prices.
Note: Differences between totals and the sums of their component parts are due to rounding.

Within the RPI, the price of tobacco has recently been rising at well above the average rate, reflecting both higher levels of duty and increases in manufactures' prices. However, in August 1999 a number of items—including mortgage interest payments, leisure goods, consumer durables, clothing and footwear, telephone services, and gas and electricity— were cheaper than a year earlier.

Another measure of inflation is the harmonised index of consumer prices (HICP), which is calculated in each EU member state for the purposes of international comparison. In 1998 the HICP for the UK was 1.5%. During most of 1998 and 1999 the UK's HICP has been slightly above the EU average.

Labour Market

In spite of the slowdown in economic growth, employment in the UK in early 1999 was rising faster than a year previously, and economic inactivity was falling as more people found jobs or sought work. Employment in the three months to June 1999 was 27.4 million, 347,000 higher than a year earlier (see chapter 11). Unemployment has fallen in recent years and is below that in many other European countries, while long-term and youth unemployment have both declined substantially. In the three months to June 1999, according to the International Labour Organisation measure, unemployment was 1.8 million, 6.0% of the workforce.

Overseas Trade

International trade plays a key role in the UK economy (see chapter 25). The UK is the fifth largest exporter of goods and services, and exports accounted for 27% of GDP in 1998. Other EU countries took 58% of UK exports of goods in 1998 and supplied 55% of imported goods.

Although the UK's surplus on the current account (see p. 415) fell from £6.3 billion in 1997 to £0.1 billion in 1998, this was the first time since 1984 and 1985 that two consecutive annual surpluses had been recorded. The deficit on trade in goods rose to £20.8 billion, with global developments—notably the financial crisis in Asia—adversely affecting UK exports. However, this deficit was more than offset by the combined effects of record surpluses on both trade in services (£12.3 billion) and on investment income (£15.1 billion).

ECONOMIC STRATEGY

The main elements of the Government's economic strategy, which is designed to improve the underlying rate of growth and employment, are:

● ensuring economic stability, as a platform for long-term sustainable growth;

● raising productivity through promoting enterprise and investment;

● increasing employment opportunity (see chapter 11); and

● creating a fairer society.

HM Treasury is the department with prime responsibility for the Government's monetary and fiscal frameworks. It is also responsible for economic policy, which it carries out in conjunction with other government departments, such as Trade and Industry; Education and Employment; and the Environment, Transport and the Regions.

Economic Stability

The Government considers that economic stability is vital for the achievement of its central economic objective of high and stable levels of growth and employment. It has introduced new frameworks for both monetary and fiscal policies to ensure low inflation and sound public finances.

The Bank of England's Monetary Policy Committee (MPC, see p. 510) is responsible for setting interest rates to meet the

Government policy on membership of the European single currency (see p. 80) was set out by the Chancellor of the Exchequer in October 1997. The determining factor underpinning any government decision on membership of the single currency is whether the economic case for the UK joining is clear and unambiguous.

To make that assessment of the national economic interest, the Government has set out five economic tests which will have to be met before any decision to join can be taken. These are:

● whether the UK economy has achieved sustainable convergence with the economies of the single currency;

● whether there is sufficient flexibility in the UK economy to adapt to economic change;

● the effect membership would have on investment in the UK;

● the impact membership would have on the UK financial services industry; and

● whether joining the single currency would be good for employment.

The Government has said that, barring some fundamental and unforeseen change in economic circumstances, making a decision during this Parliament to join is not realistic. However, preparations should be made in this Parliament so that, should the economic tests be met, a decision to join a successful single currency can be made early in the next Parliament. In February 1999 HM Treasury issued a National Outline Changeover Plan for the UK, a consultative document setting out the practical steps that would need to be taken by business and the public sector if the UK were to join the single currency.

Government's inflation target of 2.5%, as defined by the 12-month increase in RPIX. This new framework has put monetary policy on a long-term footing, and is one of the most transparent and accountable in the world.

Between October 1998 and June 1999 the MPC cut short-term interest rates from 7.5% to 5%, although it raised the rate to 5.25% in

September 1999. However, interest rates remain at historically very low levels.

International Stability

The UK Government is playing a major part in promoting economic stability around the world. The aim is to reduce the likelihood of future global uncertainties, such as those which occurred in 1998 when the world economy was affected by exceptional movements in financial markets, initially in parts of Asia but spreading to other areas, such as Russia and Latin America. A series of reforms being adopted by G7 countries, including the establishment of a Financial Stability Forum and the implementation of codes of good practice on fiscal policy, monetary and financial policy, corporate governance, and accounting, are expected to help reduce the volatility of financial markets and increase the prospects for international economic stability and prosperity.

Fiscal Policy

Fiscal policy is guided by two strict rules designed to deliver sound public finances:

- the golden rule—over the economic cycle the Government will borrow only to invest and not to fund current spending; and
- the sustainable investment rule—public sector net debt as a proportion of GDP will be held at a stable and prudent level over the economic cycle.

These rules mean that current taxpayers pay for current spending, and they require public borrowing to be kept under firm control.

The Code for Fiscal Stability, set up under the Finance Act 1998, requires fiscal and debt management policy to be carried out in accordance with five key principles:

- transparency in setting fiscal policy objectives, the implementation of fiscal policy and the presentation of the public accounts;
- stability in the fiscal policy-making process and in the way that fiscal policy affects the economy;

- responsibility in the management of the public finances;
- fairness, including between present and future generations; and
- efficiency in the design and implementation of fiscal policy, and in managing both sides of the public sector balance sheet.

The fiscal policy framework is being strengthened by a new way of planning and controlling public expenditure (see p. 402).

The Budget

The Budget is the Government's main economic statement of the year and is usually issued in March. In a major speech to Parliament, the Chancellor of the Exchequer reviews the nation's economic performance and describes the Government's economic objectives and the tax and spending policies it intends to follow in order to achieve them. The 1999 Budget report comprised two documents:

- the Economic and Fiscal Strategy Report, setting out the Government's long-term strategy and objectives; and
- the Financial Statement and Budget Report, providing a summary of each Budget measure and an analysis of the economic and public finance forecasts.

In advance of the spring Budget, the Government now publishes a Pre-Budget Report. As well as setting out economic and fiscal developments and prospects, it describes the direction of government policy and sets out for consultation measures that are under consideration for the forthcoming Budget.

INDUSTRIAL AND COMMERCIAL POLICY

The Department of Trade and Industry (DTI) aims to increase UK competitiveness and scientific excellence in order to generate higher levels of sustainable growth and productivity. It has four specific objectives:

- to promote enterprise, innovation and higher productivity;
- to make the most of the UK's scientific, engineering and technological capabilities;

- to create strong and competitive markets; and

- to develop a fair and effective legal and regulatory framework.

Measures to help achieve these objectives are described below. DTI responsibilities on export promotion are covered in chapter 25, technology and innovation in chapter 26, and consumer protection and the regulation of financial services in chapter 30, while those on industrial relations are described in chapter 11.

Competitiveness

The Government set out its new industrial policy in the White Paper on competitiveness, *Our Competitive Future: Building the Knowledge Driven Economy*, published in December 1998. Its aim is for UK business to close the performance gap with its competitors, in terms of productivity and of the ability to produce innovative new products and create higher-value services. It envisages harnessing the UK's distinctive capabilities of knowledge, skills and creativity to achieve this objective. Among the government measures to implement this policy are:

- *measures to strengthen the UK's capabilities*, including an additional £1.4 billion to modernise the science and engineering base, promotion of the commercialisation of university research, a proposed tax credit for small and medium-sized enterprises (SMEs) on research and development (R&D), a new Enterprise Fund to support the financing of small businesses with growth potential, including a new Venture Capital Challenge for investment for early-stage high-technology businesses;

- *the promotion of collaboration*, between businesses and within regions, for example, encouraging the adoption of business 'clusters'; and

- *measures to make markets more competitive*, including implementing the Competition Act 1998, and introducing an Electronic Communications Bill and other measures to liberalise communications markets.

To measure the UK's progress in improving competitiveness, a Competitiveness Index containing a series of indicators will be published in autumn 1999. A Competitiveness Council of business people is advising on the Index and related issues.

Business Support Services

The DTI promotes enterprise and innovation through encouraging successful business start-ups and offering businesses a number of support services. Most support is designed to assist business, especially SMEs, to expand and invest, and to adopt best practice.

The main mechanism for delivering business information, advice and support in England is 'Business Link', a national network of 81 local partnerships. These provide a single local point of access for integrated information and advisory services tailored to the needs of businesses, and deploy some 650 personal business advisers and 290 specialist counsellors for export development, design, and innovation and technology. Business Link partners include Training and Enterprise Councils (TECs— see p. 152), chambers of commerce, enterprise agencies, local authorities and other providers of business support. Business Links are also developing partnerships with

In March 1999, as part of the Budget statement, the Government announced its intention to create the Small Business Service (SBS) which will act as a strong voice for small businesses within government and will ensure the provision of support programmes to suit their needs. The specific roles have not yet been finalised, but one function will be to reduce the burden of regulation on small firms and provide assistance to SMEs in complying with regulations. Its responsibilities will include the new Enterprise Fund and establishing a payroll service for new employers in order to reduce the burden of complying with the tax system. The SBS is expected to be operational by April 2000.

the new Regional Development Agencies (see p. 11).

Elsewhere in the UK similar business support arrangements apply:

- in Scotland, the Business Shops Network brings together business development organisations, local authorities and chambers of commerce to support new and growing businesses;

- in Wales, Business Connect covers all the main business support agencies and has a network of business support and front-line advice centres; and

- in Northern Ireland small firms are helped by the Local Enterprise Development Unit's network of regional offices.

Business Finance

In 1998 the DTI reviewed the methods of finance available for SMEs, such as venture capital (see p. 515). It found that there was a tendency for firms to rely on debt finance (such as bank loans) when equity finance might be more appropriate, but sometimes equity finance was difficult to obtain. It therefore plans to set up by the end of 1999 a new Enterprise Fund to provide financial support for SMEs with growth potential. Funding of £180 million will be available between 1999 and 2002 with the aim of stimulating a contribution of £500 million from the private sector for these firms.

The Fund will become responsible for the Small Firms Loan Guarantee Scheme, currently the DTI's main instrument for supporting business finance. The scheme provides a guarantee enabling authorised lenders to loan money to SMEs lacking the security to receive conventional finance (4,482 loans valued at £189 million were guaranteed in 1998–99).

Among other measures designed to encourage investment are the Enterprise Investment Scheme (EIS) and Venture Capital Trusts (VCTs). These schemes seek to encourage individuals to invest in smaller unlisted trading companies in return for various tax reliefs and are designed to help smaller UK early-stage and expanding firms.

The EIS allows 'business angels'[1] to take a position on the board of the investee company. VCTs are similar to an investment trust (see p. 517) and are quoted on the London Stock Exchange. Under a new Venture Capital Challenge scheme (part of the Enterprise Fund), funding of £20 million will be available from the Capital Modernisation Fund (see p. 402) for investment in new funds for early-stage high-technology businesses in partnership with project investors. Other measures, which will apply from 2000 and are designed to provide incentives for investors and entrepreneurs to encourage investment, include:

- an Enterprise Management Incentives scheme, which will provide tax relief for certain forms of equity-based remuneration in small higher-risk trading companies;

- a new tax incentive to promote corporate venturing through promoting inter-firm collaboration and improving the flow of investment to early-stage companies from larger firms; and

- a tax credit for spending by SMEs on R&D.

Design, Quality and Standards

Through the independent Design Council, the DTI supports the effective use of design and design management techniques, which can make a significant contribution to the creation of successful products, processes and services, and to improving competitiveness. As advocate for design at the national level, the Design Council undertakes research into design issues, and develops design tools for use by industry, business, education and government, and publicises the results. It liaises with Scottish Design, the Welsh Design Advisory Service and the Northern Ireland Design Directorate on national initiatives. A separate design service offers support for

---

[1] 'Business angels' are private investors, usually with a business background, who are willing to invest in small businesses in return for an equity stake; many also offer their management expertise to the businesses in which they invest.

> **Millennium Products**
> 'Millennium Products' is a Design Council initiative which aims to identify, encourage and promote innovative British products looking forward to the new millennium. Hundreds of products have been selected, including a new evacuation system for ships, a gas-powered lorry, a prosthetic incorporating a computer chip, a solar-powered light and a gyroscope with no moving parts. A selection of products is shown in the picture spread between pp. 260 and 261.

industry through Business Links in England, with financial support from the DTI.

Quality is important throughout the business cycle—design, production, marketing and delivery to customers. Conformity assessment, such as certification to the international standard for quality management—BS EN ISO 9000 (which includes ISO 9001, the standard embracing design development)—is a key method of improving quality and competitiveness. In order to increase customer confidence, many suppliers rely on independent conformity assessment of their management systems or products and services. The competence and performance of organisations undertaking such certification are officially accredited by the DTI-sponsored United Kingdom Accreditation Service (UKAS). Companies certified by UKAS-accredited bodies are permitted to use the national accreditation marks, including the 'tick and crown' for BS EN ISO 9000 certification.

The DTI is responsible for policy relating to the National Measurement System. This provides, through several DTI-funded standards, laboratories and other contractors, many of the physical measurement standards and associated calibration facilities necessary to ensure that measurements in the UK are made on a common basis and to the required accuracy (see p. 432).

British Standards Institution

The British Standards Institution (BSI) is the national standards body and is the British member of the European and international standards organisations. It works with industry, consumers and government to produce standards relevant to the needs of the market and suitable for public purchasing and regulatory purposes. The Kitemark is BSI's registered product certification trade mark. Government support for BSI is directed particularly towards European and international standards, which account for over 90% of its work. The Government is reviewing with BSI the action that might be taken to speed up the process of setting standards, both within the UK and internationally.

Awards

The Queen's Awards for Export, Technological and Environmental Achievement recognise outstanding performance in their respective fields. In 1999, 82 Awards were made for Export Achievement, 14 for Technological Achievement and five for Environmental Achievement. Awarded annually, they are valid for five years and are granted by the Queen on the advice of the Prime Minister, who is assisted by an advisory committee consisting of senior representatives from business, trade unions and government departments. Any self-contained 'industrial unit' in the UK with at least two full-time employees is eligible to apply so long as it meets the scheme's criteria. Following a review, from 2000 the Awards will be renamed The Queen's Awards for Enterprise, with three categories: international trade, innovation and environmental achievement.

Other awards include the Export Award for Smaller Businesses (for firms employing fewer than 200 people) and the MacRobert Award for engineering made by the Fellowship of Engineering for successful technological innovation.

The Millennium Bug

The Government is working to ensure that both the private sector and the public sector are fully aware of the 'Millennium Bug', the century date change problem which arises in information technology (IT) systems and electronic equipment where the year is represented by two digits rather than four (e.g., '99' instead of 1999). As the year changes from 1999 to 2000, there is the possibility that two-digit systems might malfunction, for example, by reverting to the year 1900, or cease to operate. Costs involved in overcoming the Millennium Bug can be substantial. The UK Government has estimated that expenditure of £430 million will be needed to fix IT systems in central government departments and agencies.

The Government has set up 'Action 2000', a company which is charged with raising awareness of the problem, providing practical advice to businesses and encouraging them to tackle the problem. Action 2000 has set up a National Infrastructure Forum bringing together the major providers of essential services to share best practice. According to Action 2000's latest assessment in July 1999, the providers of the main UK utilities (including gas, electricity and water supply), telecommunications and financial services have made significant progress to ensure that there will be no material disruption to these essential services. Other key sectors, such as food supply, health and transport, are also taking appropriate measures to ensure that services are not disrupted. However, research by Action 2000 has found that some businesses—especially SMEs—need to take further action to avoid possible disruption to their operations.

Education and Training

Education and training are central to ensuring the UK's competitiveness by creating and maintaining a flexible, highly skilled and highly qualified workforce. The Government has announced a number of measures to increase education and training opportunities and to modernise skills (see chapters 10 and 11), including:

- the new University for Industry, to be launched in 2000, which is expected to play a key role in boosting competitiveness by raising people's skill levels and employability by using modern information and communications technologies; and

- a new national information technology strategy to encourage the wider use of computers in business, education and the community—a planned network of up to 1,000 IT learning centres will be targeted at developing partnerships with business to meet future skill needs.

A network of 78 business-led Training and Enterprise Councils (TECs) in England and Wales and 22 local enterprise companies (LECs) in Scotland, run by Scottish Enterprise and Highlands and Islands Enterprise (see p. 394), provide training, vocational education and enterprise programmes on behalf of the Government and offer advisory and training services to businesses. TECs and LECs also have a role in regeneration and economic development activities locally (see chapter 21). In Northern Ireland, training schemes are run by the Training and Employment Agency (see p. 153).

Regional Development

Regional policy is designed to promote economic growth and competitiveness in all areas of the UK, working in partnership with businesses, local authorities, voluntary groups and others. Where additional help is needed, it is focused on the Assisted Areas, which cover around 34% of the UK's working population. The promotion of inward investment (see p. 422) is a key element in the Government's regional policy.

The main instrument of government support to industry in the Assisted Areas in Great Britain is Regional Selective Assistance (RSA), which is designed to help:

- create and safeguard jobs;
- attract international investment; and
- improve the competitiveness of disadvantaged areas.

In 1998–99 the DTI spent an estimated £112 million on RSA grants in England, covering around 870 projects with the expected creation or safeguarding of around 28,000 jobs; total investment in the projects is expected to be some £1.5 billion. RSA is being changed to focus support more on high-quality, knowledge-driven projects providing skilled

One important role of the new RDAs is facilitating the development of business 'clusters'. These already exist in many industries, for example, the traditional concentrations of the steel industry around Sheffield and the chemicals industry on Teesside. Businesses can benefit from shared infrastructure and close links to training and research institutions, and clusters tend to be conducive to the creation and development of small start-up firms. One example of a modern industry growing up around a series of clusters is the biotechnology industry, developing around centres of research excellence, including Oxford and Cambridge. The DTI has established a team of experts to examine the growth of biotechnology clusters in the UK and how the UK can maintain its competitive position in this fast-growing sector (see p. 474).

jobs, while new measures are being considered to support growth of smaller businesses in areas with particular needs. The Assisted Areas are being reviewed and a new map will apply from January 2000.

England

Eight new Regional Development Agencies (RDAs) became fully operational in April 1999—a ninth, for London, will come into operation in 2000 (see also chapter 2). They are developing strategies to improve their regions' economic performance and enhance competitiveness. The RDAs are working with the Government Offices for the Regions, chambers of commerce, TECs, Business Links and other economic development bodies. The activities of the RDAs include:

- encouraging innovation and the exploitation of technology, including co-ordinating the development and implementation of regional innovation and technology action plans with local partners;
- reviewing business support in their areas;
- providing finance, including establishing new regional venture capital funds to

provide equity finance to small businesses with growth potential;
- promoting inward investment; and
- promoting a strategic use of EU structural funds in their regions.

Scotland

In Scotland a range of schemes is operated by the Scottish Executive Enterprise and Lifelong Learning Department, which has overall responsibility for development of the Scottish economy, and emphasis is given to the links between education and enterprise. Scottish Enterprise and Highlands and Islands Enterprise are the lead economic development agencies in lowland and highland Scotland respectively, operating mainly through the network of LECs (see p. 152). Their duties include:

- promoting industrial efficiency and competitiveness;
- attracting inward investment and encouraging exports;
- giving financial and management support to new businesses and helping existing ones to expand;
- improving the environment by reclaiming derelict and contaminated land; and
- increasing job opportunities and skills.

In early 1999 the Government announced new economic strategies for both bodies, and these will be used as a foundation for their future operation by the Scottish Parliament. The Scottish Enterprise Strategy emphasises the importance of innovation and the value of strong domestic enterprises, and will use a cluster-based approach to help develop industries which are likely to be particularly successful. The Highlands and Islands Enterprise Strategy aims to enable the people of the Highlands and Islands to realise their full potential by strengthening communities, developing skills and stimulating businesses, while encouraging more firms to compete on an international basis. Both strategies intend to safeguard environmental and social assets and stress the importance of social inclusion.

Wales

The purposes of the Welsh Development Agency (WDA—see p. 31) are to further economic and social development, promote efficiency in business and international competitiveness, and improve the environment of Wales. It is focusing on developing stronger regional clusters (such as supply and services chains), increasing standards and efficiency, and helping Welsh companies to exploit new technology. The WDA's programmes are being developed in line with *Pathway to Prosperity: A New Economic Agenda for Wales* (see p. 31). It is co-ordinating an Entrepreneurship Action Plan, with the aim of fostering a stronger enterprise culture in Wales. Support for enterprise programmes has been raised, with a target of creating at least 1,000 new entrepreneurs in 1999–2000 by helping them to set up high-quality ventures. Three new investment schemes were announced in March 1999 to provide venture capital for SMEs, including a £6 million venture capital fund, run jointly by the WDA and National Westminster Bank, to provide support for innovative developments focusing on new technology, and a £2 million WDA small loans fund.

Northern Ireland

A review of Northern Ireland's economic strategy, *Strategy 2010* (see p. 20), has been produced by a steering group for consideration by the new Northern Ireland Assembly. Support for industrial development is currently implemented through:

- the Industrial Development Board, which deals with overseas companies considering Northern Ireland as an investment location, as well as the development of local companies with more than 50 employees;
- the Local Enterprise Development Unit, which promotes enterprise and the development of small businesses;
- the Industrial Research and Technology Unit, which provides advice and assistance on R&D, innovation and technology transfer; and

- the Training and Employment Agency, which helps with in-company training and management development.

European Union Regional Funding

The EU seeks to promote economic and social cohesion, reducing disparities between the regions and countries of the Union. The principal responsibility for helping poorer areas remains with national authorities, but the EU complements schemes by awarding grants and loans from various sources, including the European Regional Development Fund (ERDF).

EU Structural Funds, especially the ERDF, play an important role in regional development, and the UK received £9 billion from the Funds in 1994–99. The highest level of assistance is available to areas with 'Objective 1' status, where GDP is less than 75% of the EU average. Changes in the areas qualifying for help are due to take effect for the period 2000 to 2006. In the UK Merseyside has retained its Objective 1 status, while Cornwall, West Wales and the Valleys, and South Yorkshire have qualified for Objective 1 status for the first time, so that just under 9% of the UK population is now in Objective 1 areas. In recognition of the special position of Northern Ireland and the structural problems faced by the Highlands and Islands, both areas will receive special enhanced transition packages after 1999, with funding levels broadly equivalent to Objective 1 status. The funding amounts to around £900 million for Northern Ireland and £200 million for the Highlands and Islands. Substantial aid is also available to areas qualifying for 'Objective 2' status; this Objective supports the economic and social conversion of areas facing structural difficulties, in particular, areas undergoing change in the industrial or service sectors, declining rural areas, urban areas in difficulty and depressed areas dependent on fisheries. About 13.7 million people in the UK will be covered by Objective 2 funding and the Government is consulting on the areas which will qualify for Objective 2 status.

Competitive Markets

The Government seeks to improve the openness and effectiveness of markets, both within the UK and internationally, and believes that effective competition is the best stimulus to innovation and efficiency. A new competition regime is being introduced in the UK under the Competition Act 1998, which will come fully into effect on 1 March 2000, with the aim of providing better protection, both to consumers and to businesses.

Competition Act 1998

The Competition Act 1998 strengthens competition law so that it is more effective in dealing with anti-competitive practices. It is modelled on EC competition law and provides a strong deterrent against anti-competitive practices and agreements such as cartels, and against abuse of a dominant market position. The Act prohibits agreements, practices and conduct which have a damaging effect on competition. The main enforcement authority will be the Director General of Fair Trading (head of the Office of Fair Trading—OFT), who will have strong powers of investigation. The Act will also be enforced by the utility regulators in their sectors (see p. 398). Financial penalties of up to 10% of a firm's UK turnover may be imposed, and those affected by anti-competitive behaviour in breach of the law may be able to claim for damages in the courts.

Agreements will not fall within the scope of the Act unless they have an appreciable effect on competition. This, coupled with the absence of any notification requirement, will mean that the vast majority of firms will be freed from the burden of notifying to the OFT harmless, insignificant agreements, which is a feature of the existing regime. In general, an agreement is unlikely to be considered as having an appreciable effect if the combined market share of the parties to the agreement is less than 25%. Nevertheless, agreements to fix prices, to impose minimum resale prices or to share markets will generally be seen as capable of having an appreciable effect even where the combined market share is below 25%. In determining whether or not an undertaking is in a dominant market position, the OFT, as a general rule, is unlikely to consider an undertaking as dominant if its market share is under 40%.

A new body, the Competition Commission, replaced the Monopolies and Mergers Commission (MMC) in April 1999. It has two main arms:

- a reporting arm, which will take over the MMC's monopolies and mergers functions under the Fair Trading Act 1973; and
- an Appeal Tribunals arm, which will hear appeals against decisions of the Director General of Fair Trading and the regulators on the prohibitions of anti-competitive agreements and abuse of a dominant position.

Monopolies and Mergers

The framework under the Fair Trading Act 1973 for dealing with scale and complex monopolies[2] is being retained alongside the Competition Act. The Director General of Fair Trading and those utility regulators which have parallel powers to apply the monopoly provisions of the 1973 Act may examine such monopolies and make a reference to the Competition Commission to establish whether a monopoly operates, or may be expected to operate, against the public interest.

Under the current framework, a merger generally qualifies for investigation if it involves the acquisition of assets of more than £70 million or the creation or enhancement of a 25% share of the supply of a particular good or service in the UK or a substantial part of it. Qualifying mergers are considered by the Director General of Fair Trading, who then advises the Secretary of State for Trade and Industry. There is a voluntary procedure for pre-notification of proposed mergers. If there are reasonable grounds for believing that a merger could have a detrimental effect on competition, the Director General can advise the Secretary of State to refer it to the Competition Commission. Alternatively, the

---

[2] A complex monopoly is defined as a situation in which at least two firms together supply 25% or more of a particular good or service in the UK in a way that may distort competition. A scale monopoly is defined as a situation in which the action of a single firm supplying at least 25% of a particular good or service may distort competition.

A recent example of a merger that was not allowed to proceed was the proposed acquisition of Manchester United Football Club by the media group BSkyB. In April 1999 the Secretary of State accepted the findings and recommendations of the MMC and the Director General of Fair Trading that the merger might be expected to operate against the public interest (as it would affect competition and innovation between broadcasters and would damage the long-term interests of British football) and that it should be prohibited.

Director General may be asked to obtain suitable undertakings from the companies involved to remedy the adverse effects identified. Most mergers are cleared without being referred to the Competition Commission.

If the Competition Commission finds that a merger could be expected to operate against the public interest, the Secretary of State can prohibit it or allow it subject to certain conditions being met. Where the merger has already taken place, action can be taken to reverse it. There are special provisions for newspaper and water company mergers.

The DTI issued a consultative document in August 1999 on reforming the regulation of mergers, so that decisions would normally be taken by the competition authorities against a competition-based test. Ministers would only be involved in making decisions in a small minority of cases where specified public interests, such as defence and national security, are at issue.

Certain mergers with an EC dimension, assessed by reference to turnover, come under the exclusive jurisdiction of the European Commission. The Commission can ban mergers if it concludes that they would create or strengthen a dominant position which would significantly impede effective competition within the EU or a substantial part of it; alternatively, it may negotiate undertakings to correct the adverse effect.

EU Single Market

The Government is working with the EU to ensure effective competition in international markets. Within the EU it is looking to improve the operation of the single market (see p. 419) and will support further measures to strengthen competition. The Government has set a target of implementing 98% of single market measures by the end of 2000.

Information and Communications Technology

The Government is keen to ensure that the UK benefits fully from the rapid developments in information and communications technology, including the growth of the Internet and of electronic commerce ('e-commerce'). Already, the UK leads the world in some areas (such as digital broadcasting) and in the delivery of certain financial and business information on-line services, while 52% of UK firms use e-mail. The Government's strategy is to ensure that by 2002 the UK provides the best environment in the world to do business electronically, and it has appointed an 'e-envoy' to take forward this strategy and promote the UK overseas on e-commerce issues. It is working to maintain the UK's communications infrastructure and to develop a suitable regulatory framework.

An Electronic Communications Bill is planned, which will facilitate the development of electronic trading and enhance public confidence in the technologies concerned. It will make it possible to remove the legal barriers to using electronic means of communicating, instead of pen and paper, and will reduce uncertainty over the legal status of electronic signatures and writing. A statutory approvals system is to be established for businesses providing electronic signature and similar services, to ensure that suitable standards of quality and service are maintained.

The DTI is working to ensure that all UK businesses make the best use of information and communications technologies to enhance their competitiveness. Its Information Society Initiative is providing businesses, especially SMEs, with practical help and guidance to enable them to exploit the opportunities for doing business electronically. An extra £20 million is being invested over the next three years with the aim of tripling, to 1 million, the number of small businesses in the UK which can trade electronically.

CORPORATE AFFAIRS

Corporate Structure

Nearly 1.4 million companies are registered with the Registrar of Companies—all UK companies must register, as must companies incorporated overseas with a place of business or branch in the UK. Most corporate businesses are 'limited liability' companies, where the liability of members is restricted to contributing an amount related to their shareholding (or to their guarantee where companies are limited by guarantee).

Companies may be either public or private; around 13,500 are public limited companies (plcs), of which 2,450 have their shares listed on the London Stock Exchange (see p. 518). A company must satisfy certain conditions before it can become a public limited company (plc). It must be limited by shares or guarantee, have a share capital and meet specified minimum capital requirements. All other UK companies are private companies and are generally prohibited from offering their shares to the public.

Company Law and Corporate Governance

Laws relating to companies are designed to meet the need for proper regulation of business, to maintain open markets and to create safeguards for those wishing to invest in companies or do business with them. They take account of EC directives on company law, and on company and group accounts and their auditing.

During the 1990s three major committees— the Cadbury, Greenbury and Hampel committees—have reported on a range of corporate governance issues, including best practices and directors' pay. As a result, principles of good governance and a code of best practice have been added to the London Stock Exchange's listing rules. Companies listed on the Stock Exchange are required to state in their annual report and accounts whether they are complying with the code's provisions, and give reasons for areas of non-compliance.

The DTI has initiated a fundamental review of company law, with the aim of producing a modern framework which is clear and accessible, and promotes competitiveness. The review is being directed by a steering group of independent experts, and its final report is due in 2001. In February 1999 the group issued a consultative document explaining the strategy that it intended to adopt in the review and outlining its proposals for future work. Provisional proposals contained in the consultation document include:

- restructuring company law to make it more accessible for those running smaller firms;
- simplifying some technical areas of company law, such as the rules on company formation; and
- using modern methods of information and communications technology to improve communications between companies and their shareholders.

Regulation of Business

In its *Modernising Government* White Paper, issued in March 1999 (see p. 57), the Government announced a new policy on removing unnecessary regulation. The DTI works to minimise regulatory burdens on business, and considers the use of non-regulatory solutions where these may be most appropriate. An independent Better Regulation Task Force advises the Government on action to improve the effectiveness and quality of existing regulations, while making sure that they remain necessary, are fair—especially to small businesses and the consumer—affordable, and simple to understand and administer.

Utility Regulation

Special arrangements cover the privatised utilities—including telecommunications, electricity, gas, water, and railways—where independent regulators have powers and duties to promote competition and the interests of consumers. One of the regulators' duties is the setting of prices.

Following a review of the regulation of gas, electricity, telecommunications and water, the Government is introducing a number of changes to the regulatory framework, including:

- a new primary duty on the regulators to protect and promote the interests of consumers through competition wherever possible and appropriate;

- new independent consumer councils for the energy, telecommunications and water sectors;

- measures to bring about a more competitive market for gas and electricity, including provision for separate licensing of supply and distribution in electricity;

- a merger and alignment of gas and electricity regulation, and the creation of a single energy regulator; and

- measures to improve the transparency, consistency and accountability of regulation.

Industrial Associations

The Confederation of British Industry (CBI) is the largest employers' organisation in the UK, directly or indirectly representing around 250,000 companies and 180 employers' organisations and trade associations. The CBI aims to help create and sustain the conditions in which business can compete. It campaigns to lessen the administrative and regulatory burdens on business, tackle handicaps on competition and improve the performance of companies. It offers members a range of advisory services. It has 13 regional offices and an office in Brussels. The CBI is the British member of the Union of Industrial and Employers' Confederations of Europe (UNICE).

Chambers of commerce represent business views to the Government at national and local levels. They promote local economic development, for example, through regeneration projects, tourism, inward investment promotion and business services, including overseas trade missions, exhibitions and training conferences. The British Chambers of Commerce represents about 120,000 businesses, through 60 approved chambers of commerce. It offers commercial and export-related services to its members.

The Institute of Directors (IOD) has around 48,000 members in the UK. It provides business advisory services on matters affecting company directors, such as corporate management, insolvency and career counselling, and represents the interests of members to authorities in the UK and EU.

The Federation of Small Businesses is the largest pressure group promoting the interests of the self-employed and small firms. The Federation has 150,000 members, and provides them with expert information and guidance on subjects such as taxation, employment, health and safety, and insurance.

Trade associations represent companies producing or selling a particular product or group of products. They exist to supply common services, regulate trading practices and represent their members in dealings with government departments

Further Reading

Building a Stronger Economic Future for Britain: Economic and Fiscal Strategy Report and Financial Statement and Budget Report March 1999. The Stationery Office, 1999.

Our Competitive Future: Building the Knowledge Driven Economy. Cm 4176. The Stationery Office, 1998.

Trade and Industry: The Government's Expenditure Plans 1999–2000 to 2001–02. Cm 4211. The Stationery Office, 1999.

United Kingdom National Accounts—the Blue Book (annual). Office for National Statistics. The Stationery Office.

Websites
Department of Trade and Industry: www.dti.gov.uk
HM Treasury: www.hm-treasury.gov.uk

24 Public Finance

Taxes and social security contributions as a proportion of gross national product (GNP) in the UK are now lower than in the mid-1980s, in contrast to the position in many other advanced industrialised countries. Lower rates of income tax and corporation tax have been introduced in the UK. Nearly three-fifths of public expenditure is on social security, health and education. Public expenditure has been thoroughly reviewed, with more spending planned in priority areas, notably health and education. The largest single expenditure programme is on social security.

Between 1986 and 1996 taxes and social security contributions as a proportion of GNP declined in the UK from 37.5% to 35.5%, while the European Union (EU) average rose from 40.4% to 44.4%. The UK's share is also below the average for the Organisation for Economic Co-operation and Development (OECD) (see diagram). When the comparison is restricted to taxes, the share of GNP for the UK is 29.3%, slightly above the OECD average and around the average for the EU.

The Comprehensive Spending Review, completed in July 1998, set out the Government's plans for current public expenditure to grow by 2¼% a year on average in real terms over the next three years, and for public sector net investment to rise substantially over this period (see Table 24.1). A new regime for planning and expenditure has been adopted and supports the Government's fiscal policy framework (see chapter 23). It involves firm three-year plans to enable departments to plan ahead and provide a more stable foundation for managing

public services, and a distinction between current and capital spending, through separate budgets.

Taxes and Social Security Contributions as a Percentage of Gross National Product

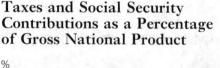

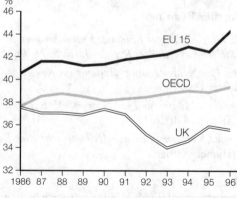

EU15 = 15 member states of the European Union
OECD = Organisation for Economic Co-operation and Development

In the first decade of the 20th century, excise duties accounted for 45% of central government tax revenue, property and income tax 21% and death duties 12%. In 1998–99 the main categories of revenue were income tax (net of tax credits), estimated at £85.5 billion (26% of current receipts), social security contributions £54.9 billion (16%), value added tax (VAT) £51.7 billion (15%), fuel, alcohol and tobacco duties £35.7 billion (11%) and corporation tax £29.8 billion (9%).

Defence accounted for over half of public expenditure in the first decade of the 20th century. For 1999–2000 its share of public spending will be around 6%, while other main components will be:

- social security—£102 billion (29%);
- health—£61 billion (17%);
- education—£41 billion (12%); and
- debt interest—£26 billion (7%).

MAIN PROGRAMMES AND PRIORITIES

The government departments with the largest spending programmes are:

- the Department of Social Security (with forecast expenditure of £99.1 billion on benefits in 1999–2000);
- the Department of the Environment, Transport and the Regions (DETR)— £43.9 billion, of which £34.2 billion is on local government (the largest part of which is spent on education) and regional policy;
- the Department of Health (£40.3 billion); and
- the Ministry of Defence (£22.3 billion).

Local authorities are estimated to spend about £82.4 billion in 1999–2000, around a quarter of public expenditure. The main categories of expenditure are education, law and order, personal social services, housing and other environmental services, and roads and transport.

Table 24.1: Current and Capital Budgets — £ billion

	Outturn 1997–98	Estimate 1998–99	Projections 1999–00	2000–01	2001–02
Public sector current budget					
Current receipts	315.7	334.2	345	364	385
Current expenditure	304.3	313.5	329	346	362
Depreciation	14.0	14.6	15	15	16
Surplus on current budget (including windfall tax)	-2.6	6.2	1	3	7
Surplus on current budget[a]	**-5.1**	**4.1**	**2**	**4**	**8**
Capital budget					
Gross investment	22.0	21.7	24	26	29
less asset sales	-4.0	-3.8	-4	-4	-4
less depreciation	-14.0	-14.6	-15	-15	-16
Net investment	4.0	3.4	5	7	10
Net borrowing (including windfall tax)	6.6	-2.8	4	5	2
Net borrowing[a]	**9.1**	**-1.0**	**3**	**3**	**1**

Source: HM Treasury: *Building a Stronger Economic Future for Britain: Economic and Fiscal Strategy Report and Financial Statement and Budget Report March 1999*
[a] Excluding windfall tax receipts and associated spending.
Note: Differences between totals and the sums of their component parts are due to rounding.

Following the Government's Comprehensive Spending Review, extra resources have been allocated to two of the Government's main priorities: education and health. Expenditure on education is planned to rise by over 5% a year across the UK in real terms, representing extra expenditure of £19 billion over the three years from 1999–2000. This involves doubling the capital budget for schools, expanding further education and higher education, and expenditure on the new University for Industry and the lifelong learning initiative (see chapter 10). Around £21 billion of additional resources are being provided to modernise the National Health Service (NHS), including a major hospital building programme (see chapter 13). Other areas receiving extra resources are:

- the regeneration of the UK's cities and housing resources, for which an extra £4.4 billion is being allocated;

- public transport, with an extra £1.7 billion to modernise the road and rail network over the next three years; and

- science, where £1.1 billion is being invested to modernise the UK's research capabilities.

A new Investing in Britain Fund has been set up to provide for the renewal and modernisation of the UK's public sector capital stock. Net public investment is planned to rise to £10 billion by 2001–02 (see Table 24.1). Over £2.5 billion of the Fund will be overseen by HM Treasury in a Capital Modernisation Fund, which will be allocated to departments on a competitive basis.

Control of Spending

A new regime for controlling public expenditure has replaced the annual spending round, under which government departments used to submit their bids for expenditure for the following year. Instead, departments have firm plans for 1999–2000 and the following two financial years. These plans will be rolled forward in 2000 in the next spending review, which is expected to be the first round of budgeting conducted on the basis of resource accounting information (see p. 403).

The March 1999 Budget contained a series of measures involving planned investment of £1.1 billion over the next three years, which will be financed from the Capital Modernisation Fund:

- up to £470 million to support the Government's national information technology strategy (see p. 393), including a challenge fund to create a network of up to 1,000 IT-based learning centres;

- £430 million to modernise accident and emergency departments in NHS hospitals and to improve patient care; and

- £170 million to tackle crime and make communities safer.

A new concept—Total Managed Expenditure—covers all public sector spending (see Table 24.2). Within this concept, current and capital expenditure are planned and managed separately. Around half of Total Managed Expenditure is managed through Departmental Expenditure Limits, involving a tightly drawn control figure for each department, which is set in cash terms. The other half is Annually Managed Expenditure, covering expenditure such as social security benefit payments, which cannot reasonably be subject to limits covering more than one year. However, this is subject to rigorous scrutiny as part of the Budget process.

Other reforms have been introduced to improve the effectiveness of public spending. Public service agreements are being adopted across the Government covering departmental objectives and measurable efficiency and effectiveness targets. By mid-1999, over 30 agreements were in force. Departmental performance against the targets is being scrutinised by a Cabinet Committee, which is chaired by the Chancellor of the Exchequer, and supported by a Public Services Productivity Panel of experts from outside government. Each department has produced its own investment strategy, which will be taken into account in the allocation of resources from the Capital Modernisation Fund.

Table 24.2: Public Expenditure Allocation £ billion

	1998–99	1999–00	2000–01	2001–02
Departmental Expenditure Limits	**167.8**	**179.2**	**189.7**	**199.5**
of which:				
Department of Health	37.6	40.3	43.3	46.2
DETR: local government and regional policy	32.8	34.2	35.4	36.9
DETR: environment and transport	9.3	9.7	10.5	11.9
Ministry of Defence	22.5	22.3	22.8	23.0
Department for Education and Employment	14.5	15.7	17.5	18.9
Scotland	13.3	13.9	14.6	15.2
Annually Managed Expenditure	**163.6**	**170.2**	**179.4**	**188.2**
of which:				
Social security benefits	93.5	99.1	101.5	106.4
Central government gross debt interest	29.5	26.0	27.6	27.1
Locally Financed Expenditure	16.1	17.0	18.3	19.8
Accounting and other adjustments	8.5	9.1	11.7	13.0
Total Managed Expenditure	**331.4**	**349.4**	**369.1**	**387.7**

Source: HM Treasury: *Public Expenditure Statistical Analyses, March 1999*

A new Office of Government Commerce will be set up as an office of HM Treasury in April 2000 with the aim of maximising the Government's buying power; this is expected to lead to substantial efficiency savings.

New Accounting and Budgeting Procedures

Cash-based government accounts are being replaced by more commercial 'resource accounting' and budgeting methods. This is designed to improve efficiency and focus more on departmental objectives and outputs in terms of resources used rather than the money available for spending. The first full set of published audited resource accounts for government departments will be for 1999–2000. The Government has announced its intention to conduct the spending review in 2000 on a resource basis. Planning and controlling public expenditure on a resource accounting basis will be fully implemented for 2001–02, subject to parliamentary approval.

Examination of Public Expenditure

Examination of public expenditure is carried out by select committees of the House of Commons. These study in detail the activities of particular government departments and question ministers and officials.

The Public Accounts Committee considers the accounts of government departments, executive agencies and other public sector bodies, and reports by the Comptroller and Auditor General on departments and their use of resources. It submits reports to Parliament.

Audit of the Government's spending is exercised through the functions of the Comptroller and Auditor General, the head of the National Audit Office (NAO). The NAO's responsibilities include certifying the accounts of all government departments and executive agencies and those of a wide range of other public sector bodies; scrutinising the efficiency and effectiveness of their operations; examining revenue accounts and inventories; and reporting the results of these examinations to Parliament.

Public-Private Partnerships

The Government sees Public-Private Partnerships as a key factor in the delivery of high-quality public services, by bringing in private sector management, finance and ownership to improve the value for money, efficiency and quality of these services. An important element is the Private Finance Initiative (PFI), introduced in 1992, in which the public sector specifies, in terms of the outputs required, the service or information technology (IT) needed, and private sector companies compete to provide these requirements. By May 1999 PFI projects with a capital value of around £12 billion in total had been signed, and £11 billion of private sector investment in PFI schemes is expected in the three years to March 2002. Many of these schemes are in the transport sector (see chapter 22), including the Channel Tunnel Rail Link; a number of 'design, build, finance and operate' road projects; and the Croydon Tramlink. Other significant projects include 22 new hospitals, six new prisons and an IT partnership project for the Employment Service.

The Government emphasises the importance of good industrial relations, and encourages consultation on projects with staff and other interested parties. New guidance on protecting the pension arrangements of staff transferring to the private sector was published in June 1999.

The Government is taking forward Public-Private Partnerships for many of the remaining commercial organisations in the public sector, including London Underground, National Air Traffic Services and British Waterways (see chapter 22); the Tote (see p. 299); and the Commonwealth Development Corporation (see p. 93).

A taskforce in HM Treasury acts as a focal point for all PFI activities and as a provider of advice and assistance to departments. From April 2000 it will form part of the new Office of Government Commerce (see p. 403). The Government will also be creating in 2000 a new body, Partnerships UK, to help increase and improve investment from private sources in the UK's public services.

DEBT MANAGEMENT

The Government finances its borrowing requirement by selling debt to the private sector. Public sector finances have improved. In 1998–99 there was a current budget surplus (excluding windfall tax and associated spending) of £7.3 billion, compared with a deficit of £5.3 billion in 1997–98, and current budget surpluses totalling £34 billion are forecast over the next five years. Public sector net debt fell from 44.1% of gross domestic product (GDP) in 1996–97 to 40.6% at the end of 1998–99—amounting to some £349 billion. It is projected to fall below 40% of GDP in 1999–2000 and to under 35% by 2003–04. Public sector net borrowing (excluding the windfall tax and associated spending) fell from £9.9 billion in 1997–98, so that there was a net repayment of £2.5 billion in 1998–99. General government gross debt was about 47% of GDP in 1998–99. The Government's financing requirement for 1999–2000 is forecast to be about £21 billion, to be met mostly from sales of gilt-edged stock ('gilts').

The Government's debt management policy is to minimise the cost of meeting its financing needs over the long term, taking risk into account. Major changes in the management of government debt are being implemented, with the transfer of government responsibility for debt and cash management from the Bank of England to HM Treasury. Responsibility for the sale of gilts and the management of the gilts market now rests with a Treasury agency, the United Kingdom Debt Management Office (DMO), which is also due to take over cash management operations in 1999–2000.

Gilt-edged Stock

The major debt instrument, government bonds, is known as gilt-edged stock ('gilts') as there is no risk of default. Gilts are widely traded; holdings of marketable gilts total almost £300 billion. Pension funds and life insurance companies have the largest holdings. The annual Debt Management Report sets out the framework for issuing gilts in the coming year.

Gilt issues are primarily by auction. This used to be broadly monthly, but the frequency has been reduced, reflecting lower government borrowing. Gilts include 'conventionals', which generally pay fixed rates of interest and redemption sums; and index-linked stocks, on which principal and interest are linked to movements in the Retail

Prices Index. The DMO is implementing a series of reforms designed to improve the efficiency of the gilts market. For example, the first auction of index-linked gilts was held in November 1998.

MAIN SOURCES OF REVENUE

The main sources of revenue are:

- taxes on income (together with profits), which include personal income tax, corporation tax and petroleum revenue tax;
- taxes on capital, which include inheritance tax, capital gains tax, council tax and non-domestic rates;
- taxes on expenditure, which include VAT (value added tax) and customs and excise duties; and
- National Insurance contributions (see chapter 12), which give entitlement to a range of benefits, including the Retirement Pension and Jobseeker's Allowance.

Taxation Policy

The general principles underlying the Government's taxation policy are that the tax system should:

- encourage employment opportunities and work incentives for everyone;
- promote savings and long-term investment; and
- be fair, and be seen to be fair.

Tax Measures in the 1999 Budget

Changes to taxation announced in the Budget in March 1999 are intended to encourage work, raise productivity, protect the environment and provide help to those who need it most (especially families and children).

Measures to Encourage Work and Support Families

Reforms to the tax and benefits system are designed to support families and ensure that work and opportunity are encouraged and rewarded rather than being discouraged, as currently happens for some people who find that their income from working is only slightly higher than it would be if they were unemployed. The main measures are:

- lower rates of income tax—a new starting rate of 10% from April 1999 (the lowest rate of income tax in the UK since 1962) and a reduction in the basic rate from 23% to 22% from April 2000;
- a major reform to National Insurance contributions (NICs), so that by April 2001 the threshold of earnings below which people do not pay NICs will be the same as that for the personal allowance for income tax—this is expected to eliminate NICs for about 900,000 people, although benefit entitlement will be protected;
- a new Children's Tax Credit, from April 2001, which will succeed the married couple's and related allowances to be abolished in April 2000; and
- a series of measures to help pensioners, including higher personal tax allowances, a rise in the winter fuel allowance from £20 to £100 and an increase in the minimum income guarantee for pensioners.

Raising Productivity

The Budget contained a number of measures designed to boost productivity through greater investment, innovation and stronger competition. A new 10% rate of corporation tax for small businesses will apply from April 2000, and the 40% capital allowance for small and medium-sized businesses has been extended until July 2000. Previously announced changes to corporation tax took effect in April 1999, reducing the main rate to 30% (the lowest main corporate tax rate among the major EU economies) and the small companies' rate to 20%. Other measures announced include a research and development tax credit for small and medium-sized firms and a new Employee Share Ownership scheme, both of which will be introduced in the 2000 Budget.

Protecting the Environment

Budget measures to protect the environment (see also p. 314) include:

- a new climate change levy from April 2001 to encourage energy efficiency in business;
- a major reform in the taxation of company cars from April 2002;
- a lower rate of vehicle excise duty (VED) for cars with small engines (up to 1,100 cc), with VED for new cars from autumn 2000 being determined primarily by their carbon dioxide emissions; and
- rises in the rate of landfill tax.

Collection of Taxes and Duties

The Inland Revenue assesses and collects taxes on income, profits and capital, and stamp duty. In April 1999 it also became responsible for NICs when it merged with the Contributions Agency, formerly an agency of the Department of Social Security. HM Customs and Excise collects the most important taxes on expenditure (VAT and most duties). The main local taxes—council tax and non-domestic rates (see p. 410)—are collected by local authorities.

Electronic transmission is already being used to a limited extent in the collection of taxes and duties; for example, some accountants and other tax practitioners submit clients' returns electronically to the Inland Revenue. The Finance Act 1999 will allow the Inland Revenue and HM Customs and Excise to develop new electronic services that can be used instead of returns on paper, so that businesses and individuals will be able to send tax information to the collection authorities via the Internet. By 2000–01 individual taxpayers should be able to file their own tax returns over the Internet.

Taxes on Income

Income Tax

Taxes on individual incomes are generally progressive in that larger incomes are subject to a greater amount of tax. Income tax is imposed for the year of assessment beginning on 6 April. The tax rates and bands for 1998–99 and 1999–2000 are shown in Table 24.3. A new 10% starting rate of income tax took effect in April 1999, while the basic rate is to be reduced to 22% from April 2000, representing the lowest basic rate for nearly 70 years. The 10% starting rate applies to income from work; the starting rate for income from savings continues at 20%, except for dividends (see Table 24.3). Of around 26 million income taxpayers, 1.8 million are expected to pay tax only at the starting rate of 10% in 1999–2000, 1.2 million at 20%, 20.7 million at 23% and 2.3 million at 40%.

Allowances and reliefs reduce an individual's income tax liability, and the main allowances are shown in Table 24.3. All taxpayers are entitled to a personal allowance against income from all sources, with a higher allowance for the elderly. One of the most significant reliefs covers employees' contributions to their pension schemes, while personal tax-free saving is encouraged through the Individual Savings Account (ISA) introduced in April 1999 (see p. 518).

In general, income tax is charged on all income originating in the UK—although some forms of income, such as child benefit, are exempt—and on all income arising abroad of people resident in the UK. Agreements with over 100 countries provide relief from double taxation, the largest network of tax treaties in the world. UK residents working abroad for the whole year may benefit from 100% tax relief.

Most wage and salary earners pay their income tax under a Pay-As-You-Earn (PAYE) system whereby tax is deducted and accounted for to the Inland Revenue by the employer, in a way which enables most employees to pay the correct amount of tax during the year.

A self-assessment system for collecting personal taxation has been introduced. Around 9 million people—primarily higher-rate taxpayers, the self-employed and those receiving investment income (particularly where this is paid without tax being deducted)—are required to complete an annual tax return for the Inland Revenue. Taxpayers may calculate their own tax liability, although they can choose to have the

In line with its policies of improving work incentives, promoting a fair and efficient tax system, and supporting families, the Government has announced a number of changes to the system of allowances. Two of the main allowances are being withdrawn:

- the married couple's allowance (MCA) and associated allowances (including the additional personal allowance) will be abolished from April 2000—however, couples in which at least one of the spouses is aged 65 or over on 5 April 2000 will be able to keep the MCA; and

- mortgage interest relief, which is available at 10% on loans used for house purchase up to a limit of £30,000, will be withdrawn from April 2000.[1]

A number of tax credits are being introduced, including:

- the Working Families Tax Credit (WFTC), which will replace Family Credit in October 1999 (see chapter 12) and is designed to provide a guaranteed minimum income for working families;

- a new Children's Tax Credit, which will take effect from April 2001 and provide an allowance worth up to £416 a year to families with one or more children under 16 living with them—to target this on the most needy families, the credit will gradually be withdrawn where the person claiming the credit is liable to tax at the higher rate; and

- a new Employment Credit for those aged over 50 who return to full-time work after six months or more on social security benefits.

---

[1] Special provisions will be made to enable relief to continue for elderly people who have taken out home income plans. These plans usually involve a loan secured on the home and enable the purchase of an annuity providing income for the rest of a person's life.

calculations done by the Inland Revenue if they return the form by the end of September.

Corporation Tax

Companies pay corporation tax on their income and capital gains after deduction of certain allowances and reliefs. The main rate of corporation tax was cut to 30% in April 1999, with a reduced rate of 20% for small companies (those with profits below £300,000 in a year). Relief is allowed for companies with profits between £300,000 and £1.5 million, so that their overall rate is between the main rate and the small companies' rate. From April 2000 a new 10% rate of corporation tax will apply to the smallest companies (those with annual profits of up to £10,000). Some capital expenditure—on machinery and plant, industrial buildings, agricultural buildings and scientific research, for example—may qualify for relief in the form of capital allowances. Expenditure on machinery or plant by small or medium-sized businesses qualifies for a first-year allowance—40% for the year to July 2000.

A new system for corporation tax payments is being phased in over a four-year period from April 1999, bringing the UK into line with other major industrialised countries. Around 20,000 large companies paying corporation tax at the main rate now pay in quarterly instalments, while advance corporation tax (which had been payable by companies distributing profits to their shareholders) has been abolished.

Windfall Tax

The windfall tax, a one-off tax on the excess profits of the privatised utilities, was payable in two instalments, in 1997 and 1998. Its estimated yield of £5.2 billion is financing the Government's Welfare-to-Work programme (see p. 154).

Petroleum Revenue Tax

Petroleum revenue tax (PRT), deductible in computing profits for corporation tax, is charged on profits from the production—as

Table 24.3: Tax Bands and Allowances		£
	1998–99	1999–2000
Income tax allowances:		
Personal allowance	4,195	4,335
Married couple's allowance, additional personal allowance and widow's bereavement allowance[a]	1,900	1,970
Allowances for those aged 65-74:		
personal allowance	5,410	5,720
married couple's allowance[a]	4,965	5,125
Allowances for those aged 75 and over:		
personal allowance	5,600	5,980
married couple's allowance[a]	5,025	5,195
Income limit for age-related allowances	16,200	16,800
Blind person's allowance	1,330	1,380

Bands of taxable income:[b]

1998–99		1999–2000	
Lower rate of 20%	0–4,300	Starting rate of 10%	0–1,500
Basic rate of 23%	4,301–27,100	Basic rate of 23%	1,501–28,000
Higher rate of 40%	over 27,100	Higher rate of 40%	over 28,000

Source: HM Treasury

[a] Tax relief for these allowances is restricted to 15% of the allowance for 1998–99 and 10% for 1999–2000. The additional personal allowance may be claimed by a taxpayer who is single, separated, divorced or widowed and who has a child at home, and by a taxpayer (with a dependent child) who has an incapacitated wife or husband living with him or her. The amounts for age-related MCAs in 1999–2000 were increased so that the value of this allowance for people aged 65 and over would be protected. For consistency, the figures shown in 1998–99 for these allowances reflect these increases. Only the further increase—in line with indexation—is shown in the Table.

[b] The rates of tax applicable to savings income are 20% for income below the basic rate upper limit and 40% above that. For 1999–2000 the rates applicable to dividends are 10% for income below the basic rate upper limit and 32.5% above that.

opposed, for example, to the refining—of oil and gas in the UK and on its Continental Shelf under licence from the Department of Trade and Industry. Each licensee of an oilfield or gasfield is charged at a rate of 50% on the profits from that field after deduction of certain allowances and reliefs. New fields given consent for development on or after 16 March 1993 are not liable to PRT.

Taxes on Capital

Capital Gains Tax

Capital gains tax (CGT) is payable by individuals and trusts on gains realised from the disposal of assets. It is payable on the amount by which total chargeable gains for a year exceed the exempt amount (£7,100 for individuals and £3,550 for most trusts in 1999–2000). Gains on some types of asset are exempt from CGT. These include the principal private residence, government securities, certain corporate bonds, and gains on holdings of Personal Equity Plans and ISAs. For individuals, CGT is payable at 20% where the gains when added to an individual's annual income are below the basic income tax rate upper limit, and at 40% where the total amount exceeds this limit.

CGT was substantially changed in the 1998 Budget, to encourage longer-term holding of assets: long-term gains are now taxed less heavily than short-term gains. Indexation relief to take account of the effects of inflation no longer applies after April 1998. Instead, a 'taper' reduces the amount of the chargeable gain depending on how long an asset has been held. For a business asset the percentage of the gain that is chargeable is reduced from 100% for assets held for less than one year to 25% for assets held for ten years or more. For non-business assets the chargeable gain falls from 100% for assets held for less than three years to 60% for assets held for ten years or longer.

Inheritance Tax

Inheritance tax is charged on estates at the time of death and on gifts made within seven years of death; most other lifetime transfers are not taxed. There are several important exemptions. Generally, transfers between spouses are exempt, and gifts and bequests to UK charities, major political parties and heritage bodies are also normally exempt. In general, business assets and farmland are exempt from inheritance tax, so that most family businesses can be passed on without a tax charge.

Tax is charged at a single rate of 40% above a threshold: £231,000 in 1999–2000. Only about 3% of estates a year become liable for an inheritance tax bill.

Taxes on Expenditure

Value Added Tax (VAT)

VAT is a broadly based expenditure tax, with a standard rate of 17.5%. A reduced rate of 5% applies on domestic fuel and power, and on the installation of energy-saving materials in low-income households under government schemes. VAT is collected at each stage in the production and distribution of goods and services. The final tax is payable by the consumer.

The annual level of turnover above which traders must register for VAT is £51,000. Certain goods and services are relieved from VAT, either by being charged at a zero rate or by being exempt.

- Under zero rating, a taxable person does not charge tax to a customer but reclaims any VAT paid to suppliers. Among the main categories where zero rating applies are goods exported to other countries; most food; water and sewerage for non-business use; domestic and international passenger transport; books, newspapers and periodicals; construction of new residential buildings; young children's clothing and footwear; drugs and medicines supplied on prescription; specified aids for handicapped people; and certain supplies by or to charities.

- For exempt goods or services, a taxable person does not charge any VAT but is not entitled to reclaim the VAT on goods and services bought for his or her business. The main categories where exemption applies are many supplies of land and buildings; insurance and other financial services; postal services; betting; gaming (with certain important exceptions); lotteries; much education and training; and health and welfare.

Customs Duties

Customs duties are chargeable on goods from outside the EU in accordance with its Common Customs Tariff. Goods can move freely across internal EU frontiers without making customs entries at importation or stopping for routine fiscal checks. For commercial consignments, excise duty and VAT are charged in the member state of destination, at the rate in force in that state.

Excise Duties

Mineral oils used as road fuel are subject to higher rates of duty than those used for other purposes, and the Government has a commitment to increase the duty on road fuels by at least 6% a year in real terms, to help to reduce carbon dioxide emissions (see p. 314). However, there are reduced rates to encourage the use of more environmentally friendly fuels, such as unleaded petrol, ultra low sulphur diesel, and gas used as road fuel. Kerosene not used as road or motor fuel, most lubricating oils and oils used for certain industrial, horticultural and marine uses are free of duty or attract very low rates. Fuel substitutes are taxed at the same rate as the corresponding mineral oil.

There are duties on spirits, beer, wine, cider and other alcoholic drinks, charged according to alcoholic strength and volume. Spirits used for scientific, medical, research and industrial processes are generally free of duty.

Cigarette duty is charged partly as a cash amount per cigarette and partly as a percentage of retail price. Duty on other tobacco products is based on weight. The Government is committed to raising tobacco duties by at least 5% a year in real terms, as part of its policy of discouraging smoking (see p. 186).

Duties are charged on off-course betting, pool betting, gaming in casinos, bingo and amusement machines. Rates vary with the particular form of gambling. Duty is levied either as a percentage of gross or net stakes or, in the case of amusement machines, as a fixed amount per machine according to the cost of playing and the prize level. On the National Lottery (see pp. 121–2) there is a 12% duty on gross stakes, but no tax on winnings.

The annual vehicle excise duty on a privately owned motor car, light van or taxi is £155, with a lower rate of £100 for small cars with engines up to 1,100 cc. The duty on goods vehicles is levied on the basis of gross weight and, if over 12 tonnes, according to the number of axles. This is designed to ensure that such vehicles at least cover their share of the full costs of road use through the tax paid (VED and fuel duty). Duty on taxis and buses varies according to seating capacity, and duty on motorcycles according to engine capacity. Lower rates of VED apply for low-emission lorries and buses. Privately owned vehicles— cars, taxis, motorcycles and non-commercial vehicles—built before 1973 are exempt from VED. A graduated VED system will apply for cars first registered after autumn 2000, based primarily on their carbon dioxide emissions.

Insurance premium tax is levied on most general insurance. The UK rate was raised from 4% to 5% in July 1999, although this remains one of the lowest overall rates in the EU. A higher rate of 17.5% applies on travel insurance and on insurance sold by suppliers of cars and domestic appliances.

Air passenger duty is charged at £10 for flights to internal destinations and to those in the European Economic Area and £20 elsewhere.

A landfill tax is levied of £10 a tonne, with a lower rate of £2 a tonne for inert waste. The Government has announced that the main rate will rise by £1 a tonne a year from April 2000 until at least 2004.

Stamp Duty

Some transfers are subject to stamp duty. Transfers of shares attract duty at 0.5% of the cost, while certain instruments, such as declarations of trust, have small fixed duties of 50p or £1. Transfers by gift and transfers to charities are exempt. Recent Budgets have raised the rate of stamp duty on the transfers of land and property (except shares) worth over £250,000, in order to encourage stability in the housing market. Duty on land and property is now payable at 1% of the total price when above £60,000, 2.5% above £250,000 and 3.5% over £500,000.

Other Revenue

National Insurance Contributions

Details of the five classes of National Insurance contribution and the rates of contribution are given in chapter 12 on pp. 172–3.

Local Authority Revenue

Local authorities in Great Britain have four main sources of revenue income: grants from central government; council tax; non-domestic rates (sometimes known as business rates); and sales, fees and charges. About 75% of expenditure (excluding sales, fees and charges) is financed by government grants and redistributed non-domestic rates.

Non-domestic rates are a tax on the occupiers of non-domestic property. The rateable value of property is assessed by reference to annual rents and reviewed every five years. The non-domestic rate is set nationally by the central bodies in England, Wales and Scotland, and collected by local authorities. It is paid into a national pool and redistributed to local authorities in proportion to their population. As part of its proposals for modernising local government (see chapter 6), the Government has suggested that local authorities should be allowed to set a supplementary local rate, subject to a maximum of 5% of the national rate and to the authorities demonstrating effective consultation and partnership arrangements with their local businesses.

Domestic property in Great Britain is generally subject to the council tax. Each

dwelling is allocated to one of eight valuation bands, based on its capital value (the amount it might have sold for on the open market) in April 1991. Discounts are available for dwellings with fewer than two resident adults, and those on low incomes may receive council tax benefit of up to 100% of the tax bill (see p. 181).

In Northern Ireland, rates—local domestic property taxes based on the value of the property—are collected by local authorities.

Further Reading

Building a Stronger Economic Future for Britain: Economic and Fiscal Strategy Report and Financial Statement and Budget Report March 1999. The Stationery Office, 1999.

Modern Public Services for Britain: Investing in Reform—Comprehensive Spending Review: New Public Spending Plans 1999–2002. Cm 4011. The Stationery Office, 1998.

Annual Report

Debt Management Report, HM Treasury.

Websites

HM Treasury: www.hm-treasury.gov.uk

Inland Revenue: www.inlandrevenue.gov.uk

25 Overseas Trade and Investment

Trade has been of vital importance to the British economy for hundreds of years. Although it has less than 1% of the world's population, the UK is the fourth largest trading nation, accounting for around 5.7% of world trade in goods and services. As one of 15 member states of the European Union (EU), the world's largest established trading group, over half of the UK's trade is with fellow EU members. The UK has a higher degree of inward and outward investment than any of the other G7 economies, relative to gross domestic product (GDP), and is second only to the United States as a destination for international direct investment. The UK is encouraging the World Trade Organisation (WTO) to take further action to reduce tariff and non-tariff barriers and to liberalise world markets, as well as supporting work on international competition policy principles, trade and investment and investment liberalisation in the Organisation for Economic Co-operation and Development (OECD).

The UK exports more per head than the United States and Japan. Its sales abroad of goods and services were about 21% of total final expenditure in 1998. Receipts from trade in services (such as financial services, business services, travel, transport and communications) and investment income make up about half of total British external earnings, and the UK consistently runs large surpluses on these accounts. The UK is the world's second biggest foreign investor and British investors have more direct investment abroad than overseas firms have in the UK.

TRADE IN GOODS AND SERVICES

In 1998, exports of UK goods amounted to £164.1 billion and imports £184.9 billion, on a balance of payments basis, giving a deficit on trade in goods of £20.8 billion, up from £11.9 billion in 1997. This represented the biggest annual deficit since 1989 and the third highest on record (see Table 25.1). The change in the deficit between the two years was largely caused by a widening in the deficit with non-EU countries, as economic difficulties in South East Asia, Russia and oil-exporting countries contributed to a fall of 4.5% in the value of exports in 1998. The value of imports rose marginally by 0.7% in 1998, reflecting the continuing strength of sterling. Between 1997 and 1998 the volume of exports of goods grew by 1.3%, while imports rose by 8.5%.

Commodity Composition

Traditionally the UK has been an exporter of manufactured goods and an importer of

At the turn of the 20th century, the United Kingdom[a] was still a large colonial power, and this is reflected in data for the period for trade in merchandise (goods). The value of total imports in 1900 amounted to £523 million, while exports were £354 million, giving a trade deficit of £169 million. Of total exports, £291 million were British produce and the remaining £63 million Foreign and Colonial produce. Some 79% of imports were from foreign countries, the remaining 21% from British Possessions. About 71% of exports were to foreign countries, the remaining 29% to British Possessions. In value terms, the largest amount of imports by far were from the United States (26.5%), followed by France (10.3%), Australasia (6.8%), Germany and Holland (both 6.0%). Germany was the UK's largest export market, taking 10.9% of merchandise, followed by the United States

(10.5%), British India (8.7%) and Australasia (8.3%).

By 'article', corn amounted to 11.3% of total imports, raw cotton 7.8%, metals 7.6%, wood and timber 5.6% and wool 4.3%. Of British produced exports, cotton accounted for 21.3%, 'coals, etc.' 13.9%, metals 12.8%, machinery 6.2% and woollen and worsted manufactures 5.4%. Of Foreign and Colonial produced exports, wool, sheep, lamb and llama accounted for 11.8%, metals 8.9%, cotton 8.5%, skins and furs 6.1% and caoutchouc (raw rubber) 6.0%.

Some more interesting or obscure imports included gutta percha—obtained from the latex of various Malaysian trees (£1.7 million), bananas (£0.5 million), opium (£0.4 million) and brimstone (£0.1 million), while exports included 'manures' (£2.4 million) and condensed milk (£0.4 million).

[a] This included the whole of Ireland.

food and basic materials. Manufactures (finished manufactures and semi-manufactured goods) accounted for 84% of UK exports in 1970. This declined with the start of North Sea oil exports in the mid-1970s, but has recovered subsequently, to stand at over 86% in 1998 (see Table 25.2).

The UK has not had a surplus on manufactured goods, however, since 1982. Machinery and transport equipment accounted for almost 48% of exports in 1998 and 45% of imports (see Table 25.3). Aerospace, chemicals and electronics have become increasingly significant export

Table 25.1: External Trade in Goods and Services, 1988–98[a]					£ million
	1988	1993	1996	1997	1998
Exports of goods	80,711	122,039	167,403	171,783	164,132
Exports of services	26,723	40,039	52,900	57,543	60,070
Exports of goods and services	**107,434**	**162,078**	**220,303**	**229,326**	**224,202**
Imports of goods	102,264	135,358	180,489	183,693	184,897
Imports of services	22,393	33,416	44,003	45,129	47,817
Imports of goods and services	**124,657**	**168,774**	**224,492**	**228,822**	**232,714**
Balance of trade in goods	−21,553	−13,319	−13,086	−11,910	−20,765
Balance of trade in services	4,330	6,623	8,897	12,414	12,253
Balance of trade in goods and services	**−17,223**	**−6,696**	**−4,189**	**504**	**−8,512**

Source: *United Kingdom Balance of Payments—the Pink Book 1999*
[a] Balance of payments basis.

UK Balance of Payments in Goods and Services, 1968–98

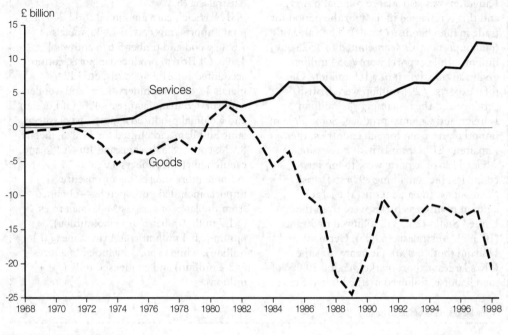

Source: Office for National Statistics

sectors, while textiles have declined in relative importance. Sectors with a positive balance of trade in 1998 included chemicals, fuels, and beverages and tobacco.

Imported manufactures have taken a greater share of the domestic market in recent decades. Between 1970 and 1998 the share of finished manufactures in total imports rose from 25% to 60%, while the share of basic materials fell from 15% to 3%. The percentage of food, beverages and tobacco in total imports has been dropping since the 1950s, down to less than 9% in 1998, as a result of the extent to which food demand has been met from domestic agriculture and of the decline in the proportion of total expenditure on food.

Geographical Distribution

The UK's external trade in goods is predominantly with other developed countries (see Table 25.4). In 1998 over 83% of UK exports were with other OECD countries,[1] and a similar percentage of imports came from these same countries. The proportion of export trade with the European Union was over 58% in 1998, while imports from the EU accounted for almost 55%. Western Europe as a whole took 63% of UK exports in 1998.

EU countries accounted for eight of the top ten export markets in 1998—the United States and Japan took the other two places— and seven of the top ten leading suppliers of goods to the UK (see Table 25.5); the other three places were taken by the United States, Japan and Switzerland. The United States maintained its position as the UK's largest

---

[1] Organisation for Economic Co-operation and Development countries comprise the 15 EU countries, Australia, Canada, the Czech Republic, Hungary, Iceland, Japan, South Korea, Mexico, New Zealand, Norway, Poland, Switzerland, Turkey and the United States.

Table 25.2: Value and Volume of Trade in Goods, 1998[a]

	Value (£ million)			Volume (1995 =100)	
	Exports	Imports	Balance	Exports	Imports
Food, beverages and tobacco	10,231	16,258	−6,027	102	121
Basic materials	2,512	5,622	−3,110	105	101
Oil	7,039	3,980	3,059	93	100
Other mineral fuels and lubricants	492	915	−423	109	110
Semi-manufactured goods	43,385	45,161	−1,776	110	118
Finished manufactured goods	98,576	111,144	−12,568	128	141
Unspecified goods	1,897	1,817	80	n.a.	n.a.
Total	**164,132**	**184,897**	**−20,765**	**118.0**	**129.1**

Source: *United Kingdom Balance of Payments—the Pink Book 1999*
[a] Balance of payments basis.
n.a. = not available.

external market for the second year running, and overtook Germany as the UK's largest single supplier.

The financial crisis in Asia caused UK exports to a number of Asia Pacific markets to decline in 1998 compared with 1997. However, there were small increases in a number of European countries, notably the Irish Republic, Italy and Spain. Total UK imports in 1998 were 1% higher than in 1997, but imports from the Netherlands showed a significant increase of over 9%.

Services

A surplus has been recorded for trade in services in every year since 1966. The £12.3 billion surplus recorded in 1998 (see Table 25.6) was slightly down on the record surplus of £12.4 billion in 1997. Exports of services grew by 4.4% to £60.1 billion, with particularly strong growth in other business services and travel. Imports of services grew by 6.0% to £47.8 billion, mainly owing to higher expenditure by UK travellers abroad.

OTHER TRANSACTIONS

Earnings on investment income on external assets increased by 3.5% to £110.6 billion in 1998, while debits fell slightly by 0.3% to £95.5 billion, giving a record surplus of £15.1 billion (see Table 25.7). This was largely

attributable to a record surplus on direct investment income and a substantial fall in the deficit on other investment income. The surplus on direct investment income was £18.0 billion, the highest on record, and an increase of £3.0 billion on 1997. This was partly offset by the deficit on other investment income, which fell by £4.5 billion to £4.7 billion in 1998, the lowest since 1990. Earnings on reserve assets for 1998 at £1.1 billion were £0.3 billion lower than in 1997.

The deficit on current transfers increased from £5.1 billion to £6.5 billion in 1998, largely owing to higher contributions to EU institutions.

BALANCE OF PAYMENTS

The UK's balance of payments statistics record transactions between residents of the UK and non-residents. In 1998 the Office for National Statistics' *United Kingdom Balance of Payments—the Pink Book*—made major changes to the presentation of the accounts, to bring them in line with international standards.

The *current account* consists of trade in goods and services, income (compensation of employees and investment income) and current transfers. In 1998, there was a small current account surplus of £136 million (see Table 25.8), a sharp decrease of £6.5 billion on the highest ever surplus recorded in 1997. An increase in income was more than offset by

Table 25.3: Commodity Composition of Trade in Goods, 1998[a]			£ million
	Exports	Imports	Balance
Food and live animals	6,280	13,244	−6,964
Beverages and tobacco	3,951	3,014	937
Crude materials	2,270	5,077	−2,807
of which: Wood, lumber and cork	56	1,099	−1,043
Pulp and waste paper	48	477	−429
Metal ores	555	1,316	−761
Fuels	7,531	4,895	2,636
Petroleum and petroleum products	7,039	3,980	3,059
Coal, gas and electricity	492	915	−423
Animal and vegetable oils and fats	242	545	−303
Chemicals	22,141	17,425	4,716
of which: Organic chemicals	4,922	4,524	398
Plastics	3,204	3,909	−705
Manufactures classified chiefly by material	21,244	27,736	−6,492
of which: Wood and cork manufactures	247	1,089	−842
Paper and paperboard manufactures	2,191	4,524	−2,333
Textile manufactures	3,264	4,865	−1,601
Iron and steel	3,326	3,212	114
Non-ferrous metals	2,437	3,719	−1,282
Metal manufactures	3,589	3,722	−133
Machinery and transport equipment	78,047	83,227	−5,180
Mechanical machinery	22,724	17,159	5,565
Electrical machinery	34,453	36,693	−2,240
Road vehicles	14,586	22,579	−7,993
Other transport equipment	6,284	6,796	−512
Miscellaneous manufactures	20,529	27,917	−7,388
of which: Clothing and footwear	3,518	8,892	−5,374
Scientific and photographic	6,687	6,112	575
Other commodities and transactions	1,897	1,817	80
Total	**164,132**	**184,897**	**−20,765**

Source: *Monthly Digest of Statistics*
[a] On a balance of payments basis.

a sharp deterioration in the deficit on trade in goods and services. The last time there were two consecutive surpluses on the current account was in 1984 and 1985.

The capital account comprises capital transfers and the acquisition and disposal of non-produced, non-financial assets. The capital account surplus fell from £0.8 billion in 1997 to £0.4 billion in 1998, reflecting lower receipts from EU institutions.

The *financial account* covers direct, portfolio and other investment and reserve assets.[2] Both UK direct investment abroad, at £64.1 billion in 1998, and foreign direct

[2] Direct investment abroad consists of investment in branches, subsidiaries or associated companies, giving the investor a significant influence on the operations of the company, unlike portfolio investment which covers investment in equity and debt securities.

Table 25.4: Distribution of Trade in Goods, 1998[a]

	Value (£ million)			%	
	Exports	Imports	Balance	Exports	Imports
European Union	95,739	101,271	−5,532	58.3	54.8
Other Western Europe	7,677	9,765	−2,088	4.7	5.3
North America	24,788	27,902	−3,114	15.1	15.1
Other OECD countries	8,777	14,959	−6,182	5.3	8.1
Oil-exporting countries	7,315	3,185	4,130	4.5	1.7
Rest of the world	19,837	27,817	−7,980	12.1	15.0

Source: Office for National Statistics
[a] Balance of payments basis.

Table 25.5: Trade in Goods—Main Markets and Suppliers, 1998[a]

	Value (£ million)	Share (%)
Main markets		
United States	21,954	13.3
Germany	20,589	12.4
France	16,450	9.9
Netherlands	12,993	7.9
Irish Republic	9,600	5.8
Italy	8,611	5.2
Belgium/Luxembourg	8,417	5.1
Spain	7,164	4.3
Sweden	4,393	2.7
Japan	3,238	2.0
Main suppliers		
United States	25,656	13.4
Germany	25,516	13.3
France	17,913	9.4
Netherlands	13,634	7.1
Italy	9,900	5.2
Japan	9,573	5.0
Belgium/Luxembourg	9,549	5.0
Irish Republic	7,920	4.1
Spain	5,836	3.1
Switzerland	5,042	2.6

Source: Monthly Digest of Statistics
[a] On an overseas trade statistics basis. Figures are not directly comparable with those in Tables 25.1–25.4.

investment in the UK, at £40.8 billion, were the highest on record. Portfolio investment abroad decreased in 1998 to £34.3 billion from £51.9 billion in 1997. Foreign portfolio investment in the UK fell in 1998 to £20.2 billion, compared with £27.2 billion in 1997. Other investment abroad fell substantially from £168.4 billion in 1997 to £16.0 billion in 1998, while investment in the UK fell sharply from £193.9 billion to £44.3 billion. Reserve assets increased by £2.2 billion in 1998.

The *international investment position* of the UK is the balance sheet of the stock of external financial assets and liabilities. At the end of 1998, direct investment in the UK stood at £207.5 billion, while direct

Table 25.6: Trade in Services, 1998 — £ million

	Exports	Imports	Balance
Transportation	11,505	13,649	−2,144
Travel	14,503	20,126	−5,623
Communications	1,210	1,454	−244
Construction	285	108	177
Insurance	3,194	570	2,624
Financial services[a]	6,318	171	6,147
Computer and information services	1,510	436	1,074
Royalties and licence fees	4,061	3,696	365
Other business services	15,673	5,651	10,022
Personal, cultural and recreational services	682	432	250
Government	1,129	1,524	−395
Total	**60,070**	**47,817**	**12,253**

Source: *United Kingdom Balance of Payments—the Pink Book 1999*
[a] Service earnings of financial institutions are recorded net of their foreign expenses. Imports of financial services only cover imports by non-financial institutions.

Table 25.7: Income and Transfers, 1998 — £ million

	Credits	Debits	Balance
Compensation of employees	**777**	**701**	**76**
Investment income	**110,588**	**95,490**	**15,098**
of which:			
Earnings on direct investment	32,426	14,407	18,019
Earnings on portfolio investment	27,161	26,477	684
Earnings on other investments	49,869	54,606	−4,737
Earnings on reserve assets	1,132	n.a.	1,132
Current transfers	**15,596**	**22,122**	**−6,526**
Central government	6,467	6,585	−118
Other sectors	9,129	15,537	−6,408
Total	**126,961**	**118,313**	**8,648**

Source: *United Kingdom Balance of Payments—the Pink Book 1999*
n.a. = not available.

investment abroad amounted to £295.0 billion, giving a net balance of £87.5 billion. Inward portfolio investment stood at £679.3 billion, while the stock of UK portfolio investment abroad amounted to £726.9 billion. In total, UK external liabilities exceeded assets by £67.5 billion.

INTERNATIONAL TRADE POLICY

The Government is committed to promoting open world markets in goods and services, to the further liberalisation of international direct investment, and to improving the transparency of international trade agreements and the WTO itself. The UK plays a leading role in achieving these objectives through work in the WTO, the International Monetary Fund (IMF) and the OECD, as well as the EU.

European Union

The single European market started trading in 1993. The Government's work on this, and on EU enlargement, seeks to create a commercial and economic environment of open markets

Table 25.8: UK Balance of Payments, 1988–98 [a]				£ million	
	1988	1993	1996	1997	1998
Current account					
Trade in goods and services	−17,223	−6,696	−4,189	504	−8,512
Income	1,291	685	8,111	11,170	15,174
Current transfers	−1,605	−4,607	−4,522	−5,051	−6,526
Current balance	**−17,537**	**−10,618**	**−600**	**6,623**	**136**
Capital account	235	309	736	804	421
Financial account	15,135	9,447	1,781	−13,186	−9,025
Net errors and omissions	2,167	862	−1,917	5,759	8,468

Source: *United Kingdom Balance of Payments—the Pink Book 1999*
[a] Balance of payments basis.

for products, services, capital and labour which encourages enterprise and supports sustainable growth. It considers that the market (see p. 81) is beneficial to the economies of all member states of the EU, and that removal of trade barriers will lead to reduced business costs and greater competition and efficiency. It is committed to making progress on issues that would lead to the completion of the single market, including removing remaining barriers to investment, opening up government procurement, making competition policy more streamlined and reducing bureaucracy. In the Government's view, specific advantages of the single market include:

- wider consumer choice;
- removal of barriers to trade through mutual recognition of standards and harmonisation;
- the right to trade financial services throughout the EU on the basis of a single authorisation 'passport';
- mutual recognition of professional and vocational qualifications; and
- a reduction in export business bureaucracy.

In 1997 a Single Market Scoreboard was introduced by the DTI and has proved effective in showing progress in implementing single market measures and in encouraging better performance among member states. Areas already identified in which the single market could operate more strongly include

financial services, public procurement and mutual recognition of standards. The Government is promoting a process of economic reform in the EU, with the goal of further improvements in productivity, investment and growth. It is also promoting the principles of competitiveness and the economic reform agenda to EU applicant countries of Central and Eastern Europe. Through the agreements each applicant has with the EU, these countries already enjoy many of the benefits of the single market in industrial goods. The Government is working to ensure that by the time of their entry each country has adopted all the measures required of EU membership, and has the administrative infrastructure to implement them.

The Government is playing an important role in partnership with the Treasury's Euro Preparations Unit in helping British business adjust to the introduction of the euro in 11 EU member states (see p. 80).

World Trade Organisation

The level of industrial tariffs in developed countries has fallen dramatically since the establishment of the General Agreement on Tariffs and Trade (GATT) in 1948. This set of agreements helped establish a strong and largely prosperous multilateral trading system that became progressively more liberal through the rounds of trade negotiations held under its auspices. The eighth GATT Round (the Uruguay round) of 1986–94 led to the formation of the World Trade Organisation and a new set of agreements. These agreements encompassed not only tariffs but also other areas covering trade in goods such as subsidies, as well as trade in services and intellectual property.

Under the WTO, trade liberalisation has continued and the Government is working towards the launching of a new trade round at the WTO Ministerial Conference in Seattle in the United States at the end of 1999. The Government wishes these negotiations to be comprehensive, covering areas such as investment, competition and trade facilitation. It also believes that they should address the needs of developing countries and least developed countries, such as better market access for their products and capacity building.

The EU and the United States and Canada are working to achieve a constructive way forward in the dispute on the EU's ban on the import of hormone-treated beef from the US and Canada (see p. 457). EU member states have asked the European Commission to draft legislation to reform the EU banana regime, following the WTO ruling that it was incompatible with world trade rules (see also p. 457)

Relations with Other Countries

The UK places great importance on developing strong relations with third countries, in particular through the EU. Examples include:

- the Transatlantic Economic Partnership (TEP), where at the US/EU summit in 1998 the two partners agreed to reinforce their close relationship (see p. 87). The TEP should be instrumental in setting the agenda for a more open and accessible world trading system and at the same time greatly improving the economic relationship between the EU and the US, by reducing bilateral frictions and promoting prosperity on both sides of the Atlantic;

- the Asia-Europe Meeting (ASEM), which provides an inter-regional forum for dialogue between 25 Asian and European countries together representing half of global wealth. The UK has worked in ASEM to build support for keeping markets open, resisting protectionism and pursuing further multilateral liberalisation; and

- the Department of Trade and Industry (DTI) works closely with the Department for International Development (DFID) in seeking to ensure developing countries participate more fully in international trade. The mandate for the successor to the current Lomé Convention (see below)—the framework for trade and aid relations between the EU and 71 African, Caribbean and Pacific (ACP) countries—includes a commitment that the new trade and economic co-operation regime should at least maintain current market access from ACP countries.

Special Trading Arrangements

The multilateral trading system provides the foundation for the EU's common commercial policy. However, the EU has preferential trading arrangements with a number of countries. These fall into three main categories:

- Those that prepare countries in Central and Eastern Europe for possible EU membership. Europe (Association) Agreements (see p. 85) are designed to facilitate closer political and economic ties and the eventual liberalisation of trade with a view to these countries becoming full members of the EU.

- The EU has association and co-operating agreements with virtually all non-member countries with a Mediterranean coastline, plus Jordan. These provide for the eventual setting up of a free trade area between the EU and these countries by 2010.

- Those that provide an economic dimension to its assistance to former dependent territories. Trade relations with these countries (known as ACP countries) are governed by the Lomé

Gas and Oil Production in the UK

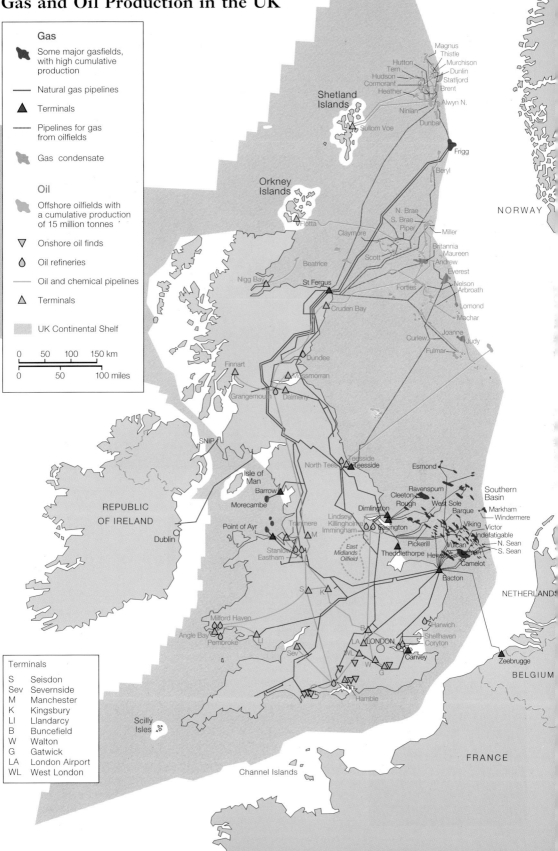

Gas

- Some major gasfields, with high cumulative production
- —— Natural gas pipelines
- ▲ Terminals
- —— Pipelines for gas from oilfields
- Gas condensate

Oil

- Offshore oilfields with a cumulative production of 15 million tonnes
- ▽ Onshore oil finds
- ◊ Oil refineries
- —— Oil and chemical pipelines
- △ Terminals

UK Continental Shelf

0   50   100   150 km
0   50   100 miles

Terminals

S	Seisdon
Sev	Severnside
M	Manchester
K	Kingsbury
Ll	Llandarcy
B	Buncefield
W	Walton
G	Gatwick
LA	London Airport
WL	West London

NORWAY

Shetland Islands

Magnus
Thistle
Hutton — Murchison
Tern — Dunlin
Hudson — Statfjord
Cormorant — Brent
Heather — Alwyn N.
Ninian
Dunbar
Sullom Voe

Frigg

Beryl

Orkney Islands

Flotta

N. Brae
S. Brae
Piper
Miller
Claymore

Scott
Britannia
Maureen
Andrew
Everest

Beatrice

Nigg Bay
St Fergus
Forties
Nelson
Arbroath
Cruden Bay
Lomond
Machar

Curlew
Joanne
Judy
Fulmar

Dundee

Finnart
Mossmorran
Grangemouth   Dalmeny

SNIP

Isle of Man
Barrow
Morecambe

REPUBLIC OF IRELAND

Dublin

Point of Ayr   Tranmere
Stanlow
Eastham

Esmond

North Tees   Teesside
Teesside

Ravenspurn
Cleeton
Rough
West Sole
Barque
Markham
Windermere

Dimlington

Lindsey
Killingholme
Immingham
Easington

Viking
Victor
Indefatigable
N. Sean
S. Sean

East Midlands Oilfield

Pickerill
Theddlethorpe
Vulcan
Hewett
Camelot

S   K
Bacton

NETHERLANDS

Milford Haven
Angle Bay
Pembroke
Ll

Sev

B
Harwich
Shellhaven
Coryton
LA LONDON
WL
W
G   Canvey

Zeebrugge

BELGIUM

Hamble

Scilly Isles

Channel Islands

FRANCE

SCIENCE

The emergence of disease-causing bacteria able to resist all current antibiotics poses a serious threat to human health. Genome analysis of microbes such as *Streptomyces*, which have provided the majority of new antibiotics over the past 50 years, will aid understanding of how antibiotics are made, and will provide tools for finding new antibiotics as well as strategies for overcoming bacterial resistance to antibiotics.

The major impact that genomics will have in biomedical research and across all biology-based industries was recognised in additional funding in the Science Budget allocations.

Colonies of *Streptomyces*.

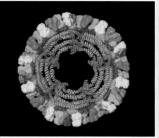

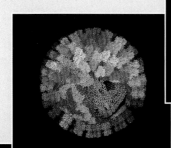

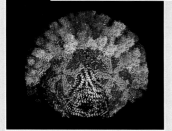

Bluetongue Virus Bluetongue virus (BTV) causes an economically important disease of cattle, sheep and deer in many countries around the world. The structure of the biochemically active core of the BTV virus particle has been studied by X-ray crystallography in a collaborative study between research groups led by Professor David Stuart at the Laboratory of Molecular Biophysics, University of Oxford, and Dr Peter Mertens at the Pirbright Laboratory of the Institute for Animal Health. The BTV core is the largest structure that has been analysed in such detail and has provided a model for the structure and assembly for other viruses within the family *Reoviridae*, including important disease-causing agents of animals, plants and humans.

Mini Lake District
A set of tanks, each one metre deep, is revealing important clues as to how bigger lakes may change as the Earth continues to warm in the next few decades. The 48 heated tanks house an ecosystem and allow the research team, all of the School of Biological Sciences at the University of Liverpool, to investigate directly the effects of global warming on fresh shallow waters.

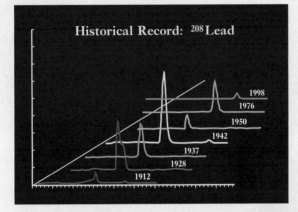

Historical Record: ^{208}Lead

1998
1976
1950
1942
1937
1928
1912

Laser Interrogation of Tree Bark
As a result of industrial emissions, potentially harmful elements are present in the atmosphere and fine airborne material can accumulate on tree bark through wet and dry deposition. During tree growth the bark can be incorporated with the trunk forming a so-called bark pocket. Interrogation and analysis of bark pockets by laser provides a new approach to measuring historic levels of air pollution. This may give an improved understanding of the impact of human activity on the environment.

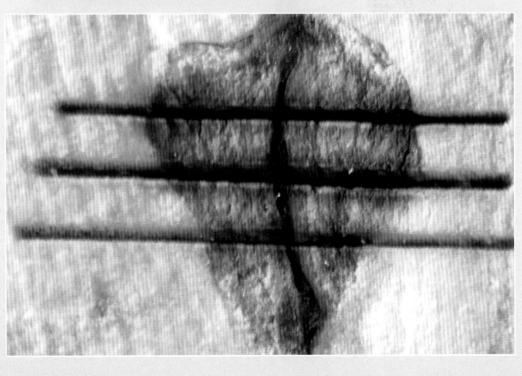

SPACE

An image of the nearby universe as seen by the NASA infrared astronomical satellite. The bright band along the middle is light from stars in our own Milky Way galaxy. The myriad of small dots are light from external galaxies in the nearby universe. A team of UK astronomers measured the distance to 15,500 of these galaxies to produce the largest map known to man.

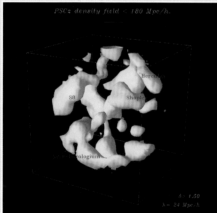

A map of the three dimensional distribution of galaxies in the nearby universe. The Earth is located at the centre of the figure. The labels indicate the names of the largest superclusters each containing several thousand galaxies. The map extends to about 1/20th of the size of the observable universe. Work on both maps is carried out by a consortium of UK universities led by Dr W. Saunders of the University of Edinburgh.

The Horsehead Nebula is one of the most famous nebulae in the sky. Like clouds in the Earth's atmosphere, this cosmic cloud has assumed a recognisable shape by chance. After many thousands of years, the internal motions of the cloud will alter its appearance. The photograph was taken by the Anglo-Australian Telescope which is funded by the Particle Physics and Astronomy Research Council (see p. 437).

Convention, which gives them tariff-free access, subject to certain safeguards, to the EU for industrial and agricultural products. The EU also operates a Generalised System of Preferences which is available to nearly all developing countries and applies to industrial products, including textiles and certain (mainly processed) agricultural products.

New trade relationships with countries and regions of Latin America are being pursued. Work is in progress on developing a free trade agreement with Mexico, and negotiations for new agreements with the Mercosur regional economic area (Argentina, Brazil, Paraguay and Uruguay) and Chile are under way.

Partnership and co-operation (non-preferential) agreements have been concluded with ten states of the former Soviet Union. Non-preferential co-operation agreements have also been made with countries in South Asia and Latin America, as well as the People's Republic of China, the Association of South East Asian Nations, the Andean Pact, and the Central American States.

Controls on Trade

Import Controls

Following the completion of the single European market, all national quantitative restrictions have been abolished. However, some EU-wide quotas have been imposed on a small range of products from the People's Republic of China, while EU imports of some steel products from Russia, the Ukraine and Kazakhstan are also restricted. Quantitative restrictions on textiles and clothing stem from the Multi-Fibre Arrangement (MFA), under which there is a series of bilateral agreements. Some quotas are also maintained for imports from non-WTO countries. The MFA restrictions will be eliminated by 2005 as part of the Uruguay Round agreement.

Imports from certain countries remain subject to sanctions or embargo agreed by, for example, the United Nations. Imports of certain other goods from all countries are prohibited or restricted in order to protect human, animal or plant life and health. These include firearms and ammunition; nuclear materials; certain drugs; explosives; endangered wildlife and derived products; pornographic material; and certain agricultural, horticultural and food products.

Export Controls

The great majority of UK exports are not subject to any government control. However, controls on certain strategic goods— conventional military goods, arms, ammunition and related materials as well as dual-use industrial goods that can be used for civil and military purposes—are imposed for a variety of reasons, including foreign policy and non-proliferation concerns, the need to comply with international treaty commitments, the operation of sanctions and national security. The scope of export controls is limited to what is necessary to meet these concerns. Most controls apply on a worldwide basis, although certain sanctions and embargoes are applied against specific countries as a result of agreement by members of bodies such as the United Nations.

The Government is strongly committed to preventing the proliferation of nuclear, chemical and biological weapons—weapons of mass destruction—and missiles capable of delivering such weapons. It works closely with the relevant international organisations in this area, while seeking to ensure that the UK meets its own international obligations without imposing unnecessary burdens on business. Licences to export arms and other goods controlled for strategic reasons are issued by the DTI acting through its Export Control Organisation (ECO). All licence applications are circulated to other departments with an interest, including the Foreign and Commonwealth Office (FCO), Ministry of Defence and DFID. The ECO is also the licensing authority for applications to export goods controlled to certain destinations only, such as Iraq, because of specific trade sanctions imposed in accordance with resolutions of the UN Security Council.

A White Paper on *Strategic Export Controls* published in 1998 contained proposals for new primary legislation and improvements to export licensing procedures, including provision for parliamentary scrutiny of the

DTI's export licensing decisions, and the introduction of powers enabling government to impose controls on the transfer of technology by intangible means such as trafficking and brokering.

Inward and Outward Investment

The UK has an open economy, and there are no restrictions on the outward flow of capital. Outward investment helps to develop markets for UK exports while providing earnings in the form of investment income (see p. 415). Inward investment is promoted by the Invest in Britain Bureau (IBB—see below), which reports jointly to the DTI and the FCO. This investment is seen as a means of introducing new technology, products and management styles to the UK, and creating or safeguarding employment.

Inward Investment

Inward investment is a significant contributor to the British economy. The UK attracts over one-third of all inward investment into the EU, and overseas businesses investing in Britain generate an estimated 50% of UK exports. Some 5,000 US, 1,000 Japanese and 3,000 French and German companies are located in the UK.

During 1998–99, the UK retained its place as the leading location in Europe for inward investment. In addition, the latest national inward investment results, for 1998–99, showed a record level of UK successes with 652 projects, creating 44,000 new jobs and safeguarding another 74,000.

The IBB co-ordinates the promotion of inward investment, operating overseas through diplomatic posts and in the UK through its partners in Scotland, Wales, Northern Ireland and the English regions:

- Regional Development Agencies in England (see p. 11);
- Locate in Scotland, operated jointly by the Scottish Executive and Scottish Enterprise;
- the Welsh Development Agency's International Division; and
- the Industrial Development Board for Northern Ireland.

About 40% of new investment in the UK comes from companies who already have a UK presence. North America continues to be the largest source of inward investment, followed by Japan. The UK receives about 23% of total EU direct investment, including 38% of investment from the United States and 40% from Japan. In addition to more established sectors, such as the automotive sector, which have traditionally brought a high number of jobs, the UK increasingly attracts high value-added investment in 'leading edge' sectors. In 1999 the UK has won the following investments with significant help from the overseas investment teams and the IBB:

- Novartis of Switzerland, a world leader in life sciences and employing over 3,000 people across 14 UK R&D sites, is investing an additional £100 million in UK properties, including £40 million on a world-class respiratory centre in Horsham, West Sussex;
- Universal Scientific Industrial of Taiwan is establishing an IT manufacturing project in Irvine, Ayrshire (creating 700 jobs);
- US-owned Pfizer has opened a new £6.2 million quality operations facility in Sandwich, Kent; and
- Toshiba established a laboratory in Bristol to work on the next generation of mobile telephones.

Advantages to overseas investors of preferring Britain include its membership of the single European market, a flexible and adaptable workforce, good labour relations, low taxation, a respected legal system and the English language.

GOVERNMENT SERVICES

The Government provides a wide range of advice and practical support to meet the needs of exporters. This support is designed to help businesses, especially small and medium-sized enterprises, through all stages of the exporting process.

British Trade International

British Trade International (BTI) has lead responsibility within government for trade development and promotion on behalf of British business. It brings together the joint work of the FCO and the DTI in support of British trade and investment overseas. It combines in a single operation all trade development and promotion work currently undertaken locally in the English regions by the Business Link network (see p. 390); trade support services provided nationally; and the commercial work overseas of over 200 embassies and other diplomatic posts.

BTI was established in May 1999 following a Cabinet Office review of all export promotion activities across government. The review involved wide consultation with industry and business organisations, and recommended some far-reaching changes in the way official support for overseas trade and investment is organised. These are being implemented over the next two years. Key priorities include:

- developing a national strategy which will provide clear direction to all parts of government on trade promotion and development;

- putting in place a new structure which will enable the team at home and overseas to function as a single organisation; and

- developing a strong brand for trade promotion services to ensure that businesses know what BTI can offer to help them win business overseas.

The Chief Executive reports to the Foreign Secretary and the Secretary of State for Trade and Industry, and to the Board of BTI, chaired jointly by FCO and DTI ministers. A majority of the Board's members are from business and have wide experience of international trade.

One of BTI's first tasks is preparation of the national strategy, which will underpin not only its own programmes and priorities but also those of other organisations working in support of Britain's exporters and overseas investors. BTI's strategy will cover the UK, and the administrations in Scotland, Wales and Northern Ireland will play a full role in its development; each of the administrations has a member on BTI's Board.

Export Insurance

ECGD (Export Credits Guarantee Department), Britain's official export credit agency, is a separate government department responsible to the Secretary of State for Trade and Industry. It helps exporters of UK goods and services to overcome the risks involved in selling and investing abroad. This is achieved primarily by providing medium and long-term export credit support (insurance and backing for finance) for capital goods and projects. It also provides reinsurance for exports sold on short terms of payment, and political risk insurance for overseas investments.

In 1997–98, ECGD issued guarantees for new business (exports and overseas investments) of £3.4 billion. It also made a cash contribution to the Exchequer of £445 million, achieved a high level of recoveries (£517 million) and experienced a continued fall in claims to £159 million. ECGD aims to be flexible and innovative in developing solutions to individual problems, and offers simple packages for the more straightforward deals. UK exporters also benefit from the extensive network of co-operation agreements that ECGD now has with export credit agencies in other countries.

Further Reading

Trade and Industry. The Government's Expenditure Plans 1999–2000. Cm 4211. The Stationery Office, 1999.

United Kingdom Balance of Payments—the Pink Book, annual report. Office for National Statistics. The Stationery Office.

Website

Department of Trade and Industry: www.dti.gov.uk

26 Science, Engineering and Technology

More Nobel Prizes for science (over 70) have been won by scientists from Britain than any country except the United States. The United Kingdom funds about 4.5% of global research and development (R&D) and produces about 8% of scientific publications. Government policy aims to reinforce the UK's international scientific standing; and maximise the contribution of science, engineering and technology (SET) to economic competitiveness and the quality of life by promoting innovation.

BACKGROUND

The public sector is the prime funder of basic science in Britain. As well as playing a crucial part in advancing scientific knowledge and producing well-trained people, such research can often lead to unexpectedly exploitable results. Business has the prime responsibility for researching and developing new and improved products and services. Government promotes the climate for the development and successful exploitation of new ideas through, for example, the Foresight Programme (which encourages partnerships between industry and the UK's science base—see p. 427), and tries to facilitate technology transfer and access. Industry is being encouraged to invest more in R&D and to take a longer-term view of R&D investment.

The Government's policies for science, engineering and technology were set out in the Competitiveness White Paper in December 1998 and were reflected in the Comprehensive Spending Review (see p. 400). This provided for an increase of 11% in real terms between 1998–99 and 2001–02 for spending in this area. The European Union (EU) launched the Fifth Framework Programme, a further round of its collaborative R&D programme, in April 1999. The objectives of this programme fit well with the UK's priorities of increased competitiveness and higher quality of life (see p. 434).

Recent pioneering work in the UK includes the discovery in 1985 by British Antarctic Survey scientists of the hole in the ozone layer over the Antarctic. Researchers at the Laboratory of Molecular Biology, Cambridge, produced the first monoclonal antibodies— proteins with enormous potential in the diagnosis and treatment of disease. Among British breakthroughs in genetics research are the identification of the gene in the Y chromosome responsible for determining sex, and of other genes linked to diseases such as cystic fibrosis and a form of breast cancer. The

At the beginning of the 20th century UK science was particularly strong in physics and chemistry, and in many branches of biology and medicine. Mathematics, psychology and philosophy were other fertile areas of scientific endeavour.

Among just a few examples of notable British discoveries around the turn of the century:

- The existence of the electron was established in 1897 by the physicist Sir Joseph Thomson, who won a Nobel Prize in 1906.

- In 1902 E.H. Stirling and W.M. Bayliss, both physiologists, isolated the hormone secretin, which aids digestion.

- Sir William Ramsay, working with Lord Rayleigh, discovered argon in 1895 and went on to identify the rest of the family of inert gases (helium, neon, krypton, xenon and radon). Ramsay and Rayleigh shared a Nobel Prize in 1904.

- Another Nobel Prize-winner was Ernest Rutherford, the New Zealand-born English physicist. He made fundamental discoveries concerning the nature of radioactivity, and deduced the existence of the nucleus in 1906.

- Sir Ronald Ross, a surgeon (Nobel Prize, 1902), confirmed the theory of the bacteriologist Sir Patrick Manson that mosquitoes transmit malaria, when he discovered the human malaria parasite in the stomach wall of an anopheles mosquito.

British engineering was also making exceptional progress: the first electric underground railway opened in London in 1890; Sir Charles Parsons, having invented the steam turbine in 1884, fitted one to *Turbinia* in 1897, making it the fastest boat of the time (35 knots); and Sir John Ambrose Fleming, an authority on electro-magnetism, constructed the first rectifying diode in 1904, which greatly stimulated the development of radio.

world's first pig with a genetically modified heart was bred by scientists at Cambridge University, an important milestone in breeding animals as organ donors for people. In 1997 scientists at the Roslin Institute in Edinburgh announced that they had succeeded in 'cloning' a sheep ('Dolly the Sheep') using a cell from an adult sheep's mammary gland. Professor Sir Harold Kroto of Sussex University shared the 1996 Nobel Prize for chemistry with two US scientists for discovering in 1985 the fullerene molecule—60 carbon atoms arranged in a symmetrical cage. Potential uses for fullerene and for materials derived from it include high-temperature superconductors, drugs, ultra-strong fibres, super-slippery lubricants, lightweight magnets and electronic superconductors.

Other notable areas of UK achievement in R&D include biotechnology, materials, chemicals, electronics and aerospace. Among the many achievements in British research reported in the first half of 1999, which may have far-reaching consequences, are:

- The discovery by scientists at Horticultural Research International at Wellesbourne (Warwickshire) of a strain of bacteria that degrades phenylureas, the most widely used herbicide family in Europe. Spraying these bacteria into the soil could greatly reduce the amount of chemicals leaking from fields into streams and harming fish.

- The development at the National Medical Laser Centre at University College London of a technique called restenosis. This uses laser light and a photosensitising chemical to make repeat surgery unnecessary for the 33% of people who, having undergone surgery to clear their blocked arteries, find that they need to return to hospital to have further blockages removed. Restenosis appears to keep the arteries clear.

- The genetic modification of tobacco plants by a team at the University of Cambridge to increase their ability to break down TNT and nitroglycerine into harmless compounds. Dangerous residues from making these explosives can leave soil highly contaminated, so much so that, in extreme cases, the ground itself can explode.

- The use of titanium dioxide and ultraviolet light by scientists at the Robert Gordon University in Aberdeen to remove dangerous toxins produced by blue-green algae, which grow in fresh water all around the world.

- A breakthrough in semiconductor memory technology by a British-Japanese team, funded by Hitachi, which paves the way for even more lightweight computers, mobile telephones and entertainment systems.

RESEARCH AND DEVELOPMENT EXPENDITURE

Gross domestic expenditure in the UK on R&D in 1997 was £14.7 billion, 1.8% of gross domestic product (GDP). Of this, £12.5 billion was on civil R&D, with the rest going to defence projects.

Industry provided 49% of total funding and government 32% in 1997; a further 15% came from abroad. Significant contributions were also made by private endowments, trusts and charities. As well as financing R&D carried out within industry itself, industry supports university research and finances contract research at government establishments. Some charities have their own laboratories and offer grants for outside research. Contract research organisations (see p. 439) carry out R&D for companies and are playing an increasingly important role in the transfer of technology to British industry.

Total spending on R&D in industry amounted to nearly £9.6 billion in 1997. Of this total, industry's own contribution was 71%, with 10% coming from government and virtually all of the rest from overseas. The chemistry and biotechnology-based sectors—chemicals, pharmaceuticals and healthcare—account for almost a third of R&D spending by listed companies; the electronics and aerospace sectors are also big investors in R&D. The three biggest investors in R&D—Glaxo Wellcome, SmithKline Beecham and AstraZeneca—all

Table 26.1: UK Company Spending on R&D

	R&D annual investment (£ million)	R&D as % of sales
Glaxo Wellcome	1,163	15
SmithKline Beecham	910	11
AstraZeneca[a]	708	13
Unilever	556	2
Shell	480	1
Ford Automotive	434	5
British Aerospace	430	6
General Electric	394	6
Pfizer	313	99[b]
BT	307	2

Source: *The 1999 UK R&D Scoreboard*, DTI
[a] AstraZeneca was formed in 1999 from the merger of Astra of Sweden and Zeneca (see p. 473).
[b] Pfizer's UK sales have been low, but much of their R&D is in Britain.
Note: R&D spending includes spending overseas.

operate in the pharmaceuticals sector (see Table 26.1).

GOVERNMENT ROLE

Science, engineering and technology base issues are the responsibility of a Cabinet minister at the Department of Trade and Industry (DTI), assisted by a Minister for Science; they are supported by the Office of Science and Technology (OST). A Ministerial Science Group has been created across government to ensure that SET are taken into account in the development of government policy. The OST, headed by the Government's Chief Scientific Adviser, is responsible for policy on SET, both nationally and internationally, and co-ordinates science and technology policy across government departments. The Chief Scientific Adviser also reports directly to the Prime Minister. An independent Council for Science and Technology advises the Prime Minister on the strategic policies and framework for science and technology in the UK. Its members are drawn from academia, business and charitable foundations/institutions.

The term 'science and engineering base' is used to describe the research and postgraduate training capacity based in the universities and colleges of higher education and in establishments operated by the Research Councils together with the national and international central facilities (such as CERN—see p. 435) supported by the Councils and available for use by British scientists and engineers. There are also important contributions from private institutions, chiefly those funded by charities. The science and engineering base is the main provider of basic research and much of the strategic research (research likely to have practical applications) carried out in the UK. It also collaborates with the private sector in the conduct of specific applied research.

The OST, through the Director General of Research Councils, has responsibility for the Science Budget, and for the government-financed Research Councils (see pp. 436–9). Through the Research Councils, the Science Budget supports research in the following ways: by awarding research grants to universities, other higher education establishments and some other research units; by funding Research Council establishments to carry out research or provide facilities; by paying subscriptions to international scientific facilities and organisations; and by supporting postgraduate research students and postdoctoral Fellows. The Science Budget also funds programmes of support to the science and engineering base through the Royal Society and the Royal Academy of Engineering. The other main sources of funds for universities are the higher education funding councils (see p. 135).

Strategy and Finance

Planned total government expenditure on SET (both civil and defence) in 1999–2000 is £7.1 billion. This represents an increase of about 7% in real terms over the estimated outturn of expenditure in 1998–99. Of the 1999–2000 total, £4.1 billion is devoted to civil science, including £1.5 billion for the Science Budget.

In 1998, the Government announced that it was providing an additional £1 billion for the science and engineering base between 1999

and 2002—£700 million through the Science Budget and £300 million through the Department for Education and Employment. A further £400 million will be provided by the Wellcome Trust. About £700 million of the extra funding, including £300 million of the Wellcome contribution, will be devoted to uprating university laboratories and other essential equipment (see p. 435). Another £400 million will be used by the Research Councils to support research in priority areas such as life sciences (including genetic research, medical science and biotechnology).

Among government departments, the Ministry of Defence (see p. 432) has the largest research budget.

The Foresight Programme

The funding and organisation of British SET aims to create a close partnership between government, industry and the scientific community in developing strengths in areas of importance to the future economic well-being of Britain. In particular, the Government's Foresight Programme encourages the public and private sectors to work together to identify opportunities in markets and technologies likely to emerge over the next ten to 20 years that would support sustainable growth, and the actions needed to exploit them. Government priorities in SET programmes, and in overall policy, regulation and education and training, are being guided by the Programme.

The Foresight Programme is co-ordinated by a joint industry/academic steering group headed by the Chief Scientific Adviser. Building on the first round (1994–99), a second Foresight round was launched in April 1999. This has three thematic panels and ten sectoral panels, made up of people from industry, academia and government. The panels will produce visions of the future which might drive wealth creation and shape the quality of life. The thematic panels will address the issues of ageing population, crime prevention and manufacturing in 2020. The sectoral panels will be focused on business sectors or broader areas, and they will carry forward the work of existing panels and tackle new issues.

Government departments, universities and higher education funding councils, as well as the Research Councils, are reflecting Foresight priorities in their research spending allocations. The private sector is being encouraged to take account of the priorities both in its participation in collaborative research programmes and in its own strategic planning. The Government provided £30 million over four years for the first round of the Foresight Challenge Competition, to fund collaborative R&D projects which address priorities identified by the Foresight panels. This was complemented by a further £62 million from private sector project participants. In addition, more than £300 million or so has already been channelled into other Foresight initiatives.

A 'Knowledge Pool' has been established as an integral part of the second round of Foresight. This is an electronic library of strategic visions, information and views about the future. It is believed to be the world's first professional knowledge management service freely accessible to the general public. Its aim is to help build new partnerships and stimulate new thinking by bringing together people with complementary and conflicting views of the future. It provides a fully searchable, single point of access to the work of Foresight panels and to most government scientific information available on the worldwide web. It also includes information from many other UK and overseas sources. The Knowledge Pool can be accessed through the Internet at the www.foresight.gov.uk website.

EQUAL—Extend Quality Life

One of the principal issues facing the UK in the years ahead is a growing elderly population (see p. 107). Life expectancy has risen, but has not been matched by an increase in years free from disability or illness. The EQUAL scheme focuses research and develops technologies to improve the quality of life of an ageing population. It spans the activities of all the Research Councils, from medical and life sciences to social and materials research, drawing together issues identified in the Foresight Programme.

ROPA and CASE

The Realising Our Potential Award (ROPA) scheme, administered by the Research Councils, is designed to encourage academic researchers to develop strategic links with industry and to stimulate new areas of 'blue skies' or 'curiosity-driven' research. Since the introduction of the ROPA scheme in 1994, 1,373 projects have been approved involving a total research investment of £123 million. The Government also makes funds available through the Research Councils for the Co-operative Awards in Science and Engineering (CASE) scheme, which supports postgraduate students on research projects jointly supervised with industry.

LINK

The LINK scheme, including Foresight LINK Awards, provides a government-wide framework for collaborative research in support of sustainable growth and improvements in the quality of life, in line with Foresight priorities. LINK aims to promote partnerships in commercially relevant research projects between industry and higher education institutions and other research base organisations. Under the scheme, government departments and Research Councils fund up to 50% of the cost of research projects, with industry providing the balance.

Since 1988, 62 LINK programmes have supported over 1,000 projects with a total value of more than £500 million (over half of which comes from industry) and involving over 1,500 companies. The latest programmes deal with: Food Quality and Safety; Oil and Gas Extraction; Management of Information for Fraud Control; and Ocean Margins. Eighteen new Foresight Link Awards, with a total value of £20 million, include: use of small-scale reactors in chemical and biochemical analysis and synthesis;

researching spectral imaging tools for the evaluation of contaminated sites; and fuel-control sensors to help reduce aircraft pollution.

Joint Research Equipment Initiative

The Joint Research Equipment Initiative brings together the higher education funding councils, the Department of Education for Northern Ireland and the Research Councils. It directs funds for research equipment in strategic priority areas. Since 1996 over £200 million of public and private money has been committed for 'leading edge' equipment for UK universities and colleges. A further £27 million was announced for a fourth round in 1999.

Joint Infrastructure Fund

The Joint Infrastructure Fund (JIF) is a 'one-off' programme to address the infrastructure problems of universities and was created by the Wellcome Trust and the DTI, each contributing £300 million. The Higher Education Funding Council for England has also contributed £100 million, raising the total fund to £700 million. In the first round of awards in May 1999, £150 million was allocated to over 20 universities. Successful bids ranged from an optical/infrared telescope capable of mapping huge tracts of the universe to a state-of-the-art vaccine centre. There will be further rounds of awards in late 1999 and in 2000 and 2001.

University Challenge Fund

The University Challenge Fund is a competitive scheme which offers financing to universities to help them in the early stages of turning research into commercial products. The first round involves over £60 million of investment funds: the Government has contributed £20 million, the Wellcome Trust up to £18 million and the Gatsby Charitable Foundation £2 million, with the remainder to be raised by the universities themselves. Following a large number of high-quality applications, the Government announced an additional contribution of £15 million: £5

million for the first round and £10 million for a second round. So far 15 university-based consortia, involving more than 30 universities and research institutes, have been awarded up to £45 million for projects aimed at turning their science base into valuable products, processes and services.

Science Enterprise Challenge

The Science Enterprise Challenge was launched in February 1999 as a £25 million competition to establish up to eight centres of enterprise in UK universities. Universities were invited to submit proposals for establishing world-class centres that would foster the commercialisation of research and new ideas, stimulate scientific entrepreneurialism, and incorporate the teaching of enterprise into the science and engineering curricula. Winners of the competition are due to be announced in autumn 1999; the centres are expected to make a significant contribution to the development of the enterprise culture in the UK.

Public Awareness

The Government seeks to raise the status of SET among the general public, by increasing awareness of the contribution of SET to the UK's economic wealth and quality of life. Raising awareness is important in encouraging young people to pursue careers in science and engineering. To this end, the Government supports activities such as the annual science festival of the British Association for the Advancement of Science (BAAS) and the National Week of Science, Engineering and Technology. The Committee on the Public Understanding of Science (COPUS), set up by the Royal Society, the BAAS and the Royal Institution (see p. 440), acts as a co-ordinator for those fostering public understanding and promotes best practice in the field.

Science festivals are also a growing feature of local co-operative efforts to further understanding of the contribution made by science to everyday life. Schools, museums, laboratories, higher education institutions and industry contribute to a variety of special events. The longest-established single-location science festival is the annual Edinburgh International Science Festival.

Activities such as these are important in assuring continued interest in SET among young people making educational and career choices. They also help to enhance the public's ability to relate to scientific issues in general and to make informed judgments about scientific developments. DTI has started to investigate public attitudes through a Public Consultation on Developments in Biosciences and will continue with a broader, fundamental review of public understanding in late 1999 and early 2000.

More than 150,000 people visited the Edinburgh Science Festival in April 1999. Presentations included an enormous bazooka made from a drainpipe which fired a potato at 250 kilometres per hour through a tennis racquet strung with titanium wire to produce the world's fastest French fries; and a bicycle anyone could ride across a tightrope—the 85 kg counterweight slung below the rope made it impossible to fall off. Other attractions popularising science and engineering included Formula One racing cars, and demonstrations of uses of artificial intelligence and the solar eclipse.

Women

The Promoting SET for Women Unit within OST at the DTI was established in 1994 in response to a report which found that women were under-represented in the SET sectors, especially at senior levels. The Unit has highlighted the benefits to business of providing a working environment sensitive to the needs of women scientists and engineers who combine a career and family responsibilities. It seeks to ensure that careers information for girls and women is widely available and to promote good employment practices, such as the provision of childcare facilities and job sharing. A website (www.set4women.gov.uk) has been launched promoting SET for girls and women and giving details of the Unit's activities.

Industrial and Intellectual Property

The Government supports innovation through the promotion of a national and international system for the establishment of intellectual property rights. These matters are the responsibility of the Patent Office, an executive agency of the DTI. The Office is responsible for the granting of patents, and design and trade mark registrations. The Patent Office encourages worldwide harmonisation of rules and procedures, and the modernisation and simplification of intellectual property law. International patenting arrangements include the European Patent Convention and the Patent Co-operation Treaty. For trade marks the European Community Trade Mark System and the Madrid Protocol provide means of extending rights beyond the borders of the United Kingdom.

R&D's important role in a knowledge-driven economy is further recognised in an intellectual property rights action plan set out in the Competitiveness White Paper (see p. 390), which focuses on making these rights more affordable and accessible. The Patent Office website offers detailed information about all aspects of intellectual property rights and is a major link between the Office and its customers.

GOVERNMENT DEPARTMENTS

Department of Trade and Industry

In 1999–2000 DTI's planned expenditure on SET is £340 million, including £62 million on technology transfer and access. This covers innovation and technology, aeronautics, space (see p. 433), and nuclear and non-nuclear energy. DTI is committed to helping UK businesses successfully exploit their ideas, and to promoting a business environment to encourage this. To this end, the Government has increased DTI's Innovation Budget over the next three years by more than 20%, rising to £230 million by 2002.

Innovation embraces the development, design and financing of new products, services and processes, exploitation of new markets, creation of new businesses and associated changes in management of people and organisational practices. Through its Innovation Unit, a mixed team of business secondees and government officials, DTI seeks to promote a culture of innovation in all sectors of the economy. In Northern Ireland the Industrial Research and Technology Unit has a similar role to that of the DTI, supporting industrial R&D, technology transfer and innovation.

Technology and Knowledge Transfer

DTI aims to increase collaboration and the flow of knowledge between the science, engineering and technology base and businesses; improve access to sources of technology and technological expertise; improve the capacity of business to use technology effectively; and increase the uptake of the latest technology and best practice techniques.

One example of a technology and knowledge transfer mechanism is TCS (formerly known as the Teaching Company Scheme); this is funded by six government departments and five Research Councils as well as by the participating companies. At any one time there are nearly 700 TCS programmes, each involving one or more graduates working in a company on a project that is central to its business needs. Each TCS programme lasts for at least two years and projects are jointly supervised by personnel from the knowledge base and the company. Small and medium-sized enterprises (SMEs) are involved in around 90% of TCS programmes. The Competitiveness White Paper announced a commitment by DTI to double its expenditure on TCS. The TCS scheme now has a common advisory board with LINK (see p. 428) to help increase the number of TCS programmes following on from LINK-funded research.

To help UK companies remain competitive in an increasingly global market, the DTI's International Technology Service (ITS) enables UK companies to become aware of and gain access to new technological developments and management practices not present in the UK. The ITS highlights developments and opportunities overseas through a monthly publication; and assists companies to access technology, set up licensing agreements and collaborative ventures, and to gain first-hand experience of new technology and leading management practices.

Smart—Small Firms Merit Award for Research and Technology

Smart helps individuals and SMEs research, develop or acquire the technologies needed to bring innovative products to the market. Help is available for feasibility studies into innovative technology and for development projects, to develop up to prototype stage new products and processes. During 1999, three new elements have been introduced to Smart: micro-projects to help very small firms and entrepreneurs develop low-cost prototypes and secure intellectual property rights; technology reviews using external expertise to improve use of technology; and technology studies with external expertise to identify technology opportunities. Business Links (see p. 390) have an important role in generating suitable feasibility studies and development projects, and in helping firms to submit applications. Separate Smart schemes are operated in Scotland, Wales and Northern Ireland.

Aeronautics

The DTI's Civil Aircraft Research and Technology Demonstration Programme (CARAD) supports research and technology demonstration in aeronautics. In 1999–2000, the CARAD budget is £20 million. The programme is an essential part of a national aeronautics research effort, with almost half of the supported research work being conducted in industry, and around a third at the Defence Evaluation and Research Agency (see p. 432). Universities and other research organisations receive about 10% of funding. The remainder represents the UK's contribution (shared with MoD) to the European Transonic Windtunnel in Cologne. CARAD and earlier programmes have supported a range of projects, including: aluminium and composite airframe materials;

more efficient and environmentally friendly engines; and advanced aircraft systems.

Measurement Standards

The DTI finances the maintenance and development of new measurement standards under the National Measurement System (NMS—see p. 392) and materials metrology programmes. Most of the work is carried out at the National Physical Laboratory (NPL), the Laboratory of the Government Chemist (LGC) and the National Engineering Laboratory (NEL). Spending about £38 million a year, the NMS provides the infrastructure to ensure that measurements can be made on a consistent basis throughout the UK. The accelerating pace of technological change and the greater awareness of the importance of quality and innovation have led to increasing demands for measurement standards and calibrations.

Ministry of Defence

The MoD has the largest government research and development budget—£2,619 million for 1999–2000, of which about £600 million is for medium- and long-term applied research relevant to military needs. Since the end of the Cold War, the Government has been committed to achieving a gradual reduction in real terms in spending on defence R&D.

The Defence Evaluation and Research Agency (DERA) is the largest single scientific employer in the UK. Its role is to supply scientific and technical services primarily to the MoD but also to other government departments. DERA has set up five dual-use (civil-military) technology centres in subjects ranging from structural materials to high-performance computing, to enhance the degree of collaboration between DERA, industry and the academic science base.

DERA subcontracts research to industry and universities, and works closely with industry to ensure that scientific and technological advances are integrated at an early stage into development and production. This technology transfer is not just confined to the defence industry but has also led to important 'spin-offs' into civil markets, in fields ranging from new materials and electronic devices to advanced aerodynamics. The latter in particular has helped to give the UK a leading role in civil aircraft design.

Department of the Environment, Transport and the Regions (DETR)

The DETR funds research in response to the requirements of all its major policy responsibilities: environmental protection; housing; construction; regeneration; the countryside; local and regional government; planning; roads and local transport; and railways, aviation and shipping. Total expenditure for 1999–2000 is £169 million (including spending by executive agencies and non-departmental public bodies—NDPBs). Major programmes of industrial support aim to benefit the construction sector and to help British industry's adoption of energy-efficient technologies. Through the Darwin Initiative (see p. 326), British expertise is being made available to assist countries that are rich in biodiversity but have insufficient financial or technical resources to implement the Biodiversity Convention.

Ministry of Agriculture, Fisheries and Food (MAFF)

MAFF co-ordinates its research programme with devolved administrations, the Research Councils and other public bodies in related areas. The programme supports the Ministry's wide-ranging responsibilities for protecting the public, especially in food safety and quality; protecting and enhancing the rural and marine environment; flooding and coastal defence; animal health and welfare; and improving the economic performance of the agriculture, fishing and food industries. The budget for research expenditure in 1999–2000 is £142 million, including support for the Royal Botanic Gardens, Kew (see p. 441).

Department of Health (DH)

The DH's R&D strategy aims to provide the evidence needed to inform policy and practice in public health, healthcare and social care. It delivers this objective through two complementary programmes: the Policy Research Programme (PRP), and the National Health Service (NHS) R&D Programme. The DH also oversees the research programmes of the health-related NDPBs. The Department expects to spend about £141 million in 1999–2000 (£70 million on the NHS R&D Programme, £31 million on the PRP, £34 million by the NDPBs and about £6 million from other DH R&D budgets). In addition, through the NHS R&D levy, the Department supports NHS providers involved in research, helping to underpin the research, including clinical trials, of other funding bodies such as the Medical Research Council and research charities, taking place in the NHS. This expenditure is expected to be £360 million in 1999–2000.

Tackling inequalities in health is one of the Government's top priorities (see p. 185). Research projects with a particular focus on children and young people are now under way funded through DH's health inequalities research programme.

Department for International Development (DFID)

DFID commissions and sponsors knowledge generation in natural resources, environment, health and population, engineering, education and social sciences. Financial provision for this in 1999–2000 is £119 million, covering research projects addressing particular development problems and projects to improve research, and research capacity relevant to particular countries. DFID also contributes to international centres and programmes generating knowledge on development issues. These contributions include support for the EU Science and Technology for Development programme, which sponsors research in renewable natural resources, agriculture, health and information technologies, and for the Consultative Group on International Agricultural Research (CGIAR).

Scottish Executive

The Scottish Executive has a budget of about £250 million for research-related spending.

Some £75 million of this encourages and funds agricultural and fisheries research, and related biological, food, environmental, economic and social science—most goes to the Scottish Agricultural and Biological Research Institutes, the Fisheries Research Services and the Scottish Agricultural College. In many areas—electrical and electronic engineering, medicine, agriculture and biological sciences, fisheries and marine science—Scotland's science base has an international reputation for research excellence. About £135 million goes to Scottish research institutions from the UK Research Councils.

The Scottish Executive Enterprise and Lifelong Learning Department encourages the development of science-based industry, for example, by promoting and administering government and EU industrial R&D schemes. The enterprise network in Scotland—Scottish Enterprise, Highlands and Islands Enterprise and LECs (see chapter 23)—addresses the need for innovation and technology transfer, both through grant support for innovation and through a wide range of initiatives.

Space Activities

The UK's civil space programme is brought together through the British National Space Centre (BNSC), a partnership of government departments and the Research Councils. BNSC's key aims are to develop practical and economic uses of space, to promote the competitiveness of British space companies in world markets and to maintain the UK's position in space science. These are realised primarily by collaboration with other European nations through the European Space Agency (ESA).

Through BNSC, the Government spends around £200 million a year on space activities. About two-thirds of this is channelled through ESA for collaborative programmes on Earth observation, telecommunications and space science, much of which returns to the UK through contracts awarded to British industry. The remaining one-third of the space budget is spent on international meteorological programmes carried out through the European Meteorological Satellite Organisation (EUMETSAT) and on the national programme, which is aimed at complementing R&D supported through ESA. Around half of the British space programme is concerned with satellite-based Earth observation (remote-sensing) for commercial and environmental applications.

The UK is also a major contributor to ESA's latest Earth observation satellite, ENVISAT, due to be launched in 2000. This will carry a new generation of radar and radiometer systems as well as other scientific environmental instruments, some of which have been either designed or constructed in Britain. The complete satellite was assembled by the UK-French space company, Matra Marconi Space. British companies are also leading the development of microsatellites.

A quarter of the UK's space budget is devoted to space science, in support of astronomy, planetary science and geophysics. Contributions have been made to missions ranging from the Hubble Space Telescope to the Ulysses solar space probe. The UK is contributing substantially to the SOHO mission to study the Sun; to the Infrared Space Observatory, which is investigating the birth and death of stars; and to the Cassini Huygens mission, a seven-year programme to send a probe to Saturn and its moon Titan, launched in 1997. It is also participating in XMM, ESA's 1999 X-ray spectroscopy mission, which will investigate X-ray emissions from black holes.

The UK is taking a leading role in the largest current international project in ground-based astronomy. The Gemini project involves building two 8 m telescopes at Mauna Kea (Hawaii) and Cerro Pachón (Chile): the former became operational in June 1999 and the latter is expected to be completed in 2000. The other partners are the United States, Canada, Argentina, Brazil and Chile. The UK has a 25% stake in the work, with major responsibility for the primary mirror support system and much of the control software.

The UK has many bilateral agreements for scientific research with other countries, such as Russia, Japan and the United States. For example, British scientists developed the high-resolution camera for Chandra (the NASA X-ray satellite).

Another major area of British space expertise is satellite communications and

In May 1999, the ESA Ministerial Council adopted the £400 million *Living Planet* environmental research programme, to help scientists understand and predict the Earth's environment and humankind's effects upon it. For example, it will measure soil moisture and other factors that are essential to the accurate modelling of climate systems. The BNSC will contribute £67 million to this programme. The first project to benefit from the programme will be the British CRYOSAT mission, to be launched in 2002, which will study the effects of global warming on the polar ice caps.

navigation. In Europe, the UK is both a leading producer and user of satellite communications technology (see p. 484). It is taking a leading role in preparations for future ESA satellite communications missions, including ARTEMIS, which will provide important communications links for the ENVISAT programme. Britain is also contributing to the development of a global navigation satellite system within Europe, which will augment the United States GPS system to provide increased accuracy and reliability for civil aviation global navigation.

INTERNATIONAL COLLABORATION

European Union

Since 1984 the EU has operated a series of R&D framework programmes, across a range of disciplines and sectors, to strengthen the scientific and technological basis of European industry and support the development of EU policies. About half of all projects have included British participation, which has been particularly strong in biomedicine, agriculture, transport, and social and economic research. The Fifth Framework Programme was agreed in December 1998 and will run for four years (1999–2002). It will support strategic and applied multidisciplinary research targeted at tackling pressing European problems, such as land transport, marine technology and the 'city of tomorrow'.

Other International Activities

Over 800 UK organisations have taken part in EUREKA, an industry-led scheme to encourage European co-operation in developing advanced products and processes with worldwide sales potential. There are 27 members of EUREKA, including the 15 EU countries and the European Commission. Some 700 projects are in progress, involving firms, universities and research organisations. Over 300 projects have finished, and among the successful ones is *E! 147 DAB*, where UK companies have helped pioneer the development of a digital radio system, resulting in new products on the market, as well as an international standard.

The COST programme (European Co-operation in the field of Science and Technical research) encourages co-operation in national research activities across Europe, with participants from industry, academia and research laboratories. Transport, telecommunications and materials have traditionally been the largest areas supported. New areas include physics, chemistry, neuroscience and the application of biotechnology to agriculture, including forestry. There are 32 member states and the UK takes part in 157 out of 176 current COST actions.

Another example of international collaboration is CERN, the European Laboratory for Particle Physics, based in Geneva, where the proposed Large Hadron Collider is due to be completed by 2005. Scientific programmes at CERN aim to test, verify and develop the 'standard model' of the origins and structure of the universe. There are 20 member states. The Particle Physics and Astronomy Research Council (PPARC— see p. 437) leads UK participation in CERN. Britain also contributes to the high-flux neutron source at the Institut Laue-Langevin and to the European Synchrotron Radiation Facility, both in Grenoble.

The PPARC is a partner in the European Incoherent Scatter Radar Facility within the Arctic Circle, which conducts research on the ionosphere. The Natural Environment Research Council (NERC) has a major involvement in international programmes of research into global climate change organised through the World Climate Research Programme and the International Geosphere-Biosphere Programme. It also supports the UK's subscription to the Ocean Drilling Program.

Through the Medical Research Council (MRC), the UK participates in the European Molecular Biology Laboratory (EMBL), at Heidelberg. The European Bioinformatics Institute, an outstation of the EMBL, at Hinxton near Cambridge, provides up-to-date information on molecular biology and genome sequencing for researchers throughout Europe. The MRC pays Britain's contribution to the Human Frontier Science Programme, which supports international collaborative research into brain function and biological function through molecular-level approaches. It also pays Britain's subscription to the International Agency for Cancer Research.

The UK is a member of the science and technology committees of such international organisations as the OECD and NATO, and of various specialised agencies of the United Nations, including UNESCO. The Research Councils, the Royal Society and the British Academy are members of the European Science Foundation, and a number of British scientists are involved in its initiatives.

The British Government also enters into bilateral agreements with other governments to encourage closer collaboration in science, engineering and technology. Staff in British Embassies, High Commissions and British Council offices (see p. 97) conduct government business on, and promote contacts in, science, engineering and technology between the UK and overseas countries; and help to inform a large number of organisations in the UK about developments and initiatives overseas. There are science and technology sections in British Missions in Paris, Tokyo, Washington, Beijing (Peking), Bonn, Moscow, Pretoria, Seoul, Rome and Ottawa, and a number of British Council offices have designated Science Officer posts.

The British Council promotes the creativity and innovation of cutting-edge UK science through events, partnership programmes, seminars, exhibitions and information provision. It balances one-to-one scientific links with projects aimed at raising awareness of scientific issues among overseas public audiences through popular communication. The Research Councils and the British Council maintain a joint office in Brussels to promote UK participation in European research programmes.

RESEARCH COUNCILS

Each Research Council is an autonomous body established under Royal Charter, with members of its governing council drawn from the universities, professions, industry and government. The Councils support research, study and training in universities and other higher education institutions, and carry out or support research, through their own institutes and at international research centres, often jointly with other public sector bodies and international organisations. They provide awards to about 15,000 postgraduate students in science, social sciences, engineering and technology. In addition to funding from the OST, the Councils receive income from research commissioned by government departments and the private sector.

Engineering and Physical Sciences Research Council (EPSRC)

The EPSRC, the Research Council with the largest budget (£404 million in 1999–2000), has responsibility to promote and support high-quality basic, strategic and applied research and related postgraduate training in engineering and the physical sciences. It also has responsibility to provide advice, disseminate knowledge and promote public understanding in these areas. Its remit is delivered through nine programme areas: physics, chemistry, mathematics, the generic technologies of information technology and materials, three engineering programmes (general engineering, engineering for manufacturing and engineering for infrastructure, the environment and healthcare) and the life sciences. This last programme was set up in 1999 to cover research and training on the borders of EPSRC's responsibilities and the life sciences.

EPSRC 'Partnerships for Public Understanding' awards were launched in 1998

The relentless miniaturisation of electronic products, from palmtop computers to portable phones, has resulted in the search for ways of storing sufficient charge to power these devices in ever smaller batteries. Scientists at the University of St Andrews, with support from EPSRC, have made an important advance in the science underpinning rechargeable batteries. By successfully synthesising a new type of lithium compound, the researchers have opened up the prospect of a new generation of more efficient, smaller batteries.

to improve public awareness of leading research and its possible impact on society. The awards encourage researchers to communicate the value of their work to the public. In the first year, 25 projects received awards totalling £570,000. Electronic help for the blind, a virtual tour of Whitehall and an animated character that explains human movement were three of the topics chosen. The awards bring together scientists with industry specialists, schools, artists, poets, community groups and the media in a wide range of activities.

Medical Research Council (MRC)

The MRC, with an overall budget of £325 million for 1999–2000, is the main source of public funds for biomedical and related sciences research. It supports research and training aimed at maintaining and improving human health. The MRC advances knowledge and technology to meet the needs of user communities, including the providers of healthcare and the biotechnology, food, healthcare, medical instrumentation, pharmaceutical and other biomedical-related industries. About half the MRC's expenditure is allocated to its own institutes and units, the rest going mainly on grant support of research in universities, including training awards. The Council has two large institutes—the National Institute for Medical Research at Mill Hill in London and the Laboratory of Molecular Biology in Cambridge; it also runs the Clinical Sciences Centre at the Royal

Postgraduate Medical School. It has more than 40 research units and a number of smaller scientific teams.

The first genetic 'blueprint' of an animal was completed by British scientists at the Sanger Centre on the Wellcome Trust Genome Campus in Hinxton and funded by the MRC, in collaboration with scientists in the United States. Results were published in December 1998 from a 15-year project to sequence the complete genome of the nematode worm *C. elegans*. Although containing fewer than 1,000 cells and only about 1 mm in length, *C. elegans* is built using remarkably similar principles to those of humans. The completed gene sequence gives scientists and health practitioners worldwide valuable information to aid the study of the human body in health as well as in illness and may, for example, lead to new treatments for disease.

A team of UK researchers made a major advance in understanding how the brain protein involved in bovine spongiform encephalopathy (BSE) in cattle and Creutzfeldt-Jakob Disease (CJD) in humans causes so much damage. Prion diseases, such as BSE and scrapie in animals, and CJD in humans, all involve conversion of a normal cell protein, known as the prion protein, into an abnormal or rogue form. The researchers captured this mysterious change in a test tube, using a genetic modification of normal soluble prion protein. The research provided, for the first time, an explanation of how these prions replicate. This has led to the development, by the same team of researchers, of new diagnostic tests for prion disease in humans and animals.

Natural Environment Research Council (NERC)

The NERC is principally concerned with the themes of sustainable development, environmental protection (see p. 340), and the quality of life. In 1999–2000 it will spend most of its budget of £220 million in the following areas: biodiversity; environmental risks and hazards; global change; natural resource management; and pollution and waste.

The Council supports research in its own and other research establishments as well as research and training in universities. It also provides a range of facilities for use by the wider environmental science community, including a marine research fleet. NERC establishments include the British Geological Survey, the British Antarctic Survey, the Centre for Coastal and Marine Sciences and the Centre for Ecology and Hydrology, together with a number of university-based units. The Southampton Oceanography Centre, a partnership with Southampton University, undertakes research, training and support activities in oceanography, geology and aspects of marine technology and engineering. The NERC's Research Vessel Services are located at the Centre.

Biotechnology and Biological Sciences Research Council (BBSRC)

The BBSRC has a budget of £195 million for 1999–2000. It supports basic and strategic research and research training related to the understanding and exploitation of biological systems, which underpin the agriculture, bioprocessing, chemical, food, healthcare, pharmaceutical and other biotechnology-related industries. The scientific themes are biomolecular sciences; genes and developmental biology; biochemistry and cell biology; plant and microbial sciences; animal sciences; agri-food; and engineering and biological systems. As well as funding research in universities and other research centres throughout the UK, the BBSRC sponsors eight research institutes.

Particle Physics and Astronomy Research Council (PPARC)

The main task of the PPARC, which has a budget of £190 million for 1999–2000, is to sustain and develop basic research into

Fundamental research into the nature of genes, how they work and how they can be transferred between organisms, has underpinned the development of the technology of genetic modification (GM). As well as driving new applications of GM, the research is providing basic information about the behaviour of genes, and of genetically modified organisms (GMOs). This information addresses many concerns about the safety of GMOs and their impact on the environment. In May 1999 the Government announced a new framework for overseeing developments in biotechnology, including the establishment of new strategic and long-term commissions to advise on human genetics and agricultural and environmental issues.

competitiveness, quality of life, and the effectiveness of public services and policy. All research funded by the ESRC is conducted in higher education institutions or independent research establishments. The Council has nine priority themes: economic performance and development; environment and sustainability; globalisation, regions and emerging markets; governance, regulation and accountability; technology and people; innovation; knowledge, communication and learning; lifespan, lifestyles and health; and social inclusion and exclusion.

The ESRC is planning a £2.2 million longitudinal study of people born in the year 2000—the Millennium Cohort—which will collect lifetime data on all aspects of people's lives, providing a unique insight into the effects of change over the next half century and beyond. It will also greatly enhance the capacity of current longitudinal studies to chart social change.

fundamental physical processes. Its three main areas of research are:

- particle physics—theoretical and experimental research into elementary particles and the fundamental forces of nature;

- astronomy (including cosmology and astrophysics)—the origin, structure and evolution of the Universe, stars and galaxies; and

- planetary science (including solar and terrestrial physics)—the origin and evolution of the solar system and the influence of the Sun on planetary bodies, particularly Earth.

The PPARC provides research and training grants to universities, and access to major facilities including observatories on La Palma (Canary Islands) and Hawaii. The Council is responsible for the UK's contributions to international collaborations, including ESA and CERN (see pp. 433 and 435).

The ESRC has recently launched a Centre for Longitudinal Studies to ensure effective implementation, co-ordination and analysis of the Millennium Cohort study and other longitudinal data. This Centre will complement three other Centres set up for the Study of Knowledge, Skills and Organisational Performance; for the Analysis of Social Exclusion; and for the Study of Globalisation and Regionalisation.

A research agenda has been drawn up for institutional, social and political change in the regions, which will include developments in England, the UK as a whole and in the EU. A series of short-term studies of immediate institutional changes in Scotland and Wales are planned along with a major research programme on Devolution and Constitutional Change in the UK, for which up to £5 million will be provided.

Economic and Social Research Council (ESRC)

The ESRC, with an R&D provision of about £70 million for 1999–2000, supports research and training to enhance the UK's economic

Council for the Central Laboratory of the Research Councils (CCLRC)

The CCLRC promotes scientific and engineering research by supplying facilities and technical expertise primarily to meet the needs of the other Research Councils. Its R&D budget for 1999–2000 is £112 million, of which £83 million comes through agreements with other Research Councils and another £24 million comes from contracts and agreements with the EU, overseas countries, and other industries and organisations. It covers a broad range of science and technology, including materials, structural and biomolecular science using accelerators, synchrotrons and lasers, satellite instrumentation and data processing, remote-sensing, electronics, sensor technology, computing, mobile communications, micro-engineering, microsystems and particle physics.

The CCLRC is responsible for three research establishments: the Rutherford Appleton Laboratory in Oxfordshire; the Daresbury Laboratory in Cheshire; and the Chilbolton Observatory in Hampshire. These centres provide facilities too large or complex to be housed by individual academic institutions. Among the facilities are ISIS (the world's leading source of pulsed neutrons and muons), some of the world's brightest lasers and the United Kingdom Synchrotron Light Source.

RESEARCH IN HIGHER EDUCATION INSTITUTIONS

Universities carry out most of the UK's long-term strategic and basic research in science and technology. The Higher Education Funding Councils in England, Scotland and Wales (see p. 135) provide the main general funds to support research in universities and other higher education institutions in Great Britain. These funds pay for the salaries of permanent academic staff, who usually teach as well as undertake research, and contribute to the infrastructure for research. The quality of research performance is a key element in the allocation of funding. In Northern Ireland institutions are funded by the Department of Education for Northern Ireland.

Basic and strategic research in higher education institutions are also financed by the Research Councils. Institutions undertaking research with the support of Research Council grants have the rights over the

commercial exploitation of their research, subject to the prior agreement of the sponsoring Research Council. They may make use of technology transfer experts and other specialists to help exploit and license the results of their research. The other main channels of support are industry, charities, government departments and the EU. The high quality of research in higher education institutions, and their marketing skills, have enabled them to attract more funding from a larger range of external sources, especially in contract income from industry and charities.

Science Parks

The UK has a range of Science Parks—property-based initiatives having formal or operational links to a higher education institution or other major research centre. The UK Science Park Association numbers 55 such initiatives, which between them host over 1,400 firms employing about 27,000 people in total. Many of these firms are spin-offs from the associated institution or are start-up enterprises in fields of high-technology such as software, biotechnology, analytical services or consultancy.

OTHER ORGANISATIONS

Research and Technology Organisations (RTOs)

RTOs are independent organisations carrying out commercially relevant research and other services on behalf of industry, often relating to a specific industrial sector. Others are contract research organisations undertaking specific projects for any client. The Association of Independent Research and Technology Organisations has some 45 members which together employ about 9,000 people.

Charitable Organisations

Medical research charities are a major source of funds for biomedical research in the UK. Their combined contribution in 1998–99 was about £440 million. The three largest were from the Wellcome Trust, the Imperial Cancer Research Fund and the Cancer Research Campaign.

Professional and Learned Institutions

There are numerous technical institutions, professional associations and learned societies in the UK, many of which promote their own disciplines or the education and professional well-being of their members. The Council of Science and Technology Institutes has ten member institutes representing biology, biochemistry, chemistry, environment, food science and technology, geology, hospital physics and physics.

The Engineering Council promotes and regulates the engineering profession. It represents 120 industry affiliates, which include large private sector companies and government departments, and 36 professional engineering institutions. In partnership with the institutions, the Council accredits higher education courses and advises the Government on academic, industrial and professional issues. It also runs a number of promotional activities. Some 286,000 individuals are on the Council's Register, through their institution, as either Chartered or Incorporated Engineers or as Engineering Technicians.

Royal Society

The Royal Society, founded in 1660, is the UK's academy of science and has about 1,200 Fellows and 100 Foreign Members. Many of its Fellows serve on governmental advisory councils and committees concerned with research. The Society has a dual role, as the national academy of science and as the provider of a range of services, including research fellowships and grants, for the scientific community. It offers independent advice to government on science matters, acts as a forum for discussion of scientific issues, and fosters public awareness of science and science education. Its government grant for 1999–2000 is £23.8 million.

Royal Academy of Engineering

The national academy of engineering in Britain is the Royal Academy of Engineering, which has 1,125 Fellows and 77 Foreign Members. It promotes excellence in engineering for the benefit of society, and advises government, Parliament and other official organisations. The Academy's programmes are aimed at attracting first-class students into engineering, raising awareness of the importance of engineering design among undergraduates, developing links between industry and higher education, and increasing industrial investment in engineering research in higher education institutions. It has a government grant of £3.7 million in 1999–2000.

Other Societies

In Scotland the Royal Society of Edinburgh, established in 1783, promotes science by offering postdoctoral research fellowships and studentships, awarding prizes and grants, organising meetings and symposia, and publishing journals. It has been engaged with Scottish Enterprise in developing a strategy to increase the extent of commercial use of the products of the Scottish research base (see p. 433), and has been active in the Foresight process. It also acts as a source of independent scientific advice to the Government and others.

Three other major institutions publicise scientific developments by means of lectures and publications for specialists and schoolchildren. Of these, the British Association for the Advancement of Science, founded in 1831, is mainly concerned with science, while the Royal Society of Arts, dating from 1754, deals with the arts and commerce as well as science. The Royal Institution, founded in 1799, also performs these functions and runs its own research laboratories.

Zoological Gardens

The Zoological Society of London (ZSL), an independent conservation, science and

The Royal Institution, which is celebrating its bicentenary in 1999, began as an 'Institution For diffusing the Knowledge, and facilitating the general Introduction, of Useful Mechanical Inventions and Improvements; and for teaching, by Courses of Philosophical Lectures and Experiments, the application of Science to the common Purposes of Life'. It acquired its current premises (at Albemarle Street in London) in 1799 and a Royal Charter, granted by King George III, early in 1800. In the Institution's laboratory, Humphrey Davy, Michael Faraday and John Tyndall carried out their fundamental research. Fifteen Nobel Laureates, including William and Lawrence Bragg, have worked in the Institution's Davy Faraday Research Laboratory, which has been the base for an extraordinary series of scientific discoveries. Today, nearly 40 scientists are concentrating on aspects of solid state chemistry.

In 1826 Faraday started two programmes to bring the excitement of science to a wider public: the *Christmas Lectures* and the *Friday Evening Discourses*. Both programmes continue today, in the famous Albemarle Street lecture theatre. The *Christmas Lectures* now reach a worldwide audience, being broadcast in Britain, other parts of Europe, Japan and the United States.

education charity founded in 1826, runs London Zoo, which occupies about 15 hectares (36 acres) of Regent's Park (London). It also owns and runs Whipsnade Wild Animal Park (243 hectares/600 acres) in Bedfordshire. ZSL is responsible for the Institute of Zoology, which carries out research in support of conservation. The Institute's work covers topics such as ecology, reproductive biology and conservation genetics. ZSL also operates in overseas conservation projects, and is concerned with practical field conservation, primarily in East and Southern Africa, the Middle East and parts of Asia. Other well-known zoos in the UK include those in Edinburgh, Bristol, Chester, Dudley and Marwell (near Winchester).

Botanic Gardens

The Royal Botanic Gardens, Kew, founded in 1759, covers 121 hectares (300 acres) at Kew in south-west London and a 187-hectare (462-acre) estate at Wakehurst Place (Ardingly, in West Sussex). They contain one of the largest collections of living and dried plants in the world. Research is conducted into all aspects of plant life, including physiology, biochemistry, genetics, economic botany and the conservation of habitats and species. During 1998–2000 Kew is building the Millennium Seed Bank, containing the world's most comprehensive collection of seeds of flowering plants, at Wakehurst Place (see p. 326). The Millennium Commission is donating up to £30 million towards the estimated £80 million cost of the project and the Wellcome Trust is granting £9 million. Staff are also active in programmes to reintroduce endangered plant species to the wild. Kew participates in joint research programmes in some 50 countries.

A major new classification for flowering plants has been developed by an international team led by scientists at the Royal Botanic Gardens, Kew, where most of the work was conducted. The new classification is based on DNA sequence analysis of the plants and will supersede 200 years of plant taxonomy built on the comprehensive work of Linnaeus. It has caused a complete rethink of the relationships between plants. It shows, for example, that the closest relative of the lotus, the sacred flower of Buddhism, is not the water lily it so closely resembles but the plane tree seen in many London squares and streets.

The Royal Botanic Garden in Edinburgh was established in 1670, and is the national botanic garden of Scotland. Together with its three associated specialist gardens, which were acquired to provide a range of different climatic and soil conditions, it has become an internationally recognised centre for taxonomy (classification of species); for the conservation and study of living and preserved plants and fungi; and as a provider of horticultural education.

A national botanic garden and research centre for Wales is to be developed on a 230-hectare (570-acre) site on the Middleton Hall estate at Llandeilo, near Swansea (see p. xii).

Scientific Museums

The Natural History Museum is one of Britain's most popular visitor attractions, with exhibitions devoted to the Earth and the life sciences. It is founded on collections of 68 million specimens from the natural world, has 350 scientists working in 60 countries, and has 500,000 historically important original works of art. It also offers an advisory service to institutions all over the world. The Science Museum promotes the public understanding of the history of science, technology, industry and medicine. An ambitious construction scheme, the new Wellcome Wing, will add 10,000 sq metres of display space to the Museum from June 2000. This new wing will contain galleries on biomedical science and information technology and a 450-seat 3D IMAX (large format screen) theatre. These two museums are in South Kensington, London. Other important collections include those at the Museum of Science & Industry in Manchester, the Museum of the History of Science in Oxford, and the Royal Scottish Museum, Edinburgh.

Further Reading

Science, Engineering and Technology Statistics 1999. DTI/OST. Cm 4409. The Stationery Office, 1999.

Blueprint for the Next Round of Foresight. DTI/OST. 1998.

The Forward Look 1999. DTI/OST. Cm 4363. The Stationery Office, 1999.

Our Competitive Future: Building the Knowledge Driven Economy (the Competitiveness White Paper). DTI. Cm 4176. The Stationery Office, 1998.

The Public Consultation on Developments in the Biosciences (available from OST).

Website

Office of Science and Technology: www.dti.gov.uk/ost

27 Agriculture, Fishing & Forestry

The downturn in British agriculture continued in 1998. The value of gross output fell by 9% (£1.68 billion) and of gross value added by 11%. Total income from farming fell for the third year in succession—by 29% (32% in real terms). The UK has won its 40-month battle to lift the worldwide ban on its beef exports owing to the BSE crisis, which has cost more than £5 billion in eradication measures and lost exports. During 1998–99 the Government announced two aid packages, worth a total of £270 million, to help the livestock sector. It has also stressed its commitment to sustainable and environmentally sensitive agriculture.

Agriculture

The slump in world farm prices in 1998, contrasting with the much higher returns of the early and mid-1990s, reflects the collapse of demand for imported foods in south-east Asia and Russia following periods of economic crisis, and the consequent oversupply in commodity markets. The European Union (EU), after discussing the problem of how to bring its farm support system closer to market prices, has agreed cuts of up to 15% in guaranteed returns for milk and cereals, and 20% for beef. It has also demanded a freeze on traditional Common Agricultural Policy (CAP) spending at an annual level of 40.5 billion euros (£27 billion), thus cutting the overall cost of the farm package from 297.7 billion euros (£196 billion) to 296.6 billion euros (£195 billion) during 2000–06.

In 1998 the British farming industry employed 2.3% of the total workforce (615,000 people). Agriculture's contribution to GDP fell from £8.22 billion in 1997 to £7.3 billion in 1998, 1% of the total. Food, feed and beverages accounted for 9% of Britain's imports by value and for 5.6% of exports. Self-sufficiency in food continued to decline in 1998 as the value of home production fell in relation to the value of imports and exports: during 1997–98 self-sufficiency in all food fell from 69.8% to 68.1% and in indigenous-type food from 83.1% to 82.3%.[1]

[1] These figures cannot be compared with those for previous years as improvements in the method of calculating self-sufficiency were introduced in 1998 to take account of the higher proportion of processed foods, as opposed to unprocessed commodities imported in recent years.

Table 27.1: Agriculture in the EU

Country	Area farmed ('000 hectares)	Number of farms ('000 holdings)	UAA[a] per holding (hectares)	Total CAP receipts (£ billion)
	1997	1996	1996	1997
United Kingdom	15,358	235	70.1	3.17
Austria	3,412	222	15.4	0.62
Belgium	1,375	71	19.1	0.70
Denmark	2,721	69	39.6	0.89
Finland	2,150	101	21.7	0.41
France	30,168	735	38.5	6.59
Germany	17,335	567	30.3	4.16
Greece	3,465	802	4.5	1.97
Irish Republic	4,325	153	28.2	1.47
Italy	14,685	2,482	5.9	3.69
Luxembourg	127	3	39.9	0.02
Netherlands	1,848	113	17.7	1.27
Portugal	3,967	451	8.7	0.47
Spain	29,649	1,278	19.7	3.31
Sweden	3,177	89	34.4	0.54
EU	**134,261**	**7,370**	**17.4**	**29.28**

Sources: Eurostat; European Commission Directorate-General of Agriculture; MAFF
[a] Average utilised agricultural area.
Note: There are 100 hectares to a square kilometre; 1 hectare = 2.471 acres.

In 1851 farming was still Britain's largest industry and employed 1.8 million people. There were few constraints on trade, however, and by 1900 the UK had become the world's foremost food importer, with the land under cultivation reduced by over 30% since 1871. On 1 January 1901 *The Times* newspaper, quoting a prominent contemporary figure on an agricultural tour of England, printed the following appraisal: 'The year 1900 would drive the farmer to utter despair did he not look forward with faith and hope to better crops and remunerative prices in the years of the 20th century.' It added that the great danger to English farms was the lack of labour, with many youngsters leaving the country in search of livelihoods in the towns. However disastrous to British farmers, though, increased quantities of cheap and imported food were considered of inestimable benefit to England's crowded population—some 30 million.

Land Use

In 1998, agricultural land made up 76% of the UK's total land area, with 11.66 million hectares (28.8 million acres) under crops and grass. A further 5.8 million hectares (14.4 million acres) were used for rough grazing, most of it in hilly areas. Soils vary from the thin poor ones of highland Britain to the rich fertile soils of low-lying areas, such as the fenlands of eastern England. The climate is generally temperate, though rainfall distribution over Britain is uneven (see p. 3).

Farming

In 1998 there were some 237,900 farm holdings in the UK (excluding minor holdings too small to be surveyed on a regular basis). These main holdings have in 1999 an average area of 71 hectares (175 acres), again excluding minor holdings. About 45% of them are smaller than eight European size units

Agricultural Land Use, 1998

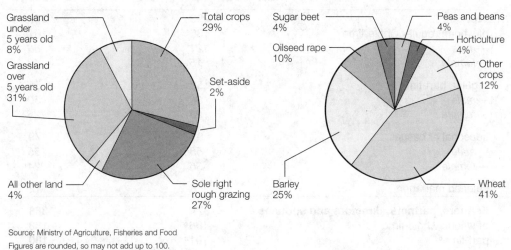

TOTAL AREA ON AGRICULTURAL HOLDINGS

CROPS

Source: Ministry of Agriculture, Fisheries and Food
Figures are rounded, so may not add up to 100.

(ESUs).[2] About two-thirds of all agricultural land is owner-occupied; the rest is tenanted or rented.

Since 1973 the productivity of UK agriculture has increased by over 40%, largely as a result of declining labour input. Total income from farming (representing income to those with an entrepreneurial interest in the agricultural industry—see Table 27.2) was estimated at £2.2 billion in 1998, 29% lower (at current prices) than in 1997, or 32% less in real terms. In 1998 the net value added of UK agriculture (which measures the income generated from production to all those employed in the industry) was 14% lower than in 1997—the prices for most agricultural commodities having fallen sharply in 1998. For example, between September 1996 and September 1998 the prices producers received fell by 17% for cattle, by 37% for sheep, by 33% for eggs, and by 57% for pigmeat. The main reasons were oversupply of commodity

markets, economic difficulties in Russia and Asia, and the strength of sterling. A similar indicator, calculated on a slightly different basis, showed a fall of 16% in the UK, but of 4% in the EU as a whole.

PRODUCTION

Home production of the principal foods is shown in Table 27.3 as a percentage by weight of total supplies. Total new supply is home production plus imports less exports.

Livestock

About half of full-time farms are devoted mainly to dairy farming or to beef cattle and sheep. Most of the animals are reared in the hill and moorland areas of Scotland, Wales, Northern Ireland and northern and south-western England. Among world-famous British livestock are the Hereford and Aberdeen Angus beef breeds, the Jersey, Guernsey and Ayrshire dairy breeds, Large White pigs and a number of sheep breeds. Livestock totals are given in Table 27.4.

[2] ESUs measure the financial potential of the holding in terms of the margins which might be expected from stock and crops: 8 ESU is judged the minimum for full-time holdings.

Table 27.2: Agricultural Employment[a]

	'000 persons 1987–89 average	'000 persons 1998
Workers	**293**	**247**
of whom: regular whole-time	136	101
—*male*	*121*	*88*
—*female*	*15*	*13*
regular, part-time[b]	58	54
—*male*	*30*	*30*
—*female*	*28*	*25*
seasonal or casual	91	79
—*male*	*55*	*55*
—*female*	*36*	*24*
salaried managers	8	12
Farmers, partners, directors and spouses	**377**	**368**
of whom: whole-time	196[c]	188
part-time[b]	101[c]	180
Total labour force (including farmers and their spouses)[d]	**670**	**615**

Source: *Agriculture in the United Kingdom 1998*
[a] In 1998 changes to the labour questions on the June Agricultural and Horticultural Census in England, Wales and Scotland may have led to the recording of additional labour not previously included in returns. There has also been redistribution of labour between the various categories.
[b] Part-time is defined as less than 39 hours a week.
[c] Excludes spouses (79,000 in 1987–89).
[d] Excludes schoolchildren and most trainees
Note: Differences between totals and the sums of their component parts are due to rounding.

Table 27.3: British Production as a Percentage of Total New Supplies

Food product	1987–89 average	1998 provisional
Beef and veal	93	83
Sheepmeat	89	100
Poultrymeat	98	93
Pork	101	113
Eggs	98	96
Milk for human consumption (as liquid)	100	102
Cheese	67	65
Butter	91	77
Sugar (as refined)	57	64
Wheat	116	123
Barley	147	126
Oats	100	107
Oilseed rape	106	98
Potatoes	89	88

Source: MAFF

Table 27.4: Livestock and Livestock Products

	1987–89 average	1996	1997	1998 provisional
Cattle and calves ('000 head)	12,134	12,040	11,633	11,519
Sheep and lambs ('000 head)	41,429	42,086	42,823	44,471
Pigs ('000 head)	7,911	7,590	8,072	8,146
Poultry ('000 head)[a]	118,282	n.a.	n.a.	152,886
Milk (million litres)	14,528	13,975	14,138	13,915
Hen eggs (million dozen)[b]	837	775	794	793
Beef and veal ('000 tonnes)	1,013	709	696	700
Mutton and lamb ('000 tonnes)	349	383	351	386
Pork ('000 tonnes)	782	801	888	930
Bacon and ham ('000 tonnes)	205	241	239	236
Poultrymeat ('000 tonnes)	1,102	1,462	1,508	1,534

Source: MAFF

[a] Includes ducks, geese and turkeys. In England and Wales a new approach to collecting poultry information has been used. The 1998 figures are not therefore directly comparable with previous years.
[b] For human consumption only; does not include eggs for hatching.
n.a.= not available.

Cattle and Sheep

Cattle and sheep constitute about 42% of the value of Britain's gross agricultural output. Dairy production is the largest part of the sector, followed by cattle and calves, and then sheep and lambs. Most dairy cattle in the UK are bred by artificial insemination. In 1998 the average size of dairy herds was 66 (excluding minor holdings), while the average yield of milk for each dairy cow was 5,793 litres (1,274 gallons).

More than half of home-fed beef production originates from the national dairy herd, in which the Holstein Friesian breed predominates. The remainder derives from suckler herds producing high-quality beef calves, mostly in the hills and uplands. The traditional British beef breeds, (see p. 445) and, increasingly, imported breeds, such as Charolais, Limousin, Simmental and Belgian Blue, are used for beef production. The size of the beef-breeding herd expanded by 36% during 1988–98, while the dairy herd decreased by 17%.

The value of beef and veal production fell by 14% in 1998 to £1,943 million, because of lower cattle prices and a fall in compensation payments after the BSE crisis (Bovine Spongiform Encephalopathy—see p. 451). Domestic use of beef and veal went up by 1%.

The UK has more than 60 native sheep breeds and many cross-bred varieties. The size of the British breeding flock rose by nearly 3% in 1998, and production of sheepmeat by nearly 9%, although the value of production fell by 5% to £1,142 million. A wet summer, which delayed the fattening of lambs for slaughter, and the collapse of the Russian market for skins contributed to the sharp fall in lamb prices, with lowland lamb producers losing between £10 and £15 a lamb. Hill farmers in Scotland and Wales have been particularly badly affected.

Pigs

Pig production is especially important in East Anglia, Yorkshire and north-east Scotland. Over 20% of holdings with breeding sows account for 84% of the national breeding herd, which comprises some 705,000 sows. The value of pigmeat production in 1998 was £873 million, 27% down on 1997, because increases in the breeding herd led to a larger number to sell in 1998, when prices collapsed owing to cheap imports. In late September 1998 average producer prices were the lowest for 20 years, with pig rearers estimated to be losing at least £20 for each pig sold.

Poultry

The total UK bird population in 1998 consisted of 98 million chickens and other table fowls; 29.5 million birds in the laying flock; 10 million fowls for breeding; and 15 million turkeys, ducks and geese.

Poultry production in 1998 was 1.53 million tonnes, a 2% increase on 1997, but prices continued to decrease, partly because of lower feed prices, but also because of oversupply and low-price imports. The value of hen eggs for human consumption was 8% down.

Farm Animal Welfare

The UK has taken the lead in pressing for improved welfare standards throughout the EU. The Welfare of Animals (Staging Points) Order 1998 lays down standards for the construction and operation of staging points from 1 January 1999. New EU standards for vehicles carrying animals for over 8 hours were implemented in the Welfare of Animals (Transport) (Amendment) Order 1999, which came into effect on 1 July 1999.

The Welfare of Animals (Transport) Order 1997 is being reviewed. On 31 May 1999 new arrangements for pre-export inspections of food animals destined for other EU member states were introduced, to ensure that all animals are healthy and fit to travel. Certifying

Table 27.5: Main Crops

	1987–89 average	1996	1997	1998 provisional
Wheat				
Area ('000 hectares)	1,988	1,975	2,035	2,045
Production ('000 tonnes)	12,575	16,103	15,018	15,423
Yield (tonnes per hectare)	6.33	8.15	7.38	7.54
Barley				
Area	1,788	1,269	1,359	1,255
Production	8,693	7,789	7,828	6,496
Yield	4.86	6.14	5.76	5.18
Oats				
Area	113	96	100	98
Production	510	590	577	587
Yield	4.53	6.14	5.78	5.98
Potatoes				
Area	178	178	166	164
Production	6,660	7,225	7,125	6,415
Yield	37.40	40.60	42.90	39.10
Oilseed rape				
Area	352	415	473	531
Production	1,101	1,412	1,527	1,575
Yield	3.13	3.41	3.23	2.97
Sugar beet				
Area	200	199	196	189
Production	8,086	10,420	11,084	9,802
Yield	40.47	52.36	56.55	51.94

Sources: *Agriculture in the United Kingdom 1998* and *Agricultural Census, June 1998*

veterinarians are provided with clearer and more transparent instructions, including minimum inspection times. The State Veterinary Service assessed compliance with current legislation at livestock markets and the Government began a review of the Welfare of Animals (Markets) Order 1990. In June 1999 the EU voted to ban the use of the barren battery cage from 2012, to introduce improved standards in the interim and, for the first time, to set minimum welfare standards for non-cage systems.

Crops

The farms devoted primarily to *arable crops* are found mainly in eastern and central-southern England and eastern Scotland. The main crops are shown in Table 27.5. In the UK in 1998, the area planted to cereals totalled 3.42 million hectares (8.45 million acres), a decrease of 3% on 1997, despite the set-aside rate remaining at 5% (see below). This was owing to a shift towards more economically advantageous oilseeds. Production was down by 740,000 tonnes (3%). Over 1998 the value of production was 14% lower than in 1997 and the price of cereals fell by a further £10 to £15 a tonne on already low 1997 prices. Despite small increases in area, yield and output, even the value of wheat production, at £1,647 million, was 11% lower than in 1997.

Large-scale *potato and vegetable cultivation* takes place on the fertile soils throughout the UK, often with irrigation. Principal areas are the peat and silt fens of Cambridgeshire, Lincolnshire and Norfolk; the sandy loams of Norfolk, Suffolk, West Midlands, Nottinghamshire, South Yorkshire and Lincolnshire; the peat soils of south Lancashire; and the alluvial silts by the river Humber. Early potatoes are produced in Shropshire, Pembrokeshire (Wales), Cornwall, Devon, Essex, Suffolk, Kent, Cheshire and south-west Scotland. Production of high-grade seed potatoes is confined mainly to Scotland, Northern Ireland, the northern uplands and the Welsh borders. Although prolonged rainy weather in 1998 caused delays for both planting and lifting, with yields down by 8%, the total

value of potato production increased by 67% (£257 million) on 1997.

Sugar from *home-grown sugar beet* provides just over half of home needs, most of the remainder being refined from raw cane sugar imported under the sugar protocol to the Lomé Convention (see pp. 420–1).

Arable Area Payments Scheme (AAPS)

The AAPS, of which set-aside is a part and which originally aimed to cut cereals support prices, helps compensate farmers for these cuts. They are paid for the land under arable production, not the quantity of crop. To qualify for subsidy, all but the smallest farmers must set aside a proportion of their land (10% for the 1999 harvest) to reduce cereals production. Where land is eligible, the subsidy is paid on cereals, oilseeds, proteins (including peas for harvesting dry) and linseed.

Set-aside payments compensate farmers for leaving part of their land fallow, while keeping it in good agricultural condition. They are encouraged to maximise the environmental benefit of the scheme and are allowed to count land entered into various environmental schemes (see p. 455) against their set-aside obligation. In addition to the compulsory set-aside rate (10% in 1999) growers may set aside, on a voluntary basis, more than 50% of the area claimed under the AAPS provided all of the set-aside land is used for the production of multiannual crops, such as short-rotation coppice, for biomass production. Farmers may also get grants of up to 50% of the costs associated with the establishment of such crops on set-aside land.

In 1998, 61,263 AAPS claims for 4.6 million hectares (11.3 million acres) were received in the UK; nearly £1,180 million was paid out.

Horticulture

In 1998 the land used for horticulture (excluding hops, potatoes, and peas for harvesting dry) was 176,797 hectares (436,883 acres), compared with 184,000 hectares in 1997. Vegetables grown in the open accounted for 69.5% of this, orchards for 16%, soft fruit for 5.6%, ornamentals (including hardy nursery stock, bulbs and flowers grown in the open) for 8% and glasshouse crops for 1%. More than one vegetable crop may be taken from the same area of land in a year, so that the estimated area actually cropped for horticulture in 1998 was 213,500 hectares (527,580 acres).

The output value of horticultural products (including seeds and peas harvested dry) was £1,752 million. Some £3,859 million of fruit and vegetables was imported.

Under the reformed EU fruit and vegetables regime, EU grants (up to 50% of eligible expenditure) are payable to producer organisations (POs) which aim to improve cultivation techniques, with emphasis on environmentally sound practices, quality improvements and marketing. Of 92 POs recognised in the UK, 76 have programmes running in 1999, with a total value of about £31 million.

Agri-Industrial Materials

The Agri-Materials Branch (formerly Alternative Crops Unit) of the Ministry of Agriculture, Fisheries and Food (MAFF) seeks to encourage the marketing of renewable energy raw materials from crops. It funds about £1.1 million of R&D each year. It has promoted short-rotation coppice as an energy crop; miscanthus as a crop for energy and industry; hemp and flax for fibre; and herbs for oil.

Genetically Modified Crops

The first trials of genetically modified (GM) crops in the UK were completed in the late 1980s. These and subsequent trials have been small-scale releases into the environment. Before general cultivation is allowed to take place, a managed programme of farm-scale trials of three herbicide-tolerant crops began in 1999. This programme will continue for four years so that their effect on wildlife can be assessed. The sites are to be closely and independently monitored; the contracts, worth £3.3 million, have been awarded to

research organisations. In October 1998 the Government came to an understanding with the plant-breeding industry that there would be no commercial planting of insect-resistant GM crops for three years and none of herbicide-tolerant GM crops for at least one year in the first instance, and then only if it were satisfied that they would be unlikely to pose a risk either to human health or to the environment. It has also stated that should the trials show a threat to the environment, commercial planting would not be allowed.

An EU-wide regulatory framework, designed to protect human health and the environment, covers all stages of work with GM organisms (GMOs). All GMOs (which include GM crops) are subject to safety evaluation before a consent for release into the environment is agreed. In the UK, the Advisory Committee on Releases into the Environment (ACRE) considers applications to release and market GMOs. The UK regulations implement the EC Directive which covers the deliberate release of GMOs into the environment for research and marketing purposes. Consent applications for the sale of GMOs throughout Europe are considered by all EU member states before a consent is issued.

Whether GM crops pose a danger to human health and the environment has been the subject of wide debate in the UK. ACRE has published details of breaches of consents, most of which concern failures by companies to stick to procedures designed to prevent GM crops straying outside their plots or hybridising with neighbouring plants. Some companies have been forced to end trials.

Before GM foods are approved for sale in the EU they must be assessed for safety in accordance with the EC Novel Foods Regulation of 1997, which established an EU-wide pre-market approval system for all novel foods—those which have not been used for human consumption in the EU before, including those containing or produced from GMOs. The regulation prescribes specific labelling when an item is judged not to be equivalent to an existing food. Food will also need labelling if there are any health or ethical concerns or if it contains a GMO. In the UK, assessment of novel foods is carried out by the independent Advisory Committee on Novel Foods and Processes. In 1998 the EU agreed on rules for labelling Monsanto's GM soya and Ciba Geigy's GM maize, approved before the Novel Foods Regulation came into force. An EC Regulation of September 1998 requires all foods containing GM soya or maize to be labelled except when neither protein nor DNA resulting from the modification is present. It also provides for the formulation of a list of ingredients which member states agree do not contain novel protein or DNA. In March 1999 the UK was the first member state to enforce the Regulation, so that all food businesses, including restaurants, cafés, bakers and delicatessens, must (from September 1999) make clear to customers whether they are selling foods containing GM ingredients. Outlets selling foods containing GM material that is not properly labelled may be prosecuted and fined up to £5,000.

Since 1992 the Government has spent £3.2 million on research to underpin the safety assessment of GM foods. It is also committed to the adequate labelling of GM animal feed throughout the EU, although there is as yet no evidence of carry-over of genetic material from animal feed to the food chain.

Several European supermarket chains have formed a consortium to eliminate GM crops and derivatives from their own-label food products. J. Sainsbury, one of the UK's largest supermarket groups, has led the initiative, which also includes Marks & Spencer and members from France, Belgium, Switzerland, the Irish Republic and Italy.

An EC Directive of June 1998 on the legal protection of biotechnological inventions aims to clarify and harmonise those aspects of national EU patent laws which concern genetic materials, plants and animals, and to balance the needs of the food industry to gain patents to foster research and the ethical concerns which surround biotechnology. The Directive affirms the possibility of patenting GM plants and animals; but if modification is likely to cause suffering to the animal, no patent should be granted, unless it can be

shown that there is substantial medical benefit to humans or the animal.

FOOD SAFETY

In June 1999 the Government introduced legislation for a Food Standards Agency (FSA), as a non-ministerial government department with powers to protect food safety and standards throughout the food chain, and with its own research budget. The aim is to launch the FSA in the first half of 2000. EU food law harmonisation covers food safety, fair trading and informative labelling. For example, the Beef Labelling Scheme provides information on fresh and frozen beef (including mince) which may be confirmed through improved traceability systems.

BSE

The government announcement in March 1996 of a possible link between BSE in cattle and a new variant of Creutzfeldt-Jakob disease (nvCJD) in humans[3] led to an immediate EU worldwide ban on exports from the UK of all live bovine animals, beef and beef products, bovine embryos, and mammalian meat and bonemeal (MBM). Reopening of the export market has been of paramount importance for the future of the beef industry and, following the Florence agreement of June 1996, various steps were taken to achieve this, including:

- a selective slaughter programme, to accelerate eradication of BSE from the national herd;

- introduction of an effective animal identification and movement recording system;

- legislation for removal of all mammalian MBM from farms and feedmills;

- strengthening and tightening controls on slaughterhouses to ensure removal of specified risk materials (SRM); and

---

[3] By the end of February 1999 some 40 people had died from nvCJD in the UK. BSE has been detected in more than 175,000 cattle across Europe, 99.7% of them in the UK.

- effective implementation of the Over Thirty Months Scheme to remove meat from older bovine animals from the food chain and destroy it.

In 1997 a risk from beef bones to consumers was identified and their use in food manufacture, and the retail sale of bone-in beef, were banned. Since June 1998 the Export Certified Herds Scheme has enabled the export from Northern Ireland of deboned beef and its products from animals qualifying under the Scheme. From 1 August 1999 export from the UK of deboned beef produced under the Date-based Export Scheme (DBES), which lays down criteria for beef to be eligible for export, has been permitted. A DBES precondition was that the UK must slaughter all offspring born to confirmed BSE cases between 1 August 1996 and 25 November 1998, a process completed by June 1999. The UK is further required to slaughter offspring of BSE cases confirmed since 25 November 1998 without delay.

Application of the EU Decision of 1997 prohibiting the use of SRMs from cattle, sheep and goats over 12 months has been postponed until 31 December 1999 because of the unforeseen impact of the legislation on the supply of pharmaceuticals and cosmetics, and the failure of subsequent Commission proposals to achieve qualified majority support from member states. In the absence of Community rules, the UK introduced national controls prohibiting the import of SRMs except when delivered to approved premises for manufacture of technical products, such as bone china. Imports of certain animal products for food or animal feed must be accompanied by additional veterinary certification confirming that they do not contain any SRMs.

The decline in the number of BSE cases in Britain continues. By mid-1999 about 55 cases were being reported each week, compared with over 1,000 a week at the height of the epidemic in 1993.

Tighter hygiene rules on the production and marketing of fresh meat, designed to help restore public confidence in food safety, were announced in March 1999. These implemented EU rules updated to allow hygiene controls to adapt to modern production methods and to make it possible to trace meat products back to the point of production for public health control. The Meat Hygiene Service (MHS) and its 1,700 veterinary surgeons and inspectors are responsible for enforcing legislation on meat hygiene, inspection, animal welfare at slaughter and SRM controls in all licensed abattoirs and cutting premises in Great Britain. The MHS Hygiene Assessment System score is a published guide to the hygiene performance of plants measured over a period. Irrespective of a plant's score, however, before any meat produced there enters the food chain, it must be inspected and health-marked as fit for human consumption. In addition, businesses making, selling or using animal feed additives have to apply for official approval or registration.

The Animal By-Products Order 1999 consolidates the rules on the processing and disposal of animal by-products and the processing of catering waste for feeding to pigs or poultry. It also introduces construction and hygiene standards for knackers' yards in line with EU rules.

EXPORTS

Food, feed and drink exports in 1998 were provisionally valued at £9.2 billion, 7% less than in 1997 (compared with £17.2 billion for imports, a fall of 3%). The main EU markets in 1998 were France (£1.2 billion), the Irish Republic (£1.1 billion), Spain (£728 million) and Germany (£700 million). There was a 20% increase in exports to Italy, worth some £416 million in 1998. Other key markets were the United States (£724 million) and Japan (£241 million).

Drink exports showed a decrease of 13% to £2.9 billion in 1998, largely as a result of a fall in demand in Far East countries. Cereals (including cereal products) were the largest category of British food exports, worth £1.3 billion in 1998. Only sugars and fish showed an increase on 1997. Meat exports fell by 21%, to £763 million, primarily as a result of lower prices.

Export promotion for food and drink is headed by Food from Britain (FFB), an organisation funded by MAFF on behalf of the four agricultural departments (£5.3 million in 1998–99) and industry (£7.2 million), which provides a range of business development services for food and drink companies seeking expansion in international markets and within the UK speciality food and drink sector. It co-ordinates the British presence at ten or more international food and drink exhibitions each year and organises seminars to highlight the benefits of successful exporting to particular markets and the annual FFB Export Awards. For all other agricultural products, services, livestock, machinery and processing equipment, MAFF co-ordinates export promotion, participates in overseas trade fairs and arranges ministerial trade missions to other countries. During 1999 MAFF attended ten trade events overseas, providing a platform for UK companies and attracting export business. Exports of agricultural machinery and tractors in 1998 were worth £1,419 million.

In 1999 MAFF unveiled a promotional British cheese map, featuring 60 different cheeses from more than 400 produced in the UK. British cheese production has increased by 18% since 1991, to 366,000 tonnes in 1998. The total volume of exports in 1998 was 55,063 tonnes, compared with 52,987 tonnes in 1997. During 1998 MAFF also highlighted the opening of Wendy's Baltic Bread Wholesale Bakery in St Petersburg, to produce bread, cakes and pastries to traditional British recipes. It also praised Crantock Bakery, which supplies 4 million Cornish pasties a year; and Rodda's Creamery, makers of traditional Cornish cream, whose export markets include Hong Kong and Japan. FFB has helped introduce more than 600 products to Japan in the past three years and the Feast of Britain exhibition at Tokyo in November 1998 displayed not only popular British exports such as Scotch whisky, tea, jam and biscuits, but also chocolate, cereals and ready-made foods.

The annual Royal Agricultural Show, held at Stoneleigh in Warwickshire in early July, enables visitors to see the latest techniques and improvements in British agriculture. Some 172,000 visitors attended in 1999, of whom 10% were from overseas. Other major agricultural events include the Royal Smithfield Show, held every other year in London, which exhibits agricultural machinery, livestock and carcases; the Royal Highland Show (June; 160,000 visitors in 1999) in Edinburgh, the largest trade exhibition of agricultural machinery in Great Britain; the Royal Welsh Show (late July) in Builth Wells; and the Royal Ulster Agricultural Show (May) in Belfast.

ROLE OF THE GOVERNMENT

MAFF; the Scottish Executive Rural Affairs Department (SERAD); the National Assembly for Wales; and the Department of Agriculture for Northern Ireland have joint responsibility for agriculture and fisheries matters; in 1999 agriculture was devolved to the Scottish Parliament and the National Assembly for Wales. Subject to the outcome of a formal Implementation Review of the Good Friday Agreement in Northern Ireland, agriculture will be devolved to the new Northern Ireland Assembly (see p. 18). Concordats between MAFF and the new administrations cover arrangements after devolution. The work of MAFF's nine Regional Service Centres in England and SERAD's eight areas in Scotland relates to payments under domestic and EU schemes, licensing and other services for farmers and growers.

Reform of the Common Agricultural Policy (CAP)

The CAP was originally established in the Treaty of Rome (1957) at a time when high agricultural productivity was considered essential to ensure secure, plentiful and cheap food supplies. Its mechanisms of support prices, import duties and market intervention, however, are now held instead to have distorted incentives for farmers, raised food prices and encouraged surplus production.

Public Expenditure under the CAP by the Intervention Board and the Agricultural Departments

FORECAST 1998–99

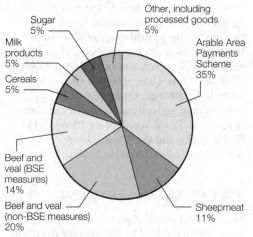

Source: Ministry of Agriculture, Fisheries and Food

The reforms of 1992 have helped to cut food mountains to manageable levels and restrained expansion of the CAP budget, at times over 70% of the EU budget. Further reforms, as part of the EU's Agenda 2000 and agreed in March 1999, represent an acceleration of the 1992 changes, with a further shift in encouraging agriculture to be more market-orientated and competitive.

- cereal support prices will fall by 15%, half in 2000–01, and half in 2001–02;

- the basic price of beef will fall by 20% in three steps, and the intervention price[4] by 25% from 2,780 to 1,560 euros a tonne;

- dairy support prices will fall by 15% in three steps, beginning in 2005, and quotas for milk production will increase by 1.5% over three years from 2005, with extra increases for the UK (for Northern Ireland only), the Irish Republic, Spain, Italy and Greece;

---

[4] The price at which intervention authorities in member states buy commodities when their prices fall below certain agreed levels and store them for later resale.

- direct payments to farmers are being increased to help compensate them for the price cuts and, at the UK's urging, a Commission proposal to impose a mandatory EU-wide ceiling on large farms was withdrawn; and

- the creation of an integrated rural development policy, including agri-environment measures, provides a framework for a shift in emphasis from production support to environmental and rural economy measures, and allows less-favoured area (LFA) compensation to be replaced by area payments with a more environmental focus.

The compromise agreement reached at the Berlin summit between member states in March 1999 did not provide for direct payments to farmers to be made degressive (a gradual reduction in value over time), which the UK has advocated as a means to bring down the cost of the CAP. The cuts in price support, however, do aim to bring market forces to bear on EU agriculture and make farmers more responsive to consumer wishes. Reductions in cereals support prices will set the normal rate of compulsory set-aside at 10% during 2000–06. The cut of 20% for beef, though significant, is not, in the UK's view, enough to bring EU beef prices to world levels, although at the new level the EU will provide private storage facilities, while not guaranteeing to buy in meat as in the existing intervention arrangements.

Under a system of 'national envelopes', a small part of the increase in direct payments to farmers will be given to member states to distribute according to national criteria suiting farmers' needs.

Agrimoney

Since 1 January 1999 CAP payments, hitherto set in ECUs, have been paid in euros or its sub-denominations (participating currencies) in the 11 member states which have adopted the European single currency. The new agrimonetary regime has therefore abandoned the 'green rate' and uses daily market rates to convert CAP payments into national currencies in the four non-participating countries: the UK, Denmark, Greece and Sweden. There is provision for payment under CAP schemes to be made in euros to these four countries, and the Government plans to make such an option available in the UK from autumn 2000 on market support measures, such as export refunds and intervention buying, with the possibility of extending this choice to direct farm payments. Ending the freeze on green rates, which benefited UK farmers more than any others, will be subject to a three-year transition period, during which compensation (in 1999 compulsory and 100% EU-funded) will be paid.

Special Aid to Farmers

In 1998–99 the Government announced extra aid of £270 million to UK farmers to help them through an especially difficult period:

- an extra £48.3 million of agrimonetary compensation to suckler cow producers;

- a £60 million increase for each of the years 1998–99 and 1999–2000 in Hill Livestock Compensatory Allowances (HLCAs—see p. 457), allowing average increases in payments of 55%; and

- an extension of the Calf Processing Aid Scheme (part of the BSE slaughter programme, originally due to lapse in November 1998) at about 70% of the current rate—or about £55 a head.

This aid is in addition to other recent government steps, including £85 million of agrimonetary aid for suckler cow and sheep producers in 1998 and a private storage aid scheme for pigmeat in the face of a 50% fall in the producer price of pigs, worth more than £150 million to the agricultural industry.

Agri-Environment Schemes

The UK's agri-environment programme provides schemes to encourage environmentally beneficial farming and public enjoyment of the countryside. All are voluntary and offer payments to farmers who agree to manage their land for the positive benefit of wildlife, landscape, resource protection, historic features or public access. The payments are based on the agricultural income which farmers forgo by participating in the schemes and are partly funded by the EU. The Government normally evaluates and reviews these schemes every five years. The 1998–99 payments (provisional) made to farmers on agri-environment schemes in the UK were about £97 million. An additional £40 million is to be made available for the major schemes in England over three years from 1999.

Environmentally Sensitive Areas (ESAs)

By the end of 1998 over 18,000 farmers throughout the UK had signed ESA management agreements to promote environmentally beneficial farming. Payments covering these agreements and conservation plans totalled some £57.8 million in 1998–99. Sums range between £8 and £500 a hectare, and are designed to compensate for reduced profitability as a result of adopting less intensive production methods. They are generally funded half by the Government and half by the European Agricultural Guidance and Guarantee Fund. In addition to the revised schemes for 11 of the English ESAs, designed to conform with the UK's Biodiversity Action Plan and relaunched in 1998, six further schemes in England, reviewed in 1998, were relaunched in 1999.

Countryside Stewardship

Countryside Stewardship is the main government incentive scheme for farmers in England for the wider English countryside outside the ESAs. Payments on over 8,600 agreements covering 143,842 hectares (355,434 acres) in operation at 31 March 1999 are expected to total some £26.5 million in the 1999–2000 financial year. Taking effect from August 1998, 78 agreements in the Arable Stewardship pilot scheme aim to reverse the decline in a number of wildlife species in East Anglia and the West Midlands, with £0.5 million set aside for new agreements in each of the three years of the scheme. Two more experiments, aiming to test an integrated

Table 27.6: ESAs at 31 March 1999

	Number of ESAs	Farmers with agreements	Land designated '000 hectares	Areas covered by agreements '000 hectares	Payments to farmers in 1997–98 (£'000)
England	22	10,000	1,100	500	36,376
Wales	6	2,156	519	160	6,553
Scotland	10	2,054	1,439	639	7,500
Northern Ireland	5	4,424	247	142	5,192

Sources: MAFF, National Assembly for Wales, SERAD and Department of Agriculture for Northern Ireland

approach to economic and environmental issues in the uplands, are taking place in Bodmin Moor (Cornwall) and Bowland (North West).

Organic Aid

During 1992–97 sales of organic food in the UK increased by about 250%, and in 1998 were valued at £400 million, but 70% is imported. The area of UK farmland organically managed rose from 54,834 hectares (0.3% of the agricultural area) in April 1998 to 274,519 hectares (1.6%) in April 1999—compared with an EU average of 1.7%. The Organic Farming Scheme in England and Northern Ireland, launched in 1999, raised the payment rates to those farmers wishing to convert to organic methods from £250 to £450 a hectare over five years for most arable land and temporary grass, and from £50 to £350 for most improved land in the uplands. It also removed the current ceiling of 300 hectares on the area of land that can receive payments on any one organic unit.

The Government also funds the Organic Conversion Information Service, which provides Helpline (0117 922 7707) information and advisory visits to prospective organic farmers in England and Wales. The UK Register of Organic Food Standards is charged with overseeing standards of organic food production.

Other Schemes

The final round of the Nitrate Sensitive Areas (NSA) Scheme in England (to run until September 2003) attracted applications covering 3,000 hectares (7,413 acres) and brought the total area of land subject to NSA

undertakings to 28,000 hectares (69,190 acres), with payments of £6.2 million forecast in 1999–2000. Under the UK Habitat Schemes 1,534 farmers entered 16,210 hectares (40,055 acres) into agreements. Proposals have been made to incorporate the English Habitat Scheme into the Countryside Stewardship Scheme from 1 January 2000. The Welsh, Scottish and Northern Ireland schemes have been closed to new applicants.

In Scotland there are three agri-environment schemes: the ESAs, the Organic Aid Scheme (OAS) and the Countryside Premium Scheme, with provision for £18.8 million expenditure in 1999–2000. Wales has the ESAs, the OAS and Tir Gofal, with provision for £12.4 million of expenditure over 1999–2002. Northern Ireland has the ESAs, the OAS and the Countryside Management Scheme.

The UK-wide Farm Woodland Premium Scheme encourages farmers to convert agricultural land to woodland by providing annual payments for ten or 15 years to compensate for income forgone. Payments are 50% funded by the European Commission under the CAP (75% in disadvantaged areas). From April 1992 to March 1999 nearly 9,000 applications were approved to convert over 60,000 hectares (148,258 acres). Nearly 75% of planting is broadleaved trees.

The Rural Economy and EU Structural Funds

Northern Ireland, the Highlands and Islands of Scotland and Merseyside qualified for assistance under Objective 1 of the EU Structural Funds for the period 1994–99.

This aims to help those regions whose economic development lags behind the EU average. For the period 2000–06, four areas have been designated for Objective 1 support—Merseyside, Cornwall, South Yorkshire and West Wales and Valleys (see p. 395).

Eleven areas in Great Britain (including South West England, the English Northern Uplands, 70% of the landmass of Wales, and Borders, Dumfries and Galloway in Scotland) were eligible to receive funds under Objective 5b of the EU Structural Funds for the period 1994–99. This aims to promote the economic development of rural areas. To be eligible, areas must have a high share of agricultural employment in total employment, a low level of agricultural income and a low population density. In England by the end of June 1999, 345 Objective 5b projects had been approved and over £101 million in EU and national public funding had been allocated to them. This included £4.83 million, comprising EU and MAFF and other public and private sector funding, to go towards the Bowland and Bodmin Moor upland pilot projects (see p. 456). In Scotland by the end of 1998, 228 projects had been approved and over £4.3 million committed. For the period 2000–06 the designation of rural areas will fall under the new Objective 2 programme.

Integrated Administration and Control System (IACS)

The IACS, an EU-wide anti-fraud measure, requires farmers claiming payment under area-based CAP schemes to submit an annual application for aid giving field-by-field details of their farmed land. This provides the basis for administrative and on-farm checks on their entitlement to aid and for cross-checks between claims under the agri-environment and IACS schemes. Administrative checks involve the use of a computerised database, and on-the-spot checks are carried out through farm visits by field officers and the use of observation satellites.

Hill Livestock Compensatory Allowances

In Less Favoured Areas (LFAs), generally hills and uplands, farmers have traditionally received headage payments on breeding cattle and sheep to support the continuation of livestock farming, thus conserving the countryside and encouraging people to remain in the LFAs. Under the EU Agenda 2000 reforms, this support must switch from headage to area payments which are conditional on the use of sustainable farming practices. Details of the new area-based scheme have yet to be finalised.

Agricultural Trade Liberalisation

The next round of negotiations on agricultural trade liberalisation under the World Trade Organisation (WTO—see p. 419) is due to start in January 2000. These are likely to consider further commitments to improve access for agricultural products, cuts in subsidised exports and reductions in domestic support.

In April 1999 the WTO upheld a complaint by Ecuador, the world's largest banana exporter, that the EU banana regime, despite changes in January 1999, was still incompatible with world trade rules. At the same time the WTO ruled that the damage suffered by United States companies because of the discriminatory elements of the EU regime amounted to almost $120 million a year; the United States subsequently imposed retaliatory duties to this value against selected EU exports. EU member states have asked the Commission, after consultation with all interested parties, including the United States, Latin American and African, Caribbean and Pacific suppliers, to draft legislation for reform of the EU banana regime.

In July 1999 the United States and Canada announced retaliatory measures against the EU over its import ban on meat from animals treated with hormone growth promoters, which in 1998 the WTO had found inconsistent with its rules because it did not follow from a properly conducted risk assessment. The UK, which has consistently voted against the ban on the grounds that it is not scientifically justified, continues to work for a resolution of the dispute which is based on sound science.

Price Guarantees, Grants and Subsidies

Expenditure in the UK in 1998–99 under the CAP was £3,293 million, compared with

£3,321 million in 1997–98; expenditure by the agriculture and other departments (including funding for special areas) on conservation measures was £262 million, slightly less than in 1997–98. The net decrease occurred mainly because fewer animals entered schemes introduced to support the industry during the initial stages of the BSE crisis.

Smallholdings and Crofts

In England and Wales county councils let smallholdings to experienced people who want to farm on their own account. Councils may lend working capital to them. At 31 March 1997 there were approximately 4,500 smallholdings in England and 787 in Wales. Land settlement in Scotland has been carried out by the Government, which still owns and maintains 105,000 hectares (259,455 acres) of land settlement estates, comprising 1,400 crofts and holdings.

In the Highlands and Islands of Scotland, much of the land is tenanted by crofters, who enjoy the statutory protection provided by crofting legislation and can benefit from government agriculture and livestock improvement schemes. Most crofters are part-time agriculturalists, using croft income to supplement income from other activities. The Crofters Commission has a statutory duty to promote their interests and to keep all crofting matters under review. The Transfer of Crofting Estates (Scotland) Act 1997 allows the Government to move some of its own crofting land to trusts set up by resident crofters, with the aim of giving them more responsibility for their own affairs.

Agricultural Landlords and Tenants

About 34% of agricultural land in England and 22% in Wales is rented. The Agricultural Tenancies Act 1995 provides a simplified legal framework for new tenancies entered into on or after 1 September 1995, known as farm business tenancies, on which landowners benefit from full income tax relief.

There is a similar proportion of rented land in Scotland, much of it under crofting tenure, including common grazings.

Most farms in Northern Ireland are owner-occupied, but the conacre system allows owners not wishing to farm all their land to let it annually to others. Conacre land, about one-fifth of agricultural land, is used mainly for grazing.

Professional, Scientific and Technical Services

In England and Wales the Farming and Rural Conservancy Agency provides services to government on the design, development and implementation of policies on the integration of farming and conservation, environmental protection, rural land use and the diversification of the rural economy. In England and Wales ADAS provides professional, business, scientific and technical services in the agriculture, food and drink, and environmental markets. In 1997–98 MAFF wholly or partly funded over 3,600 initial visits made to farmers by ADAS and the Farming and Wildlife Advisory Group (FWAG). In Scotland the Scottish Agricultural College (SAC) provides professional, business, scientific and technical services in the agriculture, rural business, food and drink, and environmental markets. In 1997–98, 450 visits were made by staff of the Department of Agriculture for Northern Ireland to farmers in the Province. CAIS, a free and integrated service for Wales, made 5,820 advisory visits in 1995–98.

Lantra is the UK National Training Organisation for the land-based sector. It represents about 1.5 million individuals and 400,000 businesses, mostly in rural areas. It aims to increase competitiveness and develop the skills and enterprise of those who work in, or provide specialist services to, the sector. It receives government support under contracts to MAFF and the Scottish Executive.

CONTROL OF DISEASES AND PESTS

Farm Animals

Britain enforces controls on imports of live animals and genetic material, including checks on all individual consignments originating from outside the EU and frequent checks on those from other EU member states at destination points. Measures can be taken to prevent the import of diseased animals and genetic material from regions or countries affected by disease. Veterinary checks also include unannounced periods of surveillance at ports.

The campaign to eradicate BSE is described on p. 451–2. As a further precaution, the British Cattle Movement Service (BCMS) for Great Britain, at Workington, has provided about 2.5 million cattle with 'passports' since its launch in 1998. It has also processed 2 million passports of slaughtered cattle and entered 1.75 million cattle movements on to the Cattle Tracing System (CTS). The Government has met all BCMS and CTS start-up and first-year running costs, a benefit of about £35 million to the farming industry, and will provide a further £45 million to fund the CTS until 2002–03.

Traditional measures aimed at preventing the spread of TB in cattle, such as regular testing, culling and restricting movements into and out of affected herds, have not been able to check a marked increase in the incidence of the disease in recent years. The Government is therefore spending over £11 million each year over 1999–2002 on research and other work for a better understanding of what causes the disease and how it is transmitted; on developing a cattle vaccine; and on investigating the contribution that badger culling can make to its effective control.

Professional advice and action on the statutory control of animal disease and the welfare of farm livestock are the responsibility of the State Veterinary Service. It is supported by the Veterinary Laboratories Agency (VLA), which also offers its services to the private sector on a commercial basis. A similar service is provided in Scotland by the SAC and in Northern Ireland by the Department of Agriculture's Veterinary Sciences Division.

Rabies

Following the recommendations of the Advisory Group on Quarantine in 1998, the Government intends to change the law to allow most pet animals coming from EU and other European countries, and rabies-free islands, to enter the UK without quarantine. Pets from other countries will continue to be subject to quarantine, though the position of those from the United States and Canada will be reviewed once the scheme is in full operation, in April 2001 (with a pilot scheme by April 2000). To enter the UK under the scheme animals will need to have been resident in a qualifying country and have been:

- microchipped;
- vaccinated against rabies;
- blood-tested at an approved laboratory;
- issued with an official health certificate detailing the fulfilment of these precautions; and
- treated against exotic infections.

MAFF provides Helpline information on 020 8330 6835.

Pesticides

The Pesticides Safety Directorate, an executive agency of MAFF, is responsible for the evaluation and approval of agricultural pesticides in England. It also carries out evaluations and approvals on behalf of the devolved administrations in Scotland and Wales. There is rigorous evaluation of new and existing pesticides under UK and EU legislation. Regulations to strengthen enforcement and provide greater public access to information will be laid before Parliament in autumn 1999. New arrangements for buffer zones applied to certain pesticides to protect aquatic life from spray drift were introduced in March 1999 for the arable sector. These allow farmers greater flexibility in the way buffer zones are applied while maintaining high environmental protection. The scheme encourages the development of low-drift spray technology. A similar scheme for orchard and hop uses is currently being considered.

Veterinary Medicinal Products

The Veterinary Medicines Directorate, another executive agency of MAFF, is responsible for ensuring that veterinary medicines are marketed only if they meet statutory standards for safety, quality and efficacy. The Government is advised by the independent scientific Veterinary Products Committee, one of whose tasks is to keep the use of organophosphorus (OP) compounds in veterinary medicines under review. Purchasers of all OP or other sheep dips must have a certificate of competence.

In response to concern about the increase of micro-organisms resistant to antibiotics, the EU has recently banned the use of four used as growth promoters in animal feed.

The Fishing Industry

Scientists at the International Council for the Exploration of the Sea (ICES) have advised the European Commission on a management plan for 1999 for fishing quotas in accordance with agreements signed at meetings of ministers from North Sea countries at Esbjerg in 1995 and at Bergen in 1998. The plan involves drastic cuts in catch limits to protect stocks from extinction.

The UK is one of the EU's largest fishing countries, taking about a quarter of the total catch in major species and committing £36.8 million in 1998 to fisheries science and to monitoring and developing stocks. It also has an interest in more than 100 allowable catches set by the Commission (see p. 461). In 1998 the British fishing industry provided about 53% by quantity of total UK fish supplies, and household consumption of fish in the UK was provisionally estimated at 448,000 tonnes.

Fisheries departments are responsible for the administration of legislation, in partnership with the European Commission, concerning the fishing industry, including fish and shellfish farming. The Sea Fish Industry Authority (SFIA), an industry-financed body, undertakes R&D, provides training and promotes the marketing and consumption of sea fish.

Fish Caught

In 1998 demersal fish (caught on or near the bottom of the sea) accounted for 58% by weight of total landings by British fishing vessels, pelagic fish (caught near the surface) for 20%

and shellfish for 22%. Landings of all types of fish (excluding salmon and trout) by British fishing vessels into the UK totalled 552,234 tonnes compared with 602,692 tonnes in 1997. Cod and haddock represented 25% and 18% respectively of the total value of demersal and pelagic fish landed. The quayside value of landings of all sea fish, including shellfish, by British vessels in 1998 was £484 million.

The Fishing Fleet

The UK fisheries departments currently spend some £24 million a year on fisheries enforcement, primarily on monitoring the application of the Common Fisheries Policy (CFP—see p. 461) and ensuring that measures designed to conserve fish stocks are effective.

All British vessels fishing for profit must be licensed by the fisheries departments. To help conserve stocks and contain the size of the fleet, only replacement licences are issued. Quotas are allocated annually between producer organisations and other groups of fishermen, primarily on the basis of historic catches.

A satellite monitoring system, to track the movements of EU vessels over 24 m in length, as well as those from third countries fishing in EU waters, will be fully operational from 1 January 2000. New controls over the landing of fish were introduced from 5 January 1999. It is a condition of UK fishing licences that, subject to derogations for landings at designated ports, at least four hours' notice must be given of all landings of whitefish and shellfish into UK ports by vessels 20 m in length and above. Measures to strengthen and improve standards of fisheries control throughout the EU were also adopted in December 1998, providing for greater transparency of action taken by member states to monitor compliance with the CFP, and are being phased in from July 1999.

Britain aims to achieve the EU target for reducing its fleet through cutting its numbers and limiting the time some vessels spend at sea. At the end of 1998 the UK fleet consisted of 7,644 registered vessels, including 270 deep-sea vessels greater than 27 m (88.5 ft) overall length, of which 233 are registered. There are an estimated 14,000 professional fishermen in Britain.

Fish Farming and Shellfish Production

There are over 1,000 fish and shellfish farming businesses in the UK, on 1,400 sites and employing more than 3,000 people. Total value is about £290 million at first sale. The main finfish species are salmon (115,000 tonnes, mainly in Scotland) and rainbow trout (16,000 tonnes), with a limited production of other species, such as carp and brown trout. There is also interest in farming marine species such as turbot and halibut. Public subsidy during 1992–98 amounted to nearly £16 million. Considerable government funds have also been spent on aquaculture research, particularly on disease control. A five-year LINK programme (see p. 428), worth over £10 million, for collaborative research between government and industry on fish and shellfish farming, was launched in 1995 to stimulate further innovation and wealth creation in this sector.

The UK's first commercial lobster hatchery, a £400,000 project funded by fishing groups, local authorities, commercial organisations and the EU, plans to open in 1999 at Padstow (Cornwall). The project aims to reverse a century-long decline in lobster numbers in Cornish waters—from 253 tonnes in 1927 to a low of 63 tonnes in 1991 and 85 tonnes in 1998—by producing 80,000 juvenile lobsters a year to seed the lobster fishing grounds around Cornwall. About 350 Cornish boats rely on shellfish catches for a significant proportion of their earnings.

Fishery Limits

British fishery limits extend to 200 miles or the median line (broadly halfway between the UK coast and the opposing coastline of another coastal state), measured from baselines on or near the coast of Britain.

Common Fisheries Policy (CFP)

The EU's CFP system for the management of fishing resources sets total allowable catches (TACs) each year in order to conserve stocks.

TACs are then allocated as quotas between member states, taking account of traditional fishing patterns. In December 1998, the EU agreed large cuts in the number of fish caught in the North Sea and other UK waters to help rebuild stocks for the future. These included a 27% cut in the TAC for North Sea whiting (from 60,000 tonnes in 1998 to 44,000 tonnes in 1999); a 26% cut in the TAC for Scottish West Coast haddock; and 23% cuts in Scottish West Coast herring, North Sea haddock and Irish Sea cod. The quota for North Sea cod was reduced by 5%, from 140,000 tonnes to 132,000 tonnes.

In 1998–99, eight new North Sea TACs (including for anglerfish, megrin and dogfish) were introduced to help conserve stocks, with the UK fishermen receiving the lion's share of quotas.

Since 1997 the number of over 10 m UK vessels partly or wholly owned by overseas interests has fallen from 160 to 140. From 1999 all vessels fishing against UK quotas are required, with Commission approval, to show that a satisfactory economic link is maintained with British coastal communities, for example:

- by landing at least 50% of their catch of quota stocks in the UK;
- by employing a crew of whom 50% are resident in a UK coastal area; or
- by spending money in UK coastal areas for goods and services.

As a contribution to the economic link requirements, 50 extra tonnes of sole quota is being made available to the UK's inshore fishing fleet by UK-Dutch boats.

British vessels have exclusive rights to fish within 6 miles of the British coast. Certain other EU member states have historic rights in British waters between 6 and 12 miles. British vessels have similar rights in other member states' 6 to 12 mile belts. Between 12 and 200 miles, EU vessels may fish wherever they have access rights. Non-EU countries' vessels may fish in these waters if they negotiate reciprocal fisheries agreements with the EU.

Technical conservation measures supplement TACs and controls on the time spent at sea. They include minimum mesh sizes for nets and net configuration restrictions, minimum landing sizes and

Table 27.7: Imports and Exports of Fish			tonnes
	1996	1997	1998 provisional
Imports			
Salt-water and shellfish	476,556	448,335	486,702
Freshwater fish	56,613	54,836	47,230
Fish meals	242,834	285,969	239,000
Fish oils	86,182	70,937	49,454
Exports and re-exports			
Salt-water fish			
and fish products	276,124	253,229	294,550
Freshwater fish	34,241	46,550	51,659
Fish meals	19,112	22,623	19,470
Fish oils	6,787	6,049	4,000

Sources: MAFF, SERAD and Department of Agriculture for Northern Ireland

closed areas designed mainly to protect young fish. Conservation measures in English and Welsh waters have increased stocks of sea bass. There are 37 nursery areas around the coasts, where fishing for bass for all or part of the year is prohibited.

Each member state is responsible for enforcement of CFP rules on its own fishermen and those of other member states in its own waters. EU inspectors monitor compliance. In December 1998, new measures were introduced to increase the effectiveness of EU enforcements.

Fisheries Agreements

CFP provisions are supplemented by a number of fisheries agreements between the EU and third countries, the most important for the UK being with Norway (for cod, haddock, saithe, redfish and Greenland halibut), Greenland and the Faroes. EU catch quotas, especially for cod, have also been established around Spitsbergen (Svalbard). In January 1999 the moratorium (since 1992) on the issue of external waters licences (EWLs) came to an end and new EWLs are available to enable UK vessels to fish in those external waters not fully subscribed, in accordance with international conventions and agreements.

Salmon, Freshwater Fisheries and the Aquatic Environment

In 1998 the ICES advised that stocks of multi-sea-winter salmon (MSW) in the North Atlantic had fallen to unprecedented low levels and recommended that the level of exploitation of MSW should be significantly reduced in 1999. The Environment Agency, responsible for day-to-day management in England and Wales, submitted a number of measures to reduce exploitation by both nets and rods. The Agency by-laws, confirmed by the Government with modifications in April 1999, included a delay in the opening of the netting season until 1 June, with certain exemptions, and mandatory catch and release by anglers until 16 June.

Scottish salmon farmers have been offered up to £9 million of government funds over three years as compensation for their costs in eradicating Infectious Salmon Anaemia (ISA), a viral disease which has been confirmed at ten sites in Scotland and is suspected at 15 more, out of a total of 335 farms. Some 3,100 tonnes of fish have been withdrawn from the ten sites.

There is no public right to fish in freshwater lakes and non-tidal rivers in Great Britain. Those wishing to fish such waters must first obtain permission from the owner of the fishing rights and, in England and

Wales, a licence from the Environment Agency. In Scotland salmon fisheries are managed locally by District Salmon Fishery Boards. In Northern Ireland fishing for freshwater species is licensed by the Fisheries Conservancy Board for Northern Ireland and the Foyle Fisheries Commission in their respective areas, and 62 public angling waters, including salmon, trout and coarse fisheries, are available to Department of Agriculture permit holders.

Research

Departmental funding of commissioned R&D in agriculture, fisheries and food in 1998–99 included £121 million from MAFF and £5.3 million from the Department of Agriculture for Northern Ireland. In Scotland about £50 million is invested in the Agricultural and Biological Sciences-related research programme. Priority areas in the MAFF programme are public health (covering food safety, transmissible spongiform encephalopathies and zoonoses) and protection of the environment (improved sustainability in production methods, with benefits for the environment and agricultural efficiency).

Research Bodies

The BBSRC (see p. 437) supports research in biotechnology and biological sciences related to food and agriculture. The Natural Environment Research Council includes some agricultural aspects in its remit. Research institutes sponsored by these councils receive income from work commissioned by MAFF, industry and other bodies.

ADAS carries out R&D, at a network of research centres and on clients' premises, for MAFF and other organisations and companies. There are research centres across England and Wales. MAFF receives scientific expertise and technical support from its other agencies, the VLA and the Central Science Laboratory. Horticulture Research International, a non-departmental public body, transfers the results of its R&D to the British horticulture industry and the wider public. It is in its third year of a five-year project on forecasting productivity, quality

and availability in outdoor flower crops, at a total cost of £385,000.

SERAD support for agricultural, biological and related sciences is achieved primarily through sponsoring the five Scottish Agricultural and Biological Research Institutes, the SAC and the Royal Botanic Garden in Edinburgh. It contracts additional research through these bodies and provides funding for Education and Advisory Services at the SAC. In Northern Ireland the Department of Agriculture maintains an integrated Science and Technology programme to improve the economic performance of the agri-food, fishing and forestry sectors, to conserve the rural environment and to strengthen the economy and social infrastructure of disadvantaged rural areas.

Forestry

Woodland covers an estimated 2.5 million hectares (6.2 million acres) in the UK: a little less than 8% of England, nearly 16% of Scotland, 12% of Wales and 6% of Northern Ireland. This is about 10% of the total land area and well below the 30% average for the whole of Europe. The EU's forests are estimated to be increasing by about 486 million cubic metres (17.16 billion cubic feet) a year, while the annual harvest has fallen to 313 million cubic metres (11.05 billion cubic feet) owing to cheaper imports and an over-supply of timber.

Britain's forestry programme aims to protect and expand forest resources and conserve woodland as a home for wildlife and for public recreation. The UK imports 85% of its timber and wood products, which costs about £8 billion a year. Promoting the market for home-grown timber is an important part of the forestry programme.

The area of productive forest in Great Britain is 2.2 million hectares (5.5 million acres), 35% of which is managed by the Forestry Commission. The rate of new planting (including natural regeneration) in 1997–98 was 131 hectares (324 acres) by the Commission and 15,912 hectares (39,319 acres) by other woodland owners, with the help of grants from the Commission. In 1997–98, 11,585 hectares (28,628 acres) of broadleaved trees were planted—both new planting and restocking.

Forestry and primary wood processing employ about 35,000 people. Great Britain's woodlands produced 9.05 million cubic metres (320 million cubic feet) of timber in 1997, 15% of total UK consumption. The volume of timber harvested on Commission lands in 1997–98 was estimated at 4.66 million cubic metres (164 million cubic feet).

The Commission's Woodland Grant Scheme pays grants (£35.5 million in 1997–98) to help create new woodlands and forests, and regenerate existing ones. Under the scheme a management grant is available for work in woods of special conservation and landscape value or where the public are welcome.

The Forestry Commission and Forestry Policy

The Forestry Commission, established in 1919, is the government department responsible for forestry in Great Britain. With 1.06 million hectares of land (2.6 million acres), it is the UK's largest land manager and the biggest single provider of countryside recreation. The Commissioners advise on forestry matters and are responsible to the Scottish First Minister, the Minister of Agriculture, Fisheries and Food, and the National Assembly for Wales.

The Commission provides grants to private woodland owners for tree planting and woodland management, controls tree felling, and sets standards for forestry as a whole. Forest Enterprise, an agency of the Commission, develops and manages the Commission's forests and forestry estate, supplying timber and opportunities for recreation, and enhancing nature conservation and the forest environment. Forest Research is the R&D agency of the Commission.

Financed partly by the Government and partly by receipts from sales of timber and other produce, and from rents, the

Table 27.8: International Forestry Comparisons

Country	Forest area (million hectares)	Total land area (million hectares)	Forestry as % of land area
United Kingdom	2.5	24.2	10
Austria	3.9	8.3	47
Belgium/Luxembourg	0.7	3.3	22
Denmark	0.4	4.2	10
Finland	20.0	30.5	66
France	15.0	55.0	27
Germany	10.7	34.9	31
Greece	6.5	12.9	51
Irish Republic	0.6	6.9	8
Italy	6.5	29.4	22
Netherlands	0.3	3.4	10
Portugal	2.9	9.2	31
Spain	8.4	49.9	17
Sweden	24.4	41.2	59
EU	102.9	313.2	33
Norway	8.1	30.7	26
Switzerland	1.1	4.0	29
Russian Federation	763.5	1,688.9	45
China	133.0	932.6	14
Japan	25.0	37.7	67
United States	212.5	915.9	23
World	3,454.4	12,981.0	27

Source: UN Food and Agriculture Organisation *State of the World's Forests 1997*

Commission's grant in aid for 1997–98 was £58 million, from which £9 million was deducted for reimbursement of EU co-financing of private woodlands grants.

As part of its strategy, announced in 1998, to restore Britain's woodland heritage, the Government plans to spend £40 million a year planting new trees in England. Emphasis is on the right mix of trees in the right place, with a ban on commercial planting of conifers.

During 1981–98, 233,440 hectares (583,600 acres), worth £258.1 million, of Forestry Commission land were sold, of which over 60% was forest land. The Government has imposed a moratorium on large-scale forest sales.

Forestry Initiatives

With an estimated 1,000 sq km (386 sq miles) of damaged land to be developed, the initial focus of the Forestry Commission's Land Regeneration Unit is on the creation of new woodlands (of 30 hectares—74 acres—or larger) in the central English coalfields and on wider plans to create working forests of about 800–1,200 hectares (1,980–2,970 acres). It has identified 175,000 hectares (432,400 acres) of derelict land suitable for trees that will stabilise and decontaminate the soil. The planned National Forest in England (520 sq km—200 sq miles) covers parts of Staffordshire, Derbyshire and Leicestershire, with the aim of increasing woodland from 6% to a third of its area—16,500 hectares (40,775 acres). For Community Forests, see p. 326.

Forestry in Northern Ireland

Woodland and forest cover about 82,000 hectares (203,000 acres) of Northern Ireland. State-owned forest constitutes 61,000 hectares (150,700 acres).

The Forest Service is an executive agency within the Department of Agriculture and is responsible for promoting the interests of forestry. It achieves this through sustainable management and expansion of State-owned forests and the encouragement of private forestry through grant aid for planting. The Forest Service offered 290,500 cubic metres (10.3 million cubic feet) of timber for sale during 1998 and receipts from this sale totalled £4.78 million. Forestry and timber processing employ about 1,100 people.

Further Reading

Agriculture in the United Kingdom 1998. MAFF and the Agriculture Departments. The Stationery Office, 1999.

Economic Report on Scottish Agriculture 1999. The Stationery Office, 1999.

Environmental Effects of Agriculture. DETR, 1998.

Scottish Agriculture Facts and Figures 1999. Scottish Executive, 1999.

United Kingdom Sea Fisheries Statistics 1998. MAFF. The Stationery Office.

Annual Reports

MAFF and the Intervention Board. The Stationery Office.

Forestry Commission. The Stationery Office.

Websites

MAFF: www.maff.gov.uk

Forestry Commission: www.forestry.gov.uk

28 Manufacturing and Construction

Manufacturing continues to play an important role in the modern economy, although services now generate about three times as much gross domestic product (GDP) and four times as much employment. The UK excels in industries such as chemicals, plastics, pharmaceuticals, electronics, motor vehicles and components, aerospace, offshore equipment, and paper and printing, where British companies are among the world's largest and most successful. Britain's construction industry has made its mark around the world and continues to be involved in some of the most celebrated building projects both at home and abroad.

Introduction

Manufacturing accounted for 19.7% of gross value added (at current basic prices) in 1998 and for 16.8% of employment (4 million people) in the UK in 1999. The East Midlands and West Midlands have the highest proportion of manufacturing employees and London the lowest. Almost all manufacturing is carried out by private sector businesses. Overseas companies have a strong presence (see p. 422), being responsible for a quarter of manufacturing output in the UK.

The recession in the early 1990s led to a decline in manufacturing output, but it began to rise again in 1993. By 1998, the volume of output was 10% above the level in 1991 and 1992, but has declined a little since. Some industries, including chemicals, rubber and plastic products, electrical and optical equipment, and transport equipment, have achieved substantial growth following the recession, but output of other sectors,

including textiles, leather and wood products, remains well below their 1990 levels.

The construction industry contributed 5.3% of gross value added in 1998. Following a period of marked decline as recession affected the industry in the early 1990s, output has picked up since 1993 and was 9.2% higher in 1998 than in 1993, although still below pre-recession levels.

Sectors of Manufacturing

Relative sizes of enterprises are shown in Table 28.1. An outline of the main manufacturing sectors is given below. A brief statistical summary is included for most sectors, taken from the appropriate Office for National Statistics (ONS) sector review. In some circumstances, statistics in these summaries may differ from figures in the text where these have been obtained from the Department of Trade and Industry or the appropriate trade association. The variations

The manufacturing base at the turn of the 20th century was much larger than it is now. In 1901, statistics for employment in textile factories showed that over 1 million people were employed in this industry alone, over half of whom worked in cotton factories. Almost twice as many women as men were employed, as were over 36,000 children under 14 (as half-timers).

	Males	Females	Total
Cotton	193,830	328,793	522,623
Wool, worsted and shoddy[a]	106,598	153,311	259,909
Flax, jute, hemp, and china grass	45,732	104,587	150,319
Silk	8,966	22,589	31,555
Hosiery	9,587	28,962	38,549
Lace	10,462	7,440	17,902
Elastic, cocoa-nut fibre and horsehair	4,036	4,460	8,496
All materials	379,211	650,142	1,029,353

[a] An inferior cloth made partly from the shredded fibre of old woollen cloth.
Source: *Statistical Abstract for the United Kingdom*

Table 28.1: Manufacturing—Size of Businesses by Turnover and Employment 1999

Annual turnover (£'000)	Number of businesses	Employment size	Number of businesses
1–49	25,175	1–9	110,595
50–99	25,960	10–19	19,295
100–249	33,290	20–49	12,400
250–499	21,805	50–99	4,715
500–999	17,295	100–199	3,115
1,000–1,999	12,130	200–499	2,050
2,000–4,999	9,450	500–999	650
5,000–9,999	4,150	1,000+	475
10,000–49,999	4,155		
50,000+	1,160		
Total	**154,570**	**Total**	**153,295**

Source: *Size Analysis of United Kingdom Business*. Business Monitor PA 1003
Note: Not all businesses covered by the inquiry have been allocated by employment size—this accounts for the difference in totals.

usually reflect differences in coverage of the industry concerned. In addition, the value of exports can include that of re-exports of imported and factored goods, and can exceed the sales values quoted.

Food, Drink and Tobacco

Food and Drink

The UK's food and drink manufacturing and processing industry has accounted for a growing proportion of total domestic food supply since the 1940s. The largest concentration of enterprises is to be found in the production of bread, cakes and fresh pastry goods, followed by those engaged in processing and preserving fruit and vegetables. The greatest number of food-based jobs are in Yorkshire (15.7% in 1997), the South East and London (12%), and the North West (11.4%). Spirits production gives Scotland the highest concentration of employment in the alcoholic and soft drinks manufacturing industry (about 30% of drinks manufacturing employment), with a significant proportion of jobs in its economically deprived rural areas; the South East has the second highest concentration (about 20%) of drinks-related jobs. By far the

Table 28.2: Output and Investment in Manufacturing, 1998 £ million

1992 Standard Industrial Classification category	Gross value added at current basic prices	Gross fixed capital formation
Food, beverages and tobacco	19,905	2,737
Textiles and textile products	6,747	531
Leather and leather products	728	40
Wood and wood products	1,928	254
Pulp, paper and paper products, publishing and printing	17,592	2,428
Coke, petroleum products and nuclear fuel	2,416	313
Chemicals, chemical products and man-made fibres	15,228	3,118
Rubber and plastic products	7,497	1,046
Other non-metal mineral products	5,158	562
Basic metals and fabricated metal products	15,752	1,882
Machinery and equipment not elsewhere classified	13,259	1,051
Electrical and optical equipment	18,970	2,456
Transport equipment	16,246	3,107
Other manufacturing	5,880	537
Total	**147,306**	**20,062**

Sources: *United Kingdom National Accounts 1999—the Blue Book; Quarterly Capital Expenditure Inquiry* (ONS)

Food, Drink and Tobacco—statistics for 1998 unless indicated

	Sales[a] (£ million)	Index of production (1995 = 100)	Exports (£ million)	Number of enterprises	Investment (£ million, 1995 prices)
Sector of which:	57,927	102.3	9,288	7,510[b]	2,656
Food and drink	*55,339*	*103.2*	*8,239*	*7,500* [c]	*2,505*
Tobacco	*2,622* [d]	*97.8*	*1,049*	*15*	*151*

Source: ONS Sector Review: *Food, Drink and Tobacco*
[a] 1996.
[b] The difference between the total and the sums of the component parts is due to rounding.
[c] Of these, 665 were drink enterprises.
[d] 1997.

biggest food and drinks export category is alcoholic drinks, which account for nearly a third of the value of total food and drink sales overseas; the largest food exporting sector is biscuits and confectionery.

Among the biggest companies involved in food manufacturing and processing are Unilever, Cadbury Schweppes, Nestlé, Associated British Foods, Tate and Lyle, Unigate, Northern Foods, United Biscuits, Hillsdown Holdings, Hazlewood Foods and Ranks Hovis McDougall (RHM). Diageo (formed by the merger of Guinness and Grand Metropolitan) had a turnover of £17.7 billion in the 18 months to June 1998 and around 70,000 employees. As well as being one of the world's leading producers of spirits, it has other extensive food and drink interests, including Burger King, the world's second largest restaurant chain. Allied Domecq is also among the world's leading alcoholic drinks companies, with significant operations in wines and spirits. Specialist small and medium-sized firms in the food and drink manufacturing industry thrive alongside these large concerns, supplying high-quality 'niche' products, often to small retail outlets, such as delicatessens.

Frozen foods and chilled convenience foods, such as frozen potato products and ready-prepared meals, fish and shellfish dishes, salads and pasta, together with yogurts, desserts and instant snacks, have formed some of the fastest-growing sectors of the food market in recent years. The range of ready-cooked meals is expanding rapidly. Many new low-fat and fat-free items are being introduced, ranging from dairy products to complete prepared meals, and organic foods are also becoming more widely available. There has been a substantial rise in sales of vegetarian foods (both natural vegetable dishes and vegetable-based substitutes of meat products, where soya plays a big role). For genetically modified foods, see chapter 27.

Around 29% of liquid milk in the UK is distributed through a doorstep delivery system employing about 21,000 people; the proportion is, however, declining as supermarkets increase their share of the market. Household consumption of liquid milk per head—2.23 litres (3.93 pints) a week—is among the highest in the world. Consumption of skimmed and semi-skimmed milk accounted for 64% of total milk sales in 1998. The British dairy industry accounts for about 79% of butter and 67% of cheese supplies to the domestic market, and achieves significant sales in overseas markets.

Bread production in 1998 was over 1.8 million tonnes. The two largest producers are Allied Bakeries, owned by Associated British Foods, and British Bakeries which is part of RHM, owned by the Tomkins Group. The UK's largest plant cake producer (Manor Bakeries/Mr Kipling/Lyons) is also part of RHM. A recent innovation—long-life bread—now accounts for more than 4% of the plant bread market. Production of bagels grew by 57% between 1996 and 1998. The morning goods market (including rolls, croissants, scones and teacakes) grew by 5% in 1998, with an estimated retail value of £417 million. A feature of the bread-making market is a move towards production in in-store bakeries, notably in supermarkets. Part-baked bread (which allows newly baked bread to be available throughout the day in a matter of minutes) is sold, for example, to in-store bakeries and restaurants. Other trends have been a steady increase in the varieties available, and the growth of the sandwich market. Sales of ready-made sandwiches through major multiples and sandwich bars, etc. are now worth £2.8 billion a year.

The brewing industry has four major national brewery groups—Scottish Courage, Bass, Whitbread and Carlsberg-Tetley—and 500 regional and local brewers of beer. British malt, which is made almost entirely from home-grown barley, is used by brewers throughout the world. Lager now accounts for 60% of all beer sales, but there is still a demand for the vast range of traditional cask-conditioned and brewery-conditioned ales and stouts. Recently there has been a shift towards stronger bottled beers, a significant proportion of which are imported. Another recent trend has been a sizeable import of beer bought on the continent, mainly in Calais, by British travellers. The main brewers are modernising and rationalising their brewing and distribution facilities to meet the changing pattern of demand, while also taking action to develop their public houses (pubs) and restaurants, concentrating increasingly on 'branded' or 'themed' pubs and restaurants.

The Scotch whisky industry is one of the UK's top export earners, with overseas sales worth £2.0 billion in 1998. About 90% of production is exported to 200 markets worldwide, the European Union (EU) taking 45%, the United States 13% and Japan 6% by volume. Some 12,000 people work in the Scotch whisky industry and a further 48,000 are employed in associated sectors, for instance supplying ingredients and materials. There are over 90 Scotch whisky distilleries in Scotland, producing either malt whisky or grain whisky. Most Scotch whisky consumed is a blend of malt and grain. Examples of well-known blended brands are J & B, Johnnie

Walker, Chivas Regal, Ballantine's Famous Grouse, Bell's and Teacher's. Glenfiddich, Glenmorangie, Glen Grant and Macallan are some of the best-known single malt Scotch whiskies. Gin and vodka production are also important parts of the spirits industry.

In a highly competitive market, English and Welsh wines have a distinctive local identity. Some 386 vineyards and 134 wineries, mainly in the south, produce an average of 1.5 million litres of wine a year, most of which is white. Quality continues to improve with a combination of more experienced winemakers, modern technologies and better winemaking equipment. Cider is made primarily in south-west England, and in Gloucestershire, Herefordshire and Worcestershire.

The soft drinks industry produces still and carbonated drinks, dilutable drinks, fruit juices and juice drinks, natural mineral waters, and spring and table waters. The UK market is worth more than £6.8 billion a year, with Coca-Cola and Schweppes Beverages the largest supplier. It is one of the fastest-growing sectors of the grocery trade, responsible for introducing many innovative products each year. Bottled waters have experienced the fastest growth within the sector during the past five years, averaging increases in value of 10% a year. In 1998 the British consumed 175 litres of soft drinks per person, compared with 128 litres in 1988—an increase of 37%; there was an increase in 1998 in the volume of the still fruit drinks market of 50%.

Tobacco

The British tobacco industry manufactures around 90% of the cigarettes and tobacco goods sold in the UK. The market is supplied by three major manufacturers—Imperial Tobacco Ltd, Gallaher Ltd and Rothmans (UK) Ltd (which recently became part of British American Tobacco). British American Tobacco is also a major manufacturer, which mainly markets its products outside the UK, providing 16% of the world's cigarette supply—900 billion cigarettes in 1998. The industry specialises in the production of high-quality cigarettes made from flue-cured tobacco, and achieves significant export sales—£1.1 billion in 1998. Europe, the Middle East and Africa are important overseas markets. The UK tobacco industry is one of the top ten balance-of-payments earners in UK manufacturing industry.

Textiles, Clothing and Footwear

Annual turnover in the UK textiles, clothing and footwear industry is around £20 billion, and about 308,000 people are employed. The sector has been significantly affected by competition from imported goods, and in 1998 the volume of sales was 11% below the level in 1995. To meet the intense competition, UK textile and clothing manufacturers have modernised and rationalised their domestic operations, and in some cases have invested in production facilities abroad. In addition, firms are shifting into higher-value products, to benefit from the UK's strengths in fashion, design and information technology. New technologies, largely designed to improve response times and give greater flexibility in production, are being used throughout the industries. British textile firms remain world leaders in wool and worsted and technical textiles.

For textiles, there is a high degree of regional concentration: cotton textiles in the North West, fine knitwear in Scotland, linen in Northern Ireland, woollens and worsteds in Yorkshire, and knitwear in the East Midlands. The clothing industry is more dispersed throughout the UK, with significant concentrations in the West Midlands, and north and east London. The principal textile and clothing products are spun textile fibres, woven and knitted fabrics, household and industrial textiles, carpets based chiefly on wool, cotton and synthetic fibres, as well as a full range of clothing and footwear.

The UK textile and clothing industries comprise a few substantial multi-process companies, but are mainly dominated by small and medium-sized firms, some of which subcontract work to other companies or to home workers. Two of the world's major groups are Coats Viyella, and Courtaulds Textiles, with turnover of almost £2.4 billion and £0.9 billion, respectively, in 1997. Raw wool is scoured and cleaned in the UK in preparation for woollen and worsted spinning

Textiles, Clothing and Footwear—statistics for 1998 unless indicated

	Sales (£ million)	Index of production (1995 = 100)	Exports (£ million)	Number of enterprises	Investment (£ million, 1995 prices)
Sector	n.a.	89.0	6,543	14,200	633
of which:					
Textiles	9,094[a]	92.2	3,207	5,765	375
Clothing	5,343[b]	82.8	2,386	7,295	213
Footwear and leather goods	1,964[c]	89.2	950	1,140	45

Source: ONS Sector Reviews: *Textiles and Clothing, Footwear and Leather Goods*
[a] 1997.
[b] 1995.
[c] 1996.
n.a. = not available.

and weaving. (Worsted is a fine wool fabric often used for making suits.) British mills also process rare fibres such as cashmere and angora. Production includes yarn and fabrics of cotton, synthetic fibres and cotton-synthetic mixes, with large-scale dyeing and printing of cotton and synthetic fibre fabric. The high quality and variety of design make the UK one of the world's leading producers of woven carpets.

Industrial textiles account for an increasing proportion of textile industry output, covering such items as conveyor belting and geotextiles used in civil engineering. Many of these are non-woven. Synthetic polypropylene yarn is used in the manufacture of carpet backing and ropes, and woven into fabrics for a wide range of applications in the packaging, upholstery, building and motor vehicle industries.

The clothing industry is more labour-intensive than textiles. While a broad range of clothing is imported from Europe and Asia, British industry supplies nearly two-fifths of domestic demand. Until 1997 exports rose consistently through the 1990s, since the British fashion designer industry regained prominence during the 1980s, and traditional design and high-quality production enable branded clothing companies such as Daks Simpson and Jaeger to compete successfully overseas. UK firms have had success in the growing market for branded street and club wear. Exports have, however, fallen both in 1997 and 1998.

Output of footwear has been particularly affected by the strength of sterling and increasing competitiveness of imports. Footwear manufacturers, with around 18,000 employees, are predominantly found in Northamptonshire, Somerset, Leicestershire and Lancashire. Nearly 50% of production by value is exported, with the UK particularly renowned for classic men's formal shoes and youth street fashion footwear.

Paper, Printing and Publishing

The UK paper and board sector has a relatively small number of medium and large firms—97 paper and board mills, employing 22,000 people—whereas printing in particular has a very large number of small businesses. Paper and board are produced for further industrial processing, corrugated paper, sacks, bags, cartons, boxes, household goods, stationery and a host of other articles. Production has been increasingly concentrated in large-scale units to enable the industry to compete more effectively; between 1987 and 1998 output in the pulp and paper industry increased by 6.5%. Over half the industry is made up of forestry product companies from Scandinavia, North America, Australia and elsewhere. Among the biggest British-owned groups in terms of production are St Regis, BPB Paperboard and Arjo Wiggins. There has been a significant trend towards waste-based

Paper, Printing and Publishing—statistics for 1998 unless indicated

	Sales[a] (£ million)	Index of production (1995 = 100)	Exports[a] (£ million)	Number of enterprises	Investment (£ million, 1995 prices)
Sector	36,312	98.2	4,507	30,320	n.a.
of which:					
Pulp, paper and paper products	12,378	89.5	2,210	2,725	803 [b]
Publishing and printing, etc.	23,934	101.7	2,297	27,595	1,786

Source: ONS Sector Review: Paper, Publishing and Printing
[a]1996.
[b]1997.
n.a.= not available

packaging grades. Usage of recycled waste paper is increasing, and recycled paper made up 52.4% of the raw material for UK newspapers in 1998.

Much publishing and printing employment and output is carried out in firms based in south-east England. Mergers have led to the formation of large groups in newspaper, magazine and book publishing. Pearson, with turnover of almost £2.4 billion in 1998, controls some of the world's leading educational publishing businesses. The British book-publishing industry is a major exporter; in 1998 it issued almost 103,000 new titles.

The UK printing industry has an annual turnover of around £12.5 billion and employs 203,000 people in Great Britain. It is undergoing significant technological change, with digital technology enabling much greater automation and standardisation, while colour printing is becoming cheaper and more widely available. The UK runs a notable trade surplus in printing and publishing—£824 million in 1998. Exports are dominated by books and periodicals, and imports by books and trade advertising.

Chemicals and Chemical Products

The chemicals industry is one of the UK's major manufacturing sectors, directly employing 249,000 people in over 3,600 companies. It had total product sales of £33 billion in 1997, of which two-thirds was exported. The sector does, however, also underpin much of the rest of UK manufacturing industry, with chemicals being essential feedstocks for most other industrial processes.

It is a diverse industry, with important representation in all primary chemical sectors— ranging from bulk petrochemicals to low-volume, high-value specialised organics. It includes key industrial materials such as plastics and synthetic rubber, and other products such as man-made fibres, soaps, detergents, cosmetics, adhesives, dyes and inks, and intermediates for the pharmaceutical industry.

Bulk Chemicals

The UK's North Sea oil and gas provide accessible feedstocks for its large organics

Chemicals and Chemical Products—statistics for 1998 unless indicated

	Sales[a] (£ million)	Index of production (1995 = 100)	Exports (£ million)	Number of enterprises	Investment (£ million, 1995 prices)
Sector	32,688	103.4	22,498	3,645	3,156

Source: ONS Sector Review: Chemicals, Rubber and Plastic Products
[a] 1997.

sector, including such products as ethylene, propylene, benzene and methanol. These provide the basic building blocks for the manufacture of many downstream chemical products, including polymers used for the manufacture of plastics products; and synthetic fibres such as nylon, polyamide, polyester and acrylics used in the textiles, clothing and footwear industries.

There is substantial inorganics production, with sales of some £2 billion a year—including sulphuric acid, chlorine and caustic soda, based upon minerals such as salt, sulphur, and phosphate ores or reaction between gases. These also serve many other downstream chemical processes.

Formulated Products

The UK is also strong in the 'formulation' of chemical products, in areas such as paints, inks, soaps and detergents, and cosmetics and perfumes. The coatings industry on its own has annual sales of around £2 billion. Home decorative products include household names such as Dulux and Crown Paints. The industrial coatings sector includes decoration on cans, and anti-fouling marine coatings.

Specialty Chemicals

For the chemicals industry, the last few years have brought increasingly rapid market and technological changes. Imperial Chemical Industries plc (ICI) is one of the world's largest specialty chemicals groups, with turnover of more than £9 billion in 1998, and is one of the world's largest paint producers (with manufacturing in 25 countries and sales in over 120). The development of specialty chemicals to meet specific needs through the application of sophisticated 'chemistry' illustrates this dimension. The pharmaceutical and agrochemical sectors are at the forefront of such innovation. In recent years, the application of chirality[1] in synthesis has allowed firms such as AstraZeneca to make drugs that are more closely tailored to targets.

Pharmaceuticals

The British pharmaceuticals industry, which is largely based in the South East and North West, is the world's second largest exporter of medicines, accounting for about 11.5% of the world export market. It manufactures the complete range of medicinal products—human and veterinary medicines, medical dressings and dental materials. In recent times, the largest growth has been in medicines that act on the respiratory system, followed by cardiovascular, muscular and skeletal, anti-infective and alimentary tract remedies. Pharmaceutical exports in 1998 reached £6.3 billion. The main overseas markets are North America, Japan and Western Europe.

Over 400 pharmaceutical manufacturers and research organisations operate in the UK, including several British and US parent multinationals which dominate production. Glaxo Wellcome (employing about 53,100 people and operating in 57 countries), SmithKline Beecham and AstraZeneca feature in the top ten UK-based companies (see p. 385). The merger in April 1999 between Zeneca and the Swedish company Astra is the biggest European merger to date in this sector, and with annual sales of £6.25 billion AstraZeneca has become the world's third biggest pharmaceuticals company.

Some 60,000 people work in the pharmaceuticals industry, of whom about a third are engaged in R&D; another 250,000 are employed in related sectors. The industry invested £2.5 billion in R&D in 1998, about one-fifth of British industry's total R&D expenditure. Glaxo Wellcome, SmithKline Beecham and AstraZeneca are the UK's top three companies in terms of R&D expenditure (see Table 26.1, p. 426). US multinational group Pfizer has invested in expansion of its medicines research centre at Sandwich, Kent. Pfizer is also to site its new UK and European corporate headquarters at Walton Dales, Reigate, Surrey in a £50 million investment.

---

[1] Chiral compounds are mirror images of each other, analogous to left and right handed forms. One form may be more effective, or safer, than the other.

Major developments pioneered in the UK are semi-synthetic penicillins and cephalosporins, both powerful antibiotics, and new treatments for ulcers, asthma, arthritis, migraine, coronary heart disease and erectile dysfunction (Viagra was developed in the UK by Pfizer). The UK pharmaceuticals industry has discovered and developed more leading medicines than any other country apart from the United States, including 13 of the world's current top 50 best-selling drugs. UK laboratories put about 20 new pharmaceutical products on the market each year. Among the best-selling drugs produced by the three largest UK-owned companies are:

- Glaxo Wellcome—Zantac (for treating ulcers), Imigran (migraine), Zofran (for countering the unpleasant side-effects of cancer treatment), Serevent (respiratory disease) and Epivir (HIV/AIDS);

- SmithKline Beecham—Augmentin (for treating a wide range of infections), Seroxat/Paxil (for depression) and Relifex/Relafen (for arthritis); and

- AstraZeneca—Losec (an anti-ulcer drug), Zestril (heart disease), Tenormin (beta blocker), Zoladex (a prostate cancer therapy), Nolvadex (a breast cancer treatment), Diprivan (an anaesthetic), Pulmicort (for asthma), Plendil (heart disease/angina), Seloken (beta blocker) and Xylocaine (local anaesthetic).

Biotechnology

The UK biotechnology industry is second only to that of the United States, employing an estimated 14,000 people directly. As well as AstraZeneca, Glaxo Wellcome and SmithKline Beecham, there are some 270 smaller specialist dedicated biotechnology firms—about a quarter of the number in Europe—with particular strengths in biopharmaceuticals. The industry benefits strongly from British universities' considerable expertise in the biosciences and related disciplines. Important R&D activities include gene therapy, genomics, bioinformatics, combinatorial chemistry, regulation of the cell cycle, and the development of transgenic animals as sources of organs and as bioreactors.

Man-made Fibres

Synthetic fibres are supplied to the textiles, clothing and footwear industries. The main types of synthetic fibre are still those first developed in the 1940s: regenerated cellulosic fibres such as viscose, and the major synthetic fibres like nylon polyamide, polyester and acrylics. Extensive research continues to produce a variety of innovative products; antistatic and flame-retardant fibres are examples. More specialist products include the aramids (with very high thermal stability and strength), elastanes (giving very high stretch and recovery) and melded fabrics (produced without the need for knitting or weaving).

Courtaulds (acquired by Akzo Nobel of the Netherlands in 1998) is one of the biggest chemical companies in the UK. It was responsible for developing the first new artificial fibre for decades, Tencel, a solvent-spun, biodegradable fibre, which is twice as strong as cotton but soft enough to be used by designers of luxury garments.

Rubber and Plastics Products

Over 234,000 people are employed by over 6,800 enterprises in the rubber and plastics industries. Rubber products include tyres and tubes, pipes, hoses, belting and floor coverings, and many have applications in the automotive industry. The largest firms in this sector are major tyre manufacturers such as Goodyear and Michelin. The highest concentrations of plastics employment are in the West Midlands (with 16.4% of total employment), the North West, the East Midlands and the South East. Plastics have a multitude of applications in the packaging, building, electrical and electronic, transport, medical, household goods and clothing industries. The UK's plastics industry continues to be a world leader in material specification and design, with new processes allowing stronger plastics to replace traditional materials and develop new applications.

Rubber and Plastics Products—statistics for 1998 unless indicated					
	Sales[a] (£ million)	Index of production (1995 = 100)	Exports (£ million)	Number of enterprises	Investment (£ million, 1995 prices)
Sector	16,289	101.1	4,116	6,835	1,040

Source: ONS Sector Review: *Chemicals, Rubber and Plastic Products*
[a] 1996.

Among the larger firms in a sector characterised by many small and medium-sized businesses is British Polythene Industries, manufacturing products such as carrier bags, sacks and shrink film. In the moulded plastics sector, Linpac's output includes food packaging and components for the automotive sector.

Glass, Ceramics and Building Materials

The UK is a world leader in the manufacture of glass used in windows, doors and cladding. Flat glass is made through the float process, developed by Pilkington plc and licensed to glassmakers throughout the world. About half of Pilkington's sales are in glass products for buildings, while the company is the world's largest supplier of glass for cars, with about one-quarter of vehicles containing its glass. Total industry turnover in 1997–98 was £2.7 billion. The manufacture and supply of windows and doors are carried out by a large number of other companies operating in one of three basic product sectors—timber, metal (aluminium and steel) and UPVC. The UK also has several leading lead crystal suppliers such as Wedgwood, Dartington, Edinburgh Crystal and Royal Brierley.

The ceramics industry manufactures domestic ceramic tableware, as well as durables such as sanitaryware, tiles and clay pipes for the building trade. It is heavily concentrated in the West Midlands. Domestic tableware production includes fine china, bone china, earthenware and stoneware. Tableware is produced predominantly in Stoke-on-Trent. The UK is one of the world's leading manufacturers and exporters of fine bone china: Wedgwood, Spode and Royal Doulton are among the most famous names. Research is being conducted into ceramics use in housebuilding and diesel and jet engines. Important industrial ceramics invented in the UK include some forms of silicon carbide and sialons, which can withstand ultra-high temperatures.

Most crushed rock, sand and gravel quarried by the aggregates industry (with a total volume of 220 million tonnes in Great Britain in 1997) is used in construction. The brick industry, one of the UK's oldest, is regarded as the world's most technically advanced. In 1998 some 3 billion bricks were produced in Great Britain. Portland cement, a 19th-century British innovation, is the most widely used chemical compound in the world. Blue Circle is the UK's largest producer of cement. Almost 85 million sq m of concrete building blocks were produced in Great Britain in 1998.

The UK is a major exporter of china clay (kaolin—1.9 million tonnes in 1998), three-quarters of which is used as coatings and

Glass, Ceramics and Building Materials—statistics for 1998 unless indicated					
	Sales[a] (£ million)	Index of production (1995 = 100)	Exports (£ million)	Number of enterprises	Investment (£ million, 1995 prices)
Sector	9,388	96.8	1,954	4,880	542

Source: ONS Sector Review: *Glass, Ceramics and Building Materials*
[a] 1996.

fillers in paper-making, the remainder going into the ceramic, paint, rubber and plastics industries. The main producer is English China Clays International (ECCI), part of the English China Clays Group, which had turnover of £834 million in 1998. ECCI is being taken over by a French company; the combined company would, subject to regulatory agreement, control some 35% of the world market in high-quality kaolin.

Metals and Fabricated Metal Products

The Industrial Revolution in the UK was based to a considerable extent on the manufacture of iron and steel and heavy machinery. These sectors remain important parts of the industrial economy. The major areas of steel production are now concentrated in south Wales and northern England, with substantial processing in the Midlands and Yorkshire. Major restructuring in the steel industry took place during the 1980s and 1990s. Metals can be recycled many times; every year the British metals recycling industry processes about 10 million tonnes of scrap metal.

From total crude steel output of 17.3 million tonnes, British producers delivered 15.5 million tonnes of finished steel in 1998, of which 54% was exported to well over 100 countries. Nearly three-quarters of UK steel exports go to other EU member states. Germany is the UK's biggest market. Since 1990 annual steel industry exports have increased by 21.5%—they were worth £3.6 billion in 1998. In 1998, British Steel was the sixth largest steel producer in the world, employing 44,000 people worldwide (of whom 34,000 are in the UK) and producing 86% of the UK's total crude steel. In 1999, British Steel announced a proposed merger with

Hoogovens, the large Dutch metals producer, which would create Europe's biggest steelmaker and the third largest in the world. British Steel's output is based on semi-finished steel, strip mill products, plate, heavy sections, bars, wire rods and tubes. These are used principally in the construction, automotive, engineering, transport, metal goods, packaging and energy industries. British Steel is Europe's biggest producer of engineering steels—specialist grades used to make components for the automotive and aerospace industries. It owns 51% of Avesta Sheffield, one of Europe's leading stainless steel producers.

Products manufactured by other UK steel companies include reinforcing bars for the construction industry, wire rod, hot rolled bars, bright bars, tubes, and wire and wire products. The production of special steels is centred on the Sheffield area and includes stainless and alloy special steels for the aerospace and offshore oil and gas industries.

Steel has had a notable success in UK construction, with its market share of buildings of two or more storeys more than doubling from 30% in the early 1980s to 65% today. It has 90% of the single storey market. Total iron and steel sector sales are about £3.3 billion a year and consumption of constructional steelwork over 1 million tonnes.

Several multinational companies, including Alcan, Norsk Hydro, Kaiser, MIM and Quexco, have plants in Britain producing non-ferrous metals. The aluminium industry, which has raised its productivity and competitiveness significantly in recent years, supplies customers in the aerospace, transport, automotive and construction industries. Other important non-ferrous metal sectors are copper and copper alloys, used for electrical

Metals and Fabricated Metal Products—statistics for 1998 unless indicated

	Sales (£ million)	Index of production (1995 = 100)	Exports (£ million)	Number of enterprises	Investment (£ million, 1995 prices)
Sector	28,263[a]	98.6[b]	10,017	30,750	1,891

Source: ONS Sector Review: *Metals and Fabricated Metal Products*
[a] 1996.
[b] Also includes other non-metallic mineral products.

wire, cables and machinery, connectors, automotive components, plumbing and building products, and heat exchangers, boilers, tubing and electrical gear; lead for lead acid batteries and roofing; zinc for galvanising to protect steel; nickel, used principally as an alloying element to make stainless steel and high temperature turbine alloys; and titanium for high-strength, low-weight aerospace applications. Despite an overall decline in the castings industry, some foundries have invested in new melting, moulding and quality control equipment.

Fabricated metal products include pressure vessels, heat exchangers and storage tanks for chemical and oil-refining plant; steam-raising boilers; nuclear reactors; water and sewage treatment plant; and steelwork for bridges, buildings and industrial installations. Other products include central heating radiators and boilers, cutlery, tools and general hardware.

Machinery and Domestic Appliances

The highest concentration of employment in these industries is to be found in the West Midlands (with 16.1% of total employment), followed by the South East (12.4%) and the Eastern region (11.4%). Mechanical machine-building is an area in which British firms excel, especially internal combustion engines, power transmission equipment, pumps and compressors, wheeled tractors, construction and earth-moving equipment, and textile machinery.

The UK is a major producer of industrial engines, pumps, valves and compressors, and of pneumatic and hydraulic equipment. The Weir Group is the world's sixth biggest producer of pumps. Companies such as Mitsui-Babcock manufacture steam generators and other heavy equipment for power plants.

Alstom, which shares a joint venture with ABB in power generation, is one of only a handful of firms in the world which can supply the major components for a complete power station project and the transformers and switchgear needed in transmission and distribution of electricity. In the UK the company's strengths are steam turbine manufacture, switchgear manufacture, industrial gas turbines, and project design and management. The mechanical lifting and handling equipment industry makes cranes and transporters, lifting devices, escalators, conveyors, powered industrial trucks and air bridges, as well as electronically controlled and automatic handling systems. The commercial heating, ventilation, air-conditioning and refrigeration sector is served to a great extent by small and medium-sized firms, although several large multinational companies have sites in Britain.

Tractors and equipment used in agriculture, horticulture, forestry, sportsturf and gardens achieved export sales of £1.7 billion in 1998. This is largely due to three major multinationals with tractor plants in Britain which, together with JCB Landpower, export to nearly every country in the world. A range of specialist and innovative golf, parks and sports field machinery, lawn and garden products, and agricultural equipment complement the tractor business.

Most machine tools—mechanically operated tools for working on metal, wood or plastics—are bought by engineering, aerospace, automotive and metal goods industries, both at home and overseas (exports of just over £1 billion in 1998 accounted for 42% of turnover). Computer numerical-controlled machines make up an increasing proportion of output. Overseas-owned manufacturers (including those from the

Machinery and Domestic Appliances—statistics for 1998 unless indicated				
	Sales[a] (£ million)	Index of production (1995 = 100)	Exports[a] (£ million)	Number of enterprises	Investment (£ million, 1995 prices)
Sector	27,327	95.4	17,913	13,275	1,118

Source: ONS Sector Review: *Machinery and Domestic Appliances*
[a] 1996.

United States, Japan and Germany) have a significant involvement in the UK machine tool industry, in which half of the top 20 companies are British; the 600 Group is the biggest British company.

The mining and tunnelling equipment industry leads the world in the production of coal-cutting and road-heading (shearing) equipment, hydraulic roof supports, conveying equipment, flameproof transformers, switchgear, and subsurface transport equipment and control systems. JCB, Europe's biggest construction equipment manufacturer, is the world's largest producer of backhoe loaders and telescopic handlers, and a major exporter. The UK possesses the second largest engineering construction sector in the world. It serves the whole spectrum of process industries, although oil, gas and related industries are areas of particular strength. Most sales of textile machinery are to export markets. British innovations include computerised colour matching and weave simulation, friction spinning, high-speed computer-controlled knitting machines and electronic jacquard attachments for weaving looms. British companies also make advanced printing machinery and ceramic processing equipment, and other types of production machinery.

The domestic appliance sector manufactures major appliances, such as washing machines, cookers, refrigerators and dishwashers, as well as heating, water heaters and showers, ventilation products, floor cleaners and vacuum cleaners, and small appliances for the kitchen and bathroom. There are around 100 companies of all sizes in the UK. Energy efficiency and water conservation are progressively improving in home laundry products, and new technology is being applied to tumble dryers, frost-free refrigeration, cookers and microwave ovens. Visual design of what were traditionally 'white goods' is changing, giving a new look to kitchens, and modern design is also being applied to small appliances such as kettles and toasters. The UK is Europe's largest manufacturer of tumble dryers, with a trade surplus in this product of around £40 million.

Electrical and Optical Equipment

Production of office machinery and computers has more than trebled since 1990, while radio, television and communications equipment output is up by about 51%. However, output of medical and optical instruments fell by 6.5% during the 1990s, while that of electrical machinery and apparatus has fallen by about 10%.

Southern England provides a substantial proportion of employment (especially sales

Electrical and Optical Equipment—statistics for 1998 unless indicated					
	Sales[a] (£ million)	Index of production (1995 = 100)	Exports[a] (£ million)	Number of enterprises	Investment (£ million, 1995 prices)
Sector	41,886	113.3	39,169	14,000	2,535
of which:					
Office machinery and computers	10,573	154.6	12,558	1,375	248
Electrical machinery and apparatus	11,399	97.1	6,537	5,465	851
Radio, television and communications equipment	12,375	118.5	13,634	2,660	1,068
Medical, precision and optical instruments	7,539	93.8	6,440	4,500	368

Source: ONS Sector Review: Electrical and Optical Equipment
[a] 1996.

and administrative jobs) in these sectors, with Scotland and Wales having become important areas for inward investors. Scotland's electronics industry ('Silicon Glen'—in reality all of central Scotland) directly employs about 40,000 people. In 1998 electrical and instrument engineering accounted for exports worth £10 billion, 54% of Scotland's manufactured exports.

Many of the world's leading electronics firms have manufacturing plants in Britain. IBM, Sony, Compaq, Panasonic, Toshiba, NEC, Nortel, Seagate and Hewlett-Packard are among overseas-based multinationals with substantial manufacturing investment in the UK. The main electronic consumer goods produced are television sets (one-third of television sets made in the EU come from the UK). High-fidelity audio and video equipment is also produced. British-manufactured products have a worldwide reputation as high-quality goods aimed at the upper end of the market.

The computer industry in the UK is the largest in Europe, producing an extensive range of systems for all uses. For information on software, see chapter 30, p. 529. The multinational computer manufacturers in the UK include IBM, Compaq and Sun. Other companies, such as Psion (a pioneer of the 'palmtop' computer), have concentrated on developing new lines for specialised markets.

A broad range of other electrical machinery and apparatus is produced in the UK: power plant, electric motors, generators, transformers, switchgear, insulated wire and cable, and lighting equipment. Rolls-Royce Industrial Power Group produces highly efficient aero-derivative gas turbines in smaller applications. The UK is a world leader in the manufacture of generating sets. In the cables sector, AEI and Pirelli produce high-voltage transmission cables and optical fibre cables for telecommunications. TLG is the UK's largest manufacturer of lighting products.

The past ten years have seen the development of electronic service providers (contract electronic manufacturers) which manufacture and assemble products to the specification of another company. This global trend has encouraged some multinational producers to move away from manufacture to become solely designers, developers, marketers or sellers of their products. The UK is one of the leading locations in Europe for this type of business. Industry giants like SCI, Celestica, Solectron, AVEX, and Jabil already have UK facilities.

Communications Equipment

The domestic telecommunications equipment market is worth some £3.2 billion a year. Manufacturers have been investing heavily in facilities to meet the rapidly increasing demand for telecommunications services (see chapter 22). The main products are switching and transmission equipment, telephones and terminals. Marconi Communications is the UK's foremost telecommunications manufacturer. It is now wholly owned by the British GEC group. Its range includes PBXs (private branch exchanges), payphones, transmission systems and videoconferencing equipment. Other prominent manufacturers in the UK include Nortel and Alcatel. Transmission equipment and cables for telecommunications and information networks include submarine and high-specification data-carrying cables.

There has been remarkable growth in mobile communications (see p. 378), where the UK is among Europe's leading markets and manufacturing bases. The main producers—Motorola, Nokia, Ericsson and Lucent—all have UK production and design centres. Fibre optics (invented in the UK) and other optoelectronic components are also experiencing rapid growth, where Hewlett-Packard, Nortel, Pirelli and Corning have considerable UK facilities.

Another sector of the industry manufactures radio communications equipment, radar, radio and sonar navigational aids for ships and aircraft, thermal imaging systems, alarms and signalling apparatus, public broadcasting equipment and other capital goods. Radar was invented in the UK and British firms are still in the forefront of technological advances. Racal Avionics' X-band radar for aircraft ground movement control is in use at airports in several overseas countries. Solid-state secondary surveillance radar, manufactured by Cossor Electronics, is being supplied to numerous overseas civil aviation operators.

Medical Electronics

The high demand for advanced medical equipment in the UK stems from its comprehensive healthcare system and extensive clinical research and testing facilities in the chemical, biological, physical and molecular sciences. Important contributions have been made by British scientists and engineers to basic R&D in endoscopy, CT (computerised tomography) scanning, magnetic resonance imaging (MRI—pioneered in the UK), ultrasonic imaging, CADiagnosis and renal analysis. UK medical electronic firms—in total more than 1,000, employing about 35,000 people—continue their tradition of developing and manufacturing a range of medical equipment for domestic and overseas health sectors. Companies such as GEC and Oxford Instruments produce, among other things, ultrasound scanners, electromyography systems and patient monitoring systems for intensive and coronary care and other uses. Other British-owned companies include Invensys (created from the merger of BTR and Siebe), Smith and Nephew and Smiths Industries. About two-fifths of the medium to large companies have a US or other overseas parent.

Instrumentation and Control

A variety of electronic measurement and test equipment is made in the UK, as well as analytical instruments, process control equipment, and numerical control and

indication materials, all for use in machine tools. The instrument engineering industry makes measuring, photographic, cinematographic and reprographic items; watches, clocks and other timing devices; and medical surgical instruments. This sector has annual exports of about £4 billion and a positive trade balance of £910 million. Some 2,700 enterprises employ about 105,000 people.

Motor Vehicles

New car registrations increased by 3.5% in 1998 to 2.25 million, the second highest figure on record. Car production, at 1.75 million, was at its highest level since 1972. Output of motor vehicles and components has risen by about 16.5% since 1990. Vehicle manufacturers are increasingly pursuing a global market, with production no longer dominated by their traditional home markets. This is reflected in the rise in both UK exports and imports of motor vehicles. Exports (including components) were valued at £16.2 billion in 1998. A total of 1.02 million passenger cars were produced for export in 1998, well over twice as many as in 1990. Commercial vehicle production in 1998 was 227,000, slightly down on the last few years; 103,000 units were for export. Production is dominated by light commercial vehicles.

Around 810,000 jobs are dependent on the UK automotive industry, including 222,000 engaged in vehicle and component production and manufacturing activities. There are 490 motor vehicle manufacturers in the UK. Car output is dominated by seven overseas groups, accounting for 99% of the total: Rover (a subsidiary of BMW), Ford (including Jaguar),

Motor Vehicles—statistics for 1998 unless indicated					
	Sales[a] (£ million)	Index of production (1995 = 100)	Exports[a] (£ million)	Number of enterprises	Investment (£ million, 1995 prices)
Sector	30,869	110.1	16,232	2,440[b]	2,296

Source: ONS Sector Review: Vehicles and Other Transport
[a] 1996.
[b] Does not cover all firms regarded as being in the motor industry—the components sector (see p. 481), for example.

Vauxhall/IBC, Peugeot-Talbot, Honda, Nissan and Toyota. The remainder is in the hands of smaller, specialist producers such as Rolls-Royce (now owned by Volkswagen), whose cars are renowned for their quality and durability.

Capital investment continues on a large scale. Motor vehicle manufacturers invested more than £3 billion in the UK in 1998. Since their arrival in the mid-1980s, Nissan, Toyota and Honda have invested substantial sums in the UK, which is their main base for the European market. All three are now producing at least two models of car in the UK. A period of major change has accompanied the arrival of the three Japanese car manufacturers. Their management approach, high productivity, quality, workforce commitment and co-operative partnerships have had a positive effect on established car and component manufacturers alike. In the last decade UK vehicle production per person has increased by over 70%.

Rover Group ranges includes the highly successful Land Rover four-wheel drive vehicles and a full range of family cars. In 1998 Rolls-Royce began producing its first totally new model for nearly 20 years—the Silver Seraph—at its Crewe plant.

The main truck manufacturers are Leyland Trucks and Volvo. Dennis, based in Guildford, is also an important bus manufacturer. British-based bus companies achieve considerable sales in overseas markets. London Taxis International has recently launched a new version of the famous London taxi.

The automotive components manufacturing sector, with an annual turnover of £8 billion and employing 100,000 in Great Britain, is a major contributor to the UK motor industry. There are 1,245 companies (some 91% of them small and medium enterprises) involved, many of which also supply other sectors. Well-known British companies such as GKN, Pilkington, Unipart, Automotive Products, Invensys, Johnson Matthey and BBA have large automotive plants, as do other multinationals such as LucasVarity, Federal Mogul, Valeo, Bosch and Johnson Controls. In recent years the sector has enjoyed strong growth and rising productivity.

Recent investments and announcements of investment plans include Toyota's £150 million at its engine plant in Deeside, raising capacity to 400,000 engines a year; four Unipart joint ventures totalling over £80 million; Visteon's £128 million on four facilities in the UK; and Toyoda Gosei's £32 million on a Weatherstrips plant in Rotherham, Yorkshire creating 400 jobs by 2002.

Shipbuilding and Marine Engineering

The UK merchant shipbuilding industry, located mainly in Scotland and northern England, consists of 14 yards producing ships ranging from fishing vessels to large specialist craft for offshore exploration and exploitation work. At the end of March 1999 the industry's order-book was for 28 ships. The merchant ship repair and conversion industry, which has a strong presence in the market for small to medium-size craft, consists of 66 companies employing between 4,000 and 8,000 people, depending on activity levels. The turnover of the sector amounted to some £300 million in 1998. The three warship building and three refit and repair yards are looking to extend their area of interest into the merchant vessel sector. Together they employ about 17,000 people.

In addition, 455 firms are engaged in the manufacture and repair of pleasure and sporting boats. A few internationally known builders dominate the sector. The UK marine equipment industry has an annual turnover of over £825 million and employs about 9,500 people. (Few companies, however, are totally dedicated to marine equipment manufacture.) It tends to concentrate around the former major shipping and shipbuilding centres in London, Southampton, Liverpool, Newcastle upon Tyne, Glasgow and Belfast, and production includes sophisticated navigational and propulsion systems. About two-thirds of output is exported.

Over 25 years of oil and gas exploitation in the North Sea have generated a major offshore industry (see p. 493). Shipbuilders and fabricators build floating production storage and offload vessels (FPSOs) and semi-submersible units for drilling, production and emergency/maintenance support; drill ships;

jack-up rigs; modules; and offshore loading systems. Harland and Wolff of Belfast is a world leader in the FPSO and drill ship fields. UIE Scotland, Highlands Fabricators, John Brown and McDermott Scotland are among the larger contractors employed by the oil operators for the design and manufacture of jack-up oil rigs and semi-submersibles. Many other firms supply equipment and services to the offshore industry, notably diving expertise, consultancy, design, project management and R&D. A number have used their experience of North Sea projects to establish themselves in oil and gas markets throughout the world.

Railway Equipment

There are several hundred UK companies engaged in the manufacture of railway equipment for both domestic and overseas markets, mainly producing specialist components and systems for use in rolling stock, signalling, track and infrastructure applications. Three large multinational train builders, Adtranz (German-owned), Alstom (UK-French) and Bombardier (Canadian-owned), have UK bases. British Steel Railway Products is one of the world's leading manufacturers of steel rail.

Aerospace and Defence

The UK's aerospace industry is one of only three in the world with a complete capability across the whole spectrum of aerospace. Turnover in 1998 was about £17.3 billion, of which approximately 67% was exported, compared with £8.4 billion in 1987. The industry contributed £1.6 billion to the UK's balance of payments in 1998. On a wider definition of the aerospace industry, exports

are as much as £11.7 billion. Some 109,000 people are directly employed, with the North West, South West and East Midlands providing the highest number of jobs. The biennial Farnborough International Exhibition and Flying Display, organised by the Society of British Aerospace Companies, is one of the world's premier airshows.

Among the leading companies are British Aerospace (BAe), with turnover of over £7 billion in 1998, and Rolls-Royce, both of which are among the UK's top five exporters. BAe produces both civil and military aircraft, as well as aircraft components and guided weapons, employing 43,000 people altogether. At the end of 1998 its order book was £8.6 billion, of which £6.3 billion represented defence-related orders.

The industry's activities cover designing and constructing airframes, aero-engines, guided weapons, simulators and space satellites, materials, flight controls including 'fly-by-wire' and 'fly-by-light' equipment (see p. 484), materials, avionics and complex components, with their associated services. In order to improve fuel economy, engine and airframe manufacturers use lighter materials such as titanium and carbon-fibre composites, combined with advanced avionics and improved aerodynamic techniques.

The UK is the second largest defence supplier after the United States. Exports were estimated at £4.7 billion in 1998, and the sector supports some 418,000 jobs.

Civil Aircraft

British Aerospace has a 20% share of the European consortium Airbus Industrie, with responsibility for designing and manufacturing the wings for the whole family of Airbus

Aerospace and Defence—statistics for 1998 unless indicated				
	Sales[a] (£ million)	Index of production (1995 = 100)	Exports (£ million)	Number of enterprises	Investment (£ million, 1995 prices)
Sector	9,755	130.5	9,944	545	n.a.

Source: ONS Sector Review: *Vehicles and Other Transport*
[a] 1996.
n.a. = not available.

airliners, from the short- to medium-haul A320 series (the first civil airliner to use fly-by-wire controls—see p. 484) to the large long-range four-engined A340. Airbus and its related businesses support 40,000 UK jobs and contribute about £1.5 billion a year to the UK's balance of payments. In 1998 Airbus received firm orders for 556 new aircraft worth a total of US $39 billion from 36 customers around the world, and in the first half of 1999 it had 65% of the world market for large civil aircraft. Airbus is planning to revise its structure, with the intention of eventually becoming a single corporate entity.

Short Brothers is owned by Bombardier Inc. of Canada and employs about 6,500 people, mainly in Belfast. The company is mostly engaged in the design and production of major civil aircraft sub-assemblies, advanced engine nacelles and components for aerospace manufacturers as well as the provision of aviation support services.

Military Aircraft and Missiles

Among British Aerospace's military aircraft is the Eurofighter Typhoon, the world's most advanced multi-role combat aircraft, built by the British Aerospace, Daimler-Chrysler, Alenia and CASA consortium. The company also has the Harrier, a vertical/short take-off and landing (V/STOL) military combat aircraft, and the Tornado combat aircraft (built jointly by British Aerospace, Alenia and Daimler-Benz Aerospace). British Aerospace is involved with Lockheed Martin of the United States in the US Joint Strike Fighter programme. It also produces the Hawk fast-jet trainer, being supplied to 17 customers worldwide.

British Aerospace is a major supplier of tactical guided weapon systems for use on land, at sea and in the air, having merged its missile business with that of France's Matra Corporation to form Europe's largest guided weapons concern, Matra Bea Dynamics. Shorts Missile Systems Ltd (SMS) is a joint venture between Shorts and Thomson-CSF of France in the area of very short-range air defence systems.

Marconi Electronic Systems achieved sales of £3.8 billion in 1997–98, with 65% representing sales to customers outside the UK. The company is prime contractor for the PHOENIX unmanned aerial vehicle project and for the Brimstone missile for the Eurofighter Typhoon, the Tornado and the Harrier.

Helicopters

GKN-Westland Helicopters manufactures the Sea King, Lynx and Apache military helicopters, and, in partnership with Agusta of Italy, the multi-role EH101 medium-lift helicopter at its Somerset facilities. Over 1,000 Westland helicopters are in service in around 20 countries. GKN-Westland recently announced a joint venture agreement with Agusta.

Land Systems

The UK's main armoured fighting vehicle capability is concentrated in two companies: Vickers Defence Systems and Alvis. Royal Ordnance, owned by British Aerospace, is the UK's only indigenous ordnance company.

Engines and Other Aviation Equipment

Rolls-Royce is one of the world's three prime manufacturers of aero-engines, with a turnover in 1998 of £3.5 billion for its aerospace business. More than 53,000 Rolls-Royce engines are in service, one of the largest fleets in the world. Over 1,000 RB211-535 engines are in service, and 80% of Boeing 757 operators have selected it. The company's latest large engine, the Trent, has achieved a significant share of the world market for the new generation of wide-body twin-engined airliners, such as Boeing's 777 and the Airbus A330. Rolls-Royce is a partner in the four-nation International Aero Engine consortium, which manufactures the low-emission V2500 aero-engine, now in service on the Airbus A320 and A321. Rolls-Royce produces military engines for both fixed-wing aircraft and helicopters, and is a partner in the EJ200 engine project for the Eurofighter and in the US Joint Strike Fighter programme.

Manufacturers such as Dowty, Marconi Electronic Systems, TRW (Lucas Aerospace),

Smiths Industries, Racal, Meggitt, Cobham, Hunting, Ultra, Normalair-Garrett and British Aerospace provide equipment and systems for engines, aircraft propellers, navigation and landing systems, engine and flight controls, environmental controls and oxygen breathing and regulation systems, electrical generation, mechanical and hydraulic power systems, cabin furnishings, flight-deck controls and information displays. Marconi Electronic Systems is the world's largest manufacturer of head-up displays (HUDs). British firms have made important technological advances, for example, in developing fly-by-wire and fly-by-light technology, where control surfaces on the wings and elsewhere are moved by means of automatic electronic signalling and fibre optics respectively. UK companies provide radar and air traffic control equipment and ground power supplies to airports and airlines worldwide (see also p. 479).

Space Equipment and Services

Over 400 organisations employing more than 6,000 people are engaged in industrial space activities (see pp. 433–4), with annual turnover now more than £700 million. Through its participation in the European Space Agency, the British National Space Centre (see p. 433) has enabled UK-based companies to participate in many leading space projects covering telecommunications, satellite navigation, Earth observation, space science and astronomy. The industry is strong in the development and manufacture of civil and military communications satellites and associated Earth stations and ground infrastructure equipment. In the field of Earth observation, it plays a major role in manufacturing platforms, space radar and meteorological satellite hardware, and in the exploitation of space data imaging products.

The largest British space company is Matra Marconi Space UK. Together with its French partner, it is one of the world's major space companies. It has become the leading provider of direct broadcast television satellites, and is involved in nearly all of Europe's space science projects. Discussions on further consolidation of the industry with the German company Dornier and the Italian company Alenia are continuing.

Other firms, such as EEV, Sira, Pilkington, Com Dev, ERA and AEA Technology, supply satellite subsystems, and IGG is Europe's leading procurer and tester of space qualified components. UK companies such as Surrey Satellite Technology and Space Innovations are leaders in the field of micro and mini satellites, which provide relatively quick and cheap access to space. Major suppliers of satellite ground stations and space software include Logica, Science Systems, SEA and Vega.

Construction

The total value of work done in the UK construction industry during 1998 was worth £62 billion. The level of output for the year grew by 2%, with the private commercial sector accounting for a large share of this growth. The main areas of construction work within the UK industry are:

- building and civil engineering—ranging from major private sector companies with diverse international interests to one-person enterprises carrying out domestic repairs;

- specialist work—companies or individuals undertaking construction work ranging from structural steelwork and precast concrete structures to mechanical and electrical services (including the design and installation of environmentally friendly building control systems);

- the supply of building materials and components—ranging from large quarrying companies, and those engaged in mass production of manufactured items, to small, highly specialised manufacturers; and

- consultancy work—companies or individuals engaged in the planning, design and supervision of construction projects.

Some 1.1 million people were employed in construction in 1998. Around 8% of all male employee jobs are in the construction industry, but the number of women working in the industry is relatively low. A large

JUBILEE LINE EXTENSION

When the Jubilee Line Extension opens it will connect central London with Docklands and Stratford in east London, and provide easy access to the Millennium Dome site at North Greenwich. The new stations have been designed with uncomplicated layouts and use natural light wherever possible. Stations below ground level have glass platform edge doors for greater comfort and safety.

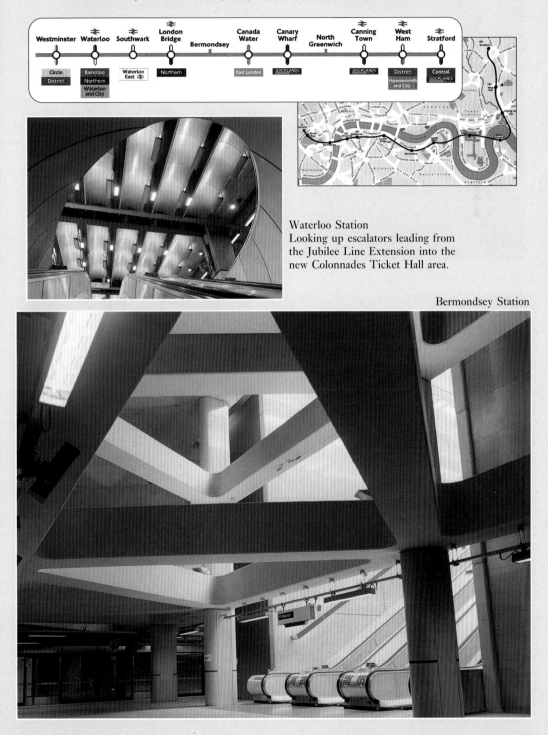

Waterloo Station
Looking up escalators leading from the Jubilee Line Extension into the new Colonnades Ticket Hall area.

Bermondsey Station

Canada Water Station

The award-winning
North Greenwich Transport
Interchange building

Canary Wharf Station

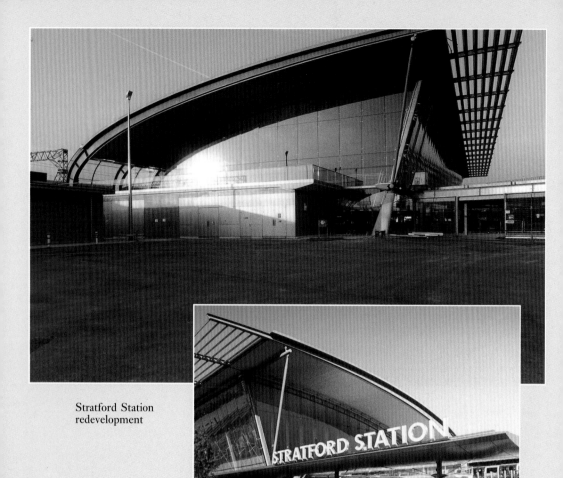

Stratford Station
redevelopment

Stratford Market Depot

number—over 600,000—of people working in construction are self-employed.

Project Procurement, Management and Financing

Private and public sector projects are managed in a variety of ways. Most clients invite construction firms to bid for work by competitive tender, having used the design services of a consultant. The successful contractor will then undertake on-site work with a number of specialist sub-contractors. Alternative methods of project procurement have become more common in recent years— for example, contracts might include subsequent provision of building maintenance, or a comprehensive 'design-and-build' service where a single company oversees every stage of a project from conception to completion.

Financing of major projects has also been changing. Traditionally, clients raised the finance to pay for schemes themselves. Today, they often demand a complete service package which includes finance; as a result, larger construction companies are developing closer links with banks and other financial institutions. In public sector construction the Government's Private Finance Initiative/Public-Private Partnerships (see p. 403) have also heralded a move away from traditional financing.

Major Construction Projects in the UK

Major building schemes in hand or recently completed include the express rail link from central London to Heathrow Airport; the London Underground Jubilee Line extension connecting the centre of the capital with the new commercial and residential areas in London's Docklands (see photographs between pp. 484 and 485); the Channel Tunnel Rail Link (see p. 371); the M60 motorway in Manchester; the Millennium Dome project (see p. ix), in the London Borough of Greenwich; and development at several major UK airports (see pp. 376–7).

The Channel Tunnel (see p. 370), which opened to traffic in 1994, remains the largest single civil engineering project ever undertaken in Europe. It is about 50 km (31 miles) long and 70 m (230 ft) below sea level at its deepest. Associated projects included new international stations at Waterloo in London and Ashford (Kent), and an international terminal at Folkestone (on the Kent coast).

In 1998, the public sector accounted for 40% of construction industry contracts in the UK.

Housing

During 1998 there was a downturn in the housing market, and the total value of new housing orders in Great Britain was just under £6 billion, 4% less than in 1997. In 1998 construction of some 189,250 dwellings was started in the UK. Starts by private sector concerns were 165,300, by housing associations 23,500, and in the public sector 500. Around 179,000 dwellings were completed: 153,600 by the private sector, 24,300 by housing associations and 1,000 by the public sector.

Overseas Contracting and Consultancy

UK companies are engaged in major undertakings throughout the world and have been in the forefront of management contracting and of 'design and build' operations. Contractors and consultants undertake the supervision and all or part of the construction of a project.

British companies have a reputation for integrity and independence. UK contractors are active in over 100 countries. In 1997 they won new international business valued at £4 billion. North America remains the most valuable market, accounting for about 38% of all new contracts. Important international contracts won in 1998 include:

- Oakland International Airport, United States;
- eight 37-storey apartment blocks in Hong Kong;
- the design and construction of a major pumping station in Egypt; and
- a power station in Hungary.

UK engineering consultants are engaged in projects in 140 countries. In 1998 members of the Association of Consulting Engineers were engaged in new programmes overseas with a total value of £28 billion. The capital value of projects under way at the end of 1998 was £101.7 billion. UK consulting engineers had estimated gross earnings in 1998 of £879 million from overseas commissions. The largest categories of work covered include structural/commercial; roads, bridges and tunnels; railways, hydro-electric and water-supply projects. The most important markets were the Far East (although the value of projects was lower than in 1997 as a result of the region's economic crisis), Africa, the EU, the Middle East and the Indian subcontinent. Major new international projects include:

- airports in the United States;
- railways in Thailand and Hong Kong;
- structural/commercial work in Singapore, Hong Kong and Poland;
- motorways in Australia and South Africa; and
- thermal power stations in Hong Kong.

The Government has a role to play in promoting the construction industry overseas, offering advice and support for individual companies. In 1998, nearly 100 companies were involved in construction trade promotion visits to Poland, the Philippines, Egypt and Brazil.

Further Reading

ONS Sector Reviews.

Websites

Department of Trade and Industry: www.dti.gov.uk

Department of the Environment, Transport and the Regions: www.environment.detr.gov.uk

29 Energy and Natural Resources

UK energy production was up by 1.9% and primary energy demand by 1.4% in 1998. Production of petroleum increased by 3.2% to a new record level, while production and consumption of gas rose by 5.0% and 3.9% respectively, mainly because of further use of gas in electricity generation. In its determination to reduce greenhouse gas emissions and to promote energy efficiency, the Government has announced its intention to levy an energy tax on industry from April 2001 and has set a target for renewables to provide 10% of the UK's electricity needs by 2010.

Great Britain has become the first country in the world to offer all of its 26 million electricity and gas customers (industrial, commercial and domestic) the choice of which company supplies their energy.

Energy Resources

Production of coal continued to fall in 1998, by 14.7% on 1997. However, production of crude oil reached a record level, exceeding the previous record set in 1995 by 2.1%. Nuclear electricity output went up by 2%, also to reach a record level. The increase in the production of natural gas, a feature of recent years, has been caused not only by the growing demand for gas for electricity generation, but also by significant exports to the Irish Republic and to the rest of Europe, and by falling imports. Coal still supplied a considerable proportion of the country's primary energy needs: 33% of the electricity

supplied in 1998 was from coal, while gas supplied 32.5% and nuclear 26%.

Provisional figures for 1998 show that, in value terms, total imports of fuels were 29.8% lower than in 1997, largely as a result of a 40.5% fall in the value of crude oil imports. Exports were 28.3% lower, mainly because of a 28.7% fall in the value of exports of crude oil and petroleum products. Overall the UK remains a net exporter of fuels, with a surplus on a balance of payments basis of £3.4 billion in 1998, £1.1 billion lower than in 1997 owing to the impact of lower crude oil prices on the international market. The surplus of crude oil and petroleum products was £4.1 billion. In volume terms, imports of fuel in 1998 were

4.5% lower than in 1997, while exports were 4% higher. The UK had a trade surplus in fuels of 39.1 million tonnes of oil equivalent—the sixth year in succession that the UK has had a trade surplus in volume terms.

In 1900 coal was virtually the country's sole source of energy. In the 19th century it gave the UK a unique advantage in establishing and sustaining British industrial leadership. In 1866 Chancellor Gladstone had forecast that demand for coal in Britain would reach 2,607 million tons in 1960. Nearly two-thirds of all coal entering world trade was mined in Britain, whose exports were nearly a quarter of output. In 1850 the mining labour force was 200,000, a figure which was to peak in 1913 at over 1 million. Gas, produced by the carbonisation of certain types of coal, was used for lighting streets, public buildings and the houses of the well-to-do, although its domestic market was extending to cooking and heating. In 1900–05 electricity was used for little more than lighting.

ENERGY POLICY

The Government's energy policy is to ensure secure, diverse and sustainable supplies at competitive prices. It is introducing major reforms aimed at achieving more effective competition in the electricity market to provide a fair deal:

- for consumers, so that they have access to energy at affordable prices;
- for producers and suppliers, so that the market in which they operate does not give unfair advantage; and
- for the environment.

In the 1999 Budget the Government announced plans for an energy tax ('climate change levy'). It will come into force in April 2001 and be paid by energy suppliers who can be expected to pass it on to industrial and commercial customers. The tax is designed to encourage businesses to use energy more efficiently, cutting carbon emissions by an estimated 1.5 million tonnes a year and playing a significant role in meeting the Government's target under the Kyoto Protocol to reduce greenhouse gas emissions by 12.5% by 2008–12.

Since June 1999 the Director General of Electricity and Gas Supply has headed a new energy regulatory body, the Office of Gas and Electricity Markets (OFGEM). Many electricity and gas companies now sell both products in the liberalised markets. The primary duty of the Director General has shifted from the regulation of monopoly suppliers to ensuring fair play in an increasingly competitive market.

International Developments

Research, development and demonstration of energy technologies in the European Union (EU) are carried out within the Fifth Framework Programme of Research and Technological Development, which started in 1999 (see p. 434), with a non-nuclear budget of £119 million a year. In November 1998 the EU Energy Council adopted four main components of the Energy Framework programme: ETAP (shared studies and analyses); SYNERGY (international co-operation); CARNOT (clean and efficient use of solid fuels); and SURE (safe transport of nuclear materials and safeguards). ALTENER (renewable energy) and SAVE (energy conservation) will continue, but as part of the Energy Framework programme. Seventeen agencies, which conduct research into, and promote, energy conservation, have been established in the UK under the SAVE II programme, which usually provides up to 150,000 euros of start-up funding.

Changes in the Oil Stocks Directive, which requires all EU member states to hold contingency oil stocks, are to come into force at the latest by January 2000. As an oil exporter, the UK is eligible for a reduction in its stocking obligation, which could save its oil industry about £10 million a year.

The EU collaborates with specialist international organisations, such as the International Energy Agency, which monitors world energy markets on behalf of

Table 29.1: Inland Energy Consumption (in terms of primary sources)
Million tonnes oil equivalent

	1988	1994	1995	1996	1997	1998
Oil	74.7	77.6	75.7	77.9	75.3	74.8
Coal	70.0	51.3	48.9	46.2	41.0	41.3
Natural gas	51.3	64.8	69.2	80.9	82.3	85.3
Nuclear energy	16.6	21.2	21.2	22.1	23.0	23.6
Hydro-electric power[a]	0.4	0.5	0.5	0.3	0.4	0.5
Net imports of electricity	1.1	1.5	1.4	1.4	1.4	1.1
Total[b]	214.4	218.5	218.7	230.3	225.6	228.9

Source: Department of Trade and Industry

[a] Excludes pumped storage. Includes generation at wind stations.

[b] Total includes renewable fuels.

industrialised countries and whose membership consists of all OECD members (see p. 414) except Iceland and Mexico.

In February 1999, 12 EU members were required to open at least 26.5% of their electricity supply markets to competition, and all must reach at least 33% by 2003. (The majority have, however, gone further: the European Commission estimated that some 60% of EU power markets were open in 1999.) By May 1999 the electricity market in Great Britain had been fully opened up, along with the electricity markets of Finland, Germany and Sweden. In August 2000, EU member states are due to open at least 20% of their gas supply markets, rising to 28% by 2003 and 33% by 2008. The UK gas market has been fully open to competition since May 1998.

ENERGY CONSUMPTION

In 1998 consumption of primary fuels in the UK was only 7.8% higher than in 1970, despite an 85% increase in gross domestic product (at constant market prices). Energy consumption by final users in 1998 amounted to 169 million tonnes of oil equivalent[1] on an 'energy supplied' basis, of which transport took 31.6%, industrial users 20.6%, residential users 27.2%, commerce, agriculture and public services 12.8% and non-energy uses 7.7%.

[1] 1 tonne of oil equivalent = 41.868 gigajoules.

Primary energy demand was 1.4% higher than in 1997, but 0.8% lower than in 1996. Primary demand for coal was 0.8% higher than in 1997; primary demand for oil fell by 0.8%; but gas rose by 3.9%, following marked increases in 1995–97. On a temperature corrected basis—which shows what the annual intake might have been if the average temperature during the year had been the same as the average for 1961–90—energy consumption grew by 1.5% in 1998, following increases in every year since 1995.

ENERGY EFFICIENCY

Government funding on energy efficiency programmes in the UK in 1998–99 was about £109 million. They are an essential part of its strategy for reducing greenhouse gas emissions (see p. 337). It has been estimated that by 2010, in the domestic sector, savings of up to 6.5 million tonnes of carbon a year could be achieved by improving the energy efficiency of buildings. The potential contribution of commercial and industrial buildings could be 5 million tonnes and of public sector buildings 1.1 million tonnes. These savings correspond to a reduction of 15%–20% on the estimated carbon emissions for 2010 for these sectors.

The Energy Efficiency Best Practice Programme advises energy managers, production managers in industry, and those involved in commissioning and designing buildings, new industrial plants, and combined heat and power (CHP—see p. 498) and community heating projects. Its target is savings of £800 million a year (at 1990 prices) by the end of 2000, or about 5 million tonnes of carbon, and it is currently saving about £650 million (about 3.25 million tonnes).

The Energy Saving Trust (EST) concentrates on domestic consumers and small and medium-sized enterprises. It received government funding of £19 million in 1998–99. In that year the EST's programmes attracted a further £28 million of funding from industry and local authorities towards the programmes run for the Department of the Environment, Transport and the Regions. Up to the end of 1998–99 more than 250,000 installations of energy saving measures, such as central heating controls, condensing boilers, cavity wall insulation, high-frequency lighting and small-scale CHP, had been made and advice given to some 660,000 individuals and organisations.

The Home Energy Efficiency Scheme (HEES), with a budget of £75 million in 1999–2000, gave insulation grants worth up to £315 to 400,000 low-income, disabled or elderly householders in 1998–99, thus reducing household fuel costs by up to £100 million a year. Its role and operation were included in the Government's review of fuel poverty policy.

The Government's Market Transformation programme promotes domestic equipment which does less harm to the environment, particularly by using less energy. It seeks to cut back on 2 million tonnes of carbon dioxide (CO_2) by 2010. Energy labels are mandatory for fridges, washing machines, washer/dryers and tumble dryers, dishwashers and light bulbs.

OIL AND GAS EXPLORATION AND PRODUCTION

Oil and gas are the most important natural resources to be discovered in the UK in the 20th century. The occurrence of vast amounts of oil and gas, in particular beneath the North Sea and the Irish Sea, is a result of a remarkable set of geologic circumstances involving the deposition and maturing of an oil-rich source rock, the timely migration of

oil and gas into porous reservoir rocks and their containment in these reservoirs beneath impermeable seals. The result has been diverse major oil and gas provinces around the UK Continental Shelf (UKCS). In 1998, output of crude oil and natural gas liquids (NGLs) in the UK averaged over 2.7 million barrels (about 363,350 tonnes) a day, making it the world's ninth largest producer. Despite the longevity of the UKCS as a petroleum province (onshore oil was first discovered in 1919 and the first major offshore find was made in 1967), there is still potential in both mature and frontier areas.

Taxation

The Government grants licences to private sector companies to explore for and exploit oil and gas resources (see below). Its main sources of revenue from oil and gas activities are petroleum revenue tax (see p. 407), levied on profits from fields approved before 16 March 1993; corporation tax, charged on the profits of oil and gas companies—the only tax on profits from fields approved after 15 March 1993; and royalty, which applies only to fields approved before April 1982 and is paid at 12.5% of the value of petroleum 'won and saved'.

Licensing

The 18th seaward licensing round since 1964 was completed in December 1998, when 47 licences were awarded covering 78 blocks in the North Sea—some on fallow blocks relinquished by previous licensees; others in hitherto unexplored areas. By the end of 1998, 6,935 wells had been, or were being, drilled in the UKCS: 2,058 exploration wells, 1,239 appraisal wells and 3,638 development wells. The Government must approve all proposed wells and development plans.

Production and Reserves

A record 204 offshore fields were in production in March 1999: 109 oil, 79 gas and 16 condensate (a lighter form of oil). Production started at 12 new offshore oilfields

Table 29.2: Oil Statistics						Million tonnes
	1988	1994	1995	1996	1997	1998
Oil production						
land	0.8	4.6	5.1	5.3	5.0	5.2
offshore	113.7	114.4	116.7	116.7	115.3	119.1
Refinery output	79.8	86.6	86.1	89.9	90.4	87.1
Deliveries	72.3	75.0	73.7	75.4	72.5	72.0
Exports						
Crude, NGL, feedstock	73.3	82.4	84.6	81.6	79.4	84.6
refined petroleum	15.8	22.2	21.6	23.7	26.7	24.2
Imports						
Crude, NGL, feedstock	44.3	53.1	48.7	50.1	50.0	48.0
refined petroleum	9.2	10.4	9.9	9.3	8.7	11.3

Source: Department of Trade and Industry

during 1998, and 24 new development projects were approved. Offshore, these comprised ten oilfields and eight gasfields; onshore, two gasfields and four oilfields. In addition, approval for 14 incremental offshore developments (elaborations to existing fields) and one onshore was granted.

Cumulative UKCS stabilised crude oil production to end-1998 was 2,202 million tonnes. The fields with the largest production totals are Forties, Brent, Ninian and Piper. Britain's largest onshore oilfield, at Wytch Farm (Dorset), produces 84.4% of the total crude oils and NGLs originating onshore. Possible maximum remaining UKCS reserves of oil are estimated at 1,800 million tonnes.

Offshore Gas

Natural gas now accounts for 38% of total inland primary fuel consumption in the UK. In 1998 indigenous production amounted to a record 95,503 million cubic metres.

Production from the three most prolific offshore gasfields, Leman, Indefatigable and the Hewett area, has accounted for 38% of the total gas produced so far in the UKCS. Associated gas,[2] delivered by pipeline to land via the Far North Liquids and Associated Gas System (FLAGS) and from the Scottish Area Gas Evacuation System (SAGE), makes

additional contributions. The Southern Basin fields and the South Morecambe field in the Irish Sea produce more gas in winter to satisfy increased demand, with the North Sean and South Sean fields also augmenting supplies to meet peak demand on very cold days in winter. The partially depleted Rough field is used as a gas store for rapid recovery during peak winter periods (see map opposite p. 420).

Cumulative gas production to end-1998 is 1.38 million million cubic metres. Maximum possible remaining gas reserves in present discoveries now stand at 1.8 million million cubic metres.

Pipelines

Some 9,435 km (5,863 miles) of major submarine pipelines transport oil, gas and condensate from one field to another and to shore.

Six terminals on the North Sea coast bring gas ashore to supply a national and regional high- and low-pressure pipeline system some 273,000 km (170,625 miles) long, which transports natural gas around Great Britain. Since 1996 a pipeline (40.4 km; 25 miles) has taken natural gas from Scotland to Northern Ireland; exports to the Irish Republic are conveyed by the Britain–Ireland interconnector. The pipeline (232 km; 145 miles) from Bacton to Zeebrugge in Belgium, opened in 1998 and costing £420 million, has a capacity of 20,000 million cubic metres a year.

---

[2] Mainly methane, produced and used mostly on oil production platforms.

Economic and Industrial Aspects

Oil prices fell sharply at the end of 1997, mainly because of the economic crisis in the Far East (combined with unseasonable mild weather in the Northern Hemisphere), and hit a 50-year low in real terms in December 1998. The average oil price received by producers from sales of UKCS oil was just under £60 a tonne, compared with £87 a tonne in 1997. In 1998 UKCS oil and gas production accounted for 1.7% of the UK's gross value added. Total revenues from the sale of oil (including NGLs) produced from the UKCS in 1998 fell to £8 billion, while those from the sale of gas rose slightly to £5.3 billion. Taxes and royalty receipts attributable to UKCS oil and gas fell to £2.6 billion in 1998–99.

The Oil and Gas Task Force, set up by the Government, with industry support, in November 1998, is developing strategies to enable the UK offshore industry to remain competitive under low international oil prices.

Since 1965 the oil and gas production industry has generated operating surpluses of some £237 billion, of which over £102 billion (including £23 billion of exploration and appraisal expenditure) has been reinvested in the industry, £89 billion paid in taxation, and about £46 billion left for disposal by the companies. However, total income of the oil and gas sector fell from £19 billion in 1997 to some £17 billion in 1998.

Production investment in the oil and gas extraction industry rose to some £5.1 billion in 1998. Including exploration and appraisal it formed about 17% of total British industrial investment and just over 4% of gross fixed capital investment. Some 28,400 people were employed offshore by the industry (which also supports about a third of a million jobs in related sectors) in 1998.

The Offshore Environment

Environmental assessment regulations introduced in 1998 aim to increase protection of the offshore environment and allow the public greater access to information. In 1999 regulations implementing a 1997 EC Directive were introduced, which require certain activities to be subject to an environmental impact assessment. In March 1999 the Government published a consultation paper seeking views on how its offshore environmental regime could be further improved.

During 1998 over 300 hours of unannounced aerial surveillance of oil and gas rigs detected minimal amounts of oil on the surface of the sea. Between April 1998 and March 1999, 57 offshore environmental inspections were carried out. The 1998 figure for accidental oil spills (137 tonnes) was significantly lower than that for 1997 (866 tonnes).

The Petroleum Act 1998 places a decommissioning obligation on the co-venturers of every offshore installation and the owners of every offshore pipeline on the UKCS. Companies have to submit a programme for ministerial approval and ensure that its provisions are carried out. In 1998 the OSPAR Commission (see p. 334) agreed rules for the disposal of offshore installations at sea. Dumping or leaving offshore installations wholly or partly in place is now prohibited, and the topsides of all installations must be returned to shore, for recycling or re-use. The presumption is in favour of land disposal and all installations with a jacket weight of less than 10,000 tonnes must go back to shore. Rare exceptions to the main rule will make allowances for the footings of large steel jackets above 10,000 tonnes and concrete installations, whose cases are to be considered individually. All installations put in place after 9 February 1999 must be completely removed.

The topsides of Shell's Brent Spar storage and loading buoy are being recycled. The hull sections are being used to build a ferry quay at Mekjarvik in Norway, due for completion at the end of 1999.

Offshore Safety

Offshore health and safety are the responsibility of the Health and Safety Executive (HSE—see p. 162). Aberdeen

University's Petroleum and Economic Consultants Ltd has evaluated the offshore health and safety regime and will recommend how it should be developed over the period up to 2010.

Suppliers of Goods and Services

The Infrastructure and Energy Projects Directorate (IEP) within the Department of Trade and Industry (DTI) is responsible for helping UK-based contractors and suppliers to win as high a share as possible of the provision of goods and services to the oil, gas and petrochemicals industry—a worldwide market estimated to be worth £200 billion a year.

The competitiveness of UK engineering designers, fabricators and local supply chains has enabled them to win an average 70% of the goods and services needed for recent development projects on the UKCS. The IEP's Target Market group focuses on 12 markets, including Brazil, Angola, Nigeria, Qatar, China and Norway.

DOWNSTREAM OIL

Oil Consumption

Deliveries of petroleum products for inland consumption (excluding refinery consumption) in 1998 included 21.8 million tonnes of petrol for motors, 15.1 million tonnes of DERV (diesel-engined road vehicles) fuel, 9.2 million tonnes of aviation turbine fuel, 7.3 million tonnes of gas oil (distilled from petroleum) and 2.9 million tonnes of fuel oils (blends of heavy petroleum).

Oil Refineries

In 1998 the UK's 14 refineries processed 93.6 million tonnes of crude and process oils. About 80% of output by weight is in the form of lighter, higher-value products, such as gasoline, DERV and jet kerosene. The UK is much more geared towards petrol production than its European counterparts—about a third of each barrel of crude oil, compared with a European average of just over a fifth.

Trade

In 1998, the UK exported 24.2 million tonnes of refined petroleum products, worth £2,328 million. Virtually all exports went to its partners in the EU and in the International Energy Agency, especially France and Germany, and the United States.

Some 2,965 million cubic metres of UKCS gas were exported in 1998. Most went to the Netherlands, from the British share of the Markham transboundary field and neighbouring Windermere, and to the Irish Republic. However, from October 1998 there were some exports to Belgium through the UK–Belgium interconnector. About 993 million cubic metres were imported from Norway, representing 1.1% of total supplies in 1998, compared with 1.5% in 1997.

GAS SUPPLY INDUSTRY

Structure of the Industry

The holder of a public gas transporter's licence may not also hold licences for supply or shipping in a fully competitive market.[3] British Gas, the former monopoly supplier to customers taking less than 2,500 therms a year, demerged in 1997 into two entirely separate companies. The supply business is now part of the holding company Centrica plc (which still trades under the British Gas brand name in the UK), while the pipeline and storage businesses, most exploration and production, and R&D have been retained within British Gas plc, renamed BG plc.

The national and regional gas pipeline network is owned by Transco, part of BG plc, which retains responsibility for dealing with leaks and emergencies, and also has a current monopoly in gas metering, which the energy regulator (see p. 488) plans to open to competition. In 1999 the Government also announced various arrangements to make gas trading more competitive, after problems in

---

[3] Suppliers sell piped gas to consumers; public gas transporters (PGTs) operate the pipeline system through which gas will normally be delivered; shippers arrange with PGTs for appropriate amounts of gas to go through the pipeline system.

1997 in balancing gas supply and demand, which led to an increase in the costs borne by shippers:

- the removal of Transco's monopoly over the flexibility mechanism that ensures supply always matches customers' demands;

- the introduction of an independently managed screen-based market, to reduce Transco's residual market balancing role;

- no more regulation of the prices charged by BG Storage at its Rough (see p. 491) and Hornsea facilities, to enable BG to auction its underground gas storage; and

- separating Transco into three businesses (transportation, providing and maintaining meters, and meter reading).

Competition

Since 1994 independent suppliers have captured 75% of the industrial and commercial gas market. By May 1999 over 4.5 million (out of 20 million) domestic customers had changed their gas supplier, switching from British Gas, which still has about 80% of the market, to one of the 26 other companies now in it, and also between these companies. In 1998 the changes were estimated to have brought each standard credit customer average savings of £56 a year on an annual bill of about £320.

Only companies which have been granted a supplier's licence are allowed to sell gas. The licence carries various conditions, which include providing gas to anyone in the licence area who requests it and is connected to the mains gas supply. Special services must be made available for elderly, disabled and chronically sick people. Suppliers must offer customers a range of payment options; they are able to set their own charges, but have to publish their prices and other terms so that customers can make an informed choice.

The Director General of Electricity and Gas Supply (see p. 488) has powers to set price controls for British Gas Trading and Transco, to set and enforce standards of performance, and to see that competitive practices continue.

Consumption

Natural gas consumption, at an estimated 1,006 terawatt[4] hours (TWh) in 1998, was up nearly 4% on 1997, with gas supplied for electricity generation (amounting to 258 TWh) up 6%. Sales to industry (176 TWh) were 3.8% up and to the commercial sector (118 TWh) 0.8% up, while domestic sales (356 TWh) were 3.0% up. There has been a steady fall in gas prices since 1982. In 1998 industrial gas prices were the lowest among the EU countries. Between 1988 and 1998 average industrial gas prices fell by 51% in real terms; domestic prices were reduced by 19% (including VAT). In Great Britain a typical standard credit household's annual gas bill fell in real terms from £350 in 1988 to £290 in 1998.

COAL

The UK coal industry is entirely in the private sector. The main deep-mine operators in the UK are RJB Mining plc (in England); Mining (Scotland) Ltd; and Betws and Tower (a pit at Hirwaun in Rhondda, Cynon and Taff, sold in 1996 to a 'buy-out' team of former employees). RJB Mining, Mining (Scotland) Ltd and Celtic Energy, which operates in Wales, are the main opencast operators. In spring 1999 there were 41 underground mines in production, including 19 major deep mines, employing some 10,500 workers and 59 opencast sites, owned by various companies throughout the UK, employing about 4,000. Opencast accounts for most of the relatively low sulphur coal mined in Scotland and south Wales, and contributes towards improving the average quality and cost of coal supplies. Government policy guidance for opencast coal-mining, published in 1999, puts concern for communities and the environment at the heart of decision-making on new developments. Planning authorities must subject all proposals to tough scrutiny; if consent is granted, the highest environmental standards will apply.

---

[4] 1 TW = 1,000 gigawatts (GW). 1 GW = 1,000 megawatts (MW). 1 MW = 1,000 kilowatts (kW).

Market for Coal

The UK produces the lowest-cost deep-mined coal in the EU. In 1998 inland consumption of coal was about the same as in 1997, at 63 million tonnes, of which 77% was used by the electricity generators, 14% by coke ovens and blast furnaces, 1% by other fuel producers, 4% by industry and 3% by domestic consumers. Exports were 944,000 tonnes, while imports amounted to 21 million tonnes—mainly of steam coal for electricity generation and coking coal. Total production from British deep mines fell by 17%, from 30.3 million tonnes in 1997 to 25.0 million tonnes in 1998. Opencast output fell by 10% to 15.0 million tonnes.

In 1998 the five-year concessionary contracts struck in 1993 before privatisation between the then nationalised industry and the three principal coal-fired generators ended. In December, Eastern Group, the third largest fossil fuel electricity generator, agreed to buy an additional 28 million tonnes of coal, worth £800 million, from RJB Mining during 1999–2009, to bring its total purchases for the period to almost 50 million tonnes (£1.4 billion). PowerGen, the second largest fossil fuel generator, agreed to buy 35 million tonnes (worth £1 billion) during 1999–2003. These orders go some way towards replacing the 1993 contracts.

> The Government insists on a fair single market for coal in Europe, in which UK coal can compete on level terms with other producers. It has challenged both the European Commission and the governments concerned on unfairly subsidised competition from other European countries and considers that the ensuing market distortion has to be removed quickly if it is not to do lasting damage to UK producers.
>
> Midlands Mining has announced the closure at the end of 1999 of Britain's oldest colliery, Annesley-Bentinck in Ashfield (Nottinghamshire), started in 1865. This will leave four deep mines operating in the East Midlands, compared with 50 when the industry was nationalised in 1947.

Clean Coal

Cleaner coal technologies reduce the environmental impact of coal used for power and industrial applications by increasing the efficiency of converting it to energy and reducing harmful emissions of particulates, oxides of nitrogen and sulphur, the cause of acid rain. Improvements in the efficiency of coal-fired power stations lead directly to reductions of CO_2, a major contributor to climate change. The DTI contribution of £12 million over three years to the cleaner coal R&D programme aims to encourage collaboration between UK industry and universities in the development of the technologies and expertise. It expects that the programme will give rise to projects worth over £60 million in R&D.

The Coal Authority

The Coal Authority licenses coal-mining; holds, manages and disposes of interests in unworked coal and mines; provides information about mining plans and geological data; and deals with subsidence damage claims and pollution to groundwater arising from former coal-mining.

ELECTRICITY

England and Wales

In December 1998, 71 companies held generation licences in England and Wales, of which the principal ones are National Power, PowerGen, Eastern Group, British Energy, and the publicly owned Magnox Electric. They sell electricity to suppliers through a marketing mechanism known as the 'Pool'. The National Grid (NGC) owns and operates the transmission system, and is responsible for calling up generation plant to meet demand.

Distribution—transfer of electricity from the national grid to consumers via local networks—is carried out by the 12 regional electricity companies (RECs) in England and Wales. Supply—the purchase of electricity from generators and its sale to consumers—is fully open to competition; since June 1999 all consumers in Great Britain, including

22 million homes and 2 million small businesses, have been able to choose from whom they can buy electricity.

Eight of the 12 RECs are owned by overseas companies. With British Energy's acquisition of SWALEC's supply businesses, all the main UK generators are being vertically integrated through ownership of supply businesses. British electricity companies continue to invest overseas. In December 1998, for example, the NGC bought the New England Electricity System in the United States for £2.7 billion.

Reform of Electricity Trading

The Government's Energy White Paper of October 1998 detailed action to remove distortions in the electricity market and introduce more competitive trading arrangements which do not feature a compulsory Pool. Key points of its programme included:

- divestment by the major generators, to ensure competition in, and more intensive use of, coal-fired flexible plant;

- radical overhaul of the Pool to ensure keen prices;

- full competition among supply companies;

- separating supply and distribution in electricity markets;

- resolving technical issues about the growth of gas, including the proper remuneration of flexible plant; and

- continuing to press for open energy markets in Europe.

Subject to time being available, it is hoped that Parliament will enact a Utilities Bill, which will allow the improved market to function, in autumn 2000.

Electricity suppliers have also been asked by the Government to improve the ways in which they treat poor and indebted customers, by, for example, reducing the gaps between tariffs for the better-off (generally those who pay by direct debit, which costs less) and the poor (those on pre-payment meters or who do not have bank accounts).

Scotland

ScottishPower plc and Scottish and Southern Energy plc generate, transmit, distribute and supply electricity within their respective franchise areas. They are also contracted to buy all the output from British Energy's two Scottish nuclear power stations (Hunterston B and Torness), until 2005. The over-100-kWh market in Scotland comprises about 6,750 customers and accounted for about 45% of all electricity consumed. ScottishPower and Scottish and Southern Energy have second-tier licences which allow them to compete in each other's area. Some customers choose to buy their electricity from the competing Scottish public electricity supplier. In 1998–99, 18% of customers in the over-100-kWh market obtained their power from holders of second-tier supply licences. OFGEM has asked generators, suppliers and customers to submit views on the future of Scotland's power-trading arrangements.

Northern Ireland

Three private companies, Nigen, Premier Power and Coolkeeragh Power, generate electricity from four power stations. They are obliged to sell to Northern Ireland Electricity plc (NIE), which has a monopoly of transmission and distribution, and a right to supply. Supply to all customers is open to competition, but the small scale and relative isolation of a system in which consumers pay an average 20% more for electricity than their counterparts in Great Britain, have prevented the introduction of competitive energy trading. Implementation of the EC Electricity Directive in February 1999 has provided the largest consumers, who comprise 25% of the total market, with the chance to contract directly with independent power producers.

The Province has a power surplus, with a peak demand of 1,500 MWh. The energy regulator for Northern Ireland combines responsibilities for electricity and gas.

Regulation and Other Functions

Regulation of the industry in Great Britain is primarily the responsibility of the Director

General of Electricity and Gas Supply (see p. 488). The Electricity Association is the principal trade body for the industry. It carries out representative and co-ordinating functions for all the major companies and has a number of overseas members.

Among companies operating in more than one market is ScottishPower, Britain's largest utility, which has electricity, gas, water and telecommunications interests. British Gas claims 1.5 million electricity customers. Eastern Electricity is the second largest seller of gas to the domestic market. Affinity deals include Alliance & Leicester's joint venture with London Electricity, offering new home loan borrowers up to three years' free gas and electricity.

Consumption

In 1998 sales of electricity through the distribution system in the UK amounted to 305 TWh. Domestic users took 36% of the total, industry 30%, and commercial and other users the remainder.

In 1998 the average industrial electricity price was lower in real terms than for any year since 1970. UK prices have fallen in real terms by 23% for domestic customers and by 28% for large industrial users since privatisation in 1990. In 1998 an annual electricity bill for a typical household was £275. Average UK domestic electricity prices, including taxes, in 1998 were the fifth lowest within the EU and industrial prices the eighth lowest.

Generation

The shares of generating capacity during 1997–99 are shown in Table 29.3.

Non-nuclear power stations owned by the UK's major power producers consumed 50.6 million tonnes of oil equivalent in 1998, of which coal accounted for 57%, natural gas 40% and oil and hydro 3%. Other power companies (for which gas is the most widely used fuel), and an increasing number of small autogenerators (which produce power for their

Table 29.3: Shares of Generating Capacity in England and Wales

%

	Winter 1997–98	Winter 1998–99
National Power	27.3	25.2
PowerGen	24.7	23.3
Eastern Group	10.8	10.5
Magnox Electric/BNFL	5.3	5.1
British Energy	11.8	11.5
Pumped storage	3.4	3.3
Interconnectors	5.1	5.0
Others	11.7	16.1
Total	**100.0**	**100.0**
Total (GW)	61.4	62.3

Source: NGC Seven Year Statements and Updates

own use), have equal access with the major generators to the grid transmission and local distribution systems. A ten-year programme to control emissions of oxides of nitrogen (NO_x) through the installation of low-NO_x burners at 12 major power stations in England and Wales is in progress. ScottishPower has fitted low-NO_x burners at Longannet power station.

Combined Cycle Gas Turbines (CCGT)

In 1998, CCGT stations accounted for 28% of the electricity generated by major power producers, compared with 7% in 1993. This increase has been balanced by a fall in coal- and oil-fired generation. CCGT stations, favoured by the smaller, independent producers and using natural gas, offer cheap generation, and give out almost no sulphur dioxide and some 55% less CO_2 than coal-fired plant per unit of electricity. At the end of March 1999, 22 such stations in the UK (with a total registered capacity of 15.6 GW) were generating power. Although new natural gas-fired generation would normally be inconsistent with the Government's energy policy relating to diversity and security of supply, the Energy White Paper of 1998 indicated that certain types of generating station may have benefits that outweigh

Table 29.4: Generation by and Capacity of Power Stations Owned by the Major Power Producers in the UK

	Electricity generated (GWh)[a]			%	Output capacity
	1988	1993	1998	1998	(MW)[b]
Nuclear plant	63,456	89,353	100,140	30	12,956
Other conventional steam plant	222,867	187,786	134,317	40	35,039
Gas turbines and oil engines	464	359	210	—	1,492
Pumped storage plant	2,121	1,437	1,624	—	2,788
Natural flow hydro-electric plant	4,121	3,522	4,240	1	1,327
CCGTs	—	22,811	93,832	28	14,680
Renewables other than hydro	1	165	609	—	108
Total	**293,100**	**305,434**	**334,972**	**100**	**68,390**
Electricity supplied (net)	270,871	285,316	315,907	—	—

Source: Department of Trade and Industry
[a] Electricity generated less electricity used at power stations (both electricity used on works and that used for pumping at pumped-storage stations).
[b] At end December 1998.
Note: Differences between totals and the sums of their component parts are due to rounding.

government concerns. It has therefore raised no objections to a new 500 MW CCGT station at Baglan Bay in south Wales because of its positive impact on employment and economic regeneration.

Combined Heat and Power

Combined Heat and Power (CHP) plants are designed to produce both electricity and usable heat. They can be up to three times more efficient than conventional generation, because they retain and utilise the heat produced in the generating process, rather than discarding it, as conventional generation does. This benefits the environment by reducing emissions of greenhouse gases. CHP is also used for cooling and chilling.

CHP can be fuelled by a variety of energy sources. It offers particular benefits in applications where there is a regular need for heat as well as electricity—such as hospitals, leisure centres and housing developments—and can be provided on a local scale. In 1998 over 1,300 CHP schemes supplied 4,000 MW of generating capacity, 6% of the UK's total electricity (and 15% of that used by industry), with 400 schemes under construction; the Government is considering an increased target of 10,000 MW by 2010. EU strategy is to double CHP's share of the electricity market from 9% to 18% by the same year.

Trade

The NGC and Electricité de France run a 2,000 MW cross-Channel cable link, allowing transmission of electricity between the two countries. The link has generally been used to supply 'baseload' power—which needs to be generated and available round the clock—from France to England. Imports met about 4% of the UK's electricity needs in 1998.

Scotland has a peak winter demand of under 6 GW and generating capacity of over 9 GW. This additional available capacity (see p. 496) is used to supply England and Wales through transmission lines linking the Scottish and English grid systems. This interconnector's capacity is now 1,600 MW, with plans to increase it to 2,200 MW. NIE and ScottishPower have put out to tender the construction of a 60-km (37.5-mile) 250 MW undersea interconnector, costing £150 million, to supply electricity to the Northern Ireland system.

Nuclear Power

Nuclear power generates about one-sixth of the world's energy and over a third of

Europe's, the world's largest market. It substantially reduces the use of fossil fuels which would otherwise be needed for generation—in the UK by over 30% in 1998. Such an amount would cause annual emissions of up to 20.5 million tonnes of CO_2. In the EU as a whole the amount avoided is some 700 million tonnes. However, public concern about the disposal of spent fuel and nuclear safety has proved a deterring factor. There are currently no plans to build new nuclear power generation plants in the UK or in France, while Germany and Sweden plan to phase out nuclear power investment; and Belgium and Spain have imposed moratoriums on building new nuclear stations. Worldwide only 30 nuclear stations were being built at the end of 1998, under 1% of global nuclear capacity.

The privatised nuclear industry in Great Britain is run by British Energy plc, which owns and operates advanced gas-cooled reactors (AGRs) at seven power stations and the pressurised water reactor (PWR) at Sizewell B. The British nuclear power generation industry achieved record output of 91 TWh in 1998, as well as contributing, at 30%, its highest ever proportion of total electricity generation. British Energy's reactors have an aggregate capacity of 7,200 MW in England and about 2,400 MW in Scotland, where electricity needs are also met by hydro, coal, oil, gas and new renewables, which, with nuclear have a total output capacity of approximately 9,300 MW. In Scotland, all British Energy's output is sold to ScottishPower (74.9%) and to Scottish and Southern Energy.

A segregated fund was established on the privatisation of British Energy, with a £228 million initial endowment from it, to cover the eventual cost of decommissioning its reactors. British Energy contributes a further £16 million a year. British Nuclear Fuels (BNFL; see below) and Magnox Electric, which merged in 1999, operate eight magnox power stations, together with a further three magnox stations that are being decommissioned. The Government has undertaken to pay BNFL £3.7 billion to decommission reactors in the 21st century.

The Fossil Fuel Levy Act 1998 ensures that nuclear electricity from licensed suppliers, or imported from France, is subject to the fossil fuel levy (see p. 500).

British Nuclear Fuels (BNFL)

BNFL is Britain's primary provider of nuclear products and services to both UK and international customers. It currently operates in 17 countries, employs about 20,000 people and has some £15 billion in future orders. It is a public limited company, wholly owned by the Government, which has announced the introduction into it of a Public-Private Partnership (see p. 403).

BNFL has also strengthened its reactor services and fuel manufacture operations with the purchase of Westinghouse in the United States. A recent government announcement means that uranium commissioning of BNFL's Mixed Oxide fuel fabrication plant at Sellafield may commence while a further consultation on the economic case for the plant is carried out.

United Kingdom Atomic Energy Authority

UKAEA's main function is to maintain and decommission safely and cost-effectively its redundant nuclear facilities used for the UK's nuclear R&D programme. UKAEA owns the sites at Dounreay (Caithness), Culham and Harwell (Oxfordshire), Windscale (Cumbria) and Winfrith (Dorset), and is also responsible for Britain's fusion programme (see below).

Nuclear Research

Nuclear fusion in the UK is funded by the DTI and Euratom (75% and 25% respectively). The Government spends £15 million a year on fusion research, of which the main focus is magnetic confinement, based at Culham, where Britain's own nuclear fusion research is carried out. The UK is also a partner in the experimental EU JET (Joint European Torus) project, also at Culham, extended to the end of 1999, and, through the EU, of the proposed ITER (International Thermonuclear Experimental Reactor), which aims to show the scientific and technological feasibility of power production from fusion energy for peaceful purposes.

Nuclear Safety

Responsibility for ensuring the safety of nuclear installations falls to nuclear operators within a system of regulatory control enforced by the HSE.

The international Convention on Nuclear Safety, in force since 1996, has been ratified by 46 countries, including the UK, and each has reported on how it has progressed towards meeting its nuclear safety obligations. The UK's main contribution to the international effort to improve safety in Central and Eastern Europe and in the former Soviet republics is channelled through the EU PHARE and TACIS nuclear safety programmes.

NEW AND RENEWABLE SOURCES OF ENERGY

In March 1999 the Government published a White Paper on the future of renewable energy, reaffirming its commitment to developing it and increasing expenditure on R&D to £43.5 million during 1999–2002. Renewables are essential to the UK's climate change programme and play a vital role in enabling it to meet its environmental targets of reducing greenhouse gases by 12.5% by 2012 and CO_2 emissions by 20% by 2010. The Government's aim is for renewable energy to provide 10% of UK electricity supplies by 2010. Over 700 British companies are involved in renewables, directly employing some 3,500 people. The White Paper states that, if the contribution of renewables to energy supply in Europe were to double from the current 6% to 12% by 2010, it would create at least 500,000 jobs. UK renewables exports are estimated to have risen from £10–£15 million a year in the early 1990s to about £80–£100 million in 1998–99. The Government's new and renewable energy R&D programme covers biofuels (including wastes), fuel cells, hydro, solar and wind. These accounted for 2% of all electricity generating capacity in Britain in 1998; natural flow hydro schemes provided about three-quarters of this total.

The main government support measure for the commercialisation of renewables is the non-fossil fuel obligation (NFFO), which requires each public electricity supplier (PES)

Three photovoltaics (PV) initiatives announced in 1999 and receiving £5 million in government support include a field trial for at least 100 houses to test PV installations under actual conditions and a scheme demonstrating the use of PV in large-scale building applications. To date, 119 landfill gas (mostly methane) schemes have been commissioned under the NFFO, the SRO (see p. 501) and in Northern Ireland with a total capacity of over 230 MW. Ecotricity, a joint venture between the Renewable Energy Company and Thames Water, is a green tariff which aims to offer consumers electricity from sewage gas, waste to energy, landfill gas, hydro, solar and wind power, at market prices. The UK's first significant power station to be fuelled by specially grown willow and agricultural and forestry wastes is under construction at Eggborough (West Yorkshire) and will be capable of generating 8 MW of electricity, enough to power about 8,000 homes. Eastern Electricity, the UK's biggest power supplier, with more than 3 million customers in eastern England, allows them to pay a 5%–10% supplement under its Ecopower scheme which goes towards supporting generation from renewable energy. These contributions are matched pound for pound by Eastern. Britain's first solar-powered pub, the Jolly Gardener at Wandsworth (south-west London), is fitted with solar panels, energy-efficient glass and terrace lights fuelled by PV cells. Britain's first offshore wind farm is currently being developed 1 km off the coast at Blyth (Northumberland), under NFFO-4 and an EU THERMIE grant, and will generate up to 4 MW, enough to satisfy 4,000 homes.

to reserve capacity for a certain amount of electricity to be generated from non-fossil and non-nuclear sources. PESs must then buy renewables-sourced power at a premium price, above the market price for conventionally generated electricity, and are reimbursed the difference through the fossil fuel levy, which is paid by all electricity consumers through their bills. Since 1990 the NFFO has provided over £600 million of support for renewables. (In Scotland the term Scottish Renewables Obligation—SRO—is used.)

Five Renewables Orders have been made for England and Wales, three for Scotland and two for Northern Ireland. At 31 March 1999, 933 projects had been contracted under these Orders, with a net capacity of 3,639 MW; 261 of these were 'live' and generating 677 MW. The cost of renewable energy under successive Orders has fallen significantly—from 6.4 pence a kilowatt hour under NFFO-1 to an average 2.73 p/kWh under NFFO-5.

Interest in wave energy has been boosted by its inclusion in SRO-3, and the DTI intends to include new work on wave energy technology in its new and renewable energy programme. North Atlantic waves pound much of Britain's shoreline, a significant part of a theoretical resource of about 50 TWh of electricity. There are at present about 700 onshore wind turbines in Britain, mostly in Wales and south-west England, producing 330 MW.

Non-energy Minerals

Output of non-energy minerals in 1997 came to 312 million tonnes, valued at £2,355 million. The total number of employees in the extractive industry was about 27,000.

The UK is virtually self-sufficient in construction minerals, and produces and exports several industrial minerals, notably china clay, ball clay, potash and salt. The Boulby potash mine in north-east England is the UK's most important non-energy mineral operation. Production in 1997 was down from a record 1.03 million tonnes in 1996 to 941,000 tonnes in 1997, of which 53% was exported. Sales of china clay (or kaolin), the largest export, increased by 3.4% to £243 million, of which 87% of output was exported.

The largest non-energy mineral imports are metals (ores, concentrates and scrap—valued at £1.6 billion in 1997), refined non-ferrous metals (£3.7 billion) and non-metallic mineral products (£4.7 billion, of which rough diamonds account for £2.8 billion).

Table 29.5: Production of Some of the Main Non-energy Minerals in the UK

	1992	1997	Production value 1997 (£ million)
	(million tonnes)		
Sand and gravel	98.9	98.4	533
Silica sand	3.6	4.7	58
Igneous rock	57.7	48.7	253
Limestone and dolomite	107.9	105.0	627
Chalk[a]	9.2	9.6	53
Sandstone	14.9	18.5	94
Gypsum and anhydrite	2.5	2.0	16
Salt, comprising rock salt, salt in brine and salt from brine	6.1	6.7	232
Common clay and shale	12.2	11.3	18
China clay	2.5 [b]	2.4	280
Ball clay	0.7	0.9	44
Fireclay[a]	0.6	0.4	2
Potash	0.9	0.9	86
Fluorspar	0.1	0.1	8
Fuller's earth	0.2	0.1	12

Source: British Geological Survey, United Kingdom Minerals Yearbook
[a] Great Britain only.
[b] Moisture-free basis.

Some Minerals Produced in Britain

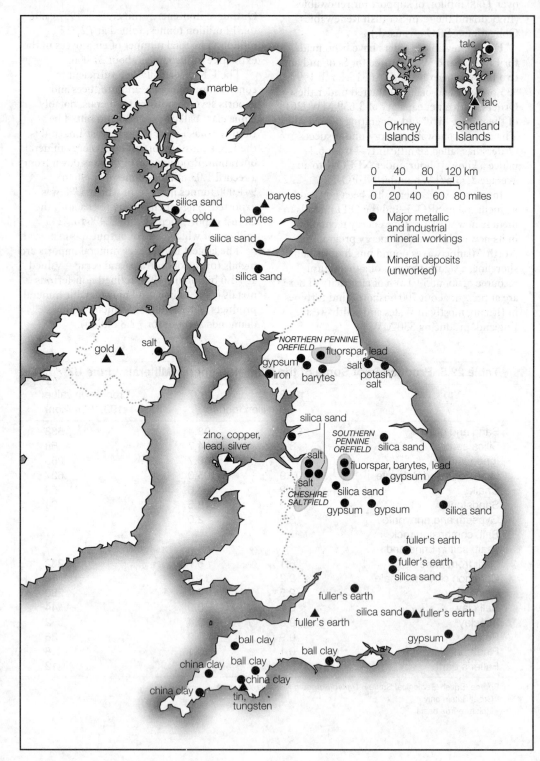

Orkney Islands

Shetland Islands

talc

talc

0   40   80   120 km
0   20   40   60   80 miles

● Major metallic and industrial mineral workings

▲ Mineral deposits (unworked)

marble

silica sand
gold
barytes
barytes
silica sand
silica sand

gold
salt

NORTHERN PENNINE OREFIELD
gypsum   fluorspar, lead
iron   salt
barytes   potash/salt

silica sand

zinc, copper, lead, silver

SOUTHERN PENNINE OREFIELD
salt   silica sand
salt   fluorspar, barytes, lead
gypsum
CHESHIRE SALTFIELD   silica sand
gypsum   gypsum   silica sand

fuller's earth
fuller's earth
silica sand

fuller's earth
silica sand   fuller's earth
fuller's earth
gypsum

ball clay
china clay   ball clay   ball clay
china clay   china clay
china clay   tin, tungsten

Value of United Kingdom Minerals Production, 1997

Total value: £20.3 billion

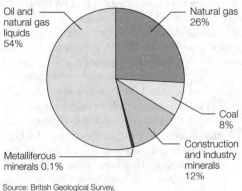

Oil and natural gas liquids 54%

Natural gas 26%

Coal 8%

Construction and industry minerals 12%

Metalliferous minerals 0.1%

Source: British Geological Survey,
United Kingdom Minerals Yearbook 1998

Water Supply

About 75% of the UK's water supplies are obtained from mountain lakes, reservoirs and river intakes; and about 25% from underground sources (stored in layers of porous rock). South-east England and East Anglia are more dependent on groundwater than any other parts of the UK. Scotland and Wales have a relative abundance of unpolluted water from upland sources. Northern Ireland also has plentiful supplies for domestic use and for industry.

Water put into the public supply system (including industrial and other uses) in England and Wales averaged 15,981 megalitres a day (Ml/d) in 1997–98, of which average daily consumption per head was about 160 litres. An average of 2,336 Ml/d was supplied in Scotland in 1997–98. In Northern Ireland the figure was 690 Ml/d.

Some 30,273 Ml/d were abstracted from rivers in England and Wales in 1997, of which public water supplies accounted for 11,822 Ml/d. The electricity supply industry took 11,880 Ml/d; fish farming, cress growing and amenity ponds 3,887 Ml/d; and agriculture 8 Ml/d, with spray irrigation accounting for a further 151 Ml/d.

By 1870, in preference to entire or partial reliance on cesspools, 146 out of 178 larger towns in England and Wales removed their household wastes through sewers, but only 46 treated the sewage before disposal into watercourses. Victorian Britain strove to develop an institutional and regulatory water regime to facilitate the emergence of a modern water supply industry, with an emphasis on municipal enterprise. Private companies were held to lack the resources to contemplate works on the scale carried out by municipal management. In 1901, 90% of provincial towns provided their own water. The achievements of Glasgow, Liverpool, Birmingham and Manchester in providing a full supply of water from distant sources, free from contamination, were much admired. By 1904 undertakings in the water industry in England and Wales numbered 870 local authorities, eight water boards and joint committees, and 221 water companies.

England and Wales

Water Companies

Ten water and sewerage companies in England and Wales have statutory responsibilities for water supply, its quality and sufficiency, and for sewerage and sewage treatment. The supply-only companies, after various mergers since 1989, have decreased in number from 29 to 17. They supply water to nearly a quarter of the population.

The Water Industry Act 1999 implements government policy in three key areas:

- removing the threat of disconnection, which could be a danger to their health, from very poor households who have difficulty in paying their water and sewerage bills;

- protecting households on low incomes, and people with medical conditions for whom high use of water is a necessity, by offering them special tariffs; and

- promoting increased customer choice on whether they have a water meter or not.

Since 1989 water bills have risen by more than a third in real terms. While the Government requires the water companies to invest between £8 billion and £8.5 billion in improvements in water quality and in meeting new UK and EU environmental standards up to 2005, it wants to ensure that customers do not have to face unreasonably high bills. Although it has been argued that higher water prices, combined with metering, would control demand for water and reflect the environmental costs of water use, the Government considers that people and firms must be able to afford the water they need, and families should face neither hardship because of water bills nor disconnection. It does not favour compulsory metering.

In April 1999 the water companies submitted their business plans for 2000–05 to the Director General of Water Services, who heads Ofwat, the industry's regulatory body. The plans include the minimum prices they believe they need to finance continued provision of services and deliver the environmental and water quality programmes that the Government has requested.[5] The companies have been asked to develop charging arrangements which distinguish between water for essential and discretionary purposes.

About 14% of households and 80% of commercial and industrial customers are charged for water on the basis of consumption measured by meter. Most homes are charged according to the rateable value of their property. Fifteen water companies supply free meters to households on request. Average water and sewerage bills for households without a meter have risen from £245 in 1998–99 to £255 in 1999–2000; for those with a meter by less than £1 to £205.

The overall quality of UK drinking water is high: nearly 99.8% of some 2.8 million tests in England and Wales in 1998 met standards that are in some cases more strict than those in the 1980 EC Drinking Water Directive. A new EC Directive, adopted in 1998, requires member states to meet a number of even more stringent standards, for example an obligation to ensure maximum concentrations of lead in water of 25 microgrammes per litre within five years and 10 µg/l within 15 years.

The Drinking Water Inspectorate (DWI) checks that water companies meet the drinking water quality regulations. Enforcement action is taken when there are infringements of standards. The DWI also investigates incidents and consumer complaints about quality, and initiates prosecution if water unfit for human consumption has been supplied.

> The roof of the Millennium Dome (see p. ix) will be used to collect rain for a water recycling system, developed by Thames Water. Rain falling on the 20-acre roof will be collected and treated in a reed bed, then used for flushing lavatories around the site.
>
> The Government is backing Thames Water's plan to pump out about 68 million litres of groundwater a day from 50 new boreholes around London to stop the capital flooding from a water table rising by up to 10 feet a year—which could affect foundations of buildings within five years. Some of the cleaner water would be used for drinking, industrial use, watering London's parks or cleaning streets. The rest would go into the sewerage system for discharge into the Thames in east London. The initial cost is estimated at £10 million, with costs of £2 million a year thereafter.

Ensuring Supplies

The Government will bring forward legislation to put time limits on water abstraction licences. It plans to bring to an end, by 2012, compensation for curtailment of licences if they damage the environment by drying up rivers and harming wetlands. All future licences would be limited to about 15 years.

About 25% of the public water supply is lost through leakage. The Director General of Water Services has set the companies mandatory targets to reduce overall leakage between 1996–97 and 2000 by 26%—enough to provide 14 million baths a day. The industry is committed to spending £816 million on leakage repair over 1998–2000 and £1.7 billion on mains rehabilitation and replacement.

All the companies except one offer a free leak-repair service for customers' supply pipes. Tougher regulations for water efficiency of equipment and fittings are being introduced.

Scotland

Responsibility for the provision of water and sewerage services rests with three public bodies—the North, West and East of Scotland Water Authorities. The Water Industry Act 1999 established a Water Industry Commissioner for Scotland who promotes customer interests and advises the Scottish Executive about the level of the authorities' charges. Water Industry Consultative Committees for each of the authorities advise the Commissioner about customer interests.

Modernisation of the water industry is in progress, with the authorities investing more than £1.7 billion over three years, including projects worth £600 million in partnership with the private sector. New water treatment plants are being built and all major towns are expected to benefit from new sewerage works by the end of 2000. Prices for water services depend on the type of consumer: domestic consumers pay amounts based on their council tax band (see p. 411) or metered charges, and non-domestic consumers pay non-domestic water rates, or metered charges.

Northern Ireland

In November 1998 the Government issued a consultation paper on water and sewerage services in Northern Ireland, in which it envisaged expenditure of up to £2.5 billion over 15–20 years to bring services up to standard and to meet increasing demand. (Some of the main sewers of Belfast date from Victorian times and may be at risk of collapse.) An extra 10% in water rates bills would be necessary to pay for these improvements. Decisions would be a matter for the Northern Ireland Executive and Assembly

Further Reading

Annual Publications

Digest of Environmental and Water Statistics. Department of the Environment, Transport and the Regions. The Stationery Office.

Digest of United Kingdom Energy Statistics. Department of Trade and Industry. The Stationery Office.

Energy Report (the Blue Book). Department of Trade and Industry. The Stationery Office.

Oil and Gas Resources of the United Kingdom (the Brown Book). Department of Trade and Industry. The Stationery Office.

United Kingdom Minerals Yearbook. British Geological Survey.

Websites

Department of Trade and Industry: www.dti.gov.uk

Department of the Environment, Transport and the Regions: www.environment.detr.gov.uk

Scottish Executive: www.scotland.gov.uk

Ofwat: www.open.gov.uk/ofwat

Water Conservation Research Database: www.databases.detr.gov.uk/water/index.htm

30 Finance and Other Service Industries

The service sector in the United Kingdom is continuing to grow and now contributes about 66% of gross value added at constant 1995 prices and 75% of employment. Around 20.8 million people have jobs in the service sector, a rise of nearly 800,000 in the last two years.

Competition in many financial services, such as personal savings, consumer credit and mortgages, has intensified as existing providers have extended their services and as new entrants, such as supermarkets, have begun to offer financial services. Telephone-based services are becoming much more widespread, for example in banking and in motor and household insurance, and some providers (such as banks and stockbrokers) are offering Internet-based services. The UK has the highest level of credit card usage in Europe. A major reform of the system of financial regulation and supervision is in progress.

As a result of rising real incomes, consumer spending on financial, personal and leisure services has increased considerably. Travel, hotel and restaurant services in the UK are among those to have benefited from the growth in tourism, and the UK is one of the world's leading tourist destinations. Computer services, business services and recreation activities are among the non-financial sectors which experienced strong growth in turnover in 1998 (see Table 30.1).

Financial Services

The UK's financial services sector accounts for 7% of gross domestic product (GDP) and employs over 1 million people. Historically the heart of the industry has been in the 'Square Mile' in the City of London, and this remains broadly the case. Among the major financial institutions and markets in the City are the Bank of England, the London Stock Exchange, Lloyd's insurance market, and the London

During the 19th century there was a process of consolidation in the banking industry, and many of the private banks were acquired by joint stock banks. Consolidation continued during the early 20th century, so that by the 1920s and 1930s there were five large retail banking groups. By contrast, in 1900 there were over 2,200 incorporated building societies, with assets of £46 million. Since then, the number of societies has contracted through mergers and takeovers and is now around 70, although membership (the number of savers and borrowers) of building societies has risen considerably. The number of people holding a Post Office savings account rose substantially from 4.8 million at the end of 1890 to 8.4 million by the end of 1900. The Stock Exchange made a growing contribution to financing development during the 19th century, for example, for the growth of railways—both in the UK and overseas— and by 1899 the value of the securities of companies quoted on the Exchange was £5,411 million.

International Financial Futures and Options Exchange. The City is one of the world's three leading financial centres, along with Tokyo and New York, and by far the biggest in Europe. An important feature is the size of its international activities. It is noted for having:

- more overseas banks than any other financial centre;
- the biggest market in the world for trading foreign equities, accounting for 59% of global turnover;
- by far the world's biggest foreign exchange market, actively trading the largest range of currencies and handling about 32% of worldwide dealing;
- the largest fund management centre, with around US $1,808 billion of institutional equity holdings;
- the fourth largest insurance market and the leading international insurance centre;
- the major international centre for primary and secondary dealing in the Euromarket;
- the most important centre in the world for advice on privatisation; and
- a full range of ancillary and support services, including legal, accountancy and management services.

Scotland (Edinburgh and Glasgow) is the fifth largest centre in the EU, in terms of institutional equity funds managed. Manchester, Cardiff, Liverpool and Leeds are also important financial centres.

British Invisibles (BI) promotes the UK as the world's foremost international centre for financial and related services, and seeks to promote a better understanding within Britain of the role of financial services and their

Table 30.1: Turnover in Selected Services, 1998

	£ million	% increase on 1997
Motor trades	121,558	6.0
Hotels and restaurants	47,501	7.2
Renting	14,218	8.7
Computer and related activities	30,313	31.7
Research and development	5,095	15.2
Business services	127,579	16.9
Education[a]	20,667	5.4
Sewage and refuse disposal, etc	6,584	5.7
Recreation[b]	21,680	11.8

Source: Office for National Statistics—annual data derived from short-term turnover inquiries
[a] Excludes public sector activities.
[b] Excludes sporting, betting and gaming activities.

contribution to the economy. BI also helps businesses to develop commercial opportunities internationally, and works to achieve greater liberalisation of international trade in financial and related services. Net overseas earnings of the UK financial sector have nearly trebled in the last five years, reaching a record £31.9 billion in 1998.

REGULATION

Government proposals for a major reform of the regulation of financial services were announced in 1997, when a new Financial Services Authority (FSA) was established. Following extensive consultation on draft legislation, the Financial Services and Markets Bill was introduced into Parliament in June 1999, with the intention of becoming law in spring 2000. As well as formally establishing the FSA, the Bill provides for:

- replacement of the system based in part on self-regulation by a fully statutory system;
- a new single compensation scheme;
- a single ombudsman system;
- a single tribunal; and
- powers to tackle market abuse.

FSA Objectives and Functions

The Bill sets out statutory objectives for the FSA, including maintaining confidence in the UK financial system and promoting public understanding of it, protecting consumers and reducing financial crime. In delivering these objectives, the FSA will have to be efficient and economic, facilitate innovation in financial services and take account of the international nature of financial services business. To ensure that the new regime will be open and accountable, the FSA will be required to maintain consumer and practitioner panels (which will have a role in assessing the FSA's performance against its statutory objectives), to hold a public meeting each year to discuss its annual report, and to consult on its arrangements for independent investigation of complaints against itself.

The FSA will eventually be a single regulator for all financial firms and markets, bringing together the functions previously handled by nine regulatory bodies. In 1998 it acquired from the Bank of England responsibility for banking supervision, and the Treasury has contracted out to the FSA the exercise of the majority of its functions under legislation on insurance. The FSA also supervises the UK's six recognised investment exchanges (such as the London Stock Exchange), and is responsible for recognising and supervising the clearing houses, which organise the settlement of transactions on these exchanges. In addition, it is currently supplying regulatory and other services under contract to a number of bodies which it will replace when the Bill takes effect:

- the Building Societies Commission;
- the Friendly Societies Commission;
- the Registry of Friendly Societies; and
- three self-regulating organisations—the Investment Management Regulatory Organisation (regulating about 1,100 fund management firms), the Securities and Futures Authority (covering most aspects of securities trading and having about 1,300 members) and the Personal Investment Authority (PIA, regulating about 4,000 firms, including product providers and independent financial advisers).

In May 1999 the FSA issued its consumer education strategy to meet the objective of promoting public understanding of the financial system. A key priority will be ensuring that managing money is taught in more schools. Impartial information will be provided by the FSA to help consumers plan their finances and make informed choices. In the March 1999 Budget the Chancellor of the Exchequer announced that the FSA would publish 'league tables' of costs and charges in savings, insurance and pensions products, so that consumers would be better able to assess the products available. The Government hopes that this will help to avoid the problems of mis-selling which have arisen on certain financial products, such as personal pensions.

Banking Supervision

Banks are required to meet minimum standards on the integrity and competence of directors and management, the adequacy of capital and cash flow, and the systems and controls to deal with the risks they experience. If a bank fails to meet the criteria, its activities may be restricted, or it may be closed. These arrangements are intended to strengthen, but not guarantee, the protection of bank depositors, thereby increasing confidence in the banking system as a whole.

Compensation Schemes

Various compensation schemes, funded by the financial services providers, currently exist to protect investors and depositors if authorised firms are unable to meet their liabilities:

- the *Deposit Protection Scheme*, for bank customers, and the *Building Societies Investor Protection Scheme*, which both provide customers with protection of up to 90% of their deposits, subject to a maximum for each scheme of £18,000;

- the *Policyholders Protection Scheme*, which provides protection for certain insurance company policyholders of 100% of claims on specified compulsory insurance policies and 90% on other policies, with no maximum limit; and

- the *Investors Compensation Scheme*, which can make payments of up to £48,000 to private investors if a regulated firm is unable to meet its investment business liabilities—since 1988 it has helped customers of about 1,050 firms, and paid out £154 million to more than 13,500 investors.

Under the Financial Services and Markets Bill, a single Compensation Scheme will be set up.

Financial Services Ombudsman

The Bill provides for the creation of a new Financial Services Ombudsman as a single point of access for complaints. With an annual budget of around £15 million, it will be the largest ombudsman scheme in the world. It will bring together eight main schemes, including those covering banking, building societies, insurance and firms conducting investment business. All firms authorised by the FSA will have to observe the Ombudsman's procedures.

International Agreements

The UK plays a major role in efforts to maintain global prosperity and prevent financial crises. The Group of Seven (G7) leading major industrialised countries agreed in 1998 on measures to reform the international financial system, including enhanced global financial supervision and regulation. A new Financial Stability Forum has been set up, bringing together G7 national authorities, international regulatory bodies and leading financial institutions, such as the Bank for International Settlements. The Forum has established three working groups—on hedge funds, offshore centres and capital flows—to examine areas where global financial regulation might be improved.

The UK has ratified a World Trade Organisation agreement, which came into force in March 1999, on liberalising trade in financial services. This is expected to result in improved access to financial services markets around the world.

HM Treasury represents the UK in negotiating EC Directives on the financial services sector, co-ordinating as necessary with the FSA, the Bank of England and other bodies. The Directives aim to provide a regulatory framework to allow banking, investment and insurance firms to operate throughout the European Economic Area (EEA, see p. 81) on the basis of their home state authorisation.

BANK OF ENGLAND

The Bank of England was established in 1694 by Act of Parliament and Royal Charter as a corporate body. Its capital stock was acquired by the Government in 1946. Fundamental changes to the Bank's role took effect under the Bank of England Act 1998. The most significant was the acquisition of operational responsibility for setting interest rates.

As the UK's central bank, the Bank's overriding objective is to maintain a stable and efficient monetary and financial framework for the effective operation of the economy. In pursuing this goal, it has three main purposes:

- maintaining the integrity and value of the currency;
- maintaining the stability of the financial system; and
- seeking to ensure the effectiveness of the financial services sector.

Monetary Policy Framework

The Bank's monetary policy objective is to deliver price stability, as defined by the target stipulated by the Government (see p. 388), by setting short-term interest rates. This responsibility rests with the Bank's Monetary Policy Committee, which comprises the Governor, the two Deputy Governors and six other members. The Committee meets monthly and interest rate decisions are announced as soon as is practicable after the meeting. The Committee is accountable to the Bank's Court of Directors as regards its procedures and to Parliament.

Financial Stability

Under the Memorandum of Understanding between the Bank, HM Treasury and the FSA, the Bank is responsible for the overall stability of the financial system, and has set up a Financial Stability Committee to oversee its work in this area. In exceptional circumstances, it may provide financial support as a last resort to prevent problems affecting one financial institution from spreading to other parts of the financial system. The Bank also oversees the effectiveness of the financial sector in meeting the needs of customers and in maintaining the sector's international competitiveness. It assisted the City of London in preparing its wholesale markets for the introduction of the euro in January 1999 and contributed to the Treasury's national changeover plan outlining the practical steps which would be necessary if the UK decided to join the single currency (see p. 388).

Other Main Functions

The Bank's money market operations are designed to smooth out fluctuations in the flow of cash between the Government and the private sector, and to steer short-term market interest rates to levels required to implement monetary policy. Through its daily operations in the money market, the Bank supplies the funds which the banking system as a whole needs to achieve balance by the end of each settlement day. It also acts as the Treasury's agent in managing the Government's reserves of gold and foreign exchange and its foreign currency borrowing.

The Bank provides banking services to its customers, principally the Government, the banking system and other central banks. It plays a key role in payment and settlement systems, and has sole right in England and Wales to issue banknotes, which are backed by government and other securities. The profit from the note issue is paid directly to the Government. Three Scottish and four Northern Ireland banks may also issue notes, but these have to be fully backed by Bank of England notes.

Court of Directors

The Court of Directors, which meets at least once a month, is responsible for managing the affairs of the Bank other than the formulation of monetary policy. It comprises the Governor, the two Deputy Governors and 16 Directors. The Directors form a sub-committee; functions include reviewing the Bank's performance in relation to its objectives and strategy, and the internal procedures of the Monetary Policy Committee. The Court is required to report annually to the Chancellor of the Exchequer.

BANKING SERVICES

At the end of March 1999 there were 335 institutions authorised under the Banking Act 1987, including retail banks and investment banks; 515 institutions were permitted to take deposits in the UK, including building societies. A further 110 branches of banks from other EEA countries were entitled to accept deposits in the UK on a cross-border basis.

'Retail' banking primarily provides deposit, withdrawal and loan facilities for personal customers and small businesses. Services generally provided include current accounts, deposit accounts, loan arrangements, credit and debit cards, mortgages, insurance, investment products—including pensions, unit trusts and the new Individual Savings Accounts (see p. 518)—and share-dealing services. Nearly all banks engage in some 'wholesale' activities, which involve taking larger deposits, deploying funds in money-market instruments, and making corporate loans and investments. Some banks, such as the merchant banks and overseas banks operating in the UK, concentrate on wholesale business. Many dealings are conducted on the inter-bank market, among banks themselves.

Access to Retail Banking Services

Between 91% and 94% of households in the UK have access to some form of bank account. However, the Government is concerned that many people, especially those in the most deprived neighbourhoods, do not have access to these basic financial services. Two policy teams in the Treasury are examining the problems of financial exclusion: one on the lack of access to personal financial services, and the other on finance and support for small firms.

> The Government has set up an independent review of UK banking services, excluding investment banking, which is looking at the levels of competition, efficiency and innovation, and examining how these compare with international standards. The review's remit was widened in April 1999 to cover the effects of the rapid expansion in electronic money, especially on money transmission services.

Retail Banks and Banking Groups

Banks feature prominently among the UK's biggest companies (see p. 385). Among the largest banks, in terms of market capitalisation, are Lloyds TSB, HSBC (including its subsidiary Midland), Halifax, National Westminster, Barclays, Abbey National, Royal Bank of Scotland, Bank of Scotland, Woolwich, Alliance & Leicester and Northern Rock. Standard Chartered, which mainly operates overseas, has a network of around 500 offices in nearly 50 countries, notably in Asia, Africa and the Middle East. Most major UK banks own finance houses, leasing and factoring companies, insurance companies and unit trust companies. Some also have overseas subsidiaries or branches.

The number of banks has been increasing, as several large building societies have joined the banking sector. In addition, other businesses, notably insurance companies and supermarkets, have begun to offer banking facilities and have attracted large numbers of depositors. For example, the Prudential insurance company launched its Egg direct banking service in October 1998, which attracted £5 billion of deposits from 500,000 customers in its first six months of operation.

Traditionally, the major banks have operated through their bank branches, but the number of branches has been falling as costs have been cut and as competition has intensified, notably with the extension of telephone and computer banking. Through direct banking services, customers use a telephone to obtain account information, make transfers and pay bills, or conduct transactions via a personal computer; services are often available throughout the day and night. Banking services using the Internet are gradually becoming more widely available. Other steps taken by the banks to contain costs include the introduction of self-service kiosks containing automated teller machines (ATMs) for dispensing and depositing money, and reductions in staffing, especially through centralising 'back-office' operations and reducing head office and support functions.

Investment Banks

Investment banks offer a range of professional financial services, including corporate finance and asset management. They have an important role in equity and debt markets, and are increasingly trading in securities and in futures and options. A major activity is the provision of advice and financial services to companies, especially in the case of mergers, takeovers and other forms of corporate reorganisation. Investment banks have considerable expertise in advising governments on privatisation. Several UK-owned investment banks have been acquired by overseas concerns.

Overseas Banks

The UK, with around 20% of cross-border bank lending, is the world's largest single market for international banking. Banks from around 80 countries have subsidiaries, branches or representative offices in London. France has the greatest number—48—followed by Japan, Italy and the United States. Like the major UK banks, these overseas banks offer a comprehensive banking service in many parts of the world, and engage in financing trade not only between the UK and other countries but also between third-party countries.

Building Societies

Building societies are mutual institutions, owned by their savers and borrowers. As well as their retail deposit-taking services, they specialise in housing finance, making long-term mortgage loans against the security of property—usually private dwellings purchased for owner-occupation. Some of the larger societies provide a full range of personal banking services. Following the Building Societies Acts 1986 and 1997, societies can undertake, with a few exceptions, an unrestricted variety of activities, enabling them to respond quickly to developments in the financial services and housing markets. The chief requirements for societies are that:

- their principal purpose is making loans which are secured on residential property and are funded substantially by their members;
- at least 75% of lending has to be on the security of housing; and

- a minimum of 50% of funds must be in the form of shares held by individual members.

There are 70 authorised building societies, all of which are members of the Building Societies Association, with assets of around £156 billion. The largest is the Nationwide, with assets of £52 billion. Other large societies are Bradford & Bingley, Britannia and Yorkshire.

The sector has been contracting as a result of several large societies abandoning their mutual status and becoming banks. The most recent to leave the sector was Birmingham Midshires, the fifth largest society at the time of its acquisition by Halifax plc in 1999. In April 1999 members of the Bradford & Bingley (the second biggest society) voted in support of a motion to convert the society to a bank, and the society is working towards conversion by the end of 2000. Although building societies no longer have the largest share of the housing finance market, they are still competing fiercely with the banks and are taking a significant share of new mortgages and attracting substantial deposits from savers. Several of the biggest societies have taken steps to defend their mutual status, by changing their voting rules to raise the threshold for a successful vote on conversion, or by requiring new members to donate to charity any 'windfall' payments arising from a conversion.

Payment Systems

Apart from credit and debit card arrangements, the main payment systems are run by three separate companies operating under an umbrella organisation, the Association for Payment Clearing Services (APACS). One system covers bulk paper clearings—cheques and credit transfers. A second deals with high-value clearings for same-day settlement, namely the nationwide electronic transfer service, Clearing House Automated Payment System (CHAPS). A third covers bulk electronic clearing for standing orders and direct debits. A total of 27 banks and building societies are members of one or more clearing companies, while others obtain access to APACS clearing through agency arrangements with one of the members.

Trends in Financial Transactions

Major changes in the nature of financial transactions have included the rapid growth in the use of plastic cards (which first appeared in 1966) and of automated teller machines (ATMs). There are 112 million plastic cards in circulation in the UK, and 84% of adults have one or more cards. The use of cash and cheques has recently been declining (see Table 30.2), although cash continues to be the most popular form of payment in terms of the volume of transactions—about two-thirds of payments above £1 are made in cash.

The installation of ATMs has greatly improved consumers' access to cash, particularly outside bank opening hours; their number has risen by 72% in the last ten years, to 24,600 at the end of 1998. All the major retail banks and building societies participate in nationwide networks of ATMs; in 1999 the LINK network became the first to cover the machines of all the main banks. There were 1,850 million cash withdrawals from ATMs in 1998, the average withdrawal being £53.

Plastic Cards

The main types of plastic card are cheque guarantee cards, debit cards, credit cards, charge cards and cash cards, although individual cards frequently cover more than one use, such as a cheque guarantee and cash card. Cheque guarantee cards entitle holders to cheque-cashing facilities in participating institutions, and guarantee retailers that transactions up to a specified limit—typically £50 or £100—will be honoured. Charge cards are similar to credit cards, but are designed to be paid off in full each month; they are usually available only to those with relatively high income or assets. Several major retailers issue store cards for use within their own outlets. New electronic purse cards are being tested: cards are 'charged' with money from the card holder's bank account, and can be used to purchase goods or services at participating retailers through electronic tills.

The UK has the highest level of expenditure on credit cards in Europe, with an average expenditure per card in 1998 of £1,550. There are over 41 million credit cards (including charge cards) in use in the UK, and 49% of adults have at least one credit card. Most credit cards are affiliated to one of the two major international organisations, Visa

Table 30.2: Transaction Trends					million
	1988	1993	1996	1997	1998
Payments for goods, services and financial transfers:					
Cheque payments	3,359	3,163	2,901	2,838	2,756
Paper credit transfers	481	432	419	419	408
Automated payments	1,384	2,047	2,613	2,826	3,055
Credit card purchases	582	703	965	1,065	1,156
Debit card purchases	10	659	1,270	1,503	1,736
Travel and entertainment and store card purchases	89	126	178	191	202
Total payments and transfers	**5,905**	**7,130**	**8,346**	**8,842**	**9,313**
Cash withdrawals at ATMs and counters	1,441	1,986	2,158	2,246	2,321
Post Office Order Book payments	832	871	914	874	843
Cash payments over £1 (estimated)	14,900	14,800	14,200	14,000	14,000
Total transactions[a]	**23,100**	**24,800**	**25,600**	**26,000**	**26,500**

Source: APACS

[a] Figures rounded, so that the totals do not exactly add up to the sums of the component parts.

and MasterCard. Barclays is by far the largest issuer, with 6.8 million customers owning 9.3 million cards. Competition has increased, with a number of new providers entering the market. There are over 1,300 different types of credit card, with particularly rapid growth in the number of 'affinity' cards, where the card is linked to an organisation such as a charity or trade union.

Debit cards, where payments are deducted directly from the purchaser's current account, were first issued in 1987. Purchases using debit cards are rising rapidly, up by 16% in 1998. Over 42 million cards have been issued, and some 77% of adults in the UK hold a debit card, often combined with cheque guarantee and ATM facilities. There are four debit card schemes in operation: Switch, Solo, Visa Delta and Visa Electron.

Banks have been concerned at the level of fraud on plastic cards, which was estimated to cost £135 million in 1998. In April 1999 they began to replace existing cards (which have a magnetic strip) with 'smart' cards, in which information is contained on a microchip embedded in the card; these are more difficult to counterfeit. Smart cards also store much more information than was previously possible.

National Savings

National Savings, an executive agency of the Chancellor of the Exchequer, is a source of finance for government borrowing and offers personal savers a range of investments. Since April 1999 most National Savings operations—including its three main sites in Blackpool, Durham and Glasgow—have been run by Siemens Business Services under a 15-year contract, with National Savings retaining responsibility for policy and marketing. In March 1999, £63.8 billion was invested in National Savings. Sales of National Savings products totalled £12.2 billion in 1998–99. After allowing for repayments, the net contribution to government funding was £363 million.

Important products include:

- Premium Bonds, which are held by 23 million people and are entered in a monthly draw, with tax-free prizes ranging from £50 to a single top prize of £1 million;

- Savings Certificates, which pay either a fixed rate of interest alone or a lower fixed rate of interest combined with index-linking (rising in line with the Retail Prices Index);

- Income and Capital Bonds;

- Pensioners' Bonds;

- Children's Bonus Bonds, designed to accumulate capital sums for those under 21;

- Ordinary and Investment Accounts, where deposits and withdrawals can be made at post offices throughout the UK; and

- FIRST Option Bonds, which provide a guaranteed rate of interest fixed for one year.

Friendly Societies

Friendly societies have traditionally been unincorporated societies of individuals, offering their members a limited range of financial and insurance services, such as small-scale savings products, life insurance and provision against loss of income through sickness or unemployment. The Friendly Societies Act 1992 enabled friendly societies to incorporate, take on new powers and provide a larger variety of financial services through subsidiaries. In May 1999 the Government announced proposals to give societies greater flexibility in extending the range of services available to their members.

There are around 270 friendly societies, with total funds of £12 billion and an estimated membership of over 5 million. By far the largest society is Liverpool Victoria, which has over 1 million members and manages some £3.3 billion of funds. Other big societies include Royal Liver Assurance, Family Assurance, Police Mutual Assurance, Homeowners Friendly, and Tunbridge Wells Equitable.

Special Financing Institutions

Several specialised institutions offer finance and support to personal and corporate sector borrowers:

- *Finance houses and leasing companies* provide consumer credit, business finance and leasing, and motor finance. The 100 full members of the Finance and Leasing Association undertook new business worth £62 billion in 1998.
- *Credit unions*—non-profit-making savings and loans bodies which mainly serve poorer members of the community—are less widespread in the UK than in some other countries. However, they have grown rapidly during the 1990s, and are particularly strong in Northern Ireland. There are nearly 770 credit unions in the UK, with a membership of about 475,000 and total share capital of £376 million. The Government has issued a consultation document containing measures to encourage the expansion of credit unions in Great Britain, for example, by widening the range of services, such as allowing them to offer interest-bearing accounts, and extending the range of organisations from which they are allowed to borrow.
- *Factoring* comprises a range of financial services, including credit management and finance in exchange for outstanding invoices. The industry provides working capital to more than 24,000 businesses a year. Member companies of the Factors & Discounters Association handled business worth £57 billion in 1998, 14% higher than in 1997.
- *Venture capital companies* offer medium- and long-term equity financing for new and developing businesses, management buy-outs and buy-ins, and company rescues. The UK sector is the largest and most developed in Europe. The British Venture Capital Association has 214 full members, which represent virtually every major source of venture capital in the UK. During 1998, a record £4.9 billion was invested by UK venture capital companies in 1,332 businesses; investment in the UK accounted for £3.8 billion. US pension funds are the largest investors in the UK venture capital industry.

INSURANCE

London is one of the world's leading centres for insurance and international reinsurance. It handles an estimated 20% of the general insurance business placed on the international market. As well as UK companies and the Lloyd's market (see p. 516), many overseas firms are represented, with which UK companies have formed close relationships.

Main Types of Insurance

There are two broad categories of insurance: long-term (such as life insurance), where contracts may be for periods of many years; and general, where contracts are for a year or less. Most insurance companies reinsure their risks; this performs an important function in spreading losses and in helping insurance companies to manage their businesses.

Long-term Insurance

Around 220 companies handle long-term insurance. In addition to providing life cover, life insurance is a vehicle for saving and investment as premiums are invested in securities and other assets. About 65% of households have life insurance cover. Total long-term insurance assets under management by companies in 1997 were £640 billion on behalf of their worldwide operations.

General Insurance

General insurance business is undertaken by insurance companies and by underwriters at Lloyd's. It includes fire, accident, general liability, motor, marine, aviation and other transport risks. Competition has intensified in areas like motor and household insurance, with the growth of telephone-based operations, such as Direct Line (which is now the largest insurer of private motor vehicles in the UK). Total worldwide premium income of members of the Association of British Insurers (ABI) in 1997 was £40 billion, of which £26 billion was earned in the UK.

Structure of the Industry

At the end of 1998, around 800 companies were authorised to carry on one or more classes of insurance business in the UK. Over 400 companies belong to the ABI.

The industry includes both public limited companies and mutual institutions—companies owned by their policyholders. Among the biggest insurance companies are Prudential, CGU, Standard Life (the largest mutual insurer in Europe), Royal & SunAlliance, and Norwich Union. There have been a number of mergers and takeovers affecting the large insurers. For example, Sun Life and Provincial (the UK arm of the French insurance group AXA) acquired Guardian Royal Exchange in 1999, becoming the third largest group in both general insurance and life insurance. The mutual insurer Scottish Widows is to be acquired by the banking group Lloyds TSB for £7 billion.

Lloyd's

Lloyd's is an incorporated society of private insurers in London. It is not a company but a market for insurance administered by the Council of Lloyd's and Lloyd's Regulatory and Market Boards.

The net premium income of the market in 1996 was approximately £4.8 billion. For 1999 the market has a total projected allocated capacity of £9.87 billion, of which some £7.17 billion (73%) will be capacity supplied by nearly 670 limited liability members, representing both companies and individuals who have converted to limited liability. The number of individual 'Names'—wealthy individuals who accept insurance risks for their own profit or loss, with unlimited liability—has fallen from a peak of 34,000 in the late 1980s to 4,700 in 1999. Members underwrite through 139 syndicates. Each syndicate is managed by an underwriting agent responsible for appointing a professional underwriter to accept insurance risks and manage claims on behalf of the members of the syndicate.

Insurance may only be placed through 133 active Lloyd's brokers and 12 'umbrella' brokers, which negotiate with Lloyd's syndicates on behalf of the insured. Reinsurance constitutes a large part of Lloyd's business—more than 5% of the world's reinsurance is placed at Lloyd's. Around one-sixth of Lloyd's current work is in its traditional marine market, and it has a significant share of the UK motor insurance market. Lloyd's is also a major insurer of aviation and satellite risks, and underwrites in all other areas of insurance except long-term life insurance.

Under the Financial Services and Markets Bill (see p. 508), the FSA will have extensive supervisory powers over Lloyd's, and it has consulted on how it will exercise these powers. The FSA's primary concern will be the protection of Lloyd's policyholders against the risk that valid claims may not be met.

Insurance Brokers and Intermediaries

Medium to large insurance brokers almost exclusively handle commercial matters, with the biggest dealing in worldwide risks. Smaller brokers deal mainly with the general public or specialise in a particular type of commercial insurance. Some brokers specialise in reinsurance business, transferring all or part of an insurer's risk to a reinsurer. A statutory regime of professional standards currently governs the registration and regulation of individuals and firms who use the title 'insurance broker'. However, this will be abolished under the Financial Services and Markets Bill. The Government envisages that there will be a new self-regulating regime for intermediaries arranging general insurance business. For intermediaries arranging life insurance constituting an investment (such as a personal pension), regulation will be by the FSA.

Some 16,000 individual insurance brokers are currently registered, the majority of whom are employed by about 2,000 limited companies. Nearly 2,000 individuals carry on business in their own right. A further 6,000 independent intermediaries operating under the ABI's code of practice may also arrange insurance, but are currently not allowed to use the title 'insurance broker'.

INVESTMENT

The UK has considerable expertise in fund management, which involves managing funds on behalf of investors, or advising them how best to invest their funds. The industry is estimated to contribute £2.7 billion a year to GDP and to generate £425 million in overseas earnings. London is the largest fund management centre in the world. The main types of investment fund include pension schemes, life insurance, unit trusts, investment trusts and new open-ended investment companies.

Pension Funds

Total net assets of UK pension funds were estimated at about £743 billion at the end of 1998. Pension funds are major investors in securities markets, holding around 22% of securities listed on the London Stock Exchange. Funds are managed mainly by the investment management houses. Among the largest are Mercury Asset Management, Phillips & Drew, Schroders and Gartmore.

Unit Trusts

Nearly 1,800 authorised unit trusts and open-ended investment companies (oeics) pool investors' money, and divide funds into units or shares of equal size, enabling people with relatively small amounts of money to benefit from diversified and managed portfolios. In the five years to 1999 total funds under management have nearly doubled, to around £205 billion, of which £56 billion represent funds in Personal Equity Plans (see p. 518). Most unit trusts are general funds, investing in a wide variety of UK or international securities, but there are also many specialist funds.

Over 50 unit trust management groups had total fund values of more than £1 billion in May 1999. The three largest groups are Schroders, Fidelity and M & G (which was acquired by Prudential in 1999), all of which have fund values exceeding £10 billion. Unit trust management groups are represented by the Association of Unit Trusts and Investment Funds.

Oeics, which became available in 1997, are similar to unit trusts, but an investor in an oeic buys shares in the fund rather than units. They are designed to enable UK companies to compete on an equal footing with similar schemes operating elsewhere in the EU. By May 1999, 171 oeics had been set up by 23 management groups, while several other groups are considering the conversion of some or all of their unit trust funds to oeics.

Investment Trusts

Investment trust companies, which also offer the opportunity to diversify risk on a relatively small lump-sum investment or through regular savings, are listed on the London Stock Exchange and their shares are traded in the usual way. They must invest principally in securities, and the trusts themselves are exempt from tax on gains realised within the funds. Assets are purchased mainly out of shareholders' funds, although trusts are also allowed to borrow money for investment. There were 300 members of the Association of Investment Trust Companies in June 1999, with £65 billion of assets under management by the industry. The three largest trusts are the venture capital company 3i Group, Foreign & Colonial Investment Trust, and Edinburgh Investment Trust.

Share Ownership

In the last 30 years a notable feature of the pattern of share ownership has been the growth in the proportion held by financial institutions—including pension funds and insurance companies—and a decline in the proportion held by individuals (see Table 30.3). At the end of 1997 financial institutions held ordinary shares valued at £669 billion (53% of the total), with the largest share held by insurance companies (£299 billion).

Recent research conducted for the London Stock Exchange and ProShare (an independent organisation encouraging share ownership) showed that 27% of UK adults owned shares: an estimated 12 million shareholders, although nearly half owned shares in just one company. Individual share

Table 30.3: Share Ownership in the UK

	% by type of shareholder at 31 December		
	1969	1989	1997
Overseas	6.6	12.8	24.0
Insurance companies	12.2	18.6	23.5
Pension funds	9.0	30.6	22.1
Individuals	47.4	20.6	16.5
Unit trusts	2.9	5.9	6.7
Investment trusts	} 10.1	1.6	1.9
Other financial institutions		1.1	2.0
Charities	2.1	2.3	1.9
Private non-financial companies	5.4	3.8	1.2
Other	4.3	2.7	0.2

Source: *Share Ownership: A Report on the Ownership of Shares at 31st of December 1997*

ownership rose as the result of the demutualisation in 1997 of five building societies and the Norwich Union insurance company. Eight companies each have over 1 million shareholders, with the Halifax bank having the largest number (3.5 million). The number of investment clubs—groups of individuals, usually about 15 to 20 people, who regularly invest in shares—has risen to around 3,800. Privatisation (see p. 386), employee share schemes and Personal Equity Plans (PEPs) have also led to increased share ownership. PEPs allowed tax-free investment in shares, unit trusts and certain corporate bonds. Between 1987 and April 1998, an estimated £53 billion was invested in 15.5 million PEPs.

FINANCIAL MARKETS

The City of London's financial markets include the London Stock Exchange, the foreign exchange market, the financial futures and options market, Eurobond and Eurocurrency markets, Lloyd's insurance market (see p. 516), and bullion and commodity markets.

London Stock Exchange

The London Stock Exchange is one of the top four global exchanges and the biggest centre for trading foreign equities. At the end of

PEPs and TESSAs (Tax Exempt Special Savings Accounts) were succeeded in April 1999 by Individual Savings Accounts (ISAs), which will run for at least ten years. The Government has introduced ISAs to help encourage savings, especially among those on more modest incomes, and to distribute the tax relief on savings more fairly. They allow tax-free saving of up to £5,000 a year (£7,000 in 1999–2000). There are three main elements of an ISA:

● cash—up to an annual total of £1,000 (£3,000 in 1999–2000)—such as in a bank or building society ISA account;

● stocks and shares—up to a maximum of £5,000 a year (£7,000 in 1999–2000); and

● life insurance—up to £1,000 a year.

There are two main types of ISA:

● a maxi ISA, which can include all three elements in a single ISA with one manager; and

● mini ISAs—an individual can have three mini ISAs each year, from different managers, for cash, stocks and shares, and life insurance, but is not allowed to take out both a mini ISA and a maxi ISA in the same tax year.

Early indications are that cash mini ISAs have proved particularly popular with savers.

1998, 2,087 UK and 522 international companies were listed on the main market, with a market capitalisation of £1,423 billion and £2,804 billion respectively. A further 312 companies, with a total capitalisation of £4.4 billion, were listed on AIM, the Alternative Investment Market, primarily for small, young and growing companies. Over £2.2 billion has been raised on the AIM since its establishment in 1995. CREST, a computerised settlement system for shares and other company securities, now handles the settlement of all company securities traded in the UK.

The value and volume of equity business on the Exchange reached record levels in 1998. Turnover in international equities was 51% higher than in 1997, at £2,183 billion, while turnover in UK equities was up by 2%, to £1,037 billion. About 83% of international equity business represented trades in European shares, in particular those of France, Germany, Switzerland and Italy.

In 1997 the Exchange introduced an electronic order book, through which share transactions between buyers and sellers are matched automatically, rather than being passed through market-making firms under the 'quote-driven' system. The order book covers the largest UK shares, including the 100 biggest companies in the FTSE 100 ('Footsie') index. By the end of 1998, about 56% of the number of trades in FTSE 100 shares were being handled through the new order book.

A variety of other products for raising capital are handled, including Eurobonds (see below), warrants, depositary receipts and gilt-edged stock (see p. 404). The London Stock Exchange provides a secondary or trading market where investors can buy or sell gilts. Preparations for the introduction of the euro in January 1999 (see p. 80) included the development of a new range of euro-denominated products, which are designed to help maintain London's prominent position among international exchanges.

In May 1999 London and seven other leading European exchanges—Amsterdam, Brussels, Frankfurt, Madrid, Milan, Paris and Zurich—signed an agreement to work towards harmonising the markets for their leading securities and developing a pan-European equity market. The aim is to create a single electronic trading platform, with common rules and regulations, for the top European 'blue chip' equities. In July 1999 the Exchange announced its intention to change the basis of its ownership, under which it is owned by its 294 members, to a new structure designed to equip the Exchange's business to meet in a more appropriate way the changing nature of the electronic marketplace in equities.

Euromarket

The Euromarket began with Eurodollars—US dollars lent outside the United States—and has developed into a major market in a variety of currencies lent outside their domestic markets. London is at the centre of the Euromarket and houses most of the leading international banks and securities firms. Its share of trading in the two main types of international bonds—Eurobonds and foreign bonds—is around 70% of the market of about £8,450 billion in 1997.

Foreign Exchange Market

London is the world's biggest centre for foreign exchange trading, accounting for about 30% of global net daily turnover in foreign exchange. A survey by the Bank of England in 1998 found that daily turnover in the UK was US $637 billion, 37% up since the previous survey in 1995. Dealing is now conducted entirely through telephone and electronic links between the banks, other financial institutions and a number of firms of foreign exchange brokers which act as intermediaries. The institutions keep close contact with financial centres abroad and quote buying and selling rates throughout the day for both immediate ('spot') and forward transactions in many currencies. Turnover is increasingly in forward rather than spot transactions.

Financial Futures and Options

Financial derivatives, including 'futures' and 'options', offer a means of protection against changes in prices, exchange rates and interest rates. 'Futures' are contracts to deliver or take delivery of financial instruments or physical commodities at a future date, while 'options' give the right but not the obligation to buy or sell financial instruments or physical commodities on a stated date at a predetermined price. Financial futures and options are traded at the London International Financial Futures and Options Exchange (LIFFE), which has 230 members, including many of the world's leading financial institutions. LIFFE is in the process of gradually converting to electronic trading, which will eventually replace the 'open outcry' trading facilities, under which members execute their business through a system of hand signals and shouting on the trading floor.

LIFFE handled 194 million futures and options contracts in 1998, and currently it is handling an average of 482,000 contracts a day, with a nominal average value of £203 billion. LIFFE also handles commodity trading, following its merger in 1996 with the London Commodity Exchange. Coffee, cocoa and sugar are the most frequently traded commodities, while trading also takes place in grain, potatoes and the dry freight index.

Other Exchanges

Other important City exchanges include:

- the *London bullion market*—around 60 banks and other financial trading companies participate in the London gold and silver markets;
- the *London Clearing House*, which clears and settles business on a number of exchanges;
- the *London Metal Exchange*—the primary base metals market in the world, trading contracts in aluminium, aluminium alloy, copper, lead, nickel, tin and zinc;
- the *International Petroleum Exchange*; and
- the *Baltic Exchange*—the world's leading international shipping market.

Other Services

The distribution of goods, including food and drink, to their point of sale is a major economic activity. The large wholesalers and retailers of food and drink operate extensive distribution networks, either directly or through contractors.

WHOLESALING

In 1999 there were over 113,000 businesses (see Table 30.4) engaged in wholesaling and dealing in the UK. About 27% were sole proprietors and 15% partnerships. Some 1.1 million people in the UK were employed in this sector in March 1999. Turnover in 1996, the latest year for which information is available, was almost £344 billion.

In the food and drink trade almost all large retailers have their own buying and central distribution operations. Many small wholesalers and independent grocery retailers belong to voluntary 'symbol' groups (for example, Spar, Cost Cutter, Londis and Mace), which provide access to central purchasing facilities and co-ordinated promotions. This has helped smaller retailers to remain relatively competitive; many local and convenience stores and village shops would not otherwise be able to stay in business. Booker, Batleys and Makro are the major 'cash and carry' wholesalers. Palmer and Harvey McLane is the principal food services delivery wholesaler, now that Booker Wholesale Foods has sold the remainder of its business to them. London's wholesale markets play a significant part in the distribution of fresh foodstuffs. New Covent Garden is the main market for fruit and vegetables, London Central Markets for meat and Billingsgate for fish.

The Co-operative Wholesale Society (CWS) is the principal supplier of goods and services to the Co-operative Movement and was a founder member of the Co-operative Retail Trading Group. The latter was formed in 1993 to act as a central marketing, buying and distribution partnership for retail co-operative societies. The Group now accounts for around 90% of Co-op food trade. The CWS is also the largest co-operative retailer in Europe, with 680 stores located in Scotland, Northern Ireland, the east and south Midlands, and south-east and north-east England; 644 of these are food stores. Retail co-operative societies are voluntary organisations controlled by their members,

Table 30.4: Wholesale and Retail Enterprises in the UK 1999

Number of businesses

Annual turnover (£'000)	Wholesale Total	of which: Sole proprietors	Partner- ships	Retail Total	of which: Sole proprietors	Partner- ships
1–49	18,655	9,360	2,790	21,665	13,055	5,260
50–99	16,440	7,690	2,985	49,870	29,475	14,950
100–249	22,920	7,560	4,565	71,830	31,560	29,430
250–499	15,135	3,035	2,965	33,320	10,090	14,665
500–999	13,305	1,470	2,150	15,835	3,290	5,715
1,000+	26,600	865	1,945	10,305	940	2,170
of which:						
1,000–1,999	10,350	n.a.	n.a.	6,300	n.a.	n.a.
2,000–4,999	8,890	n.a.	n.a.	2,540	n.a.	n.a.
5,000–9,999	3,505	n.a.	n.a.	675	n.a.	n.a.
10,000–49,999	3,150	n.a.	n.a.	545	n.a.	n.a.
50,000+	705	n.a.	n.a.	245	n.a.	n.a.
Total	113,055	29,980	17,400	202,820	88,410	72,185

Source: Office for National Statistics. *Size Analysis of UK Businesses 1999*. Business Monitor PA1003
n.a. = not available.
Notes: Turnover relates mainly to a 12-month period ending in spring 1998. Differences between totals and the sums of their component parts are due to rounding.

membership being open to anyone paying a small deposit on a minimum share. The Co-operative Movement, which comprises 48 independent societies, has nearly 4,650 stores.

RETAILING

The retail sector accounts for 37% of all consumer expenditure. In 1999 there were nearly 203,000 retail businesses in the UK (see Table 30.4); 44% were sole proprietors and 36% partnerships. Nearly 2.4 million people in the UK were employed in this sector in March 1999. Turnover in 1996, the latest year for which information is available, was over £193 billion, of which retail turnover represented £181.5 billion. Businesses range from national supermarket and other retail chains to independent corner grocery shops, hardware stores, chemists, newsagents and a host of other types of retailer. During recent years the large multiple retailers have grown considerably, tending to increase outlet size and diversify product ranges. Some, such as Marks & Spencer, J. Sainsbury and Tesco, also operate overseas, through either subsidiaries or franchise agreements. Small

independent retail businesses and co-operative societies have been in decline for some time. Sunday trading laws have been relaxed to allow retailers to open for specified periods on Sundays; smaller retailers are permitted to open on Sundays for longer hours than the larger supermarkets and department stores, to help their competitive position. The main supermarket chains are experimenting with 24-hour opening on selected days. They are also looking closely at different forms of home shopping (by telephone, fax and Internet) and delivery. Iceland was among the first to start home deliveries on a national basis.

The four biggest supermarket chains by sales value are Tesco (with about 586 stores), J. Sainsbury (391, excluding 13 Savacentre stores), Asda (210, excluding Dales)—which is to be acquired by the US retailing group Wal-Mart—and Safeway (451, excluding Presto and Wellworths). They accounted for 47% of total grocery sales, worth £43.8 billion in 1998, including over 45% of UK food sales. In April 1999 the Director General of Fair Trading asked the Competition Commission (see p. 396) to investigate the supply of groceries from multiple stores in the UK.

This follows an inquiry in 1998 which looked at profit levels of the 'Big Four'. Other significant food retailers are Somerfield, Marks & Spencer, Waitrose, Iceland and Morrisons which account for 17% of grocery sales. Morrisons, Britain's sixth-largest supermarket chain, is currently expanding into the south of England. Alcoholic drinks are sold mainly in specialist 'off licences' and supermarkets. The principal off-licence specialists are Threshers and Victoria Wine (both owned by First Quench Retailing), Parisa Group, Unwins and Oddbins.

The leading mixed retail chains are found in high streets nationwide. Among them are Marks & Spencer (mainly selling clothing and food and drink), Boots (pharmaceuticals and cosmetic goods), F. W. Woolworth (over 750 branches selling a variety of products, from clothing to kitchenware), W. H. Smith (newspapers, books and stationery), Great Universal Stores and its Argos subsidiary (which keeps in stock an extensive range of goods ordered in the stores from a catalogue and then taken away by customers), and John Lewis and Debenhams (a variety of wares, including clothing, furniture and electrical goods). Several chains of DIY (Do-It-Yourself) stores and superstores cater for people carrying out their own repairs and improvements to their homes and gardens; they stock tools, decorating and building materials, kitchen and bathroom fittings, and garden products. The three biggest are Kingfisher's B&Q, J. Sainsbury's Homebase and Wickes.

The large multiple groups have broadened their range of goods and services. Large food retailers are also placing greater emphasis on selling own-label goods (which now account for over half of sales) and environmentally friendly products (including organic produce), together with household wares and clothing. In-store pharmacies, post offices, customer cafeterias and dry-cleaners are now a feature of large supermarkets, which have also begun selling books, magazines, newspapers, pre-recorded videos, cassettes and compact discs. 'Stores within stores' are common; for example, sportswear and sports goods retailers are to be found in several of the big mixed department stores. The major supermarket chains have their own petrol stations at some of their bigger outlets (see p. 523). Several large retailers offer personal finance facilities in an attempt to encourage sales, particularly of high-value goods, while others, including Marks & Spencer and Boots, are diversifying into financial services. Some supermarkets now offer banking facilities. Boots announced in May 1999 that it was opening its first 'in-house' dental surgery. 'Loyalty' cards were introduced in the mid-1990s by supermarket and other retail groups, giving regular customers cash discounts related to the size of their purchases and providing the stores with detailed information on shoppers' buying habits.

A recent survey by NatWest and the British Franchise Association (BFA) estimates that there are 596 fully-fledged business-format franchises, with around 30,000 outlets, accounting for 300,000 direct jobs in Britain and with an annual turnover of £7.4 billion. Franchising is a business in which a company owning the rights to a particular form of trading licenses them to franchisees, usually by means of an initial payment with continuing royalties. Franchised activities operate in many areas, including cleaning services, film processing, print shops, fitness centres, courier delivery, car rental, engine tuning and servicing, and fast food retailing. Among the large-scale franchise operations are McDonald's, KallKwik (fast printing) and Alldays (with over 800 convenience stores). About 200 franchisers are members of the BFA.

In March 1999, 558,000 people were employed in the UK in retailing motor vehicles and parts, and in petrol stations. Many businesses selling new vehicles are franchised by the motor manufacturers. Vehicle components are available for sale at garages which undertake servicing and repair work and also at retail chains like Halfords and at independent retailers. Drive-in fitting centres sell tyres, exhaust systems, batteries, clutches and other vehicle parts; the largest chains include Kwik-Fit and ATS. There were 13,756 retail outlets for petrol at the end of 1998; the three companies with the highest number are Esso, BP Amoco and Shell. The number of petrol stations has declined by about 32% in the last decade, reflecting intense competition in the sector, relatively low profit margins and consolidation among operators. This is particularly so in rural areas. Petrol stations are increasingly offering other retail services, such as shops, car washes and fast food outlets, with the aim of attracting more business. Over one-fifth of petrol sold in the UK comes from the 977 supermarket forecourts operated at the end of 1998.

All kinds of goods and services can be purchased through mail order catalogues from such firms as Great Universal Stores, Littlewoods, Freemans, Grattan and Empire. In 1997 sales by direct and agency mail order totalled almost £5 billion. The largest-selling items are clothing, footwear, furniture, household textiles and domestic electrical appliances.

Shopping Facilities

Government policy is to focus new retail development in existing centres. This is to ensure that everyone has easy access to a range of shops and services, whether they have a car or not; and to enable businesses of all sizes and types to prosper. The Government aims to revitalise town centres by focusing new shopping, leisure and other facilities in these centres. One of the most significant trends in retailing has been the spread of superstores, many of which were built away from urban centres until recently. Since 1996, social, economic and environmental considerations have led the Government and local planning authorities to limit new retail developments outside town centres, which had in particular undermined the viability of existing town and district centres, encroached on the countryside and encouraged greater car use. All new retail development requires planning permission from the local planning authority, which must consult central government before granting permission for most retail developments of 2,500 sq m (27,000 sq ft) or more. Retailers' attentions are now being turned back to town centres, redeveloping existing stores and building smaller outlets. A chain of Tesco 'Metros' (1,000 sq m) has been followed by the opening of J. Sainsbury 'Central' stores (1,000 sq m) and 'Local' stores (300 sq m).

Regional out-of-town shopping centres, of which there are eight, are located on sites offering good road access and ample parking facilities. The latest is the Bluewater shopping centre near Dartford, Kent which opened in March 1999. It is the largest out-of-town retail development in Europe, covering 160,000 sq m (1.7 million sq ft), and has created some 7,000 jobs. Built on the site of old chalk quarries, and surrounded by seven lakes, it has 320 shops and parking for 13,000 cars, and is expected to attract about 30 million shoppers a year. It is likely to be the last such out-of-town centre, as government policy is now to encourage regeneration of town and city centres. Apart from Bluewater, other out-of-town regional shopping centres are: the Metro Centre at Gateshead in north-east England; Meadowhall near Sheffield; Trafford Centre in Manchester; Merry Hill at Dudley in the West Midlands; Cribbs Causeway at Bristol; Lakeside at Thurrock in Essex, and Braehead, near Glasgow. About half of total food sales are accounted for by superstores away from town centres, compared with a fifth at the beginning of the 1980s.

Retailers of non-food goods, such as DIY products, toys, furniture and electrical appliances, sportswear, and office and computer products, have also built outlets away from urban centres. There is a continuing trend towards grouping retail warehouses into retail parks, often with food and other facilities, although planning controls are limiting approvals for new parks.

Information Technology (IT)

Computers monitor stock levels and record sales figures through electronic point-of-sale (EPOS) systems. These systems read a bar-code printed on the retail item that holds price and product information and can be used to generate orders for stock replenishment as well as totalling up bills and providing a receipt for customers. Techniques such as 'just-in-time' ordering, in which products arrive at the store at the last possible moment before sale, have become widespread as a result. Leading retailers have set up electronic data interchange (EDI) systems; these enable their computers to communicate with those of their suppliers, and transmit orders and invoices electronically, so reducing errors and saving time.

'Superscan' technology—where customers use an electronic scanning device to work out their own bills, thus avoiding the need to queue at a check-out—is undergoing trials in a number of supermarkets. Electronic home shopping, using a television and telephone, and 'online' shopping, where personal computers are linked to databases, are also being introduced. In 1997, 'e-commerce' accounted for only £125 million of the £9.6 billion home shopping sales market, but it is growing rapidly.

CONSUMER PROTECTION

The Government aims to maintain and develop a clear and fair regulatory framework which gives confidence to consumers and contributes to the competitiveness of business.

It works closely with outside bodies which have expert knowledge of consumer issues to develop policies and legislation.

Consumer Legislation

Under the Trade Descriptions Act 1968, it is a criminal offence to apply false or misleading statements to goods, services, accommodation or facilities. False or misleading advertisements can also be acted against by the Director General of Fair Trading under the Control of Misleading Advertisements Regulations 1988.

Existing legislation covers the sale and supply of goods and services. The Sale of Goods Act 1979 (as amended in 1994) ensures that consumers are entitled to receive goods which fit their description and are of satisfactory quality. The Trade Descriptions Act 1968 prohibits misdescriptions of goods,

---

In July 1999, the Government issued a White Paper, *Modern Markets: Confident Consumers*, setting out a range of initiatives to improve protection for consumers. The main proposals include:

- a hallmark for consumers to identify companies that have signed up to a code of practice guaranteeing high standards of customer service, including proper redress when things go wrong;

- a digital hallmark for Internet traders who abide by codes guaranteeing security of payment and privacy of information to enable customers to shop on the net with confidence;

- the publication of international price comparisons;

- stronger powers for trading standards officers and the Office of Fair Trading to deal with dishonest traders;

- new powers for the courts to ban from trading those who continually cheat consumers;

- a speedy procedure to introduce secondary legislation to outlaw new scams;

- the development of a new advice network, building on existing advice agencies, to give people easier access to high-quality advice;

- a consumer 'gateway' on the Internet and a trial local customer helpline which will direct people to the best sources of advice;

- new measures to ensure information is accurate, comprehensive and easy to understand, including clearer prices and tougher controls on misdescriptions of services;

- a review of all consumer protection legislation, to see whether it is still effective in meeting the needs of consumers or whether it has become a burden on business with no apparent benefit;

- the relaunch of the National Consumer Council as a more effective voice of consumers; and

- a full review by the Director General of Fair Trading of his consumer protection functions.

services, accommodation and facilities. This Act enables regulations to be made requiring information or instructions relating to goods to be marked on or to accompany the goods or to be included in advertisements.

Misleading indications about prices of goods are covered by the Consumer Protection Act 1987. This Act also makes it a criminal offence to supply unsafe products, and provides product liability rights for consumers. The regulatory framework to control product safety is a mixture of European and UK legislation, voluntary safety standards and industry codes of practice. The Department of Trade and Industry (DTI) runs a programme of safety awareness initiatives. This aims to reduce accidents by increasing consumer awareness of potential hazards in the home and by encouraging them to change their behaviour.[1]

The marking and accuracy of quantities are regulated by weights and measures legislation. Another law provides for the control of medical products, and certain other substances and articles, through a system of licences and certificates. New regulations have also been recently introduced to strengthen the protection of consumers from unscrupulous doorstep sellers.

The Director General of Fair Trading promotes good trading practices and acts against malpractice. Under the Fair Trading Act 1973, the Director General can recommend legislative or other changes to stop practices adversely affecting consumers' economic interests; encourage trade associations to develop codes of practice promoting consumers' interests; and disseminate consumer information and guidance. The Director General can also demand assurances as to future conduct from traders who persistently breach the law to the detriment of consumers.

The Consumer Credit Act 1974 is intended to protect consumers in their dealings with credit businesses. Most businesses connected with the consumer credit or hire industry or which supply ancillary credit services—for example, credit brokers, debt collectors, debt counsellors and credit reference agencies—require a consumer credit licence. The Director General is responsible for administering the licensing system, including refusing or revoking licences of those unfit to hold them. The Director General also has powers to prohibit unfit people from carrying out estate agency work; to take court action to prevent the publication of misleading advertisements; and to stop traders using unfair terms in standard contracts with consumers.

The EU's consumer programme covers activities such as health and safety, protection of the consumer's economic interests, promotion of consumer education and strengthening the representation of consumers. The views of British consumer organisations on EU matters are represented by a number of organisations including the Consumers' Association (see p. 526) and the Consumers in Europe Group (UK). Numerous British consumer bodies also have a voice on the European consumer 'watchdog' body, the Bureau Européen des Unions de Consommateurs.

Consumer Advice and Information

Advice and information on consumer matters is given by 1,200 outlets of around 700 Citizens Advice Bureaux. Their work is co-ordinated by a national association linked to the bureaux via local and regional committees (Scotland has its own Association). Similar assistance is provided at trading standards and consumer protection departments of local authorities (in Northern Ireland the Department of Economic Development) and, in some areas, by specialist consumer advice centres.

The National Consumer Council (and associated councils for Scotland and Wales), which receives government finance, gives its view to government, industry and others on consumer issues. The General Consumer Council for Northern Ireland has wide-ranging duties in consumer affairs in general.

Consumer bodies for privatised utilities investigate questions of concern to the consumer. Some trade associations in industry and commerce have established codes of practice. In addition, several organisations

---

[1] DTI's Home Accident Surveillance System shows that, every year, there are just under 4,000 deaths and nearly 3 million medically treated injuries as a result of home accidents, which also cost the country about £30 billion.

work to further consumer interests by representing the consumer's view to government, industry and other bodies. The largest is the Consumers' Association, funded by the subscriptions of approximately 1 million members to its various *Which?* magazines.

HOTELS AND CATERING

The hotel and restaurant trades, which include public houses (pubs), wine bars and other licensed bars in addition to all kinds of businesses offering accommodation and prepared food, employed nearly 1.9 million people in the UK in March 1999 and their total turnover was about £43 billion. There are about 10,935 hotels and motels in the UK, ranging from major hotel groups—the largest, Forte Hotels, owned by the Granada Group, has 323 hotels in the UK—to small guest houses, individually owned. Holiday centres, including holiday camps with full board, self-catering centres and caravan parks, are run by Butlins, Holiday Club, Center Parcs, Warner Holidays and Pontin's, among others.

In 1998 there were around 44,420 restaurants, cafés and take-away food shops in the UK, with a total turnover of £13.5 billion. Restaurants offer cuisine from virtually every country in the world; they cater for the whole spread of income groups and several of the highest-quality ones have international reputations. Chinese, Indian, Thai, Italian, French and Greek restaurants are among the most popular. 'Fast food' restaurants are widespread, many of which are franchised. They specialise in selling hamburgers, chicken, pizza and a variety of other foods, to be eaten on the premises or taken away. Well-known nationwide chains include McDonald's and Burger King (hamburgers), KFC (chicken), Pizza Hut and Pizza Express. Traditional fish and chip shops are another main provider of cooked take-away food. Sandwich bars are common in towns and cities, typically in areas with high concentrations of office workers. In 1997 sandwiches accounted for 33.8% of the fast food market, hamburgers 23.6%, ethnic food (Chinese and Indian) 13.8%, fish and chips 12.5%, pizzas 10.3% and chicken 6%.

About 51,500 pubs sell beer, wines, soft drinks and spirits to adults for consumption on the premises, and most also serve hot and cold food. Many pubs are owned by the large brewing companies, such as Whitbread and Bass, which either provide managers to run them or offer tenancy agreements; these pubs tend to sell just their own brands of beer, although some also offer 'guest' beers. Others, called 'free houses', are independently owned and managed, and frequently serve a variety of different branded beers. Wine bars are normally smaller than pubs and tend to specialise in wine and food; they more closely resemble bars in other parts of Europe. 'Themed' pubs, for example Irish bars, are becoming increasingly popular.

TRAVEL AGENTS

Most British holiday-makers travelling overseas buy 'package holidays' from travel agencies, where the cost covers both transport and accommodation. The most popular package holiday destinations are Spain and France. Long-haul holidays to places like the United States, the Caribbean and Australia have gained in popularity as air fares have come down. Some people prefer to travel more independently, and there are travel firms which will make just travel arrangements for customers.

Around 80% of high street travel agencies are members of the Association of British Travel Agents (ABTA). Although most are small businesses, a few large firms, such as Lunn Poly and Thomas Cook, have hundreds of branches. Nearly 670 tour operators are members of ABTA; about half are both retail agents and tour operators. Major tour operators include Thomson, Airtours and First Choice. ABTA operates financial protection schemes to safeguard its members' customers and maintains codes of conduct drawn up with the Office of Fair Trading. It also offers a free consumer affairs service to help resolve complaints against members, and a low-cost independent arbitration scheme for members' customers. The British Incoming Tour Operators' Association is the leading body representing tour operators engaged in incoming tourism to the UK.

TOURISM AND LEISURE

Tourism is one of the UK's key long-term growth sectors, with total spending on tourism in 1998 estimated at £61 billion. In the region of 1.78 million people are employed in tourism and related activities; of these, around 154,000 are self-employed. About 159,000 businesses, mainly independent small ones—hotels and guest houses, restaurants, holiday homes, caravan and camping parks and so on—are responsible for providing the bulk of tourism services; about 8.5% of small businesses are engaged in tourism.

The number of overseas visitors to the UK increased by 1% in 1998 to reach an estimated 25.7 million, spending £12.7 billion. The UK's share of world tourism earnings reached 4.8%. Visitors from North America increased by 11% to 4.6 million, while those from Western Europe were unchanged at 16.6 million and from other areas fell by 4%. The highest proportion from a single country was from the United States (15%). Business travel accounts for about £3.9 billion, 30% of all overseas tourism revenue. London's Heathrow and Gatwick airports, the seaport of Dover and the Channel Tunnel are the main points of entry.

Some 48% of overseas tourists spend all or most of their visit in London, while others venture further afield to see the many attractions in the English regions as well as Scotland, Wales and Northern Ireland.

Domestic tourism generated approximately £45 billion in 1998. Of British residents opting to take their main holiday in the UK, 47% choose a traditional seaside destination, such as Blackpool (Lancashire), Bournemouth (Dorset), Great Yarmouth (Norfolk) and resorts in Devon and Cornwall. Short holiday breaks (up to three nights), valued at £3.1 billion in 1998, make up an increasingly significant part of the market.

The UK's historic towns and cities and its scenic rural and coastal areas continue to have great appeal for British and overseas tourists alike. There is a growing interest in heritage, arts and culture; attractions include museums, art galleries, historic buildings and monuments, and theatres, as well as shopping, sports and business facilities. Domestic and foreign tourists play an increasingly important role in supporting the UK's national heritage and creative arts, in addition to the large financial contribution they make to hotels, restaurants, cafés and bars, and public transport.

Business travel, which accounts for a growing share of the tourism market, includes attendance at conferences, exhibitions, trade fairs and other business sites. Activity holidays—based on walking, canoeing, mountain climbing, or artistic activities, for example—are becoming more popular. The Youth Hostel Association operates a comprehensive network of hostels offering young people and families a range of affordable facilities, including self-catering.

'Leisure parks' attract over 37 million visitors a year. Alton Towers (Staffordshire), Chessington World of Adventures and Thorpe Park (both in Surrey) are three of the biggest; 2.78 million people visited Alton Towers in 1998, the second largest number of visitors for any paid-for tourist attraction (see Table 30.5). Legoland near Windsor in Berkshire is the newest theme park; it attracted 1.6 million visitors in 1998. Attractions in these parks include spectacular 'white knuckle' rides and overhead cable cars and railways, while some parks also feature domesticated and wild animals.

Tourism Promotion

The Department for Culture, Media and Sport is responsible for tourism in England, and the Scottish Parliament, Welsh Assembly and Northern Ireland Offices have responsibility for tourism in their respective countries. The government-supported British Tourist Authority (BTA)—which is receiving £35 million in grant in 1999–2000—boosts tourism spending in Britain by focusing its marketing resources on 27 key markets worldwide (which in total generate 90% of all visitors to Britain) and encourages the development of tourist facilities in the UK to meet the needs of overseas visitors. The tourist bodies for England, Scotland, Wales and Northern Ireland, which also receive government finance, support domestic tourism and work with the BTA to promote Britain overseas. In July 1999, the English Tourism Council (ETC) replaced the English

Table 30.5: Attendances at UK Tourist Attractions, 1998		million
Blackpool Pleasure Beach	F	7.1
British Museum, London	F	5.6
National Gallery, London	F	4.8
Palace Pier, Brighton	F	3.5
Westminster Abbey	P	3.0
Eastbourne Pier	F	2.8
Alton Towers, Staffordshire	P	2.8
Madame Tussaud's, London	P	2.8
Tower of London	P	2.6
Tate Gallery, London	F	2.2
Pleasureland, Southport	F	2.1
York Minster	F	2.0
Natural History Museum, London	P	1.9
Chessington World of Adventures, Surrey	P	1.7
Science Museum, London	P	1.6

Source: British Tourist Authority
F = Free admission.
P = Paid-for admission.

Tourist Board. The ETC is responsible for developing and promoting a sustainable and competitive industry in England.

The Government is working with the tourism industry to raise standards of accommodation and service, and to address certain key issues facing the industry. These include its communications strategy; improving visitor attractions; boosting business tourism; encouraging best practice for the development of workforce skills; and government-industry communication. The Government is also considering how best to support tourism growth which is economically, socially and environmentally sustainable. The BTA and the national tourist boards inform and advise the Government on issues of concern to the industry. They also help businesses and other organisations to plan by researching and publicising trends affecting the industry. The national tourist boards work closely with regional tourist boards, on which local government and business interests are represented. There are about 800 local Tourist Information Centres in the UK. Accommodation classification and quality grading schemes are operated by the national tourist boards in conjunction with motoring organisations such as the AA and RAC.

EXHIBITION AND CONFERENCE CENTRES

The UK is one of the world's three leading countries for international conferences—the others being the United States and France. London and Paris are the two most popular conference cities. Other British towns and cities—including several traditional seaside holiday resorts diversifying to take advantage of the growing business tourism market—have conference and exhibition facilities.

Among the most modern purpose-built conference and exhibition centres are the International Conference Centre in Birmingham; the Queen Elizabeth II and Olympia Conference Centres, both in London; Cardiff International Arena, a 5,000-seat multi-purpose facility; and the Belfast Waterfront Hall. In Scotland, Edinburgh, Glasgow and Aberdeen have major exhibition and conference centres. Brighton (East Sussex), Harrogate (North Yorkshire), Bournemouth (Dorset), Manchester, Nottingham and Torquay (Devon) all have exhibition and conference centres. Other important exhibition facilities in London are at the Barbican, Earls Court, Alexandra Palace and Wembley Arena.

RENTAL SERVICES

A varied range of rental services, many franchised, are available throughout the UK. These include hire of cars and other vehicles; televisions, video recorders and camcorders; household appliances such as washing machines; tools and heavy decorating equipment (such as ladders and floor sanders); and video films and computer games. Retailing of many types of service is dominated by chains, although independent operators are still to be found in most fields. In addition, there is a thriving sector renting to businesses—all sorts of machinery and other types of equipment, together with computers and other office appliances. In 1998 turnover of the rental sector amounted to £14.2 billion.

COMPUTING SERVICES

The computing services industry comprises businesses engaged in software development; systems integration; IT consultancy; IT 'outsourcing'; processing services; and the provision of complete computer systems. It also includes companies that provide IT education and training; independent maintenance; support, contingency planning and recruitment; and contract staff. Turnover of companies in this sector amounted to nearly £35 billion in 1998, 17% higher than in 1997.

British firms and universities have established strong reputations in software R&D. A number of international IT conglomerates have set up R&D operations in the UK—among them are Hitachi, IBM, Nortel, Philips and Sharp. US software company Computer Associates is building a new £100 million European headquarters at Datchet, near Heathrow Airport. Microsoft has made a major R&D investment at Cambridge and Sun Microsystems will be opening a new corporate headquarters in summer 2000. Academic expertise is especially evident in such areas as artificial intelligence, neural networks, formal programming for safety critical systems, and parallel programming systems.

Software firms have developed strengths in sector-specific applications, including systems for retailing, banking, finance and accounting, medical and dental industries, and the travel and entertainment industries. For example, Misys is a market leader in financial services software, and Sage in accounting and payroll software. Specialist 'niche' markets in which UK software producers are active include artificial intelligence, scientific and engineering software (especially computer-aided design), mathematical software, geographical information systems, and data visualisation packages. Some firms specialise in devising multimedia software. Distance learning, 'virtual reality' and computer animation all benefit from a large pool of creative talent.

One of the biggest users of software is the telecommunications industry (see p. 479). The provision of almost all new telecommunications services, including switching and transmission, is dependent on software.

MARKET RESEARCH

The UK's market research profession has grown strongly in the last five years and there are now over 500 companies, with a total UK revenue of over £1 billion a year. UK-owned market research companies include the largest international customised market research specialists. Well-known names include TaylorNelson Sofres, Research International, NOP, Millward Brown and MORI.

MANAGEMENT CONSULTANCY

The UK's 35,000 management consultants supply technical assistance and advice to business and government clients. The 32 members of the Management Consultancies Association account for more than half of management consultancy work carried out in the UK. The largest consultancy firms include Andersen Consulting, CMG Management, CSC, Deloitte & Touche, Ernst & Young, KPMG, PA Consulting, PricewaterhouseCoopers and Sema. In 1998 member firms earned £5.5 billion in the UK and £1 billion abroad.

ADVERTISING AND PUBLIC RELATIONS

The UK is a major centre for creative advertising, and multinational corporations often use advertising created in the UK for marketing their products globally. British agencies have strong foreign links through overseas ownership and associate networks. Advertising expenditure in the UK increased by 7.7% to £14.3 billion in 1998. The press accounted for 52% of the total, television for 28%, direct mail for 12%, and posters, transport, commercial radio and cinema for the rest. The largest advertising expenditure is on food, household durables, cosmetics, office equipment, motor vehicles and financial services. Among the biggest spenders in 1998 were BT, Dixons, Procter and Gamble, Kellogg, Unilever, Cable & Wireless, the major car manufacturers and the Government. British television advertising receives many international awards.

Campaigns are planned by around 1,100 advertising agencies. Leading agencies include Abbott Mead Vickers BBDO, J. Walter Thompson, Saatchi & Saatchi, and Ogilvy and Mather. In addition to their creative, production and media-buying roles, some agencies offer integrated marketing services, including consumer research and public relations. Many agencies have sponsorship departments, which arrange for businesses to sponsor products and events, including artistic, sporting and charitable events. In return for financial or other support, the sponsoring company is associated with a worthy product or occasion, thereby raising its profile with consumers.

Government advertising campaigns—on crime prevention, health promotion, armed services recruitment and so on—are often organised by the Central Office of Information, an executive agency of the Government.

The UK's public relations industry has developed rapidly, and there are now many small specialist firms as well as some quite large ones, such as Shandwick and Citigate Dewe Rogerson. About 26% of the earnings of UK public relations firms represents overseas work.

BUSINESS SUPPORT SERVICES

One of the major growth areas in the services sector is in support services, reflecting the trend among more and more firms to 'outsource' non-core operations. Initially, operating areas which were outsourced or contracted out were in cleaning, security and catering. However, firms are now outsourcing other activities, such as IT and personnel support services. A study for the DTI in 1996 found that the annual turnover of business support services in the UK was around £10 billion, and the sector employed 675,000 people. Turnover in the business services sector has risen by around 10% a year since 1996. Among the largest firms providing these services are Rentokil Initial, OCS Group, Hays and Serco Group.

Further Reading

Modern Markets: Confident Consumers. Cm 4410. The Stationery Office, 1999.
Bank of England Annual Report.
Financial Services Authority Annual Report.
London Stock Exchange *Fact File* (annual).

Websites

Bank of England: www.bankofengland.co.uk
Financial Services Authority: www.fsa.gov.uk

Appendix 1: Government Departments and Agencies

An outline of the principal functions of the main government departments and a list of their executive agencies is given below. UK Cabinet ministries are indicated by an asterisk. Executive agencies are normally listed under the relevant department, although in some cases they are included within the description of the department's responsibilities.

The principal address, telephone, fax number and website of each department are given. A major change in UK telephone numbers, to overcome a growing shortage by the year 2000, is in progress, affecting certain areas including Cardiff, London, Northern Ireland and Southampton. Telephone and fax numbers in this Appendix show the new numbers, starting, for example, with 020 for London, 028 for Northern Ireland, or 029 for Cardiff. The old codes are running in parallel and can be used up to 22 April 2000.

More detailed information, including e-mail addresses and the addresses of executive agencies and the Government Offices for the Regions, can be found in the annual *Civil Service Year Book*. Through the website www.open.gov.uk the websites of many departments and agencies can be reached.

The work of many of the departments and agencies covers the United Kingdom as a whole and is indicated by (UK). Where this is not the case, the abbreviations used are (GB) for functions covering England, Wales and Scotland; (E, W & NI) for those covering England, Wales and Northern Ireland; (E & W) for those covering England and Wales; and (E) for those concerned with England only.

Cabinet Office

70 Whitehall, London SW1A 2AS
Tel: 020 7270 3000   Fax: 020 7270 0618
Website: www.cabinet-office.gov.uk
See p. 55.

Executive Agencies

The Buying Agency[1]
CCTA: Central Computer and
   Telecommunications Agency[1]
Civil Service College
Government Car and Despatch Agency
Property Advisers to the Civil Estate[1]

ECONOMIC AFFAIRS

*Ministry of Agriculture, Fisheries and Food

Nobel House, 17 Smith Square, London SW1P
3JR Tel: 020 7238 3000   Fax: 020 7238 6591
Website: www.maff.gov.uk
Policies on agriculture, horticulture and fisheries; responsibilities for related environmental and rural issues (E); food policies (UK).

Executive Agencies

Central Science Laboratory
Centre for Environment, Fisheries and
   Aquaculture Science
Farming and Rural Conservation Agency
Intervention Board[2]
Meat Hygiene Service
Pesticides Safety Directorate
Veterinary Laboratories Agency
Veterinary Medicines Directorate

*Department of Trade and Industry

1 Victoria Street, London SW1H 0ET Tel: 020
7215 5000   Fax: 020 7222 0612
Website: www.dti.gov.uk

---

[1] From April 2000 these agencies will form part of the new Office of Government Commerce (see p. 403) which will be a distinct organisation within HM Treasury.

[2] The Intervention Board is a department in its own right as well as an executive agency. Responsibility for it is shared jointly by the four agriculture ministers in the UK.

Competitiveness; relations with business; science and technology; promotion of new enterprise and competition; consumer affairs. Specific responsibilities include innovation policy; regional industrial policy and inward investment promotion; small businesses; spread of management best practice; business/education links; employment relations; international trade policy; commercial relations and export promotion; company law; insolvency; radio regulation; patents and copyright protection (GB); the development of new sources of energy and relations with specific sectors of business (UK).

Executive Agencies

Companies House
Employment Tribunals Service
Insolvency Service
National Weights and Measures Laboratory
Patent Office
Radiocommunications Agency

*HM Treasury

Parliament Street, London SW1P 3AG Tel: 020 7270 3000 Fax: 020 7270 4574
Website: www.hm-treasury.gov.uk
Oversight of the framework for monetary policy; tax policy; planning and control of public spending; government accounting; the quality of public services; international financial relations; the regime for supervision of financial services, management of central government debt and supply of notes and coins (UK).

HM Customs and Excise

New King's Beam House, 22 Upper Ground, London SE1 9PJ Tel: 020 7620 1313
Website: www.hmce.gov.uk
A department reporting to the Chancellor of the Exchequer. Responsible for collecting and accounting for Customs and Excise revenues, including VAT (value added tax); agency functions, including controlling certain imports and exports, policing prohibited goods, and compiling trade statistics (UK).

ECGD (Export Credits Guarantee Department)

PO Box 2200, 2 Exchange Tower, Harbour Exchange Square, London E14 9GS
Tel: 020 7512 7000 Fax: 020 7512 7649
Website: www.ecgd.gov.uk
A department reporting to the Secretary of State for Trade and Industry. Access to bank finance and provision of insurance for UK project and capital goods exporters against the risk of not being paid for goods and services; political risk insurance cover for UK investment overseas (UK).

Office of Fair Trading

Fleetbank House, 2–6 Salisbury Square, London EC4Y 8JX Tel: 020 7211 8000
Fax: 020 7211 8800
Website: www.oft.gov.uk
A non-ministerial department, headed by the Director General of Fair Trading. Administers a wide range of competition and consumer protection legislation, with the overall aim of promoting the economic interests of customers (UK).

Government Offices for the Regions

Government Offices Central Unit

1/C1 Eland House, Bressenden Place, London SW1E 5DU. Tel: 020 7890 5157 Fax: 020 7890 5019 (from 22 April 020 7944 5157 and 020 7944 5019 respectively)
Website: www.detr.gov.uk
Resources, personnel policy, planning and administration for the nine Government Offices for the Regions.

Inland Revenue

Somerset House, Strand, London WC2R 1LB
Tel: 020 7438 6622 Fax: 020 7438 6971
Website: www.inlandrevenue.gov.uk
A department, reporting to the Chancellor of the Exchequer, responsible for the administration and collection of direct taxes; valuation of property (GB).

Executive Agencies

National Insurance Contributions Office
Valuation Office

National Savings
Charles House, 375 Kensington High Street, London W14 8SD Tel: 020 7605 9300 Fax: 020 7605 9438 Website: www.nationalsavings.co.uk
A department in its own right and an executive agency, reporting to the Chancellor of the Exchequer. Aims to raise funds for the Government by selling a range of investments to personal savers (UK).

Royal Mint

Llantrisant, Pontyclun, Mid-Glamorgan
CF72 8YT   Tel: 01443 222111   Fax: 01443 623190
Website: www.royalmint.com
An executive agency with primary responsibility for
the production of UK coinage. It also manufactures
ordinary circulation coins and coinage blanks for
around 58 countries overseas as well as collector
coins and commemorative and official medals.

LEGAL AFFAIRS

*Lord Chancellor's Department

Selborne House, 54–60 Victoria Street, London
SW1E 6QW   Tel: 020 7210 8500
Website: www.open.gov.uk/lcd
Responsibility for procedure of the civil courts and
for the administration of the Supreme Court and
county courts and a number of tribunals under the
Court Service; overseeing the locally administered
magistrates' courts and the Official Solicitor's
Department; work relating to judicial
appointments; overall responsibility for legal aid
and for the promotion of general reforms in the
civil law (E & W). The Lord Chancellor also has
responsibility for the Northern Ireland Court
Service.

Executive Agencies

Court Service
Public Trust Office

Two further agencies—HM Land Registry and the
Public Record Office—report to the Lord
Chancellor but are departments in their own right
(see pp. 536 and 537).

Legal Secretariat to the Law Officers

Attorney General's Chambers, 9 Buckingham Gate,
London SW1E 6JP   Tel: 020 7271 2400
Fax: 020 7271 2430
Supporting the Law Officers of the Crown
(Attorney General and Solicitor General) in their
functions as the Government's principal legal
advisers (E, W & NI).

Treasury Solicitor's Department

Queen Anne's Chambers, 28 Broadway, London
SW1H 9JS   Tel: 020 7210 3000   Fax: 020 7210
3004   Website: www.open.gov.uk/tsd
A department in its own right and an executive
agency reporting to the Attorney General. Provides
legal services to most government departments,
agencies, and public and quasi-public bodies.
Services include litigation; giving general advice on
interpreting and applying the law; instructing
Parliamentary Counsel (part of the Cabinet Office)
on Bills and drafting subordinate legislation; and
providing conveyancing services and property-
related legal work (E & W).

Executive Agency

Government Property Lawyers

Crown Prosecution Service

50 Ludgate Hill, London EC4M 7EX   Tel: 020
7976 8000   Fax: 020 7976 8651
Website: www.cps.gov.uk
Responsible for deciding independently whether
criminal proceedings begun by the police should be
continued, and for prosecuting those cases it
decides to continue (E & W). The CPS is headed
by the Director of Public Prosecutions, who is
accountable to Parliament through the Attorney
General.

Serious Fraud Office

Elm House, 10–16 Elm Street, London WC1X 0BJ
Tel: 020 7239 7272   Fax: 020 7837 1689
Website: www.sfo.gov.uk
Investigating and prosecuting serious and complex
fraud under the superintendence of the Attorney
General (E, W & NI).

EXTERNAL AFFAIRS AND DEFENCE

*Ministry of Defence

Main Building, Horseguards Avenue, London
SW1A 2HB   Tel: 020 7218 9000
Fax: 020 7218 6460   Website: www.mod.uk
Defence policy and control and administration of
the Armed Services (UK).

Defence Agencies

Armed Forces Personnel Administration Agency
Army Base Repair Organisation
Army Personnel Centre
Army Technical Support Agency
Army Training and Recruiting Agency
British Forces Post Office Agency
Defence Analytical Services Agency
Defence Aviation Repair Agency
Defence Bills Agency
Defence Clothing and Textiles Agency

Defence Communication Services Agency
Defence Dental Agency
Defence Estates
Defence Evaluation and Research Agency
Defence Housing Executive
Defence Intelligence and Security Centre
Defence Medical Training Organisation
Defence Procurement Agency
Defence Secondary Care Agency
Defence Storage and Distribution Agency
Defence Transport and Movements Agency
Defence Vetting Agency
Disposal Sales Agency
Duke of York's Royal Military School
Hydrographic Office
Joint Air Reconnaissance Intelligence Centre
Logistic Information Systems Agency
Medical Supplies Agency
Meteorological Office
Military Survey
Ministry of Defence Police
Naval Bases and Supply Agency
Naval Manning Agency
Naval Recruiting and Training Agency
Pay and Personnel Agency
Queen Victoria School
RAF Logistics Support Services
RAF Personnel Management Agency
RAF Signals Engineering Establishment
RAF Training Group Defence Agency
Service Children's Education
Ships Support Agency

*Foreign & Commonwealth Office

King Charles Street, London SW1A 2AH   Tel:
020 7270 3000   Website: www.fco.gov.uk
Conduct of the UK's overseas relations, including
advising on policy, negotiating with overseas
governments and conducting business in
international organisations; promoting British
exports and investment into the UK; presenting
British ideas and policies to overseas countries;
administering the remaining Overseas Territories;
and protecting British interests abroad, including
the welfare of British citizens (UK).

Executive Agency

Wiston House Conference Centre (Wilton Park)

*Department for International Development

94 Victoria Street, London SW1E 5JL
Tel: 020 7917 7000   Fax: 020 7917 0019
Website: www.dfid.gov.uk

Responsibility for promoting development and the
reduction of poverty; managing the UK's
programme of assistance to poorer countries.

SOCIAL AFFAIRS, THE ENVIRONMENT AND CULTURE
*Department for Culture, Media and Sport

2–4 Cockspur Street, London SW1Y 5DH
Tel: 020 7211 6000   Fax: 020 7211 6270
Website: www.culture.gov.uk
The arts; public libraries; national museums and
galleries; tourism; sport; the built heritage (E);
broadcasting; press regulation; film industry;
export licensing of antiques; the Millennium; music
industry; the National Lottery (UK).

Executive Agencies

Historic Royal Palaces
Royal Parks

*Department for Education and Employment

Sanctuary Buildings, Great Smith Street, London
SW1P 3BT   Tel: 020 7925 5000
Fax: 020 7925 6000   Website: www.dfee.gov.uk
Overall responsibility for school, college and
university education; Careers Service (E).
Employment Service; youth and adult training
policy and programmes; sponsorship of Training
and Enterprise Councils; European social policies
and programmes and equal opportunities issues in
employment.

Executive Agency

Employment Service

*Department of the Environment, Transport and the Regions

Eland House, Bressenden Place, London
SW1E 5DU   Tel: 020 7890 3000 (from 22 April
020 7944 3000).
Website: www.detr.gov.uk
Policies for environmental protection; planning;
housing; construction; regeneration; the
countryside; local and regional government; roads;
local transport; aviation; shipping (E); railways and
the Civil Aviation Authority (UK). Also
responsible for sponsoring 33 executive non-
departmental public bodies, including the
Environment Agency, the Countryside Agency,
and the Health and Safety Executive and
Commission (E).

Executive Agencies

Driver and Vehicle Licensing Agency
Driving Standards Agency
Highways Agency
Maritime and Coastguard Agency
Planning Inspectorate
Queen Elizabeth II Conference Centre
Vehicle Certification Agency
Vehicle Inspectorate

*Department of Health

Richmond House, 79 Whitehall, London SW1A
2NS Tel: 020 7210 3000 Fax: 020 7210 5661
Website: www.doh.gov.uk
National Health Service; personal social services
provided by local authorities; and all other health
issues, including public health matters and the
health consequences of environmental and food
issues (E). Represents UK health policy interests in
the EU and the World Health Organisation.

Executive Agencies

Medical Devices Agency
Medicines Control Agency
NHS Estates
NHS Pensions Agency

*Home Office

50 Queen Anne's Gate, London SW1H 9AT
Tel: 020 7273 4000 Fax: 020 7273 2190
Website: www.homeoffice.gov.uk
Administration of justice; criminal law; treatment
of offenders, including probation and the prison
service; the police; crime prevention; fire service
and emergency planning; licensing laws; regulation
of firearms and dangerous drugs; the voluntary
sector; electoral matters (E & W). Gaming (GB).
Passports, immigration and nationality; race
relations; royal matters (UK). Responsibilities
relating to the Channel Islands and the Isle of
Man.

Executive Agencies

Fire Service College
Forensic Science Service
HM Prison Service
United Kingdom Passport Agency

*Department of Social Security

Richmond House, 79 Whitehall, London SW1A
2NS Tel: 020 7238 3000 Fax: 020 7238 0831
Website: www.dss.gov.uk
The social security system (GB).

Executive Agencies

Benefits Agency
Child Support Agency
Information Technology Services Agency
War Pensions Agency

REGULATORY BODIES

Financial Services Authority

25 The North Colonnade, Canary Wharf, London
E14 5HS Tel: 020 7676 1000 Fax: 020 7676 1099
Website: www.fsa.gov.uk
New regulatory body for the whole of the financial
services industry (see p. 508) (UK). Will be
formally established under the Financial Services
and Markets Bill now before Parliament.

National Lottery Commission

2 Monck Street, London SW1P 2BQ
Tel: 020 7227 2000 Fax: 020 7227 2005
Website: www.natlotcomm.gov.uk
See p. 122.

Office of Gas and Electricity Markets (OFGEM)

Stockley House, 130 Wilton Road, London
SW1V 1LQ Tel: 020 7828 0898
Fax: 020 7932 1600 Website: www.ofgem.gov.uk
The regulatory body for gas and electricity
following the merger of the Office of Gas Supply
(OFGAS) and the Office of Electricity Regulation
(OFFER). The Office is responsible for regulating
the gas and electricity markets, protecting
customers' interests and encouraging competition.

Shadow Strategic Rail Authority (SSRA)

Golding's House, 2 Hay's Lane, London SE1 2HB
Tel: 020 7940 4200 Fax: 020 7940 4210
Website: www.opraf.gov.uk
See p. 368.

Office of the Rail Regulator (ORR)

1 Waterhouse Square, 138–142 Holborn, London
EC1N 2TQ Tel: 020 7282 2000
Fax: 020 7282 2040 Website: www.rail-reg.gov.uk
See p. 369.

Office for Standards in Education (OFSTED)

33 Kingsway, London WC2B 6SE
Tel: 020 7421 6800 Fax: 020 7421 6707
Website for inspection reports: www.ofsted.gov.uk
Responsible for arranging the regular inspection of
schools, nursery education providers, teacher
training colleges and local education authority
central services. Providing informed advice to
government and those in education (E).

Office of Telecommunications (OFTEL)

50 Ludgate Hill, London EC4M 7JJ
Tel: 020 7634 8700 Fax: 020 7634 8943
Website: www.oftel.gov.uk
Protecting the interests of customers; promoting
competition in fixed and mobile telephony markets;
ensuring that telephone and cable companies meet
their licence obligations; and regulating access to
digital television services (UK).

Office of Water Services (OFWAT)

Centre City Tower, 7 Hill Street, Birmingham
B5 4UA Tel: 0121 625 1300 Fax: 0121 625 1400
Website: www.open.gov.uk/ofwat
Monitors the activities of companies appointed as
water and sewerage undertakings; regulates prices,
promotes economy and efficiency, protects
customers' interests and facilitates competition
(E & W).

OTHER OFFICES AND AGENCIES

Central Office of Information

Hercules Road, London SE1 7DU
Tel: 020 7928 2345 Fax: 020 7928 5037
Website: www.coi.gov.uk
A department in its own right and an executive
agency reporting to the Chancellor of the Duchy of
Lancaster. Main responsibilities are procuring
publicity material and other information services on
behalf of government departments, agencies and
other public sector clients (UK).

Office of the Data Protection Registrar

Wycliffe House, Water Lane, Wilmslow, Cheshire
SK9 5AF Tel: 01625 545745 Fax: 01625 524510
Website: www.open.gov.uk/dpr
Maintains a public register of electronic data users
and computer bureaux; enforces the data protection
principles; and considers complaints about breaches
of the Data Protection Act. Data users must be
registered with the Data Protection Registrar (UK).
On 1 March 2000, when the Data Protection Act
1998 is implemented, the Registrar's title will
change to the Data Protection Commissioner.

HM Land Registry

Lincoln's Inn Fields, London WC2A 3PH
Tel: 020 7917 8888 Fax: 020 7955 0110
Website: www.landreg.gov.uk
An executive agency responsible to the Lord
Chancellor. Main purpose is to register title to land
in England and Wales, and to record dealings once
the land is registered. It grants guaranteed title to
interests in land for 16.5 million registered titles,
providing a system for the transfer and mortgage of
land and access to up-to-date and authoritative
information (E & W).

Office for National Statistics

1 Drummond Gate, London SW1V 2QQ
Tel: 020 7233 9233 Fax: 020 7533 6224
Website: www.ons.gov.uk
A department and an executive agency accountable
to the Chancellor of the Exchequer. Collects,
compiles and provides a range of statistical
information and population estimates and
projections, and carries out research on behalf of
government departments concerned with social and
economic issues. Also responsible for the
administration of the marriage laws and local
registration of births, marriages and deaths; and
taking the ten-yearly Census of Population (E & W).

Ordnance Survey

Romsey Road, Southampton SO16 4GU
Tel: 023 80 792000 Fax: 023 80 792452
Website: www.ordsvy.gov.uk
An executive agency, which reports to the
Secretary of State for the Environment,
Transport and the Regions, providing official
surveying, mapping and associated scientific work
covering Great Britain and some overseas
countries (GB).

Public Record Office

Ruskin Avenue, Kew, Richmond, Surrey TW9 4DU Tel: 020 8876 3444 Fax: 020 8878 8905
Website:www.pro.gov.uk
The National Archives: a department in its own right and an executive agency reporting to the Lord Chancellor. Responsible for the records of the central government and courts of law dating from the 11th century. Advises government departments on the selection of records for preservation and makes records available to the public (UK).

NORTHERN IRELAND

*Northern Ireland Office

Castle Buildings, Stormont, Belfast BT4 3SG
Tel: 028 9052 0700 Fax: 028 9052 8473
Website: www.nics.gov.uk
11 Millbank, London SW1P 4QE Tel: 020 7210 3000 Fax: 020 7210 8254
Website: www.nio.gov.uk
The Secretary of State for Northern Ireland is the Cabinet minister responsible for Northern Ireland. Through the Northern Ireland Office, the Secretary of State has direct responsibility for political and constitutional matters, law and order, security, and electoral matters.

Executive Agencies

Compensation Agency
Forensic Science Agency of Northern Ireland
Northern Ireland Prison Service

At present the Northern Ireland civil service departments, whose functions are listed below, are subject to the direction and control of the Secretary of State. Responsibility for all these functions will transfer to the new Northern Ireland Assembly (see p. 18)

Department of Agriculture for Northern Ireland

Dundonald House, Upper Newtownards Road, Belfast BT4 3SB Tel: 028 9052 0100
Development of agri-food, forestry and fisheries industries; veterinary, scientific and development services; food and farming policy; agri-environment policy and rural development.

Executive Agencies

Rivers Agency
Forest Service and Agency

Department of Economic Development for Northern Ireland

Netherleigh, Massey Avenue, Belfast BT4 2JP
Tel: 028 9052 9900 Fax: 028 9052 9550
Promotion of inward investment and development of industry (through the Industrial Development Board); promotion of enterprise and small business (through the Local Enterprise Development Unit); training and employment services; promotion of industrially relevant research and development and technology transfer; promotion of tourism (through the Northern Ireland Tourist Board); energy; mineral development; company regulation; consumer protection; health and safety at work; industrial relations; equal opportunity in employment; and co-ordination of deregulation.

Executive Agencies

Industrial Research and Technology Unit
Training and Employment Agency (Northern Ireland)

Department of Education for Northern Ireland

Rathgael House, Balloo Road, Bangor, County Down BT19 7PR Tel: 028 9127 9279 Fax: 028 9127 9100
Control of the five education and library boards and education from nursery to further and higher education; youth services; sport and recreation; the arts and culture; and the development of community relations within and between schools.

Department of the Environment for Northern Ireland

Clarence Court, 10 Adelaide Street, Belfast BT2 8GB Tel: 028 9054 0540
Most of the Department's functions are carried out by executive agencies. These include: planning, roads, water and construction services; environmental protection and conservation services; land registries, public records, ordnance survey, rate collection, driver and vehicle testing and licensing. Core departmental functions include: overall responsibility for housing and transport policies; fire services; certain controls over local government; disposal and management of the Department's land and property holdings; and urban regeneration.

Executive Agencies

Construction Service
Driver and Vehicle Licensing (Northern Ireland)

Driver and Vehicle Testing Agency
Environment and Heritage Service
Land Registers of Northern Ireland
Ordnance Survey of Northern Ireland
Planning Service
Public Record Office of Northern Ireland
Rate Collection Agency
Roads Service
Water Service

Department of Finance and Personnel

Rathgael House, Balloo Road, Bangor, County
Down BT19 7PR Tel: 028 9052 0400
Control of public expenditure; personnel
management of the Northern Ireland Civil Service;
provision of central services and advice.

Executive Agencies

Business Development Service
Government Purchasing Agency
Northern Ireland Statistics and Research Agency
Valuation and Lands Agency

Department of Health and Social Services for Northern Ireland

Castle Buildings, Stormont, Belfast BT4 3SG
Tel: 028 9052 0500
Health and personal social services and social
legislation. Responsibility for the administration of
all social security benefits and the collection of
National Insurance contributions.

Executive Agencies

Northern Ireland Child Support Agency
Northern Ireland Health Estates Agency
Northern Ireland Social Security Agency

SCOTLAND

The Scottish Executive

St Andrew's House, Edinburgh EH1 3DG
Tel: 0131 556 8400   Fax: 0131 244 8240 (for all
departments)
Website: www.scotland.gov.uk
The Scottish ministers and Scottish Executive are
responsible in Scotland for a wide range of
statutory functions. These are administered by six
main departments: the Scottish Executive Rural
Affairs Department, the Scottish Executive

Development Department, the Scottish Executive
Education Department, the Scottish Executive
Enterprise and Lifelong Learning Department, the
Scottish Executive Health Department and the
Scottish Executive Justice Department. These
departments (plus Corporate Services, Finance
Group and Executive Secretariat) are collectively
known as the Scottish Executive. In addition, there
are a number of other Scottish departments for
which the Scottish ministers have some degree of
responsibility: the department of the Registrar
General for Scotland (the General Register Office),
the National Archives of Scotland and the
department of the Registers of Scotland. Other
government departments with significant Scottish
responsibilities have offices in Scotland and work
closely with the Scottish Executive.

Scottish Executive Rural Affairs Department

Pentland House, 47 Robbs Loan, Edinburgh
EH14 1TY
The promotion and regulation of agriculture: food
safety, plant and animal health and welfare; land
use and forestry; livestock subsidies and
commodities. Environment, including
environmental protection, nature conservation and
the countryside; water and sewerage services;
sustainable development. Promotion and regulation
of fisheries; protection of the marine environment;
research on, and monitoring of, fish stocks;
enforcement of fisheries laws and regulations.

Executive Agencies

Scottish Agricultural Science Agency
Scottish Fisheries Protection Agency
Scottish Fisheries Research Services

Scottish Executive Development Department

Victoria Quay, Edinburgh EH6 6QQ
Housing and area regeneration, social inclusion,
local government organisation and finance;
transport and local roads, National Roads
Directorate, co-ordination of Scottish Executive
European interests; land-use planning; building
control.

Scottish Executive Education Department

Victoria Quay, Edinburgh EH6 6QQ
Administration of public education; science and
technology; youth and community services; the arts;

libraries; museums; galleries; Gaelic; broadcasting and sport. Protection and presentation to the public of historic buildings and ancient monuments.

Executive Agencies

Historic Scotland
Scottish Public Pensions Agency
Student Awards Agency for Scotland

Scottish Executive Enterprise and Lifelong Learning Department

Meridian Court, Cadogan Street, Glasgow G2 7AB
Responsibility for selective financial and regional development grant assistance to industry; for the promotion of industrial development and for matters relating to energy policy; urban regeneration and training policy. It is also responsible for policy in relation to Scottish Enterprise, Highlands and Islands Enterprise and the Scottish Tourist Board.

Scottish Executive Health Department

St Andrew's House, Edinburgh EH1 3DG
National Health Service; Chief Scientist's Office; and public health.

Scottish Executive Justice Department

Saughton House, Broomhouse Drive, Edinburgh EH11 3XD
Central administration of law and order (including police service, criminal justice, legal aid and the Scottish Prison Service); civil law, fire, home defence and civil emergency services.

Executive Agency

Scottish Prison Service

Corporate Services

Corporate services to the six Executive departments. Directorate of Administrative Service, Finance and Personnel Groups.

Executive Secretariat

Matters relating to powers and functions of the Scottish Parliament and Executive; constitutional policy, Scottish Parliament elections; Information Directorate and the Office of the Solicitor to the First Minister.

*Office of the Secretary of State for Scotland

Scottish Executive, Dover House, Whitehall, London SW1A 2AU
Tel: 020 7270 3000 Fax: 020 7270 6812
Represents Scottish interests within the UK Government.

Lord Advocate/Crown Office

25 Chambers Street, Edinburgh EH1 1LA
Tel: 0131 226 2626   Fax: 0131 226 6910

WALES

National Assembly for Wales (Cynulliad Cenedlaethol Cymru)

Cathays Park, Cardiff CF10 3NQ and Cardiff Bay, Cardiff CF99 1NA Tel: 029 2082 5111
Fax: 029 2082 3807 Website: www.wales.gov.uk
The National Assembly for Wales (see p. 27) is responsible for many aspects of Welsh affairs, including agriculture, forestry and fisheries; education; health and personal social services; local government; Welsh language and culture, including the arts, museums and libraries. Also responsible for housing; water and sewerage; environmental protection; the countryside and nature conservation; sport; land use, including town and country planning; transport issues; tourism; training and enterprise; regional selective assistance to industry; equal opportunities; public appointments and civil emergencies. The Assembly also has oversight of economic affairs, EU issues and non-departmental public bodies.

Executive Agency

CADW: Welsh Historic Monuments

*Office of the Secretary of State for Wales

Gwydyr House, Whitehall, London SW1A 2ER
Tel: 020 7270 3000   Fax: 020 7270 0561
The Secretary of State for Wales is the member of the UK Cabinet who takes the lead in matters connected with the Government of Wales Act and the transfer of functions to the Assembly. The Secretary of State is responsible for consulting the Assembly on the Government's legislative programme.

Appendix 2: Obituaries

Ronald Alley
Keeper of the Modern Collection at the Tate
Gallery
Born 1916, died April 1999

Eric Ambler
Novelist
Born 1909, died October 1998

Robin Bailey
Actor
Born 1919, died January 1999

Lionel Bart
Composer and songwriter
Born 1930, died April 1999

Dorothy Barton
Surgeon
Born 1898, died December 1998

Lord Beloff (Max)
Historian, polemicist and politician; Gladstone
Professor of Government and Public
Administration, Oxford, 1957–74; founding
Principal of University College, Buckingham
Born 1913, died March 1999

Svetlana Beriosova
Ballerina
Born 1932, died November 1998

Molly Bishop (Lady George Montagu
Douglas Scott)
Portrait painter
Born 1911, died November 1998

James Blades, OBE
Percussionist
Born 1901, died May 1999

Sir Dirk Bogarde
Actor
Born 1921, died May 1999

Betty Box, OBE
Film producer
Born 1915, died January 1999

Marion Boyars
Publisher
Born 1927, died February 1999

Sir Ashley Bramall
Leader of the Inner London Education Authority,
1970–81; former Labour MP
Born 1916, died February 1999

Peter Brough
Ventriloquist (Archie Andrews)
Born 1916, died June 1999

Nicholas Budgen
Conservative MP for Wolverhampton South-West,
1974–97
Born 1937, died November 1998

George Butler
Oldest living member of Royal Watercolour Society
Born 1904, died April 1999

Sir Michael Caine
Chairman of Booker, 1979–83, and guiding spirit of
the Booker Prize for Fiction
Born 1927, died March 1999

Sir Alec Cairncross, KCMG
Head of Government Economic Service, 1964–69;
Master of St Peter's College, Oxford, 1969–78
Born 1911, died October 1998

John Chadwick
Perceval Maitland Laurence Reader in Classics,
Cambridge, 1969–84; decipherer of the Mycenaean
script, Linear B, in 1953
Born 1920, died November 1998

Sir Christopher Cockerell, CBE, FRS
Inventor of the hovercraft
Born 1910, died June 1999

Peter Cotes
Theatrical producer and director; first director of
The Mousetrap
Born 1912, died November 1998

Thora Craig
Founder of first trade union for nurses
Born 1910, died January 1999

Quentin Crewe
Writer and traveller
Born 1926, died November 1998

Iain Crichton Smith, OBE (Iain
Mac A'Ghobhainn)
Poet
Born 1928, died October 1998

Earl of Dalhousie, KT, GCVO, GCB, MC
(Simon Ramsay; 16th earl)
Governor of Rhodesia and Nyasaland, 1957–63;
Lord Chamberlain to Queen Elizabeth the Queen
Mother, 1965–92
Born 1914, died July 1999

Lord Dean of Beswick (Joe)
Labour MP for Leeds West, 1974–83; front bench
spokesman in House of Lords
Born 1922, died February 1999

Lord Denning, OM (Alfred Thompson)
Master of the Rolls, 1962–82
Born 1899, died March 1999

Karl Denver
Pop singer
Born 1931, died December 1998

Earl of Devon (Charles Christopher Courtenay;
17th earl)
Owner of Powderham Castle, near Exeter
Born 1916, died November 1998

Viscount Eccles, CH, KCVO (David)
Former Conservative minister; Chairman of the
British Library, 1973–78
Born 1904, died February 1999

Arthur Ellis
Football referee
Born 1914, died May 1999

Godfrey Evans, CBE
Kent and England wicketkeeper and batsman
Born 1920, died May 1999

Derek Fatchett, MP
Minister of State, Foreign & Commonwealth
Office, 1997–99; Labour MP for Leeds, Central
Born 1945, died May 1999

Amaryllis Fleming
Cellist
Born 1925, died July 1999

Tim Forster, OBE
National Hunt trainer
Born 1934, died April 1999

Christina Foyle
Bookseller
Born 1911, died June 1999

Leslie French
Actor and director
Born 1904, died January 1999

Rowel Friers, MBE
Artist and cartoonist; President of Royal Ulster
Academy, 1994–98
Born 1920, died September 1998

Christopher Gable, CBE
Dancer, actor and director of Northern Ballet
Theatre
Born 1940, died October 1998

Andrew Gardner
Newscaster
Born 1932, died April 1999

Christopher Gilbert
Furniture historian, biographer of Thomas
Chippendale
Born 1936, died September 1998

Frank Gillard, CBE
Broadcaster and former BBC war correspondent
Born 1908, died October 1998

Ruth Gipps, MBE
Composer and conductor
Born 1921, died February 1999

Christine Glanville
Puppeteer
Born 1924, died February 1999

John Glasham
Cartoonist
Born 1927, died June 1999

Rumer Godden, OBE
Writer
Born 1907, died November 1998

Marius Goring, CBE
Actor
Born 1912, died September 1998

Margaret Gowing, CBE, FRS
Founding Professor of the History of Science,
Oxford, 1973–86
Born 1921, died November 1998

Lord Grade (Lew)
Showbusiness tycoon
Born 1906, died December 1998

Patrick Heron
Painter and critic; member of St Ives school of
artists of 1950s
Born 1920, died March 1999

Joan Hickson, OBE
Actress; celebrated as TV's Miss Marple
Born 1906, died October 1998

Valerie Hobson (Mrs John Profumo)
Actress
Born 1917, died November 1998

Sir Alan Hodgkin, OM, KBE, FRS
Professor of Biophysics, 1970–81, and Master of
Trinity College, Cambridge, 1978–84; Nobel
prizewinner, 1963
Born 1914, died December 1998

Lord Howard de Walden (John Osmael Scott-
Ellis; 9th baron)
Racehorse owner and London estate owner
Born 1912, died July 1999

Rod Hull
Entertainer with 'Emu'
Born 1935, died March 1999

George Basil Hume, OSB, OM
Cardinal Archbishop of Westminster
Born 1923, died June 1999

Lord Hunt, KG, CBE, DSO (Henry Cecil John)
Leader of British expedition which climbed Mount
Everest in 1953
Born 1910, died November 1998

Joe Hyman
Textile magnate, creator of Viyella International
Born 1921, died July 1999

Megs Jenkins
Actress
Born 1917, died October 1998

Rosamund John
Actress
Born 1913, died October 1998

Sarah Kane
Playwright
Born 1971, died February 1999

Lord Killanin, Bt, MBE (Michael Morris; 3rd
baron)
President of International Olympic Committee,
1972–80
Born 1914, died April 1999

Sir Laurence Kirwan, KCMG
Director of Royal Geographical Society,
1947–75
Born 1907, died April 1999

Sir David Lane
Conservative MP for Cambridge, 1967–76;
Chairman of Commission for Racial Equality,
1976–82
Born 1922, died November 1998

Geoff Lawson
Car designer
Born 1944, died June 1999

**Admiral of the Fleet Lord Lewin, KG, GCB,
LVO, DSC** (Terence Thornton)
Chief of the Defence Staff, 1979–82
Born 1920, died January 1999

Lord Lowry (Robert)
Lord Chief Justice of Northern Ireland, 1971–88
Born 1919, died January 1999

Mary Lutyens
Writer
Born 1908, died April 1999

Pipe Major Angus MacDonald, MBE
'Finest bagpiper of the century'
Born 1938, died June 1999

Roddy McDowall
Actor
Born 1928, died October 1998

Mick McGahey
Vice-president of National Union of Mineworkers,
1973–87
Born 1925, died January 1999

Paul McKee
Deputy Chief Executive of ITN, 1977–86;
Managing Director of Yorkshire Television,
1986–88
Born 1939, died November 1998

Elspeth March
Actress
Born 1911, died April 1999

Sir William Mars-Jones, MBE
Judge of the High Court, 1969–90
Born 1915, died January 1999

Lord Menuhin, OM (Yehudi)
Violinist, conductor and philanthropist
Born 1916, died March 1999

Naomi Mitchison, CBE
Author
Born 1897, died January 1999

Brian Moore
Novelist
Born 1921, died January 1999

Johnny Morris
TV presenter, traveller and animal lover
Born 1916, died May 1999

Dame Iris Murdoch, DBE
Novelist and philosopher
Born 1919, died February 1999

Anthony Newley
Actor and singer
Born 1931, died April 1999

Derek Nimmo
Actor
Born 1932, died February 1999

Kathleen Nott
Critic, novelist and poet
Born 1905, died February 1999

Sir Anthony Nutting, Bt
Minister of State for Foreign Affairs, 1954–56: 'the
most prominent political casualty of the Suez
crisis'
Born 1920, died February 1999

David Ogilvy, CBE
Founder of advertising agency Ogilvy & Mather
Born 1911, died July 1999

Andrew Osmond
Writer, co-founder of *Private Eye*
Born 1938, died April 1999

Bill Owen, MBE
Actor
Born 1914, died July 1999

Bob Peck
Actor
Born 1945, died April 1999

Jim Peters
Marathon runner
Born 1918, died January 1999

Lord Phillips of Ellesmere, KBE, FRS
(David Chilton)
Professor of Molecular Biophysics, Oxford,
1966–90
Born 1924, died February 1999

William Pleeth, OBE
Cellist
Born 1916, died April 1999

Sir Leo Pliatzky, KCB
Permanent Secretary, Board of Trade, 1977–79;
Whitehall troubleshooter
Born 1919, died May 1999

Colin Purbrook
Jazz pianist and bassist
Born 1936, died February 1999

Sir Alf Ramsey
England football manager, 1963–74; manager of the
World Cup winning side, 1966
Born 1920, died April 1999

Freddy Randall
Jazz trumpeter and bandleader
Born 1921, died May 1999

Dame Kathleen Raven, DBE
Chief Nursing Officer of the UK, 1958–72
Born 1910, died April 1999

Robin Ray
Actor, broadcaster and writer
Born 1935, died November 1998

Oliver Reed
Actor
Born 1938, died May 1999

Sir Robert Rhodes James
Historian; Conservative MP for Cambridge,
1976–92
Born 1933, died May 1999

Tony Rivers
Architect and journalist
Born 1944, died March 1999

Lord Robens of Woldingham (Alf)
Chairman of National Coal Board, 1961–71; former
Labour minister
Born 1910, died June 1999

Jim Rose, CBE
Cryptanalyst, journalist and publisher
Born 1909, died May 1999

Duke of Rutland (Charles John Robert Manners; 10th duke)
Owner of Belvoir Castle and Haddon Hall
Born 1919, died January 1999

Marion Ryan
Popular singer
Born 1931, died January 1999

Dadie Rylands, CH, CBE
Shakespearean scholar and director
Born 1902, died January 1999

Lord Sainsbury (Alan John)
Former chairman of J. Sainsbury
Born 1902, died October 1998

Olive Shapley
Broadcaster
Born 1910, died March 1999

The Rev. Lord Soper (Donald)
Methodist minister and preacher
Born 1903, died December 1998

Dusty Springfield, OBE
Pop and soul singer
Born 1939, died March 1999

Alfred Stephenson
Polar explorer and surveyor
Born 1908, died July 1999

Lawrence Stone
Historian
Born 1919, died June 1999

Dame Elizabeth Sumner, OSB
Abbess of Stanbrook, 1953–83
Born 1911, died May 1999

Screaming Lord Sutch (David Edward)
Pop singer, head of Monster Raving Loony Party,
parliamentary candidate
Born 1940, died June 1999

Tony Tanner
Professor of English and American Literature,
Cambridge, 1989–98
Born 1935, died December 1998

Liz Tilberis
Fashion editor
Born 1947, died April 1999

Rachel Trickett
Principal of St Hugh's College, Oxford, 1973–91
Born 1923, died June 1999

Frank Tuohy
Writer
Born 1925, died April 1999

Dennis Viollet
Manchester United and England footballer
Born 1933, died March 1999

Cyril Washbrook, CBE
Lancashire and England cricketer
Born 1914, died April 1999

Bernard Watney
Ceramics expert and physician
Born 1922, died September 1998

Violet Webb
Athlete
Born 1915, died May 1999

Viscount Whitelaw, KT, MC, CH (William
Stephen Ian; 1st and last viscount)
Former Conservative cabinet minister
Born 1918, died July 1999

Ernie Wise
Comedian
Born 1925, died March 1999

Douglas Wright
Kent and England cricketer, 'most feared leg-break
bowler of his day'
Born 1914, died November 1998

Appendix 3: Principal Abbreviations

ACAS: Advisory, Conciliation and Arbitration Service

ACE: Arts Council of England

AIDS: Acquired Immune Deficiency Syndrome

AONB: Area of Outstanding Natural Beauty

ASA: Advertising Standards Authority

ASEM: Asia-Europe Meeting

ATMs: Automated teller machines

BA: Benefits Agency

BAFTA: British Academy of Film and Television Arts

BBC: British Broadcasting Corporation

BBSRC: Biotechnology and Biological Sciences Research Council

bfi: British Film Institute

BSC: Broadcasting Standards Commission

BSE: Bovine spongiform encephalopathy

BT: British Telecom

CAA: Civil Aviation Authority

CAP: Common Agricultural Policy

CBI: Confederation of British Industry

CCGT: Combined Cycle Gas Turbine

CCLRC: Council for the Central Laboratory of the Research Councils

CCW: Countryside Council for Wales

CFCs: Chlorofluorocarbons

CFP: Common Fisheries Policy

CFSP: Common Foreign and Security Policy

CHP: Combined heat and power

CJD: Creutzfeldt-Jakob disease

CO$_2$: Carbon dioxide

CPS: Crown Prosecution Service

CRE: Commission for Racial Equality

CSA: Child Support Agency

DCMS: Department for Culture, Media and Sport

DENI: Department of Education for Northern Ireland

DERA: Defence Evaluation and Research Agency

DETR: Department of the Environment, Transport and the Regions

DfEE: Department for Education and Employment

DFID: Department for International Development

DH: Department of Health

DNA: Deoxyribonucleic acid

DOENI: Department of the Environment for Northern Ireland

DPP: Director of Public Prosecutions

DSS: Department of Social Security

DTI: Department of Trade and Industry

EAZ: Education Action Zone

EC: European Community

ECGD: Export Credits Guarantee Department

EEA: European Economic Area

EMU: Economic and monetary union

EPSRC: Engineering and Physical Sciences Research Council

ERDF: European Regional Development Fund

ESA: Environmentally Sensitive Area; European Space Agency

ESRC: Economic and Social Research Council

EU: European Union

FA: Football Association

FCO: Foreign & Commonwealth Office

FHE: Further and higher education

FSA: Financial Services Authority

G8: Group of Eight leading industrial countries (including Russia; otherwise G7)

GCSE: General Certificate of Secondary Education

GDP: Gross Domestic Product

GLA: Greater London Authority

GM: Genetically modified

GMOs: Genetically modified organisms

GNP: Gross National Product

GNVQ: General National Vocational Qualification

GOs: Government Offices (for the Regions)

GP: General Practitioner

HSC: Health and Safety Commission

HSE: Health and Safety Executive

IBB: Invest in Britain Bureau

IEA: International Energy Agency

ILA: Individual Learning Account

ILO: International Labour Organisation

IMF: International Monetary Fund

IPC: Integrated Pollution Control

ISA: Individual Savings Account

IT: Information technology

ITC: Independent Television Commission

JNCC: Joint Nature Conservation Committee

JP: Justice of the Peace

JSA: Jobseeker's Allowance

km/h: Kilometres per hour

kW: Kilowatt

LEA: Local education authority

LEC: Local Enterprise Company

LFS: Labour Force Survey

LT: London Transport

m (mm, km): Metre (millimetre, kilometre)

MAFF: Ministry of Agriculture, Fisheries and Food

MEP: Member of the European Parliament

Ml: Megalitre

MoD: Ministry of Defence

MP: Member of Parliament

mph: Miles per hour

MRC: Medical Research Council

MSP: Member of the Scottish Parliament

MW: Megawatt

NATO: North Atlantic Treaty Organisation

NDPBs: Non-departmental public bodies

NERC: Natural Environment Research Council

NFFO: Non-fossil fuel obligation

NGC: National Grid (Company)

NGLs: Natural gas liquids

NHS: National Health Service

NI: Northern Ireland; National Insurance

NIE: Northern Ireland Electricity

NIHE: Northern Ireland Housing Executive

NMEC: New Millennium Experience Company

NO_x: Oxides of nitrogen

NTOs: National Training Organisations

nvCJD: new variant Creutzfeldt-Jakob disease (sometimes vCJD)

NVQ: National Vocational Qualification

OECD: Organisation for Economic Co-operation and Development

OFGEM: Office of Gas and Electricity Markets

OFSTED: Office for Standards in Education

OFTEL: Office of Telecommunications

ONS: Office for National Statistics

OSCE: Organisation for Security and Co-operation in Europe

OST: Office of Science and Technology

PEP: Personal Equity Plan

PFI: Private Finance Initiative

plc: Public limited company

PM_{10}: Particulate matter

PPARC: Particle Physics and Astronomy Research Council

R&D: Research and Development

RABs: Regional Arts Boards

RAF: Royal Air Force

RDAs: Regional Development Agencies

RECs: Regional Electricity Companies

RNT: Royal National Theatre

RPI(X): Retail Prices Index (excluding mortgage interest payments)

RSC: Royal Shakespeare Company

RSL: Registered social landlord

RSPB: Royal Society for the Protection of Birds

RUC: Royal Ulster Constabulary

SAC: Scottish Arts Council

SEN: Special educational needs

SEPA: Scottish Environment Protection Agency

SERPS: State earnings-related pension scheme

SET: Science, engineering and technology

SIP: Social Inclusion Partnership

SMEs: Small and medium-sized enterprises

SNH: Scottish Natural Heritage

SO_2: Sulphur dioxide

sq km: Square kilometre

SRA: Strategic Rail Authority

SRB: Single Regeneration Budget

SRO: Scottish Renewables Obligation

SSRA: Shadow Strategic Rail Authority

SSSI: Site of Special Scientific Interest

SVQ: Scottish Vocational Qualification

TA: Territorial Army

TAC: Total Allowable Catch

TEC: Training and Enterprise Council

TUC: Trades Union Congress

UfI: University for Industry

UK: United Kingdom of Great Britain and Northern Ireland

UKCS: United Kingdom Continental Shelf

UKSI: United Kingdom Sports Institute

UN: United Nations

US: United States

VAT: Value added tax

V&A: Victoria and Albert Museum

VED: Vehicle excise duty

WDA: Welsh Development Agency

WEU: Western European Union

WTO: World Trade Organisation

Appendix 4: Public Holidays, 2000

Monday 3 January	New Year Holiday	UK
Tuesday 4 January	Public holiday	Scotland only
Friday 17 March	St Patrick's Day	Northern Ireland only
Friday 21 April	Good Friday	UK
Monday 24 April	Easter Monday	UK
Monday 1 May	May Day Bank Holiday	UK
Monday 29 May	Spring Bank Holiday	UK
Wednesday 12 July	Orangemen's Day	Northern Ireland only
Monday 7 August	Public holiday	Scotland only
Monday 28 August	Summer Bank Holiday	UK
Monday 25 December	Christmas Day	UK
Tuesday 26 December	Boxing Day	UK

Appendix 5: Calendar of Main Arts Events in the UK, 2000

January: London International Mime Festival.

January: London Book Fair.

January: Celtic Connections, in Glasgow.

February–March: Bath Literary Festival.

February–May: RSC London season, at the Barbican.

March: London Handel Festival.

March–October: RSC Summer Festival, at Stratford-upon-Avon.

April and September: Chelsea Antiques Fair in London.

May: Bath Festival, including Clerical Medical Jazz Weekend (European jazz) and Bath Contemporary Music Weekend.

May: Brighton Festival. The largest in England, including theatre, music, opera, street arts, etc.

May–June: Urdd National Eisteddfod. Europe's largest youth arts festival, at Lampeter (Dyfed).

May–June: Salisbury Festival. Various events, including sculpture and street arts.

May–August: Glyndebourne Festival. Opera.

May–September: Shakespeare summer season at the Globe (London).

May–September: Shakespeare at the Open Air theatre in Regent's Park (London).

May–September: Chichester Festival. Theatre.

June: Singer of the World competition in Cardiff.

June: St Magnus Festival (Orkney). Music.

June: Aldeburgh Festival (Suffolk). Music, visual arts, film.

June: Spitalfields Festival (London). Music.

June: Glastonbury Festival. Pop and rock.

June–July: City of London Festival. Concerts in churches, livery halls and open spaces.

June–July: Lufthansa Festival of Baroque Music in London.

June–July: Opera at Garsington (Oxfordshire).

June–July: Opera at Longborough (Gloucestershire).

July: International Music Eisteddfod at Llangollen.

July: Cheltenham International Festival. Modern British music.

July: Fishguard (Pembrokeshire) International Music Festival.

July: WOMAD at Reading. Festival of world music and dance.

July–August: Edinburgh International Jazz and Blues Festival.

July–September: Henry Wood Promenade Concerts ('the Proms') at the Royal Albert Hall (London).

August: Brecon Jazz Festival.

August: Machynlleth Festival. Music.

August: Three Choirs Festival. Rotates between Hereford, Gloucester and Worcester. Founded in 1724, the oldest choral festival in Europe.

August: Royal National Eisteddfod, alternating each year in south and north Wales.

August: Edinburgh International Book Festival.

August: Edinburgh International Film Festival.

August–September: Edinburgh International Festival. Opera, dance, theatre, music, and the famous Fringe.

September: North Wales International Music Festival at St Asaph (Denbighshire).

September: Leeds International Pianoforte Competition.

September–October: Windsor Festival of Music.

October: Royal National Mod (Am Mod Naiseanta Rioghail). At a different venue each year in the Highlands. Music, dance, drama and literature.

October: Canterbury Festival. Various art forms.

October: Malvern Festival. Exhibitions, music, literature, drama and film.

October: Cheltenham Festival of Literature.

October: Chelsea Crafts Fair.

October–December: Glyndebourne Touring Opera, at various places in England.

November: Oris London Jazz Festival.

November: London Film Festival, hosted by the *bfi*, which shows some 250 new international films.

November–December: Huddersfield Festival. Contemporary music.

Index

Passenger Railway Network in the UK